We Will Remember Them

The Front Cover

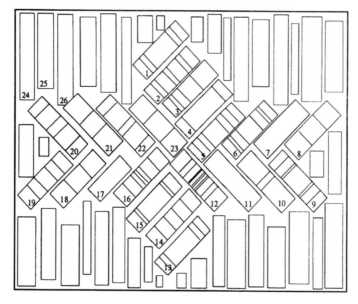

The front cover shows the memorial window which is a striking feature of the AJEX Museum. Designed by Abram Games, OBE, RDI, the emerging Star of David is composed of British medal ribbons dating back to the Boer War.

Photograph by
John Gumpright

1. British War Medal, 1914–20
2. Second World War Pacific Star
3. Second World War Africa Star
4. General Service Medal 1962
5. Second World War Burma Star
6. Defence Medal, 1939–45
7. Korean Medal (UNO), 1950–53
8. South Africa Medal, 1901–02
9. Naval General Service, 1915–60
10. Mercantile Marine Medal, 1914–18
11. 1914 and 1914–15 Stars
12. Vietnam Medal, 1964
13. Territorial Force War Medal, 1914–15
14. Second World War France and Germany Star
15. Indian General Service Star, 1936–39
16. War Medal, 1939–45
17. Second World War Star, Air Crew Europe
18. Second World War Star, 1939–45
19. Korean Medal (British), 1950–53
20. Second World War Star, Italy
21. General Service Medal, 1918–64
22. Victory Medal, 1914–18
23. Second World War Star, Atlantic
24. Royal Navy
25. Army
26. Royal Air Force

We Will Remember Them

A Record of the Jews Who Died in the
Armed Forces of the Crown from 1939

Henry Morris
and
Martin Sugarman

VALLENTINE MITCHELL
LONDON · PORTLAND, OR

The publication of this book would not have
been possible without the generous
support of The Pears Foundation.

First published in 2011 by Vallentine Mitchell
Middlesex House
29/45 High Street, Edgware
Middlesex HA8 7UU, UK

920 NE 58th Avenue, Suite 300
Portland, Oregon
97213-3786 USA

www.vmbooks.com

British Library Cataloguing in Publication Data
An entry can be found on request

ISBN 978 0 85303 621 0

Library of Congress Cataloging-in-Publication Data
An entry can be found on request

Typesetting by FiSH Books.
Printed by CPI Antony Rowe, Chippenham, Wiltshire

Dedication to the First Edition

I have tried wherever possible to register in the Roll of Honour the place where each man and woman is buried. War in every aspect is so destructive that often no information exists, and in those cases I have failed.

So many died: drowned at sea, blown out of the skies or literally destroyed on the battlefield – they were never seen again. Their families and loved ones must feel a special pain that is hard to endure.

Nearly fifty years on from the beginning of this titanic struggle against tyranny and oppression, new generations may not understand or appreciate what a great victory was won for freedom and at what a huge cost. The seeds of that victory have yet to ripen into fruits of peace, tolerance, understanding of people and the right to live a free life anywhere on earth.

I believe that we all have a right to a known last resting place where kin can come to mourn, pay their respects and, often I hope, recall fond memories.

I want to dedicate this book to those of all nations and creeds who helped to sow those seeds but have no known grave, so that it may bring some small comfort to those who loved them.

Henry Morris
London, 1989

We Will Remember Them

And the Lord spake unto Moses and unto Aaron saying:
Every man of the children of Israel shall pitch by his own standard,
with the ensign of their father's house: far off about the tabernacle
of the congregation shall they pitch.

Numbers Chapter 2 v.2

They shall grow not old
as we that are left grow old
Age shall not weary them
nor the years condemn
At the going down of the sun
and in the morning we will
remember them

Laurence Binyon, 'To the Fallen'

April 22nd 1943, Longstop Hill

That April day
Seems far away
The day they decided to kill
Lt. Tony Goldsmith R.A.
On the slopes of Longstop Hill

At Toukabour
The dawn lights stir
Whose blood today will spill?
Today it's Tony Goldsmith's
Seeping out on Longstop Hill

One can't complain
Nor ease the pain
Or find someone to fill
The place of Tony Goldsmith
Lying dead on Longstop Hill

In Germany
There still could be
A Jochem, Fritz or Will
Who did for Tony Goldsmith
That day on Longstop Hill.

Spike Milligan
(by kind permission of Spike Milligan Publications.
Lt Anthony Goldsmith was Spike Milligan's
much-loved officer – see Army Section)

Contents

List of Figures .... *xi*
Foreword by Trevor Pears .... *xxiii*
Acknowledgements to First Edition .... *xxv*
Acknowledgements to First Edition of Addendum .... *xxvii*
Author's Introduction to the First Edition, 1989 .... *xxix*
Author's Introduction to the Addendum to the First Edition .... *xxxiii*
Authors' Introduction to the Second Edition .... *xxxvii*
Introduction by Sir Martin Gilbert .... *xxxix*
Acknowledgements and Tributes to First and Second Editions .... *xliii*

PART ONE: REMEMBRANCE
The Proud War Record of British Jews 3
Special Tributes and Messages 7
Awards for Bravery in the Field 11
Amongst the Bravest of the Brave 17
The Enemy Aliens who Fought for Britain 23
Jewish Clergy in Uniform, by the Reverend Dr Isaac Levy, OBE 27
Tributes to the Fallen by their Families and Friends in Proud Remembrance 31
Memories of a Japanese Prisoner of War, by David Arkush 39
A Note on the Jewish Headstones in Commonwealth War Graves
Commission Cemeteries, by Martin Sugarman 43

PART TWO: THE ROLLS OF HONOUR
The Royal Navy, Merchant Navy and Royal Marines 49
The Army 59
The Royal Air Force 149
The Palestine Jewish Volunteers 191
The Fire Service, by Martin Sugarman and Stephanie Maltman 215

Jewish Brothers Who Died on Service in the British and Commonwealth
Forces in the Second World War, by H. Pollins and M. Sugarman.................219
Additional Killed in Action, Commonwealth and Allied...................227
A Note on Jews in the Polish Armed Forces During the Second World War,
by Dr Leonard Kurzer, Leon Fait and Ludwik Kleiner....................233
When Britain Turned to the Jewish 'Private Armies' 239
A Parachute Hero and Two Heroines.......................253
The Jewish Infantry Brigade Group: Jewish Volunteers from Palestine
in the Second World War, by Meir de Shalit 261
How the Jewish Brigade was Born, by S. Levenberg 269

PART THREE: AWARDS AND DECORATIONS 1939–1945 AND AFTER
Awards and Decorations Gained by Jews Serving in HM Forces 275
A Different May Day 327
Hevel Yami Le'Yisroel (Israeli Merchant Navy) 331

PART FOUR: POWs AND OTHER LISTS, by Martin Sugarman
British and Commonwealth Jewish POWs of the Germans, 1939–1945 335
Jewish POWs of the Japanese in the Second World War.............................361
Jews Who Served in Special Forces in the Second World War and After........383
Jews Who Served in the Commandos and Paratroopers 387
Jews Who Served with Wingate's Chindits in Burma...............................405
British and Commonwealth Jews in the Korean War 409
British and Commonwealth Jews in Kenya................................413
British and Commonwealth Jews in Malaya 415
Jewish Personnel Who Served in Cyprus during the Emergency 421
The VCs and GCs 425

Appendix *443*
Location of Cemeteries *447*
Glossary of Abbreviations *451*

Figures

1. Field Marshal Sir Gerald Templer GCB GCMG KBE DSO unveiling the Memorial to Jewish Servicemen with no known graves in the United Synagogue's Willesden Cemetery on Sunday 14 March 1960.
2. Beaten pewter plaque in the RAF Church of Saint Clement Danes, Strand, London.
3. Roll of Honour in Childwall Synagogue, Liverpool.
4. Warrant Officer Sidney Cohen.
5. A poster from the Yiddish Theatre advertising 'The King of Lampedusa'.
6. This plaque, in memory of some of our women members of the Special Operations Executive (SOE), executed at Ravensbrück Concentration Camp, was unveiled by 'Odette' in the spring of 1993.
7. Four companies – Alien Pioneer Corps.
8. Citation for Capt Goldstone.
9. Citation for Lt Grennan.
10. Citation for Capt Herbert.
11. Citation for Maj Rosenheim.
12. Citation for Cpl Rosenfield.
13. Citation for Cpl Shutz.
14. Capt A. Rabinovich.
15. Mauthausen – the wall bearing the memorial tablets to those who died.
16. The Tablet erected by the Dutch War Graves Commission bearing Newman's name. It also bears the name of Marcus Bloom, SOE.
17. Brig F.H. Kisch, Chief Engineer 8th Army.
18. Chaplains in the Middle East 1942.
19. The River Kwai Cemetery, Kanchanaburi, Thailand.
20. Leading Supply Assistant Geoffrey Berney RNVR.
21. Rad/O Aubrey Lionel Bernstein MN.
22. OS Ellis Cohen RN.
23. Telegraphist Solomon Cornbleet RN.

24. CPO D. Cowan RN.

25. Smn H. Huntman MN.

26. AB David Jackson RN.

27. Ldg/Smn Laurence Lobell (Lobinsky) RN.

28. The Grave of AB David Jackson.

29. Stwd S. Messer MN.

30. AB C. Newman RN.

31. Stkr J. Phillips RN.

32. Stwd J. Phillips RN.

33. Stwd L. Phillips MN.

34. Lt Leonard A. Teff RNVR and Ldg Air/Mech Cyril Laurence Edelman.

35. Tpr A. Aaron 18th Reconnaissance Regt (The Loyal Regt).

36. The Grave of Tpr Aaron in Chung Kai Military Cemetery, Thailand.

37. The Grave of Gnr S. Abrahams RA, in Cassino.

38. Pte Abram Abramson, RASC.

39. Pte Barnet Abramson, 2nd Btn The Duke of Wellington's Regt (West Riding).

40. The Grave of Capt P.S. Adler MRCS, LRCP, RAMC, in Rangoon.

41. The Grave of Pte Barnet Abramson in Rangoon.

42. Gnr Max Alexander, RA (formerly The Queen's Own Royal Regt).

43. The Jewish Ex-Servicemen's Armistice Service and Parade, Horse Guards Parade 1930.

44. Cpl Sam Baderman, PC.

45. The Grave of Gnr H. Baum, RA.

46. The Grave of Fus L. Bartell, The Lancashire Fus, in Rangoon.

47. The Grave of Gnr L. Basco, RA, in Chung Kai Military Cemetery, Thailand.

48. Gnr Cyril Reuben Baum, RA.

49. The AJEX Remembrance Parade 1963.

50. Pte Leonard Blashky.

51. Gnr Bernard Blyweiss, RA.

52. Capt P.M. Bogod, RA.

53. The Grave of Gnr M. Bolter, Singapore RA.

54. Pte Woolf (Willy) Bresler, The Queen's Own Cameron Highlanders.

55. Pte M. Brown, The Welch Regt.

56. Fus Solomon Chapman, lst/8th Btn, The Lancashire Fusiliers.

57. Pte Barnet Chenovitch, 2nd Btn, The Suffolk Regt.

58. Lt Paul Clompus, 107th Regt, RA.

59. The Grave of Pte A.L. Cohen, The South Lancashire Regt, in Rangoon.

60. Pte E.I. Cohen, The King's Own Regt.

61. Dvr Ephraim Cohen, RASC.

62. The Grave of Gnr Harry Cohen, RA, in Kuala Lumpur.

63. Cpl Harry Cohen, 2nd Btn, The Black Watch (Royal Highland Regt) (Commando).

64. L/Cpl Ronald Cowan, RASC.

65. Lt Leonard Arthur David, The Royal Sussex Regt (Seconded to the Royal Hampshire Regt).

66. Sgmn Leslie Davidson, Royal Corps of Signals.

67. The Grave of Capt M. Dean, RAMC, in Rangoon.

68. Cpl Henry Dehond, Royal Army Dental Corps.

69. The Grave of Pte C. Denby-Dreyfus, Para Regt, AAC.

70. The Grave of Pte S.S. Duque, The King's Regt, in Rangoon.

71. Cpl Sidney Eisbruch, 'A' Squadron 1st RTR, RAC.

72. Pte Hyman Feldman, RAMC.

73. Sgt Hillier Field, 9th Btn, KRRC (The Rangers) (TA).

74. Cpl E. Fine, RASC.

75. Craftsman Alexander Fisher, REME.

76. S/Sgt Cyril Fisher, The Glider Pilot Regt, AAC.

77. Cpl Stanley Fishman, The Green Howards (Alexandra, Princess of Wales's Own Yorkshire Regt).

78. The Grave of Pte Alec Forman, 2nd Btn, The Essex Regt, in Bayeux.

79. Sgt Ronald Franks, The Glider Pilot Regt, AAC.

80. L/Cpl Mark Fredlieb, The Duke of Wellington's Regt (West Riding).

81. Pte Henry Freeman, The East Yorkshire Regt (The Duke of York's Own).

82. Pte Leslie Freeman, Buffs.

83. The Grave of Gnr M.L. Golab, RA.

84. AO S. Goldman.

85. Israel Averback.

86. Fus Leslie Bartell.

87. Rev H. Bornstein.

88. Lt D.L. Cohen.

89. Pte S.S. Cohen.

90. Lt V.L. Cooper.

91. Sgt A. Goldman.

92. Pte L. Greenberg.

93. Pte H. Gross.

94. Pte B. Lassman.

95. Sgt R. Levy.

96. Pte G. Litwin.

97. Tpr A. Mendik.

98. Pte A. Rosenblum.

99. Gnr R. Segal.

100. Pte Sydney Goldberg, RASC.

101. Capt Lionel Stanley Goldstone MC, 8th Btn, Roy Fus (City of London Regt).

102. Pte Sidney Goodman, 'C' Company 7th Btn, The Royal Berkshire Regt.

103. Rfmn Morris Greenberg, The Tower Hamlets Rifles, RB.

104. Gnr Harry Greenstein, RA.

105. Maj Alexander Philip Greene RA.

106. Tpr H. Haft, RTR, RAC.

107. The Grave of Tpr H. Haft.

108. The Grave of Lt H. Haltrecht, RA, in Rangoon.

109. The Grave of Pte S. Halom (Israel), RASC.

110. The Grave of Pte S. Harbert, Para Regt, AAC.

111. The Grave of Tpr Charles S. Harris, 3rd County of London Yeomanry, RAC, in the Sangro River Cemetery, Italy.

112. Princess Alexandra at the AJEX Remembrance Parade 1967.

113. Sgt W. Hollman, 20th Company, RAMC.

114. Guardsman Samuel Huntman, Welsh Guards.

115. Pte Harold Iduas, The Argyll & Sutherland Highlanders (Princess Louise's), 51st Highland Division.

116. Capt Jacob Hyman Joseph, RAMC, Regimental Medical Officer, 4th Btn, The Dorset Regt.

117. L/Cpl Henry P. Kaufman, 9th Btn DLI.

118. The Grave of Pte J. Kahn, The Lincolnshire Regt, in Rangoon.

119. The Grave of L/Cpl Henry Kaufman in the Brit Military Cemetery, Catania, Sicily.
120. The Grave of Brig F.H. Kisch CB CBE DSO, Chief Engineer 8th Army, in Tunisia.
121. Lt Jack Aaron Kleinman, Buffs (Seconded to 5th Btn The Wiltshire Regt) (Duke of Edinburgh's).
122. The Grave of Pte Krieger, The Sherwood Foresters (Nottinghamshire & Derbyshire Regt), in the British War Cemetery in Kanchanaburi, Thailand.
123. Fus Harry Krimhorn, 9th Btn, Roy Fus (City of London Regt).
124. Sgt Louis Kushin, Army Educational Corps.
125. The Grave of Fus Krimhorn in the Minturno Military Cemetery, near Naples.
126. The Grave of Pte C. Laine, Buffs, in Rangoon.
127. Pte Sam Landy, The West Yorkshire Regt (The Prince of Wales's Own).
128. Gnr Moishe J. Larner, 11th Regt, RHA (HAC).
129. Pte Henry Layman, 1st Btn, The Northamptonshire Regt.
130. The Grave of Pte Henry Layman in Taukkyan War Cemetery, Rangoon.
131. Pte Bill (Wolfie) Letwin, The Green Howards (Alexandra, Princess of Wales's Own Yorkshire Regt).
132. The Grave of Capt M. Leigh, Young Men's Christian Association, in Kranji War Cemetery, Singapore.
133. The Grave of Pte Jacob Lempert, The South Staffordshire Regt (Chindits).
134. The Grave of Sgt A.E. Levin, RCOS, in Rangoon.
135. Pte Benjamin Levy, lst/4th Btn, The Essex Regt.
136. The Grave of L/Cpl H.L. Levitton, RASC.
137. Pte M. Levy, 5th Btn, The South Staffordshire Regt.
138. Dvr Philip Levy, RE.
139. Fus Mervyn David Levy, The Royal Welch Fusiliers.
140. The Grave of Dvr (Dick) Lipman, RE.
141. The Grave of Pte I. Litveen, The South Wales Borderers, in Rangoon.
142. L/Sgt Cyril David Litwack, RAC.
143. Pte Woolf Walter Loew, 2nd Btn, The Bedfordshire & Hertfordshire Regt.
144. The Grave of Sgt Cyril Litwack.
145. The Grave of Pte H. Marcus, KOYLI, in Salerno.
146. The Grave of Tpr Felix Mondschein Martin, 3rd Carabiniers, RAC, in Rangoon.
147. Cpl Moss Mendelle, Recce Corps.

148. The Grave of K. Meyer, who served as Lance Cpl P. Moody, The Hampshire Regt (Number 10 Commando).

149. The Grave of Pte N. Miller, The Worcestershire Regt, in Rangoon.

150. The Grave of Bdr Joseph Milrood, RA, in Ranville Brit Military Cemetery, Normandy.

151. The Grave of Lt John J. Morris, The Sherwood Foresters (Nottinghamshire & Derbyshire Regt) (attached to The Lincolnshire Regt).

152. The Grave of Pte H. Moss, The Northamptonshire Regt, in Rangoon.

153. The Grave of M. Mutsemaker, a Dutch Soldier in Chung Kai Cem, Thailand.

154. Lt Peter Nathaniel Myers, 4th Recce Regt, Recce Corps.

155. Fus Harry Newman, 8th Btn, Roy Fus (City of London Regt).

156. Sgt Maurice Nichols, 519 Battery, RHA (Essex Yeomanry).

157. The Grave of Pte E. Norton, The Queen's Own Royal West Kent Regt (Number 10 Commando).

158. Sgt David Olsberg, 2nd Btn, The Lancashire Fus.

159. The Grave of Sgt David Olsberg at Castel-del-Rio, Santerno.

160. The Grave of Pte M. Pavlotsky, The Yorks & Lancaster Regt, in Rangoon.

161. Lt Asher Pearlman MB, RAMC.

162. The Grave of Sgt J.D. Perry, The Welch Regt, in Rangoon.

163. Gnr Harry Phillips, RA.

164. Pte Monty Pincus, The Queen's Roy Regt (West Surrey).

165. The Grave of Pte Norman Pinsky, The West Yorkshire Regt (The Prince of Wales's Own), in Rangoon.

166. The Grave of Gnr Simon Rabinovitch, 42nd Battery, RA, in the Commonwealth Cemetery, Yokohama, Japan.

167. The AJEX Remembrance Parade, Whitehall 1980.

168. Bandsman Benjamin Ritterbrand, 1st Btn, The Herefordshire Regt.

169. The Grave of Capt A. Robson, RAMC, in Rangoon.

170. The Grave of Rfmn Solomon Rodkoff, 8th Btn, The Rifle Bde, in Tourneville.

171. The Grave of Dvr A.J. Rose, RASC, in Kranji.

172. Admiral of the Fleet Sir Peter Hill-Norton reviews the AJEX Memorial Parade, 1971.

173. The Grave of Pte N. Rosewood, The South Staffordshire Regt, in Rangoon.

174. Dvr Mark Rothberg, 672 Company, RE.

175. Cpl Leonard Rubin, 2 Commando.

176. The Grave of Cpl Leonard Rubin in Salerno.

177. The Grave of Dvr Mark Rothberg in the Communal Cemetery at Veurnes, Belgium.

178. Sgt Theodore Albert Rubinstein, The Glider Pilot Regt, AAC.

179. The Grave of Cpl H. Samberg, The South Lancs Regt (The Prince of Wales's Vol), in Rangoon.

180. Pte Harry Saperia, The West Yorks Regt (The Prince of Wales's Own).

181. L/Cpl Louis Saunders, 4th Btn, The Royal Norfolk Regt.

182. Lt Laurence Savitt, 31st LAA Regt, RA, Central Mediterranean Force.

183. Tpr Leslie E. Schalit, 1st Recce Regt, Recce Corps.

184. Pte Philip Scheffer, 7th Btn, The Black Watch (Royal Highland Regt).

185. Sgt David Bernard Schneider, REME.

186. Sgt Emanuel Schreiber, Recce Corps.

187. The Grave of Sgt Emanuel Schreiber, Recce Corps, in the Phaleron War Cemetery, Athens.

188. The Grave of Pte Pinkus Schul, The Royal Sussex Regt, in Rangoon.

189. Capt Henry Samuel Segarman, RAMC.

190. The Grave of Capt Henry Segarman at El Alamein.

191. Pte Frank Shapiro, The HLI (City of Glasgow Regt).

192. Gnr Isidore Aaron Shapiro, RA

193. The Grave of Pte H. Silkman, The Dorsetshire Regt, in Rangoon.

194. Rflmn Ben Silver, 2nd Btn, KRRC.

195. Pte Benjamin Silver, KRRC.

196. The Grave of Pte S. Shulton, The Queen's Royal Regt.

197. The Grave of Lt P. Silvert, 4th Company, 716 Btn, RASC, at Ranville.

198. The Grave of Maj R.H. Simpson, RA, in Rangoon.

199. The Grave of Gnr M. Sirkin, RA, in Rangoon.

200. Pte A. Skry, The Queen's Own Royal West Kent Regt.

201. Gnr Alfred Sorsky, 97th Anti-Tank Regt, RA.

202. The Grave of Gnr L. Stone, RA, in Kuala Lumpur.

203. Maj R. Stuppel FRCS, RAMC.

204. Tpr Cyril Symons, 13/18th Royal Hussars, RAC.

205. Whitehall 1983. General Sir John Stanier takes the salute.

206.   Pte Norman Alexander Vine, Para Regt, AAC, 6th Airborne Division.

207.   Pte Harold Wald, KOSB.

208.   Pte Sidney Wald, The South Wales Borderers.

209.   Gnr Mark Weinstock, 99th LAA Regt, RA.

210.   Grave of Gnr Mark Weinstock, in Sangro River Cemetery, Italy.

211.   Lt Max Mendel Wolpert, GM, The Cheshire Regt.

212.   Gnr Daniel (Don) Woolf, RA.

213.   Cpl D Wynne, 8th Btn, Roy Fus (City of London Regt).

214.   Sgt Albert Yudin, 10th Royal Hussars.

215.   Gnr A. Zemmill, RA.

216.   L/Cpl Harry Zimmerman, The Somerset L/I.

217.   Flt/Sgt S.S. Aarons (RAF Memorial Runnymede).

218.   Flt/Sgt Lionel David Anderson.

219.   Sgt (Wireless Operator) Mark Azouz.

220.   The Grave of LAC Michael Barry in Calcutta.

221.   Sgt (Flt/Eng) Leon Bassman.

222.   Flt/Lt Dennis J. Baum, Bomber Command.

223.   Flt/Sgt (Nav) Edward Bashi, Bomber Command.

224.   Flt/Sgt H.M. (Mick) Bluston, 18 Squadron, Central Mediterranean Force.

225.   This scroll commemorates Sergeant H. Bronsky, RAF.

226.   Sgt (Pilot) Harold Bronsky, 49 Squadron.

227.   F/O Meyer Caplan DFM.

228.   The Roll of Honour in Cardiff Synogogue.

229.   WO (Pilot) Sidney Cohen, 249 Squadron.

230.   Sgt Lionel Cornbloom.

231.   Grave of LAC Moshe Danino, in Geneifa War Cemetery, Egypt.

232.   Flt/Sgt Robert Dansby.

233.   Sgt (AG) Dennis Davies, 158 Squadron.

234.   Cpl Nathan Daren.

235.   Flt/Sgt Samuel Easton.

236.   LAC Roffer James Eden.

237.   Flt/Sgt (WO/AG) Sydney Feldman, 57 Squadron.

238.   Marshal of the Royal Air Force Sir John Grandy at the Cenotaph 1987.

239.   AG Ferneaux Jordan Van Guen.

240. Flt/Sgt Gingold.
241. Sgt Hyman Goldberg.
242. Sgt N.M. Goldberg.
243. Cpl Cyril Hyman Goldman.
244. Sgt (AG) Jacob (Jack) Goldstein.
245. Flt/Sgt N. Gordon, 49 Squadron.
246. P/O (Navigator) Sydney Goulston, 77 Squadron.
247. Last Letter of FO Peter Greenburgh, p.1
248. Last Letter of FO Peter Greenburgh, p.2
249. F/O Peter Harold Greenburgh, 39 Squadron, Fleet Air Arm.
250. Flt/Sgt Sidney Henry Greene.
251. Cpl Abe Grunis.
252. Sgt Alfred Harris.
253. Grave of LAC Geoffrey M. Harris in the RAF Cemetery, Terrel, Texas, USA.
254. Grave of Sgt (Pilot) Robert Hart in Kleve British Military Cemetery.
255. Sgt (AG) T. Hazan.
256. Sgt Sidney Helper.
257. LAC Jack Hymans, Transport Command.
258. Sgt (Flt/Eng) H.C.M. Kahler.
259. Grave of Sgt Kahler in Gram Churchyard, Denmark.
260. Sgt (Flt/Eng) Michael Kalms.
261. Sgt Harry Kaye, DFM.
262. W/Cdr J. Kemper, OBE, Medaille Militaire.
263. W/Cdr J. Kemper in the First World War.
264. A Wings for Victory Parade (W/Cdr Kemper second from right).
265. Flt/Sgt Zdenek Launer, 311 Squadron.
266. LAC Alfred Lazarus.
267. P/O Jack Leewarden.
268. Flt/Sgt H. Levene.
269. Grave of AC1 H. Levinson in the River Kwai Cemetery, Chung Kai.
270. Sgt (Pilot) Sidney S. Levitus.
271. Grave of AC1 A. Levy in the River Kwai Cemetery, Chung Kai.
272. Flt/Sgt (Navigator) H.K. Levy, 47 Squadron.
273. Sgt (Pilot) Nat Luben, Coastal Command.

274. Sgt Nathan Max, 178 Squadron.
275. Sgt (WO/AG) Samuel Miara, 38 Squadron, Bomber Command.
276. Flt/Sgt (Pilot) Michael Frederick Nathan.
277. Sgt Aaron Ottolangui.
278. Sgt Roy (Isenstein) Phillips.
279. Flt/O John David Pincus.
280. Fus S. Solomons MM, RF.
281. Pte P. Sunderland, Y and L Reg.
282. Maj L. Wigram, RF.
283. Sgt J.M. Cantor, RAF, killed.
284. Sgt Henry Cohen, RAF, killed.
285. Sgt S.L. Ford, RAF.
286. Sgt/Pilot Simon Hirsch.
287. Flt/O Leslie Israel.
288. Flt/O A.R.F. Jonas.
289. Sgt Louis Lazarus, RAF.
290. Cpl Lemberger, Green Howards, lost at sea.
291. Sgt Paul Herman, Koflik Polish RAF.
292. AJEX and British Legion Standard Bearers at a Commonwealth War Graves Cemetery in Israel 1988.
293. Flt/O Vera Rowson, WAAF.
294. Sgt (AG) Edward Shatz, 929 Squadron.
295. Sgt (Nav) Sidney Smith.
296. Flt/O Stuart Jack Smith.
297. P/O Gerald Stephens.
298. Sgt/AG Jack Davis 1352674 RAFVR, 158 Squadron.
299. Flt/Sgt Philip Silverman 158 Squadron RAF.
300. Sgt (Air Gunner) Ronald Marcus Sutton.
301. F/O (Pilot) Arthur David Walford.
302. Sgt Alan Abraham Waller.
303. Sgt (Flt/Eng) Lionel Walters (Cohen).
304. Sgt (Rad/O) Marks Wayne, 153 Squadron.
305. Sgt Wayne as a private in the Queen's Royal Regiment.
306. The Grave of Sgt Lionel Walters at Goirle, Tilburg, Holland.

307. Sgt (WO/AG) Samuel Williams.
308. The entrance to the Military Cemetery at Ravenna.
309. Graves of Pal Jewish Volunteers at Ravenna Military Cemetery.
310. Joseph Reinhold, killed in pre-invasion manoeuvres, 8 May 1944.
311. Grave of Cad/O Alexander Greenberg in Monte Cassino.
312. Commemorative prayers, conducted by Rabbi Ruebner at the Great Synagogue in Rome, in memory of Polish Jewish soldiers killed in action in Italy.
313. Jewish graves at the Polish Military Cemetery, Monte Cassino.
314. Anatol Bier.
315. A British Army recruiting poster, Tel Aviv, 1944.
316. Jewish Volunteers show the flag, Tel Aviv, 1940.
317. Jewish recruits in a Tel Aviv street, 1941.
318. Jewish contingent of the ATS, Tel Aviv, 1942.
319. Jewish soldiers of the RASC laying a telephone cable in the Western Desert, 1942.
320. The Flag Revolt – October 1943.
321. ATS Volunteers in Tel Aviv, 1942.
322. Three Palestinian Jewish Parachutists, 1944.
323. A Palestine Jewish volunteer in the Stevedores' unit, Libya, 1943.
324. Enzo Sereni with two colleagues in the army in Italy.
325. Enzo Sereni's commemorative stamp, 1988.
326. The special cancellation introduced for the Kibbutz Nezer Sereni.
327. Hannah Senesh. Executed by the Nazis in 1944 at the age of 23
328. Hannah Senesh with some of her group during the war.
329. Havivah Reik. Executed by the Germans in Slovakia.
330. Havivah Reik's commemorative stamp 1988.
331. The special cancellation introduced for Kibbutz Lavahot Havivah.
332. Bergen Belsen 1946.
333. Soldiers of the RASC dancing a *Hora* with refugees 'adopted' by the unit at Giovinazzo, Italy 1944.
334. A soldier of the Brigade at the entrance to the ruined Warsaw Ghetto in June 1945.

335. A Brigade rabbi officiates at a wedding between a Brigade soldier and a Dutch Jewish Woman in Holland.
336. Soldiers of the Brigade beside a crematorium at Bergen Belsen, 1945.
337. A Seder service organized by the Eretz Israel Volunteers in the Bari Refugee Camp, Italy 1944.
338. Posters announcing a football match between the Brigade team and a Belgian club Maccabi-Belgique in Brussels, October 1945.
339. A party given by the Brigade for Jewish children found in monasteries and Christian homes. Nijmegen, Holland, 1946.
340. Registration for the Jewish Brigade Group in Britain.
341. Four prominent veterans of the Jewish Brigade.
342. The Second Division Memorial, Kohima.
343. Arthur Louis Aaron, VC.
344. Tommy Gould, VC.
345. John Kenneally, VC.
346. Harry Errington, GC.
347. Harold 'Pop' Newgass, GC.
348. Simmon Latutin, GC.

Foreword

I am greatly appreciative of the opportunity to pay tribute to the brave individuals who fell fighting to protect the freedom that I and the post-war generation enjoy today.

I am proud of my Jewish heritage. The source of my pride is in no small part due to the great contribution made by such heroes as the Jewish serviceman and women who are remembered in this book.

I will, and do, remember them and will ensure that my children do so as well.

Trevor Pears
Pears Foundation, 2010

Acknowledgements to First Edition

I began to collect the material for this book in January 1986, forty years after the end of the Second World War. I am most grateful to all the many individuals and organisations who have given me so much help. If I were to list them all, that list would be a very long one for, apart from receiving information from every corner of the United Kingdom, I have had letters from the United States, Canada, Israel, Burma, Hong Kong, South Africa, Australia and Gibraltar. My warmest thanks go to each one of them but there are some, in particular, without whose work this labour of remembrance could not have been performed.

Researching all the published detail involved the writing of hundreds of letters and making endless telephone calls; in this task the staff at AJEX Headquarters, Sydney Davis (then General Secretary), Esther Goddard and Rosalind Roth, were ever patient in dealing with my requests and (almost) never failing. I will always be in their debt.

To the families and friends who wrote, telling me their sad stories and sending precious photographs (I think I kept my word and returned them all), to Peter Fisher who copied the pictures, and Sylvia McCallum, who computerised the Roll of Honour (coping so patiently with endless additions and changes as new material came in) – I will always be grateful.

I would like to acknowledge the help given by AJEX Branches and synagogues and by Simon Corney, who went through every issue of the *Jewish Chronicle* published between 3 September 1939 and the end of the war, checking the 'In Memoriam' columns; Her Majesty's Forces Jewish Committee, whose card index casualties revealed so much; Mr Tim Ward and his staff at the Prince Consort's Library in Aldershot, who checked the detail of the Army Roll; Mr David Spector and the late Mr Zvi Dagan (Israel War Veterans), who were largely responsible for material relating to the Palestine Jewish volunteers and the Jewish Infantry Brigade Group; Mr Basil Greenby, who allowed me to reprint his Yiddish poster advertising 'The King of Lampedusa' and to Dannie Abse for his poem about his cousin Sidney – both, perhaps, providing a little light relief in an otherwise solemn work; and the distinguished men who have written dedications and articles. The sacrifice of their time is much appreciated.

Of necessity, I have spent very many hours away from my wife during the writing of this book. I know she understood what it meant to me and I appreciate and thank her for that understanding.

Lastly, I have to offer my sincere thanks to my publishers, Brassey's, who made it all possible and to the editorial team of Gerald Smith of AJEX and Brigadier Bryan Watkins of Brassey's whose combined expertise transformed what was a compilation of articles, pictures and lists into a record which I hope will take a proud place in the archive of Anglo–Jewish history.

Henry Morris
London, May 1989

Acknowledgements
to First Edition of Addendum

In addition to Peter Sharpe, I am most grateful to Geoffrey Negus of Solihull for sending me names and details of casualties which did not appear in the original publication. I would also like to thank Martin Sugarman of Hackney for photographs and details of graves of Jewish Servicemen buried in the Military Cemetery at Ravenna, Italy, and those who died in the Far East.

I also have to thank Terry Shelley for her typing assistance, the Israel Maritime Merchant Service for information concerning the SS *Epinura* and the SS *Har Zion* and Ian Nissin who kept his father's press clippings and photographs, collected from wartime issues of the *Jewish Chronicle*.

Since the publication of *We Will Remember Them* in November 1989, I have received many enquiries from relatives of those listed in the book, particularly from Israel and the USA, some even referring to the First World War! In dealing with them, I could always rely on the help of Esther Goddard, Sheila Sieff and Harry Farbey at AJEX HQ and, especially, the Commonwealth War Graves Commission.

Finally to Hilary and Lionel Halter, their daughter, Mrs Sharon Drucker, and Martin Stead go my sincere thanks for their patience and cooperation in carrying out an exacting and unusual job.

Henry Morris
London, 1994

Author's Introduction
to the First Edition, 1989

There were several reasons why I compiled this record, but I think the most important is the regrettable fact that more than forty years after the war against Germany and Japan ended, there has been no official tribute to those of the Jewish faith who died while serving in the Armed forces of the Crown.

I hope that this book, written with the consent of the Association of Jewish Ex-Servicemen and Women, will go some way towards correcting this neglect.

Perhaps a lesser reason was my own view that after serving four years in the Royal Navy, surviving whole and uninjured and able to rejoin my wife and family and start a life of my own, I felt it was not enough to parade each year at the Cenotaph in Whitehall, in silent tribute to the fallen and to take part in a service of Remembrance.

Somewhere, details of those who paid the supreme sacrifice had to be written down with pride for all to see and to indicate poignantly that Jewish Servicemen, Servicewomen and civilians, played their part.

I was warned, when I set out on my task, that to obtain information so long after the war, would be very difficult. However, I was determined to see it through. It meant such a lot to me. Somewhere there had to be brothers and sisters, nephews, nieces, cousins of those who died, who remembered and mourned. There had to be newspaper reports, even an official file, not complete perhaps, but available. I found as much material as was possible.

The initial response to my letters in the Press, requesting information and photographs was most encouraging. People were kind enough to send me pictures they had treasured for decades. I copied and returned them with my sincere and grateful thanks. I read stories that were heartbreaking and dramatic, the stuff of books, films and plays, but they were real, life and death war. My researches uncovered many strange stories.

The grim irony of men sometimes being killed by their own side in the heat and confusion of battle has happened many times. The death of one, Private Sidney Cohen, held prisoner of war by the Japanese outside Nagasaki when the atom bomb was dropped, was one example. He died of leukaemia, a hazard of war that could not have been foreseen.

The Holocaust and the murder of six million European Jews lives with us all. Captain Maurice Pertschuk, MBE, a British officer, was hanged at Buchenwald. Captain Isadore Newman was shot at Mauthausen.

I have, in a separate section, referred to the experience of Warrant Officer Sidney Cohen in Lampedusa, and in a separate chapter to the story of Hannah Senesh, that brave young woman who was born in Hungary and emigrated to Palestine. She later volunteered to parachute into Yugoslavia as a member of the British SOE. Courage such as hers deserves special tribute.

I am sure that hidden away among the names and details listed are many other stories yet untold, but for now, let it be enough that their names are recorded.

The men in the photographs looked so young. I say men, though so many were really boys. Often during the year or so it took me to obtain the details I needed, my feelings while writing them down, got the better of me. Several times I came across boys with whom I was at school, with some of whom I spent the happiest days of my youth at the West Central Boys' Club. For them I needed no pictures. I saw their faces clearly and I felt sad, so sad.

'Missing, believed killed, air operations' became a frequent and familiar phrase, as did 'killed in action'. Sometimes there was a citation for bravery, a mention in despatches. Most times not, but they all served and died. Where I obtained details of their places of burial, I have recorded them briefly. Further facts are available. It is only right that a man's last resting place should be known. There are so many with no known graves. They have their memorials, and while AJEX exists, they will be remembered and honoured. I hope that those who come after us will continue to pay them tribute. I have not listed the names by rank. In death, all are equal.

The Records Department of the Ministry of Defence, the Commonwealth War Graves Commission (CWGC) and the many Regimental Associations kept no records; the CWGC does not specify the religion of the deceased on their Central Register.

The Rolls of Honour which form Part Two of this book are based upon my researches and information provided by some of the relatives of those listed. Such information was inevitably sketchy in many cases and such things as unit titles were often vague or inaccurate. Thus the rolls represent the best information I was able to obtain but I cannot pretend that they are anywhere near as complete or accurate as one would wish in a work of this sort. However the choice was clear: to publish what was available as a very sincere, if incomplete, tribute to the fallen or to abandon the project – which was not to be contemplated. I know that those nearest to the names listed will feel that the important thing to them was that their relative's name should be recorded, even if some detail was missing or uncertain.

One of the first things given to us on joining the Services was our identity disc or 'Dog Tag' as we familiarly called it. This disc was clearly embossed with one's religion. Many graves whose headstones carry the Star of David are evidence that the Commission are to be thanked many times for their tremendous help and co-operation in seeing that Jewish graves in every theatre of war, were properly dedicated.

On the advice of the Reverend Dr Isaac Levy, a war-time Chaplain and for many years Honorary Chaplain to AJEX, I searched the records of the Jewish Committee for His Majesty's Forces. There, high on a top shelf, perhaps unlooked at since the end of the war, I found dozens of card index files containing the names of most of the men and women who served, and some of those who died. This was to be my main source of information, though more was to come from individuals, from the *Jewish Chronicle* and from Israel. In addition to those in the British Forces, there were names of some from the Commonwealth, Czechs, Poles, a few from the United States and almost 700 from what was then Palestine and under the administration of the British Mandate. This was plainly a large proportion of the Jewish population at that time. I wonder how widely this is known and appreciated.

There is a chapter in Part Two of this book describing the history of the Jewish Infantry Brigade, its operations and how, after the war, it helped to bring relief to the survivors of the concentration camps.

Just under 3,000 British Jews died in the Armed Forces – about 1,900 in the Army; 900 in the Royal Air Force and 200 in the Royal Navy and Merchant Navy. Some 65,000 Jews fought, just under 20 per cent of the Jewish population.

There are those today on the extreme Left and Right of politics who distort history with false accusations and revisionist lies. They would better spend their time learning how, as true citizens, we shared in the struggle against Fascism while so many who voted against the Nazis in pre-war Germany were sucked into the maw of the evil Hitler regime. Rather than accuse the founders of modern Israel of 'collaboration' they would realise the tremendous sacrifices made by the youth of that country, even while some Socialists were justifying the pact between Nazi Germany and Soviet Russia.

The war against Japan did not end until later in 1945, thus prolonging the misery of those who were prisoners in places such as Changi, or who slaved on the infamous Burma-Siam railway and died from disease, largely as a result of malnutrition, forced labour and privation. Many of the Jewish graves have been visited and photographed by members of AJEX and I am most grateful to Mr Maurice Kingston for his help in this connection.

I have tried to give extra information where I had it, but in some cases, all I could find were names, taken from a synagogue 'Roll of Honour'. I have selected the stories of a few individuals to reflect the courage and spirit of all those Jews who fought. There will be many other such stories to match them.

I hope this work will serve its purpose as a lasting written memorial to those of the Jewish faith who died serving their country.

The message on the 2nd Division's Memorial at Kohima perhaps says it best: *'When you go home, tell them of us and say: "For your tomorrow, we gave our today".'*

Henry Morris
London, 1989

Author's Introduction to the Addendum to the First Edition

We Will Remember Them was published in November 1989 by Brasseys, and launched with the great help of Norman Morris and the Balfour Jubilee Trust. It was well received by reviewers in Britain and Israel, has sold well and has found a place on the bookshelves of many prestigious libraries. These include the Wiener, Mocatta, Imperial War Museum, the Library of Congress Washington USA, Monash University, Melbourne Australia, President Herzog of Israel, Houses of Parliament and Her Majesty The Queen to name but a few.

It took me nearly four years to research and it proved a difficult task so many years after the war had ended. I said, in the introduction, that I knew the book was incomplete and not an absolute and comprehensive record of every Jew who had died while in the Armed Forces from 1939–45. The uncertainties and incomplete recording of events and facts make it impossible to achieve the very last name. However, this did not deter me from the project and I tried to obtain as full a Roll of Honour as I possibly could. I hope that the families and friends of those mentioned have derived some consolation from the fact that the names of their loved ones, and the sacrifice they made, are now part of recorded Anglo-Jewish history. To those who have not found the names for which they were looking, I humbly apologise and hope that this Addendum will correct the omission. To those few who, despite my very many proof readings, have found a misspelt name or a wrong rank or date, again, I say "sorry" but there are reasonable explanations, bearing in mind that there are more than 3,700 listings gathered from every theatre of war. I hope they will understand and forgive.

The formula I used to determine a probable figure for Jewish casualties was based on the proportion of the Anglo-Jewish community compared with the population of the United Kingdom in 1939 – approximately one half of one per cent. When applied to the 295,000 UK casualties, this provided a probable figure of about 1,800 Jews. The eventual figure far exceeded this – it totalled now almost 3,000 British and 700

Palestinian Jews. However, as I have said above, time has shown that these were not really the final figures. This Addendum lists nearly 400 additional names, for which I am largely indebted to Peter Sharpe of Chatham for the tremendous help he gave me.

He has collected a vast number of records of those who died in the 1939–45 war and, after borrowing my book from Chatham Public Library, he wrote to me offering his help. On behalf of AJEX and the Jewish community, I offer my sincere thanks to him for providing additional information about deaths, burial sites etc. and making this booklet possible.

In *We Will Remember Them* I had hoped to include the story and Roll of Honour of the Polish Jews who served with the British Armed Forces but a number of difficulties prevented this. It was a story that needed to be told, for their country was brutally invaded by the Nazis and Soviets and ravaged by both. Theirs was an epic story of escape to freedom and the chance to fight their oppressors. I am grateful to Dr Leonard Kurzer, Chairman of the Polish Jewish ex-Servicemen's Association, for his contribution to this Addendum. I know he has been anxious to place on record the part played by Polish Jews, despite the huge odds against them, in defeating the forces of tyranny.

For many years, various AJEX publications have included the numbers of decorations and awards won by Jews. For the first time, the Addendum contains a comprehensive, detailed list, by name, of the men and women who died, and those who survived, who distinguished themselves by their courage, bravery and devotion to service. For this, I offer my thanks to W/Cdr Wally Zigmond who spent many hours searching our records for those who had been rewarded for their heroism. There are more than 2,500 names and awards and many stories are revealed – too many to tell them all, but here are just a few.

Little is known in this country of the tragedy of the sinking of the SS *Erinpura* on the 1st May 1943 with the loss, in ten minutes, of 148 Palestinian Jews of 462 Coy RASC en route across the Mediterranean from Alexandria to Malta. We are now familiar with the story of how Petty Officer Tommy Gould, of the Submarine HMS *Thresher*, won his VC – risking his life to remove two unexploded bombs from the forward casing, knowing that his submarine might submerge at any moment.

Not so well known, however, is the story of Pilot Officer Eric Stitcher, of the RAF, who, in June 1944, was performing embarkation duties in the Port of London. A flying bomb exploded near railway wagons, loaded with petrol, ammunition and other stores which were being despatched to Normandy. With complete disregard for his own safety, he uncoupled the burning wagons and isolated them, even though he was soaked in petrol and his clothes were burning. He was awarded the MBE.

Flying Officer William Tregar was awarded the DFC for performing 53 operational missions, during one of which he scored a direct hit on an 8,000 ton tanker in Tripoli. And my last example, the Military Cross awarded to Capt J. Segal for his part in the 8th Army capture of Derna.

Since publication, I have spoken to many different groups and organisations, describing how the book was compiled and some of the background history of the Jewish contribution to the British Armed Forces in times of war. The audiences have covered all ages, ranging from my contemporaries to the one to which I most wanted to speak, even if I felt nervous and apprehensive, the Upper Sixth Form of the Jewish Free School in North London. I need not have been afraid for, once they had grasped and understood that they were almost the same ages as the men and women about whom I was talking, and that they, too, could suffer the same experience, they were most attentive and asked many interesting questions.

It often comes as a surprise to audiences when they learn that British Jews served in the Boer War. Indeed, one of the valued items of memorabilia in the Memorial Room in AJEX House is the honourable discharge certificate of Louis Enoch. They are also surprised that five VCs were won by Jews in the First World War and the story of the Zion Mule Corps, which served at Gallipoli in 1915. They are also interested to learn about the great names in Jewish history, such as the Australian, General Sir John Monash, one of the most distinguished generals of the First World War, as well as Ben Gurion, Jabotinsky and Trumpeldor who served in the 38th – 42nd Judean battalions of the Royal Fusiliers.

An interesting spin off to this book has been a closer interest in the clandestine organisation known as the Special Operations Executive, known, more familiarly, as the SOE and learning that many Jews served in it. I have already referred to

Captains Newman, Pertschuk and Rabinovitch who were executed. I have now discovered others – Lt Edward Levine was among thirteen allied officers executed at Flossenburg Camp in 1945; Robert Boiteaux (Nicholas), who survived the war. Gaston Cohen, Bernard Uptaker and Denise Bloch, executed at Ravensbruck, and Marcus Bloom are others about whom I have, so far, learned.

In my introduction to *We Will Remember Them*, I set down the thoughts and feelings that prompted me to compile the Roll of Honour and which are paralleled in the spirit and work of AJEX. Being able to look back nearly fifty years, it is possible to see clearly just how near we came to losing the precious gifts of liberty and freedom, and how close the Jews of Europe came to extermination. It has been said that the price of liberty is eternal vigilance, and recent upheavals in Europe have, once again, shown just how true this is. The 1939–45 war caused the deaths of more than twenty million people and yet there are still some who say that Hitler was right, and that the Holocaust was a hoax. The slaughter of the six million was not only a tragedy for the Jews but for all mankind, for it showed that there is no end to the depth to which man's inhumanity to man can descend.

It is right never to forget that it took the combined armed forces of many nations to bring to an end the horrors let loose by the Germans and Japanese. Among these many nations, no small part was played by the Jews who served their countries, including the Jews of Palestine. I hope that by recording the names of the Jewish men and women who died in that epic struggle, I will have served their families. I also hope that I will have instilled, in the generations to come, an awareness of how we helped to secure victory over those who would have turned free men into slaves.

Henry Morris
1994

Authors' Introduction
to the Second Edition

For this updated version the additional names to those killed have come from many and varied sources: scouring back issues of the *Jewish Chronicle*, AJEX surveys, surfing the CWGC website, letters from AJEX members, books and articles. There may be errors in name spellings caused by transliteration from Polish, Hebrew or German names. Harold Pollins of Oxford was also a great help to our work and Gerald Bean of AJEX, whose astonishing survey of AJEX members, carried out before he died, added many more names to the roll of honour. We had some technical assistance from James Pyman, Joel Sugarman, Ron Goldstein and Saul Issroff. We also thank Shelley Hyams for her painstaking and meticulous editing skills, and Heather Marchant of Vallentine Mitchell for her guidance throughout.

Some post-war deaths have also been included, as have some in the Auxiliary Services such as the Fire Brigade and ARP during the Blitz, but this remains an area requiring further research. We know that over fifty Jewish firemen and one woman were KIA in the Second World War; their names are remembered in *Fighting Back* by Martin Sugarman (London and Portland, OR: Vallentine Mitchell, 2010), the companion volume to this one, and are recorded on the Fire Brigade Memorial at St Paul's.

The surname 'Marks' has 122 entries on the CWGC web site, 100 or so of which are military. Some we know are Jewish from the chaplains' cards but whilst this is certainly a Jewish name and all are probably of Jewish origin, there are many we have been unable to verify and so had to exclude.

The hundreds of additional Jewish awards found by the authors have also come from similar sources, including back issues of *The Jewish Year Book* and assistance from Harold Pollins surfing *The London Gazette* over several years. Some Commonwealth and Polish citizens have been included as they were serving in British Forces at the time, but the actual awards to Commonwealth Jewish servicemen and women are generally here excluded as they have their own Books of Honour, especially the Canadian, Australian and South African Communities. Palestinian Jews (Israel) have been included as they were integral to UK Forces. We have also included some post-war awards such as for Korea and Kenya and also awards to the auxiliary services such as the AFS and ARP.

Whilst we have attempted to make this book a 'definitive' one, we are sure that over the years more names will be found – as has been the case with the First World War Jewish Book of Honour. We appreciate that it is likely that further names will be identified in the future and would ask that any names be forwarded to AJEX where they will be inserted on the AJEX website in their Record of Honour (http://www.ajexroh.org.uk). It has been a case of 'the art of the possible' and we present it warts and all as a final tribute to those who never came home and those whose bravery was recognised in the awards they received during the Second World War in Britain. It is an astonishing record of achievement of a Jewish Community which endured sacrifices and performed deeds, out of proportion to our tiny numbers in the general population. We can be justly proud.

Henry Morris
Martin Sugarman
London, 2011

Introduction
Sir Martin Gilbert

The facts in this book present a remarkable picture of the contribution of British Jews to the fighting forces of Great Britain. The material has been compiled with extraordinary care and vigilance, to present a comprehensive, informative and deeply moving picture of the Jewish contribution to the fighting power and survival of Britain in the Second World War.

Among the lists are those of Jewish prisoners of war of both the Germans and the Japanese, of Jews who served as paratroopers and commandos, of Jews in the Special Forces such as the Long-Range Desert Group and SAS (Special Air Service). There are also lists of Jews who fought in the post-war conflicts in Korea, Kenya, Malaya and Cyprus. At the heart of the book are the lists of all those Jews killed on active service in the Second World War and in post-war campaigns and service.

In the First World War, British Jews had fought in all the war zones: on the Western Front, in Mesopotamia, in Italy, in East Africa, at Gallipoli and in Palestine. In all, around 3,000 British Jews were killed and 6,500 wounded fighting for Britain in that war. In the Second World War, the contribution of British Jews spanned every aspect of the conflict. Of the 350,000 Jews then in Britain, including children and old people, 65,000 men and women served the Crown. This was a far higher percentage than for any other minority. In addition, 70,000 of the half million Jews then living under the British mandate in Palestine volunteered for active duty, and 30,000 served.

In all, 3,700 Jews were killed on active service with the British land, sea and air forces in the Second World War. Of these dead, about 700 were from Palestine. Jews fought in the British Army in France in 1940, in Greece and Crete in 1941, and from 1941 to 1945 in North Africa, Sicily, Italy, France, northern Europe, Germany and in the Far East, including Hong Kong, Singapore and Burma, wherever British forces were in action. There were Jewish soldiers at Dieppe, Monte Cassino and Arnhem, and in all the naval and air battles of the war, including those in the Far East against Japan. Jews were among the prisoners of war and escapees at the notorious Colditz Castle. Among the Jewish prisoners of war of the Japanese was my own cousin, Simmy Gordon.

Each individual story adds lustre to the record of British Jewry. A leading British Army engineer, Brigadier Kisch, was a Jew. He was killed by a mine in the Western Desert. Len Crome, who had been a leading medical officer in the Spanish Civil War against Franco in which many British Jews fought, served in 1944 as a British officer at the battle of Monte Cassino. He was awarded the Military Cross for his help to the wounded. After D-Day, Ken Adam, a pre-war refugee from Berlin, was an RAF pilot in the battle that sealed the fate of the German army in Normandy. Later, as artistic director of the Bond films, he won two Academy Awards.

A Jewish submariner, Tommy Gould, won the Victoria Cross for removing a German shell from the casing of his submarine, saving the lives of its crew.

Brigadier E.C.H. Myers, commanding the Royal Engineers of the 1st Airborne Division, was among those dropped at Arnhem. In Italy, the Jewish Infantry Brigade Group, commanded by Brigadier E.F. Benjamin, fought with its own Star of David insignia. Winston Churchill insisted that the Brigade Group be allowed to fight under the Star of David.

Behind the lines Jews were also active. Among those organising escape lines was Victor Gerson, who had volunteered to be parachuted into German-occupied France. His 'Vic Line' sped hundreds of Allied airmen who had been shot down over France to the safety of Spain, from where they returned to Britain, to fight and fly again. The legendary Vera Atkins, who prepared British agents for work inside Nazi-dominated Europe, was Jewish. Many of the agents were also Jews. Among them, Lieutenant Edward Levine was murdered after capture at Flossenburg, Captain Marcus Bloom at Mauthausen and Denise Bloch at Ravensbruck.

The Palestinian parachutists were members of the British armed forces. Best known among them is Hannah Senesh. She was one of seventeen who were captured, and killed after being taken captive. A Palestinian Jew from Haifa, Peretz Rosenberg, was the first radio operator to be parachuted into Tito's headquarters in the mountains of Croatia, at the very moment when the Germans were attacking. He survived the war. Hannah Billig, an East End doctor, won the George Medal for bravery during the Blitz, when she attended to the wounded even after she herself had been wounded.

These are only a few of the individuals who contributed to Britain's war-making capacity, or who fought for freedom wearing British uniforms. This book is a tribute to their memory, and will be used in every generation to show how much the Jews of Britain were at the forefront of national effort at a time of danger.

Sir Martin Gilbert
London, 2010

Acknowledgements and Tributes
to First and Second Editions

BUCKINGHAM PALACE.

Henry Morris and Martin Sugarman could not have chosen a better time to publish this second edition of 'We Will Remember Them'.
The commemoration of the 65th anniversary of the liberation of Auschwitz has drawn the attention of many millions of people to the dreadful fate of so many Jews during the War. I hope this book will help to remind people of the service and sacrifice of the many Jews who fought with the Armed Services of the Crown. It is a remarkable record and the authors deserve every credit for their diligence and persistence.

Headquarters: AJEX House, 5A East Bank,   Stamford Hill, London, N16 5RT. Tel: 01-800 2844

A Necessary Reminder

(From the First Edition)

As President of AJEX, I record the grateful thanks of all Jewish ex-Servicemen and Women to Henry Morris, who in his introduction explains his reasons for compiling this record.

There were many of us who joined the Territorial Army or Auxiliary Services prior to the War and saw service in many different theatres of this conflict. Sadly, when hostilities ended with the signing of the unconditional surrenders, there was still so much to do to rehabilitate and resettle the pitiful remnant of those who survived the Holocaust.

Not all who served were in the front line, but if it had not been for the efforts of those who looked after us in the heat and dust of battle, I do not think we could have pulled through.

The Division I was in was the first to enter Rome, and later I was privileged to be the first British officer to have a private audience with Pope Pius XII. I informed him about what was going on in the concentration camps and he said: 'We must see that this never happens again'. He repeated this sentence twice.

When our great war leader, Winston Churchill, authorised the establishment of the Jewish Infantry Brigade Group, I was given command of one of its Batteries. My men came from all parts of Europe and a large number from Palestine. We were engaged in many battles including the crossing of the Senio River and the liberation of Bologna. Another memory is of the guard of honour mounted by my Battery for Field Marshal Alexander of Tunis when he took the salute at a march-past of Yugoslav patriots. When we met again on a later occasion, he recalled the smartness of this remarkable Guard.

I also remember when my Battery took charge of a German engineering unit, lifting mines at Venlo, Holland. Earlier, when crossing Austria and Germany, I was in an armoured car which was leading the entire Brigade when we approached an archway before the City of Mannheim. On it was inscribed the word 'Judenrein' (No Jews here). The town was in ruins and as the guns and trucks rumbled by, the German survivors emerged from the debris and the word spread 'Die Juden Kommen' (the Jews are coming). More and more people gathered to watch us pass. When we came to the central square before crossing the Rhine, suddenly there was a scuffle. From the crowd emerged a number of people dressed in Belsen garb. They threw themselves down in front of my truck and kissed the Magen David (Star of David) proudly displayed on it and on all our vehicles.

The Anglo-Jewish contribution to the military effort and sacrifice required to win the war, and by those who fought and died in the Jewish Infantry Brigade Group, is given ample testimony in 'We Will Remember Them'. The Rolls of Honour inscribed within these pages is a necessary reminder that indeed we will do so.

Major Edmund de Rothschild, TD
President of AJEX
1989

FIELD MARSHAL THE LORD BRAMALL, GCB, OBE, MC, JP.

Lieutenancy Office
Westminster City Hall
PO Box 240
Victoria Street
London SW1E 6QP
Tel : (01) 798 3260

The contribution in all ranks of the British Armed Forces of the
Crown by Jewish servicemen and servicewomen in World War II has gone
too long without a fitting literary tribute. I am delighted,
therefore, to commend 'We Will Remember Them' by Henry Morris as an
inspiration not only to new generations of the Jewish Faith but to
everyone who values the cause of peace with honour and the need for
sacrifice and vigilence to defend it.

Bramall
Field Marshal

1989

בס״ד

OFFICE OF THE CHIEF RABBI

TELEPHONE:
01-387 1066
CABLES:
CHIRABINAT LONDON W C 1

ADLER HOUSE,

TAVISTOCK SQUARE,

LONDON, WC1H 9HN

'A TIMELY RE-AFFIRMATION'

Jewish loyalty and service to King and Country during the Second World War against the monster German War machine and its satellites, cannot be measured nor comprehended merely as a statistic; as a mere proportion of the rest of the population's figures. This applies equally to Jews who served in the Allied Forces.

There was always the haunting additional danger facing Jews, that the Nazis, in their frenzied pursuit of death and destruction, were especially geared to the annihilation of all Jews, and for Jewish troops who might become prisoners of war, the Geneva Convention was but little comfort.

Yet the role of honour of those who volunteered, those who fought and those who fell, is truly a glorious reminder of the matchless courage and bravery of our sons and daughters, both in the military and in the civil defence of their country.

'WE WILL REMEMBER THEM' is a timely re-affirmation of our deepest sentiments.

Lord Jakobovits of Regents Park
Chief Rabbi of the United Hebrew Congregations
of the British Commonwealth
1989

ADMIRAL OF THE FLEET SIR JOHN FIELDHOUSE GCB GBE

MINISTRY OF DEFENCE
MAIN BUILDING ROOM 6173
WHITEHALL LONDON SW1A 2HB

Telephone 01-218 2116/6190

CHIEF OF THE DEFENCE STAFF

Dear Mr. Morris,

    I am writing on behalf of my Chiefs of Staff colleagues, to whom you extended an invitation to write tributes to be incorporated in your forthcoming record of those members of the Jewish faith in the Armed Forces who died during the Second World War.

    With my colleagues agreement I enclose a tribute from us all which I hope you will be able to include in your book.

Yours sincerely,

John Fieldhouse

1989

A Moving Act
of Remembrance
(From the First Edition)

On behalf of the Chiefs of Staff, it gives me great pleasure to write a short tribute for this book which records those of the Jewish faith who gave their lives in the cause of freedom while serving in the Armed Forces of the Crown during the Second World War.

The appalling suffering by European Jews, on an almost unimaginable scale, is, of course, well documented and will never be forgotten by those of us who lived through those dark days. But it is important that those who were born in the second half of this century, who have no personal experience of the horrors, deprivations and human waste of war, and who are able to live in the peace and freedom which was won for them at so high a personal cost, do so with ever present testimonies to the ultimate sacrifice of their forebears. Our role in the Services today is to preserve peace by deterring war, and to continue to do this effectively each of the Services depends upon young men and women who, inspired by the supreme example set by those who served before them, are committed to maintaining a free world.

Books such as this by Henry Morris, thus serve an important function, not just in honouring our dead, but in actively focusing the minds of their children and their children's children on why they died and why we live. As can be seen in these pages, there were very many of the Jewish faith who served country, cause and mankind in every corner of the globe and in every part of the Armed Forces; many did not return. I am honoured to have this opportunity to pay tribute to them and I commend this book which in itself is a moving act of remembrance.

Admiral Sir John Fieldhouse
1989

From:- General Sir Edward Burgess

THE ROYAL BRITISH LEGION

48 PALL MALL, LONDON SW1Y 5JY   TELEPHONE 071-973 0633   FAX 071-973 0634
071-930 8131

Patron: Her Majesty The Queen
President: General Sir Edward Burgess.
Chairman: E.R. Jobson, OBE
Vice-Chairman: G.G. Downing
General Treasurer: R.E. Hawkes, FCA
General Secretary: Lt. Col. P.C.E. Crea·
Assistant Secretary: Lt. Col. R.D. Hans

Our Reference:

Your Reference: *29 Aug*

WE WILL REMEMBER THEM

In the Spring of 1990, I went to Kohima in North East India with a party of war widows and veterans to visit the War Cemetery and remember those who gave their lives. One of the party. a veteran of the Royal Norfolk Regiment was Jewish and he had bought with him a list of all Jewish graves in the war cemeteries we visited. Over each one he said Kaddish. It was a very moving act. He was remembering.

This addendum to "We Will Remember Them" comes as no surprise to me. In recent years I have seen much of AJEX and the Jewish ex-servicemen and there is a deep bond of comradeship amongst them. Add this to the deep family bond of the Jewish people and it is easy to understand why Rememberance is a way of life. As President of the Royal British Legion I commend this book and salute all Jews who died for Britain.

With best wishes
yours. ever
General Ted

General Sir Edward Burgess, K.C.B., O.B.E.

1994

ב״ה

OFFICE OF
THE CHIEF RABBI

Adler House Tavistock Square London WC1H 9HN
Telephone: 071-387 1066 Fax: 071-383 4920

WE WILL REMEMBER THEM - Henry Morris

The Association of Jewish Ex-Servicemen and Women carries out a number of functions; it maintains the comradeship engendered in times of shared danger; supports those who, either through battle or advancing years, have found it difficult, if not impossible, to withstand on their own the pressures of daily life; it attempts to ensure that war is abolished for ever.

Pervading its work there is a painful awareness that many who left homes and loved ones did not return from the struggle for human rights and dignity.

AJEX carries out its self-imposed duties with efficiency and sympathy and by its actions has earned a well deserved niche in the framework of Anglo-Jewry.

Henry Morris, in a labour of love, has recorded for future generations the roll of honour of those who made the supreme sacrifice in the Second World War. He has completed the work with care and devotion and the community owes him a debt of gratitude.

The world still teeters on the brink of military conflict and the lessons of the past still remain to be learned and implemented.

May we, through this volume of remembrance, be encouraged to work towards the vision of Isaiah, when swords will be refashioned into ploughshares and spears into pruning hooks; when nations will not lift up weapons of destruction against one another and war will be taught no more. May that time come soon.

1994

חדש ימינו כקדם

The Rt. Hon. The Lord Weatherill, P.C., D.L.
Former Speaker of the House of Commons.

"For Your Tomorrow We Gave Our Today".

As an ex-Serviceman who served in the war I pay tribute to any book that
records the names of those men and women who died while serving in the
Armed Forces defending liberty and freedom.   It was my pleasure a few
years ago to be the guest speaker at the AJEX Annual Remembrance Parade
and Rally where the warmth and loyalty of those present gave me a strong
feeling of comradeship with the veterans.

The teaching of the events of the 1939-45 war and the horror of the Holocaust
will now be part of the national education curriculum, andIam pleased that
thislegislation passed through the House of Commons during the time I was
Speaker.   It is most important that those who, mercifully, have not known
war - its deprivation, pain and human waste - and are able to live in peace
and freedom gained at such human cost, should have written testimony to
those who died in the defence of the freedoms they now enjoy, and perhaps
too lightly take for granted.

"We Will Remember Them" by Henry Morris is just such a testimony, completed
by this Addendum, that should inform generations yet to come of the contributions
made by men and women of the Jewish faith in all theatres of war in overcoming
the forces of tyranny.   The book itself is an act of remembrance and I commend
it to you.

Bernard Weatherill

1994

CHIEF RABBI

We Will Remember Them

I welcome the publication of the enlarged second edition of 'We Will Remember Them'.

The first edition was an invaluable document, not only remembering those who did not return but also commemorating and paying tribute to the contribution of the Jewish Community to British society in so many ways.

Now we are privileged in the new edition to have additional information which shows that one in twenty Jewish servicemen made the supreme sacrifice – a very high proportion indeed.

Henry Morris and Martin Sugarman have between them performed a great service by producing this second volume, reminding us of our debt of gratitude, and bringing to the wider community an appreciation of the part played by the Jewish community in a war that engulfed us all.

I thank the authors and AJEX for this wonderful work, a living memorial to the courage and dedication of so many men and women for whom Jewish and British identity combined in a sense of duty in the battle for freedom, of which we are daily the beneficiaries.

Jonathan Sacks

Chief Rabbi Sir Jonathan Sacks
February 2005/Adar 1 5765

Adler House 735 High Road London N12 0US Tel: 020 8343 6301 Fax: 020 8343 6310 info@chiefrabbi.org www.chiefrabbi.org

Patron Her Majesty The Queen

The Royal British Legion
48 Pall Mall
London SW1Y 5JY

Telephone 020 7973 7200

Legion*line* (Helpline) 08457 725 725
www.britishlegion.org.uk

'We Will Remember Them'

This new and updated edition of 'We Will Remember Them' is being published in the year when the whole nation is commemorating the 65th Anniversary of victory in World War II and must surely take its place among the authoritative records of the war. In providing a list of members of the Jewish Faith, who sacrificed their lives in the conflict, it will be a source of reference for relatives and their descendants, as well as researchers and historians.

We in The Royal British Legion hold Remembrance to be an important facet of our tradition and we commend the Jewish community, who ensure that their lost ones will never be forgotten.

The book also provides an insight to the great contribution made by Jewish Service men and women in the Armed Services of the Crown, towards achieving that victory and the civilized way of life, which we all enjoy sixty-five years later.

Effingham.

The Earl of Effingham
National President
The Royal British Legion
2010

Tribute to We Will Remember Them

I am delighted to write a Foreword to this second edition of We Will Remember Them. Since the original publication twenty-one years ago, Henry Morris and Martin Sugarman, the authors, have researched and now include the names and details of 600 more Jewish men and women who served and died in the Second World War, together with hundreds more with citations for bravery and a complete list of honours and awards. The second volume is now therefore a comprehensive record of the contribution made by Jewish servicemen and women, in all ranks of the British Armed Forces in the Second World War.

I believe that like its predecessor it will provide a worthy tribute to those of the Jewish faith who valued the cause of peace with honour and were prepared to make the ultimate sacrifice to secure it; and that it will also act as an inspiration to future generations of their brothers and sisters.

Bramall

Field Marshal

Field Marshal The Lord Bramall, KG GCB OBE MC
2010

March 2010

The year 2010 marks the sixty-fifth Anniversary of the end of the
Second World War. As we commemorate those momentous
events, we will remember all those who served in our Armed
Forces during the conflict and who did so much to preserve our
Nation's freedom; we will honour especially those who gave their
lives. It is particularly fitting, therefore, that this revised edition of
'We Will Remember Them' is being published at the same time. It
represents a vital record of those Jewish men and women who
died while serving in the Armed Forces during the War and also
provides an important insight into the campaigns in which Jewish
personnel were engaged. We are therefore pleased and proud to
commend 'We Will Remember Them' as a tribute to the individual
personnel whose names it records as an inspiration to succeeding
generations.

**Former Minister
for Veterans**

**Former Chief of the
Defence Staff**

3RD BATTALION THE PARACHUTE REGIMENT

Candahar Barracks
Tidworth
Hants

14 July 1982.

Dear Mr & Mrs Burt.

I am writing this short letter to the memory of your son. It weighs very heavily on my shoulders that as their company commander I had so little time to get to know the young soldiers who died during the battle for Mount Longdon. As long as I live I will never forget the courage and spirit of the soldiers it was my honour and privilege to lead and fight besides, and it was the sort of courage and example shown by your son that enabled us to win against great odds.

I note with great satisfaction that it looks as if you will be able to bring him home now for I know that is what you dearly want.

I know that no matter how much I write your sorrow will not be lessened but I would only ask that we who remain in B company may be allowed to share your grief for the memory and example of your son will live on with us.

Yours Mike Argue

Pte Jason Stuart Burt, B Comp., 3 Para, KIA Mt Longdon, Falklands, 12/6/82 (exactly 27 years before Lt Paul Mervis). Aged 17 years, he was the youngest British casualty of the Falklands War.

Letter sent to Jason's parents by his CO

Lt Paul Mervis was born on 30 September 1981. After a gap year in Israel and university, Paul became a journalist with *The Spectator* but was attracted to the army by a keen sense of duty and adventure. He was a natural leader, highly respected by fellow soldiers, peers and superiors. His Company Commander Major Alastair Field described him as one in a million: 'I have never met a more passionate or engaged young officer in my career in the army', he said.

Paul, from London, was on foot patrol in Afghanistan with his Regiment, 2nd Rifles, on 12 June 2009 when he was killed by an Improvised Explosive Device.

He was buried with full military honours at a Jewish ceremony at Aldershot Military Cemetery.

PART ONE
Remembrance

The Proud War Record of British Jews

Their Full Share

British Jews bore their full share of the war in every quarter of the globe in the operations on sea, on land, and in the air, as they continued to do in the Korean conflict.

About 10,000 Jewish refugees, who had sought refuge here from Hitlerism just before the war, enlisted in Alien Pioneer companies and so proved their worth, trust and martial qualities that many were transferred to first-class fighting battalions, some becoming Commandos and Paratroopers, and not a few being commissioned, and awarded decorations.

Palestinian Jews served with the Royal Navy, Army and Royal Air Force. They were in France in 1940, in the campaigns in Greece and Crete, in the Western Desert, and again in Europe.

The Jewish Infantry Brigade Group, commanded by Brigadier E F Benjamin, CBE, fought in Italy, and its members won four MCs, seven MMs, two OBEs, four MBEs, two American awards, and sixty-eight Mentions in Despatches.

65,000 Served

Of the estimated Jewish population of 350,000 in the United Kingdom, something like 65,000 Jewish men and women served during the last war in the British Armed Forces, of whom 14,000 were in the Royal Air Force, and 2,000 in the Royal Navy. The figures are those of men and women actually contacted by Jewish Chaplains or whose names have appeared in authentic and checked nominal rolls. They do not include Dominion personnel or the 30,000 Jewish men and women who voluntarily enlisted in the British Forces in Palestine.

Casualties and Honours

According to the records in the office of the Senior British Jewish Chaplain, just under 3,000 Jews gave their lives, and just under 700 Palestinian Jews.

Killed or Died on Service

Army 1867
Royal Navy (including Royal Marines and Merchant Navy) 215
RAF 909
Palestinian Jews 684

Awards

VC	3	Bar to MM	3
GC	3	DFM	64
CB	6	Bar to DFM	5
CBE	28	AFC	19
OBE	98	GM	20
MBE	165	BEM	96
DSO	44	Mention in Despatches	1,105
DSC	25	US Legion of Merit	6
Bar to DSC	4	American DSO	1
MC	168	American DFC	7
Bar to MC	3	US Bronze Star	12
DFC	190	Legion D'Honneur	9
Bar to DFC	44	Croix de Guerre	40
DCM	30	Cert. of Gallantry	40
DSM	35	Other Foreign Awards	38
DSM & Bar	1	Colonial Police Medal	14
CGM	3	Air Force Medal	5
MM	153	Air Efficiency Award (AEA)	3

As at December 2010

The Sacrifice

Many ask about the percentage of Jews in the Second World War who participated or were killed, in comparison with the general population. This was attempted in the British Jewry Book of Honour for the First World War. According to the research assistants at the Imperial War Museum, from the Central Statistical Office (CSO), *Fighting with Figures*, intro. Anthony M. Brown (London: HMSO, 1995), numbers are as follows:

■ Servicemen and Women from the UK killed – 295,000.

■ John Ellis, *The WW2 Databook* (Aurum Books, 1993), states that 5,900,000 were under arms out of a population of 45,000,000.

■ We know that in the UK just under 3,000 Jews were killed in the Armed Services and about 65,000 served as a conservative estimate, from a population of about 350,000 – this from the Jewish Chaplains cards and also the CWGC website.

■ Thus simple arithmetic shows that 3,000 Jewish killed out of 65,000 served is about 4.6 per cent, approximately the same as 295,000 out of 5,900,000 in the general population. But 3,000 Jewish dead out of the Jewish population of 350,000 is 0.86 per cent, whereas 295,000 out of 45,000,000 in the general population is 0.66 per cent – a sacrifice in the Jewish community which is proportionally about 30 per cent greater, and for the small size, had a greater impact on the small Jewish community.

■ For those serving, 65,000 out of 350,000 in the Jewish population is 18.6 per cent; 5,900,000 out of 45,000,000 is 13 per cent, so the Jewish response was greater.

Leaving aside possible slight distortions such as differences in the population structure of the Jewish population compared to the national population, and luck of the draw as to where any Service Personnel were sent to fight, these numbers still remain a great tribute to the patriotism, determination and courage of British Jewry, mirrored incidentally in all Allied Forces in the Second World War in which Jews fought, and especially from Mandate Palestine/Israel.

These figures are thus offered in a spirit of showing that the Jewish contribution was by any standard very significant, from a very small ethnic British minority, and dispels the hateful and deceitful lies and myths, perpetrated and perpetuated by anti-Semites that Jews did not fight or sacrifice.

Special Tributes and Messages
IN MEMORIAM

Figure 1. Field Marshal Sir Gerald Templer GCB GCMG KBE DSO unveiling the Memorial to Jewish Servicemen with no known graves in the United Synagogue's Willesden Cemetery on Sunday 14 March 1960. This was the first Jewish National War Memorial to be erected by the Commonwealth War Graves Commission to a design approved by AJEX and the United Synagogue.

Figure 2. Beaten pewter plaque in the RAF Church of Saint Clement Danes, Strand, London, bearing the twelve Jewish tribal signs and inscribed in Hebrew and English: 'Dedicated to the Memory of Those Who Fell 1939–1945, by the Israel Branch, Royal Air Force Association'.

Figure 3. Roll of Honour in Childwall Synagogue, Liverpool.

Sidney Abse

As a boy, Sidney Abse lived with his parents in Cardiff before they moved to Birmingham.

Joining the Army under age – saying he was older than he was – Sidney died at Dunkirk with a Bible in his hand.

His cousin Dannie, the poet, wrote these verses about him and they are reproduced here with Dannie's kind permission. They were first published in his *Collected Poems 1948–1976* and later in *Ash on a Young Man's Sleeve* in which Sidney is given the name 'Clive'.

Cousin Sidney

Dull as a bat, said my mother
of cousin Sidney in 1940 that time he tried
to break his garden swing, jumping on it,
size 12 shoes at fifteen the tallest boy
in the class, taller than loping Dan Morgan
when Dan Morgan wore his father's top hat.

Duller than a bat, said my father
when hero Sidney lied about his age
to claim rough khaki, silly ass;
and soon, somewhere near Dunkirk,
some foreign corner was forever Sidney
though uncle would not believe it.

Missing not dead please God, please,
he said, and never bolted the front door,
never string taken from the letter box,
never the hall light off lest his one son
came home through a night of sleet
whistling, We'll meet again.

Aunt crying and raw in the onion air
of the garden (the unswinging empty swing)
her words on a stretched leash
while uncle shouted, Bloody Germans.
And on November llth, two howls of
silence even after three decades

till last year, their last year,
when uncle and aunt also went missing,
missing alas, so that now strangers
have bolted their door and cut the string
and no-one at all (the hall so dark)
waits up for Sidney, silly ass.

Dannie Abse

Warrant Officer Sidney Cohen 'The King of Lampedusa'

Even the tragedy of war has its lighter side, as reflected in the remarkable experience of Warrant Officer Sidney Cohen of the Royal Air Force to whom the people of the Mediterranean island of Lampedusa surrendered when the aircraft he was piloting force-landed there in June 1943. The incident was to become the subject of the longest running play in the history of the Yiddish Theatre, staged at the Grand Palais in London's East End. Sergeant Cohen, as he then was, will forever be identified by the title of the play – 'The King of Lampedusa'. Sadly, he never saw it, as he was killed in a plane crash on his way home to England.

Figure 4. Warrant Officer Sidney Cohen.

Figure 5. A poster from the Yiddish Theatre advertising 'The King of Lampedusa'.

Figure 6. This plaque, in memory of some of our women members of the Special Operations Executive (SOE), executed at Ravensbrück Concentration Camp, was unveiled by 'Odette' in the spring of 1993. Odette, GC, later Mrs Hallowes, and Peter Churchill directed behind-the-lines activities in wartime France. After conversation with Mrs Hallowes and Joe Day, who first drew attention to the absence of a British memorial on the camp site, AJEX approached government offices and Gervase Cowell Former Chair of the Special Forces Club Historical Committee. It is known that Denise Bloch was Jewish.

Figure 7. Four companies – Alien Pioneer Corps. Information from Phineas May.

Awards for Bravery in the Field

Authors' Note

Copies of the original citations for the awards to these gallant men have been used here. Produced as they were, in the field, the originals have inevitably suffered and are damaged or blurred. Nevertheless, they have been included because they bear the endorsements of so many famous commanders including Field Marshals Montgomery and Alexander. Those endorsements in themselves set a special seal upon them and are a fitting tribute to the gallantry of the recipients.

CAPTAIN L S GOLDSTONE MC *The Royal Fusiliers*

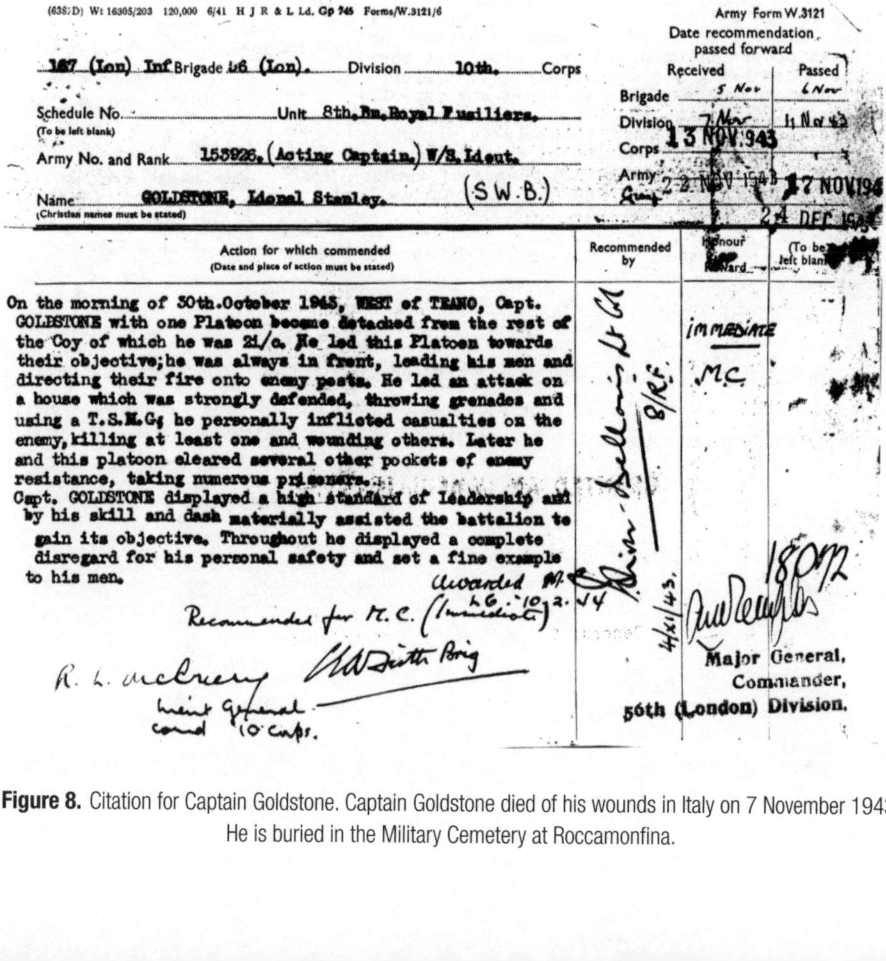

Figure 8. Citation for Captain Goldstone. Captain Goldstone died of his wounds in Italy on 7 November 1943. He is buried in the Military Cemetery at Roccamonfina.

LIEUTENANT J GRENNAN MC *The London Irish Rifles*

485

6281. W.41236/577. 240M. 12/42. Wy.L.P. 56. Form./W.3121/8.		Army Form W.3121

Date recommendation passed forward

			Received	Passed
167 Brigade 56 (Lon) Division 5 Corps		Brigade	22 Jan	23 Jan
Schedule No. _____ (To be left blank)	Unit 1/London Irish Rifles/RUR	Division	9 Feb 45	10 Feb 45
Rank and Army or Personal No. W/Lieut 233303		Corps	1 FEB 1945	1 5 FEB 1945
		Army	17 FEB 45	18 FEB 45
Name GRENNAN ~~GEOFFREY~~ Jeffrey		AFHQ.	2 0 SEP 1945	
(Christian names must be stated)				

Action for which commended (Date and place of action must be stated)	Recommended by	Honour or Reward	(To be left blank)

On the night of 24/25 Dec 44 Lieut Grennan was in command of a fighting patrol detailed to destroy the enemy in and around the house at 333284 (FAENZA, Sheet 99 I NE). During the approach to the house the enemy was encountered in several previously unlocated weapon pits about one hundred yards from the house. With great determination and despite the fire from two enemy MGs (one on each flank) Lieut Grennan led his patrol straight into close quarters, the patrol thereby killing three of the enemy and wounding one, two others being probably killed. The enemy in the house being now thoroughly on the alert Lieut Grennan successfully withdrew his patrol. The exact information which he brought back of the enemy's dispositions was invaluable in planning the subsequent Coy attack, which captured this position. The determination and powers of leadership of this officer were entirely responsible for this successful patrol action.

M.C.
Immediate

Lt Col J A Sperling DSO
Comd
1/LIR.RUR

M.C
21.6.45

Brig
Comd
167 Inf Bde

Lt-Gen

Lieutenant-General
Commander, 5 Corps

N. Whitfield
Major General
Commander
56th (London) DIVISION

35632.

P.T.O.

Figure 9. Citation for Lieutenant Grennan. He died from the effects of head wounds received in Italy, on 24 November 1947, shortly after his marriage to Miss Josephine Druker. He is remembered on the Brookwood Memorial (from *JC* 5/12/47 – thanks to Harold Pollins). Lt Grennan's burial place is not known.

CAPTAIN L HERBERT MC *Royal Army Medical Corps*

```
69 Bde.                          Substitute A.F. 3128
50 (H) Div.                      Date recommendation  used forward
13 Corps                         Bde .............
                                 Div 24/2/43...27/7/43
No.   101517                     Corps 27.43.5.8.43
Rank.WS/Captain                  Army 29/7/43.......
Name.  HERBERT, Leopold          ArmyGp 11 Aug 43   6 - 9 - 43
RAMC att. 6th Green Howards.
```

Action for which recommended	Recommended by	Honour or Reward	To be left blank
On the night of 17/18 July 1943, 6th Green Howards put in an attack following up 168 Inf. Bde. to extend the bridgehead over the Simeto river. Captain Herbert the medical officer, followed his Bn. into the attack and established his R.A.P. well forward of the river and close to the main road in order to ensure that no casualties could miss the R.A.P. no matter from what unit they came. Throughout the night the whole area of the road on which the R.A.P. was situated was under really heavy arty. fire and Captain Herbert continued to work unceasingly and to evacuate successfully casualties from all the units in action in that area. His coolness under the arty. fire and his untiring efforts gave tremendous confidence and encouragement to his staff and orderlies and his excellent work under most hazardous conditions undoubtedly saved the lives of the many casualties who passed through his R.A.P. that night.		M.C. (Immediate)	

Lieut. General, Commander, 13 Corps.
Major-General, Commander, 50 Div.

Granted an Immediate *M.C*

H.R. Alexander.
General,
General Officer Commanding-in-Chief,
15 Army Group.

Figure 10. Citation for Captain Herbert. Captain Herbert, who was Regimental Medical Officer to the 6th Battalion The Green Howards, was killed by a mortar bomb which scored a direct hit on his Regimental Aid Post in Sicily in August 1943.

MAJOR C S ROSENHEIM MC *The Welch Regiment*

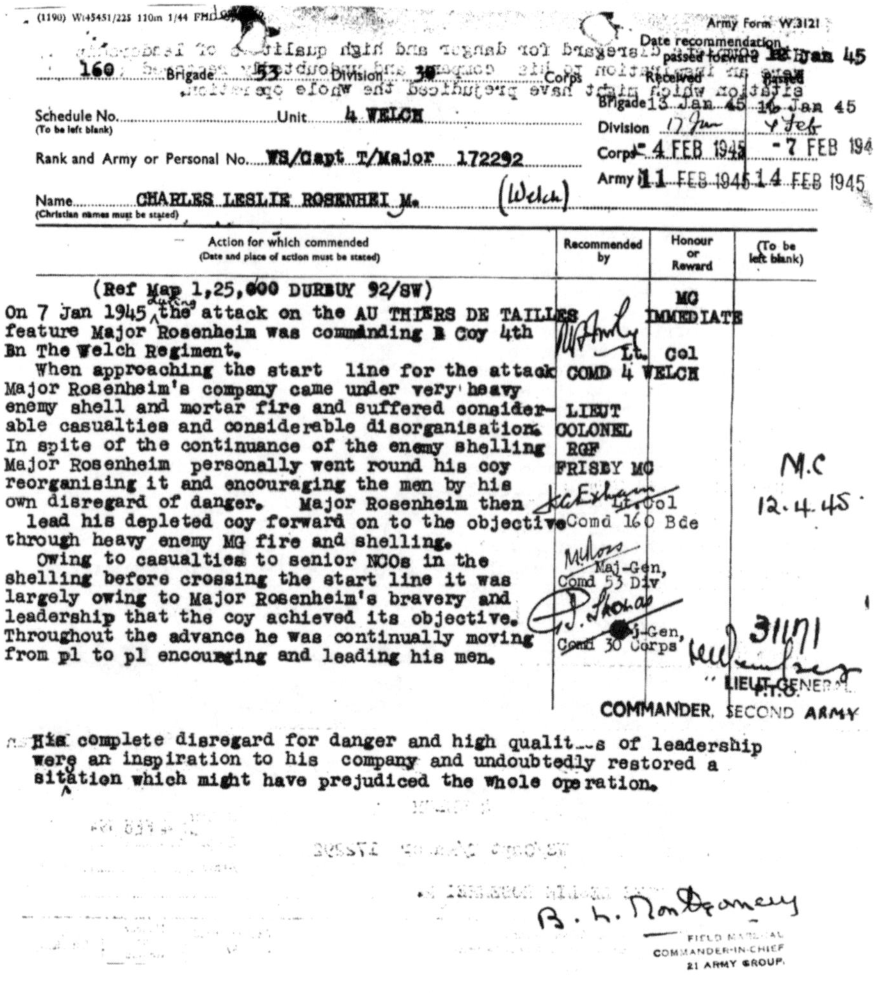

(1190) W/45451/225 110m 1/44 FMD   Army Form W.3121

Date recommendation passed forward Jan 45

160 Brigade 53 Division 30 Corps   Received

Brigade 13 Jan 45 16 Jan 45

Schedule No.............   Unit......4 WELCH   Division 17 Jan 4 Feb
(To be left blank)

Rank and Army or Personal No. WS/Capt T/Major 172292   Corps 4 FEB 1945 - 7 FEB 194

Army 11 FEB 1945 14 FEB 1945

Name.............. CHARLES LESLIE ROSENHEIM M. (Welch)
(Christian names must be stated)

Action for which commended (Date and place of action must be stated)	Recommended by	Honour or Reward	(To be left blank)
(Ref Map 1,25,000 DURBUY 92/SW) On 7 Jan 1945 the attack on the AU THIERS DE TAILLES feature Major Rosenheim was commanding B Coy 4th Bn The Welch Regiment. When approaching the start line for the attack Major Rosenheim's company came under very heavy enemy shell and mortar fire and suffered considerable casualties and considerable disorganisation. In spite of the continuance of the enemy shelling Major Rosenheim personally went round his coy reorganising it and encouraging the men by his own disregard of danger. Major Rosenheim then lead his depleted coy forward on to the objective through heavy enemy MG fire and shelling. Owing to casualties to senior NCOs in the shelling before crossing the start line it was largely owing to Major Rosenheim's bravery and leadership that the coy achieved its objective. Throughout the advance he was continually moving from pl to pl encouraging and leading his men.	MC IMMEDIATE Lt. Col COMD 4 WELCH LIEUT COLONEL RGF FRISBY MC Lt-Col Comd 160 Bde Maj-Gen, Comd 53 Div D.Thomas Lt-Gen, Comd 30 Corps LIEUT-GENERAL COMMANDER, SECOND ARMY	M.C 12.4.45. 31/1/71	

His complete disregard for danger and high qualities of leadership were an inspiration to his company and undoubtedly restored a situation which might have prejudiced the whole operation.

B. L. Montgomery

FIELD MARSHAL COMMANDER-IN-CHIEF 21 ARMY GROUP.

Figure 11. Citation for Major Rosenheim. Major Rosenheim was killed in action in North West Europe in February 1945.

CORPORAL M ROSENFIELD MM *The Loyal Regiment*

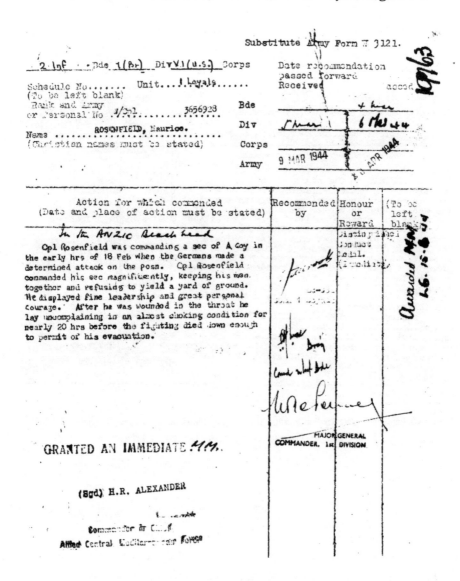

Substitute Army Form W 3121.

2 Inf Bde 1(Br) Div VI(U.S.) Corps

Schedule No....... Unit...1.Loyals......
(To be left blank)

Rank and Army
or Personal No .A/Cpl...... 3656928

Name ...... ROSENFIELD, Maurice.
(Christian names must be stated)

Date recommendation
passed forward
Received   accod

Bde   + hrs

Div   9 Mar   6 Mar 44

Corps

Army   9 MAR 1944   6 APR 1944

Action for which commended (Date and place of action must be stated)	Recommended by	Honour or Reward	(To be left blank)
In the ANZIO Beachhead Cpl Rosenfield was commanding a sec of A Coy in the early hrs of 18 Feb when the Germans made a determined attack on the posn. Cpl Rosenfield commanded his sec magnificently, keeping his men together and refusing to yield a yard of ground. He displayed fine leadership and great personal courage. After he was wounded in the throat he lay uncomplaining in an almost choking condition for nearly 20 hrs before the fighting died down enough to permit of his evacuation.		Distinguished Conduct Medal. (Immediate)	Awarded MM L.G. 15.8.44

GRANTED AN IMMEDIATE *MM*.

(Sgd) H.R. ALEXANDER

Commander in Chief
Allied Central Mediterranean Force

MAJOR GENERAL
COMMANDER, 1st DIVISION

Figure 12. Citation for Corporal Rosenfield. Corporal Rosenfield was killed in action whilst saving a wounded comrade in Italy in September 1944.

CORPORAL H. J. SHUTZ MM *The Rifle Brigade*

In lieu of A.F.W. 3121.
Date recommendation
passed forward
Received | Passed

...29. Armd... Brigade...11 Armd..Division .30..........Corps

Schedule No................... Unit.8th Bn.The Rifle Brigade
(To be left blank)

Rank and Army or Personal No...6923825 A/Cpl.

Name................ Shutz, Harold, Jack.
(Christian names must be stated)

Brigade /..... /..... /12 Sep 44
Division ...... 18 Sep 44
Corps 20 SEP 44 2 8 SEP 194
Army 28 OCT 194 6 NOV. 1944

Action for which recommended (Date and place of action must be stated)	Recommended by	Honour or Reward	(To be left blank)
At BOUVAIN on the night of Sept 2/3, 1944 the platoon in which CPL.SHUTZ commanded a section was holding a bridge. During the night the enemy began to mortar the bridge, the platoon commander and platoon serjeant were both killed and several men wounded. CPL.SHUTZ immediately took command of the platoon and reorganised it. The mortar fire continued and the enemy put in an infantry attack. CPL.SHUTZ showed a complete grasp of the situation and commanded the platoon so well that the enemy attack was broken up and beaten off. He continued to control the situation in spite of continuous enemy fire until relieved the following morning. During the whole night CPL.SHUTZ's conduct was an inspiration to the platoon and there is no doubt that his initiative and gallantry under difficult circumstances prevented the enemy from destroying a bridge which was of great value to us in our subsequent advance. 7 Sept 44	(Sgd) A.Hunter, Lt.Col. Comd 8 Rifle Brigade. C.B.Harvey Brigadier, Comd.29 Armd Bde. Maj.Gen. Comd 11 Armd Div BG Horrocks Lt.Gen. GOC 8 Corps LIEUT-GENERAL COMMANDER SECOND ARMY.	M.M. (Immed- iate) M.M 1-3.45 28392	

Figure 13. Citation for Corporal Shutz. Corporal Shutz was killed in action in Holland in September 1944. He is buried in the Burg Leopold Military Cemetery in Belgium.

Amongst the Bravest of the Brave

We pay special tribute to the memory of three of the many British Jews who joined the Special Operations Executive (SOE) and served with 'Odette' and Captain Peter Churchill. All three died at the hands of the Nazis after capture.

Captain A. Rabinovich, Croix de Guerre ('Arnaud')

Captain A. Rabinovich Croix de Guerre. A Russian-Egyptian Jew, Captain Rabinovich who was recognised to be tough and rough, devoted to his work and very courageous. He was one of the best individual agents put into the field by the Special Operations Executive. He worked as a wireless operator in France under the direction of Captain Peter Churchill and was given the code-name 'Arnaud'. He was an associate of 'Odette'.

In March 1944, he was captured after a shoot-out with a group of Germans who were waiting for him and a colleague on their drop-zone. Later that year, he was shot by the Gestapo.

Figure 14. Captain A. Rabinovich, Croix de Guerre 'Arnaud'.

Figure 15. Mauthausen – the wall bearing the memorial tablets to those who died.

Captain Isadore Newman, MBE ('Julien')

Captain Isadore Newman, who took an arts degree at King's College, Newcastle with honours in French, spent some time in France during the uneasy years 1938–39.

He joined the Royal Signals at the outbreak of war, but his outstanding gifts were needed elsewhere and he joined the French Section of the Special Operations Executive. He underwent a vigorous training in the art of living and operating in an enemy-occupied country, and was eventually sent to France where he was given the code-name 'Julien'.

He worked there as a wireless operator with Captain Peter Churchill and 'Odette'. In his book *Duel of Wits*, the late Captain Churchill writes: 'Newman was not the only Jew to cover himself with glory. They were legion.'

Having successfully completed his first mission in South-East France, he returned to London and again volunteered for similar service in another part of France. He returned there shortly before D-Day. After carrying out invaluable work in reconstructing a resistance group in Normandy, he was betrayed and arrested by the German Security Forces.

Figure 16. The Tablet erected by the Dutch War Graves Commission bearing Newman's name. It also bears the name of Marcus Bloom, SOE.

His activities are described in a letter from Colonel Buckmaster, head of SOE, who wrote:

> At great personal risk, he continued for many months to transmit and receive Morse messages to and from Supreme Allied Headquarters. These were essential to the successful execution of our part of the war effort, which consisted of supplying liaison officers, arms and ammunition and explosives to French patriots.

> After his capture he never divulged any information, despite intense pressure upon him to do so.

> I am happy to record this tribute to a very brave man of whom the French Resistance chiefs, as well as his British compatriots, are and always will be proud.'

Official records show that Captain Newman was one of 47 officers shot at Mauthausen concentration camp by the Germans when they realised that they were facing defeat.

The MBE was awarded to him posthumously and received at Buckingham Palace by Joseph Newman, his father. (The full story of Isidore Newman is told in *Fighting Back* by Martin Sugarman [London and Portland, OR: Vallentine Mitchell, 2010].)

Captain Maurice Pertschuk, MBE ('Martin Perkins' and 'Eugene')

Captain Maurice Pertschuk was trained as a member of the Special Operations Executive, under the command of Colonel Buckmaster to work in occupied France. He was the leader of a group that cooperated with 'Odette' and Captain Peter Churchill. His second-in-command was caught by the Gestapo and, under severe torture, betrayed him. Maurice was captured and spent three years in Buchenwald.

Three days before the Americans entered the concentration camp, a Tannoy message blared out 'Achtung, achtung!' and Captain Pertschuk was called to the camp office. Calls of this type nearly always ended in the death of those called. His friend tried to stop him, but he replied: 'You know what happens when someone refuses to go. They take 100 hostages and murder them'. He was hanged on 29 March 1945 in Buchenwald, where he was found by the American Army.

There is a tragic footnote.

Maurice's father (who lived in France), was told by the doctors to go to the Unoccupied Zone as the air there would be good for his tuberculosis. As fate would have it, he went to live in the very village from which Maurice operated, but his son could not contact him. For over two years Maurice could see his father who had no idea he was there. When he learned of his son's death later, the father died instantly.

Though born in France, Maurice spent most of his youth in the United Kingdom. His code-names in SOE were 'Martin Perkins' and 'Eugene'. A younger brother survived him and is now living in the United States. He too had received similar training to Maurice's but the war ended before he could see action.

(With acknowledgement to Squadron Leader David Dattner OBE AFC RAF (Retd), Israel).

Brigadier F.H. Kisch, CB CBE DSO

Brigadier F.H. Kisch, CB CBE DSO, a veteran of the First World War, was killed in the Second World War by a landmine near Tunis in April 1943. At the time of his death, Kisch was Chief Engineer of the British 8th Army.

Born in India, he was the son of a British official, and became a professional soldier in the Royal Engineers. During the First World War, he served mainly in Mesopotamia and worked in military intelligence in London while convalescing from wounds. After the war, he was a military adviser with the British delegation to the Paris Peace Conference. From his father he had imbibed Jewish traditions and a Zionist attachment.

Figure 17. Brigadier F.H. Kisch, Chief Engineer 8th Army.

Dr Weizmann considered that Kisch could serve as a bridge between the Zionist leadership and the Palestine Administration and, in 1922, offered him the post of head of the Jewish Agency's Political Department in Jerusalem, with a seat on the Executive. At first there were difficulties, as the Zionist leaders from Europe were suspicious of his ultra-British image, while for British officials he was one of their own kind who had 'gone native'. However, his moderation, tact and honesty of purpose gained him trust in both camps. He also tried hard to develop areas of Jewish–Arab cooperation. This is illustrated in his *Palestine Diary*, published in 1938 with a foreword by Lloyd George. But the odds were against him. Some of the Jews thought he courted the Arabs too much; others thought the opposite. The Arab riots of 1929 led to a crisis over British policy in Palestine.

In 1931 Brigadier General Kisch resigned and went into business in Haifa, settled on Mount Carmel and actively supported non-political institutions such as the Haifa Technion and the Philharmonic Orchestra.

With the outbreak of the Second World War in 1939, he immediately volunteered for military service and was appointed Chief Engineer of the British 8th Army in the Western Desert, with the rank of Brigadier.

His name is commemorated in Israel by the Galilee moshav, Kfar Kisch, founded by ex-soldiers of the 8th Army, and by a forest in Lower Galilee.

The Enemy Aliens who Fought for Britain

By 3 September 1939, the day on which war was declared against Nazi Germany, thousands of refugees from Germany and Austria were living in Britain. The large majority were Jewish. Although they had fled from racial and political persecution, because they were subjects of countries with which we were at war, they were defined as enemy aliens. After being interned in special camps (a story in itself), about 6,000 (some say 10,000) of these men were later released to join the British Army.

At first, they were only allowed to join the Auxiliary Pioneer Corps. Teachers became bricklayers, merchant bankers were trained to be carpenters, a philosopher became a navvy. The fifteen Alien companies formed comprised nearly 6,000 men, and though but a small part of the whole Corps, their numbers were in proportion to the British population. This brief account of their services shows that the authorities were correct in giving them the opportunity to prove themselves. There was nothing in existing legislation to stop them joining any branch of the Armed Forces but, for security reasons, the military were unwilling to admit them into fighting units. Though unfamiliar with the manual tasks, and despite being legally regarded as enemy nationals, they showed a devotion to duty that in time led them to become known as the Kings Own Loyal Enemy Aliens. Besides those who enlisted in Britain, another three companies (1,000 men), were recruited in North Africa in 1943.

The story of the Alien Companies is mostly unexciting, although five did go to France after the invasion of Belgium and two, hastily armed, fought with distinction. Most, however, were engaged in non-combatant duties defending the country against an invasion that did not come.

Significantly there was a gradual recognition of the aliens as reliable soldiers. They were later to perform a valuable service when allowed to leave the Pioneers for other branches of the Forces. Their only complaint was that they wanted the chance to fight, and in 1943 it came.

The call came for volunteers for the Commandos, the Parachute Regiment, and finally the Infantry, the Royal Armoured Corps, the Royal Artillery and Intelligence. Those who joined the fighting units understood clearly the risk they ran of being executed by the Germans if captured. They were nationals of the country against which they were fighting and even if that country was an evil and tyrannical dictatorship, they were traitors as defined by international law.

By 1944, most of the refugees had left the Alien Companies of the Pioneer Corps. Many became airborne troops and joined the special services. The commander of one of the original Pioneer Companies, Major B A Wilson, MC helped to raise the 21st Independent Parachute Company designed to form a spearhead of attack by dropping flares, radio guidance, local reconnaissance, taking prisoners and immediate interrogation. They served in North Africa, Sicily, Italy, Southern France, Palestine, Holland and Greece.

The Company was part of the 6th Airborne Division. It went into action for the last time at Arnhem, suffering many losses.

Number 3 Troop of the 10th Inter-Allied Commando was a special refugee unit composed exclusively of enemy aliens from the Pioneer Corps. The particulars of many were known to the Gestapo, their capture and identification would have meant execution and reprisals against their families. Nevertheless they took part in many daring Commando actions, offering a special contribution with their knowledge of German, Germany and the Germans. They were used for specialised reconnaissance and small-scale raiding parties, questioning German prisoners taken in the action. They saw service at Dieppe and St. Nazaire, North Africa and Italy and later in the landings in Normandy and Holland.

An illustration of the contribution made by these men is to be found in the story of Elie Nathan, taken from the book *I Understand the Risks* by Norman Bentwich, with the kind permission of the publishers Gollancz.

In 1942 Elie Nathan volunteered for the Commandos and was accepted. He had been struggling for many months to get into a fighting unit. He was a member of 3 Troop of the Inter-Allied Commando which was composed almost entirely of German and Austrian refugees and which was to gain a reputation for intelligence, bravery, enterprise and devotion. They were trained in a battle school in Wales (Aberdovey) for special service, to be conversant with their own and the enemy's weapons and organisation, capable of moving unseen and unheard by day or night, with or without a map or compass, and to carry out reconnaissance or sabotage tasks.

Elie Nathan rose to the rank of sergeant and on D-Day 1944 was renamed Howarth for security reasons. He was dropped in Normandy near the beaches. Seriously wounded, he was returned to England. On his recovery and without the medical officer's permission, he returned to France, but collapsed and was sent back again. For a time, as Troop Sergeant Major, he trained Commandos. Because he did not want to leave his troop, he turned down the offer of a commission, and as soon as he was fit went out again, this time to Holland.

The story is told in the book *Commando Men* by Captain Brian Samain, of an attempt to take an island in the River Maas in January 1945 with a small party that included Howarth. He and another refugee soldier, Captain Griffith, were to recover the dead and wounded. 'Sergeant Major Howarth', runs the record, 'who speaks fluent German, set the flag of truce upon the bank, then shouted to the Germans to hand us back our wounded and surrender the dead ... A young German cadet officer told Howarth to come back the following morning when he would give the answer of his commander. On the next day Howarth and the party returned to the river's edge. The cadet officer said we could have our dead but not the wounded.' The truce, the record adds, continued for another 24 hours during which time Captain Griffith and Sergeant Major Howarth tried hard to convince the German cadet officer that it would be better to surrender whilst there was a chance of coming out of the war alive. The young German replied that much as he and his comrades would like to go to England as prisoners-of-war, their honour and their captain would not permit them to do so.

Howarth was given a commission in the field for bravery. In April, he was with the Commandos as they advanced from the Rhine and attacked Osnabruck, the largest German town yet to be attacked by British troops. He fell in that attack and was buried in a field by the road. He loved England and he died for her.

In *The Spectator* of 8 June 1945, Sir A. Patterson wrote: 'The most natural and sincere of men, he won the hearts of all by the two great gifts of courage and honesty. We shall not see again a happier combination of all that is best in England and Germany and all that is bravest in Jew and Christian.'

When final victory came, the refugee soldiers worked in Military Government, the Control Commission, and as experts and interpreters at the Nuremberg War Crimes trials. Some thousands remained in the Army until 1947 in the armies of occupation in Germany, Austria and the Far East. After the war, the great majority stayed in Britain, were naturalised and took their part in national life.

The story of the aliens in the Forces began with the recruitment of brains for work which did not require brains, and ended with the use of brains and bravery in many special fields.

The names of those who died are listed in Rolls of Honour, those who won awards for bravery – there were six MCs, three DCMs, ten MMs, and twenty-three other decorations.

(The full story can be read in Helen Fry's *The King's Most Loyal Enemy* Aliens [Stroud: Sutton, 2000], and Peter Leighton-Langer's *The King's Own Loyal Enemy Aliens* [London and Portland, OR: Vallentine Mitchell, 2006]. The details and members of 3 Troop – the 'Jewish' Troop – are in Martin Sugarman's *Fighting Back* [London and Portland, OR: Vallentine Mitchell, 2010].)

Jewish Clergy in Uniform

Reverend Dr Isaac Levy, OBE

In this article, the Reverend Dr Isaac Levy OBE TD, a former Senior Jewish Chaplain to the Forces and to the Middle East Land Forces and for many years an Honorary Chaplain to AJEX, discusses the duties and problems of Jewish Chaplains on Active Service in the Second World War.

Figure 18. Chaplains in the Middle East 1942. Seated 2nd from left. The Reverend Dr Israel Brodie, Chief Jewish Chaplain to the Forces. Standing (left to right) Simeon Isaacs, Saul Amias, Leslie Hardman, Arthur Saul Super, Barnet Joseph, Louis Rabinowitz, Woolf Morein, Leslie Edgar, I.K. Cosgrove, I.N. Fabricant, Arthur Barnett, Jacob Israelstam, Phillip Cohen, Bernard Casper, Henry Chait, Joseph Weintrobe.

The role of Jewish Service chaplains was well-established in the First World War. Thus, when the Second World War broke out, it was an accepted fact that they would be recruited from the ranks of the clergy who volunteered for service. The late Dayan M. Gollop had been a Territorial chaplain and was immediately accepted as Senior Jewish Chaplain. He gathered round him a number of Synagogue Ministers who were commissioned and posted to the training depots and local commands scattered throughout the United Kingdom. As the war developed and troops were sent overseas, Chaplains were duly posted to the various theatres of operation in Europe, the Middle East and the Far East.

One particular problem faced Jewish Chaplains, which created a fundamental difference between them and their Christian counterparts. Whereas the latter were attached to regiments, divisions and base hospitals, because Jewish personnel were scattered throughout every arm of the Service, Jewish Chaplains had to be attached to area commands and needed to be supplied with Nominal Rolls in order to meet their flock and minister to their needs. This invariably demanded a great deal of travelling, often in difficult situations, especially as the constant mobility of units required that the Chaplain go in search of his flock. All too frequently, he would arrive at a given destination, only to learn that the unit he sought had moved.

Despite these inherent difficulties, the Chaplains managed to organize services, particularly for special religious festivals and occasions, when Commanding Officers would grant facilities for Jewish personnel to assemble at some convenient spot. Here they would not only meet their Chaplain, but derive pleasure from making the acquaintance of fellow Jews from other units.

Chaplains attached to base areas had a special advantage in that they could visit the major military hospitals there, to give encouragement to the sick and wounded. The visit of the Chaplain to Jewish personnel, who invariably were thinly distributed amongst many units, was always warmly welcomed as it served to bolster morale, often in a low state because of the absence of Jewish companions. These visits made his men feel that they were not deserted by their own people and that their presence in the Services was recognized and acknowledged. An even greater source of encouragement were the messages sent by the Chaplains to the men's next of kin at home, informing them when they had seen their loved ones. These letters were so gratefully received that often they were kept until after the war as a testimony to the well-being of their menfolk during their period of service overseas.

To the Chaplain in the field fell the unenviable duty of officiating at burials. The fallen were wrapped in a blanket, when one was available, and interred in a hastily-dug grave upon which some form of marker was erected. On it was inscribed the name and number of the deceased and his religious affiliation. The relevant map reference of the grave was duly noted for ultimate reference to the appropriate authorities. On very rare occasions, a Jewish Chaplain might be called upon to perform a burial for a non-Jewish soldier and a non denominational form of service would be used in such an emergency.

In due course, the bodies of the fallen were transferred to permanent military cemeteries where Jewish graves were marked by the appropriate Magen David. The Imperial War Graves Commission, to their abiding credit, has been most meticulous in paying regard to the sensitivities of differing religious denominations. Hence the next of kin of Jewish fallen were permitted to include three lines of Hebrew in the inscription on the tombstone. The texts of all such inscriptions prior to their being engraved, were submitted to the Senior Jewish Chaplain to ensure their correct rendition.

The differing characteristics after various theatres of operation imposed special responsibilities on Chaplains. Thus in the Middle East, where some 35,000 Palestinian Jews (as they were called) were enlisted in the British Army, the Chaplains had to converse with them in Hebrew and become involved in the many problems which the Palestinian element created. Often these were politically motivated. The Palestinians felt resentment at their deployment in the ancillary services or on guard duties, when they claimed that they enlisted for combatant duty. Frequent clashes with the authorities occurred regarding the use of the Jewish flag which, they demanded, should be displayed together with the Union Jack. Whilst their loyalty to the Service was never questioned, they felt that they had a special identity which should be recognised. It often fell to the Chaplain to act as intermediary between the Army authorities and the Jewish Agency which had been responsible for their recruitment.

As the war progressed in Europe and the enemy retreated before the advancing Allies, the Chaplains came face-to-face with a new phenomenon – the remnant of Jewry which had survived the Nazi terror. The liberation of the concentration camps and the horrors which they revealed afforded the Chaplains the opportunity of tendering whatever humanitarian service would help the inmates and encourage them to face their future.

Thus the role of the Chaplain was as varied as were the circumstances in which he found himself.

He was a friend to the Servicemen and women, a counsellor who would deal with personal problems, an officiant at services, an intermediary with the authorities when required, a bearer of good tidings to people and communities who had previously been forced to live under the heel of the enemy. It was, indeed a unique role, which though sometimes fraught with logistical problems, was one which fell to the privileged few.

Tributes to the Fallen by their Families and Friends in Proud Remembrance

FLIGHT SERGEANT BASIL GANTZ, RAF

Flight Sergeant Basil Gantz served with 227 Squadron, Royal Air Force. He was killed over Yugoslavia.

'Basil was always crazy about planes. After leaving school, he worked in a reserved occupation. After volunteering seven times, he was accepted for aircrew training, most of which took place in Canada. Returning briefly to London, he was posted to Egypt. I see from letters dated in August 1944, that he was reported missing "as a result of air operations when a Beaufighter aircraft set out to bomb a target in Yugoslavia". On 5 July 1945, we were told that he was to be presumed killed. His body was ultimately found and he is buried in the British Military Cemetery, Belgrade.'

Norman Gantz (Brother)

LEWIS SOLOSKY, Army

Lew, or Lewis, Solosky served in the British Army and was killed in Burma.

'He was aged about twenty, possibly a private soldier, and I understand that he was amongst a number of soldiers who lost their lives when their Army camp was bombed by the Japanese Air Force.

'My late grandmother's cousin's son served in the Royal Air Force as a bomber pilot. His name was Pilot or Flying Officer Krish. I am sorry that I am unable to recollect his first name. Returning from a raid on enemy territory, his aircraft, which was damaged, crash landed and sadly, he lost his life. His father, Serge Krish conducted orchestras in BBC programmes and his brother, John Krish, produced documentary films.'

Leonard Levison (Cousin)

SERGEANT (FLIGHT ENGINEER) WALTER COHEN, RAF

'As far as I can ascertain, Lionel's last flight was with a Canadian crew who were shot down near the Belgian/German border on their return from a successful bombing raid over Dresden. I think one crew member may have been rescued and, although injured, survived. This was a mission of fate for Lionel as he was not scheduled for that flight – a friend wanted to get married at that time and they changed places!

'As he apparently took steps to conceal his Jewish identity, his grave was initially marked with a cross. After his parents' visit, this was speedily replaced by a Magen David.'

Corinne Van Colle (Mrs)

SERGEANT NORMAN GORFUNKLE, RAF

Sergeant Norman Gorfunkle, aged 22, of 76 Squadron, Royal Air Force, died on 7 November 1942. He is buried at Chaumont en Bassigny, near Dijon, in France.

'His grave, No. 320, is the only one from the last war which lies beside three graves of British soldiers killed in the First World War. His Wellington bomber was shot down on only his second operational flight to Genoa. Although the rest of the crew survived, regrettably, my brother was injured while baling out and he died on the following day.

'My cousin, Professor M. Maizels, at the request of my late mother, wrote to the Mayor of Chaumont requesting any details available and I have a most moving letter from a member of the Resistance who visited the hospital and was allowed by the Germans to attend Norman's funeral. He wrote that the people of Chaumont (which is a tiny village) have adopted the grave as a tribute to a British hero. My mother and I visited the grave as soon as possible after the war. It is kept immaculately and apparently on Bastille and Liberation Day, the people of the village make a procession to it.'

Mrs N. Gellman (Sister)

FLIGHT SERGEANT ZDENEK LAUNER, RAF

'Zdenek Launer was born in Prague in 1925 and came to London in 1939 with his parents and elder brother (my father) after Hitler invaded Czechoslovakia. In 1942 or 1943, he joined the Czech (No. 311) Squadron of Coastal Command, Royal Air Force. He attained the rank of Flight Sergeant. He and the rest of his crew failed to return from a reconnaissance flight and were found dead on 1 January 1945 near Rackwick Bay, Orkney. His death certificate, which is in my possession, gives the cause of death as "War Operations" and under "Informant" gives the details 'Registered on the information of CAT Chatwin, RN, Captain HMS *Prosperine*.

'His parents were not observant at that time and his body was not buried but cremated at Golders Green Crematorium.'

Dr John Launer (Nephew)

GUNNER H. COHEN, RA

Gunner H. Cohen, 137th Field Regiment Royal Artillery died as a prisoner of war in a camp near Kuala Lumpur on 6 April 1942. He is buried in the civil cemetery there.

'The Far East were certainly a forgotten Army. I am delighted that somebody is taking an interest.'

Chanie Shine (His widow)

LANCE CORPORAL LOUIS SAUNDERS,
The Royal Norfolk Regiment

Lance Corporal Louis Saunders of the 4th Battalion The Royal Norfolk Regiment died on 21 September 1944 aged 24. The son of Simon and Annie Saunders of Edgware, Middlesex, Louis was captured in Singapore and became a prisoner of war in Japanese hands.

'He was being transferred from a camp in Malaya to Japan when the hospital ship he was on was bombed by the Americans. He was subsequently reported missing and consequently has no known grave.'

Arthur Saunders

SERGEANT HENRY CONRAD, RAFVR

Sergeant Henry Conrad served with 49 Squadron Royal Air Force at Fiskerton. He died on 2 January 1944.

'Flying in Lancaster JB 727 of 49 Squadron, he failed to return from an operational flight to Berlin. He was buried in or near Retzow near Mirow, twelve miles South East of Neustrelitz.

'Henry registered as Church of England as he did not want to be picked up over Germany as a Jew. Understandable at the time. He is commemorated on the RAF Memorial at Runnymede. I am very glad you have undertaken this memorial to our boys.'

Renee Levy (Sister)

AIRCRAFTMAN FIRST CLASS E.S. SAMUELS, RAF

'The circumstances of his death are particularly tragic. He was the oldest of seven children and volunteered to fight as he had some knowledge of what was happening to Jews in Germany.

'He left a young widow and two children, a son aged 7 and a daughter of 2.

'He died in Slough on 15 August 1941, aged thirty-three. Someone was cleaning a loaded gun which went off accidentally, shooting him in the head.'

Mrs Barbara Gilmore (Daughter)

LIEUTENANT MAX MENDEL WOLPERT, The Cheshire Regiment

Lieutenant Max Mendel Wolpert was killed in Germany with the 2nd British Army whilst crossing the Rhine on 14 April 1945. He was 22 years old and left a widow and a son of six months.

'The circumstances of his death, I understand, were these. He was leading his platoon towards the Rhine when he was shot through the neck. Although badly wounded he refused medical attention, preferring to stay with his men. It was then found that he had lost an enormous lot of blood and had to be carried back to the medics. On this hazardous journey, he was sniped by a German and killed.'

Mrs Joy Fletcher (His widow)

CORPORAL SIDNEY EISBRUCH, Royal Tank Regiment

'My Uncle was one of the original Desert Rats of Montgomery's Army and was with him throughout the war until he got shot and killed just before the end. His tank was knocked out by a self-propelled gun. He is buried in Bremen, Germany.'

Mrs Monica Slater (Niece)

STAFF SERGEANT ALFRED COHEN, RASC

Staff Sergeant Alfred Cohen, Royal Army Service Corps, was killed in an enemy air raid on Portsmouth on 9 March 1941, whilst stationed in Cambridge Barracks.

'He was 46 at the time of his death and the circumstances are rather unusual. Having been mentioned in despatches in the First World War and, by nature, being a very patriotic Englishman (albeit a naturalized one as a young man), he volunteered for service with the Royal Army Service Corps in a clerical capacity in 1940 and was immediately sent to Portsmouth.

'I well remember him just at the outbreak of war, when I was a young girl, and his intense despair at the treatment of the Jews in Germany, and his wish to do something to combat Nazism.'

Mildred Elton (Daughter)

LIEUTENANT JACK AARON KLEINMAN, The Buffs (Royal East Kent Regiment)

Lieutenant Jack Aaron Kleinman of the Buffs was reported 'Missing, presumed killed' on 5 November 1944 whilst seconded to the 5th Battalion The Wiltshire Regiment. He has no known grave but his name is recorded on the Groesbeek Memorial to the Missing in Groesbeek Canadian War Cemetery, Nijmegen.

'The information about his death, conveyed to us by the Commanding Officer, was that Jack was returning from a patrol with his platoon and came under mortar fire. He instructed his platoon to return to base while he went to investigate. He never returned. Although a search was made, no trace of Jack was ever found.'

Hilda Bell (née Kleinman)

LEADING AIRCRAFTMAN JACK HYAMS, RAF

At 9 a.m. on 1 January 1945 an attack was made by the Luftwaffe on Melsbroek Airfield, Brussels. Leading Aircraftman Jack Hyams of 271 Squadron Royal Air Force was killed whilst servicing an aircraft out in the open. He had no chance of escape.

'He is buried in the Military Cemetery of Brussels on the Louvaine Road. I hope your efforts meet with success and a lasting tribute made to LAC "Lofty" (so called because he was six feet tall) Jack Hyams.'

Joseph Jackson (Ex-Corporal, RAF)

SERGEANT ALAN ABRAHAM WALLER, RAF

Sergeant Alan Abraham Waller Royal Air Force Volunteer Reserve was a member of the Pathfinder Force of Bomber Command.

'He was the rear-gunner of a Lancaster aircraft which was shot down over Berlin on the night of 2–3 January 1944. It was his thirty-second mission and he was just 22 years of age when he was killed.'

Mrs Ruby Hilburn (Sister)

SERGEANT (NAVIGATOR) HARRY NAIMAN, RAF

Sergeant Navigator Harry Naiman Royal Air Force died in June 1942, aged 21 years.

'He had completed twenty-nine runs over the Ruhr and had only one more to do before being grounded. He gave his life trying to save the rear-gunner who had been hit by flak.

'One man came out alive; he was taken prisoner and afterwards visited the families of all the crew and told the story.'

Moss Green

SAPPER ELI GOLDMAN, RE

Sapper Eli Goldman Royal Engineers was killed on 1 November 1944 on the Island of Walcheren.

'He was blown up and, as far as we know, has no grave.'

Mrs Dorothy Cutler (Sister)

SERGEANT (FLIGHT ENGINEER) H.C.M. KAHLER, RAFVR

Sergeant Flight Engineer H C M Kahler Royal Air Force Volunteer Reserve was 21 years old when he died.

'His plane was shot down over Denmark on 19 April 1944 while on a mine-laying operation over the North Sea. Four members of the crew were killed. The other three were taken prisoner by the Germans. The dead were buried in one grave in the churchyard at Gram in South West Jutland, near the town of Ribe.

'They could not be separated which is why my late parents could not bring his body home for a Jewish burial after the war.

'My sister and brothers and I have visited the grave and prayed there and sprinkled holy sand from Israel upon it.'

Miriam Cohen (Sister)

LANCE CORPORAL RONALD COWAN, RASC

'Quite unknown to me, my brother and I crossed the Channel to Normandy on the same day: D + 6. I learned from home later that we were both in the same theatre of war.

'Prior to the assault over the Rhine my Recce (Corps) unit went ahead of the Division, playing our usual role. Our convoy was held up at a village which had been badly damaged and was being cleared to enable us to pass through. As we were waiting by the roadside, I noticed a group of soldiers "brewing up". My eye was caught by their shoulder flashes denoting their arm of the service and I realised that my brother could have been among them.

'I called out and asked if anyone knew Ronnie Cowan, to which one of them replied, "He was killed yesterday". With that, my convoy moved on. We crossed the Rhine in the early hours of the following morning. I had not seen by brother since he volunteered in 1939.'

Horace Cowan

CORPORAL ABRAHAM DAVID WANSOFSKY, (Served as WYNNE), Royal Fusiliers

Corporal Abraham David Wansofsky of 'X' Company 8th Battalion Royal Fusiliers (Tower Hamlets Rifles), who served under the name of Wynne, was killed in action at Enfidaville on 9 May 1943 aged 22, having joined the Territorial Army whilst at school.

'He read many foreign newspapers, particularly German ones, which I remember seeing about his room. He was 17 when he joined the Territorials and under age, so changed his name for the privilege of joining His Majesty's Forces.

'He was shipped to France in 1940 to fight in the rearguard action and was one of those soldiers who spent a horrifying time lying on the Mole at Dunkirk waiting to be rescued by one of the boats or ships that managed to get through. That nightmare, from which he had hardly recovered before he insisted on returning to his unit, lives on in history, as we know.

'He was again sent overseas, this time to Paiforce (Persia and Iraq Force), and then moving gradually to the North African Campaign and joining the 8th Army in Tunisia. He was killed in action outside Enfidaville while attempting to take a German machine-gun emplacement. This was on the day after the surrender of the Germans in Tunis itself, a bit further north. I often wonder sadly what would have been the outcome if they had had the message a day earlier and had not had to battle for that position.

'He was an Acting Sergeant, using his German language facility and his knowledge of German arms and equipment (which he used to practise on me when I was only 15 and firing questions at him for him to answer from the knowledge he had got from his books and papers) to interrogate prisoners and so getting valuable information to help his unit win its battles.

'After thirty years, I could no longer bear the thought that he lay in a land that we had been unable to visit. I went on a four day visit to Sousse, where I was given the utmost help from the Commonwealth War Graves Commission. At the cemetery I was shown four other Jewish graves including that of Brigadier Kisch. I have twice visited that cemetery of 1,500 souls, so young. It reminded me of Israel and the Kiryat Shaul Soldiers' Graves. At least, I felt, he was near the same sky as Israel.'

Freda Stone (Sister)

Memories of a Japanese Prisoner of War
David Arkush

I arrived in Singapore in August 1941, as a Captain in the Army Dental Corps. When Singapore surrendered on 15 February 1942 I was serving in a General Hospital on the waterfront, helping with the many battle casualties. One week later, all who could walk made their way to the Changi area, where some 70,000 British and Australian Army prisoners were held in appalling, overcrowded conditions.

At first, we only had the food we brought in ourselves. Later, minimal rations, mainly of rice, were issued by the Japanese. I found there were a number of Jewish POWs, mainly from the 18th Division, the last troops to reach Singapore before capitulation. I attended a Friday night Jewish service in 18th Division area, conducted by Captain Silman, RAMC from Leeds. I realised that there should be a central Jewish service available for all Jews in Changi and arranged with the Assistant Chaplain-General for a Saturday morning service to be held in the bombed camp arena in the hospital area, to which all had access. Some fifty Jews attended the fine service in June 1942, conducted by myself and Corporal J. Brodie.

Very soon afterwards I was sent away from Changi as part of a medical party, on a train packed in cattle trucks for four horrific days and nights, ending up in Banpong in Thailand. There were 1,800 prisoners in this squalid camp.

'Railroad of Death'

We were the advance party for the construction of the Burma-Siam Railway – the 'Railroad of Death'. There were eleven Jews in the camp and I held regular Jewish services each Friday night and on Rosh Hashana and Yom Kippur. In October, we left Banpong and marched 30 miles north to the River Kiori and to our new camp – Chungkai, where I was to spend the next three years. Soon, thousands more prisoners arrived from Changi to begin building the railway. As work proceeded,

Figure 19. The River Kwai Cemetery, Kanchanaburi, Thailand.

many fell ill from very inadequate food, exhaustion, ill treatment, endemic diseases such as Beri-Beri and Pellagra, and from injuries caused by beatings from our captors, accidents from blasting and so forth. Soon Chungkai became a vast hospital camp and, at the peak, there were about twenty deaths a day. As Senior Jewish Officer, I had to officiate at the funerals of three Jewish soldiers as well as continuing Friday night and Festival services. On Pesach 1943, soon after the arrival of many more Jews from the Dutch Forces captured in Java, we had a service after which we served rice cakes and rice coffee in lieu of a Seder. More than fifty allied prisoners attended, including many brought on stretchers. At these Services, Kaddish was recited for those killed in action or who had died on the Railway. I must say that in no way did we suffer because we were Jews and the Japanese certainly knew that I was Jewish.

'Hell Ships'

Once the Railway was completed at the end of 1943, most of the workers returned to camps like Chungkai and conditions were much improved. In 1944, many were sent to Japan, travelling in appalling conditions in 'Hell Ships'. One such ship, with many from Chungkai on board including eight Jews from my *minyan*, was bombed and sunk by the Americans in Manila Bay and all were killed.

In August 1945, after the atom-bombing of Hiroshima and Nagasaki, Japan surrendered. This saved our lives as we were due to be killed when Allied troops neared us from 'Operation Zipper', the Allied attack on Thailand and Malaya timed for September 1945.

Tailpiece

There is no visual reminder of the service and heroism given by Jewish men and women to the Allied cause during the course of the Second World War. Names on tablets of the fallen cannot portray the remarkable stories emanating from those perilous years. Jews played an extensive role in the fight against Nazism on every front and the evidence should be on permanent display for all to see.

There is now in Israel an intention to build an extension to the Bet Hagedudim Museum in Netanya for just such a purpose. The building will be erected by the Museums Authority under the aegis of the Israel Ministry of Defence. The fitting-out and setting up of the permanent Exhibition will devolve upon the country, community or organisation to be represented.

A Note on the Jewish Headstones in Commonwealth War Graves Commission Cemeteries

Martin Sugarman

Towards the end of the First World War, the Imperial (now Commonwealth) War Graves Commission agreed with the Chief Rabbi of the Empire/Commonwealth on the design of Jewish headstones for those of the Jewish faith killed on active service. Besides name, rank, number and age, with Regimental or Corps badge, it consists of the Star of David within which are the initial letters in Hebrew (Ivrit) – used also on most civilian Jewish headstones – taken from a line in Samuel 1, 25:29, 'Let their souls always be bound up with those of the living'.

In common with all casualties, relatives were also able to choose a dedicatory inscription of a certain number of letters which could be in English or Hebrew (Hebrew inscriptions are more common on First World War Jewish graves) which they could choose themselves or could take from a suggested list. For Jews the suggestions came from the Chief Rabbi's office, and a common one for those who did not wish or were unable to compose their own or for a casualty with no family, was 'Their name shall not be blotted out' (Ecc.44:13). Again this is more commonly seen on many First World War war graves and possibly because many parents at that time may not have been able to read English in order to make an informed choice, and a Rabbi or the Commission staff chose a set format for them.

Some families chose not to have any dedicatory inscription; others refused a Star of David and just wanted the headstone with no religious symbol at all, often because they were declared atheists. Although of Jewish birth, the grave of Pte Nathan Lerner, of the Dorsetshire Regiment, at Tilly in Normandy is an example of this. Others were Jews but had converted, especially among some German Jewish refugees in Second World War, and have crosses on their graves, such as Paratrooper Walter Loewy-Lingen/Landon, buried at Arnhem, Oosterbeek, in Holland. But many graves had crosses in error and Jewish visitors need to be vigilant about this and inform AJEX, the Jewish Chaplain to the Forces and the

CWGC if they feel errors have been made when there is an obvious Jewish name on a headstone, but no Star of David inscribed. Since 2000 alone, we have had many First World War and Second World War graves changed in this way, after sufficient evidence was presented to the Commission, who have been very helpful in these matters. In earlier years, many more have been changed to Stars of David.

Finally, through various errors in 'the fog of war', the CWGC often did not commemorate some war dead at all, and there are many in this book. These may have been men or women who died of wounds later, or moved to another country and died abroad with no wartime recognition. Again, with careful research and evidence, the CWGC will place war grave headstones on civilian graves if it can be shown that somebody died as a result of war service, from disease or wounds. This was achieved in 1998 for a First World War grave at Marlowe Road Jewish Cemetery (East Ham, London) for Pte Wolf Stecklyn, RAMC, who died of illness at home in 1917, of TB contracted whilst in the army. He is remembered on the First World War memorial at Hackney Synagogue and his name has been added to the RAMC Book of Honour at the Pyx Chapel in Westminster Abbey, as well as to the CWGC registers.

Those with no known grave and whose names are inscribed on the many CWGC Memorials around the world, have no religious symbol against their name. The only clue to Jewish casualties then is the name itself, which is often far from reliable, as many Anglicized or completely changed their names in both wars for a variety of reasons. Our records in this book, then, are likely to be an under-estimate.

PART TWO
THE ROLLS OF HONOUR

The Royal Navy, Merchant Navy and Royal Marines

The Army

The Royal Air Force

The Palestine Jewish Volunteers

הֲלֹא צִוִּיתִיךָ חֲזַק וֶאֱמָץ אַל־תַּעֲרֹץ וְאַל־תֵּחָת כִּי
עִמְּךָ יְהוָה אֱלֹהֶיךָ בְּכֹל אֲשֶׁר תֵּלֵךְ: י

Be strong and of a good courage;
be not afraid, neither be thou dismayed:
For the Lord thy God is with thee
withersoever thou goest.

Joshua, Chapter 1:9

The Royal Navy

The Merchant Navy

The Royal Marines

The Royal Navy, Merchant Navy and Royal Marines

Advances in the use of the internet means that readers who wish to acquire further details of any of the men and women listed here (regiment, ship, squadron, number, date of death, place of burial etc.) need only consult the Commonwealth War Graves Commission web site on *www.cwgc.org* for information. For awards, many details may be found on the web site of the *London Gazette*. NB: Many Palestinian Jews are included in this first section rather than separated out. This is due to the order in which their names were first researched.

Abrahams, Abraham
MN
SS *Arandora Star*

Abrahams, Lt Alphonse Nathaniel
RN
                              25.7.41
Killed on active service

Abrahams, OS Harry
RN
HMS *Kelly*
                              23.5.41
Died on board, in Crete

Albert, Leonard
MN
                              25.9.42

Allan, Herbert (aka Abraham)
MN
MV *Accra*
                              26.7.40

Altman, Ship's Cook Henry
RN
HMS *Voltaire*
                              9.4.41

Anglo, 1st Rad/O Albert
MN
MV *Cornish*
Age 23   29.7.43

Asher, AB L.A.
RN
                              -.-.41

Augsburger, Stoker 2nd Class Stanley George
HMS *Bickerton*
Age 18   22.8.44

Beheman, AB Gerald
MN

Benjamin, Chief Wren Cecilly M.B.
WRNS
                              -.-.41

Benstock, Cook Emanuel
MN
Scotland
Age 35   25.3.43

Benton, AB alias Goulstine Leonard
HMS *Hood*

Berg, Fireman/Trimmer Abraham Moss
SS *Samala*
Age 37   30.9.40

Berney, Ldg Supply Assistant Geoffrey
RNVR
HMS *Barham*
Age 20   21.11.41
Lost at sea when his ship was sunk by a submarine

Bernstein, Rad/O Aubrey Lionel
MN
Age 20   7.7.45

Bernstein, Steward Louis
MN
SS *Oropesa*
Age 19   -.1.40
Torpedoed on his first voyage

Biderman, Telegraphist George
MN
SS *Anking*
Age 28   -.3.42
Missing after his ship was torpedoed in the Far East

Binderman, Surg/Lt Sidney Lewis
RNVR
HMS *Vortigern*
Age 27   15.3.42

Black, OS Sidney
RN
HMS *Odyssey*
                         20.7.43
Went down with his ship in Mediterranean

Block, Cook Joel
MV *Rio Bravo*
Age 34   2.11.44

Blondel, Ldg/Smn
RN
HM Submarine *Triad*
Age 24   20.10.40

Bloom, Stkr Sidney
RN

Brinberg, Robert
MN
(formerly SVC, Shanghai)

Brodie, Temp Sub/Lt Norris S.
RNVR
Killed flying off HMS
Illustrious as observer in Barracuda Torpedo Bomber
Age 22
No known grave

Brookner, Wireman Henry
RN
HMS *Drake*
Age 38   16.9.47
Buried East Ham Jewish Cem

Brown, AS Phillip
RN
HMS *Fiji*
No known grave

Calton, Air/Mech (Ordnance) Morris (aka Carlton)
Fleet Air Arm
                         26.7.44
Killed by an explosion whilst on duty
Buried in Emel Burial Cem

Coe, AB Kenneth Benjamin
RN
HMS *Ashpodel*
Age 21   9.3.44

Cohen (Conn), Asst Stwd Benjamin
SS *Almeda Star*
Age 23   17.1.41

Cohen, OS Aaron
RN
Missing presumed killed

Cohen, Stkr Albert/Aaron
RN
HMS *Glorious*
Age 23   9.6.40

Cohen, OS David
RN
HMS *Raleigh*
                         29.3.43
Buried in Blackley Cem

Cohen, Air/Mech Douglas
RN
HMS *Bambara*
                         5.10.45
Trincomalee War Cem

Figure 20. Leading Supply Assistant Geoffrey Berney RNVR.

Figure 21. Rad/O
Aubrey Lionel Bernstein MN.

Cohen, OS Ellis
RN
HMS *Kelly*
Age 23   23.5.41
Died on board at Crete

Cohen, Sub-Lt Isaac Jack
RNVR
HMS *Merlin*
Killed on active service
                         26.3.45
Buried in Willesden

Cohen, Ord Telegraphist Irving (aka Coleman)
RN
Missing presumed killed
                         -.-.45

Cohen, Cpl Isaac
RM
Age 23   15.7.44

Cohen, Ivan Ephraim
MN
SS *Jamaica Progress*
30.7.40

Cohen, Donkeyman John
MN
Age 38   14.3.42

Cohen, Raymond M. Gerald
HM LCT 2454
13.10.44

Cohen, Stwd Maurice Meyer
RN
HMS *Veteran*
26.9.42

Cohen, Storekeeper Morris
MV *Arthur F. Corwin*
Age 35   13.2.41

Cohen, Eng/Off Walter Reginald
MN
Age 23   1.12.40

Colman, O/Sig Aaron
RN
Missing presumed killed

Cornbleet, Telegraphist Solomon
RN
Age 19
Torpedoed

Cowan, CPO D.
RN
HMS *Dasher*
Age 31   27.3.43
Served in the Pacific, on Russian convoys and in the naval actions off Norway and North Africa
Killed in an explosion in the Firth of Clyde

Crystall, OS Leonard
RN
HMS *Birmingham*
Age 17   28.11.43
Torpedoed in the Mediterranean and killed in action
Buried in Alexandria

Davies, Seaman Gnr Gerald (aka Orlofsky)
MN
15.5.43
Buried in East Ham

Davis, Harry
Died in action
19.12.41

Dawood, Lt Albert
Roy Indian NVR
HMIS *Hooghli*
Age 29   1.11.45
Buried Rangoon Jewish Cem

Ebstein, Evert
MN
MT *Nina Borthen*
Norwegian
5.10.40

Edelman, Ldg Air/Mech Cyril Laurence
Fleet Air Arm
Killed in a flying accident
14.11.42
Buried in Willesden

Falk, John
HMT *Canna*
5.12.42

Fibiger, Ch Eng/O Louis John
SS *Fort Pine*
Age 55   13.7.46

Fisherman, Stwd Joseph
MN
SS *Laconia*
Age 29   12.9.42

Fishwick, Cook Leslie
SS *Samala*
Age 24   30.9.40

Fleisher, Alan
MN
SS *Almeida Star*
17.1.41

Frankel, AB Albert Ernest
RN
CJX236508
Age 32   26.3.43

Franks, Rad/Off Leonard
SS *Jonathan Holt*

Freedman, Paymaster Lt Basil Kenneth
HMS *Welshman*
Age 28   1.2.43
Buried El Alamein War Cem

Freedman, 2nd Rad/O David
SS *Arletta*
Age 22   5.8.42

Freeman, Sub/Lt Frank
RNVR LCT
Age 20   D Day 6.6.44
No known grave

Friedman, Tor Abraham
MN
DS *Hop*
Norwegian
20.2.40
Believed buried in unknown grave in Shetlands

Geller, 2nd Wireless Officer Kenneth
MN
Age 19   -.2.43

Gish, Asst Stwd Joseph Lionel
SS *Melrose Abbey*
Age 18   27.12.42

Goldenberg, WO I.L.
Hong Kong RNVR
23.12.41
Plymouth Naval Mem

Goldman, Stwd Harry
RN Patrol Service
HMT *Lord Wakefield*
27.7.44

Goldman, Jack H.
HMS *Panther*
9.10.43

Goldman, Apprentice Officer Simon
MN

Goldstein, Lt/Cdr Lewis
RN
HMS *Lanka*
Age 59   27.06.42

Goldstone, AB George
CSSX29126
HMS *Ibis*
10.11.42

Goldstone, Stkr Harry
RN
PKX121535
HMS *Hartland*
Age 26   8.11.42

Goldstone, Sub Lt M.
Malayan RNVR
                          15.2.42

Goldstone, Master Thomas Cecil (aka Golstone)
MN
MV *Richmond Castle*
Age 60   10.8.42

Goran, AB J
MN
Age 29

Gottschalk, Stwd Ian E.
MN
SS *Ascot*
Age 27   29.2.44

Gould, AB Barry Barnett
RN
HMS *President III*
Age 20   8.6.42

Grunberg, Moses
MN
SS *Nailsea Court*
                          10.3.43

Haniford, CPO Barnet BEM
RN
                          8.5.43
Twice mentioned in despatches
Missing, believed killed, off the coast of West Africa

Harris, Writer Moss Leslie
RN
HMS *Dunedin*
Age 39   24.11.41

Heaton (Heyman) Peter Hans (aka Hugh Peter)
RCN

Figure 22. OS Ellis Cohen RN.

Figure 24. CPO D. Cowan RN.

Hefferman, AB Nelson Joseph
RN
HMS *Encounter*
                          11.2.45
Taken prisoner by the Japanese in February 1942 when his ship was sunk in the Java Sea
Buried in Malassar Cem

Hefferman, Fireman/ Trimmer John
MN
SS *Wayfarer*
Age 35   19.8.44

Figure 23. Telegraphist Solomon Cornbleet RN.

Figure 25. Smn H. Huntman MN.

Herman, 3rd Rad/O Sidney Phillip
Age 25
SS *Empire Jaguar*
Age 25   8.12.40

Holway, Sub/Lt Louis
RNVR
HMML 1163
Age 23   4.1.45

Horn, Barnett
MN
SS *Northwind*

Huntman (Hantman), Smn H.
MN
Age 25   -.7.40
Missing, presumed dead on his
first voyage

Hyman, Stkr/1 Bertram
RN
HMS *Glorious*
Age 30   9.6.40

Hyman, 3rd Rad/O Harry
MN
MV *Malaya II*
Age 28   -.-.42

Hyman, Ldg Wren Iris
Buried Willesden

Hyman, OS Samuel Lionel
SS *Empire Jaguar*
Age 25   8.12.40

Ionides, Lt Theodore
RNVR
Killed in action
16.6.44
Bayeux War Cem

Isaacs, Eng/O Bernard R.
MN
MV *Gisborne*
Age 30   11.10.44

Isaacs, 1st Rad/O Marcus
SS *Empire Bison*
Age 39   1.11.40

Jackson, AB David
RN
                          20.2.44
Saw action at Salerno, Taranto
and in Sicily
Died in Gibraltar

Jacob, Lt Richard F.H.
RNVR
FAA HMS *Lanka*
Age 20   9.4.42

Jacobs, 3rd Eng/O Sedonis
MN
SS *Kervegan*
                          9.2.41

Joel, MP Lt Dudley Jack Barnato
RNVR
Killed on active service
                          -.6.41
Buried in Willesden

Joel, Lt Henry Douglas

Joseph, Stwd Coleman
HMT *William Stephen*
25.10.43

Joseph/Josef, Ldg/Smn George
RN
6.3.45
MID Missing

Joseph, Stkr Jack
HMS *Bodacea*
                          13.6.44

Joseph, Marine Morris
RM
HMS *Cormorant*
                          17.1.43

Kagan, Rad/O Hymie
MN
SS *Napier Star*
Age 26   21.12.41
Gave up his place in the lifeboat
to elderly passengers when his
ship was torpedoed. After he
jumped into the sea when two
more torpedoes struck, he was
never seen again.
No known grave

Kahn, Midshipman Alan Frank
RN
                          9.7.47

Kaplan, Lawrence Bernard
SS *Kanbe*
                          8.5.43

Kassovitch, Storeman M
HMS *Khedne*
Age 18   25.3.45
Buried in Bombay Jewish Cem

Figure 26. AB David Jackson RN.

Kaye, 1st Rad/O Eric
MN
                          1.6.45
Buried in Kranji War Cem

Kleinberg, AB J.
MN
Age 24

Koester, Commissioned Gnr Lewis
RN
HMS *Southampton*
Age 39   12.11.41

Kossick, OS Louis
RN
HMS *Dunedin*
Age 27   24.11.41

Kowaski, Deck Boy Cecil
SS *Napier Star*
Age 18   16.12.40

Krebs, Emmanuel MM
HMS Drifter *Gleam On*

Kuttner, Walter
HMS *Nile*
                          21.12.44

Landsberg, P/O Ernest (aka Russell)
HMS *Quorn*
Normandy
                          6.6.44

Lazarus, OS Emanuel
MV *Alfred Jones*
Age 20   27.10.40

Lazarus, CPO Leon
HMS *Curacao*
missing
                          2.10.42

Lazarus, A/B James
RN
HMS *Achates*
Age 26   31.12.42

Leah, O/S Arthur
MV *Alfred Jones*
Age 17   28.10.40

Lenz, Canteen Asst Bernard H.
HMS *Royal Oak*
Scapa Flow

Levey, Jack/John
`The Times'` HMS *Hecla*
                          3.8.43

Levi, Coder Joseph Benjamin
RN
HMS *Vervain*
Age 20   20.2.45

Levine, F. Dennis
HMS *Lapwing*

Levine, H.I.
MN

Levine, OS Reginald Leo
RN
HMCS *Frazer*
Age 18   25.6.40

Levy, O/S Albert Edward
HMS *Galatea*
                          15.12.41

Levy, O/S Albert P.
HMS *Hood*

Levy, Stwd Joe
MV *Amerika*
Age 37   22.4.43

Levy, Ord. Tel. John Edward
HMS *Caledonia/Afridi*
                          3.5.40

Lewis, AB George
SS *Empire Amethyst*
Age 40   14.4.42

**Lewis, Bt Lt/Cdr Sir George
James Ernest**
RNVR
                          -.1.45
Killed in a plane crash
Buried in Saint Germain Cem

Lewis, Cook Hyman
MV *Adellen*
Age 40   26.2.42

Liebermann, Eng Frederick E.
MN
                          25.3.42

**Lobell (Lobinsky), Ldg/Smn
Laurence**
RN
                          -.-.43
Served as a volunteer in the Royal
Navy from 1938
Killed off the coast of Malta whilst
serving in a motor torpedo boat
Buried in Malta

Figure 27. Ldg/Smn Laurence
Lobell (Lobinsky) RN.

Louisson, Tel. Joseph R.
RNVR
HMS *Cambrian*
                          30.5.40

Mann, Ldg/Smn Sidney
RN
                          18.11.45
Died in an accident

Marcus, Gunther
MN
(Palestinian Jew)

Mark, Junior O/Eng Samuel
SS *San Florentino*
Age 26   21.10.41

Massil, Lt Lewis
RNVR
                          21.6.45
Buried at Willesden

Mayer, Marine
RM *Commandos*
                          -.4.43
Executed Sachsenhausen

Mayers, C.
MN
SS *Anastasia*
                          18.12.40

Mendleman, AB Harry
MIA/KIA (*JC*)

Messer, Stwd S
MN
SS *Lady Glanely*
Age 26   2.12.40

Michaels, Stwd John Myer
SS *Ceramic*
Age 44   7.12.42

Michaelson, Gerald
HMT *Anselm*
Lost at sea
                          5.7.41

Miller, Fireman/Trimmer James
SS *Fowberry Tower*
Age 31   13.5.41

Millet, Morris (Moishe)
MN
Killed in action on the high seas

Mocatta, J.M.
HMS *Southampton*
Age 17 yrs

Figure 28. The Grave of AB David Jackson.

Figure 29. Stwd S. Messer MN.

Morris, Fireman/Trimmer Isaac
SS *Empire Hill*
Age 46   23.2.42

Morris, Marine Morris
HMS *Stronghold*
Age 24   2.3.42

Moscovitch, Stkr 2nd Class M
RN
                             23.3.45
Buried in Bombay

Myers, George Edward
RM
HMS *Royal Oak*
Scapa Flow
                             14.10.39

Myers, Stkr/1 Isaac
RN
HMS *Courageous*
Age 46   17.9.39

Nathan, David
SS *Empire Cromwell*
                             28.11.42

Nathan, Gerald F. Joseph
HMS *Manistee*
                             24.2.41

Nathan, Marine Samuel Montague
7 Btn RM
Age 20   22.7.43
Buried Catania War Cem Sicily

Nelson, Ldg/Smn Louis Cyril
RN
                             -.9.43
Killed in a submarine on active service

Figure 30. AB C. Newman RN.

Newman, AB Cyril
RN
Age 22   11.5.42
Took part in the evacuation of Crete when his ship HMS *Glenroy* was sunk. Torpedoed off Mersa Matruh. His third ship was sunk with all hands during the Battle of Malta

Newman, Ldg Airman Derek
FAA
HMS *Saker*
                             11.10.44
Killed on active service, buried Indiana, US

Nicholas, 'Lizzie'
MN
Tower Hill Memorial (no more known)

Nirenberg, Fireman/Trimmer Alfred
SS *Storaa*
Age 20   3.11.43

Ottolangui, Asst Stewd George
SS *Empire Heritage*
Age 23   8.9.44

Pennick, Sub-Lt Robert
RN
HMNS `The Bath'
                             19.8.41
Killed in action

Perlman, Maurice Charles
MN
SS *Svend Foyn*

Phillips, Stkr John Joseph
RN
HMT *Burra*
Age 26   -.5.43

Phillips, Stwd J.
RN
Age 19   -.5.41

Phillips, Stwd L.
MN
SS *Isbjon*
Age 17?   17.12.44
Drowned at sea

Pressman, Sick Berth Att Hyman
HMS *Pembroke II*
                             19.8.42

Prober, Lt Nathan
RN
                             -.-.45
Killed on active service

Figure 31. Stkr J. Phillips RN.

Figure 32. Stwd J. Phillips RN.

Rabinovitch, Phillip
MN
SS *Almeda Star*
17.1.41

Rabinowitz, P.
MN

Rakusen, L/S Monty
RN
Coxswain of a minelayer
Failed to return after the raid on
St. Nazaire

Rish, 3rd Rad/O Bernard
SS *City of Pretoria*
Age 19   3.3.43

Roberts, J.
MN

Rogansky, Stwd Julius
MN
SS *Umona*
Age 21   -.2.40
Torpedoed

Rosen, Surgeon Lt Leon A.
DOAS
2.6.52

Rosen, AB Philip
RN
-.8.43

Rosenberg, AB Mark
SS *Winamac*
Age 34   31.8.42

Rosenthal, Marine Henry Clifford
HMS *Hood*
Age 18   24.5.41

Rosenthal, CPO Henry
HMS *Cabot*
Father of Henry Clifford
Buried Bristol
31.10.41

Rosenthal, Victor R.
HMS *Naiad*
11.3.42

Rosenthall, Smn Daniel
HMS *Ellesmere*
24.2.45

Rothman, Fireman/Trimmer Israel
SS *Fort Mumford*
Age 23   20.3.43

Rothwell, P/O Stkr Edward
RN
HMS *Dragonfly*
Age 40   14.2.42

Sakalofsky, Sam
MN
SS *Tremoda*
27.8.41

Salaman, Alfred
MN
SS *Ardanbhan*
27.12.40

Salter, C/W
-.8.42

Salter, O/S Harry
RN
-.6.42
Missing believed killed

Schneider, Donald
MN
-.-.43

Schwarz, Franz
MN
SS *Stancliffe*
22.4.40

Shaffer, P/O Rad. Max
HMS *Hulworth*
23.10.43

Shipley (Shapiro), OS
RN
HMS *Hartland*
Age 40   8.11.42
Buried Le Petit Lac Cem

Sisoff, Mess Room Boy Leonard
SS *Southern Empress*
Age 18   13.10.42

Sokolov, Smn John
Tower Hill
14.2.43

Solomon, Pantryman Jacob
SS *Gloucester Castle*
Age 58   15.7.42

Solomon, Fireman/Trimmer Lewis
SS *Belcrest*
Age 58   15.2.41

Figure 33. Stwd L. Phillips MN.

Figure 34. Lt Leonard A. Teff RNVR and Ldg Air/Mech Cyril Laurence Edelman.

Solomon, AB Sherman
D/JX1292821
HMS *Tamar/*
SS *Lisbon Mara*
                                    2.10.42

Spiro, O/S Henry William
RN
HMS *Firedrake* (Destroyer)
                                    -.1.43

Statman, Sub-Lt Montague
RNVR
                                    20.10.44
Buried in the US National Cem,
Florida

Steinberg, Airman AB Jacob
Fleet Air Arm
HMS *President III*
                                    -.-.42

Steinberg, Lionel
MN
                                    -.-.41
Bristol Synagogue Memorial

Sterne, Benjamin S.
HMS *Hood*

Sullivan, O/S Wilbur
(aka William Solomon)
RN
                                    -.8.42
Missing believed killed

Teff, Lt Leonard A.
RNVR
Fleet Air Arm
HMS *Indefatigable*
Age 22   1.4.45
Killed on active service in the
Pacific

Temple, Sub-Lt A.A.
Fleet Air Arm
                                    11.4.44
Died in a crash
Buried in Willesden

Torres, Sub-Lt David Joseph
Fleet Air Arm
HMS *Owl*
                                    -.1.44
Killed on active service

Valentine, Ldg Wren Helen M.J.
WRNS

Van Cleef, Lt Alexander
RNVR
HMS *President*
                                    10.7.45
Buried Golders Green

Volenitz, Donkeyman Max
MN
SS *Harbledon*

Wertheim, Smn Bertram T.
MN
SS *Montreal*
Age 33   21.12.42
Tower Hill Memorial

Wittenberg, Benjamin
MN
(Palestinian Jew)

Woolf, 2nd Rad/O Stanley Kay
SS *Stangarth*
Age 19   16.3.42

Woolman, Lt Wilfred C.
RN
Age 56   23.5.45
Headmaster Royal Naval Barracks,
Portsmouth

Zabner, AB Manuel
SS *Greenhead*
Age 34   2.12.41

THE ARMY

Aaron, Tpr A.
18th Reconnaissance Regt
(The Loyal Regt)
Age 32   2.6.43
Died Chung Kai POW Camp,
Thailand
Buried Chung Kai Mil Cem

**Aaron, Pte Arthur Adrien
Armand**
The Queen's Bays, RAC
Age 24   -.-.43
Died POW in Italy

Aaron, Pte Herbert
11 Btn Durham L/I
                                2.7.44
Buried Secqueville War Cem

Aaron, Gnr Isidore
10th Regt, RHA
                                1.4.42
Buried in Sidi Barani Mil Cem
(Italian)

Aaron, Gnr James
2 Med Regt RA
Age 39   27.7.43
Buried Damascus British War Cem

Aaron, Dvr Michael L.
RASC

Aaron Sion
Bombay Aux Force
                                19.4.44

Aarons, Sydney

Aarons, Vincent
Indian REME
                                8.8.44

Aaronson, Pte A.
Recce Corps

Abao, Pte Jacob
The Pal Regt
                                -.-.44

Abbot, Miss
ATS
                                -.11.39
Died in France

Abelson, Gnr Gerald S.
11th Field Regt, RA
                                28/29.6.42
Killed in action Gerawala Sector
Buried in El Alamein Mil Cem

Abelson, 2nd Lt James William
KOYLI
                                8.9.41

Abett, Pte I.B.
1st SSVF

Abraham, Constable Attias
Gibraltar Security Police
                                6.2.42
Buried Tangier

Abraham, L/Cpl Heinz
87 Coy, PC
                                28.4.42
Killed by an explosion at
Pembroke Dock
Buried in Pembroke Dock Mil Cem

Abraham, Cpl P.
RASC

Abraham, Pte Samuel
Army Intel Corps
                                9.6.44
Tobruk

Abrahamovitch, Richard
PC
                                -.-.40/41
Lost at Sea

Abrahams, Sapper B.
RE, GHQ
MEF
                                4.8.41
Buried in Old Cairo War Memorial
Cem

Abrahams, Gnr Gabriel
388 Battery 7 Batn Durham LI
Searchlight Regt, RA
Age 34   17.4.43
Buried Rainham Jewish Cem

Abrahams, Pte George
The Roy Sussex Regt
                                20.5.40

Abrahams, Gnr Henry
78 Field Regt RA
Age 22
Buried El Alamein War Cem

Abrahams, Rfmn Joseph
8th Btn, KRRC
                                17.8.41
Buried France

Abrahams, Pte M.S.
The S Lancs Regt
Killed in action. Runner for OC
                                27.2.45

Abrahams, Pte Nathan
PC
                                12.11.40
Killed by enemy action
Buried in Brookwood Cem

Figure 35. Tpr A. Aaron
18th Reconnaissance Regt
(The Loyal Regt).

Abrahams, Fus Nathan Alfred
2nd Btn Roy Fus
Age 30   4.5.40
Buried Oost-Dunkerke Communal
Cem

Abrahams, Pte Raphael
East Yorks Regt
Age 30   23.6.44
Killed in Normandy
Buried Hottot-Les-Bagues Cem

Abrahams, Tpr S.
Yorkshire Hussars ('34)
-.3.39 RAOC
                          2.4.45
Buried in Hasselt Cem

Abrahams Gnr S.
RA
Age 21   15.3.44
Buried at Cassino Cem

Abrahamson, Martin (Amson)
Paras
Rhine crossing
                          24.3.45

Abramovitz, Pte Joseph
2/5th Btn, The Essex Regt
                          1.11.45
Mentioned in Despatches in
recognition of gallant and
distinguished services in the field.
Died of wounds

Abrams, Sgt Jack Samuel
2 Btn Sussex Regt
Age 34   22.5.40
Buried Esquelmes War Cem

Abrams, Cpl Leonard
RCOS
                          18.2.47
Buried at East Ham Service Plot

Abrams, Pte Michael
Rifle Brigade
                          14.11.42

Abramson, Pte Abram
RASC
Age 20   20.5.40
Killed in action
Buried at St. Requier Cem

Abramson, Pte Barnet
2nd Btn, The Duke of Wellington's
Regt (West Riding)
Age 28   3.4.43
Buried in Rangoon War Cem

Abse, Cpl S.
RAMC
                          21.5.40

Ackerman, Sgt Leslie
1 Btn Berks Regt
Age 24   8.4.43
Rangoon War Mem

Addis, Gnr Myer
Gunner 16 Battery 2HAA Regt, RA
Age 21   26/27.4.41
Athens War Memorial

Adler, Lt Gabriel (aka Armstrong)
SOE
                          1.6.44
Cassino War Memorial; buried
Rome

Adler, 2nd Lt Harold James
The Rifle Brigade
                          10.2.42
Killed in action in Libya
Buried at El Kebir

Adler, Pte Harry
RAOC

Adler, Capt P.S. MRCS, LRCP
RAMC Attached KAFR
Age 29   5.11.44
Killed in action
Buried in Rangoon War Cem

Aizen, L.
REME

Akin, Pte David
RAMC
Age 41   14.4.45
Killed in action

Albala, Tpr J.
1st Roy Tank Regt, RAC
                          14.6.44
Killed in action

Albert, S.
                          19.9.44
Canadian Hldrs

Figure 36. The Grave of Tpr Aaron in Chung Kai Military Cemetery,
Thailand.

Figure 37. The Grave of Gnr S. Abrahams,RA, in Cassino.

Albrecht, Lt Andrew J.
RIDG
20.6.52
Killed in action, Korea

Albu, L/Cpl Frank S.
RASC
26.10.45
Buried in the Mil Cem, Ostend

Alexander, Pte B.
RE
-.5.40
Died at Dunkirk

Alexander, Gnr Max
328 Battery 99th LAA Regt RA
Age 25   14.5.44
Killed in action Cassino, Italy
Buried in Cassino War Cem

Allen, L/Cpl T. (aka Perlman)
PC
29.4.44
Buried in the Jewish section,
Kingston Cem

Allentoff, Pte Harold
The Essex Regt
20.8.46

Figure 38. Pte Abram Abramson, Royal Army Service Corps.

Allman, Pte A.G.
RASC
22.7.47
Buried Ramleh War Cem

Alman, Spr William
RE
15.7.43

Ammar, Dvr F.M.
RASC
-.-.42

Anderson, Pte R.
*The Sherwood Foresters
(Nottinghamshire
& Derbyshire Regt)*
23.9.43
Killed in Italy

Angel, Pte Mark
PC
14.1.42
Killed working in salvage
Buried in Rainborough Cem

Anson (Arnstein), Hans Pte Ian
PC
25.11.44
Buried at East Ham

Antaki, Capt. Albert
RAMC
6.9.42

Apfelbaum, Pte Norman
PC
7.8.40
Killed at sea on the SS *Arandora Star*
Buried in Brookwood Cem

Applebaum, Pte David
*PC 1015 Docks Company
RA*
Age 20   20.9.43
Cassino War Memorial

Arbib, Lt John H.
RCOS
-.10.43
Killed in action

Figure 39. Pte Barnet Abramson, 2nd Btn The Duke of Wellington's Regt (West Riding).

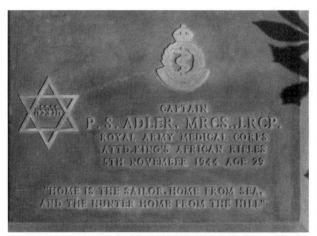

Figure 40. The Grave of Capt P.S. Adler MRCS LRCP, RAMC, in Rangoon.

Figure 41. The Grave of Pte Barnet Abramson, in Rangoon.

Figure 42. Gnr Max Alexander, RA (formerly The Queen's Own Royal Regt).

Ashbul, Gnr Pincus
RA
                                                9.5.45
Died of wounds in Italy

Asher, WO2 Alfred
RAMC
                                                13.7.46

Assous, Pte Francois
346 Coy PC
                                                8.8.44
Buried Borgel Jewish Cem, Tunis

Astley, Sgt Philip
                                                14.2.45

Attis, Bdr Joe W.
Roy Canadian Arty
                                                19.10.43
Killed in action

Auerbach, Gnr Harry
RA
                                                16.4.43
Died as a Japanese POW

Auerbach, Rfmn Nat
KRRC
                                                -.6.44
Killed in action

Arenstein (Andrews), Pte H.
The Roy Sussex Regt
                                                11.8.44
Killed in action 10 Commando
Buried at Ranville

Arlen, Pte Richard George (aka Abrahamowicz)
Sussex Regt & 10 Commando
Age 21   7.6.44
Bayeux Memorial

Arnstein, Gnr Samuel
RA
                                                29.5.40
Killed in action at Woesten near Ypres

Arthur, Gnr Ronnie
RA
Age 23   28.1.44
Killed in action
Alamein Memorial

Averback, Israel
AAC
28.9.44
Father killed in action WW1

Averback, J. (aka Avery, Joseph)
PC
Died Roehampton MH 1948

Averback, Bmdr Louis
25.12.41
Killed in action
Buried Derna Cem, Benghasi

Bachmann, Pte S.
30.7.41
Buried in Hodra Mil Cem

Baderman, Cpl Sam (George)
PC
Troopship torpedoed sunk
N African landing
-.11.42
Buried American Mil Cem Oran,
Algeria

Baigross, Paul
RAC
-.8.51
DOAS

Bailey, Cpl Jack
RM (Commando)
-.6.44
Died of wounds in France

Bailey, Spr Victor
RE
6.8.45
Killed in a motor accident
Buried in Standort Lagvett

Bakal, Pte Nathan
Queen's Roy Regt (West Surrey)
24.4.41
Buried at East Ham

Bakay, Pte A.
PC
10.7.46

Baker, Pte J.M.
Recce Corps
Died POW Camp, Thailand

Baker, Pte Louis
RAC

Baker, Sgt Norman
RAMC (Jakarta)
5.8.45

Baker, Pte S.
Queen's Roy Regt (West Surrey)
-.3.45

Balcon, Lt John
Murdered Somalia, 1948

Ballin, K..
PC

Bandell, Gnr Wolfe
RA
4.7.42

Barbalet, Pte Jack Louis
1 Btn W Yorks Regt
Age 20   21.6.44
Buried Kirkee War Cem India

Barder, Gnr Jack
RA
3.8.45

Barder, L/Cpl John
RE
-.-.45
Killed in Holland near Arnhem,
crossing the Rhine, Vehicle blown
up by mine in five feet of water
Buried in Nijmegen, Holland

Barkin, Gnr Jack
RA
3.8.45

Barnett, Lt B.C.
RAOC
3.1.41

Barnett, Pte Alfred Ian
RASC
Age 20   26/27.4.41
Athens Memorial

Barnett, Craftsman Barnet W.M.
REME
9.3.44
Buried at East Ham

Barnett, Gnr Eric Hyman John
RA
29.9.44
Killed in action in Italy
Buried in Assisi Mil Cem

Figure 43. The Jewish Ex-Servicemen's Armistice Service and Parade,
Horse Guards Parade 1930. General Sir Ian Hamilton reviews the parade.

Barnett, Gnr Ernest
3rd Regt RHA
                    26.10.42
Buried in Egypt

Barnett, Pte Moses
The Roy Sussex Regt
(tbc)   10.5.40

Barnston, Cadet Jack Emanuel
(Artists Rifles)
                    18.2.40
Buried in Dover Jewish Cem

Baron, William
Norfolk Regt
                    22.4.42

Barron, Gnr Charles Louis
Roy Canadian Arty
                    -.6.44
Buried at East Ham

**Barring, Tpr Maurice
(aka Blumenau)**
RTR, RAC
                    13.4.45
Killed in action
Buried in the Brit Mil Cem at
Soltau/Hanover near Belsen

Barron, Pte S.N.
UDF
                    1.9.42
Died at El Alamein

Bartell, Fus L.
Lancashire Fus
Age 33   19.3.43
Died of wounds
Buried in Rangoon War Cem

Bartfield, L/Cpl Harry
*2nd Btn, The Argyll & Sutherland
Highlanders (Princess Louise's)*
                    -.3.45
Killed in North West Europe

**Barth, O/Cad George Bryan
(served as Streets)**
Roy Sussex Regt/10 Commando
Age 27   29.6.44
Buried Barmouth Burial Ground,
Merioneth

Figure 44. Cpl Sam Baderman, Pioneer Corps.

Figure 45. The Grave of Gnr H. Baum, RA.

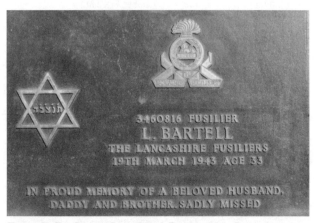

Figure 46. The Grave of Fus L. Bartell, The Lancashire Fus, in Rangoon.

Basco, Gnr L.
RA
Died in Chung Kai POW Camp,
Thailand

Bass, Sgt Emanuel
RCOS
                    -.4.42
Killed on active service

Bass, Joseph
2nd Wilts
Norwood

Bate
10 Commando
Killed in action, Dieppe

Batsman, Gnr David
RA
Killed by a mine
Buried in the Brit War Cem, Haifa

Baum, Pte Alfred
2nd Btn Buffs
                    9.7.40
Killed at St Nazaire-SS *Lancastria*
Buried in Presailles, France

Figure 47. The Grave of Gnr L. Basco, RA, in Chung Kai Military Cemetery, Thailand.

Baum, Gnr Cyril Reuben
RA
Age 26   7.1.43
Killed in action at sea (torpedoed)

Baum, Pte H.
UDF
                                         31.12.41
Buried at Capuzzo

Baum, Gnr H.
RA
Age 30   14.7.42
Buried Kranji War Cem Singapore

Bauman, Pte L.F.
UDF
                                         31.12.41
Buried South East of Bir-Er-
Regima

Beagle, Gnr Jack
RA
Cassino

Beall-Hyam, Gnr I.
Worcester Regt, RA
                                         15.7.44
Buried St Manvieu War Cem

Becker, Fritz (Benson, Fred)
SOE
                                         29.10.44

Beddington, Lt Col Claude
                                          -.8.40
Killed by a machine gun whilst commanding a yacht on Admiralty Service

**Bedrich, Pte Haim
(aka Heim)**
Singapore Def Corps

Behar, Pte Solomon
RASC
                                         20.1.47
Buried Alexandria Jewish Cem Chatby

Behrman, Dvr Gerald
RASC
Age 25   2.2.41

Behrman, Sgmn N.
Middx Yeomanry
                                         18.1.40

Behrman, Gnr S.L.
AT Regt, South African Artillery
                                         23.11.41
Buried in Knightsbridge War Cem, Acroma

Beiles, Pte O.D.
UDF
                                         24.10.42
Buried at El Alamein

Belfer, Pte Bernard
5th Btn, The Roy Berks Regt
                                         24.9.40

Bell, Pte M.
7th Btn, The Roy Norfolk Regt
                                          8.8.44
Killed on the River Arno

Belmon, Spr Abraham Isaac
                                         10.3.45
Died on active service
Buried at Evere, Brussels

Bendit, Capt A.C.
Intelligence Corps
                                          1.7.42
Buried in Willesden

Bendoff, Pte L.
*2nd Btn, Sherwood Foresters
(Nottinghamshire & Derbyshire
Regt)*
Killed in action North Africa
Buried in Massicault Mil Cem

Bendon, Gnr Elias
RA
                                         13.2.42

Benelisha, Cpl Samuel
247 Motor Boat Coy, RASC
Age 34   21.1.45
Athens Memorial

Benjamin, Pte Adron
*Nottinghamshire & Derbyshire
Regt*
                                          5.8.43

**Benjamin, Sgmn Donald
Bernard**
RCOS
Age 19   22.11.45
Buried Leeds Polish Jewish Cem

Benjamin, Pte Jack Solomon
7th Btn, KOSB
                                         18.2.44
Killed by enemy action
Buried in Edmonton

Benjamin, Pte M.
PC
                                          -.-.44

Benjamin, L/Cpl Mark
1/5th Btn, The Essex Regt
26.11.41
Buried in Belhamed War Cem

Benjamin, R.T.
PC

Benjamin, Tpr S.M.
147 Regt RAC
21.8.44
Killed in action in Normandy
Buried on the left of the road
between St.
Mauvieu and Cheux

Benjamin, Vivian
Hong Kong VDF.

Benjosef, Pte A.
The Pal Regt
30.5.42
Killed in action

Bensinger, Lt Eric Sigmund
7th Btn The Oxford and Bucks LI
-.-.43
Distinguished service in North
Africa
Mentioned in Despatches
Missing presumed killed

Figure 49. The AJEX Remembrance Parade 1963. General Sir Richard Hull takes the salute. (Tommy Gould, VC, third from the right, below.)

Figure 48.
Gnr Cyril Reuben Baum, RA.

Benson, Herbert
(info. Mrs V. Levy 2005)

Bensusan, Pte M.I.
2nd Btn, The Wiltshire Regt
21.6.44
Died of wounds in Italy in a mine
explosion
Buried at Valle Ranello in a field
Probably reburied in a Mil Cem

Berenson, Gnr Benjamin
RA
Age 35   12.5.44
Killed in action Monte Cassino
Buried near Naples

Berger, Capt Benjamin David
RAMC
18.8.44
Killed in action

Berger, Tpr Gerald
*11th Hussars (Prince Albert's
Own) RAC*
1.9.44
Killed in action in North West
Europe
Buried Bayeux

Berger, Julius Frederic Josef
PC
5.2.44

Bergman, Lt Wladyslaw
Intelligence

Berkoff, Fus Mark
9 Btn Roy Fus
Age 23   17.2.44
Buried Beach Head War Cem,
Anzio

Berkovitch, Gnr Sydney
RA
16.4.41
Killed by enemy action

Berkovitch, Pte Louis
The Suffolk Regt
8.9.41
Buried at East Ham

Berkovitch, Louis
9th RB
22.2.45

Berkowitz, Dvr S.
RASC
5.9.44
Buried Bolsena War Cemetery, Italy

Berkowitz, Pte Leslie G.
RUR
5.10.43

Berlin, Pte John
The Roy Sussex Regt
17.6.40
Missing believed killed

**Berliner, Egon Friedrich Paul
(served as O'Hara, Michael, aka
Chirgwin, F.M.)**
SOE
Age 22   4.4.45
Cassino Memorial, Italy

Berman, Spr Barnet
RE
5.5.44
Died on active service

Bernaert, Willy (aka Clement)
19.4.44
Buried in Brookwood
MID

Bernard, Rfmn Felix
Roy Ulster Rifles
Age 25   8.9.44
Killed in action in Italy
Buried in Gradara War Cem

Bernescu, Spr M.
RE
30.5.42
Buried at Tel-El-Kebir

Bernstein, Pte Fritz
PC
Age 26   4.8.42
Buried Llandilo Churchyard, Wales

Bernstein, Pte Jacob
5 Btn East Yorks Regt
13.7.43
Buried Syracuse War Cem Sicily

Bernstein, L/Cpl Joe I.
Killed in action France   -.-.40
Brady Club

Bernstein, Pte S.W.
UDF
31.12.41
Buried at Iponticelli

Beskin, Rfmn Sydney
1st Btn, KRRC
15.7.42
Buried in Egypt

Besser, Pte Alfred
RAOC
20.6.44

Besserman, Pte Jack
48th Btn, The Highldrs of Canada
19.11.43
Killed in action

Beth, Bdr Joseph
RA
29.5.40

Bialestock, Pte C.
The Roy Norfolk Regt
-.10.43
Went down with POW ship in
Manila Bay,
Philippines

Bianco, Tpr Edgar
-.9.45

Biderman, Sgt L.
2/5 Btn, The Leicestershire Regt
Age 25   2.4.43
Killed in action in Tunisia

Birk, Lt P.
RA
Western Desert
Age 21
No known grave

Birk, Lt Philip Theodore
The Beds and Herts Regt
24.12.45
Died in Burma

Bischburg, Pte L.
74th Coy PC
27.8.40
Buried in Newport Jewish Cem

Blake, L/Cpl D.J.
Roy Signals
11.9.43
Died from typhoid in North Africa

Blake, Cpl Sidney (aka Cohen)
REME
19.8.45

Blashky, Pte Leonard
Age 20   -.11.45
Killed in action

**Bleichroeder, Pte Timothy
Adolph (Bleach)**
Paras
Killed in action Arnhem

Blindt, L/Cpl J.I.
1st Btn, The Dorset Regt
Age 29   2.8.1943
Killed in action fighting in Sicily

Figure 50. Pte Leonard Blashky.

Bloch, Lt Andrei
(aka Boyd Alan George)
Croix de Guerre
SOE

Bloch, Pte A.S.
UDF
31.12.41
Buried South East of Bir-Er-
Regima, Bardia

Bloch, Ensign Denise, Croix de
Guerre
SOE

Bloch, James Charles
REME
8.6.45

Bloch, Sgt Mark
HQ Singapore Fortress RASC
Age 25   16.1.42
Singapore Memorial

Bloch, Pte Louis
4th Btn, The Roy Berks Regt
-.5.40
Killed in action

Bloom, Rfmn A.
The Kaffrarian Rifles, UDF
31.12.41
Buried at Bardia Frontier

Bloom, Lt Marcus
SOE
Executed 1944 Mauthausen

Blyweiss, Gnr Bernard
RA
3.10.43
Killed in action in Italy
Buried in the Brit War Cem
near Florence

Bogansky, Pte Hyman
3863288
7th Btn Ox and Bucks L/I
Age 30   5.10.44
Killed in action
Buried Cesena War Cem

Figure 51. Gnr Bernard Blyweiss, RA.

Bodner, Cpl William
RAOC
30.6.45

Bogod, Capt P.M.
RA
Age 22   17.5.43
Killed on active service

Bolter, Gnr M.
Singapore RA
Age 29   7.9.43
Buried Chung Kai

Bonstein, Rfmn Isidore
KRRC
30.4.43
Killed in action

Boorman, S/Sgt John Arthur
(Pilot) Ist Glider Pilot Regt
Age 26   10.7.43
Cassino Memorial

Borman, Rfmn S.
Rifle Brigade
28.6.44
Buried Assisi

Boston, H.
Liverpool Reg.
7.8.43

Figure 52. Capt P.M. Bogod, RA.

Bornstein, Rev Harry
Chaplain to the Forces
28.11.43
Died in Tunis
Buried in Tripoli Mil Cem

Botibol, 2nd Lt C.
The Leics Regt
-.5.40
Died on active service at Dunkirk

Botwinsky, Bdr C.
RA
-.4.45
Mentioned in Despatches
Killed in action in Italy

Braham, Capt Mark
RAMC
Age 26   -.10.43
Died on board POW ship before it
sank in Manila Bay, Philippines

Brattman, Pte John
7th Btn, The Roy West Kent Regt
19.11.46
Died in India
Buried at Kohima

Braun, Cpl Hans
PC

Braun, Pte Jack Francis
The Middx Regt
                                25.12.41
Killed in action

Brazil, Tpr Reuben Victor
HQ Squadron 2 Army/Brigade
RAC
                                 9.4.43
Buried Sfax War Cem

Breitman, Sgt
                                 9.5.41
Killed in action, Libya

Bresler, Pte Woolf (Willy)
The Queen's Own Cameron
Highlanders
                                 -.6.42
Killed in action at Tobruk
Buried in the Brit Cem Bir-Hakim

Bribram, Pte Vilam
(Czech Army)
                                 -.2.44
Buried at East Ham

Figure 53. The Grave of Gnr M. Bolter, Singapore RA.

Figure 54. Pte Woolf (Willy) Bresler, The Queen's Own Cameron Highlanders.

Brichta, Pte Friedrich
RAOC
                                28.11.41
Buried in the Birmingham Jewish Cem

Brier, Gnr Samuel
                                 -.7.43
Died on active service

Brodie, Dvr David J.
RASC
                                10.7.44
Killed in Normandy
Buried in Bayeux Cem

Brodie, L/Cpl J.
The West Yorks Regt (Prince of Wales's Own)

Bromberg, Pte Harold
KOYLI

Bromberg, Dvr Woolfe
RASC
                                27.2.43
Died in India
Buried in Karachi

Bronks, Gnr J.
RA

Bronsky, L/Cpl David
2 Btn Devonshire Regt
                                23.8.43
Buried Catania War Cem Sicily

Brooks, Pte Jack
PC
Age 43   -.-.45

Brooks, Pte Joseph
Buffs
                                24.10.43
Lost at sea, HMS *Eclipse* nr. Kalymnos

Brooks, Pte N.
The Queen's Roy Regt (West Surrey)
                                 3.8.44
Buried in Bayeux Cem

Brown, Pte Eric
The Gordon Highlanders
                                 -.8.43
Died of wounds

Brown, Gnr M.
RCA
                                20.9.44

Figure 55. Pte M. Brown, The Welch Regt.

Brown, Pte M.
The Welch Regt
Age 25   25.2.45
Killed in action in Holland

Brown, Pte Montague Harold
The East Surrey Regt
Died of wounds in North Africa
Buried in Beja War Cem

Brown, Sgt Phillip
          17.5.41

Browne, Capt H.
          -.6.42

Brownhood, Gnr Alec
RA
Died as POW of Japanese

Brownstone, Pte K.A.
Killed in action

Brudney, Lt Isadore
RAOC
          -.1.46
Buried in the Reichswald Brit Cem

Bubb, Pte C.
PC
          19.7.44
Killed by an anti-personnel bomb

Buchsbaum, Pte Solomon
PC
          29.12.40
Killed by enemy action
Buried at East Ham

Buckofzer, G.
PC

Budner, Sgt Harold MM
The Westminster Dragoons, RAC
          12.4.45
Killed in action in Germany
Buried in Soltau Cem

Bulmanory, Tpr Cecil
RAC
          2.4.45
Killed in action

Bunn/Bun, Sgt Walter
PC
Age 31   25.8.45
Buried Birmingham Jewish
Cemetery

Burnard, Cpl Sidney MM
The Roy Dragoons, RAC
          24.10.44
Mil Medal in Middle East
Awarded Bar in Italy
Died of wounds

Burt, Jason S.
Paras
          -.6.82
Killed in action Falklands War

Burton, Dvr J.
RASC
          6.7.43
Buried at Bizerta, North Africa

Buschbaum, S.
PC
Killed in Blitz

Byer, L/Bdr Abraham
59th AT Regt, RA
          13.2.44
Killed in France
Buried at Chateaux Fontaine

Bywood, Pte (Lazarus) Alfred
7 Btn Black Watch
Age 17   3.6.41
Buried Leeds Cem, Harhill

Cachia, Pte Carmel
PC

Caggan, Gnr L.
14th Beds Yeomanry
Age 25   9.8.45

Cahill, Rfmn David
10th Btn, The Rifle Brigade
26.7.44

Calman, Pte Albert
RASC
          19.11.44
Killed in Antwerp, Belgium
Buried in Antwerp Mil Cem

Calton, Hyman
RE Bomb Disposal
          -.12.44

Canon, L/Cpl Edward Lionel
Intel Corps
Age 42   29.5.44
Buried Willesden Liberal Cem

Cannon, Gnr Henry
RA
          10.12.41

Cannon, L/Cpl Julius
RCOS
          28.3.45
Killed by enemy action
Buried at East Ham

Cantor, Sgt J.M.
          3.2.44

Caplan, Harry
ARP
KIA Sheffield

Caplan, Sgmn Leslie
RCOS

Caplan, Pte S.
RE
Killed in action in North West
Europe
Buried in Ostend Cem

Caplin, Sgt Leon
Recce Corps
11.8.44
Mentioned in Despatches
Killed in action in Italy

Carol, Fus Leon
Roy Fus
7.10.40
Killed by shrapnel
Buried at East Ham 11.10.40

Carpen, Pte Max
RAMC
9.1.44
Found drowned
Buried at Rainham

Carpus, Cpl Philip
4 Btn Buffs
Age 29   23/24.10.43
Athens Memorial

Cashmaker, Pte Harry
332 Coy PC
16.12.44
Killed by enemy action
Buried at Schoonselhoe, Antwerp

Castle, B.V.
PC
Hampstead Synagogue Memorial

Catsell, 2nd Lt Boris Bernard
12.6.44
Died in Normandy
Buried at Rue Brasseville,
Normandy

Cembler, Lewis
Roy Scots
12.11.44

Chalk, Pte Sydney
REME
26.8.44
Buried at East Ham

Chapman, Pte Frank
6 Btn Lincs Regt
Age 21   4.3.43
Buried Tabarka Ras Rajel War
Cem

Chapman, Fus Solomon
1st/8th Btn, The Lancashire Fus
Killed in action at Wormhouldt,
France
Buried in Wormhouldt
Commonwealth Cem

Figure 56. Fus Solomon
Chapman, lst/8th Btn,
The Lancashire Fusiliers.

Charkham, Maj Sidney F.
2nd Btn, The Beds and Herts Regt
16.5.44
Mentioned in Despatches
Killed in action
Buried at Cassino

Chasin (Cousins), Pte Norman
RAOC
4.6.42
Killed in an air raid
Buried in Willesden Cem

Chencholsky, Rfmn Samuel
13 Parachute Btn/9th Btn,
The Cameronians (Scottish Rifles)
Age 23   8.2.45
Killed in action at the Battle of the
Rhine
Buried in the Reichswald Forest
War Cem, Germany

Chenovitch, Pte Barnet
2nd Btn, The Suffolk Regt
Age 23
Killed in the Imphal-Kohima battle
in Burma
Buried in Imphal Cem

Chevinsky, Tpr Wolf B.
RAC
10.6.45
Died of wounds, Apeldoorn,
Holland

Chomed, Gnr Percy
RA
-.10.44
Killed in action

Chowcat, Pte David (aka Bell)
1/7th Btn, Queen's Roy Regt
(West Surrey)
6.10.44
Killed in action
Buried at Tilly-sur-Seulles,
Normandy

Churnin, Lt Barnett
The East Yorks Regt
-.2.45
Killed in action, N.W. Europe

Clapper, Tpr Joseph
48th RTR, RAC
-.2.45
Killed in action
Buried in the Canadian Cem,
Riccioni

Clayman, Pte Harry
RAMC
11.6.45
Died in hospital in India
Buried at Jubbulpore

Clayton, Pte David
4th Btn, The Suffolk Regt
-.8.44
Died in a Japanese POW Camp
Buried at Formosa

Clompus, Lt Paul
107th Regt, RAC
Age 21   18.9.44
Killed in action
Buried in the Brit Mil Cem,
Gradara

Clyne, Gnr Reuben
65th LAA Regt, RA
         30.3.42
Drowned on the way to Malta,
body washed up
Buried at Alexandria

Coan, Spr Leonard Noel
275 Fid Company RE
Age 20   3.11.42
Buried El Alamein War Cem

Cohen, S/Sgt Alfred
RASC
Age 46   9.3.41
Served 1914/18. Mentioned in
Despatches
Killed in air raid
Buried in Willesden Cem

Cohen, Cpl A.
         16.2.42
Buried in Tobruk War Cem

Figure 57. Pte Barnet Chenovitch, 2nd Btn, The Suffolk Regt.

Figure 58. Lt Paul Clompus, 107th Regt, RA.

Cohen, Pte A.L.
The South Lancs Regt
Age 26   14.2.45
Killed in action in Burma
Buried in Rangoon War Cem

Cohen, Spr Abe
RE
         17.8.44
Killed in action in France
Buried at Tilly-sur-Seulles,
Normandy

Cohen, Rfmn Albert
6913792, Rifle Brigade
         17.9.40
Alexandria War Mem Cem

Cohen, Sgmn Alfred
RCOS 2360039
Age 26   25.4.45
Becklingen War Cem

Cohen, Sig Alfred
RCOS
Age 26   -.4.45
Killed in action
Buried in the Brit Cem Soltau

Cohen, Tpr Alfred
2nd RTR
         9.9.44
Died of wounds

Cohen, Lt B.
Womens ATS S Africa
         2.4.46
Buried Caserta war Cem

Cohen, Pte Bernard
1st Middx.
Age 27   24.12.41
Sai Wan Memorial Cem

Cohen, Cpl Bernhard
1 Btn Dorset Regt
Age 20   7.9.44

Cohen, Spr C.J.
2nd Field Company UDF
         31.5.42
Buried at Bir Chescena

Cohen, Pte Charles
         1.1.43
Killed in action

Cohen, Tpr Cyril
44th Regt, RAC
         27.6.44
Killed in action in Normandy

Cohen, Lt Daniel Lionel
Queen's Roy Regt (West Surrey)
Died of wounds received in action.
Mentioned in Despatches,
posthumously
Buried in the Sessa Arunca Mil
Cem

Cohen, S/Sgt David
RAOC
         1.9.45
Died in an ammunition ship
explosion

Cohen, Rfmn David
9th Btn, KRRC (The Rangers)
         -.6.40
Accidentally shot
Buried in Streatham

Figure 59. The Grave of Pte A.L. Cohen, The South Lancashire Regt, in Rangoon.

Cohen, Dvr Delara Henri (Haim)
325 Coy RASC (Pal.)
                                    9.12.44
Cassino Memorial

Cohen, Pte E.I.
The King's Own Regt
Age 28   27.12.44
Killed on active Service in France

Cohen, Pte Emanuel
The Queen's Own Roy West Kent Regt
                                    3.3.43

Cohen, Cpl Emmanuel
2nd Btn OBLI 6th Airborne Div (Para/Regt)
                                    24.3.45
He was the only child of widow and lived in a block of flats between Oxford St and Marylebone Rd.

Cohen, Ephraim (aka Cohn)
RAMC
NE Memorial

Cohen, Dvr Ephraim
RASC
                                    22.5.45
Mentioned in Despatches
Buried in the Brit Mil Cem
Carvignano

Cohen, Pte Ernest
The King's Regt
                                    26.12.44
Buried at Bryas near St. Pol, France

Cohen, Pte H.
2/7 Btn West Riding Regt
Age 28   6.10.42

Cohen, Sgt Harris
RAOC
Age 31   -.-.42

Cohen, Gnr Harry
137th Field Regt, RA
                                    6.4.42
Died Kuala Lumpur POW Camp
Buried in the Protestant Cem, Kuala Lumpur

Cohen, Sgt Harry
RAOC
                                    3.4.42
Killed on active service
Buried at Mosul War Cem

Figure 60. Pte E.I. Cohen, The King's Own Regt.

Figure 61. Dvr Ephraim Cohen, RASC

Figure 62. The Grave of Gnr Harry Cohen, RA, in Kuala Lumpur.

Cohen, Cpl Harry
2nd Btn, The Black Watch (Roy Highland Regt) (Commando)
                        -.-.41
Mentioned in Despatches
(posthumous)
Killed in Syria by the Vichy French.
Gave his life to save his Sgt Maj
who lay badly wounded and under
heavy machine gun fire. Cpl
Cohen left the safety of his own
position to bring him in and was
shot while doing so.
Buried in Syria

Cohen, Pte Henry
PC
                        2.5.41
Buried at Rainham

Cohen, Pte Henry
PC
                        28.4.45

Cohen, Spr Isaac George
SAEC
Age 29   26.10.41
Buried El Alamein War Cem

Cohen, Pte Isadore
REME/PAL
                        14.12.43
Buried Khayat Beach War Cem

Cohen, Pte J.
PC
                        5.12.44
Killed in Holland

Cohen, Sgt J.M.
                        15.11.41

Cohen, L/Cpl Jack
The Dorset Regt
                        -.7.40
Buried at Streatham

Cohen, Dvr Jacob
RASC
                        -.3.45
Buried in Holland

Cohen, Pte Joseph
131st Inf Brigade
Buried at El Alamein

Cohen, L/Cpl Joshua Nathan
RE
                        4.7.41
Buried at East Ham

Cohen, Gnr Julius
LAA Regt, RA
                        7.9.43
Buried at East Ham

Cohen, Pte Lazarus
11th Btn The Gordon Highldrs
                        21.7.41
Killed in France
Buried in St. Leger Ryes Brit Mil
Cem

Cohen, Rfmn Leonard
1st Btn, The London Irish Rifles
Died of wounds
Buried in Camp Verano Cem

Cohen, Pte Leslie
5 Btn Norfolk Regt
Age 32   24.1.42

Cohen, Pte Leslie James
1/7 Btn West Surrey Regt
Age 26   26.4.40
Buried Meteren Communal Cem

Cohen, Pte Lionel Henry
RAPC
                        7.1.41
Killed by a bomb

Cohen, Lt Louis Victor
Jat Regt
                        9.10.41
Buried Penang Jewish Cem

Cohen, Dvr M.
Pal Motor Transport Coy, RASC
                        -.-.42

Cohen, Pte Norman
The Middlx Regt
                        31.10.42
Died whilst a Japanese POW
Buried in the Commonwealth
Cem, Yokahama

Cohen, Capt Peter
443 Battery 61 Field Regt, RA
Age 26   8.8.44
Mentioned in Despatches
Killed in action

Cohen, Pte Reginald George
RAOC 10535108
                        20.1.42
Buried Benghazi War Cem

Cohen, Pte Reuben
The Roy Norfolk Regt
                        1.6.40
Dunkirk

Cohen, Fus Samuel
10th Lanc Fus
                        27.9.44
Buried Johannesburg Cem

Cohen, Pte Samuel Sidney
The Oxfordshire and Bucks L/I
                        -.11.43
Killed in action
Buried between Francolise and
Sparinisi

Figure 63. Cpl Harry Cohen, 2nd
Btn, The Black Watch (Royal
Highland Regt) (Commando).

Cohen, Pte Sidney
RA
Age 32
POW in a camp outside Nagasaki when the Atom Bomb was dropped. Died a year later of leukaemia in Battle Hospital, Hastings

Cohen, Capt Stephen Behrens
Upper Scinde Force India
                        10.2.43
Died at Karachi
Buried in the Jewish Cem, Karachi

Cohen, Cpl Sydney
REME 6848567
Age 26   20.8.45
Naples War Cem

Cohen, Pte W.G.
2nd Botha Regt, UDF
                        23.11.41
Buried Knightsbridge War Cem, Acroma

Cohen-Zeevi, Sgt Herzl
PAL602 RASC
                        23.11.42
Tobruk War Cem

Coleman (Kugelman), Pte H.J.
PC
                        23.10.44
Died by enemy action
Buried in Ghent Civil Cem

Collier-Bradley, Spr Michael
RE
                        18.6.43
Killed in action. Tank landing craft struck a mine
Buried Sousse Mil Cem

Collins, Rfmn C.

Collins, Eli
132 PC

Conroy, Capt Ronald
RAMC
                        -.-.55

DOAS

Comber, Spr Solomon
994 Docks Operating Coy, RE
Age 23   17.6.43
Killed when *SS Yoma* was torpedoed

Conway, Capt S.
RAMC
Age 32   21.7.44
Buried in Willesden Cem

Cooke, Richard Levi
Age 52   26.3.36
DOAS
Buried in Willesden Cem

Cooper, Lt Victor
RAMC
Age 24   26.11.43
Killed in action

Corkland, Pte Cecil
Essex Regt
                        20.12.43
Buried Sangro River War Cem

Cornell, Lt Basil Seymour
2/7th Btn, The Middx Regt
                        28.3.45
Killed in action

Cornik, Lt M.
                        -.-.48
KOAS

Cowan, Gerald
RASC

Cowan, Lt John D.
Welch Regt
                        6.9.44

Cowan, L/Cpl Ronald
RASC
Age 29   18.3.45
Died as a result of injuries received in a road accident in the forward area in Germany

Cowan, Pte Ronald David
RAMC
                        12.6.45

Cowan (Cowen), Sydney
Norwood Memorial

Craig, Cpl Anthony

Cramer, Arthur
RE
(tbc)   31.5.40

Cramer, John Dennis
                        23.3.43
KIA
Memorial at Willesden Cem

Crann, Lt Benjamin
164 Coy PC
                        8.7.44
Killed in action at sea

Da Costa, Capt Darnley Peter L.
Leic. Regt/Chindits
                        14.7.44

Da Costa, Pte Michael M.
KOSB
                        1.7.44
Buried in the Brit War Cem, St. Mauvieu, France

Da Costa, Sgt N. Mendes
Age 38   23.7.43
Died as a POW on the River Kwai

Da Costa, Patrick Clements
Irish Guards
                        31.1.44
KIA
See brothers killed

Figure 64. L/Cpl Ronald Cowan, RASC.

Davico, E.M.
PC

Davico, Pte Marco
Berks

David, Lt Leonard Arthur
*The Roy Sussex Regt, Seconded
Roy Hampshire Regt*
Age 28   29.1.44
Buried in the Brit Mil Cem, Naples

Figure 65. Lt Leonard Arthur
David, The Royal Sussex Regt
(Seconded to the Royal Hampshire
Regt).

David, L/Cpl Solomon
FMSVF
                         27.8.45

Davidson, Sgmn Leslie
RCOS
Age 29
Killed during the first landing in
Italy

Davidson, Pte Richard
Blackwatch
                         21.11.41
Buried at Knightsbridge

Davies, Gdsmn Leonard
6/Grenadier Guards
Age 22   16/17.3.43
Medjez-El-Bab Memorial

Davies, Sig Maurice
RCOS
                         6.9.45
Killed in an accident
Buried in Klagenfurt Mil Cem

Davies, Dvr Sidney
RASC
                         2.10.40
Buried at Haifa

Davies, Sgt Stanley
RA
Age 28   30.8.44
Died following a bomber raid

Davis, Bdr David
RA
Age 22
Died in a POW camp in Thailand

Davis, Cpl Henry C.
RASC
                         16.4.43
Buried at Baghdad

Davis, Capt Dudley Isaac
RCOS
                         -.1.45
Killed in Burma

Davis, Sig J.
*1st Btn, The Capetown
Highlanders*
                         -.2.42
Killed in action
Buried in Alexandria

Davis, John
Roy Fus
DOAS   -.-.70

Davis, Pte P.
The L/I
                         1.1.42
Buried in Sidi Aziz Cem

Davis, Dvr Reuben
RASC
                         21.3.44

Davis, Sig S.
*3rd Brigade Signal Coy, South
African Corps of Signals*
                         21.2.42
Buried in Hodra Mil Cem

De Groot, O/Cad Ivor Clifford

De La Fuente, Pte C.
4th Btn KSLI
Age 19   6.8.44
Buried Vire

De Pass, Alfred P.
1st RB

De Solla, Gnr Warren David
RA (TA)
                         26.11.43
Killed in an accident
Buried at Willesden

Dean, Capt M.
RAMC
Age 31   4.6.45
Killed in action in Burma
Buried in Rangoon War Cem

Dehond, Cpl Henry
RADC
Age 23   -.-.41
Killed by Italian enemy aircraft in
Libya

Denby-DreyFus, Pte C.
The Para Regt, Army Air Corps
Age 22   19.6.44

Denton, Lt P.A.
3rd Field Regt, S African Arty
                         8.1.42
Buried in Kantar West Mil Cem

Dester, Fus Samuel
Roy Fus
                         17.9.41
Killed in an accident

**Deutschkron (Dean), Sgt
Herbert John Hudson**
PC/ 7th Buffs
Age 43   27.6.45
Buried Sage War Cem, Adenburg

Figure 66. Sgmn Leslie Davidson, RCOS.

Figure 68. Cpl Henry Dehond, Royal Army Dental Corps.

Figure 69. The Grave of Pte C. Denby-Dreyfus, Para Regt, AAC.

Devries, Pte William
1 Btn Northants Regt
Age 21   20.4.44
Rangoon War Memorial

Diamond, Tpr J.L.
4th S. African Armoured Car Regt
                          2.12.41
Buried at Sollum-Tobruk

Diamondstone, Pte Jacky
The Yorks & Lancs Regt
                          -.-.44
Killed at Lanciano, Italy

Dickman, Pte R.L.
1st Btn, Capetown Highldrs
                          11.2.42
Buried in Tobruk Mil Cem

Dobbie Lt L.W.
RAOC
KIA N Ireland
                          -.10.73

Dobrozynski, Pte Frank Percy
1 Btn Para Regt
Age 26   19.9.44
Buried Arnhem Oosterbeek War Cem

Doelberg, Maj Julian Frederick
RE
                          29.4.41
Killed in Greece

Doppler, Pte Joseph
Free Czech Brigade
Age 34   9.10.44
Buried near Dunkirk

Dorf, Gnr A.
RA
Age 23   10.7.43
Buried at Willesden

Dorfberger, Tpr Myer
RCOS
                          8.8.44
Killed in action in France

Druce, Pte Abraham
RAOC
                          23.2.44
Buried in Glenduffhill Jewish Cem

Figure 67. The Grave of Capt M. Dean, RAMC, in Rangoon.

Dubovitch, Gnr Michael
519 Coast Regt, RA (Paras)
Age 26   -.8.44
Died of wounds

Ducker, Gnr Israel A.
117th Anti-Aircraft Regt, RA
                          21.10.43
Buried in Philipeville Anglo-
American Mil Cem

Duque (Duke), Pte S.S.
The King's Regt
Age 21   15.5.44
Killed in action in Burma (Chindits)
Buried in Rangoon War Cem

Duschinsky, Lt Charles
5th Middx
                          13/7/44
KIA
Willesden memorial

Dyson, Agatha Louise
Believed to have died fighting with
the Resistance

Eager, Cpl J.T. (aka Ehrlich)
RAC
                          13.5.46

Eckstein, S/Sgt Percy J.
RAOC
                          13.10.46
Killed in an accident in Nairobi

**Ekstein, Pte Anthony
(aka Edwards, Andor)**
*The Queen's Own Cameron
Highldrs*
Buried in Tourneville

Edel, L/Bdr Bernard
155 Field Regt RA
Age 23   7.1.42
Singapore Memorial

Edelstein, Pte Eric
RAOC
                          -.12.40
Killed in an air raid

Edelman, Capt J.R.
7th Rajputana Rifles, Indian Army
                          -.7.42
Missing believed killed

Ehrenfield, Lt A.H.
PC

Ehrlich, J.
13800121
6th AMPC
                          -.-.41

Eichen, Pte Hyman
*The Seaforth Highldrs (Ross-Shire
Buffs, The Duke of Albany's)*
                          -.2.45
Killed in action

Eisbruch, Cpl Sidney
*'A' Squadron, 1st Roy Tank Regt,
RAC*
                          -.4.45
Killed in action
Buried in Bremen, Germany

Elkan, Spr John
36th Btn RE
                          3.5.40

Elkind, Gnr Samuel
14th LAA Regt, RA
                          29.4.41
Killed by a bomb in Tobruk
Buried in Tobruk War Cem, Libya

Figure 71. Cpl Sidney Eisbruch,
'A' Squadron 1st RTR, RAC.

Ellerker, Pte Morris
1 Btn Lancaster Regt
Age 20   17.8.42
Buried Ramleh War Cem

Elliot, Frank
Hong Kong VDF

Figure 70. The Grave of Pte S.S. Duque, The King's Regt, in Rangoon.

Ellis, Nurse Leontine
Hong Kong VDF
b. Stanley

Elsner, Spr Harry
220 Field/Company RE
Age 36   14.12.44
Buried Forli War Cem

Emanuel, Pte George Alexander
The Para Regt
                          25.9.44
Died of war wounds, Arnhem

Emdon, R. Benjamin
Queens
DOAS

Evnine, Capt Maxim
RAMC
                          6.12.43
Died on active service

Faber, Fus S.N.
Roy Fus
                          16.9.44
Killed in action
Buried in 167 Brigade Cem,
Mulazzano

Fairman, Pte Jacob
RAOC
                          20.8.45

Falcke, Pte R.
3rd Btn, Transvaal Scottish, UDF
                          23.1.41.
Buried in Knightsbridge War Cem,
Acroma

Falk, Pte Mark
PC
Age 46   31.1.45
Buried Schoonselhof Cem,
Antwerp

Falk, Sgt Morris
RAOC
Age 18   6/7.12.42
SS *Ceramic*

Falk, Lt Rudolph Julian
The Para Regt
                          -.-.44
Killed in action, Arnhem

Falk, Corp W.
                          2.11.42
Buried in El Alamein Mil Cem

Falwasser, Gnr Peter Felix
1 Regt RHA
Age 26   22.12.42
Buried Heliopolis War Cem

Farber, Pte Hymie
The King's Own Regt
Age 28
Served with Wingate's Chindits
Missing in India, later presumed
dead

Fassenfeld, Pte Lawrence
*1st Btn The Seaforth Highlndrs
(Ross-Shire Buffs, The Duke of
Albany's)*
                          28.12.44
Buried in Bombay Jewish Cem.
Body transferred to new War Cem
in Kirkee, 100 miles from Bombay

**Feigenbaum, Rfmn Arnold
Abraham**
KRRC
                          3.10.42

Felbourne, Fus Joseph
9th Btn The Roy Fus
                          9.9.43
Killed in action
Buried at Spinetta near Salerno

Feld, Pte Mark
PC
                          20.3.46
Buried in East Ham

Feldman, Cpl Gerald
10th Roy Hussars, RAC
                          11.5.45
Killed by accident in Italy
Buried in the Jewish Cem at
Rovigo

Feldman, Pte Hyman
RAMC
                          -.6.42
Killed at Tobruk

Feldman, Gnr Louis
Pow Burma, Sunk Aboard Jap
Ship by American Sub.
                          -.9.44

Feldman, Pte Sammy
1 Btn Gloucester Regt
                          7/8.3.42
Rangoon Memoria

Felix, Cpl A.
PC
                          20.6.42
Buried at Willesden 21.6.42

**Fellous, Pte Joseph
(aka Fellows)**
364/Coy PC
Age 30   3.4.44
Buried Borgel Jewish Cem

**Fenton, Abraham
(aka Feinstein)**
Killed in action, Arnhem

Field, Sgt Hillier
9th Btn, KRRC (The Rangers) (TA)
                          3.11.42
Killed in action at El Alamein

Fieldman, Leslie
6th A&SH

Figure 72. Pte Hyman Feldman,
RAMC.

Figure 73. Sgt Hillier Field, 9th Btn, The KRRC (The Rangers) (TA).

Fierstein, Pte Sendar
General Service Corps
                              1.4.44
Buried in Glenduffhill Cem

Fileman, Pte John Myer
1st Btn, The Essex Regt
Killed in action in Burma

Finburg, Pte David M.
D/13195 DLI
                              19.2.47
DOAS
Buried Sunderland Jewish Cem

Finberg, Gnr John
RA
                              14.11.42

Fine, Dvr Eli
RASC, attached LAA Regt, RA
Age 32   12.9.44
Died at sea as a Japanese POW

Fine, Gnr Eli
127 Field/Regt RA
Age 24   24.7.43
Buried Catania War Cem

Fine, Cpl E.
RASC
                              -.6.45
Buried Sicily, Catania

Finegold, Pte Morris
The Roy Warwickshire Regt
Age 20   13.10.44
Killed in action at Overloon, Holland

Finkel, Gnr Harold
RA
                              23.4.41
Killed in air raid
Buried at West Ham

Finklestein, Pte Julius
The Roy Sussex Regt
                              27.8.42
Buried at East Ham

Finklestone-Sayliss, Capt Dr Hyman
Yorks & Lancs
                              18.5.44
DOAS

Finlay, Pte David (aka Finkelstein)
5th Btn, The Black Watch (Roy Highland Regt)
                              9.4.45
Killed in action
Buried in Rheinberg Brit Cem

Finlay, Cpl David Kenneth
Roy Army Vet Corps
                              27.3.45
Killed by a V2
Buried in Adath Yisroel Cem, Enfield

Firestone, Pte L.
Welch Regt.
                              19.9.44
Killed in action

Firth, Sgmn Charles
RCOS, Airborne
Died in India
Buried in Madras Cem

Figure 74. Cpl E. Fine, RASC.

Figure 75. Craftsman Alexander Fisher, REME.

Fisher, Cftmn Alexander
REME
Age 24   -.3.44
Killed by enemy action at sea

Fisher, S/Sgt Cyril
The Glider Pilot Regt, Army Air Corps
Age 24   20.9.44
Killed at Arnhem
No known grave

Fisher, Gnr Jack
RA
                              12.2.44
East Africa Memorial

Figure 76. S/Sgt Cyril Fisher, The Glider Pilot Regt, AAC.

Fisher, 2nd Lt Maurice
Army Cadet Force
18.11.43

Fisherman, Gnr D.
RA
27.9.44
Italy

Fishler, Cpl Sydney
PC
11.9.46
Buried at East Ham

Fishman, Pte Monty Emanuel
Essex Regt Att 1 Battery
Sherwood Foresters
Age 20   26.9.44
Buried Streatham Jewish Cem

Fishman, Cpl Stanley
The Green Howards (Alexandra,
Princess of Wales's Own Yorkshire
Regt)
Taken prisoner during the battle of
Tobruk
Not heard of again

Fleisher, Pte Solomon
RASC
17.6.40
SS *Lancastria*

Fletcher (Fleischer), Pte Fred
The Worcestershire Regt
-.6.44
Killed in action 10 Commando
Buried in a commando plot in a
farm yard north of Ranville,
Normandy

Fletcher, O/Cad Fred
RASC
22.11.45
Buried Merthyr Tydfil

Flexer, Pte Bernard
General Service Corps
Age 20   23.3.46
Buried Leeds, Geldard Road Cem

Flome, Pte Michael
RAMC
22.4.44
Buried at East Ham

Flowers, Gnr Maurice
3rd Survey Regt, RA
Age 38   25.5.44
Killed in action, Cassino

Fordonsky, Pte Joseph
The South Staffs Regt
26.12.40
Buried at East Ham

Foreman, Gnr Abraham Michael
118 HAA Regt, RA
-.6.45
Drowned on boat patrol in France

Foreman, Pte N.
2/4th Btn, KOYLI
8.12.43
Killed in Italy
Buried in Montorno Mil Cem

Forman, Pte Alec
2nd Btn The Essex Regt
19.6.44
Died of wounds in Normandy
Buried in the Brit Mil Cem, Bayeux

Fortuin, Pte Gerald
RASC

Figure 77. Cpl Stanley Fishman, The Green Howards (Alexandra, Princess of Wales's Own Yorkshire Regt).

Foster (Fraenkal), Tpr E.
1st Roy Tank Regt, RAC
12.6.44
Killed in action in Normandy
Buried at Tilly-sur-Seuilles

Foster (Fogel), Pte Harry
220 Coy PC
11.8.43
Drowned
Buried in Cheltenham Cem

Fram, Pte Richard
Army Catering Corps
12.6.44
Killed in action in Normandy
Buried in France

Frame, Pte J.
1st Imperial Light Horse
3.12.42
Buried in El Homer, Bardia

Frank (Franklyn), M.G.
10th Commando Normandy

Frankel, Lt E.S.
KSLI
24.4.43
Killed in action
Buried at Medjez El Bab, Tunisia

Frankenburg, Capt Miles
The Gurkha Riles
-.6.44
Killed in action

Franklin, Dvr Jacob
RCOS
-.11.45
Died while a POW in Thailand

Franks, Sgt Ronald
The Glider Pilot Regt, AAC
Age 25   22.10.44
Died of wounds at Arnhem

Franzblau (Fox), Pte David W.
4 Btn KSLI
Age 20   19.4.45
Buried Soltau War Cem

Fredlieb, L/Cpl Mark
*The Duke of Wellington's Regt
(W Riding)*
Age 18   17.1.45
Drowned
Buried in Ecclesfield Jewish Cem

Freed, Col/Sgt Harold
2 Btn Roy Berks Regt
Age 25   24.2.45
Buried Taukkyan War Cem
Rangoon

Freed, Sydney
RA
14.11.42

Freedlander, Fus David
Roy Fus
27.7.41
Buried at Willesden

Freedlander, Pte Gerald Eleazer
12 Btn Para Regt
Age 19   7.8.44
Buried Ranville War Cem

Freedman, Pte Alexander
7.3.44
Buried in Glasgow Jewish Cem

Freedman, David
(Harrogate)

Figure 78. The Grave of Pte Alec Forman, 2nd Btn, The Essex Regt, in Bayeux.

Figure 79. Sgt Ronald Franks, The Glider Pilot Regt, AAC.

Freedman, Pte H.J.
PC
22.3.44
Buried at Willesden

Figure 80. L/Cpl Mark Fredlieb, The Duke of Wellington's Regt (West Riding).

Freedman, Pte Israel
PC
18.10.44
Buried at East Ham

Freedman, Pte Joseph
2 Btn Lancaster Regt
Age 27   25.5.44
Rangoon Memorial

Freedman, Lt Joseph
A&SH
28.11.42

Freedman, Bdr Morris Frank
31.7.45
Died in POW Camp Kuching
Sarawak

Freedman, Pte Sydney
*16th Glamorgan (Cardiff) Btn
Home Guard*
6.10.40
Buried Cardiff Jewish Cem

Freeman, Maj Barnett
RAMC
-.11.44
Died in India
Buried at Calcutta

Freeman, Bdr David
RA
14.11.42

Freeman, Rfmn Jack
RB
                               23.5.40

Freeman, Pte Henry
*The East Yorks Regt (The Duke of
York's Own)*
Age 21   6.6.41

Freeman, Pte Leslie
Buffs
Age 22
He went down with the SS
Lancastria, which suffered a
direct hit by an enemy bomb
when evacuating Dunkirk

Freeman, Dvr Maurice Basil
2nd Middx Yeomanry
                               20.3.40
Killed in an accident

Freeman, WO2 Morris Hilliard
                               8.4.45
Buried in Zambia

Freeman, Sgt Sidney
RA
Buried H Kong

Freshwater, Rfmn Harry A.
10th Btn, The Rifle Brigade
Killed in North Africa. Shot by the
Germans on capture. Body
recovered and buried 4 miles
West of El Aronsa
Name placed in a bottle

Froewe, Dvr E.
RASC
                               -.-.42

Fuchs, Sgt Eric
PC
                               -.8.45
Buried in Wolvercote Cem, Oxford

Gabriel, Capt John P.
The Roy Berkshire Regt
                               24.2.41

Gafanowitz, Pte P.
Rhodesian L/I, UDF
                               26.7.42
Buried at El Imayid, Egypt

Figure 81. Pte Henry Freeman,
The East Yorkshire Regt (The Duke
of York's Own).

Gaffin, Cpl Merton Eugene
RCOS
                               28.3.43
Died in POW Camp Thailand

Gahtan, Pte David Solomon
5 Btn Hants Regt
Age 25   26.2.43
Buried Beja War Cem Tunisia

Galinsky, Cftmn Norman
REME
                               20.2.46
Buried at Secunderabad, India

Galman, Pte Phillip
4/Buffs
Age 27   23/24.10.43
Athens Memorial

Garfunkel, Pte
The Gordon Highldrs
*5th Btn The Oxfordshire &
Buckinghamshire L/I*
Age 18   16.8.44
Died of wounds
Buried at Tourneville

Gartin, Pte Sam
1/4th Btn, The Essex Regt
                               23.7.42
Killed in action
Buried at El Alamein

Figure 82. Pte Leslie Freeman,
Buffs.

Garvaton, M.E.
RA
                               8.3.47
Buried at Glasgow

Gavronsky, Pte Leo
7 Btn Black Watch
Age 27   18.10.42

Gavurin, Lt Harold
RAMC
                               7.1.43

Gay, Sgmn Leslie L.
RCOS
                               1.6.43
Buried in the European Cem, Souk
Ahras

Geber, Pte Jakub
Polish Army
                               -.5.41
Killed in action

Gee, Pte Joseph
8th Btn The Durham L/I
                               -.3.43
Age 22
Killed in action

Gendil, Pte J.
PC
                               -.-.42

Gerber, Spr I.R.
SAEC
                               24.10.42
Buried at El Alamein

Gergel, Sgt A.
6th Btn (Pal) Buffs
          31.12.41
Buried in Ramleh Mil Cem

Gerscovitch, Pte I.
RAOC

Gerzo, Gnr S.D.
Hong Kong V.D.F.
b. Stanley

Gibbs, Pte Gerald Gershon
PC
Age 34   8.3.44
Buried Streatham Jewish Cem

Gilbert, Fus Bert
13th Btn, Roy Fus
         13.8.40
Buried at East Ham

Gilbert, Gnr Michael H.S.
RA
         12.11.41
Buried at East Ham

Gilbert, Cpl Percy
RASC
         18.5.47
Buried Rainham

Gilbert, Gnr Samuel
RA
         19.2.45

Gilbert, Pte Sidney
RAOC
         12.8.45
Buried at East Ham

Gilbert, L/Bdr Sidney
RA
         -.2.45
Killed in action

Giles, Peter (aka Otto Hess)
10 Commando/SOE

Ginsberg, Pte F.
1st Btn, The Rhodesian L/I, UDF
         24.10.42
Buried in El Hamman Mil Cem

**Ginsberg, L/Cpl Leonard E.
(aka Winter)**
The Middx Regt
         25.12.41
Killed in action
Buried in Hong Kong

Ginsberg, L/Cpl M.
UDF
         21.7.41
Buried in Hodra Mil Cem

Ginsberg, Sgt R.
         3.12.43

Glasel, Fus William
Age 27   -.12.42
Died on active service in Africa

**Glaser, Capt J. Kurt
(aka Keith James Griffith)**
10 Commando

Glass, Pte Bruce Barnet
2nd/13th Australian Infantry Btn
         5.12.42
Buried at sea in the
Mediterranean

Glass, Rfmn Leslie R.
1st Queen Vic Rifles

Glassman, Pte Harry
1st Btn, The Bedfordshire and
Hertfordshire Regt
         12.6.44
Died in India
Buried in Dibrugarh Civil Cem

Glauber, Sgt Kurt Erich
RA
Age 42   1.4.45

Glekin, Pte Louis
*8th Btn The Roy Scots
(The Roy Regt)*
         29.9.44
Buried at Tilly-Sur-Seulles,
Normandy

Glicksman, Pte Jack
The South Staffs Regt
Age 36   -.1.41
Died of wounds

Gluck, Israel
RE

**Gluckstein, Capt Bruce
Montague**
1st Btn KSLI
         14.3.44
Died of wounds
Buried in Naples Mil Cem
Mentioned in Despatches
(posthumously)

Golab, Gnr M.L.
RA
         3.2.45

Figure 83. The Grave of Gnr M.L.
Golab, RA.

Gold, Dvr Alfred Abraham
RASC
         13.7.43
Killed in North Africa
Buried in Constantine Civil Cem

Gold, Sgt Harold
REME

Goldapple, Pte Philip
*The Roy Berks Regt (Princess
Charlotte of Wales's)*
         1.6.40
Died of wounds in Flanders
Buried at East Ham

Figure 84.
AO S. Goldman.

Figure 85.
Israel Averback, AAC.
Died of Wounds.

Figure 86.
Fus Leslie Bartell.

Figure 87.
Rev H. Bornstein.

Figure 88.
Lt D.L. Cohen.

Figure 89.
Pte S.S. Cohen.

Figure 90.
Lt V.L. Cooper.

Figure 91.
Sgt A. Goldman.

Figure 92.
Pte L. Greenberg.

Figure 93.
Pte H. Gross.

Figure 94.
Pte B. Lassman.

Figure 95.
Sgt R. Levy.

Figure 96.
Pte G. Litwin.

Figure 97.
Tpr A. Mendik.

Figure 98.
Pte A. Rosenblum.

Figure 99.
Gnr R. Segal.

Goldberg, Gnr Aaron
12th Field Regt, RA
1.5.45
Died in Italy
Buried at Argenta

Goldberg, Pte A.
3rd Monmouthshire Reg.
27.2.45

Goldberg, Rfmn D.
1st Btn, KRRC
20.4.45
Killed by a shell at Traghetto
Buried at Bocconiole

Goldberg, D.
5th Field Reg. RA
Died in Taiwan

Goldberg, Lt E.
*Army in Burma Reserve of
Officers*
27.4.42
Rangoon Memorial

Goldberg, Gnr Harry
RHA (HAC)
Died of wounds in Italy

Goldberg, L/Cpl Hyman Stanley
2nd Btn, DCLI
-.5.44
Killed in action
Buried at Amazon Bridge, Rapido
River

Goldberg, Pte J.
RASC

Goldberg, Pte Leslie
RAMC
Age 20   12.6.44
Killed in action in North-West
Europe

Goldberg, L/Bdr P.
312 Battery, 54 HAA Regt, RA
25.4.41
Buried at Willesden

Goldberg, Dvr S.
RASC
25.12.42
Died in Palestine

Goldberg, Pte Sidney
PC
6.1.46
Buried at East Ham

Goldberg, Pte Sydney
RASC
Age 19   -.2.45
Killed on active service in North-
West Europe

Goldblath, Gdsmn Leslie Harris
2 Btn Irish Guards
Age 29   9.5.45
Buried Soltau War Cem

Goldblatt, Cpl Michael Isaac
Beds & Herts Regt
31.3.48
DOAS

Goldblum, Pte Sigmond
6th Btn, KOSB
-.11.44
Killed in action

Goldfarb, Pte David Harry
Buffs
-.5.42
Buried at Edmonton

**Goldfeather, L/Bdr Israel
Joseph**
142 Field Regt RA
Age 24   9.9.43
Buried Salerno War Cem

Goldfield, Capt Munro
(A.D.C.)
14.4.46

Goldman, Sgt Alfred
*4th Btn, Para/Regt,
Army Air Corps*
-.2.44
Died of wounds

Goldman, Spr Eli
RE
1.11.44
Killed on Walcheren Island
No known grave

Goldman, Pte F.
Maritime Regt
30.9.43
Gunner aboard SS *Fort Howe*,
sunk by U Boat

Goldman, Pte Harry
-.-.41
Killed in action in the Middle East

Goldman, Bdr Jack
*1st Maritime Anti-Aircraft Regt,
RA*
-.6.44
Killed at sea

Figure 100. Pte Sydney
Goldberg, RASC.

Goldman, Rfmn Jacob
The Roy Ulster Rifles
-.6.44
Buried at East Ham

Goldman, L/Cpl Louis
*2nd Btn, The Devonshire
Regt*
6.6.44
Killed in action

Goldman, Pte Philip
RAOC
-.3.43
Killed by accident

Goldman, Reginald
Hong Kong VDC

Goldman, Stanley
RCOS
13.8.46

Goldsmith, Lt Anthony Maurice Elim
22.4.43
Killed in action in Italy
Spike Milligan wrote a poem about this officer, who was his CO in Tunisia (*see 'Longstop Hill', above*).

Goldsmith, Pte H.
RAOC
13.10.45
Killed in an accident

Goldsmith, Gnr Leslie Norman
4 Survey Regt RA
Age 36
14.11.42

Goldsmith, O.A.
RASC
DOAS

Goldstein, unknown
Paras
KIA Arnhem

Goldstein, A.M.
PC
21.1.50

Goldstein, Spr Fred
56th RE
9.1.43
Buried in Mosul, Iraq

Goldstein, L/Cpl Heinz
PC
29.12.40
Killed by enemy action
Buried at East Ham

Goldstein, Pte Hyman
The Black Watch (Roy Highland Regt)
13.5.41
Died on active service
Buried at Glasgow

Goldstein, Fus Isaac Louis
2nd Btn, The Roy Scots Fus
Age 30
-.7.43
Killed in action in Sicily

Goldstein, J. (aka Joe Stewart)
PC
21.1.50

Goldstein, J.M.
RA
Buried in Tunisia

Goldstein, Pte K.H.
31.3.42
Buried in the Jewish Civil Cem, Haifa

Goldstein, Rfmn Maurice
8 Btn Rifle Brigade
Age 18
3.9.44
Buried Lille Southern Cem

Goldstein, Gnr Samuel
LAA RA 169 Battery
Age 26
9.5.44
Cassino Memorial

Goldston, Sgmn Jack
RCOS, Attached 11th Regt, RHA (HAC)
26.10.42
Killed in action
Buried at El Alamein

Goldston, Lt Richard D.
RA
18.9.43

Goldstone, Tpr Benjamin Thomas
10th Hussars RAC
Age 33
10.6.40
Buried St. Pierre-Du-Vauvray Communal Cem

Goldstone, Capt Bernard P.H.A.
Manchester Regt
25.10.44
Buried Gent City Cem

Goldstone, Pte Bernard
1st Btn, The Manchester Regt
29.8.43
Died at Song Krai, Thailand

Goldstone, Pte Donald
Essex Regt
Age 26
23.11.43
Sangro River War Cem

Goldstone, Lt H.B.
SAEC
31.5.41
Buried at Addis Ababa

Goldstone, Lt Morris
2nd/23rd Australian Infantry Btn
26.7.42
Buried in Hodra Brit War Cem

Goldstone, Cpl Maurice
16th Btn, The Durham LI
27.9.44
Killed in action
Buried at La Villa

Goldstone, Capt Lionel Stanley, MC
8th Btn, Roy Fus (City of London Regt)
7.11.43
Died of wounds
Buried in the Brit Mil Cem, Roccamonfina

Goldstone, Gnr Sidney Walter
RA
Age 28
20.07.43
Catania War Cem

Figure 101. Capt Lionel Stanley Goldstone MC, 8th Btn, Roy Fus (City of London Regt).

Goldwater, Pte Philip
4 Btn King's Shropshire L/I
Age 26   6.9.44
Buried Schoonselhof Cem

Golombik, Pte I.
2nd Btn, Transvaal Scottish, UDF
                                        12.12.41
Buried in Figtree Wells Cem,
Sollum

Gomm, Cpl A.
                                        -.-.59
DOAS Malta

Gomperts, Lt Phillip J.
RE
                                        5.1.42
(Son of Brig Mervyn C.T.
Gomperts)

Gompertz, Pte Arthur
RASC
                                        17.6.40

Gompertz, Pte Joseph A.
3 Lancs
                                        13.6.45

Goodfield, Tpr R.
1st Derbyshire Yeomanry, RAC
                                        12.4.43
Buried War Graves Cem. Infida,
Sousse

**Goodfriend, Capt Isaac
Theodore**
RE
                                        10.5.43
Killed in a train accident whilst on
duty
Buried at East Ham

Goodman, Pte
The Essex Regt
                                        -.-.41
Died in a POW Camp in Italy

Goodman, Cpl Albert Alfred
Roy Fus (City of London Regt)
                                        -.7.44
Died of wounds

Goodman, Tpr Bernard
40th RTR, RAC
                                        31.8.42
Killed in action
Buried at El Alamein

Goodman, Dvr Harry
RAOC
                                        -.10.42
Missing presumed killed in action
at sea

Goodman, Pte Herman
RASC
                                        -.-.41
Buried at Crete

Goodman, Sgt Israel
RAOC Att Indian AOC
Age 40   9.6.43
Buried Delhi War Cem

Goodman, Pte Jack
4th Dorsets
Killed in action
Age 29   26.9.44
Vianen Protestant Cem

Goodman, Pte Lewis
1 Btn Buffs
Age 27   23.3.43
Buried Ancona War Cem Italy

Goodman, Pte M.
The Capetown Highldrs, UDF
                                        24.10.42
Buried in El Alamein Mil Cem

Goodman, Fus Mickie
*2nd Btn, Roy Fus (City of London
Regt)*
                                        -.7.43
Missing believed killed in action

Goodman, Pte Sidney
*'C' Company 7th Btn, The Roy
Berks Regt*
Age 21   -.4.43
Killed in action in Burma

Goodman, Stanley
RCMP
                                        24.5.40

Figure 102. Pte Sidney
Goodman, 'C' Company 7th Btn,
The Royal Berkshire Regt.

Gordon, Pte David
E Yorks Regt

Gordon, S/Sgt Hyman Israel
RE
                                        10.8.41
Died on active service in Bermuda

Gordon, Dvr Joseph
RASC
                                        -.-.42

Gordon, Gnr Joseph Samuel
RA
                                        -.4.44
Killed in action
Buried near Anzio, Italy

Gordon, Lt Stanley
The Gordon Highldrs
                                        17.4.45

Gorman, Fus Abraham
Lancs Fus
Age 31   12.10.44
Faenza War Cem

Gostinsky, Pte Ralph
4 Btn W Kent Regt
Age 27   11.10.42
Buried Caserta War Cem

Gottlieb, Gnr Gerald
RA
POW Thailand

Gould, Bmdr Harold
RA
                              29.5.40
Dunkirk

Gould, Sgt Montague
RA
Age 21   -.-.42
Killed in Burma
His name is on the Memorial in
Rangoon

Grab, Pte Rolf Rudi
The Jewish Inf Brigade Group
                              -.4.46
Served in Italy. Died in Palestine
Buried in Ramleh Mil Cem

Grabarsky, Samuel
Norwood Memorial

Graber, Dr Adam
Killed in action Cassino, Polish

Graetzer, Pte Fritz Eitel
PC
Age 43   12.5.44
Buried in Willesden Jewish Cem

Grad, Pte Joseph
The Seaforth Highldrs of Canada
                              -.11.43
Killed in action

Green, Sgt Sidney
56th LAA Regt, RA
                              9.5.43
Buried in the Brit Mil Cem
near Enfidaville

Greenbaum, Pte Sidney
7th Btn, The South Staffs Regt
                              -.12.43
Died on active service

Greenberg, Pte H.
*1st Btn, The Transvaal Scottish,
UDF*
                              15.12.41
Buried in the Italian Burial Ground,
Sollum

Greenberg, L/Cpl Harry
3781716 Kings Reg.
Age 30   12.8.43
Madras (St Mary's) Cem, Chennai

Greenberg, Pte Leonard
The Gloucestershire Regt
                              30.7.44
Killed in action in North-West
Europe
Buried in the Brit Cem Hottot-les-
Bagues

Greenberg, Rfmn Morris
9th Btn, The Rifle Brigade
                              17.6.42
Buried in Cyrenaica, Sollum, Tobruk

Greenberg (Burgh), Dvr Reuben
RASC
                              -.6.42

Greenberg, Capt S.
RAMC
                              -.9.41
Died on active service

Greenburg, Pte
REME
                              -.-.45
Died at Secunderabad, India

Greene, Maj Alexander Philip
RA
Age 28   21.6.45
Died in Salonika

Greenman, L/Bdr Morris
RA
                              7.12.45
Buried at East Ham

Greenstein, Gnr Harry
RA
Age 23   31.10.43
(Garnet Hill Hebrew Congregation,
Glasgow)
Taken prisoner at Singapore.
Died in a POW Camp in Thailand
Buried in the River Kwai Cem

Greenstein, Cpl Joseph
*8th Btn, Roy Fus (City of London
Regt)*
                              23.7.41
Buried at Ogliara

Grennan, Capt Jeffery L., MC
The London Irish Rifles
                              -.12.47
Died of wounds

Grew, G.C.I.L.
                              22.11.40

Figure 103. Rfmn Morris
Greenberg, The Tower Hamlets
Rifles, RB.

Figure 104.
Gnr Harry Greenstein, RA.

Figure 105. Maj Alexander Philip
Greene, RA.

Grisip, Gnr Isidore Aaron
The Essex Yeomanry
Age 23   -.-.42
Killed in Tobruk
Buried in the Halfaya Sollum Mil
Cem

Groman, Moszek
Paras
Arnhem, Polish

Grombakh, Gnr Boris
135 Fld/Regt RA
Age 33   11/14.2.42
Buried Kranji War Cem

Gronfein, Dvr Hyman M.
RASC
                            1.1.42
Buried at East Ham

Gross, Pte Herbert
6th Btn, The Cheshire Regt
                            -.2.44
Killed in Italy
Buried in Caserta Mil Cem

Gross, L. (aka Cross)
PC

Gross, Pte Willi
PC
                            16.5.42
Buried in Darlington Cem

**Grossman, Capt Adolph
Reginald**
The South Wales Borderers
                            8.8.42
Buried in Willesden

Grossman, Rfmn Jack
8th Btn, The Rifle Brigade
                            11.8.44
Killed in Normandy
Buried in Bayeux Cem

Grosvenor, Beresford
Killed in North Africa piloting a
fighter

Gruenwald, Pte Oscar
PC
Killed in Algiers by explosion
Buried in El Alia Cem

Gruskin, L/Bdr B.
South African Artillery
                            30.5.42
Buried at Gazala

**Gubby, Nurse Sallie
(aka Gubbay)**
Hong Kong Def. Corps
Age 54   1.5.43
Hong Kong Jewish Cem

Guinsberg, Sgmn T.
SACOS
                            10.6.42
Buried in Kantara West El Balloh
Mil Cem

**Gumpertz, Pte Kurt Wilhelm
(aka Graham, Kenneth
Wakefield)**
Hants Regt/10 Commando
Age 24   12.6.44
Buried in Hermanville War Cem,
Normandy

Gutfreund, Pte Leo
11th Czech Btn
                            30.10.41
Buried at Tobruk

Guttenberg, Pte S.
PC
                            23.6.45
Killed on active service
Buried in the Reichswald Forest
Brit Cem

Guzzan, Rfmn Sam
The Rifle Bde
Buried at El Alamein

Haberman, Pte Joseph
RASC-Canada
                            3.10.44
Buried at Naples

Habler, Pte Norbert
PC
                            19.2.44
Buried at East Ham

Haft, Tpr H.
RTR, RAC

Haikin, Cpl Bernard
Para/Regt
Killed in action, Arnhem

Haimovitch, Pte David
2nd/6th Btn, The East Surrey Regt
                            19.9.44
Killed in action
Buried at S. Marin Capiano

Halevy, Lt Isaiah
*2nd Btn, Roy Fus (City of London
Regt)*
Age 23   13.9.44
Killed in action
Buried at Gradara

Halford, T. (Hernstadt)
PC

Halpern, Capt David
RAMC
Age 32   -.9.44
Killed in action

Halpern, Pte Jack David
1 Btn W Yorks Regt
Age 27   12.4.44
Rangoon Memorial

Figure 106. Tpr H. Haft, RTR, RAC. (The photograph dates from his early training in the Infantry).

Figure 107. The Grave of Tpr H. Haft.

Figure 108. The Grave of Lt H. Haltrecht, RA, in Rangoon.

Figure 109. The Grave of Pte S. Halun (Israel), RASC (see p. 199.)

Haltrecht, Lt H.
RA
23.3.45
Killed in action at Puttaing in Burma
Buried in Rangoon War Cem

Hamber, Pte Norman
Killed in North Africa

Hamberger, Dvr Joseph
RASC
17.6.43
Missing at sea presumed dead

Hamdi, Pte Eliyahu
RE (Pal)

Hamilton (Weich) or Reich, Cpl Robert Geoffrey
Roy Sussex Regt 10 Commando
Age 28   1.11.44
Buried Bergen-op-Zoom War Cem

Hamley, Cpl A. (aka Baumfeld)
PC
11.4.45
Buried at Willesden

Hananel, Dvr Chaim
RASC
1.5.43
Brookwood Mem

Hanau, Col Julius, OBE
SOE
12/5/43

Handel, Dvr Benjamin
RASC
-.8.43
Missing at sea presumed killed

Harbert, Pte S.
The Para/Regt, Army Air Corps
Age 27   8.6.44

Hardman, Cpl Joseph, MM
25.3.44
Killed in action at Cassino

Hardstone, Gnr Abraham
RA
-.10.43
Killed at San Salvo

Harris, Gnr Abraham
Buried in Enfield

Harris, Pte Alfred
PC
25.11.42
Buried in Bone Cem, Annaba

Figure 110. The Grave of Pte S. Harbert, Para Regt, AAC

Harris, Tpr Charles S.
3rd County of London Yeomanry, RAC
Age 35   30.11.43
Killed in action
Buried in the Sangro River Cem

Harris, Gnr David
RA

Harris, 2nd Lt Derek Basil
Roy Fus (City of London Regt)
                              -.2.45
Killed in action in Italy
Buried East of Mezzino

Harris, Cpl E.
PC
                              6.6.44
Killed in action
Buried in the White Beach Shore Cem, Bernieres-sur-Mer

Harris, Bdr Harold
RA
                              4.7.42
Buried at El Alamein

Harris, Fus Harry
Roy Fus (City of London Regt)
                              -.10.44
Buried at East Ham

Figure 111. The Grave of Tpr Charles S. Harris, 3rd County of London Yeomanry, RAC, in the Sangro River Cemetery, Italy.

Harris, Pte Harry
6th Airborne Division
                              -.11.44
Killed on active service

Harris, Cpl Jack
PC
Died of wounds in North-West Europe
Buried in Bayeux Cem

Harris, Tpr Jack
RTR
                              27.4.43

Harris, Capt Kaynon
RAMC
                              7.12.42

Harris, L/Cpl Leslie
10th Btn, The Rifle Brigade
                              -.1.43
Died of wounds in North Africa

Harris, Sgt Mark
9th Btn, KRRC
Killed in the Middle East
Buried South of Deir El Ragil, Egypt

Harris, Rfmn P.
7th Btn, The Rifle Bde
                              26.10.44
Killed in action
Buried at Faenza

Harris, Sgnlr Ralph
10th Rifle Bde
MID

Harris, L/Cpl Ronald
Grenadier Guards

Hart, Lt Elias
SAAC att. London Regt

Hart, Gnr L.
RA
Age 21   10.12.42
Buried Bari Mil Cem

Hartman, Pte Sidney
Para/Regt, Army Air Corps
                              6.6.44
Killed in Normandy

Hartstein, Gnr Emanuel
51st AT Regt RA

Hass, Gnr Lawrence
RA
                              25.5.44
Buried in Rowe War Cem

Heinzman, Tpr F. (Darky) Heinz
(No known next of kin)
11th Hussars (7th Armoured Division)
Age 22   21.8.44
Killed in action Normandy

Heller, Maj E.G.
Intel Corps
                              3.2.46
Buried at Volmerdingsen, Germany

Hellman, 2nd Lt J.M.
South African Defence Force
                              -.5.41

Figure 112. Princess Alexandra at the AJEX Remembrance Parade 1967.

Helman, Pte Godel
PC
            17.7.44
Buried Dely Ibrahim War Cem

Henefry, Cpt Leonard
RAMC
            -.-.43

Henriques, 2nd Lt D.J.Q.
The Sherwood Foresters
(Nottinghamshire & Derbyshire
Regt)
            -.5.40
Killed in action in Belgium

Henry, Capt John Miles
Para/Regt (AAC)
Age 23   19.9.44
Buried at the Airborne Cem,
Arnhem

Herbert, Capt Leopold, MC
RAMC
            -.8.43
Killed by a mortar bomb making a
direct hit on his Regimental aid
post in Sicily

Herman, Frederick
RE
            17.6.40
SS Lancastria

Herman, Pte Mark P.
13th Btn, The Para/Regt, AAC
            4.1.45
Killed in action in North-West
Europe
Buried in the Ardennes

Herman, Pte Morris
The East Surrey Regt
          24.11.40
Killed by enemy action
Buried at Willesden

Hermann, V.
PC

Herrmann, E.B. (aka Howard)
PC

Herscott, Gnr Maurice Jack
56 Indep LAA Battery RA
            6.3.45
Buried Rainham Jewish Cem

Hersh, L/Cpl Harry
PC
            1.9.42

Hershovitz, Pte Herman
RAOC
            17.7.42
Killed in the Middle East

Hershowitz, Pte W.
The Durham L/I
          17.12.41
Buried at Ras El Manaster

Herson, Gnr Myer
5 Searchlight Regt RA
Age 30   12.2.42
Singapore memorial

Herzog, Pte Manfred
4 Welch Regt 53 Div 21 Army
Group
Age 18   8.4.45
Buried Groesbeek Memorial Cem

Hewitt, Jack (aka Reich)
Died as Japanese POW
            -.11.43

Hieger, Tpr Francis Gordon
RTR, HQ 22nd Armoured Bde
            1.11.41
Buried in Hodra Mil Cem

Higgins (Wilk), Spr Michael
RE
            30.5.45
Buried in Evere Cem

Highbloom, Rfmn Benjamin
10th Btn, The Rifle Bde
            -.2.43
Killed in action

Hildebrand, Lt Col G.L.
RA
            6.4.48
Killed in Israel

Hiller, Tpr Alex Max
7 Queens Own Hussars
Age 25   2.5.42
Rangoon Memorial

Hillman, Capt Wilfred
1st R North Fus

Hince, Fus Edward
RF
          14.12.43

Figure 113. Sgt W. Hollman, 20th Company, RAMC.

Hirsch, O/Cad David Philip
Green Howards (Yorks Regt)
(Nephew of WW1 VC)
Age 19   10.6.45
Kirkee War Cem

Hirsch, Janislaw
Polish Resettlement Corps
                          21.7.47

Hirsch, Pte John
RAMC

Hirsch, Pte Paul
The Yorks & Lancs Regt
                          -.11.43
Died of wounds in Italy

Hirschfeld, Lt Walter A.B.
RAMC
Age 36   18.4.47
Streatham Park Cem

Hirshman (Hershmann), Tpr Abraham
44th Recce Regt. Recce Corps
                          27.9.43
Killed in action
Buried in Ponte Cagnano Cem

Hockman (Hochman), Pte E.
151st Company PC
                          15.2.41
Died on active service
Buried in Glasgow

Hoffenberg, Pte J.S.
UDF
                          15.7.42
Buried at El Daba, El Alamein

Hoffman, Charles
RAMC
(tbc)   25.5.40

Hollman, Sgt W.
20th Coy, RAMC
                          -.2.40
Died in Haifa
Buried in Ramieh Mil Cem

Hollos. P.
PC, 8th Irish Hussars
Killed in action, Normandy

Homer, Pte Benjamin Harry
12th Btn Para Regt
Age 21   8.4.45
Buried Hanover War Cem

Hooker, Rev Solomon
Chaplain to The Forces
                          -.-.45
Died at Secunderabad, India

Hoppen, Gnr Harry
94 HAA RA
                          1.6.43
Buried Heliopolis War Cem

Horowitz, Cpl Moshe
Pal Unit
                          -.-.44

Horley, R. (aka Harley, Cohn)
PC
                          5.4.46

Horton, Tpr S.
RTR RAC
Age 28   8.11.43
Buried British Mil Cem Bolsena

Hoselitz, Rudolf
Hong Kong VDC

Figure 114. Guardsman Samuel Huntman, Welsh Guards.

Howard, Pte Eric Bernard (aka Nathan)
PC/10 Commando
Age 32   30.4.45
Buried Jonkerbos War Cem, Holland

Howard, L/Cpl J. (aka Honigsberg)
627 Mil Govt Detachment, Brit Army of The Rhine
Died on the Belgian-German Border
Buried in Dusseldorf Mil Cem

Howarth, RSM (WO1) Eric William (aka Nathan, E.W.)
The Buffs/10 Commando
Age 22   3.4.45
Buried Reichswald Forest War Cem

Howell, Lt Michael Alec (aka Rosenbluth)
REME
Age 25   16.3.45
Buried Naples War Cem

Figure 115. Pte Harold Iduas, The Argyll & Sutherland Highlanders (Princess Louise's), 51st Highland Division.

Huntman, Gdsmn Samuel (aka Hantman)
Welsh Guards
-.3.44
Killed in action

Huber, O.
PC
3.7.44

Hyams, Maj Harold Crozier
RAPC
24.1.45
Buried at East Ham

Hyams, Sgmn Peter
RCOS
12.7.41
Buried in Bishop's Stortford New Cem

Hyams, Pte Sidney
The Black Watch (Roy Highland Regt)
Age 18 -.10.44
Died on active service in Holland

Hyamson, Capt Theodore David
RE
15.2.42
Died of wounds in Singapore

Hyman, Lt Anthony George
RA
12.6.40
Kia France
Buried in Willesden Cem

Hyman, Pte Maurice
1/5th Btn, The Sherwood Foresters (Nottinghamshire & Derbyshire Regt)
-.3.45
Died as a Japanese POW in Singapore

Hymanson, Pte Emanuel
RAMC
15.9.41
Buried at East Ham

Iduas, Pte Harold
The Argyll & Sutherland Highldrs (Princess Louise's) 51st Highland Div
Age 19 4.11.42
Died at El Alamein

Instone, Cpl David
Intel Corps
-.3.45
Killed in action
Buried at Cesena, Italy

Irvine, Lt Ronald Nicolai
Berks Regt Att Btn S Staffs
Age 33 11.6.44
Rangoon Memorial

Isaac, Spr J.
RE
26.11.42

Isaacs, Pte Jacob
PC
Age 27 21.4.45
Buried Blackley Cem

Isaacs, WO Marcus
2.11.40

Isaacson, Gnr Joe
RA
Age 39 2.8.46
Buried Blackley Cem

Isaacson, Pte M.
The South Lancs Regt (The Prince of Wales's Volunteers) 3718349
Age 36 12.8.44
Buried Vire

Figure 116. Capt Jacob Hyman Joseph, RAMC, Regimental Medical Officer, 4th Btn, The Dorset Regt.

Isaaman, Gnr Mark
RA
Killed in North-West Europe
Buried in Eindhoven Jewish Cem

Iskovitch, Gnr Hyman Harry
68 Medium Regt RA
Age 27 14.11.42

Isky, Dvr Behr
RASC
12.8.40
Drowned

Israel, Pte C.
1st Imperial Light Horse
31.12.41
Buried in Sidi Aziz Cem, Sollum

Israel, Fus Louis
Roy Fus
Age 19 7.7.44
Buried Assisi War Cem

Israel, Pte Samuel
2/7 Btn W Surrey Regt
Age 25 2.1.45
Buried Forli War Cem Italy

Israel, Lt Walter
Jewish Brigade
Buried in Udine

Izzio, L.Cpl. Louis
Roy Berks Regt
                             23.4.44
Kohima

Jachimowitz, Pte S.
3rd Btn, The Pal Regt,
Jewish Infantry Brigade Group
Age 24   30.7.45
Buried in the Jewish Cem, Metz

Jack, Montague
74th HAA RA

Jacks, Pte A.
2nd Btn, The Transvaal Scottish,
UDF
                             11.1.42
Buried in Fort Capuzzo Cem

Jackson, Pte Heinz George
PC
Age 28   6.10.43
Glenduffhill Jewish Cem

Jackson, Pte J.
2nd Btn, The Leics Regt
                             -.7.42
Killed in action in Crete

Jacobovitch, Fus Max
15th Btn, Roy Fus (City of London
Regt)
                             26.3.43
Killed in action
Buried in Tunisia

Jacobs, Lt Bernard H.L.
RA
                             -.11.42
Killed on active service

Jacobs, L/Sgt Henry
11th Btn, KRR C (Westminster
Rifles)
Age 25   27.10.42
Died of wounds
Buried in El Alamein War Cem

Jacobs, Capt J.R.M.
UDF
                             24.10.42
Buried in El Alamein Mil Cem

Jacobs, Tpr J.E.
5th RTR, RAC
Killed in action
Buried in El Barran, Sollum,
Tobruk

Jacobs, Pte John Stanley
SLI India

Jacobs, L/Bdr Nathaniel
RA
                             11.12.42
Buried at East Ham

Jacobs, Cpl S.
PC
                             -.-.42

Jacobs, Pte T.W.
The Worcs Regt
Died of wounds

Jacobsohn, Dvr J.E.
Attached 11 South African Field
Ambulance, UDF
                             23.1.41
Buried in Knightsbridge War Cem,
Acroma

Jacobson, Pte David Jacob
2/7th Btn, The Middx Regt
                             28.1.41
Drowned
Buried at Willesden Cem

Jacobson, Pte Harold
RASC
Dunkirk

Jacobson, Lt Herbert David
                             -.1.42
Killed in action

Jacobson, 2nd Lt Lawrence
11th Hussars (Prince Albert's
Own), RAC
                             15.6.41
Buried at Sollum

Jacobson, 2nd Lt Miron
8th Field Regt, RA
                             17.6.41
Buried at Buq-Buq, Egypt

Jacobson, Spr Morris
RE
                             25.2.42

Jacobson, Spr Morris
RE 2007341
Age 22   16.12.41
Knightsbridge War Cem, Acroma

Jacoby, Tpr Ernest
8th Kings Roy Irish Hussars, RAC
                             2.9.44

Jaffe, Maj E.J.
The West Yorks Regt (The Prince
of Wales's Own)
Killed in Burma

Jakosky, Tpr Albert Max
5 Regt Recce Corps
                             1.4.44
Buried Sangro War Cem Italy

Jakubowicz, Pte Henryk
13th Company PC
                             29.1.46
Buried in Phien, Calais British
Military Cem

Jarvis, Capt Samuel S.
1st Essex
                             11.4.43

Jason, Rfmn S.
12th Btn, KRRC
                             29.8.44
Killed in Normandy

Joel, Spr Maurice Kenneth
626 Field Squadron RE
Age 20   13.7.44
Buried Ancona War Cem

Joseph, Pte H.B.
Hong Kong VDC
                             22.12.41
Sai Wan Memorial

Joseph, Maj Henry S.
RAMC
Hampstead memorial, AJEX
Museum

Joseph, L/Cpl Herbert Robert
RE
                                26.5.43
Died in West Africa in a mortar
accident

Joseph, Capt Jacob Hyman
RAMC Regt Medical Officer
4th Btn, The Dorset Regt
                                15.3.45
Killed in action
Buried in Germany

Joseph, Gnr Joseph H.
RA
                                29.11.43

Joseph, Pte Lazarus
PC
                                8.2.44
Buried in Birmingham Jewish
Cem

Joseph, Sgt Leslie
Intel Corps
                                -.4.45
Killed in action in Italy

Joseph, L/Cpl Moses
2 Btn W Yorks Regt
Age 27   23.4.44
Rangoon Memorial

Joskowicz, Pte Bernard
RAOC
                                11.1.41
Buried in Rainham Jewish Cem

Jublitzky, Rfmn Sidney
12th Btn, KRRC
                                -.8.44
Killed in action in France

Jude, Pte P.
UDF
                                22.11.41
Buried in Knightsbridge War Cem,
Acroma

Judes, Pte A.
*1st Btn, The South African Irish
Regt, UDF*
                                9.2.41
Buried at Banno, Abyssinia

Juggler, Coy QMS David
PC
                                5.7.44
Buried in Bayeux Cem

Kacev, Pte J.
*1st Btn, The Rhodesian L/I,
UDF*
                                23.10.42
Buried in El Alamein Mil Cem

Kaempfner, Pte Arpad
PC
Age 44   23.10.41
Buried Birmingham Jewish Cem
Witton

**Kagerer-Stein (Fuller) (Didi), Sgt
Eugen**
Hants Regt 10 Commando
Age 30   13.6.44
Buried Ranville War Cem

Kahler, Eli

Kahlow, Pte Thomas
4 Btn Roy Berks Regt
Age 21   28.5.40
Buried Adegem Canadian War Cem

Kahn, Lt Eddy
Roy Welch Fusiliers
                                19.8.44
Buried in Banneville-La-
Campagne War Cem

Kahn, Edgar
Leinsters Regt
b. Willesden

Kahn (Kaye), Cpl Eric
PC
Age 42   24.11.45
Buried Leeds, Geldard Road Cem

Kahn, Pte Isaac Henry
The Dorset Regt
                                27.4.44
Killed in action
Buried in Trimulgherry Cem

Kahn, Pte J.
The Lincs Regt
Age 28   3.2.45
Buried in Rangoon War Cem

Kahn, Cpl J.
1st Btn, The Pal Regt
                                7.4.45
Buried at Ravenna

Kahn, Pte Joseph
PC
                                4.12.44
Buried at East Ham

Kahn, Cpl Peter
53 Coy PC
Age 35   17.6.40
Buried Escoublac War Cem France
SS *Lancastria*

Kahn, Dvr R.J.
RASC
                                -.-.45
Died as POW

Kaits, Pte Henry
RAMC
                                28.8.44
Died in France
Buried at Beuzeville, Le Havre

Kalikoff, Sgt Maurice
2 Btn Para Regt
Age 28   27.10.44
Killed in action, Arnhem
Buried Rheinberg War Cem

Kalkstein, Pte Joachim
SAS
Killed in action
                                27.8.44
Buried at Recey Sur Ouce

Kalmus, Sgt Hans Marcus
RPC
                                6.2.47
Brookwood Memorial

Kaminiecki, Pte M.
PC (Pal)
                                9.1.42
Buried at Tel-El-Kebir

Kaminkowski, Cpl David
3rd Light Arty Regt Polish Brigade
                                25.7.45
Buried at Haifa Khayat Beach Mil
Cem

Kaminsky, Cpl Maurice MM
11th Btn, The Argyll & Sutherland Highldrs
-.10.44
Military Medal Italy
Killed in action
Buried at Santerno Valley

Kan, Pte A.
RAPC
14.10.40
Killed by enemy action
Buried at Willesden 20.10.40

Kanann, Pte J.F.
PC
6.5.43
Buried at Alexandria

Kanel, Capt Max
RAMC
24.3.46
S African

Kanter, Pte Phillip
RAMC
-.11.42
Died on active service in Malta

Kaplan, Gnr Lionel
South African Arty, UDF
25.2.41
Buried in the Mil Cem, Mombasa

Karamelli, 2nd Lt Alroy Harry
RCOS
22.11.41
Buried in Margo Jewish Cem

Karlicky, Pte Frances
Buffs
22.3.43
Buried in Sangro River War Cem

Karsberg, Pte Samuel
PC
7.7.46

Karstaedt, Capt Abraham Oscar
RAMC. Attached 2nd/8th Btn, The Lancs Fus
-.7.43

Kasolofsky, Pte Louis
1st Btn, The Devonshire Regt
10.4.43
Died in India
Buried in Colombo Kanatta Cem

Kasperovitch, Cpl Boris (aka King)
2nd SAS
26.9.44
Buried Moussey, Vosges
No symbol on grave in error

Katchoure, Pte M.
PC
-.-.42

Katz, Dvr Herbert L.
RASC
Age 23   16.7.43
Buried in Medjez-El-Bab War Cem

Katz, Pte Teddy
Queen's Roy Regt
-.9.44
Died of wounds in Italy

Kauffman, 2nd Lt Edward Crompton
28 Feld/Regt RA
Age 26   6.6.42

Kauffman, Capt Henry Benedict Crompton
Roy Fus Att 2 Btn Para Regt
Age 27   3.4.45
Buried Reichswald Forest War Cem

Figure 117. L/Cpl Henry P. Kaufman, 9th Btn DLT

Kaufman, Pte Harry
4 Btn Green Howards
Age 28   9.5.44
Missing as escaped POW Italy

Kaufman, Dvr Harry
54 Inf Brigade Gp RASC
Age 30   12.9.44
Buried Chungkai War Cem

Kaufman, L/Cpl Henry
Durham L/I
Age 22   17.7.43

Kaufman, Pte Israel
15th Btn, The Seaforth Highldrs (Ross-Shire Buffs, The Duke of Albany's)
24.6.44
Buried in Cassimode Cem, Madras

Figure 118. The Grave of Pte J. Kahn, The Lincolnshire Regt, in Rangoon.

Figure 119. The Grave of L/Cpl Henry Kaufman in the Brit Military Cemetery, Catania, Sicily.

Kaufman, Gnr Jacob
                              7.7.46

Kaufman, Pte K.
Czech Army
                              3.12.41
Buried in Tobruk War Cem

Kaufman, Tpr Kenneth
Glos Hussars
                              6.8.40

Kaufman, Tpr Louis Nathan
51st RTR, RAC
                              -.8.44
Killed in action
Buried in Italy

Kauter, Capt Herman Joseph
RAC
(tbc)   21.5.40

Kawalsky, Cpl Archie
2nd Btn, The London Irish Rifles
                              17.5.43

Kay, Pte Abram
15 Btn King's Liverpool Regt
                              22.3.41
Buried Manchester Polish Jewish Cem

Kay, Jack
RASC
(tbc)   27.5.40

Kay, Pte Samuel (aka Reeves, James)
E. Kents
                              10.4.43

Kaye, L/Cpl Stanley
Sherwood Foresters
in Italy

Keen, Pte Denzil Meyer
Para Regt, Army Air Corps
                              -.9.44
Killed at Arnhem

Keizer, 2nd Lt Max
7 Btn Beds & Herts Regt
                              10.12.42
Buried Golders Green

Kelman, Cpl Lola
Pal ATS
                              24.12.42
Tel El Kebir War Cem

Kennard, Maj Gordon C.
RE
                              10.12.43

Kersh, Gnr Isaac
360 Battery RA
40 Searchlight Regt
                              25.5.45
Buried Prestwich Jewish Cem

Kessler, Tpr S.
RAC
                              2.12.42
Buried in the Jewish Cem, Liverpool

Khytovich, L/Sgt Eric M.M.
RE 6 Commando
Age 24   10.6.44
Buried Ranville War Cem

King, Lt George Stanley (aka Cohen)
5th Btn, The Duke of Cornwall's L/I
                              12.7.44
Killed in action

Kingston, Pte Morris (Cohen)
Killed in action, Arnhem

Kirsch, Pte Jack
UDF
                              27.12.41
Buried in Heliopolis Mil Cem

Kirschenstein, Pte Ernest
PC
Age 44   19.9.45
Buried Prestwich Jewish Cem

Kirsh, L/Cpl Hyman
2 Btn KOYLI
Age 34   12.9.44
Buried Coriano Ridge War Cem

Kirsheansky, Sgt L.

Kisch, Capt Oliver Cecil
RCOS
                              -.6.43
Killed in action at sea

Figure 120. The Grave of Brig F.H. Kisch CB CBE DSO, Chief Engineer 8th Army, in Tunisia.

Figure 121. Lt Jack Aaron Kleinman, Buffs (Seconded to 5th Btn The Wiltshire Regt, Duke of Edinburgh's).

Figure 122. The Grave of Pte Krieger, The Sherwood Foresters (Nottinghamshire & Derbyshire Regt), in the British War Cemetery in Kanchanaburi, Thailand.

Kisch, Brig F.H., CB, CBE, DSO
Chief Engineer 8th Army
Mentioned in Despatches
Age 54   7.4.43
Killed whilst inspecting a minefield in North Africa. Buried Sousse Tunisia Cem

Kiwi, Pte H.J.
69th Company PC
                          29.12.40
Killed by enemy action
Buried at Willesden

Kleedorfer, Pte T.
220 Coy PC
                          20.3.42
Killed in an accident
Buried in Newport Jewish Cem

Kleinman, Lt Jack Aaron
Buffs. Seconded to 5th Btn, The Wiltshire Regt (Duke of Edinburgh's)
Age 24   5.11.44
Missing presumed dead. He did not return from a patrol after attempting to locate the source of mortar fire. His name is recorded at the Nijmegen Canadian War Cem

Klemin, Dennis Phillip
REME

Klipp, L/Cpl Samuel
REME
                          18.8.45
Buried at East Ham

Kluska, WO S.
                          14.5.44

Knapper, Lt Jack Aaron
Buffs Att 5 Btn Wilts Regt
Age 23   5.11.44

Koch, Richard
The Roy Berks Regt
(tbc)   27.5.40

Kohloff, Cpl Mervyn
SSVF
Killed in Action
                          13.2.42
Singapore

Komrower, Maj Donald Alexander
288 AT Battery, 102 AT Regt, RHA
Age 25   -.9.44
Died of wounds in Normandy

Konigsberg, Gnr Sidney
3 Fld/Regt RA
Age 28   9.5.44
Cassino War Memorial

Koplevker, Pte Joseph Leon
1 Btn Gloucs Regt
Age 22   22.3.42
Buried Ranchi War Cem

Koppel, Gnr L.
53rd AT Regt RA
                          -.5.40
Buried in the Jewish Eastern Cem, Dundee

Korklin, Sgt Benedict
RCOS – Hull
                          -.7.46

Kowalski, J.I.
PC

Kraft, Sgt Charles
A&S High
                          20.2.45

Krausz, Pte Bertha
ATS
Age 38   13.5.42
Buried Birmingham Jewish Cem (Witton)

Figure 123. Fus Harry Krimhorn, 9th Btn, Roy Fus (City of London Regt).

Kravatsky, Rfmn Barnet
2nd Btn, The Rifle Brigade
Killed in action
Buried in Faenza Cem

Krestin, Capt David
RA
22.3.45

Kretzer, Sgt Ernest, MM
RAC
23.4.43

Krieger, Pte
The Sherwood Foresters (Nottinghamshire & Derbyshire Regt)
Died in a POW Camp, Thailand
Buried in Kanchanaburi War Cem

Krimhorn, Fus Harry
9th Btn, Roy Fus (City of London Regt)
Age 23   7.11.43
Killed in action
Buried in Minturno Mil Cem near Naples

Krish, Dvr Felix M.
RASC

Kritzmer, Pte L.
2nd Botha Regt, UDF
21.6.41
Buried in El Alamein War Cem

Figure 124. Sgt Louis Kushin, Army Educational Corps.

Kruyer, John
1st Btn Berks Regt
-.4.44
Killed in action, Kohima

Kuberofsky, Gnr Hyman
21st AT Regt, RA
Age 20   2.8.44
Died of wounds in Normandy
Buried in Bayeux Cem

Kuczynski, L/Cpl Szaja
33 Company PC
11.1.48
Buried in Streatham

Kugler, Joseph
13801945
(aka Smith 6305456)

Kushin, Sgt Louis
Army Educational Corps
-.5.45
Killed on active service in India

Kushner, Pte Harry
Green Howards
Died Minturno, Italy

Kushner, Rfmn Jacob
KRRC
Age 64   4.7.46
Buried Rainham Jewish Cem

Kuttner, Pte Alfred R.
8th Paras
D-Day

Kwintner, Pte Isaac
RAOC
Age 37   14.2.44
Buried in Edmonton

Laaser, Cftmn Walther
REME
Age 37   7.8.44
Buried Rome War Cem

Ladewig, Jochen (Lawrie)
PC/RAC
-.5.45
Killed in action

Laine, Pte C.
Buffs
Age 22   12.2.45
Buried in Rangoon War Cem

Figure 125. The Grave of Fus Krimhorn in the Minturno Military Cemetery, near Naples.

Figure 127. Pte Sam Landy, The West Yorkshire Regt (The Prince of Wales's Own).

Figure 126. The Grave of Pte C. Laine, Buffs (Royal East Kent Regt), in Rangoon.

Landau, Aaron/Alan
RAOC
-.8.42

Landau, Lt E. (aka Langley)
10 Commando
-.-.43
DOAS

Landale-Landauer, Lt John David

Landauer, Walter
PC

Lander, Cpl Ronald
N. Lancs Regt
8.10.42

Landon/Langdon, Walter (aka Lewey-Lingen)
Paras
KIA Arnhem
Cross on grave in error

Landsman, Lt Joseph
Commando
14.7.44
Killed in action, Italy

Landy, Pte Sam
West Yorks Regt (The Prince of Wales's Own)
4.6.42
Killed in action at Sollum, Western Desert
Buried at El Alamein

Lang, Pte Jack
4th Btn, Army Air Corps
Para/Regt, 6th Airborne Division
-.1.46
Died in Palestine

Langer, Pte Henry Gustav

Larner, Gnr Moishe J.
11th Regt, RHA (HAC)
Age 23   -.2.42
Lost at sea

Lasker, L/Sgt J.L.
AIF
17.10.41

Laskey, Cpl Cyril
RM Commando
18.4.45
Ravenna

Lasky, Pte I.
RAMC

Lassman, Pte Bernard
PC
4.10.44
Died in Belgium

Lassman, Dvr Morris
RASC
21.9.42
Buried in Streatham

Latawick, Sgt C.
RAC
16.8.44

Latutin, Capt Simmon, GC
The Somerset L/I (Prince Albert's)
31.12.44
Died in Mogadishu, Somaliland
GC awarded posthumously for superb heroism

Laufer, S.
PC

Lauffer, G.
PC

Laufer, V.
PC

Figure 128. Gnr Moishe J. Larner, 11th Regt, RHA (Honourable Artillery Company).

Laughton, Pte Martin (Lobel)
220 Coy PC
                                11.8.43
Drowned
Buried in Cheltenham Cem

Lawrence, 2nd Lt Daniel
10th RTR, RAC
                                -.12.42
Died of wounds

Lawrence, L/Cpl Ernest Richard (aka Lenel)
The Queen's Own Roy West Kent Regt/10 Commando
Age 26   23.6.44
Bayeux Memorial

Lawrence, Lt George
RA
Cassino

Lawrence, Capt Harold
RAMC
                                21.10.46
Died in an accident

Lawrie, John F.
RIH

Lawton, Pte B.R.
PC
                                16.12.44
Killed by enemy action

Figure 129. Pte Henry Layman, 1st Btn, The Northamptonshire Regt.

Layman, Pte Henry
1st Btn, The Northamptonshire Regt
Age 20   26.1.45
Killed in action in Burma
Buried in Taukkyan War Cem

Lazarus, Lt A.M.
RA
Age 26   13.8.44

Lazarus, Pte Charles
KORR
                                18.10.42

Lazarus, Cftmn Lewis
                                -.7.44
Killed by enemy action

Lazarus, Pte N.A.
The Queen's Roy Regt (West Surrey)
                                10.9.41
Buried in the Canadian Cem near Bruges

Lazarus, Pte Victor Ernest
KSLI
                                12.9.44
Edmonton Cem

Lazarus, Pte Walter
2/5 Btn Leics Regt
Age 21   24.9.43
Cassino War Memorial

Leckerman, M.
RAMC
DOAS
                                -.-.51

Lee, Pte Hyman
Army Catering Corps
                                1.9.44

Figure 130. The Grave of Pte Henry Layman in Taukkyan War Cemetery, Rangoon.

Figure 131. Pte Bill (Wolfie) Letwin, The Green Howards (Alexandra, Princess of Wales's Own Yorkshire Regt).

Lee, Capt Lionel, MC (aka Levy)
RAC/SOE
Age 27   27.5.44
Murdered at Gross-Rosen Camp

Leibovitch, Gnr Isaac
79th Anti-Aircraft Regt, RA
                          -.10.44
Killed in an accident in Italy

Lehman, Henry
Burma – Norwood Memorial
Killed in action

Lehniger, Pte Richard
(aka Leonard)
PC/10 Commando, SSRF, SAS
Age 42   13.9.42
KIA St Nazaire
Buried at St Laurent-sur-Mer
Churchyard

Lehrer, Gnr Samuel
RA
                          21.6.40

Leigh, Capt M.
Young Men's Christian Association
                          24.12.45
Buried in Kranji, Singapore

Leigh, Sgt R.
                          1.3.45

Leitch, Spr Isaac
2 Stevedore Btn RE
Age 22   3.6.40

Lemberger, Cpl Morris
7 Btn Green Howards
Age 24   14.11.42
Lost at sea.

Lempert, Pte Jacob
The South Staffs Regt (Chindits)
Age 31   23.6.44
Killed in action in Burma

Lent, L/Cpl Joseph
11th Btn, Roy Fus (City of London Regt)
Age 22   12.5.44
Killed in action in Italy
Buried at Cassino

Lenz, Sgmn Max
RCOS
Age 35   25.3.45
Buried Taukkyan War Cem

Leon, Tpr Heinz Henoch

Leon, Cpl Samuel
RAOC
                          4.6.42
Buried in Tel-El-Kebir Mil Cem

Figure 132. The Grave of Capt M. Leigh, Young Men's Christian Association, in Kranji War Cemetery, Singapore (Centre grave in the front row of headstones).

Leonard, S/Sgt Albert
(aka Barnet Yanovitch)
RAMC
                          -.-.41
Missing presumed killed in
Singapore

Lerner, Pte Nathan
The Dorset Regt
                          28.6.44
Died of wounds in France
Inscription on headstone reads
'From Cable St., to Normandy, he
died fighting Fascism'
Buried in Jerusalem War Cem
Chouin

Lesser, Pte David
*2nd Btn, The Duke of Cornwall's
L/I*
                          -.7.43
Killed in action
Buried in Tunisia

Letwin, Pte Bill (Wolfie)
*The Green Howards (Alexandra,
Princess of Wales's Own Yorks
Regt)*
Age 31
Captured at El Alamein, taken to
prison camp in Italy and then to
Germany. Died of typhus.
Buried in Czechoslovakia

Letwin, Gnr Jack
RA
Age 34   31.8.47
Buried Rainham Jewish Cem

Leuftman, Pte N.
*The Wilts Regt (The Duke of
Edinburgh's)*
                          26.8.44

Levene, H.G.
RAPC

Levene, J. Kenneth
RAMC

Levene, James/Josh, DCM
Chindits
                          -.-.47
Died of malaria in Liverpool

Figure 133. The Grave of Pte Jacob Lempert, The South Staffordshire Regt (Chindits).

Levene, Pte L.
Beds & Herts
                                    13.6.44

Levene, Pte Louis
RASC
                                    14.6.45
Buried Rainham Jewish Cem

Levene, Spr Louis
RE
                                    13.6.44
Killed in action in France
Buried in Bayeux Brit Cem

Levene, Cpl Sam
151 Regt, RAC (King's Own Roy Regt)
Age 32   14.8.44
Buried in Bayeux Mil Cem

Levenson, Lt Yehudi
PPCLI Can
Killed in action Korea

Levenstein, Dvr Benjamin
RASC
Age 41   30.9.43
Buried Edmonton Jewish Cem

Leventhal, Pte Isaac S.
PC
                                    3.12.40

Leversuch, Pte Stanley Charles
RAOC
Age 31   17.6.43
Lost on SS *Yoma* when torpedoed

Levetin, Rfmn Hyman
2nd Btn, The Rifle Bridge
Buried at Rainham

Levey, Sgt Reginald Isidore
The Queen's Roy Regt (West Surrey)
                                    -.10.43
Killed on active service. Buried Italy.

Levin, Sgt A.E.
RCOS
Age 41   11.5.46
Buried in Rangoon War Cem

Levine, Lt Edward (Eugene)
RA SOE
                                    29.3.45
Murdered Flossenberg Camp

Levine, Cpl Israel
2nd Btn, The Gloucestershire Regt
                                    25.11.44
Killed in action in North-West Europe

Leving, Rfmn Stanley Michael
Rifle Brigade
                                    -.6.44
Killed in action in Normandy

Levison, Sgt John Oliver
Glider pilot
Age 23   19.9.44
Arnhem Oosterbeck War Cem
Cross on grave in error

Figure 134. The Grave of Sgt A.E. Levin, RCOS, in Rangoon.

Levithan, Cpl A.
10th Roy Hussars, RAC
9.1.42
Buried in El Alamein War Cem

Levitt, Capt John R.
RA
8.12.44

Levitton, L/Cpl H.L.
RASC
Age 29   3.12.44
Died in POW Camp in Thailand

Levin, Montague
Norwood Memorial

Levy, S/Sgt A.
Indian & Malay Corps
16.11.41
Buried in Dera Dun Cem

Levy, Pt A.
MEF
-.6.41
Killed in action

Levy, Cpl Albert Marco
4th Corps Signals, RCOS
18.7.44
Killed in action in Normandy

Levy, Pte Benjamin
1st/4th Btn, The Essex Regt
Age 24   -.6.42
Killed at El Alamein
Buried in Alamein Cem

Figure 136. The Grave of L/Cpl H.L. Levitton, RASC.

Levy, S/Sgt Bob Julius
The Glider Pilot Regt, Army Air Corps
Age 21   12.4.44

Levy, L/Bdr E.L.
RA
-.1.43
Killed on active service in Libya

Levy, Capt Frederick Walter
Intel Corps
Age 43   -.7.44
Buried Dely Ibrahim War Cem

Levy, Gnr Gershon
381st HAA Regt, RA
20.6.41
Killed in a driving accident

Levy, Harry
General Service
DOAS
-.-.47

Levy, Pte Harry
Fiji Infantry
28.7.43

Levy, Dvr Israel
RASC
3.1.41
Buried at East Ham

Levy, Pte Jacob
2/7 Btn Queens Roy Regt
Killed in action in Italy
Buried at Menate

Levy, Dvr John
RASC 223707
Age 24   11.4.45
Durnbach War Cem

Levy, Pte M.
5th Btn South Staffs Regt
Age 21   16.7.44
Died of burns in North-West Europe
Buried in Bayeux Mil Cem

Levy, Fus Mervyn David
The Roy Welch Fus
Age 18   -.4.45
Killed in action in Western Europe

Levy, Bdr Moss Henry
142 Field Regt, RA
20.4.44
Killed in accident in Italy
Buried in the Brit Mil Cem

Levy, Pte Neville J.
RAOC
23.6.41
Killed in action in Crete
Buried in Crete

Figure 135. Pte Benjamin Levy, Ist/4th Btn, The Essex Regt.

Figure 137. Pte M. Levy, 5th Btn, The South Staffordshire Regt.

Figure 138. Dvr Philip Levy, RE

Figure 139. Fus Mervyn David Levy, The Royal Welch Fusiliers.

Levy, Maj P.B.
NZF
                                    24.7.42
Mentioned in Dispatches
Killed in action at El Alamein
Buried in Heliopolis Mil Cem

Levy, L/Cpl Peter John
Notts Yeo

Levy, Dvr Philip
RE
Age 33   -.6.42
Killed at Gazala south of Tobruk

Levy, Ronald
W. Surrey Regt
                                    20.10.45

Levy, Pte Sidney H.
2nd Btn, The Hampshire Regt
                                    -.1.45
Killed in action
Buried in 46 Division Cem

Levy, Pte Solly
PC
                                    11.6.46

Lewin, Pte Baruch
Jewish Inf Brigade Group
                                    30.3.45
Buried at Ravenna

Lewin, Pte Martin
Pioneer Corps
Age 44   29.11.44
Buried St. Sever Cem, Rouen

**Lewinsky, Pte Max
(served as Laddy)**
The Queen's Own Roy West Kent Regt/10 Commando
Age 32   6.6.44
Buried Hermanville War Cem

Lewis, Pte Albert
Cheshire Regt
Age 38   17.10.40
Buried Pornic War Cem
SS *Lancastria*

Lewis, Pte Bernard
                                    20.10.40

Figure 140. The Grave of Dvr (Dick) Lipman, RE.

Lewis, Pte Jack
6 Company PC
                                    21.8.44
Killed in an accident
Buried in the Brit Mil Cem, Bayeux

Lewis (Lewinsohn) Pte Michael
The Special Air Service Regt
Age 24   10.4.45
Buried in Sage Cem, Oldenburg

Lewis, Harry
                                    -.-.46
Killed in action, Palestine

Leyland, Gnr J.R.
RA

Liborwich, Pte Sam
*1st Btn, The Middx Regt
(Duke of Cambridge's Own)*
                                    18.12.41
Killed in Hong Kong

Lightman, Cpl Leon

Lindheimer, Pte W.
POW
Killed in air crash
(Palestinian Jew)

Lindon, Pte J.C.
6th Btn, The Cheshire Regt
18.9.44
Killed in action
Buried in Morciano

Lipkovsky, Gnr Boris
Hong Kong VDF
25.12.41
Buried Sai Wan Mem Cem

Lipman, Dvr (Dick)
RE
Age 24 16.3.43
Struck by a bomb splinter in
Tunisia
Killed in action
Buried in Sfax War Cem

Lipman, Rfmn Joseph Robert
1 Btn Roy London Irish Rifles
Age 28 7.9.44
Buried Gradara War Cem, Italy

Lipman, Gnr Nathan
188 HAA Regt, RA
10.12.42
Died while a POW in Fukuoka
Camp, Japan
Buried at Yokohama

Lipman, Lt Ronald B.
RASC
13.4.42
Killed on active service
Buried at Willesden

Lipman, Gnr Victor
RA

Lipschild, Cpl Barnett
13.5.53
KIA Korea
born Nkana, N. Rhodesia

Lipschitz, Cpl C.
UDF
31.1.42
Buried in Tobruk Mil Cem

Liptz, Cpl Robert Israel
1st Btn, KRRC
2.10.42
Died of wounds

Figure 141. The Grave of Pte I. Litveen, The South Wales Borderers, in Rangoon.

Listinsky, Pte Saul
8th Btn, The Lancs Fus (BEF)
18.1.41
Died of wounds in France
Buried in Bethune Mil Cem

Lithauer, L/Cpl Ronald Louis
RCOS
Age 24 1.1.43
Buried Yokohama War Cem

Litveen, Pte I.
The South Wales Borderers
Age 34 18.11.44
Killed in action in Burma
Buried in Rangoon War Cem

Litwack, L/Sgt Cyril David
RAC
Age 26 16.8.44
Killed in action in the Falaise Gap,
Normandy

Litwin, Pte G.
RAPC
29.1.44
Killed by enemy action
Buried at Edmonton

Livingstone, Pte Martin
PC
-.-.43

Lobbenburg, Pte O.
PC
16.12.44
Killed by enemy action
Buried in Kerkhof van Antwerpen

**Lockmaker, B/Sgt Maj David
(aka Lackmaker)**
11th LAA Regt, RA
-.12.44
Killed in action

Figure 142.
L/Sgt Cyril David Litwack, RAC.

Figure 144. The Grave of Sgt Cyril Litwack.

Figure 143. Pte Woolf Walter Loew, 2nd Btn, The Bedfordshire & Hertfordshire Regt.

Loder, L/Cpl Hans (aka Lilienfeld)
PC
16.12.44
Killed by enemy action
Buried in Kerkhof van Antwerpen

Lodge, Sgt Robert, DCM (aka Friedlander, Rudolf)
2nd SAS
Age 36   18.8.44
Buried Moussey Churchyard, France

Loebell, Pte Leonard
13116978 RPC
Age 26   10.12.47
Buried Nottingham Jewish Cem

Loebell, Pte L.
18116978
DOAS
-.6.59

Loew, Pte Woolf Walter
2nd Btn, The Beds &Herts Regt
Age 30   22.4.42
Killed in action at Djebbel-Jaffa during the 1st Army campaign in North Africa

Loewenstein, C.
RASC

Loewenthal, Pte Anna
ATS
19.8.43
Buried in the Jewish Cem, Bristol

Loewenwirt, Pte Bernard
1st Btn, 1st Czech Brigade
9.3.41
Buried in Birmingham Jewish Cem

Lorie, Gnr M.
RA
17.3.44
Killed in action in Burma
Buried in Imphal Mil Cem

Lottenberg, Lt Louis Henry
-.6.44
Mentioned in Despatches (Italy)
Killed in action
Buried in the Mil Cem, Ornieto

Louis, Capt Percy
RAMC, HQ 1st Airborne Army
25.9.44
Mentioned in Despatches for valuable service March–June 1940
Killed at Arnhem

Low, Pte K.
RASC/PAL
17.7.42

Lowey, Sgmn Norman William
7 Armd Div RCOS
Age 25   22.11.41

Lowis, Cpl B.
RAMC
28.11.40
Buried in the Jewish Cem, Bombay

Lowy, Sgt Alexander S.
Intel Corps
30.5.44

Lowy, Lt Peter
2nd Btn, Roy Fus (City of London Regt)
4.5.43
Killed in action

Lubman, Fus Isaac
Lanc. Fus
20.10.44

Lubraniecki, Pte E.
362 Company, PC
7.12.43
Buried in El Alia Cem

Lucas, Dvr Herman
462 Coy RASC
1.5.43

Lucas, Lt Henry A.
-.10.42
Drowned on board a Japanese transport between Singapore and New Guinea

Lucas, 2nd Lt Maurice Barclay
Age 26   17.7.41
Buried in Mersa Matruh Mil Cem

Ludmer, Maj. H., MBE
MEF

Lukes, Spr Murray
RE
-.6.42
Died on active service

Lurie, Lt/Col D.
UDF
                                      17.6.42
Buried in Tel-El-Kebir Mil Cem

Lurie, Gnr Maurice
RA
                                      -.-.44
Died in Burma

Lyons, Tpr Ellis
RAC
Age 29   19.1.44
Buried Leeds, Geldard Rd Cem

Lyons, Cpl S.E.
Age 26   16.2.41

Lyons, Lt Samuel A.
RA/Airborne
                                      6.6.44
D-Day

Mackler, Capt Arthur
*RAMC Attached 57
LAA Regt, RA*
                                      -.5.43
Injured in a landmine explosion
Died later of his injuries in the
Middle East

Macklin, Sgt Robert
Army Educational Corps
                                      -.11.43
Died whilst a POW of the
Japanese

Mader, Cpl Gerszon
248 Company PC
                                      4.11.41
Buried in Darlington Cem

Magrill, L/Sgt Harold
125 AT Regt, RA
Died whilst a Japanese POW

Main, L/Cpl M.
KRRC
Age 25   19.10.42
Buried Bari Mil Cem

Maissel, Pte Jack Cecil
*2nd/6th Btn, The Queen's Roy
Regt (West Surrey)*
                                      -.9.43
Killed in action

Makofski, Sgt Aubrey Bernard
MEF
                                      -.7.42
Died of wounds

Maltz, L/Bdr David Geoffrey
48 LAA Regt, RA
                                      -.-.42
Killed in action in Java

Maltz, Cpl H.
504 Coy PC
                                      1.10.43
Buried at East Ham

Manasseh, Lt S.D.Ellis
RE
Age 23   3.8.44
242253
Killed in action in France
Buried Vire

Manis, Pte Morris
E. Surrey's Regt
                                      6.1.45
Colombo

March, Lt Leslie
*The Queen's Own Cameron
Highldrs*
                                      -.7.44
Killed in action

Marcus, Pte H.
KOYLI
Age 24   9.4.43
Buried in Salerno Cem

Marcus, Pte Leon Jack
MEF
                                      -.10.42
Killed in Egypt
Buried in El Alamein Cem

Marcus, Pte Sidney
                                      22.3.40
Drowned in boating accident

Figure 145. The Grave of
Pte H. Marcus, KOYLI, in Salerno.

Margolis, Gnr David
RA
                                      3.1.41
Buried at East Ham

Markham Lt Maurice
*The Roy Berks Regt (Princess
Charlotte of Wales's)*
                                      11.6.44
Killed in action North-West Europe

Marks, Lt A.
Home Guard
                                      17.5.42
Killed in an explosion
Buried at Willesden

Marks, Pte Arthur
Dorset Regt
                                      10.7.44
Killed in action

Marks, Sgt B.
*1st Btn, The Sherwood Foresters
(Notts & Derbyshire Regt)*
                                      13.6.42
Buried in Sollum Mil Cem

Marks, Spr Brian
RE
                                      -.-.61
Died cancer after Christmas Island
service

Marks, Dvr Casper
RASC

-.10.45

Died from injuries on active service

Marks, Fus Cecil
20th Btn, Roy Fus (City of London Regt)

Marks, Gnr D.C.
56 HAA Regt, RA
Age 27   -.6.43
Died in Southern India

Marks, Pte David
RTR

-.-.43

Died in North Africa

Marks, Tpr David W.
RAC

13.6.42

Killed in action
Buried in Sollum Mil Cem

Marks, Desmond Cecil
Died in India

10.6.43

Marks, L/Cpl G.B.
KRRC

Marks, Pte Lionel
11th Btn, The Durham L/I
10.7.40
Died by accidental gunshot
Buried in Sunderland Jewish Cem

Marks, L/Cpl Michael
The Middx Regt (Duke of Cambridge's Own)
Age 18
Died at Dunkirk

Marks, Brig Neville Robert
Chindit
Died in USA

Marks, Noah
54th RE

Marks, Pte S.

Figure 146. The Grave of Tpr Felix Mondschein Martin, 3rd Carabiniers, RAC, in Rangoon.

Marks, S/Sgt Zalich Joshua
AIF

23.8.42

Buried at Gaza

Markson, Pte N.G.
RAOC

-.10.43

Went down with a POW ship in Manila Bay, Philippines

Marmorstein, Lt M.C.
2nd Btn, The London Irish Rifles
Killed in action
Buried in Italy

Marson, L/Cpl Harry Selwyn
The Queen's Roy Regt (West Surrey)
10.7.41
Buried in Damascus Cem

Martin, Sgt Clifford
IC

-.-.47

Killed by Irgun in retaliation for hanging of 2 Irgun fighters by British.
Buried in Ramleh
Mother was Jewish

Martin, Tpr Felix Mondschein
3rd Carabiniers, RAC
Age 25   15.3.45
Buried in Rangoon War Cem

Masser, Pte Eli
Durham L/I
Age 27   4.7.44
Buried Bayeux War Cem

Master, Cpl S.

26.10.41

Buried in El Alamein War Cem

Mastring, Pte P.D. (aka Masting)
The Hampshire Regt
Buried in Bayeux

Maurice, Gnr L.
RA

28.2.43

Maxwell, Tpr Jack Stanley
13/18th Roy Hussars
Killed in action in Europe
Buried in Mook Mil Cem

Mayers, Edward
PC
SS *Lancastria*

17.6.40

Mayr (Meyer) Lt Hubert
General List
Age 32   1.1.45
Cassino Memorial

Mayslin, Gnr S.
RA
                          1.3.42
Buried in Nachlath Yitzhak Cem

McKenna, L/Cpl Harry
RE
                          7.5.45
Killed in an accident
Buried at Delhi

Melek, Meyer
RE
Died Jap POW

Melinsky, Lt Vivian
RAC
                          -.4.44
Killed in action in Burma
Plaque at Willesden

Meltzer, Tpr Harry
RTR, 8th Army
                          19.1.42
Killed in action

Melvil, A.
PC

Melville (Mayer), Tpr Frederick Peter
8 Roy Hussars
Age 27   14.8.44
Buried Fulford Burial Ground
Yorkshire

Melvin (Milch), Lt John Stephen/Steven
PC
Age 39   9.8.45
Buried Golders Green

Mendel, Pte D.
King's Own Roy Regt

Mendel, Pte Harry
RCOS
                          25.6.42
Killed in action in the Middle East

Figure 147. Cpl Moss Mendelle, Recce Corps.

Mendelle, Cpl Moss
Recce Corps
Age 29   -.8.43
Killed in action at Catania during the invasion of Sicily

Mendelovitch, S/Maj Louis
Instructor in Gunnery, RA
                          1.12.44
Buried in Morch Mil Cem

Mendelson, Pte Arthur Leonard
1st Middx
Age 30   1.2.42
Sai Wan Mem

Mendelsohn, L/Cpl J.M.
2nd Btn, the Transvaal Scottish, UDF
                          21.1.42
Buried Hodra Mil Cem

Mendik, Tpr Arthur
RAC
                          9.10.43
Accidentally drowned in India
Buried in Madras

Mendoza, Pte Evelyn Ivor
Roy W Kent
Age 32   19.3.44
Buried Taukkyan Cem

Mendoza, Pte Judah Benjamin
152 Coy PC
                          -.5.41
Killed by enemy action

Mervis, Lt Paul
The Rifles
                          -.6.09
KIA Afghanistan
Buried Aldershot

Meshkit (Maschit) Pte M.
(Palestine)
                          -.-.45
Returning POW from Germany
Killed in an air crash

Mesner, Cpl Emil
69 Coy PC
                          29.12.40
Killed by enemy action
Buried at East Ham

Messer, L/Cpl Sidney Walter Nathan
1 Btn Roy Fus
Age 29   30.11.43
Buried Sangro River War Cem

Meyer, K. (Served as L/Cpl P. Moody)
The Hampshire Regt (10 Commando)
Age 25   13.6.44
Killed in action in Normandy

Michaels, Sgt John Lewis MM
The Worcestershire Regt
                          -.6.41
Killed in action, Khartoum

Michaelson, Gnr B.
52 Field Regt, RA
                          18.8.44
Died of wounds
Buried in the Brit War Cem
Florence

Miller, Gnr Alfred
21 A/T Regt RA
                          19.9.40
Buried Hull Central Hebrew Cem

Figure 148. The Grave of K. Meyer, who served as Lance Cpl P. Moody, The Hampshire Regt (Number 10 Commando).

Figure 149. The Grave of Pte N. Miller, The Worcestershire Regt, in Rangoon.

Miller, Pte H.
The Wilts Regt (Duke of Edinburgh's Own), MEF
16.1.41
Buried in Nairobi Jewish Cem

Miller, Pte Jack
PC
Age 36   -.11.42
Buried in Bone Cem, Annaba

Miller, Gnr Mark
311 RA
9.1.44
Buried at Search Light Battery, Edmonton

Miller, Pte Maurice
RAMC
5.2.43
Imphal

Miller, Pte N.
The Worcs Regt
Age 29   8.2.45
Buried in Rangoon War Cem

Miller, Pte Nathan
7.2.44

Miller, Pte Sydney Benjamin
HLI (City of Glasgow Regt)
8.2.45
Killed in action
Buried at Nijmegen, Holland

Milrood, Bdr Joseph
RA
Age 24   25.6.44
Killed in action
Buried in Ranville Brit Mil Cem

Minden, Gnr Max Henry
8th Survey Regt, RA
Killed in action
Buried at Brezza near Capua

Minster, Pte Louis
The South Wales Borderers
4.4.42
Buried in Madras War Cem India

Miranda, Cpl Louis
KRRC
27.11.44
Died of wounds

Mirousky, Sgt Jiri
Czech Army
-.1.45

Mirsky, Pte Samuel
74 Company PC
13.10.41
Buried in Newport Jewish Cem

Mishkin, Pte Alfred
The Wilts Regt (Duke of Edinburgh's Own)
26.8.44
Buried in St Desir Brit Mil Cem

Figure 150. The Grave of Bdr Joseph Milrood, RA, in Ranville Brit Military Cemetery, Normandy.

Mitchell, Lt Edward Michael
Roy Fus (City of London Regt)
Attached 6th Btn, The South
Wales Borderers
Age 30   13.2.45
Killed in action in Burma

Mitchell, Pte Morris
11th Btn, HLI (City of Glasgow
Regt)
                         14.11.40

Mocatta, Maj William Edward
W Yorks Regt
                         25.2.44
Brookwood Mem

Moisewitch, Pte Daniel
1st Btn, The Loyal Regt (North
Lancs)
                         -.4.44
Buried in Anzio Brit Mil Cem

Montefiore, Capt Langton
RASC
                         26.4.41
Athens Memorial

Mondschein, F.
PC

Morein, Capt Wolf
Chaplain to The Forces
                         18.9.41
Buried at Willesden

Moreve, L/Sgt Lionel
RA
                         7.7.44

Morgan, Sgt Max
295 Field Company, RE
                         -.3.45
Killed in action
Buried in the Brit Empire Mil Cem,
Italy

Morrick, O/Cad Henry
                         21.2.44
Buried in Glasgow Cem

Morris, Eric (Moses)
PC

Figure 151. The Grave of Lt John J. Morris, The Sherwood Foresters
(Nottinghamshire & Derbyshire Regt) (attached to The Lincolnshire Regt).

Morris, Dvr Edward Max
RASC
                         21.6.43
Died of wounds
Buried at East Ham

Morris, Brig F. OBE MC
Chief Ordnance Officer
                         -.3.42
Killed in an aircraft crash in Delhi,
India

Morris, Fus Harold
Lancs Fus
Killed in a minefield in Tunisia

Morris, Lt John J.
The Sherwood Foresters (Notts &
Derbys Regt) Attached to The
Lincs Regt
Age 33   7.4.44
Buried in Rangoon Cem

Morris, Gnr Louis (Maurice)
116 HAA Regt RA
                         25.2.43
Buried in Willesden

Morris, Gnr Nathan
98 Field Regt RA
                         8.4.44
Killed in action
Buried in Vairano Mil Cem

Morris, Dvr Robert
RE
                         12.7.44

Morris, Pte Solomon
5 Btn Roy Berks Regt
                         15.6.40

Morton, Pte Peter John
(aka Meyer)
Intel Corps
Age 24   10.3.45

Moscovitz, Pte Elimelech
609 (Palestine) Company PC
Age 32   -.3.42
Died of wounds received in action
Buried in Heliopolis Mil Cem

Moscow, Coy S/Maj Benjamin
The Durham L/I (Commando)
                         -.8.44
Killed in France

Moseley, Cpl Sidney
9th Btn, Roy Fus
(City of London Regt)
                         9.5.43
Killed Tunisia
Buried at Enfidaville

Moser, Fus Maurice
10 Btn Lancs Fus
Age 32   9.1.43
Rangoon Memorial

Moses, L/Cpl Arthur
2nd/28th Australian Inf Btn
                          2.11.42
Buried El Alamein Mil Cem

Moses, Sgt K.J.
NZ Arty
Killed in action Crete
                          -.-.42

Moskovitch,, Maj E.
5th Roy Gurkha Rifles
                          28.12.43
Buried in Bombay

Moskowitz, Pte J.
2nd Btn, The Beds & Herts Regt
Killed in action
Buried at Cassino

Moss, Alf Aaron
RA
Died Malaya POW

Moss, Pte H.
The Northants Regt
Age 20   1.3.45
Buried in Rangoon War Cem

Moss, Pte Harry Bernard
PC
                          14.11.42
Buried at Edmonton

Moss, Spr M.
RE
                          4.5.42
Buried in Ramleh Mil Cem

Moss, Lt Percy Lawrence
Intel Corps
                          10.3.46

Mossack, Gnr Emanuel
69th Field Regt, RA
                          26.7.44
Killed on active service

Muller-Schoen
PC

Figure 152. The Grave of Pte H. Moss, The Northamptonshire Regt, in Rangoon.

Figure 153. The Grave of M. Mutsemaker, a Dutch Soldier in Chung Kai Cem, Thailand.

Munk, Pte S.
Czech Army
                          19.1.42
Buried in the Mil Cem Jerusalem

Musaphia, Gnr Joseph
206 Bty, 60 HAA Regt, RA
                          23.11.44
Drowned
Buried in Holland

Mussalim, Pioneer K.M.
Pal 11135, PC
                          19.7.41
Phaleron War Cem

Mutsemaker, M.
Dutch Inf
Age 40   11.10.43
Buried in Chung Kai Cem

Figure 154. Lt Peter Nathaniel Myers, 4th Recce Regt, Recce Corps.

Myerowitz, Pte Henry
2nd Btn The Roy Norfolk Regt
　　　　　　　　　　3.7.40
Killed in action

Myers, Pte Arthur
Cheshire Regt
Coriano Ridge
　　　　　　　　　　18.9.44

Myers, Daniel
5th Buffs

Myers, Pte Mark
The Queen's Own Roy West Kent Regt
　　　　　　　　　　6.8.42
Killed in action

Myers, Lt Peter Nathaniel
4th Recce Regt, Recce Corps
Age 22　　　　　　7.11.44
Killed near Rimini in Italy
Buried Coriano Ridge

Myers, Sgt Philip
REME
　　　　　　　　　　11.7.44
Died of injuries received in a battle accident
Buried in St Leger Ryes Brit Mil Cem

Myers, Gnr Reginald
127 Fld/Regt RA
Age 22　　　　　　22.6.41
Buried Bramley Cem Leeds

Nabarro, Pte Benjamin
1/4 Essex Regt
Age 19　　　　　　26.7.44
Buried Arezzo War Cem

Nabarro (Narbarro) Gnr Jack George
RA
　　　　　　　　　-.10.40
Died of wounds

Nagley, Pte Sidney
214 Company PC
　　　　　　　　　18.6.45
Killed in Western Europe

Nagel, P.
PC

Natborny, Sgmn H.
RCOS

Nathan, Alfred
RA
　　　　　　　　　27.11.39

Nathan, L/Cpl B.
NZ Expeditionary Force
　　　　　　　　　25.6.42
Buried in Crete

Nathan, Henry James
Black Watch
　　　　　　　　　17.8.44

Nathan, Gnr James
11th Regt RHA (HAC)
　　　　　　　　　5.1.45
Buried at East Ham

Nathan, Rfmn Leslie
KRRC 1Btn
Age 28　　　　　　27.11.42
Buried Benghazi War Cem

Nathan, Col Sidney Joseph
RAMC
Regular Officer from 1938-1972

Nathan, Lt Trevor A.
RA
　　　　　　　　　12.2.44
East Africa

Natskin, Pte Max
5th Btn, The Black Watch (Roy Highland Regt)
　　　　　　　　　18.11.44
Died of wounds

Naughton
No 3 Troop 10 Commando
DOAS

Nedas, Rfmn Lawrence
2nd Btn, The Rifle Brigade
　　　　　　　　　-.6.44
Killed in action

Needleman, S/Sgt Jack
1st Btn The London Scottish Regt/Paras
　　　　　　　　　28.4.44
Killed in an air crash
Buried in Glasgow Jewish Cem

Needleman, Spr Percy
RE
Killed in action, Normandy
　　　　　　　　　11.6.44

Needlestein, Fus Barnett (Barney)
1 Btn Roy Irish Fus
Age 21　　　　　　25.1.43
Cassino Memorial

Neirynck, Pte Leslie
Essex Regt
Age 20　　　　　　3.11.43
Buried Minturno War Cem

Neumann, L/Cpl Gerhard
PC
　　　　　　　　　29.12.40
Killed by enemy action
Buried at East Ham on 5.1.41

Newman, Fus Harry
8th Btn Roy Fus (City of London Regt)
Killed in Italy
Buried in Minterno War Cem

Figure 155. Fus Harry Newman, 8th Btn, Roy Fus (City of London Regt).

Figure 156. Sgt Maurice Nichols, 519 Battery, RHA (Essex Yeomanry).

Newman, Capt N.
RAMC
6.4.52
DOAS

Newman, L/Cpl Woolf
12.10.45
Died in accident

Newman, Capt Isidore MBE
Intel Corps SOE
Shot by the Germans in Mauthausen Camp

Newman, Cpl Michael
2nd Airborne
DOAS
Germany 1958–61

Newton, Pte Montague
6th Btn, The Manchester Regt
Age 24   -.2.44
Killed in action

Newton, Gnr Morris
RA
26.5.41
Buried at Deolali, India

Nichols, Sgt Maurice
519 Battery, RHA (Essex Yeomanry)
Age 26   7.9.42
Died at a forward observation post during the withdrawal of the 8th Army to El Alamein

Nickolay, Gnr G.A.W.
RA
Age 33   16.4.45
Buried in the River Kwai Kanchanburi War Cem

Nidzon, Pte L.
2nd Btn, Transvaal Scottish, UDF
11.1.42
Buried in Fort Capuzzo Cem

Nightingale, Pte S.
1st Btn, Buffs Central Mediterranean Force
29.3.44
Killed in action

Nirke, Sgt Eugene
Intel Corps
DOAS
-.2.57

Nishman, Pte Benjamin
17.7.42

Nissan, Lt Trevor A.
PC
13.4.43

Nissenbaum, Hyman
PC

Niznick, Lt N.
The Durham L/I
9.9.44

Norman, Capt Stephen
351 HAA Regt, RA
-.12.46

Norton, Pte Ernest (aka Nathan)
The Queen's Roy West Kent Regt/ 10 Commando
Age 21   13.6.44
Buried Ranville War Cem

Figure 157. The Grave of Pte E. Norton, The Queen's Own Royal West Kent Regt (10 Commando).

Novick, L/Cpl Harris
The Roy Norfolk Regt
Went down with a POW ship in Manila Bay, Philippines

Nyman, Pte A.H.
RAOC
19.6.43
Buried at East Ham

Figure 158. Sgt David Olsberg, 2nd Btn, The Lancashire Fus.

Nyman, Gnr Samuel
87 Field Regt RA
Age 37   21.7.43
Died on active service
Buried in Mosul War Cem

Ofner, Pte Isaac
RAPC
                      22.6.45
Buried at East Ham

Oldstein, Sgt Hyman
6th Btn Green Howards
(Alexandra, Princess of Wales's
Own Regt of Yorkshire)
                       9.9.44
Killed in action
Buried at Tongaloo -Westerloo
Cem

Olfman, Gnr Solomon
Roy Canadian Arty
                      31.7.42
Buried in Brookwood Cem

Olsberg, Sgt David
2nd Btn, The Lancs Fus
Age 27   19.10.44
Killed in action
Buried in Castel-del-Rio, Santerno

Opoczynski, Sgt Abraham
(served as Orr, Adam)
SAS
Age 23   -.12.45
Buried Durnbach War Cem

Figure 159. The Grave of Sgt David Olsberg at Castel-del-Rio, Santerno.

Oppenheim, Pte Aaron L.
1 Btn Straights Settlement
Volunteers
                      15.1.45
Singapore Memorial

Oppenheim, Lt G.W.
RASC
Age 38   -.-.45
Killed at Tripoli

Orlich, Pte
                      -.7.42
Killed in action in Keren
(Palestinian Jewish)

Ostroff, L/Cpl Mathias
PC
                       6.6.42
Killed during training

Ozareoff J.
The Home Guard
                      -.3.41
Killed by enemy action

Pack, Pte Marcus
UDF, South Africa
                      -.11.41

Park, Spr John
RE
                      11.5.42
Killed in a shooting accident
Buried at East Ham

Pasch, Pte J.
226 (Czech) Coy, PC
                      -.-. 41

Pass, Pte M.
UDF, MEF
                      31.12.41
Buried at El Homer Bardia

Paterson, T.
PC
Killed in action, Ardennes

Pavlotsky, Pte M.
The Yorks & Lancs Regt, Chindit
Age 36   26.4.44
Buried in Rangoon War Cem

Figure 160. The Grave of Pte M. Pavlotsky, The Yorks & Lancaster Regt, in Rangoon.

Figure 161. Lt Asher Pearlman MB, RAMC.

Figure 162. The Grave of Sgt J.D. Perry, The Welch Regt, in Rangoon.

Pearlman, Lt Asher
MB
RAMC
-.2.44
Killed in action
Buried at Castleforte

Pearls, Lt Ormond Israel Rodney
66 Light Regt RA
-.-.45
POW in Malaya, December 1942
Died in Japanese hands

Peer, Gnr Joseph
101 Battery 304 A/T Regt RA
Age 36   4.12.44
Buried Kohima War Cem

Pegler, Lt Herbert R.D., DCM, MM
RAC
16.6.44

Pepper, Pte Frank Robert
Norfolk Regt
Age 26   26.9.43
Buried Chungkai War Cem

Perlman, A.
formerly SVC Shanghai
Burma?

Perry, L/Bdr
RA
Killed in action Italy

Perry, Sgt J.D.
The Welch Regt
Age 31   16.2.44
Buried in Rangoon War Cem

Pertschuk, Lt Maurice MBE
SOE
-.3.45
MBE for distinguished services in the field
Hanged in Buchenwald Concentration Camp

Peskin, Capt Louis, MC (WW1)
RA
16.1.43
DOAS
Buried in Willesden Cem

Peterkosky, Gnr Harry
RA
29.10.41
Died in an accident
Buried at Leicester

Philips, Lt J.J.
RA
Killed in action in Burma

Phillips, Rfmn Alexander Alfred
2nd Btn, The Cameronians (Scottish Rifles)
31.5.44
Killed in action

Phillips, Rfmn Benjamin Yehuda
Rifle Brigade 1 Btn
Age 28   19/20.5.42

Phillips, Gnr Harry
RA
Age 32   5.3.44
Served 3 Years in Tobruk
Died in a road accident

Figure 163. Gnr Harry Phillips, RA.

Phillips, Capt Isaac Philip
KOYLI
                                    30.6.46

Phillips, Pte Henry (Pitzkoon)
'C' Company 2nd Btn, The Border Regt
                                    31.3.44
Killed in North Burma
Buried on Nippon Hill

Phillips, Lt Jacob
RAMC
                                    11.7.43

Phillips, Pte Joseph
W. Yorks Regt
                                    30.3.42

Phillipson/Phillipsohn, W.
PC
                                    17.9.42
Killed in action

Pick, A.
PC 51st Highland Div Ski Instructor
Killed in action, Walcheren

Pick, Cpl M.
PC
                                    17.3.44
Buried St Eugene Jewish Cem

Pickles, Cpl Stanley
RAMC
Age 41   11.7.45
Buried Prestwich Jewish Cem

Pieske, Sgt Hermann
RA
                                    29.5.40

Pincus, Pte Monty
The Queen's Roy Regt (West Surrey)
Age 18   -.-.40
Enlisted at 16 while under age.
Rejoined later. Killed whilst
guarding RAF North Weald,
Epping, during an air raid.
Buried with eight comrades in a
nearby church

Figure 164. Pte Monty Pincus, The Queen's Roy Regt (West Surrey).

Pinsky, Pte Norman
The West Yorks Regt (The Prince of Wales's Own)
Age 23   19.1.44
Buried in Rangoon War Cem

Pitkovsky, Cpl A.
RE
                                    11.6.40

Plaut, Cpl Ernst
PC
Age 45   2.5.45
Golders Green Cem

Podgurski, L/Cpl Alan
Durham L/I
Age 21   24.1.45
Buried Sittard War Cem

Podgurski, Pte E.
1/Roy Scots
                                    26.5.40
Buried Le Paradis War Cem

Podolsky, Cpl Barnett
8 Btn Roy Fus
Age 32   20.1.44
Cassino Memorial

Polikoff, Pte Leslie
DOAS
                                    -.3.48

Pollack, Franz
PC
                                    -.-.53

Polli, Pte Simon (aka Poliwansky)
RAPC
Buried in Glasgow

Figure 165. The Grave of Pte Norman Pinsky, The West Yorkshire Regt (The Prince of Wales's Own), in Rangoon.

Pollock, Pte Harry
4th Btn, The Dorset Regt
15.3.45
Killed in action
Buried in Germany

Popper, Pte Harry
1st Btn, The Essex Regt
15.4.44
Buried in Kohima Mil Cem

Port, Rfmn Isaac
KAFR
28.5.43
Buried Bari Mil Cem

Porter, Tpr Wilfred H. (Portner)
RTR, RAC
Age 24   2.9.44
Killed in France
Buried at Canaples, Amiens

Posener, Gnr Theodore
RA
Died of wounds in the Middle East
Buried in Tripoli Mil Cem

Posnansky, Pte Isaac
Jewish Inf Bde Group

Posner, Fus Isaac
7 Btn Roy Welch Fus
Age 41   11.7.45
Buried Prestwich Jewish Cem

Posner, Sydney
Norwood Memorial

Postan, Gnr Emanuel
75th LAA Regt, RA
11.5.44
Buried in Ganhati Mil Cem

Pottinger, Spr J.D.
RE
Buried in the Brit War Cem
Florence

Prager, Joseph
PC
SS *Lancastria*
17.6.40

Price, Fus Abraham A.
Lanc. Fus
12.1.43

Primhak, Lt Leonard P.
192 Mountain Battery, RA,
South East Asia Command
17.1.46
Killed in action in the Dutch East
Indies
Buried in Surabaya Cem

Proops, Cpl Lawrence, J.
RASC
23.11.40
Died from injuries received
removing an incendiary bomb
from a hotel

Pruim, Sgmn Bernard
RCOS
18.7.46
Buried in the Jewish Cem, New
Delhi

Purdy, L/Bdr
RA
Killed as a POW of Japs

Pyzer, L/Bdr Lewis
120 HAA Regt, RA
20.4.42
Buried at East Ham

Queskey, Lt David Denis
7th Btn, The East Yorks Regt
(The Duke of York's Own)
-.10.44
Killed in action

Rabinovitch, Gnr Simon
42nd Bty, RA
10.5.44
Buried in the Commonwealth
Cem, Yokohama, Japan

**Rabinowitz (Rabinovich), Capt
Adam**
Croix de Guerre
SOE
-.-.44
Murdered in France

**Rabinowitz, Spr Arthur (served
as Knight)**
67/69 Bomb Disposal RE
Age 21   25.8.40
Buried Toxteth Cem

Rachovitch, Gnr Louis
105 LAA Regt, RA
12.6.43
Buried in El-Alia Mil Cem,
Maison Caree, Algiers

Figure 166. The Grave of Gnr Simon Rabinovitch, 42nd Battery, RA,
in the Commonwealth Cemetery, Yokohama, Japan.

Ralstein, Tpr Clarence J.
11th Hussars, RAC, Prince Alberts Own
9.12.40
Killed in action in Egypt
Buried at Sidi Barani

Rams, Sgt Max
Paras
Killed in action Arnhem

Rapaport, Elijah (aka Butcher, Samuel Eric)
SOE
7.6.44 (tbc)
KIA at sea

Rappaport
SVC
-.-.36
Killed on active service, Shanghai

Rapstone, Bdr Fred
265 Battery 75th LAA Regt, RA
-.11.42
Died of wounds in North Africa
Buried in El-Alia Cem

Ratchkind, Dvr
RASC
18.3.40
Died in France
Buried in Fouquieres Churchyard Extension

Ratcliffe, Pte George S.
Norfolk Regt
1.3.45

Rathe, R.
PC

Raymond, Lt Archibald
9th Btn, Roy Fus (City of London Regt)
27.7.42
Killed in a mine accident

Rebek, Cpl Tony
RE

Reid, Lt Lucien Bernard
RA
2.5.43

Reisman, Pte Bernard
Hampshire Regt
11.9.43
Buried at Salerno

Redlich, Pte Leo
RAOC
26.8.43
Buried in Tripoli Mil Cem

Redwood, Pte Reuben
RAOC
28.4.43
KIA and buried in Tripoli
Plaque at Willesden Cem

Ree, CSM Eric Lionel
SOE Field Security
21.11.43
(father Jewish)

Reinhold, Cpl Joseph
Pal.
1st Btn, The Para Regt, Army Air Corps 6th Airborne Division
- .5.44
Buried in Tidworth Mil Cem

Reisman, Pte H.
1/4th Btn, The Hampshire Regt
-.1.45
Killed in action

Reisz, Pte A.
74th Company PC
17.9.42
Killed in accident
Buried in Boscombe East Cem, Bournemouth

Remer, Pte Louis
Middx Regt
10.1.42
Sai Wan, Hong Kong

Resnick, Pte M.
UDF, MEF
31.12.41
Buried at El Homer, Bardia

Reuben, Spr Hyam Solomon
RE
10.5.41
Buried in Scholemoore Cem, Bradford

Reuben, Rfmn Hyman Casper
The Roy Ulster Rifles
16.4.43
Killed in action

Rice
10 Commando
Killed in action, Dieppe

Rich, Sgt Jack
1st Btn, The Middx Regt (Duke of Cambridge's Own)
25.12.41
Killed in the Far East
Buried in Sarwan Bay War Cem

Richards, Lt/Col Terence
26.4.44
Killed in action, Italy
Buried Taranto Brit Mil Cem

Richter, Pte Jack (aka Richmond, Jacob)
13/18 Roy Hussars
6.6.44
Killed on D-Day

Ricklovitch, Pte Israel
RAOC
23.6.45
Buried Naples War Cem

Rifkin, Cpl Sydney
The Queen's Own Cameron Highldrs
Age 26   -.4.43
Killed in North Africa

Risidore, John
DLI
3.4.45

Risker, Dvr David A.
RASC
1.8.42
Buried in Glenduffhill Cem, Glasgow

Figure 167. Whitehall 1980. The Countess Mountbatten takes the salute at the AJEX Remembrance Parade.

Ritinitis, Capt P. (aka Weinberger)
General List
10.1.43
Buried Medjez-El-Bab War Cem

Ritterband, Montague
KSLI
Killed in action Korea
17.11.51

Ritterbrand, Bandsman Benjamin
1st Btn, The Hereford Regt
Age 27   19.7.44
Killed in action in the Battle of Caen

Rivers, Pte C.M. (Rothbarth)
The Suffolk Regt
Age 30   25.11.44
Buried at Overloon, Holland

Figure 168. Bandsman Benjamin Ritterbrand, 1st Btn, The Herefordshire Regt.

Rivlin, Sgt Monty
REME
16.10.43
Killed in Egypt

Robinson, L/Bdr Woolf
133 Field Regt, RA
-.8.44
Killed in action, Italy

Robson, Capt A.
RAMC
27.1.45
Buried in Rangoon War Cem

Rocklin, Capt Sidney
5th Btn, The Nigeria Regt
-.6.46
Killed in an accident

Rodin, Fus Jack (Israel)
RIF
28.12.42

Figure 169. The Grave of Capt A. Robson, RAMC, in Rangoon.

Figure 170. The Grave of Rifleman Solomon Rodkoff, 8th Btn, The Rifle Bde, in Tourneville.

Rodker, Sgmn Benjamin
RCOS
           3.10.43
Died in a mine explosion
Buried at East Ham

Rodkoff, Rfmn Solomon
8th Battalion, The Rifle Brigade
           28.6.44
Killed in Normandy by a German sniper. Having driven his commanding officer off the beach after landing, his car was shot up. He was sent to find another and was killed.
Buried in Tourneville

Rodner, Sgt Harold MM
Age 21   -.-.45
Killed in action

Rodness, D.
Regt of Canada Italy
           2.1.45

Rogers, L/Cpl Woyland
REME
           14.7.44
Buried in Great Yarmouth

Roitt, Tpr H.
RAC
           7.12.43
Killed in a tank accident
Buried at Willesden

Rokach, Allan Henry
RCOS
Buried Minturno War Cem

Rolphe, Sgt Alexander Edgar

Romain, Gnr Jack
12th Regt, RHA (HAC)
           -.-.41
Killed in action in Greece

Romano, Pte L.
The Loyal Regt
           13.6.43
Buried in Sousse Mil Cem

Rose, Pte H. (Rosinsky)
RAMC
           -.2.42
Killed in action in Singapore

Rose, Gnr Alexander
RA
           -.2.42
Killed in action in Malaya

Rose, Dvr A.J.
RASC
           25.9.45
Buried in Kranji War Memorial Cem

Rose, Fus Leon
Roy Fus (City of London Regt)
           -.-.44

Figure 171. The Grave of Dvr A.J. Rose, RASC, in Kranji.

Rose, L/Bdr Victor
83rd Field Regt, RA
           -.7.44
Died in France

Rosen, L/Cpl Manny
9th Btn, Roy Fus (City of London Regt)
Age 27   18.9.44
Died of wounds
Buried in Gradara War Cem

Rosen, L/Bdr Michael
58th AT Regt, RA
                                -.5.45
Buried in Hanover (Limmer) Cem

Rosen, Pte Morris
5 Btn West Kent Regt
Age 28   20.10.44
Buried Faenza War Cem

Rosen, Myer R.
2nd RF

Rosen, Pte Shlomo
PC (Palestine)
Age 25   -.-.45

Rosen, Gnr Solomon
LAA, RA
                           -.-.45
Died as POW in North Borneo
Buried in Labuan War Cem

Rosenbaum, 2nd Lt Alfred Manning
14th Btn, The Sherwood Foresters (Notts& Derbys Regt)
                          -.-11.42
Killed in action

Rosenbaum, Pte Hyman
RAOC
                          25.2.44
Buried Edmonton

Rosenberg, Gnr A.
RA
Age 41   26.12.43
Buried in the River Kwai Mil Cem

Rosenberg, Maj Donald
RAMC
                          14.10.46
Buried in Kirkee War Cem,
Bombay

Rosenberg, Fus Frank
2nd Btn, Roy Fus (City of London Regt)
                          14.5.43
Buried in the Bone Mil Cem,
Annaba

Rosenberg, Gnr Gerald Dennis
237 Battery 101 LAA Regt RA
Age 20   12.6.40
Buried St. Valery En Caux Cem

Rosenberg, L/Cpl Harry
RAOC
Age 23   10.7.42
Buried Alexandria (Hadra) Cem

Rosenberg, Tpr Herbert (aka Russell)
B Sq 3rd RTR
Age 21   19.7.44
Buried in Hermanville War Cem

Rosenberg, Gdsmn John
Grenadier Guards
                          -.9.40

Rosenberg, Gnr Joseph
RA
Age 33   3.12.43
Buried in the River Kwai Mil
Cem

Rosenberg, L/Cpl L.
3rd Btn, The Transvaal Scottish Regt, UDF
                          23.11.41
Buried in Knightsbridge War Cem,
Acroma

Rosenberg, Lt Maurice MD
RAMC
                          -.7.43
Missing, believed killed

Rosenberg, Pte Percy
The Lincs Regt
Age 20   14.10.44
Killed in action at Overloon,
Holland

Rosenberg, Pte Ralph
2/7 Btn West Surrey Regt
Age 24   21.1.44
Buried Minturno War Cem Italy

Rosenberg, Col Richard Louis
RCOS Att Indian COS
                          2/3.3.42
Singapore Memorial

Rosenberg, Pte Siegbert
PC
                          28.3.42
Buried in Scholemoor Cem,
Bradford

Rosenberg, Pte Woolf
2nd Btn, Roy Fus (City of London Regt)
                          -.-.43
Buried at Medjez-El-Bab, Tunisia

Rosenbloom, Rfmn Benjamin
The Rifle Brigade
Age 21   -.-.43

Rosenbloom, Pte Frederick
Attached HQ 54th Div
                          26.7.42
Died in a mine accident

Rosenblum, Pte Arnold
10th Btn, The Green Howards (Alexandra, Princess of Wales's Own Regt of Yorks)
                          -.11.43

Rosenburg, Dvr S.
RASC
                          -.11.42
Killed accidentally

Rosenfeld, Cpl Hans (P. J. Rodley)
Paras
                          -.11.44
Killed in action at Arnhem

Rosenfeld, Pte Sidney
50th Btn Buffs
                          5.9.40
Killed by a land mine
Buried at Streatham

Rosenfield, Cpl Maurice (Monty) MM
1st Btn, The Loyal Regt (North Lancashire)
                          -.9.44
Killed in action in Italy saving a
wounded comrade

Rosenheim, Maj. Charles Leslie MC
4th Btn, The Welch Regt
-.2.45
Killed in action in Western Europe

Rosenthal, Gnr Cyril
78th LAA Regt, *RA*
9.2.41
Buried in Hull Western Synagogue Cem

Rosenthal, Pte Ludwig
PC
28.4.46
Killed by an explosion
Buried at Willesden

Rosenthal, Cpl N.
1st Btn, South African Irish Regt, UDF, MEF
23.11.41
Buried in Knightsbridge War Cem, Acroma

Rosenthal, Pte S.
PC (Czech)

Rosenthal, L/Bdr William Guy
1st Canadian AT Regt,
Roy Canadian Arty
-.11.43
Killed in action

Rosenweig, Pte Maurice
RAOC
Age 26   28.10.45
Buried Manchester

Rosenzweig, Egon
PC
-.12.45
Buried at Oslo

Rosewood, Pte N.
The South Staffs Regt
Age 21   17.3.44
Buried in Rangoon War Cem

Rosner, L/Cpl H.
5th (Palestine) Water Tank Company
-.4.42
Buried in Conference Cairn Cem

Figure 172. Admiral of the Fleet Sir Peter Hill-Norton reviews the AJEX Memorial Parade 1971.

Rossen, Gnr Ellis Jack
RA
4.6.43
Buried at Willesden Cem

Roth, Gnr Maurice
64 Med Regt RA
Age 22   14.11.42

Rothberg, Dvr Mark
672 Coy RE
Age 20   30.5.40
Buried at Veurnes Communal Cem, Belgium

Rothenberg, Gnr Joseph
RA
1.8.42
Buried at Heliopolis

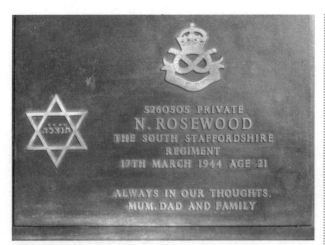

Figure 173. The Grave of Pte N. Rosewood, The South Staffordshire Regt, in Rangoon.

Figure 175. Cpl Leonard Rubin, 2 Commando.

Figure 174. Dvr Mark Rothberg, 672 Company, RE.

Rothman, Pte Mendel
The East Lancs Regt
17.8.44
Died of wounds
Buried in Banneville-La-Campagne Brit Cem

Rothschild, Maj Leonard Douglas
RTR RAC
(served 1914/18 too)
Age 53   17.3.42
Buried Cheltenham Cem

Roumania, Pte A.
-.10.43
Went down with POW ship in Manila Bay, Philippines

Rowne, Crftsmn Abram
REME, Attached HQ 30 Corps
-.7.45
Killed in an accident

Rozaner, Sgt Joseph
PC
30.9.46
Buried at East Ham

Ruben, Dvr Arthur
230534/270699 RASC
8.6.42
Died of Wounds (*Times*)
Buried in Tobruk War Cem

Rubin, Pte Albert (Ruben)
The Worcs Regt
31.3.41
Buried in Eritrea

Rubin, G.
PC

Rubin, Gnr Henry
259 Battery 83 HAA Regt RA
Age 33   14.10.42
Buried in Basra War Cem

Rubin, Cpl Leonard
2 Commando
Age 26   11.9.43
Killed in the first landing and buried at Salerno

Rubinstein, Spr Charles
306 Bomb Disposal Group, RE
18.10.42
Buried in Brookwood Cem

Rubinstein, Gnr Morris
79 Searchlight Regt, RA
2.7.42
Buried in Holy Law South Broughton Burial Ground

Rubinstein, Sgt Theodore Albert
The Glider Pilot Regt, Army Air Corps
Age 23   -.10.44
Killed in action at Arnhem
Buried in the Brit Mil Cem, Arnhem

Figure 176. The Grave of Cpl Leonard Rubin in Salerno.

Figure 177. The Grave of Dvr Mark Rothberg in the Communal Cemetery at Veurnes, Belgium.

Ruda, Pte Harry
PC
        3.7.46
Buried Leeds, New Farnley

Rudetsky, David (aka Rudelsky)
21043409
Gen. Service Corps
        17.11.47

Figure 178. Sgt Theodore Albert Rubinstein, The Glider Pilot Regt, AAC.

Rueff, Lt Marcus
The Tower Hamlet Rifles
        -.-.41
Died of wounds in the Near East
Buried in Benghazi Mil Cem

Russell, Lt M.L.
Intel Corps
Buried Kranji War Cem
        9.8.46

Ruttman, Fus Hyman
Roy Fus (City of London Regt)
        -.11.44
Killed in action

Sabel, Pte Stanley
RAOC
        24.3.45

Sachon, Gnr Joseph
94th AT Regt, RA
        13.7.45

Sachs, Pte Herbert (aka Seymour)
The Buffs/10 Commando
Age 27   23.3.45
Groesbeek Mem Cem

Sacks, Cpl I.
The Durham L/I
        17.12.41
Buried at Ras-El-Menaster

Saffer, 2nd Lt Neville Nathan
13th Btn, The King's Regt (Liverpool)
        -.8.42
Died of wounds
Buried in Ramna Forest Pathania, India

Salkel/Seeltier/Sealtiel, Pte David G.
The Roy Berks Regt (Princess Charlotte of Wales's)
        30.10.43
Buried in Santa Maria Mil Cem, Caserta

Salmon, Lt George Barnett
RA
Age 29   18.11.45
Buried Willesden (Lib)

Salmon, Lt M. Leonard
HLI
Age 26   30.4.45

Salmon, N.F.
REME
        -.8.45
Buried at Labuan

Salomon, Pte Alfred
248 Coy PC
        23.10.40
Buried in Bristol Jewish Cem

Salomon, Pte Kurt
PC
        30.1.42
Buried in Birmingham

Salomon, L/Cpl John G.
Intel Corps
        16.9.40
Newmarket Cem

Salomons, Sgt Joseph Lowden
Ox and Bucks LI
Age 28   26.11.42
Gosport Cem

Salzburg, Pte Israel
PC
Age 24   -.-.40
Killed in Greece

Saltzburg, Victor
E. Yorks
27.2.45

Samberg, Cpl H.
The South Lancs Regt (The Prince of Wales's Volunteers)
14.2.45
Buried in Rangoon War Cem

Samuel, Capt Ernest Lambert
16 Btn Mddx Home Guard
27.1.44
Buried Golders Green

Samuel, Gnr H.A.
Hong Kong V.D.F
Buried Stanley, Hong Kong

Samuels, Pte Morris
RAMC
25.3.44
Buried at Meerut, India

Samuels, Spr Sidney
RE
14.8.44

Samuels, L/Bdr Stuart
56 Medium Regt, RA
22.4.43
Killed in an accident
Buried in Edgeline Cem, Liverpool

Sander, Lt 'Gus' Gustav
Middx/Paras
Killed in action Korea
30.10.50

Sander, Dvr W.
148 Coy RASC
-.1.44
Buried in Naples

Sanders, Pte H.
AIF
30.12.42
Japanese POW
Buried Kranji

Sandford, W. (aka Zunz)
PC

Saperia, A.
RAPC

Saperia, Pte Harry
*The West Yorks Regt
(The Prince of Wales's Own)*
-.3.41
Served in 1914–18 War. Killed in an air raid in Scotland. Buried at New Farnley, Leeds

Sapiro, Gnr S.
5th Field Regt SAA
31.5.42
Buried at Gazala

Figure 180. Pte Harry Saperia, The West Yorks Regt (The Prince of Wales's Own).

Figure 181. L/Cpl Louis Saunders, 4th Btn, The Royal Norfolk Regt.

Sarfaty, Douglas Jack
Roy Sussex
14.5.40

Saunders, L/Cpl L.
The Roy Norfolk Regt
-.10.43
Went down with a POW ship in Manila Bay, Philippines

Saunders, Tpr Lawrence (Salinger)
8th King's Roy Irish Hussars
30.3.45
Killed in action at Oeding on the Dutch-German Frontier

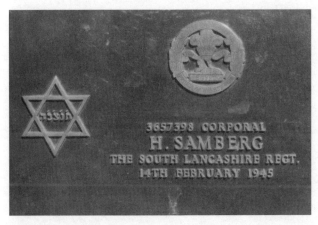

Figure 179. The Grave of Cpl H. Samberg, The South Lancs Regt (The Prince of Wales's Vol), in Rangoon.

Figure 182. Lt Laurence Savitt, 31st LAA Regt, RA, Central Mediterranean Force.

Figure 183. Tpr Leslie E. Schalit, 1st Recce Regt, Recce Corps.

Figure 185. Sgt David Bernard Schneider, REME.

Saunders, Pte Sydney
W. Surreys Regt
                                    24.10.42
Alamein

Savitt, Lt Laurence
31st LAA Regt, RA, Central Mediterranean Force
Age 29   12.5.44
Killed in action at Cassino

Sayers, Fus Harry R.
RAC
                                    5.4.45
Repatriated to US

Schaffer, Gnr Herman 'Harry'
RAC
                                    20.4.50

Schaffner, E. (Phillips)
Killed in action, Dunkirk

Schalit, Tpr Leslie E.
1st Recce Regt, Recce Corps
                                    -.9.44
Died while attempting to escape the enemy in Italy

Figure 184. Pte Philip Scheffer, 7th Btn, The Black Watch (Royal Highland Regt).

Schalitz, Pte I.
RASC
                                    9.10.44

Schanoff, Dvr M.O.
RASC GTC
                                    5.7.44
Buried Salerno Mil Cem

Scheider-Sinclair, Sgt David Bernard
REME, Attached Ensa
                                    -.9.45
Died in Palestine

Scheffer, Pte Philip
7th Btn, The Black Watch (Highland Regt)
Age 19   20.2.45
Buried in the Reichswald Forest War Cem

Schein, Tpr Solomon
2nd Derbys Yeomanry RAC
Age 26   10.2.45
Buried Milsbeek War Cem

Schifrin, Lt Aaron Edward (served as Barson)
MM Croix de Guerre
13 HAA Regt RA
Age 29   26.6.44
Buried Ryes War Cem

Schindler, Herbert
KOR, LANCS.
Dunkirk
                                    29.5.40

Schlinkman, Pte A.
                                    8.3.44

Schlesinger, Terence J.
RE
                                    17.6.40
Killed in action *SS Lancastria*
Dunkirk Memorial

Schmechel, Pte Joseph
5 Btn Manchester Regt
                                    12.9.41
Buried Liverpool Cem (Ford)

Schmidt, Bdr Alex
RA
Killed by shellfire at Tobruk

Schneider, Sgt David Bernard
*REME Orig with the Duke of
Wellington's Regt*
MID
31.8.45
Died in the Middle East

Schneider, Pte L.
UDF
13.12.41

Schneiderman, Pte Ralph
The East Surrey Regt
-.12.44
Killed in action

Schneiderson, Pte Myer
*The Queen's Roy Regt, (West
Surrey)*
6.2.44
Killed in action in Burma

**Schner, Maj F., BEM, MID (aka
Schneck)**
General List
9.1.47
Buried in Klagenfurt War Cem,
Austria

Shratsky, Pte Solomon
REME
19.10.44
Died by enemy action
Buried in Antwerp Mil Cem

Schreiber, Sgt Emanuel
Recce Corps
Died of wounds in Greece
Buried in Athens Phaleron War
Cem

Schrinski, Pte Bronnie
1 Btn Buffs
Age 20   25.1.43
Buried Tripoli War Cem

Schul, Pte Pinkus
The Roy Sussex Regt
Age 20   6.2.45
Killed in action in Burma
Buried in Rangoon War Cem

Schultz, Lt F.
RAMC
3.2.42

Schwarcz, Capt E.
RAMC
12.10.44
Buried at Miramaredi Romagna

Schwartz, Dvr David Harry
206 Coy, RASC
26.12.43
Buried in El Alia Cem, Algiers

Figure 186. Sgt Emanuel
Schreiber, Recce Corps.

Figure 187. The Grave of Sgt
Emanuel Schreiber, Recce Corps,
in the Phaleron War Cem, Athens.

Schwartz, Pte Donald Reginald
7th Paras
Age 20   6.6.44
Bayeux Memorial

Schwartz, Rfmn Solly
Central Mediterranean Force
Age 24   -.4.45
Killed in action in Italy

Figure 188. The Grave of Pte Pinkus Schul, The Royal Sussex Regt, in
Rangoon.

Schwartz, Maj Z.
AIF
Killed at Tobruk

Schwarz, Pte Victor
Czech Army
28.11.41
Buried at East Ham

Schwarze, Pte Heinz
87 Coy, PC
28.4.42
Killed in an explosion
Buried in the Mil Cem, Pembroke
Dock

Schwenk, H.
RASC
10.4.42

Schyberg, Gnr Alfred Edward
RA
14.11.42
Tripoli War Cem

Sclare, Gnr David
RA
17.8.42

**Sebag-Montefiore, Maj Geoffrey
Edmund, MBE**
-.5.43

Secunda, Pte Emmanuel
22.4.44
Cassino

Secunda, Pte Harry
*The Queen's Own Regt (West
Surrey)*
Killed in North Africa

Segal, Pte B.
*2nd Btn, The Transvaal Scottish
Regt, UDF, MEF*
27.5.42
Buried at Acroma

Segal, Pte Jack
*Argyll & Sutherland Highldrs
(Princess Louise's)*
1942/43
Killed in action in Italy

Segal, Gnr Reuben (Ben)
RA
23.1.44
Died in an explosion
Buried in Rice Lane Cem,
Liverpool

Segal, Pte Stanley
KOSB
28.7.41
Buried at East Ham

Segarman, Capt Henry Samuel
RAMC
Age 29
Killed at El Alamein
Buried in El Alamein Cem

Selby, Fus Joseph
Roy Irish Fus
-.-.44
Killed in action

Seligman, Capt Oliver R.
RA
Age 28   4.9.44
London Cem, Longueval

Seligsohn, Sgt Rabbi Rudolf
PC
-.5.43
Buried in Willesden Liberal Cem

Selzer, Lt Bernard
The Nigeria Regt
-.3.43

Selzer, Tpr Edmund
RAC
24.2.44
Buried in St Denys Cem

Shaiman, WO L.
27.4.44

Shalks, Pte Charles
RAOC
12.4.43
Buried in Moor Top Cem

Shama, Lt Clement
Intel Corps
-.1.43
Buried in Tripoli Mil Cem

Figure 189. Capt Henry Samuel
Segarman, RAMC.

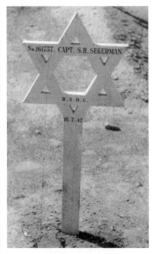

Figure 190. The Grave of Capt
Henry Segarman at El Alamein.

Shapero, Sgt Harry
RASC
6.1.46
Buried at East Ham

Shapero, Sgt Harry
RTR, RAC

Shapiro, Sgmn I.
RCOS
Died in a POW Camp, River Kwai,
Thailand

Shapiro, Fus Bertie Victor
Roy Fus (City of London Regt)
-.7.44
Died of wounds in Italy

Shapiro, Pte Frank
The HLI (City of Glasgow Regt)
Age 26 -.11.44
Killed in action in Holland

Shapiro, Gnr Isidore Aaron
RA
Age 23 1.4.42
Fought at Tobruk
Buried in Halfaya Sollum War Cem

Shapiro, Gnr Jack
341 Battery 551 Coast Regt RA
Age 36 15.11.44
Buried Edmonton

Shapiro, Pte Louis
RAOC
Age 28 27.3.45
Buried Edmonton

Share, Fus Harry
2/6th Btn, The Lancs Fus
17.8.40
Accidentally shot
Buried in Minthorpe Cem,
Middlesbrough

Sharp, Capt David
RA
2.10.47

Figure 191. Pte Frank Shapiro,
The HLI (City of Glasgow Regt).

Figure 192. Gnr Isidore Aaron
Shapiro, RA.

Sharpes, Capt Harry Arthur
RAOC
Age 37 17.11.47
Buried Edmonton

Sheinkman, Abraham
HG/Mddx Btn
5.3.44

Shepler, Gnr H.
8th Survey Regt, RA
22.9.44
Buried at Florence, Italy

Sheps, Capt Samuel B.

Sher, Pte Greg
1st Australian Commandos
-.1.09
KIA Afghanistan

Sherer, Pte Leonard
RAMC
-.2.42
Killed in Singapore

Shilofsky, Gnr Hyman
RA
-.1.44
Missing, presumed killed

Shiner, Lt Leslie W.
RA
29.10.43

Shinman, Gnr David
RA
-.6.44
Killed in action

Shinman, Pte Jack
6th Black Watch
Age 32 17.7.44
Assissi War Cem

Shock, Pte Sidney (aka Shork)
Hants Regt
30.8.44

Shonfeld, Frank
RWK
28.5.40

Shooster, Pte Barnett
1 Btn Sussex Regt
Age 25 16/18.1.44
Cassino Memorial

Shore, Gnr Solomon
RA
17.11.44
Killed in action

Shore, Gnr Theodor
RA
7.7.45
Died Japanese POW

Shriebman, Gnr H.
119 LAA Regt, RA
29.12.44
Killed in North-West Europe
Buried in Eindhoven Jewish Cem

Shulman, Sgt Herbert Norman
RASC
-.8.52

Figure 193. The Grave of Pte H. Silkman, The Dorsetshire Regt, in Rangoon.

Shulman, Fus J.
10th Btn, The Lancs Fus
12.7.42
Buried in Kohima Cem

Shulton, Pte S.
Queen's Roy Regt
Age 22   2.12.43

Shuster, Pte Stephen
7th Btn, The Essex Regt
25.8.40
Killed in an air raid
Buried in the Jewish Cem,
Rainham

Shutz, L/Cpl Harold Jack, MM
8th Btn, The Rifle Brigade
-.9.44
Killed in action in Holland
Buried in Burg Leopold

Sicklin, Pte Nathan
RASC
5.11.46

Sidman, Capt Bernard, MB
RAMC
Age 28   30.3.45
Killed in action
Buried in Bologna War Cem

Silberman, Pte W.
The Rand L/I, UDF
-.4.43

Silifonts, Para Simon Aron
Commandos
-.12.43
Killed in action

Silkman, Pte H.
The Dorset Regt
Age 28   10.3.45
Buried in Rangoon War Cem

Silosky, Pte Lewis
The Black Watch (Roy Highland Regt)
Age 20
Killed in Burma

Silver, Pte Alec
130 Field Ambulance, RAMC
7.3.45
Killed in action
Buried at Nijmegen, Holland

Silver, Rfmn Ben
2nd Btn, KRRC
Age 21   31.5.42
Despatch rider for Sir Anthony
Eden, served in France and the
Middle East, killed in action
Buried in Acroma (Knightsbridge)
Cem

Silver, QMS Harry
RAOC

Silver, Pte L.
The Essex Regt

Silver, Sgt Leslie
RAC
Age 33   14.9.44
Killed during the liberation of
Belgium

Silver, Sgt M.
6.10.44

Silver, Bugle Maj Reuben
2nd Btn, The Rifle Bde
Served 1934–1961
Died in Germany

Silver, Pte Sam
Captured in Singapore. No trace
Died as POW Singapore

Silverman, Spr Colman
RE
-.5.44
Killed in action
Buried in Naples

Silverman, Gnr John J.
230 Searchlight Regt
14.5.41
Buried Edmonton Cem

Silverman, Pte Joseph
7 Btn Worcs Regt
Age 24   14.3.45
Buried Taukkyan War Cem
Rangoon

Silverstein, Pte Leon J.
70 Btn, The Essex Regt
8.10.42
Buried at Rainham

Silverstein, Pte Max
6th Btn, The Devonshire Regt
23.2.43
Buried at East Ham

Silverstein, Robert
HLI
10.4.45

Figure 194. Rifleman Ben Silver, 2nd Btn, The KRRC.

Figure 195. Pte Benjamin Silver, The KRRC.

Figure 197. The Grave of Lt P. Silvert, 4th Company, 716 Btn, RASC, at Ranville.

Silverstein, Dvr Woolf
463 Water Tank Coy RASC
Age 20   2.3.44
Lost in HM LST 362.

Silvert, Lt P.
4th Company, 716 Btn, RASC (Airborne)
Age 27   6.6.44
Buried in Ranville Mil Cem

Simeon, Sgt E. (Simion)
PC/AAC
                          29.4.44
Glider Pilot, Arnhem

Siminsky, Pte Israel Benjamin
5 Btn East Yorks Regt
Age 27   27.7.42

Simmonds, Rfmn Samuel
2nd Btn, The Rifle Bde
                          27.10.42
Killed in action in the Western Desert

Simmons, Fus Jack (aka Dubchansky)
11th Btn, The Lancs Fus
Age 22   -.3.45
Killed in action
Buried in Faenza Brit Cem

Figure 196. The Grave of Private S. Shulton, The Queen's Royal Regt.

Simmons, Pte Jack
1st Btn, The Dorset Regt
Age 24   19.6.44
Killed near Caen
Buried in Hottot-Les-Bagues War Cem

Simon, Pte Albert
PC Pal 866
                          29.4.41
Athens Mem

Simon, L/Sgt Cyril R.
RAC
                          16.7.42

Simons, Gnr Edward
RA
                          17.6.44

Simons, Cftmn Faulk Emanuel
REME
                          11.8.46
Drowned
Buried in Wuppertal Jewish Civil Cem

Simons, Gnr Morris
61 AT Regt, RA
                          -.10.42
Killed on active service, Alamein

Simons, Sgt Reginald
RE
                          21.7.44
Killed by enemy action
Buried at East Ham

Simpson, Maj R.H.
RA
Age 33   12.2.45
Buried in Rangoon War Cem

Figure 198. The Grave of Maj R.H. Simpson, RA, in Rangoon.

Figure 200. Pte A. Skry, The Queen's Own Royal West Kent Regt.

Sinai, Sgt Frederick
RAPC
1942–1.5.68
Buried in Aldershot Jewish Cem

Sinauer, Lt/Col E.M. OBE, MC
RE
10.7.46

Singer, Pte Fred
5 Btn Seaforth Highldrs
Age 25   14.7.43
Buried Syracuse War Cem

Singer, Dvr L.
RCOS
Age 36   18.10.43
Died on the River Kwai

Singer, Pte P.
PC (Palestine)
9.7.42
Buried in Famagusta Mil Cem

Sipkin, L/Cpl Alexander
RAPC
17.11.46

Sirkin, Gnr M.
RA
Age 34   21.2.44
Buried in the War Cem, Rangoon

Sirotkin, Fus Hyman
2 Btn Roy Fus
Age 29   30.6.44
Buried Assisi War Cem

Skolnik, Pte Jack
1st Btn, The Sherwood Foresters (Notts & Derbys Regt)
15.2.41
Killed on active service in the Middle East

Skulnik, Cpl Wolfe
REME
Age 29   23.4.45

Skryzinsky, Pte Arthur (aka Skry)
7th Btn, The Queen's Own Roy West Kent Regt
-.10.43
Killed in action
Buried in Catania Brit Cem

Figure 199. The Grave of Gnr M. Sirkin, RA, in Rangoon.

Slossman, Reuven
Formerly SVC Shanghai
Burma?

Smith, Sgt M.
5th Field Coy, UDF, MEF
1.12.41
Buried in Sollum,Tobruk

Smith, Rfmn Mark
K.R.R
25.4.42
Buried at Tobruk

Smith
10 Commando
Killed in action, Dieppe

Smith, Cftmn Monty
REME
-.4.44
Died in North Africa

Smith, Cpl R.A.
2nd/12th Field Regt AIF
10.6.41
Mentioned in Despatches
Killed at Tobruk. Buried in Tobruk
War Cem

Smith, Sydney
Norwood Memorial

Smollan, Pte Harold
West Yorks Regt
-.4.45
Killed in action in Western Europe

Snowzell, Pte George Charles
1 Btn KOYLI
Age 36   30.7.44
Buried Bayeux War Cem

Sokol, Pte Alois
PC
9.6.44
Cassino Memorial

Solanskey, Fus Maurice
6th Btn, Roy Scots Fus
16.7.44

Soll, Sgmn Isidore
RCOS
22.3.42
Buried at Edmonton Cem

Solomon, Albert Victor
OBLI
Age 29   16.7.44
Brouay War Cem

Solomon, Maj David
RE
9.6.46

Solomon, Cpl Emanuel
'Q' Services Attached
5th Inf Bde
17.8.41
Buried in Hodra Mil Cem

Solomon, Pte Myer
PC
3.8.45
Buried Failsworth Jewish Cem

Solomon, Gnr Ralph
2nd Regt RHA
Age 23   8.5.43
Buried Massicault War Cem

Solomon, Lt Richard Samuel Vic
8th Btn, The King's Regt
(Liverpool)
13.6.41
Killed accidentally
Buried in Aldershot

Solomon, Pte Ronald
2 Btn Beds & Herts Regt
Age 20   23.7.44
Buried Arezzo War Cem Italy

Solomon, Lt Ronald
2nd Btn, The Royal Norfolk Regt
-.5.44
Killed in action in Burma
Buried in Kohima Mil Cem

Solomons, Benjamin
RA
Age 21   19.1.42
Brookwood Mem

Solomons, Pte Henry
Dorset Regt
-.2.45
Killed in action

Solomons, Fus Samuel, MM
Roy Fus (City of London Regt)
-.12.43
Killed in action in Italy
Buried at Capua

Solosky, Pte Louis
2 Btn KOSB
Age 24   20.1.44
Rangoon Memorial

Somberg, Sgt Instructor David
The Queen's Westminster Rifles
-.1.42
Buried at Enfield

Figure 201. Gnr Alfred Sorsky,
97th Anti-Tank Regt, RA.

Sorsky, Gnr Alfred
97th AT Regt, RA
Age 29   7.7.44
Killed in action

**Sosskind, S/Sgt Alexander J.
(Bobby)**
RE
Age 26   -.-.45

Spagowitz, Pte Ray (Rachel)
ATS
Age 21   -.-.43
Killed by enemy action
Buried Glasgow Jewish Cem

Spark, Gnr Arthur
110 HAA Regt RA
Age 36   8.5.45
Buried East Ham

Spiegel, Pte Michael
The E Yorks Regt
                                -.8.42

Spieler, Pte Franz
PC
                                1.10.41
Buried at East Ham

Spielglass, Pte Mane, DCM
(aka Spiegelglass)
Killed in action Arnhem

Spivak, L/Cpl Nathan
The Black Watch (Roy Highland Regt)
                                -.2.43
Died of wounds
Buried in Tripoli Mil Cem

Sporover, Gnr Alec
498 Battery HAA Regt RA
Age 28   31.10.44
Buried Rainham Jewish Cem

Stane, Pte S.
1st Cape Town Highldrs, UDF, MEF
                                11.2.42
Buried in Tobruk Mil Cem

Stanley, Charles A.
RASC
                                1.1.45

Stanley, Pte H.
The Worcs Regt
                                27.10.44

Stark, L/Cpl Frank
RE
                                9.6.45
Buried Hamburg Cem, Ohlsdorf

Stark, Fritz
PC

Starmont (Stormont)
(Steinberg) S.
PC
                                23.4.43

Steel, Sgt Kenneth Joseph
(Rosenstiel) (Kurt)
PC
                                13.9.45
Killed in an accident
Buried in the Jewish Cem, Lingen

Stein, Derek
RAPC
DOAS
                                -.10.57

Stein, Tpr Albert
50th RTR
Age 31   19.7.43
Cassino Memorial

Stein, Pte Theo
KOSB
                                11.6.44
Rangoon Memorial

Stein, Pte Sidney
Manchester Regt
Age 31   17.5.45
Buried Soltau War Cem,
Becklingen

Stein, Pte W.
RAOC
Died as a POW

Steinberg, Pte Bernard
1/5 Btn West Surrey Regt
Age 26   30.9.42
Buried El Alamein War Cem

Steinberg, Pte Harry
The West Yorks Regt (Prince of Wales's Own)
                                21.1.41

Steinberg, Hugo
PC
DOAS

Steinberg, Pte L.
The Cape Town Highldrs, UDF, MEF
                                11.2.42
Buried in Tobruk

Steinberg, Fus Stephan
Manfred

Steiner, Pte R.
(aka Jevons)
Intel Corps
                                7.8.44

Steingart, Sydney
78th LAA RA

Stengelhofen, Jacob
RA
                                1.6.43
b. Iver, Bucks

Stern, Pte Abraham/Aaron
4th Btn, Roy Berks Regt (Princess Charlotte of Wales's)
                                31.5.40
Killed on active service

Stern, L/Bdr Jack
RA
Age 29   -.8.43
Killed in India on active service

Stern, Fus Monty
1st Btn, Roy Fus
Age 20   12.4.45
Killed in action in Italy
Buried in Ravenna War Cem

Stern, Lt Reginald H.
RA
                                21.2.41
(Son of Maj H.J. Stern)

Sternheim, Pte Chaim
9th Btn, The Roy Sussex Regt
                                16.2.45
Killed in action, Burma

Sternshine, Pte Aubrey
1st Btn, The Tyneside Scottish
                                26.6.44
Buried in the Brit War Cem
Tilly-sur-Seulles, Normandy

Stillman, Pte Wolf
The Middx Regt (Duke of Cambridge's Own)

21.7.43

Died of wounds in the Middle East
Buried near Catania, Sicily

Stock, Tpr Edward
1st RTR, RAC

6.11.44

Died of wounds
Buried in Glenduffhill Cem, Glasgow

Stoederum, Lt Henri
RTR

7.1.42

Willesden Jewish Cem

Stoldaum, Lt Henry Judah
RAC

7.1.42

Died in an accident
Buried at Willesden

Stolerman, Dvr Jack D. (aka Stanton)

RASC

9.12.40

Stone, Gnr Louis
RA

8.4.42

Died POW Camp, Kuala Lumpur

Stone, Sgt L.A.

20.11.42

Buried Kranji War Cem

Stopler, Cpl Leonard

11.1.42

Storch, Pte Adolph G.
1st FMSVF

22.1.45

Strauss, Capt Cyril Anthony
KRRC

-.12.44

Polish Cross of Valour
Killed on active service

Figure 202. The Grave of Gnr L. Stone, RA, in Kuala Lumpur.

Strauss, L/Cpl Gordon H.
1st Btn, KRRC

-.8.44

Killed in action in Normandy

Strauss, Col Joel Nathan
RAMC
Age 34   - .-.43

Killed in action in Crete

Strauss, Pte Montague
1st Btn, Buffs
Age 26   -.10.42

Died of wounds at El Alamein

Stuppel, Maj R. FRCS
RAMC (SOE)

-.6.44

Taken POW in Tobruk, he escaped
and joined Marshal Tito's forces in
Yugoslavia
Mentioned in Despatches
Killed in Occupied Europe

Sultman, Pte M.
The Durham L/I

Sumray, Sgt Malcolm Hyman
The Para Regt, Army Air Corps
Age 25   -.-.44

Figure 203. Maj R. Stuppel FRCS, RAMC.

Sunderland, Pte Paul Hirsch
The York & Lancaster Regt
Age 26   -.-.43

Sunshine, Edward
RA

5.3.43

Suschny, Dvr J.
RASC

10.12.41

Buried in Ramleh Mil Cem

Susskind, S/Sgt Alexander J.
RE

-.5.45

Killed on active service

Swarts, Pte Samuel
Cape Corps SA

28.8.42

Alexandria

Swift, Pte Joseph
Buried in Singapore

Swirsky, Rfmn Max
2nd Btn, The Queen Victoria's Rifles

10.5.41

Died of wounds

Sykes, Lt Peter Sassoon
RA

20.1.43

Died of wounds
Buried in Medjez-El-Bab War Cem

Figure 204. Tpr Cyril Symons, 13/18th Royal Hussars, RAC.

Symons, Tpr Cyril
13/18th Roy Hussars, RAC
Age 21   28.3.45
Killed in action in Western Europe
Buried at Nijmegen

Taft, Tpr Harry
RTR, RAC
Age 31   1.12.43
Killed in action in the Middle East

Tager, L/Cpl S.
2nd Botha Regt, UDF
                      23.11.41
Buried in Knightsbridge War Cem, Acroma

Tagger, Pte Joe
PC
                      25.6.43
Buried in Manchester

Tankel, Pte S.
UDF, MEF
                      23.11.41
Buried in Knightsbridge War Cem, Acroma

Tapper, Pte Myer
4th Btn, The Roy Berks Regt, (Princess Charlotte of Wales's)
                      -.2.42
Died of wounds in France

Tash, Pte Emanuel
The Welch Regt
Age 21   -.4.45
Killed in action

Taussig, Pte I.
226 (Czech) Company, RASC
                      -.-.41

Taylor, Pte A.L.
The Dorsetshire Regt
Buried in Arnhem Mil Cem

Taylor, Pte B. (aka Tuchmann, Ben)
3 Commando
                      11.6.44
Killed in France
Buried in Ranville Mil Cem

Taylor, Pte H.
The Para Regt, AAC
                      4.1.45
Killed in action
Buried in the Ardennes

Taylor, John (Johann Schneider) DCM
Leicester Regt

Taylor, Maurice
Middx Regt
Killed in action Dunkirk

Teicher (Teichert), Pte Solomon
74 Coy, PC
                      18.3.44
Buried in Brookwood Mil Cem

Teichman, Maj Philip Raymond
2 Btn Para Regt
Age 30   1/5.12.42
Buried Massicault War Cem

Teiman, Pte Adolph
40th RTR, RAC
                      2.11.42
Buried in El Alamein War Cem

Teller, Pte Abraham
5th Btn, Buffs
                      -.12.42
Killed in Tunisia

Thal, L/Cpl Basil J.
2nd Btn, The Black Watch (Roy Highland Regt)
Killed in action and buried in Somaliland

Thomas, L/Cpl Dennis Russell
RASC

Tibber, Pte Jack
230 Coy PC
                      -.2.45
Died on active service
Buried in Antwerp Mil Cem

Tillum, Bdr M.L.
1st Anti-Aircraft Regt, S African Arty
                      2.9.42
Buried in Kantara Mil Cem

Tobias, Pte Alfred
PC
Age 23   16.10.40
Buried Edmonton

Tobias, Fus Leslie P.
11th Btn, The Roy Fus (City of London Regt)
                      2.9.44
Died of wounds at Cassino

Tondofsky, Pte Samuel Jacob
The Roy Scots (The Roy Regt)
                      23.2.45
Killed in action in North-West Europe

Touche, Sgt Sam
RAOC
Killed on active service in India

Toumayian, Dvr H.G.
RASC
                      15.12.42
Buried Ramleh War Cem

Toyk, Rfmn H.
Kaffranian Rifles
                      8.4.42
Buried in Tel-El-Kebir Mil Cem

Figure 205. Whitehall 1983. General Sir John Stanier takes the salute.

Trisker, Nurse Lea
Age 23   16.2.43
Died on duty
Buried in Willesden Cem

Tucker, Capt H.B.
RASC
                          16.7.41
Buried in Ismailia Mil Cem, Egypt

Tucker (Tuckman), Tpr Henry
46th Recce Regt, RAC
                          28.9.44
Killed in Italy
Buried in Coriano Ridge War Cem

Turkl, Pte Siegfried
137 Coy PC
Age 22   12.1.45
Buried in Schoonselhof Cem,
Antwerp

Tutasz, Samuel
PC

Unterman, Gnr Francis Réné
                          1.3.42

Vangrosky, Gnr Sydney
140 Fld Regt RA
Age 25   30.5.40
Buried Hotton War Cem

Vender, Rfmn Israel
7 Btn Rifle Brigade
Age 24   31.3.43
Buried Medjez-el-Bab War Cem

Verhoeff, Pte Anthony William
10th Btn Para Regt
Age 19   18.9.44
Killed in action Arnhem
Buried Arnhem

Victor, Pte John B. George
2/4th Btn The Hants Regt
                          14.5.44
Died of wounds
Buried in Cassino War Cem

**Villiers, Sgt Egon Ernest Robert
(aka Vogel)**
10 Commando
                          24.3.45
Buried in Reichswald Forest

Vine, Pte Norman Alexander
*The Para Regt, Army Air Corps,
6th Airborne Division*
Age 20   6.6.44
Shot down over Normandy during
the D-Day landings
Buried in Ranville War Cem

Viner, Gnr Bernard
RA
                          -.11.41
Killed in action at Sidi Rezegh

Viner, Pte Leonard Louis
*5th Btn, The Wilts Regt (Duke of
Edinburgh's Own)*
                          8.3.45
Killed in action
Buried in Germany

Vysove, Cpl Cyril
RCOS
                          18.6.45
Buried in Bruges Civil Cem

Wadel, Pte M.
*3rd Btn, The Palestine
Regt*
                          6.4.45
Buried at Ravenna

Figure 206. Pte Norman Alexander Vine, Para Regt, AAC, 6th Airborne Division.

Figure 207. Pte Harold Wald, KOSB.

Figure 208. Pte Sidney Wald, The South Wales Borderers.

Wald, Pte Harold
KOSB
Age 19   16.2.45
Died at Nijmegen

Wald, L/Cpl Leo Simon
Intel Corps
                           24.5.43
Buried at Willesden

Wald, Pte Sidney
The S Wales Borderers
Age 24   16.6.40
Buried in Swansea Jewish Cem

Waldenburg, Spr Hyman
RE
                           1.1.41
Killed on active service
Buried in Leeds Jewish Cem

Waldman, Tpr Tobias
The Roy Glos Hussars
                           -.6.44
Killed in action

Wall (Velgansky), Pte Leon
*6th Field Ambulance, 2nd NZ
Expeditionary Force*
                           20.4.41
Killed in action in Crete

Wallace (Wapnitski), Dvr Charles
RASC
                           18.11.44
Died in an accident
Buried at East Ham

Wallach, Gnr Norman N.
RA
                           28.2.45
Killed in action

Walters, L/Bdr Norman Henry
*226 Bty I/5 Btn E Surrey Regt
RA, Dunkirk*
Age 20   29.5.40
No Known Grave

Walters, Gnr Samuel
9th Field Regt, RA
Age 22   -.5.41
Died in an accident

Wank, Robert (Ward)
PC

Warburton, Pte Ostend M.
Wilts Regt
                           18.1.44
Buried in Minturno War Cem

Warndorfer, Auguste Jacques
SOE

Warschawski, Pte Alice A.
ATS
Age 41   4.9.45
Birmingham Lodge Hill Cem

Wasserman, Pte J.
1st Btn, Rhodesian LI
                           29.10.42
Buried in Tripoli

Wasserman, Pte Naphtali Simon
(Palestine)
Age 22   -.-.44

Waterman, Gnr David
RA
                           7.1.42

Watts, Lt M.
2nd Btn, The Hants Regt
Killed in an accident in Austria
Buried at Klagenfurt

**Wegener, Sgt Norbert
(served as Norman Willert)**
13805634 SOE
                           12.9.44

**Weil, Tpr Donald Meinhard
(aka Winster, aka Hamilton, S.)**
C Squadron 23rd Hussars RAC
Age 26   4.11.45
Buried Nederweert War Cem

Weill, Gnr Leon
Hong Kong VDF
                        27.4.45

Weinberger, E.G. (aka Webster)
10 Commando
KIA, Normandy

Weinblatt, Pte Raphael Leslie
4th Btn Suffolk Regt
                        14.9.43
Died in Burma

Weiner, Pte Ernst
137 Coy PC
                        7.8.40
Buried in Ridgeway Jewish Cem,
Bristol

Weiner, Gnr Hyman Bernard
240 Battery 39 LAA Regt, RA
                        27.8.44
Killed in action
Buried in the Brit War Cem,
Florence

Weiner, Pte Leonard Louis
Queen's Own Roy West Kent Regt
Age 49   30.9.47
Buried Edmonton

Weiner, Pte Max
Killed in Normandy

Weiner, Phillip
Believed to have died fighting with
the French Resistance

Weinman, J.H.A.
Capetown Highldrs
                        22.7.44

Weinman, William
RA
                        13.2.42

Figure 209. Gnr Mark Weinstock, 99th LAA Regt, RA.

Weinreich, Rfmn Vitalis
Roy Berks
Age 29   20.7.44
Banneville-La-Campagne War
Cem

Weinstein, WO Alexander
*2nd/2nd Australian Machine Gun
Btn*
                        24.10.42
Buried at El Alamein

Weinstein, Gdsmn Meyer
2721961
3rd Btn, Irish Guards
Age 31   11.8.44
Killed in France
Buried in St Charles De Percy
Cem, Calvados

Figure 210. The Grave of Gnr
Mark Weinstock, in the Sangro
River Cemetery, Italy.

Weinstock, Gnr Mark
99th LAA Regt, RA
Age 31   12.1.44
Killed in action
Buried in the Sangro River Cem

Weiss (West), Pte R. Harry/Fred
KOYLI
                        -.10.44

Weiss, Spr Fredrick
RE
                        12.5.44
Buried in Prague

Weiss, Tpr A.
*3rd South African Armoured Car
Regt, UDF*
                        6.11.42
Buried in El Alamein Mil Cem

Weiss, Capt Oliver S.
RE
                        24.9.44

Weiss (Weisz), Peter
SOE
Executed at Dachau

**Wells, Pte Peter Vernon Allen
(aka Auerhahn, W.)**
Hants Regt/10 Commando
Age 26   19.1.44
Buried Minturno War Cem

Wenzerul, Gnr Edward
RA
Killed as a POW of Japanese

Wernick, L/Cpl Cyril
The Roy Norfolk Regt
Age 28   21.9.45
Captured in Singapore. Japanese
POW. Died as a result of illness
after being liberated
Buried in Madras War Cem,
Chennai

Wertheim, Pte Gerhard
337 Coy Alien PC/SAS
Age 30   2.12.44
Buried Medjez-El-Bab, Tunisia

Wieshbinski, Pte M.
1st Btn, The Pal Regt
                          29.3.45
Buried at Ravenna

Wiseberg, Pte Mark
RAOC
                          26.11.43
Buried Medjez-El-Bab War Cem

White, Ikey
London, Glider Regt
Killed in action, Sicily
                          -.-.43

Wigram, Maj Lionel
*11th Btn, Roy Fus (City of London
Regt)*
                          -.2.44
1927/1944, Pioneer of new battle
drill. Killed in action in Italy

Wilby (Wisebad) (Wiseberg), S.
3459187
Para Regt
Buried in Tunisia

Wilchick, Pte Solomon
11th Field Ambulance, RAMC
                          31.7.43
Buried in Syracuse Mil Cem

Will, Pte H.H.
RAOC
                          20.4.42
Buried in Leeds Hilltop Jewish
Cem

Winer, Tpr Cyril
RAC
KOAS
                          -.8.51

Winer, L/Cpl Jack George
RAPC
Age 37   -.6.40
Lost in Dunkirk evacuation

Wingate, Lt John S., MC
RAC
                          25.1.44
KIA
Buried in Willesden Cem

Wingrad, L/Cpl Keva
RASC
                          2.4.45
Killed by a V2
Buried at East Ham

Winter, Dvr I.
RASC
                          26.7.45
Killed by an accidental gun shot
Buried in Kiel Mil Cem

Winter, M.
PC

Wise, Pte Asher
302 Company, PC
Age 41   -.8.44
Killed in France
Buried in La Delivrande War Cem,
Douvres

Wisebad, Sgt J.
Airborne
Killed in action at Arnhem

Wiseman, Neville S.
Intel Corps
                          11.6.44

Wittenburg, Tpr C.H.
4th S African Armoured Car Regt
                          12.2.42
Buried near Rotonda Signali, Libya

Wolfe, Lt Phil
RCOS (Times)
                          17.11.41

Wolfe, Gnr Samuel
157 Field Regt RA
Age 29   5/6.6.42

Wolff, Victor
PC

Wolpert, Lt Max Mendel, GM
The Cheshire Regt
                          14.4.45
Killed crossing the Rhine
Buried in Hamburg Mil Cem

Figure 211. Lt Max Mendel
Wolpert, GM, The Cheshire Regt.

Wolsey, Pte Sidney
6 Btn,Buffs
Age 45   6.9.40
Buried Edmonton

Wood, Rfmn Ansell L.
RB
25.10.42

Woodrow, Sgmn Samuel
RCOS
19.2.41
Buried in the Jewish Cem,
Farnley, Leeds

Woolf, Pte Alfred
1 Btn Norfolk Regt
Age 30   6.6.44
Buried Ranville War Cem

Woolf, Gnr Daniel (Don)
RA
Age 23
Wounded at Tobruk. Died on
board HMS *Chakdina* when the
ship was torpedoed en route to
Alexandria. One of 95 who
perished in this attack

Woolf, F.
RASC
14127620
Age 18   12.7.46
Suez War Mem

Figure 212. Gnr Daniel (Don)
Woolf, RA.

Woolf, Capt Frances Patrick
RA
-.9.44
MID
Killed in air operations in Italy
while attached to the RAF

Woolf, Cpl Harry Louis
617 Assault Squadron RE
Age 29   16.10.44
Buried Venray War Cem

Woolf, L/Cpl John
RASC
26.4.41
Athens

Woolfe, Fus Bernard
10th Btn, The Lancs Fus
12.12.42
Died in India
Buried in Kohima Cem

Woolffe, J.
East Af. Lab. Corps
Age 70
Nairobi Jewish Cem

Woolfson, Dvr Joel
RASC
21.3.44

Wordman, Tpr John Abraham
2nd Derbys Yeomanry, RAC
3.12.44
Killed in action
Buried in Holland

Worritzky, Pte David
130th Field Ambulance, RAMC
15.3.45
Killed in action
Buried in Holland

Wroblewski, Pte Louis
PC
24.11.45
Buried Caserta War Cem

**Wyss, Capt Edward Mariel
(Weiss)**
Killed in action, Arnhem

Figure 213. Cpl D. Wynne, 8th
Btn, Roy Fus (City of London
Regt).

Wynne (Wanofsky), Cpl D.
*8th Btn, Roy Fus (City of London
Regt)*
Age 22   9.5.43
Killed in action on Razor Back
Ridge, Enfidaville, Tunisia
Buried at Enfidaville Mil Cem

Yagernose, Pte David
The Glasgow Highlndrs
22.9.44
Killed in action in North-West
Europe

Yankelson, Cpl Benjamin
S African Tank Corps
-.1.41

Yankovsky, Pte Moss
6 Btn Roy West Kent Regt
Age 26   16.4.43
Buried Hedjez-El-Bab War Cem

Yapp, Frances 'Buster'
Paras
Killed in action, Arnhem

Yarrow, Pte Abraham
The Devonshire Regt
23.4.42
Buried at East Ham

Yasofsky, Pte Hyman
38 Company, PC
26.5.45
Buried at Brookwood Mil Cem

Yentis, Harry
Killed at Arnhem

Yospur, Pte Simon
RASC
15.8.43
Buried in Sheffield Synagogue Cem

Yudin, Sgt Albert
10th Roy Hussars
Age 30   21.4.45
Killed in action in the Argenta Gap, Northern Italy
Buried at Argenta Gap War Cem

Figure 214. Sgt Albert Yudin, 10th Royal Hussars.

Yudkin, Gnr Abraham
48 Battery LAA Regt RA
Age 29   29.11.43
Norwood Boy. Died as Japanese POW

Zack, L/Cpl M.B.
6th Btn, The Gordon Highlndrs
Age 28   4.2.44
Killed at Anzio
Buried in Anzio Mil Cem

Zackheim, Lt David Alfred
The Roy Sussex Regt
4.2.43
Killed in an accident
Buried at Willesden

Zaharoff, Pte Victor I.
Hong Kong VDF
22.12.41
Sai Wan Mem

Zaher, Dvr Shafir
RASC
17.11.44
Fayid War Cem

Zamanski, Pte J.
Queen's Own Cameron Highlndrs
-.6.43
Killed on active service
Buried Enfidaville British Mil Cem

Zapp, Sgt Victor Irving
RASC
17.6.40
SS *Lancastria*
Buried Pornic War Cem

Zatzenstein, Pte K.M.
UDF
7.6.42
Buried at Ain El Gazala, Libya

Zeidler, Pte William John
9.1.43
b. Gaza

Zemmill, Gnr A.
RA
Age 32   19.2.44

Zenftman, Pte Nathan
5 Btn Wilts Regt
Age 23   26.8.44
Buried St Desir War Cem

Figure 215. Gnr A. Zemmill, RA.

Figure 216. L/Cpl Harry Zimmerman, The Somerset L/I.

Zietman, Pte Isaac Joseph
2nd Btn, The Dorset Regt
22.4.44
Buried Kohima Mil Cem

Ziman, Sgt Arthur Myer
NZF
-.11.41
Killed in action

Zimmer, Gnr Morris
AT Regt, RA
-.9.44
Drowned in transit as a Japanese POW

Zimmerman, L/Cpl Harry
Roy Fus (City of London Regt)
1.10.44
Killed in action
Buried at Arnhem Mil Cem

Zimmerman, Sgt Wolfe
79th Assault Company, RE
9.6.44
Killed in Normandy
Buried at La Delivrande War Cem

Zimmern, Bdr A.
HKVDC
18.12.41
Of Jewish origin

Zimmern, Sgt E.
HKVDC
19.12.41
Of Jewish origin

Zissy, Lt Theodore A.L.
RAC
-.11.42
Died of wounds in the Middle East

Zlutohcavek, Pte Emile
Czech Training Depot
6.11.41
Buried in Hodra Mil Cem

Zoller, Pte Cecil
1 Btn Kings Own Roy Regt
Age 26 4.11.42
Buried Nicosia War Cem

Zorfatt, Shlomo
RE
1.10.41

The Royal Air Force

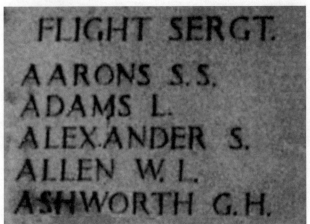

Figure 217. Flt/Sgt S.S. Aarons (RAF Memorial Runnymede).

Figure 218. Flt/Sgt Lionel David Anderson.

Aaron, Flt/Sgt Arthur Louis VC, DFM
Pilot
14.8.43
Buried Bone Mil Cem

Aaron, WO Dennis
RAFVR
Age 23   30.4.46
Rawalpindi War Cem

Aarons, Flt/Sgt S. Solomon
18.8.45
No known grave
Killed in air operation Far East

Aarons (Jackson), Sgt (Pilot) Bert
220 Squadron
19.7.41
Shot down after a raid on Norway, flying a Hudson aircraft

Abrahams, Sgt Alexander
22.1.44
Reported missing
His body was later recovered and buried in the Texel (Den Burg) War Cem

Addess, Sgt M.
22.4.43
Reported missing

Albert, Edward J.M.
RAF
7.12.42
KIA at sea
Buried in Willesden Cem

Alexander, Sgt (Pilot) Harold
15.11.41
Killed in action
Buried at Cherbourg Cem

Allman, AC2 V.E.
-.-.41

Alter, P/O L.I.
3.9.42

Altman, Sgt Leslie
Age 39   29.11.44

Amstell, Sgt R.H.
7.8.43
Missing presumed dead

Amzalak, AC2 E. Avner
Pal.
20.2.45
Killed in action

Anderson, Flt/Sgt Lionel David
Age 22   27.4.44
Buried in Moskowa Cem

Figure 219. Sgt WO Mark Azouz.

Figure 220. The Grave of LAC Michael Barry in Calcutta.

Anekstein, Sqdn/Ldr Cyril, DFC & Bar
31.8.43
Killed in action

Appleson, AC Michael Isaac
1.6.45

Arnholtz, Sqdn/Ldr H.E.
MID

Assata, AC2 S.
11.10.41
Buried in the Jewish Cem, Alexandria

Axler, Sgt David R.
RCAF
21.3.41

Azouz, Sgt (WO) Mark, DFM
06.12.44
Killed in action at Arnhem
Buried in Nijmegen Blite Cem

Baerhein, Anthony
51 Squadron
22.10.41

Baker, F/O David
24.9.44
Missing presumed killed on air ops

Baldachin, Sgt (Pilot) S.D.
16.8.41
Rhodesian. Killed in a flying accident

Balkin, Cpl Morris Ernest
Age 20   14.6.40
Killed in a flying accident
Buried in the Jewish Cem, Glasgow

Baltinester, ACW1 Golda
WAAF
20.11.43
Buried Moascar War Cem

Banikhan, Flt/Sgt L.
16.10.42

Banin, AC1 Marcus
-.9.45

Banker, ACW Leah (Lily)
WAAF
Age 21   -.-.45
Killed in an air crash in Palestine

Baras, Sgt Mark Sydney
1621592
23.8.43
Missing, presumed killed on air ops

Bardega, Sqdn/Ldr B. DFM
27.5.58

Barnard, Flt/Sgt Michael C.
14.1.44

Barnett, Sgt (Nav) Conrad A.S.
15.6.43
Buried at Oosterbeek, Arnhem, Holland

Barnett, LAC L.S.
21.4.44

Barnett, Sgt Laurence P.
14.5.43

Barnett, P/O Sydney S.
115 Squadron
4.4.41
Buried in Marham Churchyard, Norfolk

Baron, Sgt Ernest Emmanuel
101 Squadron
27.1.44

Barry, LAC Michael (aka Cohen)
12.1.45
Killed in Calcutta

Barsky, Sgt (Pilot) Gideon Gilbert
Pal
23.8.43
Killed on ops
Buried in Bristol Jewish Cem

Barss, Sgt Monty
101 Squadron
13.8.44
Missing on air ops, presumed dead
Later buried in the Russian Cem, Hann-Stohen Dispenau, Germany

Figure 221. Sgt (Flt/Eng) Leon Bassman.

Figure 222. Flt/Lt Dennis J. Baum, Bomber Command.

Figure 223. Flt/Sgt (Nav) Edward Bashi, Bomber Command.

Bartholomew, P/O Basil (aka Bloom)
17.9.41
Killed in action

Bashi, Flt/Sgt Edward
27.4.44
Born in Iraq
Presumed killed

Bassman, Sgt (Flt/Eng) Leon
Age 22   3.11.44
Killed in action on return from a bombing raid over Norway

Batzofin, P/O Hyman
24.10.41
Killed in action

Baum, Sgt Alfred J.
11.8.40

Baum, Flt/Lt Dennis J.
Bomber Command
Age 26   -.-.41
Served with the Roy Scots Regt in 1939. Transferred to the RAF
Killed in action

Baxter, ACW Patricia
WAAF
Age 19   22.2.43
Killed in an air raid
Buried at East Ham

Beagle, Sgt Charles
38 Squadron
14.5.44

Beardshaw, Flt/Sgt John George
RAFVR
Age 24   17.12.44
Runnymede Memorial

Beck, Sgt Herbert
Czech 311 Squadron
13.3.44

Becker, P/O Herman Hersh, DFC
Norwegian Squadron RAF/ 464 Squadron
-.3.45
KIA on famous raid on Gestapo HQ in Copenhagen
Buried Samso Island, Denmark

Befeler, AC V.
971 Squadron
10.5.42
Killed by a bomb
Buried in Hodra Mil Cem

Belkin, P/O (AG) P.
RCAF
Age 22   9.10.43
Buried in Rangoon War Cem

Bender, P/O Milton Harold DFC
10.4.44
Buried in Fourfelt Cem, Esbjerg

Bender, Flt/Eng Joseph
17.6.44

Benjamin, AC2 Israel P.
23.4.42
Buried in Norwich City Cem

Benjamin, Sgt Louis Lionel
31.8.40
Buried in Crooswijk General Cem

Benjamin, Sgt Morris

Benjamin, Flt/Sgt Sydney Hyman
2.8.43
Killed in action over Sicily

Bennett, Sgt Geoffrey Harcourt
6.9.42
Killed in an aircraft accident
Buried in Wallasey Cem

Bentley, Calman
10.12.42

Berg, F/O Joseph DFC
17.6.44
Missing presumed killed in action

Berger, Sgt Cyril Seymour
-.2.43
Missing presumed killed in action

Berger, Sgt/Nav David
22.7.42
No Known Grave

Berger, Flt/Sgt Herbert Otto, DFM
RAFVR
16.1.45
Berlin War Cem

Bergman, LAC M.
-.11.41
Buried in Heliopolis Mil Cem

Bergson, P/O Julius
19.1.42
Missing presumed killed in action over Algiers

Berliner, LAC Jack Joseph
Age 23   17.11.44
Died at sea on active service
Buried in Ostend Cem

Bernstein, F/O David Elias
4.11.42
Killed in action

Bernstein, AC2 Maurice
Age 20   12.11.40
Killed on active service
Buried in Blackley Jewish Cem

Bernstein, P/O Ralph Isaac
5.1.43
Killed in a crash
Buried in Manchester

Bernthal, Flt/Sgt Leslie Lawton
70 Squadron Bomber Command
Age 22   8.7.43

Besso, F/O Walter E.
25.6.45
From Newfoundland
KIA

Binderman, AC2 Sydney
16.1.42

Birley, P/O Alan F.
28.8.42
Missing believed killed in action

Bittiner, Flt/Sgt Henry Mark
5/6.6.44
Missing presumed killed in action

Black, WO/AG David
1000 bomber raid and Civil War Spain
Killed in action Cologne

Black, Sgt Harry

Black, Sgt Lionel
Age 21   3.9.41
Died in air ops over enemy territory
Buried in Dunkirk

Black, Capt Robin Alan
KOAS
-.-.53

Blake (Schwartz), Sgt Hans Heinz
101 Squadron
15.8.44
Missing presumed killed in air ops

Blitz, AC Morris
41 Squadron
13.1.40
Killed by enemy action whilst on leave with his wife

Block, Flt/Sgt David
49 Squadron
Age 30   31.5.42

Block, Sgt Samuel
83 Squadron
26.3.42
Missing believed killed during Air ops. Body found and buried at East Ham

Bloom, Sgt Benjamin
1414792, RAFVR
Lost June 16, 1944, France. Son of the late 'Kivey' and Celia Bloom, shoe manufacturers, Hackney Marshes, E5. Final resting place found. Stone setting 1998 but recognized at Runnymede only by CWGC.

Bloom, Flt/Lt M.
Hampstead memorial

Bloomfield, Sgt Mendel
Age 21   7.11.41
Missing over Norway.
Buried Oslo.

Bloomfield, Sgt/Nav Michael
Age 30   2.7.43
Buried Leeds Hebrew Cem

Blum, LAC Joseph Maurice
9.6.42
Killed in a collision whilst landing
Buried in Jewish Cem, Leeds

Blumberg, Sgt (Nav) Asrielis (aka Blumbergas)
Pal
16.3.45
Killed in an aircraft accident
Buried Suez War Memorial Cem

Blumenkanz, LAC C.
202 Group
26.3.42
Buried Suez War Memorial Cem

Bluston, Flt/Sgt H.M. (Mick)
18 Squadron, Central Med Force
28.12.44
Shot down over Italy

Boam, Sgt A.M.
17.3.43
Missing presumed dead

Figure 224. Flt/Sgt H.M. (Mick) Bluston, 18 Squadron, Central Mediterranean Force.

Bogard, Sgt Joel
50 Squadron
12.8.42

Boggatt, A/C Hugh
KOAS
-.-.54

Bolton, Sgt Sydney
21.11.44
Killed in action
Buried in the Reichswald Mil Cem

Bome, Colin Russell
KOAS
-.-.55

Boroski, Sgt F.
RCAF
2.6.41
Runnymede Memorial

Boyd, LAC Philip (aka Kupinsky)
RAFVR
21.12.45
Killed by a grenade in an Indonesian ambush, Batavia
Buried Jakarta War Cem

Braham, Cpl Michael
Age 23
31.1.44
Buried Edmonton Fed Jewish Cem

Brener, P/O Henry
22.2.42
Missing over Germany. Died of wounds in a Dutch hospital

Brenner, Sgt Sidney
2.4.43

Bressloff, LAC Sidney
13.12.42
Killed in a crash during nav training in Canada

Brodie, Flt/Lt Aubrey Norman
Killed in an aircraft accident at sea whilst travelling to Canada

Brodie, Flt/Sgt Basil
RAFVR
6.9.44
Missing over Germany

Bronsky, Sgt (Pilot) Harold
49 Squadron
26.11.43
Killed on ops, flying a Lancaster
Buried at Gransee, near Berlin

Bronstein, AC2 A.
3.7.41

Bronstein, LAC R.
SAAF
10.8.41
Buried in Ismailia War Memorial Cem

Brown, Sgt David
29.6.43
Buried in Venlo Mil Cem

Brown, Sgt Jack
9 Squadron
21.6.42

Brown, Sgt (Obs) Sydney
1322948
14.5.43
Missing presumed killed

Brown, Sgt Sydney
21.11.44
Killed in action
Buried in the Reichswald Mil Cem

Bruck, Radar Obs Edward William
Shot down over Med.
Buried in N. Africa

Bruck, WO Raymond A.
46 Squadron

Burson, Sgt Aaron
106 Squadron
3.4.43

Byck, Section Officer Muriel Tamara
SOE, WAAF
Age 26
23.5.44
Mentioned in Despatches

Camberg, AC2 David
RAFVR
Age 25
28.4.45
Buried Labuan War Cem

Cantor, Sgt Jack Marshall
30.1.44
Killed in action over Germany
Buried in Willesden

Cantor, William M.
RAF
-.-.48
Killed in action Israel War of Indep

Caplan, F/O Meyer DFM
Age 27
-.9.43
Mentioned in Despatches
Killed when his Lancaster crashed over Yorkshire

Cashman, Sgt (Obs) Simon Michael (Mick)
13.7.41
Missing presumed killed on ops

Casparius, LAC Heinz Max
Age 36
21.1.43
Buried Heliopolis War Cem

Castle, LAC Barry
-.-.41
Killed in a flying accident whilst training in Canada

This scroll commemorates Sergeant H. Bronsky Royal Air Force held in honour as one who served King and Country in the world war of 1939–1945 and gave his life to save mankind from tyranny. May his sacrifice help to bring the peace and freedom for which he died.

The Queen and I offer you our heartfelt sympathy in your great sorrow. We pray that your country's gratitude for a life so nobly given in its service may bring you some measure of consolation.

Mrs. H. Bronsky.

Figure 225. 'This scroll commemorates Sergeant H. Bronsky Royal Air Force held in honour as one who served King and Country in the world war of 1939–1945 and gave his life to save mankind from tyranny. May his sacrifice help to bring the peace and freedom for which he died. The Queen and I offer you our heartfelt sympathy in your great sorrow. We pray that your country's gratitude for a life so nobly given in its service may bring you some measure of consolation. Mrs H. Bronsky.'

Figure 226. Sgt (Pilot) Harold Bronsky, 49 Squadron.

Cherns, Sgt/Nav Harold
Missing presumed dead
-.-.43
Crew of Catalina Flying Boat. Disappeared over E Mediterranean

Clark, F/O Peter
RAF
-.7.44
KOAS
Buried in Willesden Cem

Clayden, Gerald
29/30.8.41
KIA
Memorial at Willesden Cem

Clayman, Trevor N.
DOAS
-.-.56

Cobden, Flt/Sgt Gerald
RAFVR
27.6.42
Runnymede Memorial

Cohen, Sgt Abraham
3.1.44
Missing presumed killed during air Ops

Cohen, Sgt Arnold
5.7.46
Buried in Hildersheim Jewish Cem

Cohen, Sgt (Obs) Aubrey Herbert
22.5.42
Killed on active service

Cohen, Sgt Bernhard/Benjamin
19.2.44
Missing presumed killed

Cohen, Sgt Benjamin
24.4.44
Missing presumed killed on air ops

Cohen, F/O David Anthony
Age 23   1.8.45
Buried in Madras War Cem, Chennai

Cohen, Sgt David Isadore
21.2.44
Missing on air ops, presumed killed

Figure 227. F/O Meyer Caplan, DFM.

Figure 228. The Roll of Honour in Cardiff Synogogue.

Cohen, Sgt Edward Charles
RAF/AAF 840499
Age 26   1.8.42
DOAS
Runnymede Memorial

Cohen, Lt G.
SAAF
                         13.12.43
Missing presumed killed in action

Cohen, P/O Geoffrey L.
RAAF
Age 27   3.8.42
Buried Finningley Churchyard

Cohen, AC2 Harry
                         28.3.42
Buried at Rainham Cem

Cohen, LAC Harry
                         23.12.45
Buried English/Hebrew Cem,
Leeds

Cohen, Sgt (Pilot) Henry
                         27.2.44
Died in an aircraft accident in
India
Buried at Jessore

Cohen, Sgt Herbert Cyril
76 Sqdn
Age 22   20.12.43
Runnymede Mem

Figure 229. WO (Pilot)
Sidney Cohen, 249 Squadron.

Cohen, Sgt Isaac Ivan
195 Squadron RAFVR
Age 19   4.11.44
Rheinberg War Cem

Cohen, LAC Jack
                         14.9.45

Cohen, AC1 John Laurence
                         19.1.45
Buried in Madras

Cohen, Sgt John Moss
                         15.11.41
Killed in an air crash
Buried in Willesden

Cohen, Sgt/WO/AG Leonard
100 Squadron Bombers
Age 20   1943
Buried Eelde General Cem
Groningen

Cohen, Sqdn/Ldr Lionel Rees
150 Squadron
Age 29   30.7.42
Pihen-Les-Guines War Cem

Cohen, Flt/Sgt (AG) Louis
626 Squadron
                         5.10.44
Missing on air ops believed killed
His name is recorded on the RAF
Memorial, Egham

Cohen, AC1 Maurice
Age 40   24.2.45
Buried Manchester Southern Cem

Cohen, Sgt Maurice
35 Squadron
Age 23   31.3.42
Trondheim (Stavne) Cem

Cohen, F/O Melville David
24.8.43
Killed in a flying accident

Cohen, Sgt (AG/WO) Murray
3.10.43
Killed in a flying accident

Cohen, Sgt (Pilot) Nathan
Rhodesia Squadron
4.5.43
Died during air ops off the coast
of Denmark
Buried in Denmark

Cohen, F/O Nathan
Age 33   6.12.42
Missing over Holland, presumed
killed on air ops
Buried at Eindhoven

Cohen, F/O Robert Simon DFC
RAFVR
11.8.44
Killed on air ops
Buried at Breux-sur-Avre

Cohen, Cpl Robert Sydney
21.12.41
Died as the result of an aircraft
accident
Buried in the Spanish and
Portuguese Cem, Golders Green

Cohen, Sgt/AG Samuel George
7 Squadron Pathfinders
Age 19   29.1.44
Buried Berlin War Cem

Cohen, WO (Pilot) Sydney
249 Squadron   25.9.46
Missing presumed killed
The Italians on Lampedusa Island
surrendered to him on 12.6.43

Cohen, Cpl Tovyer
-.12.44
Died in India

Coleman, P/O Gerald
Killed on ops

Conrad, Sgt Henry
49 Squadron
2.1.44
Killed on ops
Buried near Neustrelitz, East
Germany

Figure 230. Sgt Lionel
Cornbloom.

Cornbloom, Sgt Lionel
1.2.45
Killed in an aircraft accident

Cornell, Flt/Sgt M.H.
31.5.43

Cornfield, AC2 Maurice
22.2.45
Buried in Gildersome Cem, Leeds

Cousin, P/O Cyril
101 Squadron
Age 20   -.8.44
Killed in action over Stettin

Cowan, Sgt Alfred Julian
17.4.41
Killed in an air crash

Craig, Cpl A.
4.12.44
Buried in Madras, India

Cramp, F/O Douglas Louis DFC
-.1.45
Missing presumed killed on air
ops

Crystal, Flt/Sgt A.S.
27.1.45
Missing presumed killed

Cullen, Flt/Lt Richard Nigel DFC

Daitz, Flt/Sgt Leslie Bernard
Age 22
Killed in action.
Buried in the City Cem, Paris
He flew 22 operational missions

Dale, F/O George Raynor
3/4.4.43
Killed on air ops
Buried in the Mil Cem, Dusseldorf

Danino, LAC Moshe
6.10.42
Buried in Geneifa War Cem, Egypt

**Dansby, Flt/Sgt Robert (aka
Dansky)**
Age 21   16.2.46
Plane crashed when struck by
lightning
Buried in Glenduffhill Cem,
Glasgow

Daren, Cpl Nathan
Age 28   5.7.41
Reported missing presumed dead
HMT Anselm sunk by enemy
action

Davies, Flt/Sgt Dennis
8.7.44

Davies, Sgt (AG) Dennis
158 Squadron
Age 21   24.5.44
Killed in a raid over Aachen.
Although wounded earlier, he had
refused to be grounded

Davis, Sgt David Weiss
179 Squadron
(Coastal Command)
Age 22   31.12.42

Figure 231. Grave of LAC Moshe Danino, in Geneifa War Cemetery, Egypt.

Figure 232. Flt/Sgt Robert Dansby.

Figure 233. Sgt (AG) Dennis Davies, 158 Squadron.

Davis, F/O Harry Samuel
KIA
24.12.44

Davis, P/O Henry David AFM
1.8.40
Killed at St Valerie

Davis, Flt/Lt Frances Montague

Davis, Sgt Jack
1.9.43
Missing presumed killed in action

Davis, Sgt Louis L.
26.6.43

Davis, Flt/Lt Philip M.
3.11.42
Killed on active service
Buried in Brookwood Cem

Davis, Air/Mech Raymond
SAAF
-.10.41
Killed on active service

Davis, F/O Alec
Age 26   20.1.43
Lost over the Channel

Day, Sgt/Nav Frank Samuel
Coastal Command
Age 27
Wick, Scotland

De Keyser, P/O John Lionel
Coastal Command
Age 25   15.9.40
Posted missing when on patrol over North Sea, Battle of Britain

De Lange, AC2 George Ivor
Age 32   16.7.42
Died as a Japanese POW
Buried in Jakarta War Cem

De Villiers, Sgt David
SAAF
10.5.45
DOAS

De Villiers, Flt/Sgt Douglas
SAAF
17.5.44
Killed in action

Dent, P/O Harry
Killed in action
Buried near Essen

Figure 234. Cpl Nathan Daren.

Desmond, AC Sydney
2.8.44
Died in St Frances Sanatorium, Sherbrooke, Quebec
Buried in the Baron de Hirsch Cem

Dicks, Cpl Simon S.
Drowned as a result of an aircraft
accident
Buried at Brighton

Dlusy, Flt/Sgt Nathan
RCAF
Age 23   15.8.44
Buried Glenduffhill Jewish Cem

Domnitz, Sgt (Navigator) Jacob
(Son of Rev. Isaac Domnitz,
Londonderry)

Dornsaft, AC2 M.D.
Killed in an accident
Buried in the Old Cairo War Mem
Cem

Douglas, Sidney L.I.
                          -.-.60
DOAS Singapore

Dushman, Sgt David
97 Squadron
Age 22   22.3.44
Runnymede War Mem

Dvorjetz, Sgt George Arthur
2 Squadron
                          19.7.44
Killed in action
Missing presumed killed on active
service

Dymond, Sgt Derek M.
                          -.1.43
Missing presumed killed

Earle, P/O Jack
                          4.12.43
Killed in an air crash

Easton, Flt/Sgt Samuel
                          17.12.44
Killed on air ops
Buried in France with no Star of
David due to mass grave: this is
CWGC policy.

Edelman, LAC C.
                          14.11.42

Eden, LAC Roffer James
Age 31   20.9.44
Killed at Arnhem

Edwin, Edward F.
                          14.11.40
Buried Luton

Elbogen, Flt/Sgt Arnst
Czech Squadron
                          11.8.44
Missing presumed killed in air ops

Ellenbogen, Flt/Sgt P.
                          8.2.44
Rhodesian. Missing presumed
killed on air ops

Ellick, Sgt Maitland
106 Squadron
Killed in action
Buried in the Brit Mil Cem,
Hanover

Emanual, Flt/Lt William Vernon
                          -.10.40
Killed in an air raid

Engel, Gilbert
RAF
                          -.-.53
DOAS

Engelhardt, Sgt Wolf Herman
101 Squadron
                          28.7.44
Died in an air crash
Buried at Rebrechien Cem, near
Orleans

Fainer, Cpl Paul
RAF

Falkson, P/O Jack
Aircraft Carrier Glorious
                          -.-.40
Drowned at Narvik

Fass, Sgt Leonard
114 Squadron
                          19.4.41
Killed in a flying accident
Buried in the Jewish Plot at
Middlesbrough Cem

Fechtner, P/O, DFC
Czech RAF 310 Sq.
                          29.10.40
KIA, Battle of Britain

Feldman, Sgt/Obs Bernard
45 Squadron
Age 23   11.6.40
Buried Alexandria Mil Cem

Feldman, Sgt/WO/AG Israel
9 Squadron Bombers
Age 22   8.7.44

Feldman, Sgt/Bomb Aimer J.
630 Squadron
                          12.5.44

Feldman, Flt/Sgt M.H.
SAAF
                          12.8.44
Died in an accident in Italy

**Feldman (Felman), Flt/Sgt
(WO/AG) Sydney**
57 Squadron
Age 23   10.4.41
Killed on air ops over the East
Friesian Islands
Buried Rheinberg War Cem

Feldman, LAC Zelig
                          23.5.42
Buried in Kantara Mil Cem

Felix, Flt/Sgt Hyman
RAF (Pal)

Felsenstein, Flt/Sgt Basil
India Command
                          15.1.45
Died of wounds received on ops

Felsenstein, Sgt Gerald Cecil
                          12.3.43
Missing presumed killed

Fencer, AC1 A.
112 Squadron
                          15.5.43
Buried in Ramleh Mil Cem

Figure 235. Flt/Sgt Samuel Easton.

Figure 236. LAC Roffer James Eden.

Figure 237. Flt/Sgt (WO/AG) Sydney Feldman, 57 Squadron.

Fine, Flt/Sgt Bernard David
RAAF
27.5.44
Killed in a flying accident
Buried in the RAF Cem, Chester

Fink, P/O Jan Frederick
18.7.44
Missing presumed killed during air ops

Finkelstone-Sayliss, Sgt Raphael
500 Squadron
24.9.42
Killed in action. No known grave

Fishman, F/O Boris
12.8.43

Fitzgerald, P/O Maurice Isidore
75 Squadron
28.5.44

Ford, Sgt Sydney L.
-.6.43
Missing believed killed

Fordham, LAC Samuel Bernard
Age 23   21.4.45
Killed in action in Holland
Buried in the Brit Cem, Venraj

Fox, F/O Charles Lawrence
17.9.44
Missing presumed killed during air ops

Fox, Flt/Sgt Leslie Henry
101 Squadron
-.11.42
Killed in action over Germany

Fox, Flt/Sgt Leslie W.
Runnymede Mem
30.7.44

Fox, Sgt Sonny
10.2.46
Killed in an air crash
Buried at East Ham

Frankal (Frankel), Sgt Bertram Moss
8.4.45
Missing presumed killed during air ops

Frankelson, WO Nathan
Air Transport Aux
8.4.42

Franklin, Flt/Lt J.P.
28.12.43
Killed in action

Fredman, F/O Levin
615 Squadron
Age 21   12.5.40
Killed in action
Buried in Wihogne Communal Cem, Liege

Freedman, F/O Harold H.
17.1.45
Killed in an aircraft accident
Buried at East Ham

Freedman, Flt/Sgt Jack H.
6.1.44
Missing presumed killed

Freedman, F/O Leslie Morris
248 Squadron Mosquito
7.12.44

Freedman, F/O Sydney S.
-.6.44
Killed in action

Freeman, Sgt Hyman
9.12.44
Killed on air ops
His body was found and buried on the sea shore near the Derna road in the Western Desert, Libya

Freeman, Sgt Lionel Gerald
Age 21   25.4.43
Buried Rheinberg War Cem

Friedl, LAC Konstantin
14 Squadron
25.6.43
Buried at Bagrish Main, Egypt

Friend, P/O Joseph
4.3.41
First World War and Boer War
His ashes are in the Liberal Cem, Willesden

Friendly, WO Jocelyn DFM
21.5.43
Killed in action

Galkoff, LAC Leon
13.3.46

Gantz, Flt/Sgt Basil
227 Squadron
Age 21   -.8.44
Killed in action
Buried in the Brit Mil Cem, Belgrade

Garcia, Sgt Abraham
3.3.44
Missing presumed killed during air ops

Garcia, Flt/Sgt Alfred/Harry
Age 27   -.-.42
Missing presumed dead

Garcia-Webb, Sgt (WO) Joseph
109 Squadron
16.11.44
Killed in an aircraft accident
Buried in Willesden

Garshowitz, Sgt A.
653 Squadron (DAMBUSTER)
17.5.43

Gee, Flt/Lt Nathan T.
DOAS Singapore
-.-.56

Gingold, Sgt Sydney David
Age 20   31.8.44
Killed in an aircraft crash
Buried in Witton New Cem

Ginsberg, Sgt (AG) Ruby
26.11.43
Killed on bombing mission
Buried at Willesden

Figure 238. Marshal of the Royal Air Force Sir John Grandy at the Cenotaph 1987.

Glassman, Sgt (WO/AG) David
12.6.43
Missing presumed killed during air ops

Glassman, AC2 H.S.
9.11.43

Glatt, Sgt C.

Gluck, F/O Mark
23.5.43
Missing presumed killed on air ops

Godfrey, Sgt/WO/AG Harry (Val)
38 Bomber Squadron
Age 21   21.6.41
Missing presumed killed Ops.
No known grave

Gold, P/O David Allan

Gold, F/O Edward Maurice
11.6.43
Killed on air ops
Buried at Mönchengladbach

Gold, AC2 Isaac
13.8.43
Buried at East Ham

Goldberg, Charles

Goldberg, Sgt Hyman
Age 20   26.4.44
Killed on air ops
Buried in Durnbach Mil Cem

Goldberg, Sgt Louis 'Curly'
-.-.41
Canadian. Killed in a flying accident

Goldberg, Sgt N.M.
Age 22   22.5.44
Shot down over Germany

Goldberg, LAC Samuel
Killed in action
Buried in the Jewish Cem, Brighton

Figure 239. AG Ferneaux Jordan Van Guen.

Figure 240. Flt/Sgt Gingold.

Figure 241. Sgt Hyman Goldberg.

Figure 242. Sgt N.M. Goldberg.

Goldberg, F/O Woolf W.M.
6.9.43
Missing presumed killed during air ops
Later buried Cholay Mil Cem, France

Goldfarb, LAC Alfred
31.8.42
Buried at Edmonton

Goldfeather, P/O Albert Michael
9.12.40
Alamein Mem

Goldfinger, Sgt (Nav) Zangwell
24.5.43
Missing presumed killed during air ops

Goldflust, Sgt Julius
24.5.43
Missing presumed killed during air ops

Golding, Flt/Sgt Joseph A.
3.12.44
Missing presumed killed during air ops

Goldman, Cpl Cyril Hyman
24.1.43
Buried in the Jewish Cem, Cardiff

Goldman, Sgt (Pilot) Jossil
-.6.41
Killed in a flying accident

Goldman, F/O Roy Grayson
16.12.44
Died as the result of enemy action
Buried in the Kirkhof van Antwerpen

Goldsmith, Sgt Benjamin Frederick
2.10.42
Killed on air ops

Goldsmith, WO Lionel Manuel
RNZAF 40919
Age 27   22.9.43
Buried Hanover War Cem

Goldspink, Joseph
RCAF
28.3.43

Goldstein, Sgt/AG Dennis Harold
51 Squadron Bomber Command
Age 21   9.10.43
Buried Hanover War Cem

Goldstein, Sgt (AG) Jacob (Jack)
16.3.45
Missing presumed dead on bombing mission to Nuremberg
Polish by birth, he enlisted in 1943.
Buried in the Brit War Cem, Durnbach

Goldstein, Sgt Mathias Aaron
158 Squadron Bomber Command
Age 33   8.11.42

Goldstein, Morris

Goldston, Sqdn/Ldr John Raymond
Age 27   11.11.42
Alamein Mem

Goldstone, Flt/Lt Robert Michael

Goldstone, Sgt Albert Abraham
143 Squadron
1.8.43

Goldthorpe, F/O Kenneth R.
8.2.45
KIA

Gompertz (Gomperts), P/O A. Benjamin
21.8.42
Killed in a crash
Buried in Willesden

Gompertz, F/O Philip
19.8.42

Goodman, P/O George E.
Battle of Britain
KIA North Africa
Born in Haifa
May be of Jewish origin

Goodman, W/Com Hubert R.
KIA
12.5.44
Royal Hellenic Air Force Cross

Gooravitch, Sgt Jack Bernard
2.1.44
Killed on air ops
Buried at Hanover War Cem

Gordon, Flt Sgt N.
49 Squadron
Age 25   4.7.44
Killed on an operational flight with Lancaster Bombers

Gordon, Lt Nathan L.
SAAF
-.3.41
Killed in an air accident in Africa

Gorfunkle, Sgt (Nav) Norman
76 Squadron
Age 22   7.11.42
Killed in action
Buried at Chaumont

Goth, P/O Vilem
Czech RAF Squadron
25.10.40
KIA, Battle of Britain

Gottleib, WO Abe Isadore
44 Squadron Bomber Command
Age 22   6.6.42

Gotzlinger, Sgt W.
18.10.42
(Czech)
Died in an aircraft accident
Buried in Brookwood Cem

Gould, LAC Leslie
15.2.44
Buried in Gildersome Jewish Cem, Leeds

Goulston, P/O (Nav) Sydney
77 Squadron
Age 24
Killed in action over Berlin
Buried in Berlin Brit Mil Cem

Grabie, AC1 A.
24.4.41
Died of wounds in the Middle East

Granard, Cpl John
Age 34   3.1.42
Killed by enemy bombing during siege of Malta
Buried in the Roy Naval Cem, Malta

Grant, LAC Harold John
19.9.45
Killed in accident

Grant, F/O Jacob Maurice DFC
-.9.43
Killed on air ops
Buried near Cleves

Grant, F/O S., DFC + Bar
Hampstead memorial

Figure 243. Cpl Cyril Hyman Goldman.

Figure 244. Sgt (AG) Jacob (Jack) Goldstein.

Figure 245. Flt/Sgt N. Gordon, 49 Squadron.

Gravia, AC Abraham
Pal
                                -.7.41
Killed in Greece

Greenberg, F/O Albert Aaron
                        21.3.40
Killed in action at Leuchers
Aerodrome, Fife
Buried in the Christian Cem,
Leuchers, Fife, Scotland

Greenblatt, Sgt Instructor B Z
SAAF
                                -.4.41
Killed in an air accident

Greenburgh, F/O Peter Harold
39 Squadron Fleet Air Arm
Age 21   17.6.44
Killed on air ops
Buried in Salonika Mil Cem

Greene, Flt/Sgt Sidney Henry
Age 24   4.12.42
Missing presumed dead, Tunis

Greenhill, Sqdn/Ldr Ronald A.
                                -.4.44
Missing presumed dead

Grek, Lt I.
SAAF
Killed on active service Kenya

Grew, AC2 Louis
907 Squadron
                        12.11.40
Killed in an air raid
Buried in Willesden Cem

Greystoke, F/O Peter
                        22.5.44
Buried at Streatham

Grossman, F/O George Mendell
Age 22   10.10.43
Gloucester Old Cem

Gruber, Sgt Pilot Maurice
                        9.5.42
Killed in action

Gruber, Sgt Rufus Isaacs
44 Squadron
Age 21   9.11.42
Hamburg Cem

Grunis, Cpl Abe
Age 26   -.2.44
Died as a Japanese POW
The ship in which he was being
transferred sank

Guterman, Sgt Jack, DFM
'DAMBUSTER' 207 Squadron
Lancaster
                        17.5.43
Killed in action

Hacker, Cpl Cyril
                        22.2.42
Missing presumed killed on air
ops

Hainin, WO Leslie

Haley, Sgt (Pilot) John Simon Dasilva
                        9.7.42
Killed in an aircraft accident
Buried at Hoop Lane Cem

Hallows, P/O E.S.I.
79 Squadron
                        4.11.40
Killed in an accident
Buried in Willesden

Halperin, P/O Ronald, DFC
101 Squadron
                        21.2.44
Missing presumed killed on air
ops

Figure 246. P/O (Navigator) Sydney Goulston, 77 Squadron.

Halpern, LAC Wolf
10.3.43

Hamme, AC2 J.
20.4.43
Buried in Willesden

Hannah, P/O J.
RAFVR
Buried Bayeux

Hare, Sgt (AG) William George Nelson
8.6.41
Killed in action
Buried in Hull

Harris, Sgt Alfred
Age 24   1.11.44
Served Middle East as a Flight Rigger attached to the 8th Army Eight campaign medals. Killed in action over Holland
Buried at Bergen-op-Zoom, Holland

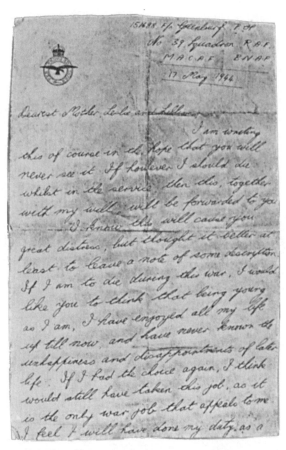

Figures 247 & 248. Last letter of FO Peter Greenburgh.

Figure 249. F/O Peter Harold Greenburgh, 39 Squadron, Fleet Air Arm.

Figure 250. Flt/Sgt Sidney Henry Greene.

Figure 251. Cpl Abe Grunis.

Figure 252. Sgt Alfred Harris.

Harris, F/O Eric John
-.3.43
Missing presumed dead

Harris, LAC Geoffrey M.
17.9.42
Killed in a flying accident
Buried in the RAF Cem, Texas

Harris, Sgt Gerald Leonard
-.3.45
Killed on air ops

Harris, Harold
582 Squadron
16.6.44

Harris, Sgt (Navigator) Jessel H.
-.3.43
Killed on an operational flight

Harris, AC2 Joseph
3.12.42
Died after being discharged
Buried at East Ham

Harris, Sgt Leslie Desmond
12 Squadron
Buried Bergen War Cem

Harris, Sgt Myer
67 Squadron
12.6.43

Harris, Sgt Norman
375 Squadron Bomber Command
Age 24   19.4.43

Harris, Sgt Stanley Louis
98 Squadron Bomber Command
Age 20   17.6.40

Harris, LAC Stanley
25.6.43
Killed in a flying accident in Canada

Hart, Jacob Maurice Stanley, DFC + Bar
-.9.43
DOAS
Memorial at Willesden Cem

Hart, Sgt (Pilot) Robert
Age 19   2.6.42
Shot down over Cologne
Buried at Kleve

Hartstein, P/O Emmanuel
23.8.44
Killed in an aircraft accident
Buried in Willesden

Hartstein, P/O Philip
-.12.43
Killed in action

Hazan, Sgt (AG) T.
Age 21   23.6.42
Shot down over the Mediterranean

Figure 253. Grave of LAC Geoffrey M. Harris in the RAF Cemetery, Terrel, Texas, USA.

Figure 254. Grave of Sgt (Pilot) Robert Hart in Kleve Brit Military Cemetery.

Figure 255. Sgt (AG) T. Hazan.

Figure 256. Sgt Sidney Helper.

Hazard, Sgt (Pilot) J.H. CGM
                              -.4.43
Killed in a flying accident

Heller, Sgt F.A.
                              18.11.43
Missing presumed killed on air ops

Helper, Sgt Sidney
Age 21   10.11.44
Killed on active service Vancouver Island, Canada
Buried in a grave at 3,600 feet, at Nitnot Lake

Henriquez, F/O Alfred George
                              16.8.44
Missing presumed killed on air ops
Buried at Risznow, Pomerania, East Germany

Herbert, F/O Dennis
India AFC, 62 Squadron
                              12.11.44
Lost in flight over Indian Ocean

Heymans, LAC David Benjamin
Age 19   25.10.43
Buried Calgary Jewish Cem

Hillelson, Sgt Leslie Henry
                              21.10.40
Died from injuries received in a flying accident
Buried in the Jewish Cem, Grimsby

Hillier, F/O Dr Donald
KOAS
                              18.10.51

Himelsztaub, LAC Maier Ben
                              13.2.42
Palestinian Jewish. Buried California

Hipps, P/O Arnold
(Dunkirk)
Age 21   19.7.41
Missing presumed killed on air ops

Hirsch, Sgt Simon
Killed on air ops
                              22.6.43
Buried in Ede General Cem

Hirschfield, Sgt Sidney Owen
754017
Age 20   5.8.41
Reichswald Forest Cem

Hirst, F/O David
26.5.43
Killed in a flying accident
Buried in the RAF Cem, Brookwood

Hoffman (aka Hoffnung)
Special Operator 214 Squadron

Hoffman, F/O David A.
RAAF
25.4.44
Killed on air ops

Holder, Flt/Sgt Norman Lionel
19.2.44
Missing presumed killed on air ops

Holme, F/O Kenneth
31.8.43

Hond, Sgt Reginald
5.10.44
Buried in Rheinberg Mil Cem

Honig, F/O Amichai, DFM
63 Squadron Palestinian Jew
30.8.43
Missing presumed killed on air ops

Horkheimer, F/O Milton
27.9.43
Missing presumed killed on air ops

Horne, P/O Aubrey Abraham
27.8.41
Killed in a plane crash
Buried in Willesden

Horner, Sgt.WO/AG Leon
49 Squadron Bomber Command
5.7.44
Romescamps Churchyard
Abancourt

Hornuny, Sgt Jan
310 (Czech) Squadron
13.7.44
Killed on air ops

Hudson, Sgt Jack
50 Squadron
25.3.42

Hyam, Sgt Alfred
214 Squadron Bomber Command
23.11.40

Hyam, Sgt Jack Louis
57 Squadron Bomber Command
13.6.43

Hyams, Flt/Sgt Joseph
119 Squadron
Age 30   2.9.44

Hyamson, Cpl Philip Henry Samuel
20.8.44
Killed by enemy action

Hyman, Flt/Sgt Basil
30.7.43
Missing presumed killed on air ops

Hyman, Sgt W.W.
-.-.41

Hymans, LAC Jack
271 Squadron
1.1.45
Killed by enemy action at
Melsbroek Airfield, Brussels
Buried at Evere Cem

Isaac, Lewis R.
Battle of Britain
-.8.40

Isaacs, Sgt Fredrick Ralph
926326
Age 20   17.1.42
Runnymede Mem

Isaacs, LAC J.M.
25.1.45
Buried in Willesden

Isaacs, Sgt (Pilot) Ralph
2.3.43

Isaacs, Richard Edward
RNZAF
Buried Wellington, NZ.
Father Jewish as confirmed by
brother David

Isaacs, Thomas Joseph
29.5.42

Isaacson, Herbert Alexander
30.9.43
Buried in Ambou

Israel, F/O Leslie
23.11.43
Killed on air ops
Buried in Willesden

Jackson, Sgt/WO Barnett Bert
751797
19.7.41

Jackson, Sgt Bernard Bernstein
4.5.42
Missing presumed killed in action

Jackson, Sgt (WO/AG) Harold
50 Squadron
12.7.41
Killed in air ops
Buried in Parish Cem, Veendam

Jackson, Sgt (Radar Obs) Irvine
4.1.43
Killed in a flying accident
Buried at Bournemouth

Jacob, Sgt/F/O H.
22.4.45
Killed in action

Jacobs, Alec
211 Squadron

Jacobs, Sgt George
70 Squadron
23.7.43

Jacobs, F/O Harold Louis, DFC
Age 20   26.1.44
Killed in action over India
Buried in Kamptee Mil Cem

Jacobs, Sgt (WO/AG) Henry Emanual
4 Squadron
25.10.41
Killed in a flying accident

Jacobs, Jack Phillip
5.11.60
Died due to radiation leak from
Windscale

Jacobs, Sgt James Sydney
17.9.41
Buried in Willesden

Jacobs, John G.
RAF
-.-.39
With Isaac Myers RN 1st
2 Jewish KIA (JC) HMS
Courageous

Jacobs, 2nd Lt K.I.
SAAF
-.5.42
Killed on active service

Jacobs, M.
4169052
-.9.55
DOAS

Jacobs, Sgt Michael Stanley
8.11.41
Killed in action
Buried in the Municipal Cem,
Crooswijk

Jacobs, Sgt William Frederick
RAF
(brother of John George, FAA/RAF)

Jacobsen, Sgt Alexander
9.1.43
Killed in action

Jacobson, L/Cpl Morris
22.4.43
Buried in the West End Chessed
V'ameth Cem

Jacques, F/O Charles R.
KIA
16.12.43

Jarvis, LAC Maurice
RCAF
5.9.53
Killed in accident, Three Rivers,
Quebec

Jarvis, Flt/Lt Ronald Austin
-.9.41
Missing presumed killed on air
ops

Figure 257. LAC Jack Hymans,
Transport Command.

Jirsak, Sgt Otto
Czech Squadron 787141
16.10.40
Oosterwolde Cem, Oldebroek

Joelson, Flt/Lt Herschel, MC
RAFVR
23.3.41
KIA
Cross on grave – records show no
religion given

Jonas, F/O Alfred Ron Falkner
-.12.43
Missing presumed killed

Joseph, Flt/Sgt Alfred
11.7.45
Died as the result of an aircraft
accident

Joseph, AC1 Cyril
5.1.44
Buried in Karachi Jewish Cem

Joseph, Sgt D.A.
-.-.41
Killed on air ops

Joseph, Sgt E.
13.1.44
Buried in Bombay Jewish Cem

Joseph, P/O Graham H

Joseph, LAC Harold H.
17.12.40

Joseph, Flt/Lt L.
10.5.44
Missing presumed killed on air
ops

Joseph, AC1 Maurice
5.7.41
Lost in SS *Anselm*

Josephs, Sgt Herbert
30.10.42

Kahler, Sgt (Flt/Eng) H.C.M.
Shot down over the North Sea.
Three of his comrades were taken
prisoner by the Germans. He and
four other members of his crew
were buried in a single grave in
the churchyard at Gram, near Ribe
in South West Jutland, Denmark

Kahn, Flt/Lt Arthur Harold
172 Squadron Coastal Command
Age 25
15.6.44

Kalensky, Flt/Sgt Josef
311 Czech
Age 25
11.4.42
Buried Bergen-op-Zoom War Cem

Kalms, Sgt (Flt/Eng) Michael
Age 18
16.3.43
Killed on active service on a
bombing mission over Stuttgart,
Germany

Kam, LAC Leib
29.7.44
Buried Heliopolis War Cem

Kaminsky, Cpl Morris
7.11.44
Missing at sea believed dead

Katz, Sgt G.

Katz, Flt/Sgt Karel
Czech 311 Squadron
3.10.44
Runnymede Mem

Figure 258. Sgt (Flt/Eng) H.C.M. Kahler.

Figure 259. Grave of Sgt Kahler in Gram Churchyard, Denmark, which he shares with four of his comrades.

Figure 260. Sgt (Flt/Eng) Michael Kalms.

Kaufman, P/O Frank Wolfgang
6.1.44
Missing presumed killed on air ops

Kaufman, Sgt John Hyman
405 Squadron Bomber Command
24.9.42
Buried Aabenraa Cem

Kawenoki, Sgt (AG) Alec
Age 22   -.-.41/2
Killed in an air crash 1941/42
Buried in Long Lane Cem, Liverpool

Kay, F/O James
26.12.44

Kay, W/Com Leslie H., DFC
KIA
2.2.45

Kaye, Sgt (Obs) Gordon
Age 21   -.5.41
Killed in action whilst bombing a convoy off the Dutch coast

Kaye, Sgt Harry, DFM
-.-.43
Shot down over Holland
Buried at Nijmegen

Kemper, W/Cdr J. OBE, Medaille Militaire
18.12.45
Mentioned in Despatches
Buried in Willesden

Kendrick, Sgt Bernard, DFM
61 Squadron
23.4.44
Missing presumed killed on air ops

Kersh, AC1 Hyman
22.5.44
Killed by enemy action
Buried at East Ham

Kesten, Sgt George
4.11.44
Missing presumed killed on air ops

Kestler, Sgt Pilot Oldrich
Czech RAF 111 Squadron
7.4.41
Czech MC
KIA, Battle of Britain

Khan, Flt/Lt Maurice Donald
23.8.44
Died in an aircraft accident

Kieff, Flt/Sgt Maurice
26.8.44
Shot down over Nordenstadt, Germany

King, Sqdn/Ldr Andrew N.
4.11.46
Cremated at Golders Green, London

King, Sgt Colin
Brady Club Memorial
Buried Delhi

King, Flt/Sgt Leonard Alfred
18.11.45
Buried at Willesden

King, G. Raymond
Buried at Malta

Figure 261. Sgt Harry Kaye, DFM.

Figure 262. W/Cdr J. Kemper, OBE, Medaille Militaire.

Figure 263. W/Cdr J. Kemper in the First World War.

King, Sgt Ronald (aka Kempner)
101 Squadron
Age 19   28.12.44
Buried Rheinberg War Cem

Kirk, Sgt (Obs) Sidney
18 Squadron
Age 22   30.3.43
Killed on an operational flight
Buried in Canrobert Cem

Kirsh, Sgt Abe
RCAF
                          -.12.41

Kissin, S.

Klein, Zygmunt 'Joe'
Czech Squadron
Bat of Britain Pilot
KIA

Kleinberg, P/O Georges
                          22.6.43
Missing presumed killed on air ops

Kleiner, Sgt (Flt/Eng) Harry
                          23.5.43
Killed in action on air ops

Kleinhorn, Maurice

Kluska, Sgt (WO) Sylvain
                          9.5.44
Killed in an aircraft accident
Buried in Willesden

Klusky, Sgt (AG) Gerald
                          28.8.41
Killed in action
Buried in Holland

Knoeson, P/O AG Benjamin Gabriel
97 Squadron Bomber Command
                          30.7.43
Buried Becklingen War Cem
Soltau

Koflik, Sgt (Obs) Paul
Polish Air Force
                          19.12.43
Killed on active service
Buried at Milltown Cem, Belfast

Kolitz, P/O Louis L.
218 Squadron
                          -.9.41
Missing presumed killed on air ops

Komaroff, Flt/Lt Lennart Alex
29 Squadron
                          19.4.44
Missing presumed killed on air ops

Koransky, Sgt (WO/AG)
                          4.9.41
Killed on air ops
Buried in the Municipal Cem, Dunkirk

Korer, Flt/Lt Ralph
Killed on air ops
Buried in the Brit Mil Cem, Rheinberg

Kosky, Sgt/Pilot Philip Kay
Bomber Command
Age 21
Failed to return from raid over Germany

Kossick, Arnold
44 Squadron
                          13.6.41

Kotkin, F/O Max
                          23.12.45
Johannesburg

Kowalski, Sgt John
419 Squadron RCAF
                          1.3.43

Kramer, Flt/Lt Marcus, DFC
92 Squadron
Age 29   -.6.41
Killed in action, Battle of Britain

Figure 264. A Wings for Victory Parade (W/Cdr Kemper second from right).

Kraus, G.W.
611 Squadron

Krish, P/O Felix Maurice
Age 26   12.2.43
Killed in a flying crash
Buried at Willesden

Kriseman, D.
SAAF
Buried in Tunisia

Kruszynski, P/O J.
                        -.-.42
Killed on active service

Kronfeld, Sqdn/Ldr (Lt/Col) Robert
Glider Expert (D-Day plans)
                        12.2.48

Kugelmass, LAC Jack
                        -.7.41
Killed in a flying accident

Landau, F/O Hyme
Age 26   17.11.42
Killed on active service
Buried Rainsough Jewish Cem

Figure 265. Flt/Sgt Zdenek Launer, 311 Squadron.

Landau, Sgt (Obs) Henry
Age 26   21.1.44
Obs in a Lancaster Bomber
Missing in a raid over Magdeburg

Langner, LAC Gordon Darcy
                        10.4.45
Died whilst driving supplies to Belsen

Lapish, AC1 Harry
126 Squadron
                        2.7.42

Lassman, AC1 Leonard
                        -.8.44
Buried at East Ham

Launer, Flt/Sgt Zdenek
311 Squadron
                        1.1.45
Czech. Killed on air ops
Cremated at Golders Green

Lawrence, LAC Sylvia
WAAF
                        4.4.44

Figure 266. LAC Alfred Lazarus.

Figure 267. P/O Jack Leewarden.

Figure 268. Flt/Sgt H. Levene.

Lawson, Sqdn/Ldr Stanley
24.1.46

Lazarus, LAC Alfred
Age 33   6.7.44
Killed on active service
Buried at Rainham

Lazarus, Sgt (AG) Louis
3.10.43
Killed in a crash
Buried at East Ham

Lazarus, Flt/Sgt S. David
19.3.45
Killed in an aircraft accident
Buried in Bergen-op-Zoom War
Cem

Lazarus, LAC Stanley Henry
-.4.45
Missing presumed killed in air ops

Le Bosse, LAC Francois Mark
Age 23   -.-.45
Died at Sans Sevaro
Buried Bari War Cem

Leckie, Sgt Norman Abraham
(Canadian)

Leder, LAC Alfred
7.1.43
Killed in aircraft accident in Canada
Buried in a Canadian Jewish Cem

Lee, Sgt Bernard Jack
115 Squadron
7.6.44

Leewarden, P/O Jack
Age 25   27.8.42
Shot down over Germany
Buried in Reichswald Forest War
Cem

Leigh, Sgt Ronald (aka Levy)
3.3.45
Killed in an aircraft accident

Lelyveld, Sgt Anthony
DOAS
-.-.68

Lens, P/O Aubrey
Age 22   23.8.43
Killed over Berlin

Lentin, Flt/Sgt Kenneth
7.7.44
Killed in an aircraft accident
Buried in Haycombe Cem

Lesser, AC1 Alan Aaron
Age 21   10.3.43
Killed in an accident
Buried in the Jewish Cem,
Calcutta

Lesser, LAC Samuel
1.8.44
Buried in Willesden

Levene, P/O David
Age 34   -.-.45
Killed on air ops
Buried in Scheirloh Cem,
Tecklenburg

Levenston, Cpl Louis Solomon
Age 31   29.6.46

Levey, Flt/Sgt J.
635 Squadron.
8.3.45

Levey, Flt Sgt Philip H.M.
RAAF
Age 20   9.10.44
Buried in Reichswald Forest War
Cem

Levi, P/O Frederick H.
4.7.43
KIA

Levin, AC2 Joseph

-.6.41

Killed in Greece

Levine, A
RCAF

Levine, Flt/Sgt H.
Age 34   -.-.43
Killed over Belgium

Levine, LAC Samuel M.
RCAF

-.1.42

Levinson, AC1 H.
Age 22   5.6.43
Murdered whilst a Japanese POW
in Thailand
Buried in the River Kwai Cem,
Chung Kai

Levinson, F/O Harold Brock
118 Squadron

4.4.43

**Levinson/Levitus, Sgt (Pilot)
Sidney S.**
Age 23   -.-.43
Killed in action
Was member of the Garnethill
Hebrew Congregation, Glasgow

Levy, AC2 A. (Jack?)

23.3.41

Levy, F/O A.J.D.
218 Squadron

21.4.44

Failed to return from a raid

Levy, AC1 Alfred
Age 25   3.10.43
Died as a Japanese POW in
Thailand
Buried in River Kwai Cem, Chung
Kai

Levy, F/O Colin Raphael

14.11.46

Levy, Sgt (Obs) David Joshua

16.3.42

Killed in an aircraft accident
Buried in Blackley Cem

Levy, F/O Frank
44 Squadron

7.9.44

Missing presumed killed on air
ops

Levy, Sgt George Arthur

21.7.44

Levy, P/O Henry
RCAF

-.3.41

Killed in an aircraft accident

Levy, Flt/Sgt (Nav) Henry K.
47 Squadron
Age 25   6.11.43
Missing presumed killed on air
ops over the Aegean Sea

Levy, Flt/Sgt Lucien G.
Free French Forces

5.10.41

Buried in Old Cairo War Memorial
Cem

Levy, P/O P. Albert
57 Squadron

28.8.43

Levy, Flt/Lt R.V., DFC
Tempsford Squadron Spec Ops
Killed in action

-.-.44

Levy, Flt/Sgt Nav Sidney
619 Squadron Bomber Command
Age 24   10.5.44

**Levy-Haarscher, AC2
Abraham L.**

28.1.41

Alamein Mem

**Levy-Haarscher, Flt/Lt Richard
Simon**
230 Squadron

15.10.45

Levyn, Flt/Sgt S.

10.3.45

Missing presumed killed on air
ops

Lewen, Sgt Ralph Hyman
144 Squadron Bomber Command
5.5.42

Lewis, Dennis

-.5.45

KIA
Memorial at Willesden Cem

Lewis, Sgt Harold
Killed on air ops
Buried in the Brit Mil Cem,
Belgrade

Lewis, Sgt Leonard James
Runnymede Mem

Lewis, Sgt (AG) Louis
Bomber Command
Age 21
Killed in action

Lewis, P/O Norman L.

13.7.40

Missing presumed killed on air
ops

**Lewis, Flt/Sgt Syd (aka
Lazarus)**
SAAF

-.12.40

Killed in action

Lewis, Sgt Ralph, DFM

-.3.43

Missing presumed killed on air
ops

Lexton, Sgt Charles

20.3.47

Missing presumed killed on air
ops

Liebermann, P/O W. Charles

2.8.43

Lieberman, AC1 Israel

-.1.43

Killed on active service in N Africa
Buried in El Alia Ceme

Linett, ACW1 Lily
WAAF
Age 19   12.9.44
Buried Streatham Jewish Cem

Figure 269. Grave of AC1 H. Levinson in the River Kwai Cemetery, Chung Kai.

Figure 270. Sgt (Pilot) Sidney S. Levitus.

Figure 271. Grave of AC1 A. Levy in the River Kwai Cemetery, Chung Kai.

Figure 272. Flt/Sgt (Navigator) H.K. Levy, 47 Squadron.

Lipiner, S.
RAF

Lipman, LAC Daniel
3.12.41

Lipshitz, Flt/Sgt Arthur, DFM
23.12.43
Killed in action
Buried at Edmonton

Lisner, Sgt (WO) Leonard
5.3.45
Killed in an aircraft accident

Litolff, Sgt Bernard Leo
207 Squadron
Age 27   12.3.42
Buried Reichswald Forest War Cem

Litvak, Flt/Sgt Barry (Wolf)

Loewenson, Sgt Louis Jack
100 Squadron Bomber Command
Age 22   3.1.44

Loewenstein, 1st Officer Robert Serge
ATA
29.3.41
Maidenhead Register

Loewi, Flt/Lt George F.
4.3.44
His ashes are buried in the Liberal
Jewish Cem, Willesden

Lowin, AC1 J.
24.4.41

Luben (Lubin), Sgt (Pilot) Nat
Coastal Command
Age 25
Killed in action

Luck, Sgt (Pilot) Leslie
-.10.44
Killed in an aircraft accident
Buried in Nigeria

Lyons, Cpl E.
11.2.41

Magasiner, AC2 Arnold
1 Squadron
22.7.40
Killed in action

Mandelson, Flt/Lt Norman
Age 26   19.11.45
Killed in an accident in Malta
Buried at Marsa Jewish Cem

Mandler, Flt/Sgt Otto
311 Czech Squadron
1.1.45

Mantus, P/O Gerald
27.3.45
Killed by a V2
Buried at East Ham

Marantz, Nathaniel
Eagle Squadron
-.7.41
Missing presumed killed on air
ops

Marcus, Sgt Derek Julius
5.12.41
Killed in an aircraft accident
Buried at Kempston Church near
Bradford

Marcus, Jack Allen
ATA Aux

Figure 273. Sgt (Pilot) Nat Luben,
Coastal Command.

Marder, Sgt (Pilot) Arthur E.
25.4.42
Killed in an aircraft accident,
Sierra Leone
Buried in Freetown Cem

Markovitch, P/O Fred Abraham
2.1.44
Killed on air ops
Buried in Holland

Marks, Sgt (AG) David Aaron
Air Transport Auxiliary
1.1.42
Buried in Willesden Cem

Marks, Grahame
17.5.42
KOAS
Memorial at Willesden

Marks, Flt/Lt Robert Alan, DFM
9.11.45

Marks, AC1 Robert George
Buried Kranji

Marks, Robert P.
426 Squadron RCAF

Marks, LAC S.G.
19.8.43
Buried Delhi

Markson, Sgt Ellis
*161 Squadron/Moonlight
Squadrons/SOE*
Age 38   9.8.44
Buried in Cugny Communal Cem

**Mason, Sqdn/Ldr Ernest
Mitchelson, DFC**
-.2.42
Author of the book *Imshi*
Killed in action

Masters, P/O Ralph
1.12.41
Killed in an air crash
Buried at Streatham

Max, Sgt Nathan
178 Squadron
19.3.44
Killed in action

Mayer, Stanley, CGM
101 Squadron
26.11.43

Mazin, Sgt Francis Montague
21.6.43
Missing presumed killed on air
ops

Mazure, Flt/Lt Ivor
9.12.44
Buried in Poona Saint Sepulchre
Cem

Meizales, LAC Wolf
294 Squadron
Age 33   9.11.44
Buried Alexandria Mil Cem

Melhado, Sgt Leslie Stanhope
6.6.42
Killed on air ops over Holland

Mendoza, P/O AG Michael Isaak
149 Squadron Bomber Command
Age 36   18.8.41

Menell, Sgt David
31.3.44
Missing presumed killed on air
ops

Figure 274. Sgt Nathan Max, 178 Squadron.

Figure 275. Sgt (WO/AG) Samuel Miara, 38 Squadron, Bomber Command.

Mercer, AC2 Israel Nathan
4.1.44
Buried at East Ham

Mermelstein, LAC Marcel
30.7.42
Buried Heliopolis War Cem

Metzger, Sgt Harold
10.2.45
Killed in an air crash
Buried at East Ham

Miara, Sgt (WO/AG) Samuel
38 Squadron, Bomber Command
Age 25   13.4.41
Killed on the last operational flight of his tour after twenty-two ops over France, Holland, Germany, North Africa and the Middle East

Michaels, Flt/Sgt Arthur
16.3.45
Missing presumed killed on air ops

Michaelson, Gerald Wilfred
5.7.41

Miller, P/O David
20.12.43
Missing presumed killed on air ops

Miller, Flt/Sgt Stanley Isadore
25.2.44
Missing presumed killed on air ops

Mindel, Sgt David Samuel
Age 24   21.6.43
Killed on a bombing mission to Krefeld, Germany

Mondschein, Flt/Lt
RAF
(Great Escape Saagan)
Murdered by SS

Morganstein, Sgt Isadore Maurice
13.9.44
Missing presumed killed on air ops

Morganstein, F/O Morris
10.11.44
Killed on air ops

Morris, W/Cdr Harry
-.6.44
Killed on active service

Morris, LAC
is this Leonard Morris?

Morris, LAC I. Leonard
-.-.42

Morris, Sgt/AG Solomon
149 Squadron Bomber Command
Age 27   5.8.41
Buried St Martens-Voeren Churchyard

Morrison, AC2 M.A.
12.7.41
Buried in Willesden

Morrison, Sgt (Pilot) Edward H.
SAAF

Morrison, LAC Samuel
12.2.42
Missing presumed killed in Singapore

Moses, LAC Arthur
Age 38   15.10.44
Buried Heliopolis War Cem

Moses, Cpl Mark
15.6.45
Killed in an aircraft accident

Moss, Norman, E.
-.7.51
DOAS

Moss, Sgt Wallace Woolf
608 Fighter Squadron
Age 27   11.11.42

Moss-Vernon, Flt/Sgt David Keith

Myer, Flt/Sgt Edward Michael
22.1.44
Missing presumed killed in air ops

Myers, Abraham
909 Balloon Squadron

Myers, F/O George W.
KIA
14.7.43

Myers, Sgt J.J.

Myers, Sgt Paul Montefiore
31.3.45

Myers, Sgt (Pilot) Solomon

Naiman, Sgt Harry
Age 21   25.6.42
Missing presumed killed on air ops

Naimas, Flt/Lt Mayer Henry Richard
226 Squadron
Age 20   20.9.41

Nathan, AC1 Gerald M.
15.2.45
Died as a Japanese POW in Sandakan Camp, Borneo

Nathan, Harry
909971
30.4.41

Nathan, Flt/Sgt (Pilot) Michael Frederick
Age 20   -.9.42
Killed in action

Nathanson, Flt/Sgt Cecil
24.5.44
Killed in action
Buried in the Reichswald Brit Cem

Neirynck, LAC Victor C.E.
235 Squadron
Age 19   8.5.40
Buried Southend-on-Sea Cem

Nelson, F/O William Henry DFC
10 Squadron
Killed in action, Battle of Britain

Nerden, LAC William Woolf
Age 23   6.2.45
Killed in an aircraft accident
Buried at East Ham

Newton, Flt/Sgt Sidney
Ferry Command
Age 23   27.7.45
Killed in an aircraft accident
Buried at Madras War Cem

Niman, AC2 Solomon Peter
-.8.42
Killed in a bombing raid

Noar, Sgt Joseph
-.9.43
Killed in an accident when returning from ops

Noble, P.

Nunez, F/O George A.
KIA
1.5.43

Nykerk, Sgt (WO/AG) Henry
28.6.41
Missing presumed killed on air ops

Nyman, AC2 M.
102 Maintenance Unit, MEF
11.10.41
Buried at Tel-El Kebir Mil Cem

O'Brart, Flt/Sgt Ernest
Age 22   -.4.43
Killed on air ops in North Africa

Ohrenstein, LAC Edward
15.3.45
Buried in Scholemoor Cem, Bradford

Omens, P/O Gilbert I.
Age 23   26.7.42
Buried Brookwood Mil Cem

Orbuck, Sgt Laurence David
RAAF
Age 20   10.4.42
Killed in action over Germany
Buried in Rheinberg War Cem

Osborne, F/O Edward Walter
15.9.44
Killed in action
Buried near Lubeck

Ottolangui, Sgt Aaron
14.4.43
Killed on air ops
Buried in the Maubeuge-Centre Cem, Nord

Figure 276. Flt/Sgt (Pilot) Michael Frederick Nathan.

Ovis, Sgt Ronald Dennis
6.12.44
Missing presumed killed on air ops

Oxenburgh, Flt/Sgt (AG) James David (Owen), DFM
3.5.44
Killed in action
Buried in Wevelghem Commonwealth Cem

Padveem, LAC A.
RCAF
-.10.43
Buried in Gildersom Cem, Leeds

Paget, Flt/Lt Stuart Harold
Age 48   7.4.45
Buried Golders Green Reform Cem

Pagin, LAC Ben
17.5.45
Buried in Delhi War Cem

Figure 277. Sgt Aaron Ottolangui.

Paisachowitz, AC1 Nissan
975 Squadron
                                    10.8.44
Served in the Jewish Legion
during First World War
Killed on active service. Buried in
Port Said, Egypt

**Pantoock, Sgt Instructor Philip
(Panto)**
                                    23.1.42
Killed in an aircraft accident
Buried in Eastbourne (Langlen)

Pareezer, P/O R.T.
Battle of Britain

**Pateman, Sgt (WO/AG) Harry
(Petrunin)**
161 Squadron, Bomber Command
Age 29   20.9.42
Killed in action over France
Buried in the East Cem, Boulogne

Patkin, Sgt L.E.
RAAF
Killed in action
Buried at Hanover

Pearce, Sgt William Ernest
RAAF
Age 23   9.4.42
Buried in St Stephen's Cem,
Trincomalee, Ceylon

Pearl, F/O Warren W.D.
                                    26.3.43
KIA
Buried in Brookwood, repat. to
USA

**Pelham, Flt/Sgt Maurice
Bernard**
15 Squadron
                                    -.-.44
Buried in Holland

Pervin, T.I.
RCAF
                                    22.9.44

Pezaro, Sgt Louis
                                    18.11.43
Missing presumed killed on air
ops

Philips, P/O John Montague
61 Squadron
                                    30.7.43
Died piloting a Lancaster Bomber
on a mission to Hamburg

Phillips, (Obs) Elias
                                    8.6.42

**Phillips, Flt/Sgt Albert Cyril
Lewis**
                                    4.3.44

Phillips, AC1 D.L.
                                    25.8.43
Killed on active service
Buried in Willesden

Phillips, F/O Maurice
                                    11.7.46
Died from an illness due to war
service

Phillips, Sgt Roy (Isenstein)
                                    -.9.43
Killed in action over England
Buried in Rice Lane Cem,
Liverpool

Figure 278. Sgt Roy (Isenstein)
Phillips.

Phillips, F/O Selwyn Guy
Killed in a flying accident in
French West Africa
Buried in St Etienne Mil Cem,
Mauritania

Pincus, F/O John David
                                    19.7.44
Killed in action
Buried in the Brit Mil Cem,
Ranville

Platt, Sgt (Pilot) Ivor Ralph
Age 21
Killed in action over Italy

Ploskin, Flt/Sgt Ralph Isaac
                                    16.12.42
Missing presumed killed on air
ops

Pogrell, Sgt/Nav Arthur
Age 24   -.-.42
Killed in action over Cologne

Politzer, Sgt Josef
Czech RAF
                                    11.4.42
Buried Bergen-op-Zoom War Cem

Politzer, Sgt Max
Czech RAF
Age 22   10.3.42
Maidenhead Register

Figure 279. F/O John David Pincus.

Polland, Sgt Joseph N.
138 Squadron Tempsford
19.12.43

Popper, Sgt Heinz George
29.8.44
Killed on air ops
Buried in the Jewish Cem, Malmo

Porter, Flt/Sgt Louis
233 Squadron
Missing presumed killed on air ops over Formia, Italy

Posener, P/O Frederick Hyman
-.3.41
Missing presumed killed on air ops

Posner, LAC Solly/Sully
3.10.43

Posner, Sgt Sydney
11.10.42
Missing presumed killed on air ops

Rabin, Sgt/Nav Jack
153 Squadron Bomber Command
Age 22   22.1.45
Buried Venray War Cem

Rabinovitch, AC2 Samuel
-.7.42

Radston, Cpl Max
8.3.41
Killed in an air raid
Buried in Willesden

Radvant, LAC Albert

Rafer, AC2 Joseph
8.3.41
Killed in an air raid
Buried at Edmonton

Raises, Brian
601 Squadron

Raphael, Gp/Capt G., DSO, DFC & Bar
85 Squadron
10.4.45
Mentioned in dispatches
Killed in an aircraft accident

Raphael, LAC Louis
16.4.41
Killed in a flying accident
Buried in Stanton St Quinton Churchyard, Wilts

Raphael, Sqdn/Ldr Alfred Sydney, DFC
467 Squadron
Age 27   18.8.43
Killed in action
Buried at Kolpin-See Mecklenburg

Rappaport, F/O John Gerald
-.5.43
Killed in action

Rathbone, F/O Harold E.
18.5.43
Buried in the Jewish Cem, Hull

Ratnowski, LAC Szymon
9.4.45
Malta Memorial

Rich, Sgt (Obs) Joseph Geoffrey
58 Squadron
13.10.41
Killed when returning from an ops flight
Buried in the Jewish Cem, Leeds

Rimmer, Flt/Lt R. Frank
21.9.40

Ritz, AC2 Harry (Hyman)
26.10.41
Buried at Birmingham

Riung, F/O Norman Moritz
Norwegian RAF Squadron 332
4.7.44
KIA over Le Havre

Robinson, P/O Peter Samuel Myer
19.8.44
Killed on ops
Buried in Ohlsdorf Mil Cem, Hamburg

Robinsohn, Rudolf

Rogers, Sgt Peter
15 Squadron
26.2.43

Roher, LAC Lionel
RCAF
Killed in an accident

Rolfe, Sgt Edgar Alexander
37 Squadron
9.2.43

Romain, Sgt Gerald E. Anijah
RAFVR
22.1.42
Buried in St Mary's Cem, Walthamstow

Rose, Sgt Maurice
Age 21   29.10.40
Died when returning from a bomber raid

Rose, P/O Harry
26.10.41
Involved in a fatal air crash
Buried at East Ham

Rosen, Sgt (Radar Obs) Anthony Ezra
101 Squadron
18.11.43
Missing presumed killed on air ops

Figure 280. Fus S. Solomons, MM, RF.

Figure 281. Pte P. Sunderland, Y and L Reg.

Figure 282. Maj L. Wigram, RF.

Figure 283. Sgt J.M. Cantor, RAF, killed.

Figure 284. Sgt Henry Cohen, RAF, killed.

Figure 285. Sgt S.L. Ford, RAF.

Rosen, Acting Sqdn/Ldr Raymond Arnold
1.7.44
Killed on air ops in France
Buried at Amiens

Rosen, AC2 Sydney I.
7.9.43
Killed in action at sea near Sicily
Buried in Catania Brit Cem

Rosen, AC2 Zvi
11.3.41
Died from an accidental gun shot
Buried in Chatby War Cem, Alexandria

Rosenberg, WO Albert

Rosenberg, Sgt/Flt/Eng Ernest Dennis
635 Squadron Pathfinder
Age 21   11.4.44
Buried Roosendaal-en-Nispen Gen Cem

Rosenberg, Cpl Richard K.W.
Age 23   2.6.43
Suez War Mem Cem

Rosenberg, P/O Stanley

Rosenberger, Sgt/Air Bomber Maurice Bernard
70 Squadron
17.11.44
Buried Ancona War Cem

Figure 286. Sgt/Pilot Simon Hirsch.

Figure 287. F/O Leslie Israel.

Figure 288. F/O A.R.F. Jonas.

Figure 289. Sgt Louis Lazarus, RAF.

Figure 290. Cpl Lemberger, Green Howards, lost at sea.

Figure 291. Sgt Paul Herman, Koflik Polish RAF.

Rosenblatt, Flt/Sgt Nathan
192 Squadron Bomber Command
6.8.43

Rosenfield, Flt/Sgt Eric
4.5.44

Rosenfield, Hyman Isaacs
24.2.46
Buried Kandy, Sri Lanka

Rosenthal, Thomas E.P.
23.4.45

Rosenthal, Sgt (Pilot) Gordon
10.8.42
Killed in a flying accident
Buried in the Jewish Cem,
Liverpool

Rosenthal, Sgt (Nav) S.
RCAF

Rosenthal, Sgt Saul Austin
10.11.43
Killed in action on air ops

Rosenthal, AC1 Sidney
RNZAF
18.11.43
Killed in an aircraft accident
Buried in the Freetown Mil Cem,
Sierra Leone

Rosenthal, Sgt Stanley
9.2.45
Killed on air ops

Figure 292. AJEX and British Legion Standard Bearers at a Commonwealth War Graves Cemetery in Israel 1988.

Rosenthall, AC2 Ronald
21.10.41
Killed in an accident
Buried at Hull

Rosofsky, P/O Harold
9 Squadron
8.9.39
From South Africa. Killed in a crash. Possibly first Jewish casualty of WW2.
Buried in the Church Cem, Honington

Ross, Flt/Sgt Harry
Age 36   30.6.43
Killed in a flying accident at Khartoum
Aerodrome. Buried Khartoum War Cem

Rossner, F/O Lewis
KIA in Greece
6.11.43

Rowe, F/O Harold
3.12.45

Rowson, Sgt (Pilot) Geoffrey Harold
18.1.43
Missing presumed killed on air ops

Rowson, F/O Vera
WAAF
5.12.42
Mentioned in dispatches
Buried at Hoop Lane Cem

Rubin, Sgt Jiri
311 Squadron, Czech
Age 24   29.8.43
Brookwood Mil Cem

Rubinstein, Sgt (Obs) John Daniel
-.9.43
Died in North Africa

Figure 293. Flt/O Vera Rowson, WAAF.

Rume, Sgt Myer
RCAF
25.5.44
Missing presumed killed on air ops

Sabin, P/O Samuel
235 Fighter Squadron
Age 24   24.5.43

Sabine, Sgt/Nav Louis
23 Fighter Squadron
Age 30   17.8.43
Buried Syracuse War Cem

Sagar, Sgt Joseph
                      16.3.44
Missing presumed killed on air
ops

Sajet, LAC Daniel
                      22.5.41
Killed in a flying accident in
Holland

Salaman, P/O Adam Herbert
                      -.7.42

Salz, Sgt Karl
                      7.8.43
Killed in a plane crash
Buried in Nassau, Brit West Indies

**Salzman, Flt/Sgt Rainard
Russell**
Age 29   5.7.43
Malta Mem

Sampson, WO Sidney
                      -.-.43
Killed in action

Samuel, F/O Bryan
KIA
                      15.1.43

Samuel, F/O F.
                      -.4.43
Missing presumed killed on air
ops

**Samuel, Sqdn/Ldr Norman D.,
DFC**
KIA
                      14.11.45

**Samuels, AC1 Emanuel
Solomon**
Age 33   15.8.41
Died in an accident
Buried in Willesden

Samuels, Sgt Reginald
RAFVR
                      15.3.44

Sandow, Sgt Alfred
                      1.3.43

Sassoon, Flt/Lt T.A.
                      -.9.43
Missing presumed killed on air
ops

**Sassoon, Flt/Sgt Joseph
Richard**

Savage, P/O WO Maurice
207 Squadron Bom. Cd.
Age 26   25.8.44
Missing presumed killed on air
ops
Buried Durnbach Mil Cem, Bayern

Savage, F/O Nav. Myer
254 Squadron Coastal Command
                      5.4.43
Killed
Air Force Memorial Runnymede

Schatzberg, P/O Seymour M.
                      -.12.43
Killed in action
Memorial at Brookwood, US
citizen.

Scheddle, Flt/Sgt Max
                      -.7.43
Killed in action
Buried in Ghent Mil Cem

Schefrin, Sgt (AG)
                      1940/41
Failed to return from a raid over
Germany
Missing presumed killed on air
ops

Schiller, AC2 Max
                      18.5.44
Died of injuries
Buried at Basrah, Iraq

Schlesinger, L.G.
RNZAF
                      10.5.44

**Schmitzler/Schnitzler, Sgt
Daniel**
KOAS
Buried Newton on Ouse 1951. No
Magen David. Parents in Israel

Schneer, Sgt Ronald Seymour
                      26.12.43
Died in an accident
Buried at Edmonton

Schneider, Sgt Maurice
Killed in a flying accident
Buried at Liverpool (Walton)
Jewish Cem

Schorr, Sgt (AG)
Age 26   23.4.44
Killed in action
Buried in the Reichswald Brit Mil
Cem

Schragger, Sgt S.
                      6.7.43
Died on active service
Buried at Madras Cem

Schumann, Sgt Pierre
                      27.8.42
Killed in an air crash
Buried in the Jewish Cem,
Bulawayo

Schumer, P/O Francis Herbert
600 Squadron
                      -.7.41
Killed in action, Battle of Britain

Schutan, AC2 Robert
DOAS
                      -.4.56

Schwind, Sgt/Obs Gordon Louis
59 Squadron
Age 21   26.5.40
Battle of Britain
Buried Warneton Communal Cem,
South of Ypres

Schwind, Lionel Harold
213 Squadron Battle of Britain

Seager, AC1 J.

Sealtiel, Sgt A.R.
                        22.5.44
Buried in Eindhoven Mil Cem

Seel, I.M.
SAAF
                        19.9.43
Buried Rhodes

Segal, Sgt Abraham
                        29.4.43
Killed in action
Buried in Graveslund Cem,
Esbjerg

Segal, Capt Leon
RAF Ferry Comm
                        3.5.42
Ottawa Mem

Segaloff, Sgt (Pilot) Louis
228 Squadron
                        12.6.44
Missing presumed killed on air
ops

Segar, Jack
                        5.7.41

Seigal, Sgt David
                        17.05.43

Seigler, R.
RCAF
                        10.8.44

**Seligman, Flt/Sgt Edouard
Zadoc**
                        8.10.45
Killed on active service

Setzkorn, 2nd Lt J.
SAAF
                        -.3.41
Killed in a flying accident at
Pretoria

**Shackman, Sqdn/Ldr Lawrence,
AFC**
                        31.10.44
Killed in action
Buried in Ohlsdorf Cem, Hamburg

Shaer, Sgt Joseph Israel
                        13.4.44
Killed on ops duties
Buried in the Jewish Cem,
Wolvercote, Oxford

Shafsby, LAC Denis S.
Age 19
Killed while training as a bomb
aimer
Buried at East London, S Africa

Shaiman, Sgt Leonard
                        23.4.44
Killed in an air crash
Buried in Willesden

Shapir, Flt/Sgt Morris William
458 Squadron, RAAF
                        15.8.42
Killed during ops in Libya

Sharp, P/O Leslie M.
96 Squadron
                        28.12.40
Killed on active service, Battle of
Britain
Buried in Carnmorey Jewish Cem

Shatz, Sgt (AG) Edward
929 Squadron
Age 23   5.3.44
Killed in action
Buried Poix de Picardie
Churchyard

Shaw, AC2 Michael
                        25.11.43
Killed in an accident
Buried in Borough Cem,
Cambridge

Shenfield, LAC James David
                        1.2.42
Killed in an aircraft accident,
South Africa

Shibko, Fl Sgt Maurice
                        4.4.43
Buried in Oxfordshire

Shieff, LAC Solomon
                        -.3.43
Killed on active service

Shire, Flt/Lt Lolly
                        10.6.45
Buried in Brookwood Mil Cem

Shovlin, F/O William
KIA
                        13.8.42

Shurman, P/O Charles
KOAS
                        -.1.52

Sidlin, AC2 Samuel
Age 23   24.9.40

Sieve, Flt/Sgt Leonard
                        -.1.42
Killed in action
Buried in Failsworth Jewish Cem,
Lancs

Sigler, Sgt Benjamin
                        31.5.42
Missing presumed killed on air
ops

Silver, Sgt/Pilot Leslie Raymond
9 Squadron Bomber Command
Age 20   29.4.42
Buried Aabenraa Cem

Silver, ACW2 Marion
WAAF
                        1.7.44
Died as the result of enemy action
Buried in Willesden

Silver, Sgt Maurice
                        30.9.44
Killed in an aircraft accident

Silverman, AC1 Anthony Myer
                        16.4.41

Figure 294. Sgt (AG) Edward Shatz, 929 Squadron.

Figure 295. Sgt (Nav) Sidney Smith.

Silverman, Sgt David Louis
102 Squadron Bomber Command
Age 21   28.4.44
Buried Maubeuge Centre Cem

Silverman, Flt/Lt Pilot Alex Louis
434 Squadron Bomber Command
Age 19   21.9.44
Buried Berlin War Cem

Silverman, P/O David Mark Claude, DFM
                                      9.11.44
DFM 18.11.43
Killed in action

Silverman, Flt/Sgt Philip
158 Squadron
                                      10.9.42
At sea off Ostend, Belgium, air operations

Silverman, Flt/Sgt Tony
                                      7.7.44
Killed in an air crash
Buried in Blackley Cem, Manchester

Simmons, LAC H.
                                      25.12.45

Simmons (Simmonds), Cpl Harold
Joined RFC in 1915 aged 16 yrs.
Served
WW2 1940–3 RAF
                                      23.5.43
Killed by enemy action
Buried at East Ham

Simmons, Sgt Robert Louis Nathaniel
                                      6.1.42
Died on ops
Buried at Feltwell, Norfolk

Singer, Sgt J.H.
Bomb Aimer

Singer, R. Maitland
RNZAF
                                      -.11.44

Sklan, Cpl Harry Samuel
                                      21.12.47
Died as the result of an accident
Buried in Willesden

Slater, Sgt (AG) Samuel
                                      24.10.41
Killed in an aircraft accident
Buried at Edmonton

Smith, Flt/Lt John Benjamin Joseph
169 Squadron
                                      8.2.45

Smith, Sgt (Nav) Sidney
Age 21   5.3.45
Killed on bombing raid over the Rhine, Germany
Buried at Heverlee War Cem

Smith, F/O Stuart Jack
Age 19   21.3.45
Killed on ops

Smollan, Sgt (AG) Dennis
(one of 3 brothers killed)
Age 21   7.2.43
Killed in action
Buried in Hazelrigg Cem, Gosforth

Smollan, Sgt/Obs Joshua (Jossy)
Age 29   1943
Missing after bomber raid Italy Anzio Beach. No known grave. He was one of family of six of whom three brothers on active service were killed.

Sober, Sgt (Obs) Ronny
                                      12.1.43
Killed in an air crash
Buried at Edmonton

Solomon, P/O Edmund
                                      3.8.43

Solomon, Air/Mech L.
SAAF
                                      7.10.41
Buried in Mersa Matruh Mil Cem

Solomon, F/O Leonard John
                                      1.6.44
Missing presumed killed on air ops

Solomon, Sgt M.
RAAF
                                      21.7.42
Died in a plane crash
Buried in the Jewish Cem, Plymouth

Solomon, Sgt Maurice Abraham
10 Bomber Squadron
Age 23   6.1.45

Solomon, P/O Neville David
                          20.8.40
Killed in action, Battle of Britain

Solomon, LAC Ronald
                          4.8.42

Solomon, F/O Sonny
                          11.9.44
Killed in action
Buried in Epinac Les Mines Cem

Solomons, Flt/Sgt Simon Stanley
RAAF
                          -.5.45
Killed in action

Somberg, Sgt David
ATC

Somers (Solomons), Sgt Louis John
                          17.11.43
Killed in an aircraft accident

Sonenthal, Sgt Alfred
                          26.11.44
Killed in an aircraft accident

Spillman, Sgt Godfrey Joseph
                          -.10.44
Killed on air ops

Stanley, Sgt (Obs) Richard B.
                          21.4.43
Buried in Willesden

Stanton, Flt/Sgt (Pilot) David
                          23.9.43
Missing presumed killed on air ops
                          23/24.9.43

Starr, F/O Joseph
                          13.6.44
Killed in an aircraft accident
Buried in the Jewish Cem, Nottingham

Figure 296. F/O Stuart Jack Smith.

Stein, Sgt Isadore
RCAF
                          8.11.41
Buried Rheinberg War Cem

Stein, F/O John F.
KIA
                          14.4.44

Stephens, P/O Gerald
Age 21   3.2.43
Killed in action over Holland

Stern, LAC Lawrence
                          7.5.42
Killed in a shooting accident
Buried in Willesden

Stern, LAC2 Morris
                          -.-.47
DOAS

Sternberg, AC1 Walter
                          21.4.43
Cremated at Golders Green, London

Stettiner, Flt/Sgt Henry F.R.
158 Squadron
                          30.3.43

Stevens, F/O Frederick
                          7.4.44

Figure 297. P/O Gerald Stephens.

Stirzacker, Cpl James Rowland
Age 33   7.11.44
Lost in HM LST 420

Stollar, Sgt Harry
                          25.2.44

Stone, Sgt Harold
                          2.9.42
Died in a plane crash when returning from a raid on Germany

Strauss, AC2 E.
                          -.3.41
Killed on active service
Suez Road, Palestine

Strauss, Flt/Lt Jacobus G.
                          11.2.45
KIA

Strauss-Leemans, P/O Georges
Czech RAF
                          18.10.42
Brookwood Mem Cem

Strock, H. Guilda
WAAF
                          15.7.46

Summers, Sgt Woolf Jack
                          24.2.44
Missing believed killed in action

Figure 298. Sgt/AG Jack Davis 1352674 RAFVR, 158 Squadron. Shot down 1 September 1943 Age 22.

Figure 299. Flt/Sgt Philip Silverman 158 Squadron RAF at sea, off Ostend, Belgium, 10 September 1942. His name is enshrined in The Book of Remembrance Royal Air Force, Church of St Clement Danes, The Strand, London.

Supkovitch, Sgt A.

19.2.44

Killed in action

Sussman, Flt/Lt Harold Edward
907 Squadron

30.5.45

Killed in an aircraft accident
Cremated at Golders Green, London

Sutton, Sgt/AG Ronald Marcus
Age 21   27.4.42
Killed in action in a Wellington bomber over Cologne
Buried in Rheinberg Mil Cem

Tabacznik, AC2 M.
274 Squadron

30.5.41

Tabner, Sgt Lawrence Harry
466 Squadron Bomber Command
Age 20   14.1.43

Tagger, AC1 Derek
DOAS

-.5.56

Body never found

Talgam, Sgt Edward
51 Squadron

3.8.43

Tallerman, F/O Bernard Edward

3.3.45

Missing presumed killed on air ops

Tankel, LAC Isadore

31.10.41

Killed in an air crash

Tannen, Sgt Leslie Marcus

5.2.45

Tattenbaum, AC2 Tobias
Age 20   22.4.41
Phaleron War Cem

Taylor, P/O David

-.2.42

Taylor, F/O H.

30.7.44

Figure 300. Sgt (AG) Ronald Marcus Sutton.

Taylor, Sgt/Pilot Irvine
104 Squadron
Age 21   21.3.43
Buried Sfax War Cem

Taylor, Sgt/WO Jack
Killed on active service
Buried in the Jewish Cem, Karachi

Tiller, P/O Henry
101 Squadron
Age 23   2.12.43
Killed during a bombing raid over Germany
Buried in Rheinberg War Cem

Toeg, F/O Joseph Philip

24.6.43

Missing presumed killed on air ops

Tofield, Sgt (Obs) Cyril

-.3.42

Killed on active service

Tomachepolsky, Sgt (Bomb Aimer) (Tomas) Favel
101 Squadron

3.11.43

Buried Reichswald War Cem

Torrance, Bernard
75 Squadron

Treister, Sgt (Pilot) Joel
RNZAF
7.8.42
Killed in an aircraft accident
Buried in Hazelrigg Cem, Gosforth

Trepp, LAC David
1.11.42
Buried Petach Tikva

Tritt (Trutt), Jack E.
RCAF
-.-.41
Buried in Southend Jewish Cem

Tym, Flt/Lt William E.
Killed on active service serving in
a Mosquito squadron
Buried in the Mil Cem, Malta

Ulrich, F/O Jack
7.3.43

Usher, Sgt Moses Lewis
(Canadian)

Valencia, Flt/Sgt R.B.
13.8.44
Killed on active service over
Germany
Buried in the Rheinberg Mil Cem

Van Gelder, Sgt Nathaniel
Age 22   28.12.42
Malta Mem

**Van Geun, Sgt (AG) Ferneaux
Montague**
RCAF
Age 21   -.-.42
Disappeared over Essen

Van Mentz, Flt/Lt Brian DFC
Battle of Britain
Age 24   26.4.41
Killed on active service
Buried in Brookwood Mil Cem

Victor, Andre Turkie
Died on Stafford RAF camp
1950–52

**Vineburg, Sgt (Pilot) Aaron
Joseph Ronnie**
1.10.42
Killed on air ops
Buried in Flensburg Mil Cem

Viner, Sgt/WO Norman
Age 22   21.1.42
Missing presumed killed on air
ops over Germany

Waldman, Sgt Sidney Solomon
78 Squadron Bomber Command
Age 26   1.10.42
Buried Kiel War Cem

Waldorf, Sgt Leonard
199 Squadron
13.5.43
Killed in action
Buried in Harderwijk Cem

Walford, F/O (Pilot) Arthur David
2.2.43
Killed in Ontario, Canada

Wallen, Sgt Emanuel
31.8.43
Buried Rheinberg War Cem

Waller, Sgt Alan Abraham
Age 22   2.1.44
Rear gunner of a Lancaster
bomber of the Pathfinder Force,
Bomber Command
Shot down over Berlin on his 32nd
mission

**Walters (Cohen), Sgt (Flt/Eng)
Lionel**
Age 22   23.4.44
Killed in action
Flew that mission so that another
member of his crew could get
married
Buried at Goirle, Tilburg, Holland

**Wayman, Flt/Lt Michael Myer
DFC**
139 Squadron
-.-.43

**Wayne, Sgt (Rad/Op) Marks
(Weinberg)**
153 Squadron
Age 27   23.7.42
Served as a War Reserve
Constable 1939
Queen's Roy Regt 1940
RAF September 1941
Killed in a flying accident in
Fighter Command
Buried at East Ham

Webb, Sgt (WO) Joseph Garcia
Age 22   18.11.44
Died on a mission
Buried in the Jewish Cem,
Willesden

Weber, Cpl Peter
16.8.46

Weinberg, LAC Alec
Age 36   7.11.44
Lost in HM LSI 420

Weiner, AC2 S.E.
16.3.41

Weinstock, AC2 Jacob
-.11.45
Died in an accident
Buried in Willesden

Weizman, Flt/Lt Michael O.
502 Squadron
-.11.42
Missing presumed killed on air
ops over the Bay of Biscay
(Son of President Chaim
Weizmann of Israel)

Weldon, Aubrey/Arnold, DFM
101 Squadron

Werner, P/O Raymond
11.6.40

White, F/O Bernard Arthur
28.5.44
Missing presumed killed on air
ops

White, Sgt Joseph Alexander
180 Squadron
27.2.43

Figure 301. F/O (Pilot) Arthur David Walford.

Figure 302. Sgt Alan Abraham Waller.

Figure 303. Sgt (Flt/Eng) Lionel Walters (Cohen).

Figure 304. Sgt (Rad/O) Marks Wayne, 153 Squadron.

Figure 305. Sgt Wayne as a private in the Queen's Royal Regiment.

Figure 306. The Grave of Sgt Lionel Walters at Goirle, Tilburg, Holland.

Wiener, F/O WO Derek Abraham
103 Squadron Bomber Command
Age 21   23.5.44
Buried in Reichswald Forest War Cem

Wilk, F/O Jack
                                16.8.40
Killed in action, Battle of Britain

Williams, LAC Nathaniel
90 Squadron
                                9.8.42

Williams, Sgt (WO/AG) Samuel
Age 22   21.1.42
Missing presumed killed in action over Germany
Buried in the Canadian War Cem, Holton

Winberg, Sgt Israel
                                -.7.40
Missing presumed killed on air ops

Figure 307. Sgt (WO/AG) Samuel Williams.

Winston, Sgt Joseph Charles
11.4.41
Missing presumed dead after evacuation of the Brit Expeditionary Force from France

Wiseman, Flt/Lt (Act. Sqdn/Ldr) Edward Wolf
142 Squadron 82176
Age 29   17.4.44
Missing over Yugoslavia
Buried Belgrade War Cem

Wixen, Capt Jack
RAF Ferry Service
-.-.41
Only Jewish grave on Isle of Arran

Wolff, AC1 Benjamin
28.6.43

Wolff, Harold Joseph
25.9.43

Wolff, 1st Officer Harry/Henry
ATA
28.10.41

Wolff, AC2 Victor
Age 33   30.5.44
Buried Golders Green Crematorium

Wolfson, F/O Leo
1.7.44
Killed on air ops
Buried in the Brit Cem, Marquise, Pas de Calais

Wolman, Sgt Morris Louis
20.11.43
Killed in an aircraft accident
Buried at Rainham

Woolf, Sgt Isaac Sidney
-.1.43
Killed on active service

Woolf, Flt/Sgt Stanley E.
502 Squadron
27.12.43

Yaffee, AC2 Norman
30.6.43

Zahl, Flt/Sgt Ronald Aaron
434 Squadron
29.9.43
Killed on air ops
Buried in Reichswald Forest Brit Mil Cem

Zalsberg, Sgt (WO/Nav) Lewis, DFM
9.7.43
Navigator of the plane which crashed when carrying General Sikorski, who was killed
Buried in the Jewish Cem, Gibraltar

Zamek, Sgt (Obs) Ian Alexander
58 Squadron
2.10.40
Killed in action

Zamek, Sgt (Pilot) Norman
-.8.42
Killed on active service
Buried in the Jewish Cem, Calcutta

Zeffert, F/O Leslie Charles
8.7.44
Missing presumed killed on air ops

Zuker, Cpl Ronald Simon
14.9.42
Killed in an accident
Buried in the Hazelrigg Jewish Cem

Ziegler, F/O
(RAF Scientist)

The Palestine Jewish Volunteers

Note: There are many problems with differential spellings of Hebrew names; only careful searches on the CWGC website will reveal them.

Abbadin, Pte K.A.
PC
           -.-.42
Died in a POW camp

Abbai (Abdo), Pte Yaacov
The Pal Regt
           15.2.44
Died in Palestine as a result of an accident

Abel, L/Cpl Shimon
RASC
           2.1.43
KIA in the Western Desert
Buried Benghazi War Cem

Abdin, Q.H.Z.
PC
Pal11005

Aber, Sgt Mordechai
RASC
           1.5.43
KIA at sea

Abramovitz, OS Kalman
MN
SS *Har Zion*
Age 21   31.8.40

Ackerman, Pte Benjamin
RASC
           1.5.43
KIA at sea

Ackerman, Pte Dov
PC
           12.4.45
Died in Germany in a POW camp

Adami, Spr A.N.
RE
           -.1.42

Akhras, Spr H.M.
RE/Pal
Buried Benghazi War Cem

Altgenug, Pte Hans C.
RASC
           1.5.43
KIA at sea

Altmann, Spr Richard
RE
           11.3.43
Died in Cracow, Poland in a POW camp

Altschul, Cpl L.
RASC
           18.7.45
Died in Italy as the result of an accident

Altschuler, Pte Yigal
RASC
           1.5.43
KIA at sea

Amami, L/Cpl Eliahu
RE
           9.2.42
Died in Syria as the result of an accident

Amar, Pte Nissim
RAMC
           16.6.40
Died in Egypt

Anikast, Pte A.
PC
           13.10.42
Died in the Western Desert

Apotin, A.
PC
           -.-.41

Arman, Eng Ernest (aka Erman)
MN
SS *Har Zion*
           31.8.40

Artal, Spr Tuvia
RE
           29.6.46
KIA

Ashkenasi
           -.-.41
Missing presumed dead in Crete

Askerov, Cpl Shimon
RASC
           1.5.43
KIA at sea

Auerbuch, L/Cpl David (aka Urboch)
RASC
           1.5.43
KIA at sea

Ausburg, Spr Bela
Jewish Inf Bde Group/RE
Age 21   -.-.46
Died in Great Britain. Buried Liverpool (Walton)
Hebrew Burial Ground

Avissar (Avizar), Spr Shlomo
RE
27.8.43
Died in Syria from illness

Avni, Cpl Shraga
RASC
1.5.43
KIA at sea

Babahikian, Dvr S.H.
RASC/Pal
29.11.43
Buried Heliopolis War Cem Egypt

Bacharach, Pte Erich
RASC
1.5.43
KIA at sea

Back, Gnr J.
RA
7.12.44
Bari War Cem

Backshi, Pte Shimon
RASC
25.11.45
Died in Egypt as the result of an accident

Bagdady, Spr
RE
21.7.41
KIA in Greece

Bahiry, Cpl Tzvi
RASC
1.5.43
KIA at sea

Bakis, Pte Ury
RASC
1.5.43
KIA at sea

Bankhalter, Spr Nathan
RE
24.6.43
Died in the Western Desert as the result of an accident

Barash, Cpl Yitzchak
Jewish Inf Bde Group
28.10.44
Died in Palestine due to illness

Barcat, Pte Avraham
RASC
7.11.42
Died in Egypt as the result of an accident

Bardicev/Berdichev, Abba (aka Lt Willis)
SOE
19.1.45
Died in Slovakia on a special mission

Barzilay, A.
SOE
Killed in action
Not commemorated by CWGC

Basat, Pte Ruth
ATS
29.4.43
Died in Palestine as a result of an accident

Baum, Theodor
12.5.44

Baum, Capt Gerard
RAMC
Age 30   24.1.45
Died in Eritrea as the result of an accident
Buried Asmara War Cem

Baumgarten, Pte Leopold
RASC
1.5.43
KIA at sea

Beck, Pte Yaacov
RA, Jewish Bde
7.12.44
Died in Italy as the result of an accident

Becker, Capt Meir D.
RAMC
23.11.43
KIA at sea

Beckierman, Pte Moshe
RASC
14.5.41
Died in Greece in a POW camp

Bein, AB Conrad
MN
SS *Har Zion*
Age 18   31.8.40

Beinstock, Greaser Yitzhak Aaron
MN SS *Har Zion*
Age 26   31.8.40

Ben-Avraham, Pte Avraham
PC
23.5.44
Died in Algeria from illness

Ben Baruch, Pte Rochela
ATS
23.11.45

Ben-Bassat, Rafael
-.12.45
Died in Palestine as the result of an accident

Ben-Hakfar, Cpl Yaakov
RASC
1.5.43
KIA at sea

Ben-Michael, Pte Y.
PC
10.5.42
Missing, presumed dead, at sea

Ben-Nun, Pte Eliahu
Jewish Inf Bde Group
25.12.42
Died in Egypt as the result of an accident

Ben-Nun, Spr Yitzchak L.
RE
19.5.44
Died in Egypt as the result of an accident

Ben-Shachar, Pte Eliezer
PC
28.4.41
KIA in Greece

Ben-Shalom, Pte Eliyahu
RASC
-.-.44
Died in Palestine as the result of an accident

Ben-Shalom, Pte Sara
ATS
29.5.42
Died in Egypt as the result of an accident
Buried Tel-el-Kebir War Cem

Ben Tzvi, Pte Yaacov
RASC
1.5.43
KIA at sea

Ben-Yaacov, Tzvi
SOE
9.1.45
Died in Slovakia on a special task

Ben-Yehuda, Spr Eliyahu
RE
-.-.41
Died in Greece in a POW camp

Ben-Yisrael, Pte Yakov
RASC
1.5.43
KIA at sea

Ben-Yossef, Pte Arye
Commando
1.5.41
KIA in Ethiopia

Berger, Pte Cornelia
ATS
3.9.44
Died in Egypt as the result of an accident
Buried el-el-Kebir War Cem

Berghausen, Eng Herbert
MN
SS *Har Zion*
31.8.40

Bergman, Pte M.
RASC
-.-.41
Missing, presumed dead, in Greece

Berlovitz, Cpl
PC
-.-.41
KIA in Greece

Betzer, L/Cpl Moshe
RASC
1.5.43
KIA at sea

Birnbaum (Buzsuka), ACW1 Elisabeth
WAAF
Age 23   19.10.44
Buried Khayat Beach War Cem

Birntzweig, Pte Victor
PC
5.10.40
KIA in the Western Desert

Bistritler, Pte Shmuel
Infantry
4.8.41
Died in Palestine as the result of an accident

Bitran, Spr Moshe Y.
RE
2.7.41
Died in Greece in a POW camp

Blank, Sgt Shoshanah Sara
ATS
20.12.44
Died in Palestine as the result of an accident

Blili, Spr Eliyah V.
RE

Bloch, Pte Oscar
PC
13.5.45
Died in Great Britain from illness after being a POW

Blustein, Pte Tzvi
Jewish Inf Bde Group
9.3.46
Died in Holland as the result of an accident

Bogri, Spr
RE
-.-.43

Bosses (Boshes),Cpl Benjamin
RE
15.7.43
Died in Libya as the result of an accident

Botnik (Butnik), Pte Yaakov
Jewish Inf Bde Group
19.3.45
KIA in Italy

Bransco, Spr M.
RE
30.5.42
Died in Egypt as the result of an accident

Braunfeld, Pte David
RASC
1.5.43
KIA at sea

Breier, Cpl Haym M.
RE
26.1.45
Died in Germany whilst escaping
from a POW camp

Breitman, Sgt Yosef
PC
-.2.41
KIA in the Western Desert

Brod, L/Cpl Chayim
Jewish Inf Bde Group
20.3.45
KIA in Italy

Bronstein, Sgt Yosef
RE
3.3.44
Died in Palestine from illness

Brull (Bruell), Spr Wilhelm
RE
23.6.43
Died in Egypt from illness

Buchbinder, Pte Reuven
RASC
1.5.43
KIA at sea

Buchs (Bucks), Pte Herman
PC
10.6.43
Died in Palestine from illness

Buchstab, Pte Alexander
Jewish Inf Bde Group
11.4.43
Died in Palestine as the result of
an accident

Busbi, Pte Meir (aka Busany)
RASC
1.5.43
KIA at sea

Butovitzky-Stein, Pte Chava
ATS
24.3.43
Died in Egypt as the result of an
accident

Caftan, Pte Aharon
PC
23.10.45
Died in Palestine from illness

Cagan, Pte A.
RAMC
13.7.42
KIA in the Western Desert
Alamein Memorial

Cahana, Pte Yosef
RASC
1.5.43
KIA at sea

Caspi, Pte Chayim (aka Kaspi)
RASC
1.5.43
KIA at sea

Chabas, Pte Salim
PC
-.-.42
Died in the Western Desert

Chagigi, L/Cpl S.H.H.
RE
25.9.41
Died in a POW camp

Chalaf, Moshe A.
RASC

Chalma, Sgt Shlomo George
PC/Pal
31.1.45
Buried Tel-el-Kebir War Cem

Changel, Sgmn Avraham
RCOS
27.4.44
KIA at sea

Changel, Pte Chayim
RASC
1.5.43
KIA at sea

Chanovitz, Samuel
SOE
18.5.41
KIA at sea

Charad, Naim
PC
Died in Greece whilst escaping
from a POW camp

Charlap, Pte Itzchak
RASC
1.5.43
KIA at sea

Chavan, A.A.
13.4.43

Chayim, Cpl Mordechai
RASC
1.5.43
KIA at sea

Cherma, Pte Israel
Pal/Rgt
20.11.46

Chibowsky, Urko
MN

Chugi, Pte Ben Tzion
RASC
12.10.42
Died in Egypt as the result of an
accident

Cohen, Pte Albert
PC
12.4.45
Died in Germany in a POW camp

Cohen, Pte Asher
RASC
1.4.43
KIA at sea

Cohen, Dvr Felix Israel
RASC/Pal
Age 19   1.5.43

Cohen, Mordechai
SOE
18.5.41
KIA at sea

Cohen, Dvr Moshe
RASC
24.2.41
KIA in the Western Desert
Buried Tobruk War Cem

Cohen, Pte Moshe
RASC
1.5.43
KIA at sea

Cohen, Dvr Raphael
462 Coy RASC
1.5.43

Cohen, Pte Yechye (Peter)
RASC
1.5.43
KIA at sea

Cohen, Cpl Yosef
Jewish Inf Bde Group
7.4.45
KIA in Italy

Czerjek, Spr Herman
1039 Port Coy RE/Pal
1.1.43
Athens Memorial

Dabach, Spr M.
RE
-.4.41
KIA in Greece

Dachbash, Pte Shmuel
RASC
28.4.41
KIA in Greece

Dagany, Pte Tzvi
RASC
3.12.41
Died in Egypt as the result of an accident

Dahan, Stkr/2 Yaakov
RN/Pal
HMS *Woolwich*
Age 20   27.5.43
Buried Hodra War Cem Alexandria

Dambovsky, Capt Shlomo
RAOC
10.4.46
Died in Egypt as the result of an accident

Daniel, N.
PC
-.4.41
KIA in Greece

Danziger, Sgt Issachar
PC
29.5.41
KIA in Greece.
Athens Memorial

Davdovitz, Pte Chayim
Jewish Inf Bde Group
-.10.45
Died as result of an accident

Davidov, Spr Chayim Y.
RE
11.10.45
Died in Iraq as the result of an accident

Dehahn, Pte Chayim
RASC
1.5.43
KIA at sea

Deutsch, Pte Fritz
RASC
1.5.43
KIA at sea

Deutsch, Cpl Yosef
RAOC
13.1.43
Died in Egypt as the result of an accident

Deutsch, Pte Zerach
PC
15.11.42
Died in Egypt as the result of an accident

Diener, L/Cpl Wolff
RE
27.4.41
Died in Egypt as the result of an accident

Digil, H.
4.9.43
Died in Germany whilst in a POW camp

Dodin (Dudin), Pte Yehuda
RAMC
21.8.43
Died in Iran as the result of an accident

Dorany, Pte Menashe
PC
-.-.43
KIA in Greece

Dovkovsky (Dobkovsky), Spr Arye
RE
4.4.44
Died in Palestine as the result of an accident

Driki, Herrman
Died in Yugoslavia whilst escaping from a POW camp

Drotman, Pte Dov
RASC
1.5.43
KIA at sea

Drucker, Pte Mordechai
RASC
1.5.43
KIA at sea

Duchan, Pte Yehoshua
RASC
10.5.43
KIA at sea

Dunda (Donda), Pte Y.
RAMC
3.3.45
Died in Italy as the result of an accident

Edri, Pte Yehoshua
RASC
1.5.43
KIA at sea

Ehrlich, Dvr K.
RASC
11.7.42
KIA in Egypt
Buried El Alamein War Cem

Ehrman (Arman), Spr Aharon
RE
                                    26.1.45
Died in Germany whilst escaping
from a POW camp

Eisen, Arye
SOE
                                    18.5.41
KIA at sea

Eisenberg, Pte Dov
Pioneer Corps
                                    28.6.44
Died in Poland escaping from a
POW camp

Elimelech, Spr Avraham
RE
                                    19.7.41
Died in Greece whilst escaping
from a POW camp

Elkind, Sgt Yitzchak
RE
                                    30.12.41
Died in Poland in a POW camp

Ellison, OS Paul
MN
SS *Har Zion*
                                    31.8.40

**Elmasor (Almazar), Lt M.
Alexander (aka Schlesinger)**
RAMC
                                    -.5.41
KIA at sea

El-Mishali, Pte Masaud
PC
                                    8.3.43
Died whilst a POW in Germany
Buried in Cracow Rakowicki Cem

Elsner, Cpl Hans
RASC
                                    1.5.43
KIA at sea

Epstein, Pte Milada
ATS
Age 37   14.6.43
Died in Egypt from illness
Suez War Memorial Cem

Ettinger, Pte Menachem
PC
Missing, presumed dead

Ettlinger, Pte Dora Liese
ATS
                                    14.10.45
Died in Egypt
Buried Heliopolis War Cem

Fabian, Pte Yaacov
RASC
                                    -.-.41
Died whilst a POW in Greece

Federmann, Pte Herbert
RA Long Range Desert Group
Age 22   24.10.43
KIA on the Isle of Kos
Buried Rhodes War Cem

Feibek, Pte Hanoch
Jewish Inf Bde Group
                                    10.7.45
Died in Germany as the result of
an accident

Feinberg, Cpl Zvi
RE
                                    6.12.44
Died in Egypt as the result of a
train accident

Feldman, Pte Israel
RASC
                                    1.5.43
KIA at sea

Fell, Dvr Akiva Kurt (aka Fehl)
RASC
                                    6.8.42
KIA in the Western Desert

Fenichel, Pte N.
PC
                                    10.3.45
Buried Cracow British War Cem
Poland

Ferber, Pte Chanan (Hans)
RASC
                                    12.11.42
Died in the Western Desert as the
result of an accident

Fernbeck, Pte Arie (Ernst)
RASC
                                    1.5.43
KIA at sea

Filo, Eliyahu
                                    -.-.43
Died as the result of an accident

Filo, Spr Shimeon
RE
                                    1.4.42
Died whilst escaping in Greece
from a POW camp

Finkelstein (Funkel), Spr Hans
RE
                                    15.3.45
Died in Egypt from illness

Fisch, L/Cpl Chaim
RASC
                                    6.8.42
KIA in the Western Desert
Buried El Alamein War Cem

Fischer, Pte Morris
Commando Pal 10750
Age 19   13.5.41
KIA in Ethiopia

Fischer (Fisher), Pte Zvi
Jewish Infantry Bde Group
                                    15.10.45
Died as the result of an accident
Buried Eindhoven Jewish Cem

Fleischman, Pte Shmuel
RASC
                                    17.5.45
Died in Palestine as the result of
an accident

Forscher, Pte M.
RAMC
                                    15.11.43
Died in Italy as a result of an
accident

Frank, Spr Siegfried
RE
9.3.43
Died in Iraq due to illness
Buried Basra War Cem

Freibach (Frack), Pte A.
RASC
1.10.40
Died in Palestine from illness

Freizer, Pte Abraham
Infantry
13.4.42
Died in Palestine as the result of
an accident

Frenkel, Reuven
8.9.45

Frenkel, Spr Yaakov Julius
RE
19.5.44
Died in Egypt as the result of an
accident

Freud, Pte Ehud
PC
10.5.42
KIA in the Western Desert

Freund, Pte Elieser (Eliyahu)
RASC
Age 20   17.7.43
KIA in Sicily
Buried Syracuse War Cem

Freund, Spr Yehoshua
RE
22.5.44
Killed in an accident in Syria

Fried, Pte Abraham
RASC
29.1.43
Died in Palestine from illness
Buried Tel Aviv (Nahlat Yitzhak)
Cem

Friedler, Pte Joseph
RASC
1.5.43
KIA at sea

Friedman, Pte Alexander
Jewish Inf Bde Group
29.3.43
Died in Palestine as the result of
an accident
Buried Tel Aviv (Nahlat Yitzhak)
Cem

Friedman, Pte Shlomo
Jewish Inf Bde Group
9.5.45
Died in Italy as the result of an
accident

Friedman, Shmuel
PC
6.6.45
Died in Switzerland from illness

Furstenfeld, Spr Aharon
RE
9.2.42
Murdered in Palestine

Furt, Pte Moshe
Commando
KIA in Italy

Futman/Furman, Cpl H.
Jewish Inf Bde Group
26.10.45
Died in Holland from illness

Gadol, Pte Yehuda
Jewish Inf Bde Group
21.10.43
Died in Palestine as the result of
an accident

Gambel, S/Sgt John Alan
Jewish Inf Bde Group
17.4.45
KIA in Italy

Gans-Schiller, AC2 Max Meir
RAF
Age 19   18.5.44
Basra War Cem

Gargal, Sgt Avraham
Infantry
31.12.41
Died in Palestine as the result of
an accident

Gavriel, Pte Norbert
PC
-.11.41
Died in Greece, escaping from a
POW camp

Gelbard, Arye
SOE
18.5.41
KIA at sea

Gelbart, Pte Avraham
PC
24.4.42
Died in Greece, escaping from a
POW camp

Gelbart, Cpl Pinchas
RASC
1.5.43
KIA at sea

Genussow, Capt Israel Solomon
Green Howards/KAR Madagascar
Age 28   30.7.44
Buried Diego Suarez War Cem

Gerber, H.
REME
Pal 64122
2.8.45
Tel El Kebir War Cem

Geshpen, Pte Yosef
RASC
1.5.43
KIA at sea

Ghatatheh, Pte A.
PC
6.5.41
Died in a POW camp in Greece

Gilinks (Gilinski), Pte Gershon Y.
Jewish Inf Bde Group
13.4.45
KIA in Italy

Gitlitz, Pte Israel
RASC
1.5.43
KIA at sea

Giyori, Cpl Itzchak (aka Trent, Michael, SOE)
RASC
Died in Greece

Gjesin, Spr Michael
RE
10.4.43
Died in Egypt from illness

Goferman, Gnr Asher
RA
2.4.45
Died in Cyprus as the result of an accident

Gold, Pte Avraham
Jewish Inf Bde Group
17.6.45
Died in Italy as the result of an accident

Goldman, Sgt Y.
PC
29.4.41
KIA in Greece

Goldman, Pte Yaacov
RASC
1.5.43
KIA at sea

Goldring, Pte Asher
Jewish Inf Bde Group
31.3.45
KIA in Italy

Goldring, Sgt Chanuch
RE
23.1.43
Died in Palestine as the result of an accident

Goldschmidt, Mordechai
PC
24.10.45
Died in Palestine from illness

Goldstein, Pte Asher
PC
24.8.41
Died escaping from a POW camp

Goldstein, L/Cpl Paul
RASC
1.5.43
KIA at sea

Goldstein (Ferenz), Peretz
SOE
1.3.45
Died in Germany on a special mission

Goldbov (Golobov), Pte Yehuda
Jewish Inf Bde Group
11.4.45
KIA in Italy

Golomb, Pte Moshe Leib
Jewish Inf Bde Group
3.2.45
Killed by mines in Italy

Gonshirovsky, Pte Herbert
PC
28.3.45
Died in Germany in a POW camp

Gorali, Pte Moshe
PC
24.4.41
KIA in Greece

Gordin, Yaacov
SOE
18.5.41
KIA at sea

Gorfein, Cpl Itzchak
Jewish Inf Bde Group
12.4.45
KIA in Italy

Gottfreund, Leo
RASC
Died in the Western Desert

Gotthelf, Spr Martin
RE
23.4.42
Died in Palestine as the result of an accident

Gottlieb, Pte Eliyahu
Commando SIG
12.6.42
KIA in the Western Desert
Alamein Memorial

Gottlieb, Cpl Tzvi
RASC
1.5.43
KIA at sea

Graber, Cpl H.
RAOC
2.8.45
Died in Egypt from illness

Grabler, Spr Itzchak
RE
29.1.45
Died in Palestine from illness

Granovsky, Cpl Emanuel
RASC
1.5.43
KIA at sea

Grav, Pte David Y.
Jewish Bde
-.4.46
Died in Italy as the result of an accident

Greenberg, Pte Moshe
RASC
1.5.43
KIA at sea

Grishenfeld, Pte Aharon
10.2.43
Killed in Palestine by Arabs

Gruber, L/Cpl Gavriel Otto
RASC
1.5.43
KIA at sea

Grundeland, Pte Aharon
RASC
1.5.43
KIA at sea

Grundich (Grunhut), Lt Jindrich
RAF – SOE Para
20.10.44

Gurevitch, Pte Baruch
RASC
1.5.43
KIA at sea

Gustin, Sgt Yosef
Jewish Inf Bde Group
29.3.45
KIA Italy

Guterman, L/Cpl Mordechai
RASC
1.5.43
KIA at sea

Haass, Cpl Peter (Hess)
Commando SIG
12.6.42
KIA in the Western Desert

Haber, Pte Yosef
RASC
1.5.43
KIA at sea

Hacker, Itzchak
SOE
18.5.41
KIA at sea

Hadjaj, Pte Shimon
PC/Pal
18.3.43
Buried Choloy War Cem

Hafou, Pte O.H.
Pal Regt
31.3.45
Buried Hodra War Cem Alexandria

Haftel, Pte Yosef
RASC
1.5.43
KIA at sea

Hahn, Spr P.
RE
7.2.43
Died in Libya from illness

Hakim, Eliahu
PC
Buried in Cairo

Halun, Pte Shlomo
RASC
11.12.44
Died in Italy as the result of an accident

Hamadani, Pte Tzion E.
PC
24.3.44
Died in Germany in a POW camp

Hananel, Sgmn Avram
RCOS/Pal
Att 106 LAA Regt RA
26.4.41
Athens Memorial

Hansel, Avraham
-.1.45
KIA in France

Harar, Pte S. M.
PC
2.4.45
Died in Palestine from illness

Harris, Aubrey MBE (aka Silver?)
Pal. Police
12.12.44

Hassan, Pte H.S.
PC
Alamein

Hauber, Pal Police Sgt Emmanuel
12.11.47

Hausknecht, Spr Meir
RE
12.1.43
Died in Palestine from illness

Heidman, Pte Gershon
RASC
1.5.43
KIA at sea

Heilbron, 4th Eng/O Mordechai
MN
SS *Har Zion*
Age 25
31.8.40

Heim, Pte Aharon
Jewish Inf Bde Group
27.7.43
Died in Palestine as the result of an accident

Heiman, Pte Paul
RASC
1.5.43
KIA at sea

Herlinger, Gnr Max
RA
3.4.45

Herman, Pte Chayim
PC
13.6.45
Died from illness in a POW camp in Germany

Hermann, Dvr Lucas
Pal. RASC

Hershkovitz, S/Sgt Eliyahu MM
Jewish Inf Bde Group
24.4.45
Killed in Italy by mines
Buried Ravenna War Cem

Hershkovitz, Pte Tzvi
RAOC
17.5.42
Died in Palestine as the result of an accident

Herzog (Herzig), Pte Tzvi A.
PC
12.5.44
Died in Germany in a POW camp

Hess, Pte Chanoch
RASC
12.5.41
KIA in the Western Desert

Hewinsohn, Dvr E.
RASC/Pal
2.11.45
Buried Benghazi War Cem

Hirshfeld, Pte Tzvi
Jewish Inf Bde Group
22.4.45
Died in Italy as the result of an
accident

Hirschler, Pte Peretz
Jewish Inf Bde Group
24.11.45
Died in Austria as the result of an
accident

Hochberg
Died prob. Pal.

Hochberg, Pte Moshe
RAOC
26.4.41
Died in Greece

Hochman, Pte Nachum
RASC
7.8.42
KIA in the Western Desert
Buried El Alamein War Cem

Hofberg, Yaacov
RASC
1.5.43
KIA at sea

Horn, Pte Moritz
PC
4.5.41
Died in Greece while escaping
from a POW Camp

Hurvitz, Cpl Moshe
RE
13.3.44
Died in Egypt as the result of an
accident
Buried Tel El Kabir War Memorial
Cem

Isber, Pte Israel
RASC
1.5.43
KIA at sea

Ismirly, Spr Yaacov
RE
19.12.44
Died in Egypt as the result of an
accident

Israel, Pte Avraham
PC
8.2.41
KIA in the Western Desert
Buried Tobruk War Cem

Isvitzky, Pte Michael
Jewish Inf Bde Group
29.3.45
KIA in Italy

Jacobs, Sgt Shlomo
PC
29.8.40
Died in the Western Desert
Buried El Alamein War Cem

Jalouskay, Marian
1.10.45
Killed by mines

Jellineck, Pte Nandor
PC
15.7.41
Died in Egypt as the result of an
accident

Jellineck, Pte Shlomo
PC
7.11.42
Died in Palestine from illness

Joudiyeh, Spr A.I.
RE/Pal
Buried Heliopolis War Cem

Kachor (Katchoure), Pte Moshe
PC
5.10.40
KIA in the Western Desert
Buried El Alamein War Cem

Kagan, A.
RAMC
13.7.42

Kahn, Dvr Peter Stefan
462 Coy RASC/Pal
1.5.43

Kalinsky, Pte Meir
Jewish Inf Bde Group
21.10.43
Died in Palestine as the result of
an accident

Kalman, Pte Carl Heinz
RASC
7.5.45
Died in Egypt from illness

Kalman, Pte L.
ATS
24.12.42
Died in Egypt as the result of an
accident

Kalter, Pte Zalman
Jewish Inf Bde Group
20.3.45
Killed in action in Italy
Buried Coriano Ridge War Cem

Kaminsky, Pte M.
PC
9.1.42
Died in Egypt from illness

Kant, Pte Arthur
PC
31.8.42
Died in Egypt from illness

Kantorovitz, Pte Chana
ATS
23.1.44
Died in Palestine from illness

Kantorovitz, Pte Zeev
RASC
28.11.42
Died in the Western Desert as the
result of an accident

Kanza, L/Cpl J.
RASC
30.12.42
Benghazi War Cem

Kaplan, Pte Moshe Alter
RASC
1.5.43
KIA at sea

Figure 308. The entrance to the Military Cemetery at Ravenna (Martin Sugarman).

Figure 309. Graves of Pal Jewish Volunteers at Ravenna Military Cemetery (Jewish Inf Bde Group) (Martin Sugarman).

Karfunkel, Spr J.G.
RE
13.12.41
Died in Palestine from illness

Karter, Pte Ervin
PC
31.12.43
Died whilst a POW in Germany

Karvany, Pte Aharon
RASC
1.5.43
KIA at sea

Kasp, Sgt Asher Yechiel, DCM, MM (aka Kasap)
Jewish Inf Bde Group
21.11.43
KIA in Italy

Katz, Pte Rozelle
ATS
15.7.43
Died in Egypt from illness

Kaufman, Pte Lieber
RASC
1.5.43
KIA at sea

Kauterman (Kortman), Pte Stephania
ATS
4.10.45
Killed in a plane crash

Kbuk, Sgmn A.
Royal Signals
-.6.42

Keller, Pte Moshe Kurt
PC
12.4.45
Died whilst a POW in Germany

Keln, Pte Helmut (aka Koln)
RASC
1.5.43
KIA at sea

Kempinsky, Pte Gavriel
RASC
1.5.43
KIA at sea

Kendil (Gendel), Pte Joseph
PC
8.2.41
KIA in the Western Desert

Kenseh, L/Cpl Joseph
RASC
30.12.42
KIA in the Western Desert

Kertesh, Pte Robert
RASC
13.7.43
KIA in the Western Desert

Kimmelman, Pte Daniel
RAOC
10.10.42
Died in Egypt as the result of an accident

Kipnis, Lt Abner Yaakov
Infantry
3.6.42
Died in Palestine as the result of an accident

Kitay, Pte Moshe
RASC
1.5.43
KIA at sea

Klariss, Spr Zalman
RE
11.5.44
Died in Palestine as the result of an accident

Klass, Spr David
RE
13.9.45
Died in Palestine from illness

Klein, Pte Joseph George
PC
12.2.41
KIA in the Western Desert

Kleiner, L/Cpl Noach
RASC
11.1.46
Died in Italy as the result of an accident

Klinger, AB Rudolph
MN
SS *Har Zion*
Age 19   31.8.40

Klorfeld, Pte Menachem
Jewish Inf Bde Group
13.5.46
Died in Holland as the result of an accident

Koffler, Gershon
SOE
18.5.41
KIA at sea

Kohn, Pte Albert
PC
12.4.45
Durnbach War Cem

Kolman, Pte Yitzchak
PC
12.4.45
Died whilst a POW in Germany

Kolodny, Spr Moshe
RE
3.11.44
Died in Egypt as the result of an accident

Kolsky, Pte Yaacov
RASC
3.4.43
Died in the Western Desert as the result of an accident

Konfino (Confino), Cpl Gavriel
PC
14.4.42
Died in Egypt as the result of an accident

Kopelick, Pte Pinchas
RASC
1.5.43
KIA at sea

Koppel, S/Sgt Shlomo
Jewish Inf Bde Group
19.7.46
Died in Great Britain from illness

Korakin, Menachem
SOE
                                    18.5.41
KIA at sea

Korichoner, Pte Shmuel
RASC
                                    1.5.43
KIA at sea

Kornitz (Kornovitz), Capt Leon
*RAMC Attached Free French
Forces*
                                    17.3.42

Koslovitz, Eliyahu
                                    -.6.44
KIA in Italy

Koslovitz, Cpl Mattatiahu
Jewish Inf Bde Group
                                    22.5.45
KIA in Italy

Kosrocha, Z.
                                    12.4.45
KIA in Italy

Kosterlitz, Cpl Rudolf
RASC
                                    1.5.43
KIA at sea

Kotter, Pte David
RASC
                                    1.5.43
Killed in action at sea

Kotz, Pte S.
RASC
                                    12.11.44
Died in Palestine as the result of
an accident

Krabchinsky, Cpl J.
PC
                                    11.11.43
Died in Egypt as the result of an
accident

Krause, Pte Eliyahu
PC
                                    17.5.44
Killed whilst escaping from a POW
camp in Germany

Kreitner, Pte Joseph
PC
                                    23.4.45
Died in Germany as a POW

Kriegel, Pavel
MN

Kurtzrock, Cpl Chaim
Jewish Inf Bde Group
                                    29.3.45
KIA in Italy

Kutas, Dvr Samuel
RASC/Pal
Age 22   12.11.44
Buried Ramleh War Cem

Landau, Pte Israel
Jewish Inf Bde Group
                                    1.1.46
Murdered in Belgium

Landau, Cpl Moshe L.
RAMC
                                    20.6.42
KIA in the Western Desert

Lange, Cpl Yaacov
RAOC
                                    13.9.44
Died in Syria as the result of an
accident

Laor (Langfuss), Spr Shimon
RE
                                    19.2.46
Died in Palestine as the result of
an accident

Lapidoth, Pte Shmarya
RASC
                                    1.5.43
KIA at sea

Latz, Pte Yoseph
RASC
                                    1.5.43
KIA at sea

Leichter, Pte Abraham
RASC
                                    19.1.42
Died in Egypt as the result of an
accident

Leizer, Sgt Shuli
Jewish Inf Bde Group
                                    31.3.45
KIA in Italy

Lev, Pte Kurt
RASC
                                    17.7.42
Died in Egypt as the result of an
accident

Levavy, Pte Irma
ATS
                                    25.11.44
Died in Egypt as the result of an
accident

Levenberg, Ilana
ATS Pal.
                                    -.4.43

Levine, Pte Baruch
Jewish Inf Bde Group
                                    30.3.45
KIA in Italy

Levine, Spr Pesach Katriel
RE
                                    16.3.43
Died in Egypt as the result of an
accident

Levinson, Pte A.
RASC
                                    2.3.45
Died in Libya as the result of an
accident

Levinson, Pte Chaim
RASC
                                    1.5.43
KIA at sea

Levite, Pte L.
RASC
                                    1.5.43
KIA at sea

Levkovitz, Cpl Yosef
RASC
                                    27.8.43
Died at sea from wounds received
in action

Levy, Pte Aharon
PC

15.5.41

KIA in the Western Desert

Levy, Pte David
RASC

1.5.43

KIA at sea

Levy, Pte Edward
RA

22.11..42

Died in Palestine as the result of
an accident

Levy, Pte Menashe
Jewish Inf Bde Group

7.4.45

KIA in Italy

Levy, Sgt Michael (Martin)
Jewish Inf Bde Group

31.3.45

KIA in Italy

Levy, L/Cpl Shmuel
Pal Regt

19.5.44

Died in Palestine as the result of
an accident

Levy (Chazmi), Spr Eliahu
RE

24.3.44

Died in Palestine from illness

Liebergott, Pte Nachman
Infantry

9.11.42

Died in Palestine from illness

Lieberman, Pte Max
RASC

1.5.43

KIA at sea

Lieberman, Sgt Meir
RE

22.4.41

KIA in Greece

Lieberman, Cpl Joseph
Jewish Inf Bde Group

11.4.45

KIA in Italy

Lindenworm, Pte Tzadik Yoseph
Infantry

1.6.45

Died in Palestine as the result of
an accident

Lipman, Spr Peretz
RE

22.12.42

Died whilst a POW in Poland

Loewensohn, Dvr Haim
RASC 462 GT

1.5.43

Brookwood Memorial

Loss, Cook Robert
MN
SS *Har Zion*

31.8.40

Lowy, Gnr Edward
RA

22.11.42

Buried Khayat Beach War Cem

Lubnitzki, Deckboy Jacob
MN
SS *Har Zion*
Age 15   31.8.40

Lubtzensky, Greaser Benjamin
MN
SS *Har Zion*

31.8.40

Lustig, Sgmn Norbert
RCOS

11.5.44

Died whilst a POW in Germany

Lutz, Pte Yitzchak
RASC

1.5.43

KIA at sea

Madurski, Cpl Shimshon
RASC

1.5.43

KIA at sea

Maimaran, Shimon Ben Yaacov
Alamein Pal. Regt

Maimon, Spr N.
RE

13.10.44

Died in Italy as the result of an
accident

Maimon, Pte Raphael
RASC

1.5.43

KIA at sea

Maimon (Yudovski), Cpl Pesach
RASC

1.5.43

KIA at sea

Malcovski, Pte Yehuda
RASC

1.5.43

KIA at sea

Maliniak, Pte Dov
Pioneer Corps

23.4.41

KIA in Greece

Mandel, Pte David
Jewish Inf Bde Group

12.4.45

KIA in Italy

Mann, Sgt Hans
RE

17.2.42

Died in Egypt as the result of an
accident

Manovela, Pte Moshe
Pal Regt

8.9.46

Murdered in Palestine

Marcus (Markos), Pte Yaakov
Infantry

22.8.42

Died in Palestine as the result of
an accident

Marcus, Pte Zvi
RASC

1.5.43

KIA at sea

Mark, Pte Tamar
ATS
                                        25.3.43
Died in Egypt as the result of an
accident

Mass, Spr Moshe
RE
                                        4.5.42
Died in Palestine as the result of
an accident

Matityahu, Spr A.B.
RE
                                        1.8.43
Died as the result of an accident
in Libya

Mazon, Pte Chaim
PC
                                        8.2.41
KIA in the Western Desert

Meichinsky, Pte Hugo
PC
                                        23.4.45
Died whilst a POW in
Czechoslovakia

Meir, Pte Zeev (Otto)
RA/Jewish Bde
                                        30.12.44
Died in Italy as the result of an
accident

Meir, Capt P.
RAMC

Meizler (Meler), Pte Meir
Jewish Inf Bde Group
                                        5.2.45
Died in Italy as the result of an
accident

Meizlin, Gnr Shmuel
RA
                                        1.3.42
Died in Palestine as the result of
an accident

Meizlish, Pte Rachel
ATS

Melamed, Pte Dov
Pal Regt
                                        13.8.42
Died in Palestine from illness

Melman, Sgt Moshe
Jewish Inf Bde Group
                                        6.4.45
KIA in Italy

Menasherov, Cpl Ephraim
PC
                                        29.10.43
Killed in Crete whilst escaping
from captivity

Meno, Pte Avraham Yehuda
PC
                                        8.2.41
KIA in the Western Desert

Meshulam, Gabriel
                                        -.-.41
KIA in Greece

Messinger, Ephraim
                                        17.8.41
Missing

Metal, Pte Carl
PC
                                        -.-.41
Missing in Greece

Meyerheim, Spr Chanan
RE
                                        8.1.44
Died in Syria as the result of an
accident

**Meyerman (Memaran), Pte
Shimeon**
                                        12.8.46
Died in Egypt from illness

Mielzynski/Meilchineski, Pte V.
Jewish Inf Bde Group
                                        10.6.46
Died in Germany from illness

Mikailovicz, Pte P.
PC
Died whilst a POW in Poland

Milkain, Pte Yaacov
RASC
                                        1.5.43
KIA at sea

Miller, Aharon
                                        -.2.45
Died in Italy as the result of an
accident

Miller, Ch Eng/O Samuel
MN
SS *Har Zion*
Age 50   31.8.40

Mitler, Pte Aharon
RASC
                                        1.5.43
KIA at sea

Mizen, Pte Yermiahu
PC
                                        22.4.41
KIA in Greece

Mizrahi, Pte Abraham
RASC
                                        28.3.43
Ramleh Memorial

Mizrahi, Spr B.B.
RE
                                        20.7.41
Died in Palestine as the result of
an accident

Mizrahi, Pte Binyamin
The Pal Regt
                                        21.10.43
Died in Palestine as the result of
an accident

Mizrahi, Cpl Yaacov
PC
                                        28.4.41
KIA in Greece

Mograbi, Cpl
RE
                                        -.-.41
Died in Egypt

Molnar, Pte R.
RASC
19.11.44
Died in Italy as the result of an
accident

Moshanof, Pte H.B.
RASC
5.7.44
Died in Italy as the result of an
accident

Moskowitz, Pte Elimelech
PC
4.12.41
Died in Egypt as the result of an
accident

Nadan (Nader), Pte Daniel
RASC
8.2.42
Died in Egypt as the result of an
accident

Nadav, Pte Yigal
RASC
1.5.43
KIA at sea

Nafcha, David
SOE
18.5.41
KIA at sea

Nasser, Spr Ezra
RE
13.2.43
Murdered whilst a POW in Poland

Neder, Pte Moshe Avraham
Jewish Inf Bde Group
26.3.46
Died in Belgium as the result of
an accident

**Neubauer, Pte Siegfried Shalom
Yehuda**
RASC/Pal
6.2.43
Buried Heliopolis War Cem

Neuberg, Pte Miriam
ATS
20.6.42
Died in Egypt as the result of an
accident
Buried Tel El Kabir War Mem Cem

Neulinger, Pte Shmuel
RASC
1.5.43
KIA at sea

Neumann, Pte Yehezkiel
PC
13.2.43

Neumark, Pte H.
RASC
16.9.45
Died in Italy as the result of an
accident

Neuwirth, Sgmn Edgar
RCOS
11.11.41
Died in Egypt as the result of an
accident
Buried Alexandria (Hadra) War
Mem Cem

Nevel, Pte Zvi (Horst)
RASC
1.5.43
KIA at sea

Niman, Nachman
4.1.45
Died in an accident

Nissim, Omar
RAMC
20.6.42

Nordon (Nordau), Israel
SOE
18.5.41
KIA at sea

Nurel (Norel), Pte Arie (Lova)
Commando
15.3.41
KIA in Eritrea
Buried Khartoum Memorial Cem

Nuriel, Avraham
SOE
18.5.41
KIA at sea

Nussbaum, Cpl Moshe
RASC
1.5.43
KIA at sea

Nussbaum, Yigal
RASC
1.5.43
KIA at sea

Ofrover (Opprower), A.
Commando Sig
-.-.42
KIA in the Western Desert

Oppenheimer, Spr Ernst
RE
25.5.46
Died in Palestine as the result of
an accident

Orbach, Pte Shaul S.H.
PC
10.2.44
Died whilst a POW in Poland

Osman, Pte I.I.S.
PC

Ossman, Peretz
-.-.45
Died whilst a POW in Germany

Osterman, Pte Werner
Commando
23.8.41
KIA in Ethiopia
Buried Asmara Civil (St Michele)
Cem

Ostrogursky, Pte Ilse
ATS
3.7.44
Died in Egypt as the result of an
accident

Otchital, Shimon
SOE
18.5.41
KIA at sea

Paglin, Nuriedl (Neri)
SOE
18.5.41
KIA at sea

Panishel, Pte Naftali
PC
10.3.45
Died whilst a POW in Poland

Parierski (Pagirsky), Capt Chaim
RAMC
9.2.41
KIA in the Western Desert

Pariss, Avraham
-.-.43
Died in Palestine

Passomnik, Pte R. Abraham
RASC
1.5.43
KIA at sea

Peretz, Spr David
RE
16.7.43
Died in an accident in Egypt
Buried Fayid War Cem

Peri, Pte Ernst
Jewish Inf Bde Group
29.5.45
Died in Italy as the result of an accident

Perlberg, Gnr Yitzchak
RA
4.1.42
Died in Palestine as the result of an accident

Perski (Friederich), Pte Julius
RASC
1.5.43
KIA at sea

Pessy, Spr Joseph
RE
2.7.41
Died in Greece whilst escaping from a POW camp

Peys, Pte Leib
RASC
15.10.44
Died whilst a POW in Germany

Pietri, Pte Mordechai
The Pal Regt
10.12.44
Killed in an accident in Palestine

Pintel, Pte Yehoshua
RASC
25.11.41
Died in Egypt as the result of an accident
Buried Suez War Mem Cem

Platzman, Dvr Israel
RASC/Pal
1.5.43

Plonchik, Mordechai
SOE
18.5.41
KIA at sea

Politzer, Pte H.P.
RASC
20.7.42
KIA in the Western Desert
Buried El Alamein War Cem

Polka (Polke), Pte Dr M.
PC
15.5.41
KIA in the Western Desert

Polkes/Polaks, Pte Nachum
RASC
1.5.43
KIA at sea
Brookwood Memorial

Poros, Pte Yitzchak
RASC
1.5.43
KIA at sea

Poulson, Spr Moshe
RE
18.11.43
Died in Syria as the result of an accident

Prober, Lt Nachum
RN
Age 33   9.2.45
Port Said War Cem

Proper, L/Cpl Joseph
RASC
1.5.43
KIA at sea

Prussak, Pte Joseph
RASC
1.5.43
KIA at sea

Rabinovitz, Pte Tanchum
Jewish Inf Bde Group
22.3.45
KIA in Italy

Rappaport, Cpl
RASC
1.5.43
KIA at sea

Rappaport, Cpl Eliyahu
Commando
7.6.41
KIA in Syria

Rasiel, Capt David
SOE
20.5.41
Died in Iraq on a mission
Not commemorated by CWGC

Rechavi, Sgmn S.S.
RCOS
-.5.43

Reichenberg, S/Sgt Peretz L.
RASC
1.5.43
KIA at sea

Reichlin, S/Sgt Zelig
RASC
1.5.43
KIA at sea

Reiffer, Pte Gideon T.H.
RASC
28.2.43
Died in Palestine as the result of an accident

Reik (Martinovitz), Chaviva (aka Ada Robinson)
SOE
                              20.11.44
Died in Slovakia on a mission
Buried Jerusalem Mt Herzl Cem

Reiss, A.
Died in Palestine

Reiss, Edgar
RASC
                              5.1.46

Reiss (Rice/Reisz), Raphael
SOE
                              -.11.44
Died in Slovakia on a mission

Reizman, Sgt Eugen
RAOC
                              15.8.45
Died in Greece as the result of an
accident

Rephan, L/Cpl Franz
RE
Age 43   15.7.43
Died in Egypt as the result of an
accident
Buried Fayid War Cem

Reuven, Spr Zacharia
RE
                              -.-.41
Died in Greece

Reznik, Pte Abraham
RASC
                              6.7.42
KIA in the Western Desert
Buried El Alamein War Cem

Rieff, Pte Joseph A.
RASC
                              1.5.43
KIA at sea

Ringo, Sgt Shmuel
RE
                              6.2.42
Died in Iraq as the result of an
accident

Rittner, Eising
MN

Rivlin, Cftmn Mordechai
REME
                              16.10.43
Buried Gaza War Cem

Rizhi (Ryzy), Sgt Yitzchak
Jewish Inf Bde Group
                              29.3.45
KIA in Italy

Rosenberg, Pte Aharon
RE
                              10.6.45
Died in Italy as the result of an
accident
Buried Milan War Cem

Rosenberg, Pte Eitan
                              -.4.42
KIA at sea

Rosenberg, Pte Shimon
RASC
                              1.8.42
Died in Egypt as the result of an
accident
Buried Moascar War Cem

Rosenstein, Pte Arno
PC
                              29.8.40
KIA in the Western Desert
Buried El Alamein War Cem

Rosenstein, L/Cpl Nathan
SAS
                              28.7.42
Died in Egypt from illness
Buried Fayid War Cem

Rosenstein, L/Cpl Uri J. (Zeno)
Commando PAL 1115
                              29.7.44
KIA in Albania
Athens Memorial Cem

Rosenwald, Pte Yerachmiel
RASC
                              1.5.43
KIA at sea

Rosenzweig, Pte David
RASC
                              1.5.43
KIA at sea

Rosin, Sgt (Hans) Zvi
RASC
                              1.5.43
KIA at sea

Rosin, Pte Shlomo
PC
                              19.9.45
Died in Palestine as the result of
an accident

Rosinov, Sgt S.H.
Intel Corps
                              10.11.44
KIA in Belgium

Rosner, Pte Zvi (Heinrich)
RASC
                              26.3.42
KIA in the Western Desert
Buried Halfaya Sollum War Cem

Roth, Sgt Alexander
Jewish Inf Bde Group
                              6.2.44
Died in Palestine due to illness
Buried Khayat Beach War Cem

Rothman, Zeev
SOE
                              18.5.41
KIA at sea

Royansky, Pte Itzchak
Jewish Inf Bde Group
                              22.8.45
Died in Austria as the result of an
accident

Ruchotz, Cpl Raphael
RASC
                              1.5.43
KIA at sea

Rusak, Pte (Wolf) Zeev
Jewish Inf Bde Group
                              19.3.45
KIA in Italy

Salem, Jacob
MN

Salomon, Elazar (Lazer)
1.3.45

Salomon, Spr Y.
RE
19.7.42
Died whilst a POW in Greece

Samet, Pte Zeev Werner
PC
10.5.42
KIA in the Western Desert

Sangrosky, Purser Moshe Yaakov
MN
SS *Har Zion*
Age 32   31.8.40

Sayeg, Pte Meir
RASC
1.5.43
KIA at sea

Schechter, Pte Arie
Jewish Inf Bde Group
31.3.45
KIA in Italy

Scheier, Pte A.
PC
-.-.41

Scheizer, Shlomo
RCOS
8.1.45
Died in the Western Desert as the result of an accident

Schiefer, Sgt Zvi
RASC
1.5.43
KIA at sea

Schleifstein, Pte Asher
Jewish Inf Bde Group
7.4.45
KIA in Italy

Schlesinger, Pte Michael
RASC
1.5.43
KIA at sea

Schlossberg, Sgt Avraham
RASC
1.5.43
KIA at sea

Schmerling (Shneur), Pte Yaakov
RASC
1.5.43
KIA at sea

Schoner, Sgt Moshe Yehuda
PC
28.4.41
KIA in Greece

Schor, Pte Gideon
Jewish Inf Bde Group
3.1.43
Alamein Memorial

Schor, Pte Zvi
PC
27.5.41
KIA in Crete

Shreier (Shrir), Pte Shlomo
Jewish Inf Bde Group
2.4.45
KIA in Italy

Schremmer (Kremmer), Rudi
SOE
18.5.41
Died in action at sea

Shremmer (Kremmer), Pte Yehuda
Jewish Inf Bde Group
Died as the result of an accident

Schulgasser, Pte Yaakov
Jewish Inf Bde Group
20.3.45
KIA in Italy

Schwartz, L/Cpl Alfred
RASC
24.10.44
Died in Italy as the result of an accident

Schwartz, Greaser Sarol
MN
SS *Har Zion*
31.8.40

Schwartzer, Pte Gad
RASC
1.5.43
KIA at sea

Schwartz, Spr Yaakov
RE
14.3.41
KIA in the Western Desert

Seevi-Cohen, Sgt Herzl
RASC
23.11.42
KIA in the Western Desert

Segal, L/Cpl Aharon
RASC
1.5.43
KIA at sea

Segal, Pte Israel
RASC
1.5.43
KIA at sea

Sekel, L/Cpl Alfred
RASC
1.5.43
KIA at sea

Sender (Sander), Pte V.
RASC
2.1.44
Killed in an accident in Italy

Senesh (Szenesh), Hannah (aka Minnie)
WAAF/SOE
7.11.44
Executed in Hungary on a mission

Senior (Sinvar), Pte
PC
-.1.42

Serbrani (Sarbonick), Pte V.
PC
17.2.42
Died as a POW in Germany

Shalom, Pte Joseph Shmuel
PC
23.4.41
KIA in Greece

Sharawski (Sharanski), Pte Itzchak
PC
12.5.40
Died as the result of an accident in Palestine

Shaw, Pte Joseph
RAOC
-.6.46
Died in Palestine as the result of an accident

Sheinfeild, L/Cpl Benyamin
RAOC
9.8.45
Died in Italy as the result of an accident

Shemesh, Spr A.
RE
8.6.43
Died in Libya as the result of an accident

Shepi (Spivak), Pte Baruch
Jewish Inf Bde Group
25.8.45
Died in Palestine from illness

Sherff, Pte Zeev (Wilhelm)
RASC
1.5.43
KIA at sea

Shiefer (Schipper), Pte Moshe
Jewish Inf Bde Group
6.4.45
KIA in Italy

Shimon, Pte Eli
RASC
-.-.41
Died in Greece as a POW

Shimon (Simon), Pte Ernst Y.
RASC
1.5.43
KIA at sea

Shitrit, Pte David
PC
15.8.41
Died as as POW in Greece

Shneur (Sznejer), Cpl Joseph Chaim
Jewish Inf Bde Group
31.3.45
KIA Italy

Shochat, Amiram
SOE
18.5.41
KIA at sea

Sholem, Pte Dan (Robert)
Jewish Inf Bde Group
2 Commando
2.4.45
KIA Italy

Shoshani, Pte Y.
RASC
10.12.41
Died in Palestine from illness

Shpirov, Pte M.
PC
Died from illness

Shtamm, Spr Uriel
RE
29.5.43
Died in Egypt as the result of an accident

Sigal, Sgt Hillel
PC
26.11.43
Died as a POW in Germany

Silber
1.5.41
Died in a POW camp in Greece

Silberstein, Jacob
MN

Sima, Pte Yitzchak
Jewish Inf Bde Group
6.4.45
KIA in Italy

Sireni (Serini), Chaim (Enzo) (aka Lt Samuel Barda)
SOE
-.-.44
Killed by the Germans in Dachau

Skorinski, Avraham
RASC
1.5.43
KIA at sea

Skrebiny, Pte Izak
PC/Pal
17.2.42
Athens War Memorial

Solomon, Seaman Pinati Marc
MN
SS *Har Zion*
31.8.40

Spaak, Pte Menachem
PC
24.1.45
Died as a POW in Germany

Spector, Zvi
SOE
18.5.41
KIA at sea

Speyer, Pte Yaacov (aka Spaier)
RASC
23.9.40
Died in Palestine from illness

Spinzel, Pte Arie (Arthur)
RASC
1.5.43
KIA at sea

Springer, Pte Ludwig
PC
15.7.41
Died in Egypt as the result of an accident

Stein, Pte Herman Zvi
RAMC
27.3.43
Died in Egypt from illness

Steinberg, Pte Moshe
RAMC
1.5.43
KIA at sea

Stengel, Sgt H.
PC

Stern, Pte Avraham
PC
9.1.42

Stern, Cpl Franz
RASC
1.5.41
Died in Greece as a POW

Stern, Pte Shlomo (Alter)
RASC
1.5.43
KIA at sea

Sternberg, Pte Robert A.
Infantry
11.6.45
Died in Palestine as the result of
an accident

Sternheim, Pte Michael
RASC
1.5.43
KIA at sea

Strizover, Pte C.H.
PC
7.3.42
KIA in the Eastern Desert

Szechter, Cpl Leon
PAL 13016
PC
4.1.44
Died as a POW in Poland

Tagar, Capt Benjamin
Free French Forces
22.8.44
KIA in France

Tagavy, Pte K.
PC
Died as the result of an accident

Tager, Pte Gershon C.H.
RASC
1.5.43
KIA at sea

Tamas, Ariel
SOE
18.5.41
KIA at sea

Tanpilov, Pte Shmuel
RASC
1.5.43
KIA at sea

Tchizik, Pte Bath-Ami (aka Yahaloumy-Chizik)
ATS
24.3.43
Died in Egypt as the result of an
accident

Tenkel (Tankelis), Pte Zelig
Jewish Inf Bde Group
13.4.45
KIA in Italy

Tepper, Pte Avraham
Infantry
29.9.45
Died in Palestine on duty

Terbas, Pte Moshe
RASC
1.5.43
KIA at sea

Tibor, Maj Adam
Jewish Inf Bde Group
16.11.45
Died in Holland as the result of an
accident

Toib, Pte Itzchak
RASC
1.5.43
KIA at sea

Tovim, Pte Yephet
PC
1.4.45
Died in Germany as a POW

Tratner, Pte Akiva
Jewish Inf Bde Group
-.8.43
Died in Palestine as the result of
an accident

Trauman, Pte Werner
RASC
1.5.43
KIA at sea

Turk, Pte Zvi (aka Turek)
RASC
1.5.43
KIA at sea

Tydhar, Spr Noach
RE
23.7.43
Died in Syria as the result of an
accident

Tzabari, Saadia
PC
-.6.41
Died in Yugoslavia escaping from
a POW Camp

Tzarfati, Cpl Shlomo
RE
1.10.41
Died in Greece escaping from a
POW camp

Tzeitlin, Spr David Chaim
RE
13.9.45
Died from illness

Tzenkar (Tzenkan), Pte Yaakov
RASC
1.5.43
KIA at sea

Tzerjeck, Spr Herman
RE
2.7.41
Died in Greece escaping from a
POW camp

Tzerner, Pte Azriel
20.11.46
Died in Palestine from illness

Tziknovsky, Pte Menahem Chaim
RASC
1.5.43
KIA at sea

Tzolner (Solner), Pte Meir J.
RASC
1.5.43
KIA at sea

Tzur (Bernstein), Lt Joseph
Jewish Inf Bde Group
4.3.44
Died in Palestine as the result of an accident

Tzwick, Pte Mordechai
51st Commando
27.7.41
KIA in Ethiopia

Tzwilling, Pte Kurt
RASC
1.5.43
KIA at sea

Tzwilling, Capt Zvi (aka Zwiling)
RAMC
8.8.45
Died in Palestine as the result of an accident

Ulrich, Pte Yitzchak
Commando
5.3.41
KIA in Eritrea

Umtza (or Omtza), Y.A.
PC
-.4.41
KIA in Greece

Urbach, Pte Saul
PC/Pal
10.12.44
Athens Memorial

Van-Gelder, Lt David A.
Jewish Inf Bde Group
6.4.45
KIA in Italy

Veiner/Weiner, Pte Avraham T.
RASC
1.5.43
KIA at sea

Vogel (Fogel), Pte David
RASC
1.5.43
KIA at sea

Wagner, L/Cpl Richard
PC
23.5.41
KIA in Crete

Walentin, Pte Yosef
PC
28.4.41
KIA in Greece

Warshadi, Pte Y.E.
PC
22.4.41
KIA in Greece

Waslovsky, Sgmn Shalom
RCOS
2.8.43
Died in Egypt as the result of an accident

Wasserman, Pte Alter
No.1 RASC
1.5.43
KIA at sea
Buried in Brookwood

Wasserman, Pte Eliezer
Infantry

Wechsler (Wexler), Cpl Eliyahu
Jewish Inf Bde Group
11.4.45
KIA in Italy

Weil, Pte Elasar
RASC
1.5.43
KIA at sea

Weil, Pte Shimon
RASC
13.6.41
Died in Palestine as the result of an accident

Weiman, Pte Ephraim
SOE
18.5.41
KIA at sea

Weingarten, Pte Avraham
Jewish Inf Bde Group
21.10.43
Died in Palestine as the result of an accident

Weinstein, Pte Shmaryahu
Commando
5.3.41
KIA in Eritrea

Weinstein, Pte Sima
ATS
25.8.45

Weinstock, Anshel
-.9.44
Murdered in Palestine

Weisel, Sgt Nadav
RA
7.12.42
Died in Palestine as the result of an accident

Weiss, L/Cpl E.
RAOC
11.5.43
Died in Libya as the result of an accident
Buried in Benghazi War Cem

Weissbein, Cpl Aharon
RASC
28.5.42
Died in Egypt as the result of an accident

Weissberg, Pte Y.
RASC
30.10.42
Died in Greece escaping from a POW camp

Weissman, L/Cpl Aharon
RE
7.7.41
Died in Greece escaping from a
POW camp

Weissman, Chayim
SOE
18.5.41
KIA at sea

Weiss-Politzer, Pte Shoshana
ATS
19.8.45
Died in Egypt as the result of an
accident
Buried in Heliopolis War Cem

Wermund, Pte Shmuel
RASC
1.5.43
KIA at sea

Whittlin, Fireman Salo
MN
SS *Har Zion*
Age 26   31.8.40

Widslavsky, Pte Simcha
RASC
1.5.43
KIA at sea

Wilentzok, Pte Pnina
ATS
17.9.43
Died in Syria as the result of an
accident

Williams, Lt Cyril Norman
Jewish Inf Bde Group
-.1.45
Died in Italy as the result of an
accident

Wirt (Wirth), Pte Bracha
ATS
28.5.45
Died in Palestine as the result of
an accident
Buried Ramleh Memorial Cem

Wissotzky, Pte Yaacov
PC
12.6.41
Died in Greece escaping from
POW camp

Witkovsky, Pte Itzchak
RASC
1.5.43
KIA at sea

Witriol, Pte Yoav
RASC
1.5.43
KIA at sea

Wohlin, Pte Shlomo
Jewish Inf Bde Group
30.5.45
Died in Italy as the result of an
accident

Wolf, 3rd Eng Off Karl
MN
SS *Har Zion*
31.8.40

Wolfhein, Pte A.
RASC
1.5.43
KIA at sea

Wolfsohn, Moshe
18.11.43

Yaacobson, Baruch
SOE
18.5.41
KIA at sea

Yaacobson/Jacobson, Pte Hans
RASC
1.5.43
KIA at sea

**Yaacobson/Jacobson, Pte
Pessach**
RASC
1.5.43
KIA at sea

Yaacoby (Yaacovi), Pte Nachum
Jewish Inf Bde Group
30.3.45
KIA in Italy

Yaffe, Catriel
SOE
18.5.41
KIA at sea

Yaffe, L/Cpl Moshe
PC
6.5.41
Died in Greece as a POW

Yaget, Pte Shlomo
RASC
1.5.43
KIA at sea

Yaglov, Pte Avraham
RASC
1.5.43
KIA at sea

Yakobovitz, Albert
-.-.40
KIA in the Western Desert

Yashim, Pte Yosef
RASC
1.5.43
KIA at sea

Yassin, Spr A.Y.
RE/Pal
5.7.45
Buried Khayat Beach War Cem

Yishuvi, Pte Gavriel
RASC
1.5.43
KIA at sea

Yokelson, Pte Moshe
Jewish Inf Bde Group
30.6.45
Died in Italy as the result of an
accident

Zack, Dvr Moshe
RASC
15.2.45
Died in Italy as the result of an
accident
Buried Florence War Cem

Zagagi, Pte Peretz
RASC
                              1.5.43
KIA at sea

Zagill, Pte M.M.
PC
                              -.-.41
Died in the Western desert

Zasler, Sgmn Israel A.
RCOS
                              25.2.43
Died as a POW in Poland

Zeitz, Pte Gershon T.
RASC
                              1.5.43
KIA at sea

Zeltzer, Pte Tzvi
Recruiting Base
                              9.11.39
Died in Palestine as the result of
an accident

Zerner, Pte Yehudi
SOE
                              18.5.41

Ziegler, Spr Arthur
RE
                              -.3.45
Died in a POW camp in Germany

Zilberberg, Pte Dov
PC
                              28.4.41
KIA in Greece

Zilberberg, Pte Moshe Yosef, MM
Jewish Inf Bde Group
                              20.3.45
KIA in Italy
Buried Ravenna War Cem

Zinger, Sgt Karl
RASC
                              1.5.43
KIA at sea

Zinger, Pte Erich
RASC
                              1.5.43
KIA at sea

Zinger, Lutz

Zinger, Pte Paul
PC
                              9.7.42
Died in Cyprus as the result of an
accident

Zion (Sion), Spr Gavriel
RE
                              9.4.46
Died in Holland as the result of an
accident
Buried Arnhem Jewish Cem

Zuckerbrodt, 3rd Officer Shimmon
MN SS Har Zion
Age 28   31.8.40

The Fire Service

by Martin Sugarman and Stephanie Maltman

The list below is a tribute to the Jewish Firemen and Women who died in the Second World War. The deaths of Firewatchers have also been included as they were trained by the Fire Service and often dealt with fires before the Fire Service arrived. The list was compiled by Martin Sugarman and Stephanie Maltman (the latter a founder of the organization Firemen Remembered) and is an abbreviated version of the study published in Martin Sugarman, *Fighting Back: British Jewry's Military Contribution in the Second World War* (London and Portland, OR: Valentine Mitchell, 2010). The authors are also compiling a list of all those who served from the Jewish community which is a work in progress, already running into several thousands of names.

Abrahams, George Isaac
Firewatcher Southampton
25.2.43

Amiel, Isaac
Firewatcher Mile End
10.5.41
Buried Edmonton, V 75 20.

Appleby, David
AFS Station, Invicta Rd
Age 33   14.4.40
KIA
Husband of N. Appleby of 432 Bancroft Rd, Mile End.
Buried 19.11.40 at East Ham Jewish Cem, grave 0.20.643

Aronowsky, Eric
Firewatcher Liverpool
4.5.41

Belinsky, Solomon
Leeds
1.4.41
WIA, died of wounds
Appears on the Fireman's Memorial website, but not on Memorial near St Paul's Cathedral

Berkon, Samuel
Manchester, AFS Despatch Rider
2.11.40

Black, Louis
Firewatcher Hull
8.5.41

Blumson, George William
Firewatcher, of Whitechapel
Age 15   10.5.41
KIA, of Jewish origin
Possibly the youngest Jewish casualty (see Coster below).

Brilleslyper, Louis
Firewatcher
10.5.41
KIA Mile End, buried Marlow Road, I 6 377
Son of Rebecca, of Leytonstone

Carason, Abraham
Firewatcher Liverpool
8.5.41
Husband of Eva

Cohen, David
3.1.43
From Edgware. Killed at Shanklin.

Cohen, George Leslie
Served West Hampstead Station
19.3.43
Death in service, buried 21.3.43 Willesden, P 1 12
JC, 2.4.43, but not on CWGC site or Fire Service memorial

Cohen, Isaac
Firewatcher Liverpool
3.6.41

Cohen, Monty
Firewatcher Stepney

Cohen, Simon
Stepney
11.8.40
Buried Marlow Road, N 20 630

Corby, Jacob Woolf
Hackney
25.9.40
Buried Marlow Road, O 12 368

Coster, Albert Victor
Firewatcher and unofficial
Volunteer Fireman
Age 14   9.4.43
Possibly youngest Jewish casualty
KIA at 71 Sutton Street
Buried Manor Park Cem
Tbc if Jewish or of Jewish origin.
Son of Harry and Alice of 70
Sheridan Street, London E1,
Nephew of J. Marks and Joseph
Harris.
Not on CWGC site.

Coster, Harry
Camberwell
3.12.42
Buried Willesden, GX 3 133,
(grave says 1943?)
Son of Benjamin and Esther

Deutsch/Deutch, Israel
(incorrectly spelt as Isreal on the
memorial) Cable and Backchurch
Street, Stepney
8.3.41
Buried Edmonton, grave V 70 24

Emden, Mrs Miriam 'Dolly'
Firewatcher, Hughes Mansions,
Stepney
10.5.41
Buried Marlow Rd, I 6 380

Feldman, Hyman
Stepney
19.3.41
Buried Edmonton, V 71 2 –
gravestone disintegrated
Of Amhurst Park, Stamford Hill.
His brother Louis was killed as
POW of the Japanese.

Friedman, Daniel
Firewatcher Westminster
16.4.41

Gaidelman, Benjamin
Fireguard Stoke Newington
16.8.44

Gevelb, Sydney
Firewatcher Stepney
Age 17   16.4.41
Buried Edmonton, V 74 19/18, in
a double grave
His cousin Morris was in St John's
Ambulance and killed in same
incident

Glantzpegel, Harry (aka Lewis)
3.1.43
From Finchley. Killed at Shanklin.
Buried Marlow Road.

Gold, David
Dundee (tbc)
24.4.44

Goldberg, John
Firewatcher Battersea
21.11.45
Died of injuries sustained 11.44

Golden, Herbert Benjamin
Paddington (tbc)
11.5.41
King's Commendation for Brave
Conduct
Son of Sydney and Annie

Goldsmith, B.
(tbc: on Fire Service Memorial but
not on CWGC website)

Goldsmith, Neil
(tbc: on Fire Service Memorial but
not on CWGC website)

**Goldsmith/Goldschmitt,
George Eric**
Killed Chelsea
16.4.41
From Finchley

Goldstein, Morris
Firewatcher Stepney
16.4.41

Goodman, Edwin
(tbc: on Fire Service Memorial but
not on CWGC website).

Goodman, Joshua
Firewatcher Leeds
16.12.43

Gordon/Cohen, Jack
Firewatcher Stoke Newington
17.4.41
KIA, Cannon St
Buried Edmonton Federation, V 74
16

Greenberg, Barnett
Killed Poplar
11.5.41
From Peckham

Greenberg, Harry
Firewatcher Stepney
19.3.41

Greenberg, Joseph
Stepney
1.1.41
Buried Marlow Road, O 26 846

Greenberg, Nat
Firewatcher/Ambulance Driver
Liverpool *JC*, 7.5.41

Gush, Emmanuel
Exeter (tbc)
25.4.42

Harris, Henry
Firewatcher Flower and Dean St
Age 16   10.3.41
Buried Marlow Road, I 5 307 –
headstone no longer exists
Possibly second youngest Jewish
casualty on duty

Harrison, Myre/Moier
13.3.41
8 Jewish firemen were pallbearers at his funeral.

Heiser, Aaron (Harry)
Firewatcher Golders Green
11.5.41
KIA Old Street, *JC*, 16.5.41
Buried Willesden, FX 19 857

Heiser, Jacob
Firewatcher
11.5.41
Brother of Aaron, killed in same incident
Buried Willesden, FX 19 856

Hyams/Hyman, Gilbert
Firewatcher Liverpool
Not on CWGC website.

Isaacs, Leslie Walter Joseph
Wandsworth
16.11.40

Jacobs, Leslie Alfred
from Shanklin (tbc)
3.1.43

Lennick, Hyman
West Ham
18.6.43
Buried Marlow Road, P 14 440 –
headstone no longer exists

Lettner/Latner, Ascher/Arthur (David) Davis
City
17.4.41
Family say correct spelling is Latner. Brother-in-law of Jack Silver (listed below).
Cremated and ashes scattered at sea.
Plaque on parents' grave in Willesden Jewish Cem

Levenson, Albert
Hackney, killed Mile End
5.11.41

Levy, Abraham
Hull
German refugee (tbc if killed – not on CWGC site)

Levy, Samuel
Firewatcher Bristol
13.4.41

Lewin, Ms Hetty
Firewatcher Stoke Newington
17.4.41
Killed at West Central Synagogue Jewish Youth Club, Alfred Place, Holborn
Buried Streatham, E 26 35
(see S. Osterer, listed below)

Lewis, Abraham (aka Bookatz)
Stepney
12.5.41
Buried Rainham, A 24 24
Also noted in the LMA records FB/WAR 4/12, no.1663.

Libbert, Samuel
Killed Glasgow
19.9.42
From Manchester

Loveman, Samuel
Greenock
19.10.40
Son of Moses and Jane, husband of Rebecca

Michaelson, Victor
Wandsworth
6.11.40
Buried Willesden, FX 13 566, headstone totally blank/worn.

Millet, Percy
Stepney
8.9.40
Buried Rainham, A 19 29.
First Jewish Fireman killed
Brother Morris KIA in Merchant Navy on 22.10.42

Morris, Harry
AFS
11.5.41
Buried Marlow Road, I 6 388
Son of Solomon of Hackney

Myers, Miss Margaret
Firewatcher,
8.3.41
Daughter of Joseph of Stepney

Nyman, Issac
Firewatcher killed Mile End Road
10.5.41
Buried Rainham, A 24 23
From Ilford
Not listed as Firewatcher on CWGC website

Osterer, Sarah
Fireguard
17.4.41
Killed West Central Synagogue Jewish Youth Club, Holborn, with Hetty Lewin.

Paul, Alexander
Manchester
24.12.40

Pearl, Pizer
Hackney Fire Station
26.9.41
Killed Tottenham Court Rd
From Surrey
Buried Marlow Road, O 13 404

Rabinowitz, Manuel (Mendel)
Edinburgh, posted to London
WIA and died of injuries in Edinburgh in 1941

Randal, Max
Firewatcher Golders Green
18.3.41

Raphael, Jack
Firewatcher Hampstead
20.6.44

Rose, Maurice Sydney
Column Officer
11.12.43
Killed Bradford
From Surrey

Roseman, Hyman
Previously in ARP
                                    12.7.44
Killed Elephant and Castle
Buried Streatham, F 28 28
From Nova Rd, Croydon

Salkeld, Frederick Charles
Section Officer, Wandsworth
                                    17.10.40
Son of Bessie and William

Schneider, Ernest Adam
Killed Finsbury
                                    14.10.40
From Stepney

Schooler, Alexander
No. 891
                                    8.5.41
Killed Albert Dock, Hull.
German refugee
First Hull Jewish Fireman casualty
Buried Hull Jewish Cem

Schwartzberg, Israel
Bethnal Green
                                    29.8.43

Share, Morris/Maurice (Mossy)
Bermondsey
                                    8.9.40
Buried Rainham, A 20 14
Killed same day as Millet, listed
above

**Sheldon, Benjamin
Joseph/John (tbc)**
Killed Woolwich
                                    11.9.40

Simeon, Harry Thomas (tbc)
Glasgow
                                    13.3.41

Simon, Harry
From Scotland
Believed buried in Manchester
(tbc) (Info. from Carl Goldberg of
Manchester)

Slipman, Alec
Firewatcher Holborn
                                    17.4.41
Buried Edmonton, V 75 23 –
gravestone disintegrated.

Smith, Alexander
AFS
                                    9.3.41
Buried East Ham Cem 11.3.41,
grave 1-2-118 Of Urswick Rd (6,
Kings Market Parade, E9)

Sussman, Miss Helen
Kensington
                                    19.6.44
Buried Edmonton, W 26 19

Tasho, Harold Alan
Southampton
Age 27   21.2.41
Died in Hertford (JC, 7.3.41 p.7)
Buried Marlow Road, 23.2.41, O
33 1086, headstone no longer
exists.
Not on Fire Service Memorial or
CWGC website, as died of illness.

Tobias, Joseph Leonard
District Officer, Marylebone
                                    17.9.40
Lived Euston

Viener, David
Hackney,
                                    23.12.45
Buried Rainham A 39 19

Wand, Myer
Marylebone
                                    18.9.40
From Stepney
Buried Marlow Road, O 10 313

Wolff, Herbert Thomas (tbc)
Camberwell
                                    28.9.40
From Deptford

Zagerman, Phillip
Firewatcher/ARP Stamford Hill
                                    13.1.41

Jewish Brothers Who Died on Service in the British and Commonwealth Forces in the Second World War

H. Pollins and M. Sugarman

The sources of information for the list that follows are:

1. Two books by Henry Morris that deal mainly with those who died while in the British forces but also include names of those who died while serving in Commonwealth forces: *We Will Remember Them: A Record of the Jews who Died in the Armed Forces of the Crown 1939–1945* (1989) and *We Will Remember Them: A Record of the Jews who Died in the Armed Forces of the Crown 1939–1945, with Addendum* (1994).

2. G. Pynt (ed.), *Australian Jewry Book of Honour* (1973).

3. *Canadian Jews in World War II* (1948).

4. *South African Jews in World War II* (1950).

I am grateful to Harold Pollins for almost all the work on this section.

Martin Sugarman

These sources normally indicate name and rank, sometimes the unit and sometimes date of death. Sometimes fuller details are obtainable from the Commonwealth War Graves Commission website. The CWGC has data which was supplied to them by the relevant forces authorities, supplemented by information obtained from next of kin whose name and address (usually the town only) is often on the website where the name is commemorated.

Sometimes the CWGC entry contains the statement that a named brother also died while in service. This is indicated in the entries below. However, this was recorded infrequently and in most cases one can conclude from the names and addresses of parents that the men were brothers. In some cases the name of a brother was found on the CWGC website which are not in the books mentioned above. The list includes at least two sets of twins and one set of three brothers.

(This is an updated version of an article by Harold Pollins which appeared in Shemot, *9, 3 [September 2001]).*

1. Adler, 2nd Lt Harold James 149325 *RF (Tower Hamlets Rifles)*. Killed 25.2.42 aged 26. Parents James and Ellen Augusta Adler of St John's Wood – col. 73 Alamein. Twin brother of –

Adler, Capt Paul Sabel 107225 *RAMC/K.A.R.*. Killed 5.11.44 aged 29. Parents James and Nellie Adler, husband of Margaret Phoebe Adler of Theydon Bois, Essex. Buried at Taukkyan, Burma.

––––––––––––––––––––––

2. Benjamin, Tpr Sidney Montagu. 7963317 *147 Regt (10 Hampshire Regt) RAC*. 18.7.44 aged 20. Buried St Manvieu War Cemetery, Cheux, France. Parents Louis, Rachel of Chapel Allerton, Leeds. Brother Donald Bernard died in the UK.

Benjamin, Sgmn Donald Bernard. 14438298 RCOS. 22.11.45 aged 19. Buried Leeds (Louis Road) Polish Jews' Cemetery. Parents Louis, Rachel Gertrude of Chapel Allerton, Leeds. Brother Sidney Montagu also died.

3. Biderman, Telegraphist George. P/LD/X 5418 HMS *Anking RNVR*. 4.3.43 aged 28. Portsmouth Naval Memorial. Parents Max, Sophie of Willesden.

Biderman, Sgt Leslie. 4750571 *2/5Bn Leicester Regt*. 22.2.43 aged 25. Enfidaville War Cemetery. Parents Max, Sophie of Willesden.

––––––––––––––––––––––

4. Flt/Sgt Block, David. 903489 *– 49 Squadron RAFVR*. 31.5.42 aged 30. Runnymede Memorial. Parents Joseph, Hettie of Salford, Lancs. Wife Phyllis. Had served in the Spanish Civil War against General Franco.

Block, Sgt/AG Samuel 1378566 *83 Squadron RAFVR*. 25.3.42 aged 33. East Ham (Marlow Road) Jewish Cemetery. Parents Joseph, Hettie. Wife Blanche of Brighton.

––––––––––––––––––––––

5. Brown, F/O AG Sydney. J/5744 *RCAF*. 15.4.43 aged 25. Mesnil-St Laurent Churchyard, Aisne, France. Parents Abraham, Leah of North Bay, Toronto.

Brown, Pte Zave. B/162744 *Roy Hamilton LI*. 9.3.45 aged 19. Groesbeek Canadian War Cemetery. Parents Abraham, Leah of North Bay, Toronto.

––––––––––––––––––––––

6. Buch, Capt Harold Julius. 4475774 *4 Squadron SAAF*. 31.12.43 aged 26. Sangro River War Cemetery, Italy. Parents Max, Annie E. of Cape Town.

Buch, Air Cpl Isadore Lionel 99548 *SAAF*. 27.11.42 aged 29. Maiduguri Cemetery, Nigeria. Parents M., Annie E. of Cape Town.

––––––––––––––––––––––

7. Calton, Spr Hyman. 2128800 *RE, 156 Bomb Disposal Coy*. Killed 31.12.44. Buried Moro River Canadian War Cemetery, Italy, XII C 1. Parents Louis and Annie, husband of Minne.

Calton, Air/Mech Officer 2nd Class Morris FX 104178 *RN*, HMS *Landrail*. Killed 26.7.44. Buried Glenduffhill Jewish Cemetery, Sec C, grave 199. Parents Louis and Annie of Glasgow.

8. Cherkinsky, Sgt Flt/Eng Arthur David. R/67557 *419 Squadron RCAF*. 2.3.42. Schiermonnikoog (Vredenhof) Cemetery, Netherlands. Mother Essie, Windsor, Toronto.

Cherkinsky, F/O Joseph. J/144677 *RCAF*. 5.5.43 aged 25. Evesham Cemetery, Worcestershire. Parents Yehudah, Essie of Windsor, Toronto.

9. Cornell, Flt Sgt/Nav Michael Henry. R.144931 *RCAF*. 31.5.43 aged 26. Willesden Jewish Cemetery. Parents Philip, Elisabeth; Wife Margaret Frances of New Jersey.

Cornell, Lt Basil Seymour. 220390 *8 Btn Middx Regt*. 29.3.45 aged 29. Reichswald Forest War Cemetery. Wife Mildred. *JC* 29 March 1946 p.4 states they were brothers, family name **Kornberg**.

10. Crotin, Sgmn Arthur. B/132344 *4 Canadian Armd Div Signals, RCIC*. 23.8.44 aged 22. Bayeux War Cemetery. Parents Harry, Sonia of Ansonville, Ontario.

Crotin, L/Bdr Walter Joseph. B/21856 *RCA*. 23.4.43 aged 29. Krugersdorf Jewish Cemetery, Ontario. Parents Harry, Sonia of Ansonville, Ontario.

11. Da Costa, Capt Darnley Peter Lamont. 121576 *Leicestershire Regt/Chindits*. Killed in action 14.7.44 aged 28. Buried Taukkyan, Burma 6 F 1. Parents Darnley and Mary of Dalkeith, Barbados.

Da Costa, Lt Patrick Clements. 156083 *1st Irish Guards*, Killed in action 30.1.44 aged 23. Buried Anzio III K 11. Parents Darnley and Mary of Dalkeith, Barbados.

12. Davis, Air/Mech Raymond. 96158 *SAAF*. 17.1.41 aged 22. Pretoria (Rebecca St) Cemetery, Gauteng, Jewish Section. Parents David, Sarah of Sea Point, Cape Province, South Africa.

Davis, Sgmn Sydney. 15962 *SACS*. 21.2.42 aged 24. Alexandria (Hadra) War Cemetery Egypt. Parents David, Sarah of Sea Point, Cape Province, South Africa.

13. Feinstein, Pte Nathan. F/3906 *N. Nova Scotia Highlanders RCIC*. 2.11.44 aged 27. Adegem Canadian War Cemetery, Belgium. Parents Isidor (sic), Fannie of Toronto.

Feinstein, Flt/Sgt AG Sam R/104215 *12 (RAF) Squadron RCAF*. 30.9.42. Bergen General Cemetery, Netherlands. Parents Isador (sic), Fannie of Inverness, Nova Scotia.

14. Feldman, Elect Artificer C13 Arthur. V/23593 HMCS *Columbine RCNVR*. 26.2.44 aged 21. St John's (Mount Pleasant) Cemetery, Newfoundland. Parents Morris, Grace Ellis Feldman, Glace Bay, Nova Scotia.

Feldman, Cpl Harold. C/14271 *Algonquin Regt, RCIC*. 8.3.45 aged 27. Groesbeek Canadian War Cemetery, Netherlands. Parents Morris, Grace Ellis Feldman, Glace Bay, Nova Scotia.

15. Feldman, Hyman. *AFS*. KIA 19.3.41 in Stepney. From Amhurst Park, Stamford Hill, buried Edmonton grave V 71 2 – headstone now disintegrated.

Feldman, Gnr Louis. 1577716 *RA 9th Coast Regt*. 12.9.44 on board Japanese POW ship. Singapore memorial Col. 18 (testimony from Mrs Stern in Enfield, daughter of Hyman) .

16. Felsenstein, Sgt Gerald Cecil 1396129 *102 Squadron RAFVR*. 12.3.43 aged 21. Runnymede Memorial. Parents Arthur, Ada of Golders Green. Twin brother Basil Saul also died.

Felsenstein, Sgt Nav/Bomber Basil Saul, 1396138 *82 Squadron RAFVR*. 15.1.45 aged 22. Buried Gauhati War Cemetery, India. Parents Arthur, Ada Felsenstein of Golders Green. Twin brother Gerald Cecil also died.

17. Finklestone-Sayliss, Capt. Dr Hyman. P283751 *Med. Officer Cadet Forces, JLB 2nd Btn Yorks and Lancs Regt, ARP Warden Officer, Divisional Surgeon St John's Ambulance*. DOAS in Sheffield 18.5.44 aged 48. Buried Ecclesfield Jewish Cemetery, Blind Lane. Husband of Lucy, father of Eric and David, son of Saul and Leah. Despite an appeal, Hyman is NOT recognized as war dead by the CWGC, despite proof of his army and ARP positions.

Finklestone-Sayliss, Sgt Raphael. 1067676 *RAFVR*. KIA 17.9.42 aged 27. Runnymede Panel 83 – from Sheffield. Son of Saul and Leah.

18. Flax, 2nd Lt Maurice.
207126 *SAAF*. 13.10.42 aged
23. Alamein Memorial. Parents
Simmy, Sarah of Johannesburg.
B.Sc (Eng).

Flax, Sgt Sydney. 31377
Technical Service Corps SAF.
20.1.43. Johannesburg (West
Park) Cemetery, Jewish Section.
Parents Mr and Mrs Simon Flax;
Wife S. of Johannesburg.

---

19. Pte Gaskin, David. D/86127
Black Watch of Canada RCIC.
8.8.44 aged 27. Bretteville-sur-
laize Canadian War Cemetery.
Parents Samuel, Gertie of
Montreal; Wife Nora Madeleine of
Montreal.

Gaskin, Sgmn Jack Hyman,
D/26890 *RCCS*. 10.5.45 aged
30. Holten Canadian War
Cemetery, Netherlands. Parents
Sam, Gertie of Montreal; Wife
Mary of Montreal.

---

20. Goldberg, Sgt/Pilot Louis,
R/56185 *RCAF*. 7.7.41. Buried
Merthyr Tydfil (Cefn) Jewish
Cemetery. Parents Joseph, Bryna
of Montreal. Brother Harry also
died.

Goldberg, Cpl Harry D/3524 *B.
Squadron 7th Recce Regt 17th
Duke of York's Roy Canadian
Hussars*. 26.4.45 aged 26. Buried
Holten Canadian War Cemetery,
Netherlands. Parents Joseph,
Bryna of Montreal. Brother Louis
also died.

**21. Goldfeather, Sgt Albert
Michael**. 747841 *RAFVR 113
Squadron*. 9.12.40. Alamein
memorial – Col. 240. Son of Mr
and Mrs George Goldfeather of 24
Adolphus Rd, Finsbury Park.

**Goldfeather, L/Bdr Israel
Joseph**. 955821 *RA, 142 Royal N
Devon Field Regt*. 9.9.43 aged
24. Salerno IV-A-40. Son of Mr
and Mrs George Goldfeather of 24
Adolphus Rd, Finsbury Park.

---

22. Gruber, Sgt Pilot Maurice.
777669 *50 Squadron RAFVR.*
9.5.42 aged 30. Buried Svino
Churchyard, Denmark. Parents
Sigmund, Annie of Mashaba,
Zimbabwe, Rhodesia. Brother
Rufus Isaacs Gruber also died.

Gruber, Sgt Rufus Isaacs.
777670 *44 Squadron RAFVR.*
9.11.42 aged 21. Buried
Hamburg War Cemetery, Germany.
Parents Sigmund, Annie of
Mashaba, Zimbabwe, Rhodesia.
Brother Maurice also died.

**23. Hantman, Fireman and
Trimmer Henry**. SS *Otterpool*
(West Hartlepool) *MN*. 20.6.40
aged 30. Tower Hill Memorial.

Hantman, Gdsman Samuel.
2736536 *3 Welsh Guards.*
11.2.44 aged 26. Cassino War
Cemetery, Italy.

[Note. *Jewish Chronicle* 17 March
1944 states that they were
brothers, using the name
Huntman. This was corrected to
Hantman in *JC* 9 June 1944].

---

24. Hartstein, P/O Philip.
158031 *7 Squadron RAFVR.*
9.10.43 aged 21. Buried Hanover
War Cemetery, Germany. Parents
Abraham, Anna of Willesden.

Hartstein, P/O Emmanuel.
184006 *RAFVR*. 23.8.44. Buried
Willesden Jewish Cemetery.
Parents Abraham, Anna of
Willesden. Brother Philip also died.

---

25. Heiser, Aaron. *Firewatcher.*
KIA 11.5.41 aged 57 at 95 Old
Street, London (*JC* 16.5.41).
Buried Willesden, grave FX 19
857. Of 5 Brookside Rd, Golders
Green, husband of Sarah,

Heiser, Jacob, *Firewatcher*. KIA
11.5.41 aged 55 at 95 Old Street,
London (*JC* 16.5.41). Buried
Willesden, grave FX 19 856. 44
Stanhope Gardens, Haringay.

**26. Hyamson, Lt Theodore
David**. 132095 *45 Army Troops
Coy RE attached Roy Bombay
Sappers and Miners*. 25.2.42
aged 28. Singapore Civil Hospital
Grave Memorial. Parents Albert
Montefiore Hyamson, Marie of
West Kensington. B.Sc.

**Hyamson, Cpl Philip Henry
Samuel**. 1012829 *RAFVR.*
20.8.44 aged 32. Buried Golders
Green Jewish Cemetery. Parents
Albert Montefiore Hyamson, Marie
Rose Hyamson of West
Kensington. B.Sc. Brother
Theodore David also fell.

[NOTE: Albert Montefiore Hyamson was the
well-known historian of Anglo-Jewry, a
President of the Jewish Historical Society of
England and author, *inter alia*, of The
Sephardim of England, 1951.]

27. Jacobs, LAC John George. 521000 *FAA RAF*. KIA 17.9.39 HMS *Courageous* aged 24. Son of Henry and Emma, Woodford, Essex. Panel 2, Runnymede/

Jacobs, Sgt Obs William Frederick. 1168909 *RAF*. 5.8.42, aged 20. Buried Berwick, St John's churchyard, Wilts. Son of Henry and Emma.

---

28. Joseph, LAC Pilot under training Harold Walter Harris. *RAFVR*. 17.12.1940 aged 24. Buried Stoke-upon-Trent (St Peter) Church. Parents Clifton Hyman Joseph, Vera Rachel of Armadale, Victoria, Australia.

Joseph, P/O Graham Harris 400415 *RAAF*. 17.6.43 aged 25. Buried Rheinberg War Cemetery, Germany. Parents Clifton Hyman Joseph, Vera Rachel of Armadale, Victoria, Australia. [Not listed in *Australian Jewry Book of Honour*].

---

29. Kauffman, 2nd Lt Edward Crompton. 184290 *28 Field Regt RA*. 6.6.42 aged 26. Alamein Memorial, Egypt. Parents Otto Jackson Kauffmann, Rosalind of Golders Green.

Kauffman, Capt Henry Benedict Crompton. 129413 *Roy Fus att 12th Btn Para Regt*. 3.4.45 aged 27. Buried Reichswald Forest War Cemetery, Germany. Mother Rosalind of Golders Green. BA (Cantab.)

---

30. Letwin, Gnr Jack. 1081522 *RA*. 31.8.47 aged 34. Rainham (Federation) Jewish Cemetery. Parents Reuben, Ada; Wife Annie of Hackney.

Letwin, Pte Woolfe. 4751940 *4 Bn Green Howards*. 28.2.45 aged 29. Prague War Cemetery, Czech Republic. Parents Reuben, Ada of Bethnal Green.

---

31. Levy, Cpl Peter John. 7905057 *RAC*. KIA 8.4.43. Buried Medjez-El-Bab. Son of J.A. Leigh of Cricklewood.

Leigh (aka Levy), Flt Sgt Ronald. 1804526 *RAF*. KIA 3.3.45. Buried Willesden Jewish Cemetery. Son of J.A. and Sarah Leigh.

---

32. Levy-Haarscher, AC2 Abraham Leopold, 775546 *RAFVR*. 28.1.41 Alamein Memorial.

Levy-Haarscher, Flt Lt Richard Simon 127181. *230 Squadron RAFVR*. 15.10.45. Singapore Memorial.

---

33. Lion, Charles. Killed 17.10.40 aged 59, of 88 Old Street. Died St Matthews' Hospital, Shoreditch.

Lion, Walter M. 42248 *RI Rifles*. KIA 10.5.18. Named at Tyne Cot, Panel 38 (First World War).

---

34. Magid, WO2 Moses. 101383V *SAAF*. 17.7.45 aged 22. Khartoum War Cemetery, Sudan. Parents Salig, Fannie of Sea Point, Cape Province, South Africa.

Magid, Lt Obs William Joseph. 104065V *SAAF*. 17.7.45 aged 26. Khartoum War Cemetery, Sudan. Parents Salig, Fannie of Sea Point, Cape Province, South Africa.

35. Millet, Percy. *Firefighter*. KIA 8.9.40 aged 28 in Buckle Street, Stepney, first Jewish Firefighter killed. Son of Annie and A. Millet of 45 Fuller St, Bethnal Green. Burial place not given.

Millet, Morris/Maurice. *Merchant Navy*. Killed 22.10.42 aged 20, MV *Primero* (Norway). Tower Hill Memorial, panel 85. Son of Michael and Anne of South Tottenham – tbc if brothers.

---

36. Morris, Gnr Nathan (aka Moranski). 969730 *RA, 98 Surrey & Sussex Field Regt*. 8.4.44 aged 27. Cassino – 1 A 17. Son of Mrs L. Morris, 22 Coronation Ct., Brewster Gdns, North Kensington.

Morris, Dvr Robert. 2121988 *RE 517 Corps Field Coy*. 12.7.44. Florence XII E 9. Son of Mrs L. Morris, 22 Coronation Ct., Brewster Gdns, North Kensington.

---

37. Neirynck, LAC WO/AG Victor Charles Edward. *235 Squadron RAF*. 8.5.40 aged 19. Buried Southend-on-Sea (North Road) Cemetery. Parents Eugene, Bertha of Westcliff-on-Sea. Brother Leslie Douglas also died.

Neirynck, Pte Leslie Douglas. 6017768 *5th Btn Sherwood Foresters (Notts & Derby) Regt*. 3.11.43 aged 20. Buried Minturno War Cemetery, Italy. Parents Eugene, Bertha of Westcliff-on-Sea. Brother Victor Charles Edward also died.

38. Ottolangui, Sgt Aaron.
1391065 *101 Squadron RAFVR*.
15.4.43. Mauberge-Centre
Cemetery.

**Ottolangui, Asst Steward
George.**. SS *Empire Heritage*
(Cardiff) *MN*. 8.9.44 aged
23.Tower Hill Memorial. Parents
Montague, Fanny of Bow.

**39. Podgurski, Pte Ernest
Edward.** 3058654 *1st Btn Roy
Scots*. 26.5.40 aged 21. Buried
Le Paradis War Cemetery, France.
Parents Ernest Edward, Sarah of
Hendon, Sunderland. Brother Alan
also died.

Podgurski, L/Cpl Alan.
14245056 *9th Btn Durham LI*.
24.1.45 aged 21. Buried Sittard
War Cemetery, Netherlands.
Parents Ernest Edward, Sarah of
Hendon, Sunderland. Brother
Ernest Edward also died.

---

40. Rich, Sgt Jack, 6202762 *1st
Bat. Middx. Regt*. 24/25.12.41,
aged 24 years, son of Abraham
and Leah Rickman. Buried Sai
Wan, Hong Kong.

Ricklovitch, Pte Israel,
10535093 *RAOC*. Killed 23.6.45
– buried Naples.

---

41. Rosenthal, Gnr Cyril.
1587192 *178 Bty 50 LAA Regt
RA*. 9.2.41 aged 27. Buried Hull
Western Synagogue Cemetery.
Parents Isadore, Nina of Hornsea.

Rosenthal, AC2 Ronald.
1479439 RAFVR. 21.10.41 aged
20. Buried Hull Western
Synagogue Cemetery. Parents
Isadore, Nina of Hornsea.

42. Savage, F/O Myer. 124230
254 Squadron RAFVR. 5.4.43.
Commemorated Runnymede
Memorial. Parents Robert Arthur,
Annie of Hampstead.

Savage, WO/AG Maurice. 56045
207 Squadron RAF. 26.8.44 aged
26. Buried Durnbach War
Cemetery, Germany. Wife Betty.

**43. Schwind, Sgt Obs Gordon
Louis.** 581353 *59 Squadron
RAFVR*. 26.5.40 aged 21. Buried
Warneton Communal Cemetery,
Belgium. Parents Charles Lionel,
Florence of Crowborough, Sussex.

Schwind, Flt/Lt Lionel Harold.
37870 *213 Squadron RAFVR*.
27.9.1940. Buried Crowborough
Burial Ground. Parents Charles
Lionel, Florence (nee Dayton) of
Crowborough; Wife Georgina (née
Trueman).

---

44. Shapiro, Lt David. *Lanark &
Renfrew Scottish Regt, RCIC*.
5.12.44. Ravenna War Cemetery,
Italy. Parents Mr, Mrs Mayer,
Toronto.

Shapiro, Pte Norman. B/76976
Toronto Scottish Regt (MG), RCIC.
21.3.41 aged 24. Toronto (Jones
Avenue) Cemetery, Ontario.
Parents Meyer, Sarah of Toronto.

---

45. Shinman, Gnr David.
1145278 *15 Field Regt RA*.
12.6.44 aged 38. Buried Moro
River Canadian Cemetery, Italy.
Parents Alexander, Jane; Wife
Alice Lillian of St Pancras.

Shinman, Pte Jack. 6145753 *6th
Btn Black Watch (Roy Highland
Regt)*. 17.7.44 aged 32. Buried
Assisi War Cemetery, Italy. Parents
Alexander, Jane; Wife Gladys
Winifred of Biggin Hill, Kent.

---

46. Shore, Gnr Solomon.
1563035 *48 Bty 21 LAA Regt RA*.
17.11.44. Singapore Memorial.

Shore, Gnr Theodore. 6472825
48 Bty 21 LAA Regt RA. 7.7.45
aged 27. Labuan War Cemetery,
Malaysia. Parents Morris, Millie of
Southgate.

[On chaplains' cards held at AJEX they had
the same address, 80 Chase Road, N14,
and their father was M. Shore.]

---

47. Smollan, AC1 Dennis.
1520153 *51 Squadron RAFVR*.
7.2.43 aged 21. Buried Hazelrigg
Jewish Cemetery,
Northumberland. Parents Henry,
Annie of Montreal. Brothers
Joshua and Harold also died.

Smollan, Sgt/Obs Joshua.
1109606 *608 Squadron RAFVR*.
30.1.44 aged 29. Malta
Memorial. Parents Henry, Annie of
Montreal. Brothers Dennis and
Harold also died.

Smollan, Pte Harold. 14820558
*West Yorks Regt attached 7th Btn
Para Regt*. 7.4.45 aged 19.
Buried Becklingen War Cemetery,
Germany. Parents Henry, Annie of
Montreal. Brothers Dennis and
Joshua also died.

---

48. Solomon, Gnr Ralph. 956379
2nd Regt RHA. 8.5.43 aged 23.
Buried Massicault War Cemetery,
Tunisia. Parents Gerald Isaacs
Solomon, Mahalath of Southgate.

Solomon, Pte Ronald.
14323981 *2nd Btn Beds & Herts Regt.* 23.7.44 aged 20. Buried Arezzo War Cemetery, Italy. Parents Gerald Isaacs Solomon, Mahalath of Southgate.

---

49. Solomons, Fus Samuel MM.
6481845 *8th Btn Roy Fus.* 8.10.43 aged 21. Buried Naples War Cemetery, Italy. Parents Laurence, Elizabeth of Clapton.

Solomons, Pte Henry.
14586576 *4th Btn Dorsetshire Regt.* 15.2.45 aged 20. Buried Reichswald Forest Cemetery, Germany. Parents Laurence, Elizabeth of Clapton.

---

50. Wald, Pte Sydney. 3911315 *1 Brecknockshire Btn S.Wales Borderers.* 16.6.40 aged 24. Buried Swansea Hebrew Congregation Cemetery. Parents Samuel, Gertie of Leeds. Brother Harold also died.

Wald, Pte Harold. 14719382 *5th Btn KOSB.* 16.2.45 aged 20. Buried Milsbeek War Cemetery, Netherlands. Parents Samuel, Gertie of Leeds. Brother Sydney also died.

---

51. Wolfson, Pte Norman.
NX79953 *55/.53 Btn Australian Inf.* 7.12.42 aged 21. Buried Port Moresby (Bomana) War Cemetery, Papua New Guinea. Parents Jacob, Rebecca of Coogee, New South Wales.

Wolfson, F/O Harold (Harry).
424253 *RAAF.* 2.3.1945 aged 29. Buried Heverlee War Cemetery, Belgium. Parents Jacob Percival, Rebecca; Wife Peggy Ruth of Bellvue Hill, New South Wales.

---

52. Zahn, L/Bdr, B.W.P. 114800 *2 Bty 1 Field Regt SAA.* 20.6.42 aged 22. Knightsbridge War Cemetery, Acroma, Libya. Parents Mr, Mrs G.A. of Knysna, Cape Province, South Africa.

Zahn, 2nd Lt Pilot John Pilgrim.
103622 *21 Squadron SAAF.* 3.10.44. Tel-el-Kebir War Memorial Cemetery, Egypt. Parents Gustav A., Kathleen P. of Knysna, Cape Province, South Africa.

---

53. Zamek, Sgt Ian Alexander.
749523 *58 Squadron RAFVR.* 3.10.40. Buried Berlin 1939/1945 War Cemetery, Germany. Parents Alfred, Kate of Bournemouth. Brother Norman Henry also died.

Zamek, Sgt/Pilot Norman Henry. 119637 *RAFVR.* 16.7.42. Buried Ranchi War Cemetery, India. Parents Alfred, Kate of Bournemouth.

---

54. Zareikin, P/O WO/AG Samuel. J/17716 *102 (RAF) Squadron RCAF.* 28.5.43 aged 26. Wieringen (Hippolytushoef) General Cemetery, Netherlands. Parents David, Pola of Los Angeles. Brother Joseph also died.

Zareikin, P/O AG Joseph,
C/88488 *433 Squadron RCAF.* 5.10.44 aged 36. Harrogate (Stonefall) Cemetery, Yorkshire. Parents David, Pola of Los Angeles. Brother Samuel also died.

Note
This list excludes civilian/forces siblings killed. For these, see http://www.jewishgen.org/jcr-uk: go to 'Databases' then 'Supplementary UK Databases' then 'Jewish Civilian Casualties of War'.

Additional Killed in Action, Commonwealth and Allied

(Not named in other Books of Honour or by the CWGC)

South Africans killed in action

(Many names have been found in the South African Jewry Book of Honour BUT not in the CWGC records. Some have been found in neither, but have war graves, for example in East Africa!)

Abramowitz, L/Cpl Joseph Barnett

Bark, Gnr Joseph
SAA

Barnet, Pte A.
1st Rand LI, SAAF

Block, Lt S.
SAAF

Cash, Lt Louis
SAAF
                                28.11.43
Alamein

Cohen, Lt B.
Womens SAAC

Cohen, Spr Isaac G.
b. Egypt (father Jewish)

Cohen, Leonard
328769V SAAF

Davis, Lt S.D.
SAAF
                                5.9.42
Buried Kenya

De Saxe, Capt Harold

De Haaf, Sgt N.C.A.
Kenya Regt
                                29.4.41
Buried Nairobi

Epstein, Sgt D.
(Rhodesian)

Evans, Cpl Jack
SAAF

Frank, Cpl D.S.G.
Natal Mtd Rifles

Frankel, N.D.
SAA
                                23.11.41

Frankel, W.E.
SAEC
                                29.12.42

Friedman, Sgt A.
21 Sqd SAAF

Friedman, Cpl Gabriel
SAAF

Friedlander, AB Cecil Arnold
HMSAS *Southern Floe*
                                11.2.41

Goldstone, Cpl R.F.
99509V SAAF
                                10.12.44
Ancona War Cem

Greenstein, Cpl W.W.
1 Cape Corps

Grosman, Cpl A.J.
SAASC

Guttman, Cpl F.
East African REME
                                12.7.44
Buried Nairobi

Hirschfeld, Capt G.W.
SAAF
                                4.12.44

Hirschman, Alf
Gren Gds

Houthhakker, Harold Sam

Hurwitz, Mechanic F.
SAAF

Jacobson, WAAF A.M.
SAAF

Kahn, Cpl L.
SAA

Karnovsky, Lt Moses
15 Sqd SAAF

Kruyer, Simon Isaac

Lenz, William
SANF

Lieberman, AC2 Stella May
S Rhodesia WAAF
Age 23   28.2.42
Buried Harare (Pioneer) Cem

Marks, Lt G.V.
SAAF 11 Squadron

Marx, Cpl P.S.
Special Service SAAF

Marx, Pte S.J.
General Service Corps

Menn, WO2 Abraham
SAASC
Age 48   18.8.46
Malmesbury Jewish Cem

Nathan, G.J.
C Town High., 19293
                           28.1.43

Newmark, Brian
Kenya Regt
                           -.4.42
KIA Abyssinia
Memorial in Nairobi

**Rosenberg, Sgt Arthur L.
(aka Lawrence)**
SAAF

Salomon, Cpl E.
Witwatersrand Rifles

Salomons, Cpl Robert
Technical Service Corps

Samuels, Pte F.
Cape Corps
                           6.11.40
Buried Nairobi

Scheinberg, Cpl Harry
SAEC

Schneider, WO2 Norman F. (Jack)
General Service Corps

Shrock, Cpl J.
SAAF
Age 26   22.2.46
Buried Cape Town Jewish Cem

Solomon, Spr J.
SAEC

Stein, Pte Sam

Steinberg, C.J.
SAAF

Susskind, Lt P.J.
4th Field Reg SAAF

Swarts, Pte Samuel
Cape Corps
Age 29   28.8.42
Buried Alexandria (Hadra) War
Cem

Ralstein, C.J.
Rhodesian Forces
Buried Egypt

Thal, Basil
Rhodesian Forces
Buried Somalia

Tren, Pte

Australia/NZ killed in action

Aarons, Sgt Francois Emanuel
RAAMC
Age 28   2.12.42
El Alamein War Cem

Cantor, Sqdn/Ldr Oswald T.
RAAF
Age 36   20.3.44
Toowoomba Cem

Cantor, P/O Colin V.
RAAF
Age 28   17.6.42
Northern Territory Memorial

Caselberg, F/O John
RNZAF
Buried New Caledonia

Cohen, Flt/Lt Colin Edward
255205 RAAF
Age 43   1.5.45
Labuan War Cem

Cohen, P/O Geoffrey Landas
402212 RAAF
Age 27   3.8.41
Finningley Churchyard

Cohen, Cpl Maxwell
NX39899 Aust Inf
Age 23   16.2.43
Port Moresby Mem

Cohen, Spr Phillip
34342 NZRE
Age 30   2.12.43
Sangro River War Cem

Cohen, Spr Reuben John
TX5609 RAE
Age 37   31.5.43
Thanbyuzayat War Cem

Cohen, Maj Richard Hugh
NX499 AIF
Age 30   9.12.42
Singapore Mem

Cohen, Pte Robert Henry
WX19697 AIF
Age 36   25.10.43
Lae War Cem

Cohen, Lt Roy David
34909 AIF
Age 26   9.2.42
Singapore Mem

Davis, Joseph (aka Davidovitz)

De Costa, Lt R.
NZEF

Faine, LAC Harry
RNZAF
Buried New Caledonia

Fienberg, Sydney H.
Aust Pay Corps

Forman, Sgt William Israel
RNZAMC
                           17.12.44
Buried Auckland

Friedman, Maurice W
RNZN

Glazer, Sol
RNZAF
Buried Groningen

Goldberg, Leslie C.
AIF 2/24

Goldburg, Pte Arthur L.
AAOC
                           7.9.43
Buried Kanchanaburi, POW

Goldman, Sgt Maurice
RAAF

Goldstone, Robert M.
RNZAF

**Grossman, Pte Edwin George
(aka Crossley)**
AIF
Age 27   20.2.42
Ambon Mem

Gubbay, Lt Alan R.
Z Force AIF Special Forces
                         13.4.45
KIA, Lae Memorial

Herman, I.
Japanese POW Kanchanaburi

Hirschfeld, Pte Werner
Aust. Labour Corps
Age 43   25.4.42
Fawkner Mem Park Cem

Hyams, Flt/Lt A. Joseph
RNZAF
Buried New Caledonia

Hyman, Lawrence F.
AIF 2/22

Israel, P/O Jack Lewis
RAAF 423752
Age 20   27.6.44
Runnymede Mem

Israel, Gnr Leonard Joseph
RAA NX37548
Age 26   20.12.44
Labuan War Cem

Lazarus, WO1 Frederick H.
NP485, Aust. Instruc. Corps
Age 62   11.12.46

Lazarus, LAC Percy R.
32408 RAAF
                         28.2.43

Lazarus, Samuel A.
AIF 2/21

Levene, WO1 Samuel
2665 RNZI
Age 45   26.9.43
Auckland (Waikumete) Cem

Levey/Levy, P/O Alan Neil
429153 RAAF
Age 22   21.3.45
Buried in Reichswald Forest War
Cem (cross on grave in error)

Levy, W. Julius
NZEF
Buried Cassino

Levy, Sub Lt Keith
RANR
HMS *Australia*
                         5.1.45

Levy, L/Cpl Walter
RNZI
Buried Cassino

Louisson, Charles Louis
NZ Artillery
Died as POW of Germans 1945

Louisson, Capt Neil M.
NZEF
                    5–27.11.43
Suicide after returning wounded
twice and found wife with another
man
Buried Auckland

Manoy, S/Sgt P.H.
NZMGC 2nd NZEF
KIA   18.11.60
Buried Auckland Cemetery Jewish
section

Marcus, Pte L.J.
NX22101, 2.17 AIF
                         28.10.42
El Alamein

Marks, Sub/Lt Frank Ernest
RNZN

Marks, Murray
RNZAF

Marks, Asst Cook Thomas Leslie
RNZN

Marx, Phillip
NZI
                         9.12.41
Buried Greece

Marx, Ray Stanley
NZASC
Son of Jacob and Alice, Auckland

Mitchell, J.J.
NZEF

Moss, Pte John
RNZMC
Buried Sfax

Myers, Alan J.
AIF

Myers, Lt Elliot
RNZEF
Buried Wellington

Myers, Sig. Ernest
RNZCOS
Buried Labuan

Myers, Ms I.L.C. ?

Nathan, Lt. Carroll Robert
NZEF

Nathan, Pte Edward David
VX96635 AIF
Age 20   4.7.47
Buried Yokohama War Cem

Nathan, George B.
NZI
Buried Athens

Neumann, Pte Herbert O.
AIF
Age 40   1.5.41
Alamein Mem

Oppenheim, Leonard Aaron
Singapore Vol
                         15.2.45
From Sydney

Rose, H.G.
NZ Artillery

Rosenberg, Alan
Japanese POW Kanchanaburi

Rosenberg, Barry
RNZAF
                         5.10.44

Sachs, Lt John MM
Z Force Commando
                              -.4/45
Executed by Japanese
Son of F. Abraham Sachs

Sanders, H.
AIF
                              30.12.42

Sole, G.
RNZAF

Urlich, Sub Lt. Joseph
RNZN

Walde, L.
Unit unknown
Wellington Synagogue memorial

Canadians killed in action

Abramson, Cpl David
RCCOS

Bigurski, Pte Walter Jack
RCIC
Age 20   3.1.44
Buried Brookwood Mil Cem

Bloch, F/O W. Roland
RCAF J21312
                              26.11.43

Bonder, AC1 Hyman
RCAF

Cherry, Capt Alex
RCAMC
Age 47   4.8.45
Lethbridge Hebrew Cem

Cohen, F/O Cyril Branston
RCAF J17619
                              3.6.44
Runnymede Mem

Cohen, Pte Murray
RCIC B498060
Age 21   24.11.40
Buried Toronto (Dawes Rd) Cem

Feldman, Electrical Artificer Arthur
RCN V23593
Age 21   26.2.44
St John's (Mt Pleasant) Cem

Feldman, Cpl Harold
C14371 Algonquin
Age 27   8.3.45
Groesbeek Canadian War Cem

Florence, AC1 Kolman
RCAF
Age 23   25.12.44
Toronto (Dawes Rd) Cem

Goldspink, Sgt Joseph J.
RCAF
                              28.3.43
Buried Escoublac-la-Baule Cem

Goldstein, Cpl K.
RCPC
Buried Brookwood

Goldstein, F/O Robert Philip
J12863
Age 25   3.10.43
Buried Hanover War Cem
Cross on grave in error

Goldston, WO2 Murray
RCAF R106050
Age 25   13.6.43
Runnymede Memorial

Halperin, Fl/Lt William Lionel
RCAF
                              6.11.43
Ottawa Mem

Klein, Pte Adam
RCIC

Klein, Pte Anthony
RCIC

Kowalski, Flt/Sgt Louis
R60959 RCAF
Age 21   11.3.42
Beck Row (St John) Churchyard

Lakser, CSM Louis M.
RCAMC

Lazarus, WO John
Can MN
SS *City of Benares*
                              17.9.40
Halifax Mem

Levine, Cpl Louis
RCCS
                              22.1.46

Levy-Despas, Fl Off. Guy
RCAF
                              9.7.42
Served as Carlet, KIA
Legion D'Honneur, Croix de
Guerre Malta Memorial

Marks, WO2 Edward R.
RCSF R134206
                              18.8.43
Killed in action
Buried Berlin War Cem

Marks, Cpl Maude Alexandra
Canadian WAC
Age 43   3.8.47
Buried Toronto (Mount Hope) Cem

Marlowe, LAC L. Chaim
RCAF
Age 22   8.5.43
Buried Detroit (Hebrew Mem) Park

Mendelson, L/Cpl Nathan (aka Leon L/Cpl Norman Cecil, aka Carl, aka Middleton)
Can Forestry Corps
                              24.8.42

Mendelssohn, Sgt Joseph
RCAC
Age 43   28.7.43
Toronto (Dawes Rd) Cem

Morris, LAC Julius J.
RCAF

Nathan, Flt/Lt Gerald
RCAF J13441
                              30.8.44

Novick, Flt/Lt Alexander
RCAF
                              22.10.43
Hanover War Cem

Rokach, Dvr Alan H.
RCCOS

Rosenberg, Cpl Carl C.
RCIC

Rosenberg, Gnr Dennis
RCA
6.9.44

Rosenberger, Pte David W.
RCIC
19.7.44

Rosenberger, Pte Joseph P.
RCIC
11.9.44

Steiner, Pte Murray
RCAMC
5.1.47

Strauss, R.H.
RCAF
20.11.43

Weinheimer, Pte Eric J.
RCIC
Age 22   19.7.44
Buried Bretteville-sur-Laize Can
War Cem

Weinstein, Pte Robert James
RCIC
18.3.45

White, Capt Julian
RCAMC

Wiener, Gnr Murray Aaron
RCA
Age 23   19.2.46
Buried Toronto (Roselawn) Hebrew
Cem

Wolf, Sgt Hiram (aka
Greenberg, Julius)
RAF/RCAF
1.1.42
Buried Rainsough Jewish Cem,
Lancs

Allied Nationals serving in forces attached to British Forces

Czech Army

Alt, Robert
18.1.41
Buried Liverpool Jewish Cem (*JC*)

Faden, Hugo
7.9.42
Buried Birmingham (*JC*)

Grunwald, Kurt
10.10.41

Mirovsky-Muller, Jiri E.
Buried East Ham (*JC*)
22.1.45
Buried Birmingham (*JC*)

Pick, Evzen Bedrich
3.3.45
Buried East Ham (*JC*)

Rosenfeld, Alexander
10.12.44
Buried Belgium

Schwarz, Maximillian
24.1.44
Buried Rainham (*JC*)

Waldstein, Hanus
22.2.45
Buried Birmingham (*JC*)

Wilhelm, Frantisek
26.11.41
Buried Birmingham (*JC*)

Dutch

De Lange, M.B.
Army
11.5.44
Buried East Ham (*JC*)

Zwarterser, Louis
MN
25.6.44
Buried Dover (*JC*)

Belgian

Edelstein, Michel
Army
31.3.42
Buried East Ham (*JC*)

A Note on Jews in the Polish Armed Forces During the Second World War

Leonard Kurzer, Leon Fait and Ludwik Kleiner

The members of the Polish Jewish Ex-Servicemen's Association have long been aware that there is no record of the contribution made by Jews to the efforts of the Polish Armed Forces during the Second World War. However, it is only recently that a few of us decided to take steps to rectify this omission. Little did we realise the enormity and difficulty of the task which we had undertaken: many Jewish ex-servicemen have died, others have emigrated to the far corners of the globe and the memories of those who are left have faded with the passing of the years. Furthermore, the War Office could not provide us with information about those killed in action because it cannot, by law, divulge details of such servicemen without the permission of their families and these were, all too often, amongst the victims of the Holocaust.

We present the little that we have been able to find out, in the form of this partial record, of those who gave their lives in the cause of the fight for freedom and we dedicate it to their memory. We thank Rabbi Pinkas Rosengarten of Jerusalem, former Chaplain to the Second Corps of the Polish Army, for his record of Polish-Jewish servicemen killed in action and Mr Norbert Sonnenblick for supplying us with details of Jews who served with the 1st Polish Independent Parachute Brigade.

We have also included in this record those of our colleagues who won the Virtuti Militari. This is the highest Polish decoration (it is the equivalent of the Victoria Cross) and is awarded for heroism on the field of battle. In addition, many Jewish servicemen won the Krzyz Walecznych, the Cross of Valour. One, Captain David Kupferman of the Polish Second Corps, received the British Military Cross.

When Poland was invaded by Germany and the Soviet Union in September 1939, most Jews realised the threat to their lives posed by a Nazi occupation and those who could tried to flee. Some of the luckier ones escaped eastwards to the Soviet-occupied zone, from where a small number managed to get to China or Japan and on to Canada and Britain; others headed southwards to Romania and Hungary, and then, in a roundabout fashion, on to France. Many of the Jews who, using these routes, escaped the Nazi terror, volunteered for the armed-forces-in-exile set up in the free world by the Polish refugees.

Figure 310. Joseph Reinhold, killed in pre-invasion manoeuvres, 8 May 1944.

Figure 311. Grave of Cad/O Alexander Greenberg in Monte Cassino.

The First Corps of the Polish Army, the Polish 1st Armoured Division, was set up in the West under the command of General Maczek. Unfortunately, we have been able to collect very little information about the Jews in this corps which took part in the Normandy landings. The casualties known to us are as follows:

Bokser, Pinchos
Army

1.7.46

Buried Glasgow

Czertok, 2nd Lt Leon, VM

31.12.44

KIA Holland and awarded the Virtuti Militari

Goldin, Cpl Michael, VM

-.8.44

Killed in action at Falaise and awarded the Virtuti Militari

Klayman, Dr Chaskiel, VM

-.8.44

Was awarded the Virtuti Militari at Falaise

Kuflik, Plutonowy
Polish Air Force

20.12.43

Buried Carmoney (*JC*)

Singer, Pte Henryk

-.8.44

Fatally wounded at Falaise

Szwarcsztajn, Josef N.
Army

20.5.44

Buried Glasgow

Zinger, Heinz
Army

15.9.44

Buried Bristol (*JC*)

The Second Corps of the Polish army was formed by General Anders in the Soviet Union and consisted of those, among them Jews, who had either been in the Gulags (labour camps), and were released after the Stalin-Sikorski agreement, or those who had been deported from Soviet-occupied Eastern Poland during 1939 and 1940. Among these was Menachem Begin, the future Prime Minister of Israel. There were also a number of Jews who had been demobilised, in 1941, from the Soviet Army into which they had previously been conscripted. As far as we have been able to ascertain, there were 838 known Jewish soldiers in the Second Corps, including 132 officers. It is, however, common knowledge that there were many more soldiers of Jewish origin who, for reasons of their own, did not admit to it.

Figure 312. Commemorative prayers, conducted by Rabbi Ruebner at the Great Synagogue in Rome, in memory of Polish Jewish soldiers killed in action in Italy.

On several occasions, General Anders expressed the highest regard for the Jewish soldiers under his command. Thirty-five Jewish soldiers were killed during the Second Corps' Italian Campaign of 1944 and 1945, and 58 were wounded.

In particular, Jewish soldiers distinguished themselves in the heroic battle for Monte Cassino which took place in May 1944. Eighteen graves in the war cemetery there are marked by the Star of David.

Our Roll of Honour of Jewish Soldiers killed in that part of the Italian campaign, which took place between 12 May and 30 July 1944, reads as follows:

Ancewicz, Rfmn Izaak

Awner, Rfmn Izrael

Baum, Cad/O Teodor
Buried at Monte Cassino

Blasenstein, Rfmn N.

Borkowski, Cpl Mieczyslaw

Chaskielewicz, Gnr Mordko
Buried at Monte Cassino

Goldin, Cpl Michael
Falaise VM 1944

Graber, Surg/Lt Adam
Buried at Monte Cassino

Grunbaum, 2nd Lt Mieczyslaw, VM
Wounded at Arnhem and awarded the Virtuti Militari

Grunberg, Cad/O Alexsander
Buried at Monte Cassino

Grunberg, Rfmn Lewi

Huttner, Rfmn Juliusz

Jekel, Cad/O, VM
Cassino

Jedwab, Janek
Pol Commandos
Italy Cross of Valour

Kleinbaum, Rfmn Marek

Kimmerman, Wladislaw, VM
Cassino

Klepfish, Michael, VM
(*JC* 17.3.44) Warsaw Ghetto

Knobloch, L/Cpl Wilhelm
Buried at Monte Cassino

Langsam, Cpl Zygmunt

Lieberman, 2nd Lt Jakub
Buried at Monte Cassino

Lipschutz, Cad/O Stanislaw
Buried at Monte Cassino

Mauer, Lt/Cpl Herman
Buried at Monte Cassino

Neufeld, Rfmn Szymon

Osterwel, Rfmn Zygmunt

Pastor, Rfmn Leon
Buried at Monte Cassino

Rapoport, VM
A/G Polish Air Force

Rosen
Pol Commandos
Italy Cross of Valour

Rozen, Cpl, MM
Italy

Rubinstein Rfmn Izrael

Simon, Rfmn Leon
Buried at Monte Cassino

Sommer, Rfmn Jozef

Sprauss, Cpl
Polish Cross of Valour

Stein, Richard
Polish Cross of Valour
Monte Cassino

Stern, Richard
Polish Cross of Valour
Monte Cassino

Sternlicht, Rfmn Samuel

Stokel, Rfmn Adolf

Stybel, Rfmn Chuna
Buried at Monte Cassino

Szapira, Rfmn Marek
Buried at Monte Cassino

Szapiro, Sgt Eljasz
Buried at Monte Cassino

Tennenbaum, Rfmn Abraham

Thieberger, L/Cpl Jozef
Buried at Monte Cassino

Trocki, 2nd Lt Adolph, VM

Unger, Cpl Maurycy
Buried at Monte Cassino

Wienner, Rfmn Szloma

Winawar, H.M.
Polish Cross of Valour

Wurzel, Rfmn Abraham
Buried at Monte Cassino

Zalzberg,Cad/O Ryszard

Zogrze, Cad/O Henryk
Buried at Monte Cassino

Zygman, Rfmn Hersz
Buried at Monte Cassino

Five of those who took part in the battle for Monte Cassino were awarded the Virtuti Militari, amongst them **Wladislaw Kimmerman** and Cad/O **Abraham Jekel. Michael Mordechai Kleinlerer** was also highly decorated for bravery. (A Cadet Officer [Cad/O] was a soldier who had undergone a course of military training open only to those who were graduates of secondary, i.e. high school, or further education.)

There was another army in the Soviet Union of which, unfortunately, we have no details at all, and that was the Kosciuszko Division, founded by Colonel (later General) Berling. This contained a large number of Jews who did not wish, for a variety of reasons, to join General

Figure 313. Jewish graves at the Polish Military Cemetery, Monte Cassino.

Anders' Army. They fought alongside the Soviet Army, entering Germany from the East, and sustained heavy losses.

There were 28 known Jewish soldiers in the 1st Polish Independent Parachute Brigade, of whom ten were officers. As in other sections of the Polish Armed Forces, there were more Jews who did not admit to their origins. The Brigade joined forces with the

21st British Army Group and took part in the battle for Arnhem, Holland, in September 1944. The casualties known by us to have been incurred by this unit are as follows:

Bier, Pte Anatol
Killed in action at Arnhem and buried in Oosterbeek

Fiakowski, Lt Jerzy Bereda
Wounded at Arnhem

Figure 314. Anatol Bier.

Groman, Cpl Moszek
Wounded at Arnhem

Czertok, 2nd Lt Leoanard
Polish Forces Cert Gallantry

Grunbaum, 2nd Lt Mieczyslaw, VM
Wounded at Arnhem

Reinhold, Cad/O Joseph
Killed in pre-invasion manoeuvres in May 1944 and buried in Newark.

Jedwab, Janek
Polish Cross of Valour Bar Italy

Kaczan, Will
Polish RAF Cross of Valour Military Courage

There were also Jews in the Polish Commandos. Of seventy-seven Commandos active behind German lines, seven were Jewish. These included **Janek Jedwab** and his brother as well as **Mr Rosen**, all of whom were in action behind enemy lines in Italy where they won the Krzyz Walecznych, the Cross of Valour. Janek Jedwab's brother was wounded and awarded the Podwojny Krzyz Walecznych, the Cross of Valour with Bar.

There were a number of Jews among the pilots, navigators and ground crew of the Polish Air Force which fought with such distinction during the Battle of Britain. A relatively high proportion were killed in action but only four (who had made their way to Britain through the Soviet Union and Japan) are known to us. They are:

Bychowski, Nav Ryszard
Killed when his damaged aircraft crashed on landing.

Glass, Nav Zygmunt
Shot down over Holland in 1943

Lipszyc, Nav Rubin
Shot down on the last day of the War while returning from a mission over Holland

Posner, Nav Eljasz
Shot down over the Channel in 1942.

Many others were decorated, including Aircraft Gunner Bombadier **Stanislaw Rapoport**, who won the *Virtuti Militari*. We regret that, for reasons already mentioned, we have not been able to give a more complete and accurate record of Jewish soldiers who served with loyalty and distinction in the Polish Armed Forces during the last War. We are, however, very happy to honour our colleagues who paid the ultimate sacrifice so that we could live in freedom.

Kleinlehrer, Michael Mordecha
Decorated Cassino

Klepfish, Michael, VM (Pos).
17.3.44
Warsaw Ghetto

Kupferman, David, MC

Klayman, Dr Chaskiel, VM
Falaise
-.8.44

Winawar, H.M.
Polish Cross of Valour

The full list of Polish Jewish killed, and POWs is published in the books by Benjamin Meirtchak, in seven volumes, in Israel.

When Britain Turned to the Jewish 'Private Armies'

Based upon articles in War Efforts by Major Wellesley Aaron, Royal Army Service Corps

In 1941, when Britain fought alone and seemed to be without a friend in the Middle East, the British military authorities turned to the Jewish 'private armies'. Those were the days when Britain was being hammered night and day by the Luftwaffe, Rommel was advancing across Libya, the Nazis had overcome Greece and Crete and in the heart of the Middle East a fifth column was at work. It was at that time that the ruling Arab classes made their greatest war effort, but in favour of the Nazis not the Allies.

The Egyptian Prime Minister, Defence Minister and Chief of Staff, were in communication with the enemy. In Iraq the British-trained armed forces rose in revolt against them. In Syria and Lebanon there was collaboration with the Germans and Italians and in Trans-Jordan the frontier force turned against the British. The British needed reliable information on the movements and plans of the enemy and Jewish agents working for Allied Intelligence were able to provide this in countries stretching from Syria to Africa.

Spearhead of the Syrian Campaign

When regular operations against Vichy Syria were about to begin, the military authorities asked the Haganah to provide reconnaissance and advance parties for the troops attacking on the eastern sector of the front. A unit of the Haganah, with 'illegal' arms, was attached to the Australian Division and formed the spearhead of the advance. A representative of Haganah was also attached to the staff of the Australian Brigade at Metulla.

Before zero hour, the unit brought the military authorities detailed information about the disposition of enemy troops and fortifications. At zero hour, the men of the Haganah were first to cross the frontier. They cut the telephone communications between the French garrisons, captured a number of pill-boxes which covered the frontier, and secured two important bridges. The purpose of these operations was to protect the deployment of the Australian Brigade which followed the Jewish spearhead. Soon after zero hour, all their objectives were achieved. More than 100 prisoners were taken and machine guns, lorries and armoured cars captured. The Haganah commander, who lost an eye during these operations, was one of the 43 young Jews previously imprisoned by the Palestine Government in Acre for membership of that organization. His name was Moshe Dayan

During a later stage of the Syrian campaign, when Vichy forces counter-attacked at Merj Ayoun and reached the Palestine frontier, members of the Haganah formed the first line of defence at Metulla. By their resistance, they discouraged the French commander from exploiting his success and covered the exposed Allied flank until reinforcements arrived. The Chief Liaison Officer with the military authorities was Mr David Hacohen, of Haifa, who rendered valuable services in connection with the Syrian campaign and in whose house on Mount Carmel the secret Free French Levant Radio Station was installed.

Formation of the Palmach

The Palmach, the striking force of the Haganah, was created during the war as a distinct formation, on the initiative of the Special Service Command of General Headquarters, Middle East. The British armies in the Middle East were in great peril. After the disasters of Sidi Rezheg and Knightsbridge, the fall of Tobruk and the loss of Mersa Matruh, General Auchinleck formed a last line of defence in front of the Nile Valley. The advance of Rommel's armies seemed irresistible and in the Egyptian cities the populace was hailing his advent with cries of 'Forward Rommel'. British troops had to surround the Royal Palace in Cairo in order to force the appointment of a government from which some measure of loyalty could be expected. But Nahas Pasha, Egypt's British-appointed Premier, later declared that he would request the Allies to evacuate his country when the Germans reached Alexandria, 'in order to spare Egypt useless suffering'.

Figure 315. A British Army recruiting poster, Tel Aviv, 1944.

Figure 316. Jewish Volunteers show the flag , Tel Aviv, 1940.

In the villages of Palestine and Syria, Arabs crowded round wireless sets, listening hungrily to Radio Bari's tales of Nazi victories. In the prisons of Acre and Jerusalem, the gang-leaders of the Arab disturbances told their fellow-prisoners of the Haganah, many of whom were kept in prison even at this period, that the day of reckoning was at hand.

This was the background against which the Palmach came into being. In the months before El Alamein, the British military authorities took a sombre view of the

Figure 317. Jewish recruits in a Tel Aviv street, 1941.

prospects. The evacuation of British institutions from Cairo was begun and staff officers and Embassy officials began to arrive in Jerusalem. It was considered that after a German break-through into Egypt, Palestine could not be held for any length of time and plans were contemplated for a strategic withdrawal to Syria and Iraq, or to the Sudan and East Africa. It was hoped that from these bases it would be possible, with the arrival of reserves and American material, to undertake the re-conquest of the Middle East.

The British staff officers working on these plans were not blind to the experience of the Russian campaign, which showed the immense value of partisans operating in enemy-occupied territory and supporting the advance of re-conquering armies.

The only community in the Middle East which could be relied upon to fulfil this task were the Jews of Palestine. Consultations took place with the leaders of the Haganah and the Palmach was established as one of the Special Service Units of the Middle East Command. An agreement was drawn up and signed between the British Special Service branch and the Staff of Haganah, defining the present and future duties of the formation, principles of its organisation and particulars of arms, equipment and stores to be provided by the military. Training centres were opened

Figure 318. Jewish contingent of the Auxiliary Territorial Service (ATS) known as the 'PATS' (Palestinian ATS), Tel Aviv, 1942.

at the towns of Yagour (raided and searched for arms in the recent operations), and at Mishmar Haemek. The existence of these centres was a 'top secret' and in order to avoid the danger of leakage, neither the Palestine Administration nor the police seem to have been informed.

The Palmach was recruited from existing Haganah units, in particular from members of Wingate's Special Night Squads and the advance and commando parties of the Syrian and other campaigns. The Palmach training camps were staffed by British instructors, although the commanders were men of the Haganah. Among the British instructors in demolition work, sniping and all forms of commando training were famous guerrilla experts. Palmach was later expanded to include this role, in addition to the original partisan nucleus. There was also a wireless section under

Figure 319. Jewish soldiers of the RASC laying a telephone cable in the Western Desert, 1942.

Jewish experts, some of whom were later taken over by General Headquarters (GHQ) as instructors in wireless operation and building for regular Army Signals Units. A network of secret Palmach wireless stations was organised throughout Palestine and Syria to ensure communications with the British Forces in the event of their withdrawal.

A further stage in the development of the Palmach was the incorporation of a special commando unit: the *Peter Haas Platoon.*

Peter Haas, after whom the platoon was named, had belonged to the famous 'Heaven Commando' (*Himmelfahrtscommando* or SIG). This was a commando unit of the British Army, almost entirely recruited from German-born Palestinian Jewish volunteers, who operated behind the lines in the Western Desert in German uniform. After distinguishing himself in a daring demolition raid on a Nazi airfield in Cyrenaica, Haas was killed in action, together with some of his friends, after being given away by a Nazi deserter.

The 'Haas Platoon' was intended to continue the work of the 'Heaven Commando' and to operate in a similar way in Palestine in the event of German occupation. Another special unit of the Palmach was the 'Balkan Platoon' which was employed mainly on parachute missions.

A detailed scheme of operations, to be put into effect in the event of German invasion, was prepared by the Staff of Palmach in cooperation with the British military authorities. This plan included the demolition of all rail and road communications and of industrial plants which could be of use to the enemy, and other types of commando and 'scorched earth' operations. A few weeks before El Alamein, units of Palmach were reviewed at Mishmar Haemek by the General Officer Commanding, Middle East Commandos, who took the salute together with Haganah leaders and complimented the men.

Palestine's Home Guard

Important military tasks were assigned to Haganah and Palmach under the alternative plans prepared by the British Staff, in case the protracted defence of Palestine, rather than its evacuation, should be decided upon. Extensive fortified zones were built in different parts of the country, and Jewish engineers, scientists and contractors (especially Solel Boneh headed by Mr David Hacohen), gave valuable assistance in their construction. But it was realised that static defence alone was not sufficient and that it would be necessary to supplement this, as had been done in Britain under the threat of invasion, by an additional network of Home Guard formations dispersed all over the country, to deal with enemy paratroops and armoured advance parties and thus give the regular forces the necessary respite to bring up reinforcements and stage a counter-attack.

It was clear that in Palestine, only the Jewish community could serve as the basis for such a Home Guard and that it could only be organised in co-operation with the Haganah. The Jewish Settlement Police Force was chosen as the framework for the development of this Home Guard and was equipped with some light and heavy machine guns, mortars and anti-tank weapons. As during the 1936 disturbances, Jewish supernumeraries were entrusted with the defence of all vulnerable and essential military objectives and took over coastal defences and air watch.

Figure 320. The Flag Revolt. Eretz Israel soldiers demanded that the Jewish flag be flown alongside the Union Jack in Benghazi – October 1943.

The Parachute Menace

When it became known that Rommel was receiving heavy paratroop reinforcements, and airborne operations against Palestine seemed to be imminent, the military authorities asked the Haganah to supply urgently a plan to meet the parachute menace throughout the entire country, both Jewish and Arab districts. An operational scheme to deal with minor airborne landings was worked out and approved. Joint British and Haganah manoeuvres were held as a preliminary step in the execution of the plan.

Figure 321. ATS Volunteers in Tel Aviv, 1942.

Another plan prepared by GHQ in the event of German invasion was to make Haifa a second Tobruk. It was to be held with a minimum of British forces, the main defenders being drawn from Jewish forces, i.e. the Palestine Regt and Jewish anti-aircraft and coastal batteries of the Artillery as well as by units of the Haganah. The then head of the Jewish security organization, the late Eliahu Golomb, was frequently in consultation with the authorities in connection with this and other schemes. *If connection with the Haganah was an offence, then the British Middle East Command was the worst offender during the war.*

Figure 322. Three Palestinian Jewish Parachutists, dressed as locals whilst on a mission behind the enemy lines for SOE, 1944.

Stalingrad and El Alamein turned the tide of the German advance. But the year that saw the beginning-of-the-end for the Nazis also saw the peak of the extermination campaign against the Jewish people. It was the year of the heroic and desperate Ghetto risings; the year when the gas chambers and crematoria worked overtime.

In Palestine, as the danger to the Middle East receded, Jewish assistance was no longer so urgently required and the allies of yesterday became the outlaws of today.

The arms so welcome during the Syrian campaign and in preparations to meet the threat of invasion, once again became 'illegal'. As the enemy began to retreat from the Middle East, the cry of 'Forward Rommel' heard in the streets of the Arab cities changed to a chorus of protestation of loyalty to the Allies.[1] While Mr Shertok was being told that there was no modern equipment available for the Jewish infantry battalions who demanded to be sent to the Front, supplies of material were lavished on the once mutinous Iraqi Army and Trans-Jordan Frontier Force.[2]

At the same time, a wave of persecution began against the Haganah and its leaders, and during the numerous arms trials which followed, the former partner of the British Army became the butt of a campaign of vilification. In passing sentence at one of these trials, the President of the Court referred to the existence in Palestine of a dangerous organisation possessing 'wide knowledge of military matters, including military organisation', as though this were a revelation, and as though the Haganah had not derived much of its military knowledge and training from the British themselves.

Despite persecution and rebuffs, the Haganah continued to offer its services to the British authorities.[3]

Enlistment

The following are extracts from *War Efforts*, a Palestinian war-time publication with acknowledgements to Major Wellesley Aaron, RASC and Dr Israel Beer.

The enlistment of Jewish volunteers in Palestine was first authorized only for the Auxiliary Military Pioneer Corps, and later on Jewish volunteers were admitted to various technical units. At first the authorities insisted on mixed Arab-Jewish units and that there should be numerical parity between Jews and Arabs. This restriction

Figure 323. A Palestine Jewish volunteer in the Stevedores' unit, Libya, 1943.

was abandoned as it limited Jewish recruitment, since Arabs did not volunteer in anything like the same number.

The urgent need for sappers and drivers led to the creation in 1940 of the first Jewish RE and RASC companies. Later, Jewish Infantry companies were formed which were incorporated in the Palestine Regt and subsequently became the nucleus of the Jewish Brigade Group which fought in the final stages of the Italian campaign.

There were Jewish contributions to the campaigns in East Africa,[4] Abyssinia, Rommel's defeat in Libya[5] and Tripolitania and the invasion of Italy.[6]

The story of one of the RASC units is given in *The Battle of the Desert*.

Notes

1. See *Arab Volunteers in the German Army*, A.J. Munoz, Axis Europa books, 5320, 207th St., N.Y. 11364, USA.
2. Anwar Sadat – later PM of Egypt - was arrested by the British on his way to meet with Rommel.
3. A final 'Redoubt' was planned on Mt. Carmel, near Haifa, as a last stand for Palestine Jewry had Rommel broken through.
4. The Jewish 51st Middle East Commando.
5. The Special Interrogation Group – S.I.G.
6. See section on the 'Parachute Heroes'.

A Parachute Hero and Two Heroines

Enzo Hayyim Sereni 1905–1944

Shot by the Germans in Dachau

Enzo Sereni was born in Rome in April 1905 into a well-established Jewish family. His father, a university lecturer, was doctor at the Royal Court and his uncle head of the Jewish communities in Italy. His mother's family also boasted a number of well-known personalities. Although deeply rooted in Italian society and culture, Enzo was very active in Zionist circles. In 1922 he became the Secretary to the movement and, on finishing his university studies in philosophy, he and his wife Ada left for Eretz Israel in 1927. There he worked in the citrus plantations in Rehovot and joined the group of Kibbutz Ha-Me'uchad that founded Givat Brenner. In 1932, he was sent to Germany to help strengthen the Zionist Youth Movement. After Hitler's rise to power, he went back to Germany to serve in the organisation of the efforts of the large Jewish Pioneer Movement to get Jewish capital out of the country. In 1936 he was sent on a mission to the United States.

In Eretz Israel, Enzo was active in the work to produce a united Kibbutz movement. Throughout his life, he was a believer in the need to reach an understanding with the Arabs and sought to establish relations with the neighbouring Arab villages. He preached non-violence. Nevertheless, the events of the Second World War influenced him deeply and he volunteered for service with the British Army. He was given an important task in Cairo by British Army Intelligence in the field of anti-fascist propaganda through the radio and newspapers and personal contact with Italian prisoners of war. He was arrested by the Egyptian police and, after an eleven-day hunger strike, was freed to return to Eretz Israel.

The year 1942 found him in Iraq organising the illegal Pioneer Movement. He later returned to Eretz Israel to serve the Mossad, helping to organise the illegal immigration of Jews from Nazi rule, even whilst the war still raged.

Figure 324. Enzo Sereni (centre) with two colleagues in the army in Italy.

Enzo Sereni was one of the initiators of the plan to parachute Jewish agents into Europe and insisted on taking part, in spite of his age. On 15 May 1944, he was dropped behind the German lines but was captured. On 18 November of the same year, he was put to death in Dachau.

Enzo was a cultured man, very learned and a great linguist. He was a deep and original thinker. Very much a man of action and possessed of great personal courage, his natural charm made him numerous friends.

A selection of his speeches is contained in the book *The Holy Spring* and his own book, *The Sources of Italian Fascism*, was published after his death.

In 1988 a commemorative stamp bearing his portrait was issued and a special cancellation, showing the insignia of the National Organisation of Hagana Veterans, was introduced to be used in the Kibbutz Nezer Sereni, which is named after him.

Figure 325. Enzo Sereni's commemorative stamp, 1988.

בחותמת מופיעים שם היישוב נצר סרני הנקרא על שמו של אגצו חיים סרני וכן סמל הארגון הארצי של חברי ההגנה.

The special cancellation, showing the insignia of the National Organisation of Hagana Veterans, will be used at Kibbutz Nezer Sereni, which is named after Enzo Hayyim Sereni.

Figure 326. The special cancellation introduced for the Kibbutz Nezer Sereni.

Hannah Senesh

Figure 327. Hannah Senesh. Executed by the Nazis in 1944 at the age of 23.

There are seven graves in the shape of a 'V' in the National Military Cemetery overlooking Jerusalem, with the outline of a parachute carved on each headstone. Buried there are seven of the 32 Palestinian Jewish parachutists, members of the British Armed Forces, who were dropped into Nazi-occupied Balkan countries during the war in a rescue bid. One of the seven was Hannah Senesh, executed at the age of 23 in 1944.

The story of how Hannah chose to leave her home and friends to become a pioneer in Israel has been written at great length. She has been described as Israel's 'Joan of Arc', a national heroine whose memory has been enshrined in many ways, not least when her body, having been brought from the Martyrs' section of Budapest's Jewish Cemetery to Israel, was buried with the highest military honours and saluted by thousands of Israeli soldiers and leading members of the government.

Hannah Senesh was born into an assimilated Hungarian Jewish family on 17 July 1921. She was part of a Jewish world that, strangely, survived relatively unharmed at a time when the rest of Europe's Jewry was being slaughtered. But even in Hungary things began to change and the mounting anti-Semitism led to Hannah becoming a Zionist in the late 1930s, as this trend led to the introduction of anti-Jewish legislation. She was determined to become a pioneer farm worker in Palestine and settled in the Kibbutz of Sdot Yam, near Caesarea in 1939.

Hannah had a secret ambition to be a writer and left diaries and poems written in Hungarian and Hebrew. She is remembered for those diaries. They include a portent for the future, written when she was already in Palestine and Hungary had joined the Nazis. 'Sometimes I feel like someone who has been sent to perform a mission. What that mission is, is not clear to me', she wrote. Again, in January 1943, we find an entry: 'I have had the sudden idea of going to Hungary. Regardless of how clearly I see the absurdity of the idea, it seems possible and necessary to me'.

In 1942, when news of Hitler's extermination policy reached the world, Hannah joined a group of Hagana members whom the British military authorities had agreed to train with the aim of dropping them into occupied Europe. She joined the British Army in 1943 at a time when the British were training a number of Jewish volunteers from Palestine as parachutists with a mission to rescue Allied pilots, organise resistance and to set up rescue operations for Jews. Hannah was amongst them.

Figure 328. Hannah Senesh with some of her group during the war.

In the Spring of 1944, a group of Jewish Palestinians, five men and a young woman, were dropped by parachute into Yugoslavia where, after a ten-day march, they reached a Partisan Corps headquarters. They established wireless communication with the British and arranged for arms and equipment to be dropped for the partisans by British planes. This was a few days before the Germans occupied Hungary and began to deport Jews on a massive scale.

Hannah Senesh crossed into Hungary with three other parachutists who were on a secret mission to Budapest. Sadly, she was captured by the Hungarian police while in possession of a wireless transmitter, but despite being tortured, she refused to give away her mission and was executed by a firing squad on 8 November 1944 within the prison courtyard in Budapest.

Shortly before she crossed from Yugoslavia into Hungary in early 1944, she passed on to Reuven Dafne, a fellow parachutist, the following poem 'Blessed is the Match'*:*

> Blessed is the match consumed in kindling flame
> Blessed is the flame that burns in the secret fastness of the heart
> Blessed is the heart with strength to stop its beating for honour's sake
> Blessed is the match consumed in kindling flame

Her last poem written in prison in Budapest was called 'One-Two-Three'.

> One, Two, Three, eight feet long
> Two strides across, the rest is dark
> Life hangs over me like a question mark
> One, Two, Three, maybe another week
> Or next month may still find me here,
> But death I fear, is very near.
> I would have been 23 next July
> I gambled on what mattered most
> The dice were cast, I lost

A Kibbutz, Yad Hanna, is named in her honour.

Haviva Reik 1919–1946

Figure 329. Haviva Reik. Executed by the Germans in Slovakia.

Haviva (Emma) Reik was one of the four members of the Hagana to be parachuted into Slovakia during the Second World War.

Born of working class parents who lived in a small village near the town of Banska Bystrica in Slovakia, she emigrated to Palestine in 1939 and joined the Hashomer Hazair Kibbutz of Ma'anit.

During the critical days of the war, she volunteered to return to Slovakia.

On 15 September 1944, parachutists from Eretz Israel were dropped into Slovakia in an area that was the scene of fighting between the Germans and the Slovakian anti-Nazi partisans. This drop marked the start of 'Operation Amsterdam' which had been planned by the British. On 20 September, Haviva Reik was dropped from an American aircraft over the heart of the fighting area, the fourth of the group of parachutists.

בחותמת מופיעים שם היישוב להבות חביבה הנקרא על שמה של חביבה רייק וכן סמל הארגון הארצי של חברי ההגנה.

The special cancellation, showing the insignia of the National Organisation of Hagana Veterans, will be used at Kibbutz Lahavot Havivah, which is named after Havivah Reik.

Figure 331. The special cancellation introduced for Kibbutz Lavahot Havivah.

Figure 330. Havivah Reik's commemorative stamp 1988.

On finding that the fighting unit of Jewish youth which they were intended to support was already fighting with the Slovakian Army or the partisans, Haviva decided to return to Banska Bystrica where she had been an active member of Hashomer Hazair and of the local branch of the Jewish National Fund before she left for Palestine. When she got there, she found very few Jews whom she knew. Most of the community, including her parents and members of her family, had been sent to concentration camps in Poland. She set about helping those who remained.

The Germans concentrated a strong force to put down the partisans and overran their position on 28 October 1944 after heavy fighting. The four parachutists, together with a group from the Jewish Youth Movement from the capital, made their way into the mountains where they set up camp. Here they were again attacked by the Germans and many of the group were killed. Three of the parachutists were captured – Haviva Reik, Zvi Reis and Zvi Ben Yakov – and were put to death; the fourth, Chaim Hermesh, was the only one to escape and to get back to Palestine after the war was ended. Havivah Reik was executed in the village of Kremenicka and buried, together with hundreds of Jews and partisans, in a communal grave. In 1952 her body was brought to Israel and re-interred on Mount Herzl in the special plot for parachutists.

A Kibbutz, Lavahot Havivah, was named in her memory and, in 1988, a commemorative stamp and cancellation were issued in her honour.

The Jewish Infantry Brigade Group: Jewish Volunteers from Palestine in the Second World War

by Meir de Shalit, Chairman, Israel War Veterans League

Thirty-five thousand young Palestinian Jews, men and woman, out of a Jewish population of just over half-a-million, volunteered in the British Armed Forces to join the fight against the Nazis in the Second World War. They served in every branch land, sea and air, in the Middle East, the Western Desert and Europe. Some served in Africa and in the Far East.

In September 1944, the British Government made the long-awaited electrifying announcement that a Jewish Brigade Group was to be formed to take part in active operations against the Nazis. Mr Winston Churchill, then Prime Minister, referring to the Jewish Brigade, stated: 'I have no doubt that they will not only take part in the struggle, but will also participate together with other Allied Forces in the occupation which will follow.'

The Jewish Brigade, consisting of over 5,000 men, joined in the battle for Northern Italy in the final phases of the war. It took up positions on the River Senio facing crack German Paratroopers. In the ensuing battle, the Brigade crossed the River Senio and pursued the enemy, flanked by Indian, Polish and Free Italian forces, until the final and total collapse of the German front.

The Jewish volunteers from Palestine made their mark in history and achieved the following:

They fought the Nazis until victory.

They were the first to meet with and assist the survivors of the Holocaust.

They provided them with food, clothing and shelter and arranged for their, then illegal, onward journey to the Homeland.

They formed the nucleus of the emerging Israel Defence Forces.

David Ben-Gurion, Israel's first Prime Minister and Minister of Defence, wrote: 'Without these soldiers and officers it is doubtful if we could have built the Israel Defence Forces in such a short period and in such a stormy hour.'

Figure 332. Bergen Belsen 1946. Soldiers welcoming Rabbi Yaffee, the Brigade Chaplain.

Figure 333. Soldiers of the RASC dancing a *Hora* with refugees 'adopted' by the unit at Giovinazzo, Italy 1944.

Figure 334. A soldier of the Brigade at the entrance to the ruined Warsaw Ghetto in June 1945.

Figure 335. A Brigade rabbi officiates at a wedding between a Brigade soldier and a Dutch Jewish woman in Holland.

Almost seven hundred Palestinian Jewish men and women died on active service and are interred in British War Cemeteries in every zone of combat. May their Memory be blessed.

Figure 336. Soldiers of the Brigade beside a crematorium at Bergen Belsen, 1945.

Figure 337. A Seder service organized by the Eretz Israel Volunteers in the Bari Refugee Camp, Italy 1944.

Figure 338. Posters announcing a football match between the Brigade team and a Belgian club Maccabi-Belgique in Brussels, October 1945.

Figure 339. A party given by the Brigade for Jewish children found in monasteries and Christian homes. Nijmegen, Holland, 1946.

JEWISH AGENCY FOR PALESTINE

Registration for the Jewish Brigade Group

". . . the Government have decided to accede to the request of the Jewish Agency for Palestine that a Jewish Brigade Group should be formed to take part in active operations. There are vast numbers of Jews serving with our forces and the American forces throughout all the armies, but it seems to me indeed appropriate that a special unit of that race which has suffered indescribable treatment from the Nazis, should be represented in a distinct formation among the forces gathered for their final overthrow, and I have no doubt that they will not only take an active part in the struggle but in the occupation which will follow." —*Winston Churchill.*

Categories of Persons Eligible for Enlistment

1. Palestinians
2. Stateless
3. Aliens (enemy)   (Age 18 - 40)
4. Allied Nationals

5. British Subjects   (Age 26 - 40)

Qualifications for Infantry and Technical Units

Note:—Application for Ministry of Labour approval will be made, where necessary, after registration.

Age – Infantry: British 26 - 35
Others 18 - 35
Technical Units: British 26 - 40
Others 18 - 40

Minimum Height – 5 feet.
Minimum Weight – 7 stone 2 lbs.
Lowest Medical Category – B.II (a).

List of Jewish Agency Registration Offices for Jewish Brigade Group:

CENTRAL REGISTRATION OFFICE:

Jewish Agency Registration Office, 25, Bloomsbury Square, W.C.1. Tel. MUS 2522. Office Hours: 10-6 weekdays, except Saturdays, and 10-1 Sundays.

MANCHESTER.—Manchester Zionist Office, 139, Cheetham Hill Road, Manchester 8. Tel. Blackfriars 8435/6. Office Hours: 10-5 weekdays, except Saturdays, and 10-1 Sundays.

LEEDS.—Leeds Zionist Offices, 17, Brunswick Street, Leeds 2. Tel. Leeds 24745. Office Hours: 10-5 weekdays, except Saturdays, and 10-1 Sundays.

BIRMINGHAM.—Birmingham Zionist Office, 61, Station Street, Birmingham. Tel. Midland 3349. Office Hours: 10-5 weekdays, except Saturdayls, and 10-1 Sundays.

LIVERPOOL.—Liverpool Zionist Office, 8, Princes Road, Liverpool. Tel. Royal 2809. Office Hours: 10-5 weekdays, except Saturdays, and 10-1 Sundays.

GLASGOW.—South Portland Street Synagogue, 95, South Portland Street, Glasgow, C.5. Tel. South 1934. Office Hours: 10-12 a.m. and 7-9 p.m. (except Fridays and Saturdays) and Sundays 3-5.

Figure 340. Registration for the Jewish Brigade Group in Britain.

The Jewish Infantry Brigade Group: Order of Battle

Infantry Brigade Headquarers formed in Egypt – 28 September 1944[1]

Commanders

Lieutenant Colonel P.F.A. Growse (acting)	6 October 1944
Brigadier E.F. Benjamin	20 October 1944
Lieutenant Colonel P.F.A. Growse (acting)	5 February 1945
Brigadier E.F.Benjamin	15 February 1945

Order of Battle

Inf

1 Palestine Regt	8.10.44–31.8.45
2 Palestine Regt	8.10.44–31.8.45
3 Palestine Regt	8.10.44–31.8.45

Arty	1 (Palestine) LAA Battery	8.10.44–5.12.44
	Jewish Field Regt	11.2.45–19.2.45
	200 Field Regt	(20.2.45–29.6.45
		(12.7.45–31.8.45
RE	643 (Palestine) Field Company	8.1.45–31.8.45
ST	178 (Palestine) Company RASC	8.1.45–31.8.45
Med	140 Field Ambulance RAMC	17.2.45–31.8.45
Ord	Jewish Inf Bde Gp Ordnance	12.1.45–31.8.45
REME	Jewish Inf Bde Workshops	13.1.45–31.8.45

Field Park Section

Pro	Jewish Inf Bde Gp Provost Section
Postal	Jewish Inf Bde Gp Postal Unit

Higher Formations

GHQ MELF	6.10.44–5.11.44
15 Army Gp	5.11.44–16.11.44
201 Sub-Area	17.11.44–27.2.45
5 Corps	28.2.45–3.3.45
8 Indian Inf Div	3.3.45–30.3.45
10 Corps	31.3.45–1.5.45
8 Army	2.5.45–15.5.45
5 Corps	16.5.45–19.5.45
78 Inf Div	19.5.45–25.7.45
13 Corps	25.7.45–30.7.45
21 Army Gp	30.7.45–2.8.45
L of C 21 Army Gp	3.8.45–31.8.45

Theatres

Egypt	6.10.44–31.10.44	At Sea	31.10.44–5.11.44
Italy	5.11.44–27.7.45	North West Europe[2]	30.7.45–31.8.45

Battles

Bologna	14.4.45–21.4.45

Notes

1. Effective date of Formation but the Brigade did not begin to function until 6 October 1944.
2. Travelled by road from Italy to join 21 Army Group.

How the Jewish Brigade was Born

S. Levenberg

The decision of the British Government in 1944 to establish a Jewish fighting force to take part in the war against Nazi Germany was an event of historic significance. On 29 August 1939, Dr Chaim Weizmann wrote to the then Prime Minister, Neville Chamberlain, stressing that the Jews felt they had 'a contribution to make to the defence of sacred values'. They were ready, he said, to place themselves, 'in matters big and small, under the coordinating direction of His Majesty's Government'. Chamberlain's reply, received on September 2, was non-committal. He thanked Weizmann for the offer and concluded: 'Your public-spirited assurances are welcome and will be kept in mind'.

It took more than five years before the Government accepted the outstretched hand of the Jewish Agency which wanted Jews in Palestine, in neutral countries, and refugees, to be able to fight under their own flag like all other peoples engaged in the struggle against the common enemy. The offer of the World Zionist Organization did not apply to the over 1 3/4 million British, American, Soviet and other Jews of the Allied lands who were either already conscripted or had volunteered to join the fighting forces of their respective countries.

While waiting impatiently for a response from the British Government, the Jewish Agency in Jerusalem organised the registration of Jews for voluntary service with British forces. Out of a Jewish community which then numbered half a million, 85,781 men and 50,262 women between the ages of 18 and 50 enlisted. Despite this evidence of enthusiasm, the British military authorities hesitated; they wanted evidence of equal willingness on the part of the Arabs. But the Arabs were lukewarm to the war effort.

The first official call to the inhabitants of Palestine to join British units was made in October 1939. The quota was small and on the strict basis of numerical parity with Arabs. A total of 680 Jews enlisted before the end of the year.

Figure 341. Four prominent veterans of the Jewish Brigade. From left: Meir Grabovsky (Argov) later Chairman of the Knesset Foreign Affairs and Defence Committee; Joseph Baratz, a founder of Kibbutz Degania; Joseph Sprinzak, General Secretary of the Histadrut and later Speaker of the Knesset; and Zeev Fainstein who became a leader in the Hagana.

In 1940, Palestinian Jews were permitted to enlist in companies attached to the East Kent Regt (the 'Buffs') but parity with Arab companies was still preserved. Besides, Jewish volunteers who later formed part of the Palestine Regt were confined to auxiliary duties. On 9 November 1941, Weizmann addressed a London conference under the auspices of the Zionist Federation. He outlined a twofold effort that the Jewish Agency had pursued since the beginning of the war: to recruit in Palestine a maximum number for Jewish units within the British Army for the defence of the country and in support of the general war effort in the Middle East; and to raise a Jewish division in the west consisting of Jewish volunteers from all free countries including Palestinian Jews, for service wherever required.

That month *The Times,* in its editorial, declared that there was no evidence that the Arabs objected to the raising of a Jewish force overseas. The *Manchester Guardian,* too, claimed that there was no justice in the refusal to let the Jews help Britain with their national 'fighting force' at a time when the Government led by Churchill had reaffirmed a policy to establish a Jewish National Home in Palestine. There was widespread support in the United States and Commonwealth for the Jewish Agency plan. In Britain, a campaign was led by a parliamentary committee under Colonel Victor Cazalet.

Figure 342. The Second Division Memorial, Kohima (Copyright Commonwealth War Graves Commission).

Indignation against the vacillating policy of the British Government grew as the Germans advanced in North Africa to threaten British positions in the Middle East. Reports about Nazi extermination of Jews, coupled with fear of a German thrust into Palestine, strengthened the case for a Jewish fighting force.

Things began to move in August 1944, when the Prime Minister informed Weizmann that he had given 'personal attention' to his suggestion. He asked for particulars about the flag of a Jewish fighting unit and Weizmann replied: 'I have the greatest pleasure in sending you a sketch of the proposed flag – two horizontal blue stripes on a white background with the Star of David in the centre. It is known to Jews all over the world as their national symbol'.

On 4 September, an official communiqué announced that the British Government had decided to accede to the Jewish Agency's request that a Jewish brigade should be formed to take part in active operations.

The brigade came into being during October 1944. After training in Egypt, it was transferred to Italy, where it became part of the famous British Eighth Army. Brigadier Ernest Frank Benjamin of the Royal Engineers, a Canadian-born Jew, was appointed Commander of the unit, which took part in active operations and suffered 40 dead and 70 wounded.

With the establishment of the State of Israel in 1948, volunteers of the Jewish units provided the State's young army with experienced officer personnel and veteran fighters.

(This article was first published in the 'Zionist Review' in October 1984 and is republished by kind permission of the Author.)

PART THREE
Awards and Decorations
1939–1945 and After

Awards and Decorations Gained by Jews Serving in HM Forces

For fine detail on awards, readers can check the *London Gazette* online. However, research has shown that many awards which we know were given are not formally recorded in the *LG*.

NB: Inevitably, some Commonwealth awards will be included as it was never really clear if personnel were in UK or Commonwealth units. Sources include back numbers of the *Jewish Chronicle*, books, articles, AJEX surveys, back issues of the *Jewish Year Book* awards, the *London Gazette* on line (thanks to Harold Pollins of Oxford), etc. Some post-war awards are included, for example Malaya and Kenya. Most Commonwealth awards are excluded (except the Palestinian Jews) – if included, the numbers would be considerably higher. For details see the Jewish Books of Honour for Canada, Australia and South Africa. Where known, wartime awards to AFS, ARP, Special Constables, etc. are included, mostly BEMs and Commendations for courage.

Some awards have been found in the *London Gazette* by Harold Pollins, of which only some had AJEX cards. They have been included because we believe they are all Jewish.

Martin Sugarman

—, **Capt Robert**
RE Bomb Disposal
Commended
Afghanistan 2008

Aaron, Flt/Sgt Pilot Arthur Louis
DFM (*Gazette* 19.10.43)
VC (Pos 3.11.43)

Aaron, Fus R.
MM

Aaronson, Cpl Leo
RAF 1024013
MID (12.1.45)

Abadee, Sgt Solomon
4193 RAAF
MID (Birthday Hons 2.6.43)

Abbecassis, Sqdn/Ldr G.E.
DFC, MID

Abbey, Lt/Col Philip E.D.
(Canada)
Efficiency Decoration for
Meritorious Service (*JC* 18.9.42)

Abdin, Pte Q.E.Z.
11005 Pal/PC
Pos MID (*Gazette* 1.6.44)

Abeles, L.
Pal
MID

Abels, Sqdn/Ldr
65517 RAFVR
DFC (*Times* 29.5.42), MID

Abraham
1282540 RAF
DFM (*Gazette* 5/2/43)
Bar (*16.2.45*)

Abrahams, Capt A.
Indian Army
MID

Abrahams, Lt Basil George
109747 RA
Territorial Efficiency Medal
(*Gazette* 12.12.46)

Abrahams, Harry
Manchester Regt
Four medals from French
Resistance – escaper

Abrahams, LACW Isobel J.E.
890404 WAAF
MID (Birthday Hons 2.6.43)

Abrahams, Cpl Joseph Louis
5574569 Glos Regt
MID

Abrahams, Flt/Sgt Julius
23652 RAF
MID

Abrahams, Cpt Keith
10267 KOSB
MID (*Gazette* 5.4.45)

Abrahams, Morris
DFM and Bar (in *WWRT* page 54)

Abrahams, Gp/Capt R.J.
OBE 1957

Abrahamson, Sgt Arthur
2346833 RCOS
BEM

Abramovich, Capt Hyman
126442 RAMC
MC, MID

Abramovitz, Pte Joseph
6021252 Essex Regt
MID

Abramsky, Capt M.
MN Pal
MBE

Addison, Maj Felix
MID (*JC* 12.7.46)

Ades, Judith
ARP Cairo
MBE

Adler, Dvr F.
31051 Pal
MID (*Gazette* 9.7.45)

Adler, F/O F.F.
DFC

Adler, Sqdn/Ldr Robert
RAF
DFC + BAR
(later fought in Israel's War of
Independence)

Aitman, Oswald
MN
MID

Alazrachi, P/O Jack
199900 RAF
AFC

Akavia, Abraham
ADC to Orde Wingate
MID

Albury, Sgt Kenneth Judah
648082 RAF
DFM (*Gazette* 14.9.43)

Album, Sydney A.
MC
(Yugoslavia)

Alexander, Lt Norman Cyril
237411 Pioneer Corps
MID

Allenbick, Pte Morris
7392912 RAMC
MM (*Gazette* 7.12.44)

Allenstein, Rfmn Herbert
7012319 London Irish Rifles
MID (*Gazette* 23.3.44)

Aloof, Sgt Percy R.
1307500L Pioneer Corps
Field Marshal Montgomery's
Certificate for
Good Service and Devotion to
Duty
(*JC* 27.7.45)

Altman, P/O Reginald Otto
DFC, DSO

Amiel, Maj Harold J.
177497 RAC
MID (*Gazette* 19.7.45)

Amholz, Sqdn/Ldr H.E.
RAF
MID (KIA)

Amswych, Lt Ivor
RE
MID (*Gazette* 29.9.42)

Andrews, AB Dennis
RN HMS *Eagle*
MID

Anekstein, F/O Cyril
RAF
DFC (*Times* 27.6.42) + Bar
First to gain award for 1,000
bomber raids
Cologne and Ruhr

Angel, Lt Solomon
300148
Croix de Guerre (*JC* 12.1.45)

Appel, H.
Pal
MID

Appell, E.
Pal
MID

Applebaum, Bdr Barnet
1096853 RA
MID twice (*Gazette*
11.1.45/14.9.45)

Applebaum, Haim
TJFF (Pal)
MBE

Aptekman, Cpl J.
774989 RAF
MID (15.12.42)

Aram, P/O J.A.
DFC

Arnstein, Lt Nachum
284382 RASC
MID (*Gazette* 11.1.45)

Arbour, CSM A.
MC

Arje, F.
MID twice

Aron, Maj Wellesley
139520 RASC
MBE (*Gazette* 20.9.45)

Aronov, Maj Eliezer
185861 RE
MBE (*Gazette* 20.9.45)

Ash, Lt/Col Sidney Hubert
192169 SAEC
OBE

Asher, Maj Joseph
28478 SACOS
MID

**Atkins/Rosenberg, 1st Officer
Vera**
SOE
CBE, Croix de Guerre
Legion D'Honneur

Azous, Sgt/WO Mark
1378796 RAF
DFM (*JC* 1.11.44)

Babiak, Cpl Edward
1444002 RAF
MID
(New Year Hons 2.1.43)

Babot, Leonard
MID (twice)

Babrow,Capt Louis
176074 SAMC
MC

Bach, WO1 Ferdinand
32529 SAMC
MID

Bacher, M.
Pal
MID

Back, WO Sidney
R72341 RCAF
DFM (*Gazette* 20.4.43)

Bagdadi, K.
Pal
MID

Baker, Sgt Cecil
RASC
MID

Baker, Flt/Lt Eli
J14781 RCAF
DFC (*Gazette* 2.6.44)

Baker, Hyman
MM

Baker, Ct Percy
RAMC
MID (*JC* 31.10.41)

Balbirsky, Gdsman Philip
2723631 Welsh Guards
MID (*Gazette* 23.5.46)

Balcon, Capt Phineas C.
RAF
MID

Bamberger, Flt/Lt Cyril
DFC + Bar
Jewish origin

**Bamberger, Mrs Florence
Woodhouse**
WVS
BEM

Banberger, Lt A.W.
RA
OBE, MID

Banks (Bonks), Solomon
RE
MID

Barbasch, Julius
PC
MID

Bard, Maj Samuel
231836 RAOC
MBE, MID
(*Gazette* 9.11.45/13.12.45)

Bardega, Sgt Ron
580633 RAF
DFM (14.9.40)

Barer, Capt. Robert
MC

Barford, Sgt H.
13041605 1st Northants Regt
MM

Barker, H. Levi
DFC

Barnard, Abraham
SAF Bomb Disposal
GM

Barnard, Sydney
MM

Barnato, Diana
ATA
MBE

**Barnes, Pte Robert
(aka Baumwolspinner)**
3 Trp. 10 Com
BEM

Barnet, Lt/Col G.
RA Vet. Corps
MC

Barnett, D.
DFM

Barnett, Capt David Anthony
RA
MID

Barnett, Capt David Solomon
RM
MC (*JC* 22.6.45)
MID (*Gazette* 23.1.45)

Barnett, CSM Edward Isaac
NZF
MM (*JC* 15.2.43)

Barnett, Sgt Eric
7522515 RAMC
Tito Medal (*JC* 14.9.45)

Barnett, Capt Frank
MID

Barnett, Sgt Isadore Morris
144128 SAF
MID (*JC* 1.5.42)

Barnett, Flt/Lt Morris
182044 RAF
MBE (Hons List 13.6.46)
Bomb Disposal

Barnett, AB Sydney
DSM

Baron, Flt/Lt Ronald J. Moss
201363 RAF
MBE
(Queen's Birthday Hons June
1952)

Baron, Capt Joseph
MC

Barrow, Capt B.W.
RN, HMS *Hare Bell*
DSO

Barton, Flt/Lt Ronald J.M.
MBE, MID

**Barwell, Sqdn/Ldr George
Charles**
RAFVR
DFC (*JC* 6.8.43)
American DFC and Air Medal
2 Oak Leaf Clusters

Bas, Dvr S.
MID

Bas/Rasch, Lt Bendel
RE Pal
MID

Bassa, Capt Charles
MN
MID

Baum, H.H.
Pal
MID

Baum, Capt Isaac Hyman
106383 RAMC
MID (*Gazette* 10.5.45)

Baum, Sec Off M.C.
WAAF
MID

Bauman, Edward L.
DFC

Bauman, Sgt N.
775398 RAF
MID (Birthday Hons 14.6.45)

Baumann, H.S.
RAF
MID

Baumgarten, Dvr S.
Pal/747 RASC
MID (Gazette 29.11.45)

Baumstein, Sgt
Pal
MM

Bayers, Flt/Lt Raphael Howard
144468 RAF
DFC (*Gazette* 23.3.45)

Bean, Col George
RASC
OBE (*JC* 1.3.46)
MBE (*JC* 5.11.43)
MID

Beautyman, Cpl Jack
RE
MID

Beber, Flt/Sgt Alfred Abraham
1282540 RAF
DFM (*Gazette* 5.2.43)
Bar (16.2.45)

Bechier, AC1 M.H.
775162 RAF
MID (18.2.43)

Becker, P/O Herman Hersh
Norwegian Squadron
DFC
KIA

Becker, Lt Dr Meier
RAMC (Palestinian Jew)
MC

Beddington, Lt/Col F.
RE
MID

Beddington, John Louis
CBE

Beddington, Lt/Col H.L.V.
RA
MID

Beddington, Lt/Col Keith Lionel
23633 RA
OBE

Beddington, Capt Richard Edward Lionel
47160 RAC
MID

Beddington, Maj/Gen William Richard
14293 The Queen's Bays
CBE (*Times* 21.12.41)
MID (*Gazette* 5.8.43)
MID (23.12.43)
MID (2.8.45)
USA Legion of Honour, Degree of Commander (*Gazette* 8.11.45)

Begger, Flt/Sgt S.
MID

Behar, Cpl Nissim
5509151 RAC
MID (*Gazette* 22.3.45)

Behr, Flt/Lt Eli
DFC

Belesario, Lt/Col J.C.
OBE, CBE

Bell, Phillip
Welsh Guards
MID

Bellis, David B.
DFC and Bar

Ben Azri, Maj Ephraim
239824 Pal/Regt
MID

Bendell, Kenneth S.
RN
MID

Bender, P/O Milton Harold
173405 RAF
DFC (*JC* 20.4.43)

Benenson, Lt/Col Israel
RAOC
MID

Benjamin, Capt A.L.
VX117096 ANF
MID (*Gazette* 23.12.43)

Benjamin, Capt Charles
Roy Fus
MID

Benjamin, Lt Edward
DFC and Bar

Benjamin, Maj B.H.
132948 RASC
MID (*Gazette* 4.4.46)

Benjamin, WO1 Cyril Baron
1431680 Intel Corps
BEM (New Year Hons 9.1.46)

Benjamin, 2nd Lt
DFC + Bar

Benjamin, Brig Ernest Frank
18035 RE
CBE (*Gazette* 13.12.45)
MID (*Gazette* 8.7.43)

Benjamin, Capt Richard Peter
121237 RUF
MID (*Gazette* 20.6.42)

Benjamin, Major W.
RA
MBE

Ben-Levi, Capt Marcus Norwood
220571 RA
MC (July 1943) MID (*Gazette* 11.1.45)
Efficiency Medal TA (*Gazette* 6.2.47)

Bensinger, Lt Eric Sigmund
235386 OBLI
MID
(Posthumous *Gazette* 23.9.43)

Benson (aka Becker, Fritz/Fred)
SOE
MID

Benson, Sqdn/Ldr Cyril
DFC + Bar

Benson, Martin
RA
MID (Dunkirk)

Bentwich, P/O Norman
OBE 1942

Benwick, LACW Helen
2130571 WAAF
MID

Benzecry, Capt Abraham
Buffs
MC

Berber, Albert Abraham
DFM

Bercovitch, Sgt M.
MID

Bercow, Flt/Lt Reuben
146629 RAF
DFC (*Times* 8.3.44)

Berens, Maj Herbert C.B.
DSO

Berenson, WO M.
MBE

Berest, Lt David Zvi
279932 RE
MID
MBE (*Gazette* 21.12.44)

Berg, F/O John Joseph
129551 RAF
DFC (*Gazette* 12.11.43)

Berger, George W.
Mosquitoes and Sunderland pilot
DFC
Austrian Jewish Refugee

Berger, Flt/Sgt H.O.
DFM

Berger, L/Bdr Joseph
6293543 RA
Fld/Mshl Montgomery Certificate (*JC* 16.9.46)

Berger, Flt/Sgt S.
994916 RAF
MID (*JC* 13.7.42)

Ber Kimche, Pte Aharon
Jewish Inf Brigade Group
MM (*JC* 22.6.45)

Berlandia, Wg/Cdr J.C.H.
DFC

Berlin, Cpl Pinhas
775258 RAF (Pal)
MID (*JC* 10.7.42)

Berliner, Lt A.
RAPC
MC

Berman, Lt H.
282466 Pal/Regt
MID (*Gazette* 23.5.46)

Berman, Sqd/Ldr Monty Morris
101767 RAF
MBE (Birthday Hons 14.6.45)
MID (New Year Hons 1.1.43)
MID (Birthday Hons 23.6.44) *JC*

Berman, Capt Myer
159709 RA Chaplain Dept
MBE (*Gazette* 21.12.44)

Berman, Maj Theodore
296385 RASC
MBE (Hons List 13.6.46)

Bermanes, L.
Pal
MID

Bernard, P/O Seymour
J15939 RCAF
DFC (*Gazette* 14.5.43)

Bernaert, William G.
MID
Died 19.9.44

Bernhardt, Pte K.
Pal/31578
MID (*Gazette* 19.7.45)

Bernstein, Benjamin
RAF
2 commendations for bravery
after crashing
at sea
MID

Bernstein, F/O Cyril
149142 RAF
DFC (*Gazette* 10.12.43)
Bar (26.10.45)

**Bernstein, Maj Hyman George
Gillis**
111999 RAMC
MBE (*Gazette* 14.10.43)

Bernstein, Cpl Joseph
23039 Pal/RE
MM (*Gazette* 29.6.44)

Bernstein, Lewis
RA
Certificate of Gallantry

Bernstein, Capt Ronald Harold
143076 RA
DFC (*Gazette* 27.4.44) serving as
air
Spotter

Bernstein, Lt Sydney M.
48066 SAAF
DFM

Bichovsky, Sgt J.
MID

Biehal, Ernest L.
Czech Armoured
Bravery Award

Bielinky, Lt Louis
251323 RAMC
MC (New Year Hons 1.1.45)

Billig, Capt Hannach
RAMC
MBE (New Year Hons 1.1.45)

Billig, Dr Hannah
GM, MBE (Civil Defence)

**Bingham, Dvr Walter
(aka Billig, Wolfgang)**
RASC
MM (*JC* 22.9.44)

Binick, Sgt Norman
4752181 Para Regt
MM (*JC* 10.11.44)

Birch, Lionel Lee
SAS N Ireland
MBE

Birnbaum, M.
PI556 RASC
MSM
MID x 3 (*Gazette* 1.5.42,
22.10.42, 24.6.43)

Blacher, Nathan
Kings Police Medal

Black, Cpl Harris
RAF
MID

Blankensee, Capt J.A.J.
32595 RE
TD (*Gazette* 17.8.44)

Blasky, Sam
MID

Blint, Maj Louis
MBE
(Hons List *JC* 9.6.50)

Blint, Sgt Wolf
North Africa Commando
WIA/POW
MID

**Bloch, Lt Andrei
(aka Boyd)**
Croix de Guerre, MID

Bloch, Denise
SOE
Legion D'Honneur
Croix de Guerre, KC for Gallantry
MID

Block, Gnr Bernard
Cert of Gallantry 1945

Block, Pte Harold
Citation Cert of Gallantry

Block, Spec Constable Ralph
GM

Blockman, David
RA
MID

Bloom, Capt Albert Edward
RASC
MID

Bloom, Alfred W.
RAF
BEM

Bloom, Lt M.
RAOC
MID

Bloom, Lt Marcus
SOE
MID

Bloom, Capt N.
RWK
MID

Bloom, Maj Neville H.
133142 RAMC
MID (*Gazette* 5.4.45)

Bloom, WO R.J.
DFC

Bloomfield, Sgt Harry
6472638 Roy Fus
BEM
MID (*Gazette* 19.7.45 and
29.11.45)

Blumenthal, Flt/Lt Stephen
87219 RAF
(Hons List 3.6.43) MID twice

Boaz, Capt Thomas Geoffrey
RA
MBE

Bodnoff, Flt/Sgt Israel Joseph
DFM

Bogard, Isaac
(WW1 MM)
Blitz stretcher bearer
Commendation for courage

Bogush, Solomon
AFS
MID

Boiteux, Capt Robert
SOE
MC, Croix de Guerre
Legion D'Honneur, MBE

Bordoley, Sgt Israel
5341132 TRASC
Croix de Guerre with Palm
(Belgium)
(*Gazette* 17.10.46)

Borkum, Jack
SAAF
MID

Bornstein, S/Sgt Leon
23033 Pal RE
MM (*Gazette* 26.3.42)

Borosh, Capt Henry
SOE
MC

Bossick, Flt/Sgt Harry
1803126 RAF
MID

Botwinsky, Bdr Coleman
945055 RA
MID (*Gazette* 29.11.45)

Bourne, Capt I.H.
RAMC
MBE, MID

Bowman, W/Cdr Nathan
103573 RAF
DSO
DFC + Bar (*Gazette* 6.11.45)

Bowman, Sgt H.
775472
MID

Boyers, Flt/Lt Raphael Howard
DFC

Brachi, Flt/Lt D.P.
MID twice

Brachi, Lt Maurice
RA
MC

Brachman, Capt Ben
RCAMC
MID (*Gazette* 2.10.42)
MM

Braham, Capt Jackson
227250 RAMC
MC
MID (*Gazette* 21.12.44)

Braham, Capt L.
PC
MID

Braidey, Sqdn/Ldr Lewis
DFC
DSO

Brakier, WO2 O.
MID

Brand, Israel
RAF
MID

Brandon, Sqdn/Ldr Lewis
116886 RAF
DSO, DFC + Bar
(*Gazette* 4.11.42, 10.11.44)

Brandt, LAC G.
774320 RAF
MID (*JC* 13.7.42)

Braun, Lt/Col Israel
29174 SAMC
OBE (*JC* 1.5.42)
MID (*Gazette* 18.2.43)

Braunstein, Sgt
MM

Bresloff, L/Lt Boris
RAF
DFC (*Gazette* 18.5.43)

Bresloff, Major S.
RE
Knight Orange Nassau
Croix de Guerre

Brennan, Lt Edward Bernard
RAMC
OBE

Brenner, Flt/Lt Alfred
DFC

Brenner, Eddie
RN
MID

Bresloff, Tpr Harry
7908499 RAC
MM (*Gazette* 18.5.43)

Brickner, F/O Ralph
146684 RAF
DFC (*Gazette* 5.6.45)

Bright, Lt/Cdr M.
RN
DSC (*Times* 2.7.41)

Brill, Maj Leopold
RAMC
MID (*JC* 21.4.44)

Brilliant, Lt Stanley
RNVR
DSC (*JC* 3.11.44)

Briscoe, Air/Cdr Abraham
RAF
CBE (*JC* 9.6.50)

Britstone, Cpl Sidney
2590185 RCOS
MID (*JC* 17.8.45)

Brockman, David
RA
MID

Brod, Capt J.
RAMC
MID

Brodie, (Rabbi) Rev Israel
RAF
MID (Birthday Hons 8.6.44)

Brodis, Sgt Samuel
3513613 RA
BEM (*Gazette* 4.8.42)

Brodsky, Flt/Lt B.K.
AFC

Brodsky, Michael
RE
MM D-Day

Bromberg, Sig Harold
30468V SACS
MID

Bromnick, Pte Myer, H.
6465423 Paratroops
(*Gazette* -.3.44) MID twice

Brown, Col D.
RAC
MID

Brown Flt/Lt David
RAF
DSO (*JC* 4.1.46)

Brown, Stanley Samuel
RN
MID Murmansk convoys

Bruser, Sqdn/Ldr David Moses
MBE

Bryanston, Mario
(aka Majzesz Brinsztejn)
Polish Armoured
MID

Buchvitz, R.A.
Pal
MID

Budner, Sgt Harold
14275750 RAC
MM (*JC* 27.4.45)

Bulka, Y.
Pal
MID

Burke, AC2 Barnet
RAF
BEM

Burke, Barnett
ARP
BEM

Burnard, Cpl Sidney
321017 1st Roy Dragoons
MM + Bar
(*Times* 26.2.43, *Gazette*
21.12.44)

Burns, Wilfred M.
RA
MID

Burton, P/O Stanley
DFC

Byck, Muriel Tamara
SOE
MID

Caen, Flt/Lt A.E.
MID (Birthday Hons 8.6.44)

Calvalthorac, Capt Bryan H.N.
MBE

Camrass, Capt Isaac
RAMC
MBE, MID (*Gazette* 19.7.45,
20.9.45)

Camrass, Maj Richard Hersh
W Yorks Regt
MBE (*Gazette* 21.12.45)
Croix de Guerre & Palm
Efficiency medal (TA)
(*Gazette* 21.2.47)

Canter, Capt Archibald Miles
RAMC
MC (*JC* 28.4.42)

Canter, P/O Wilfred Lloyd
RCAF
DFM (*Gazette* 27.8.43)
KIA Israel War Ind   25.10.48

Cantor, Cpl Albert
RAMC
MM (*Gazette* 1.10.45)

Caplan, LAC B.
RAF
MID (New Year Hons 1.1.45)

Caplan, David
MID

Caplan, E.
ACC
MID

Caplan, Sgt E.M.
RAF
SEAC Cert of Good Service
(*JC* 11.44)

Caplan, Nursing Member Fay
VAD (Naval)
BEM (*Gazette* 1.12.42)

Caplan, P/O Maynard Mayer
RAF
DFM (*Gazette* 20.4.43)
MID (*Gazette* 14.1.44)

Caplin, 2nd Lt Alfred
RA
MID

Caplin, Pte Arthur
S Wales Borderers
MM (*JC* 8.6.45)

Caplin, Maj A.T.
Intel Corps
MID

Caplin, Cpl C.T.
RE
MID

Caplin, Sgt Leon
Recce Corps
MID (*Gazette* 10.5.45)

Caplin, Maj Dr Max
OBE

Caplin, Cpl P.
RASC
MID (*Gazette* 10.5.45)

Caras, Pte Lewis
RAMC
MM (*JC* 11.6.43)

Cardozo, Maj F.H.
MC

Carlebach, Col Sir Philip
CMG CBE HG
(Birthday Hons 2.6.43)

Carmi, Israel
*SNS (Special Night Squads
1936–39), SIG*
Col. Pol. Medal
Jewish Brigade

Carlton, Cpl Donald
Rifle Bde
MM (*JC* 1.9.44)

Carson, P/O T. Alexander
DFC

Carvalho, Capt Bryan
MBE

Caselberg, Myer
MN
MID

Casper, Capt Bernard Moses
Sen Chap, Jewish Inf Bde
MID (*Gazette* 29.11.45)

Castello, Maj E.J.
RA
MC

Castello, F/O WT A.
DFC

Cates, Capt Laurence Edgar
RE
MBE (*Gazette* 13.11.45)

Ceen, Emmanual
RA
MM

Chafri, Sgt E.
MID

Chaplin, Sgt
DFC

Chapman, Eddie
MI5 Double Agent 'Zig-Zag'
German War Merit Cross!

Charkham, Maj Sidney F.
Beds & Herts Regt
MID (*Gazette* 27.1.44)

Chasanoff, Flt/Lt Joseph
RCAF
MID (*Gazette* 14.1.44)

Chayan, Capt Markham Sydney
RAMC
MC (*Gazette* 28.1.43)

Chazen, Capt Stanley Harold
RAMC
MID (*Gazette* 8.11.45)

Chester, Pte Ben
Cert of Gallantry

Chester, Capt Miss Ellie
RAF/RE
July 2005 bombings - MID

**Child, Kenneth Joseph
(aka Burleigh)**
RCOS
MID (FEPOW)

Chittis, Sgt
Pal
MID

**Chowcat, Pte Myer/Michael
(aka Bell)**
Roy Berks Regt
MM (*Gazette* 31.8.44)

Citron, Capt Samuel
RAMC
MID

Clark, P/O Denis
DFC

Clynes, Lt Donald
RAMC
MID (*Gazette* 23.5.46)

**Clarke, Cpl K.E.
(aka Goldschlaeger)**
3 Trp 10 Com
MID Osnabruck 1945

Coen, Flt/Lt O.H.
DFC
MID

Cohen, Sgt A.P.
AIF
MID

Cohen, Maj Aaron
RE
MID (*Gazette* 23.5.46)

Cohen, F/O Anthony Lawrence
RAAF
DFC (*JC* 25.8.44)

Cohen, L/Cpl Bernard
Roy Sussex Regt
MID (*Gazette* 19.9.46)

Cohen, Sgt Bernhard
MM

Cohen, Cpl C.
RCOS
MID

Cohen, Pte Chaim
MM

Cohen, Clifford T.
MC

Cohen, Pte Daniel
MM

Cohen, Lt Daniel Lionel
Queen's Roy Regt
MID (*Gazette* 11.1.45)

Cohen, Capt Dennis Hart
RAOC
MID (*Gazette* 24.8.44)

Cohen, WO2 E.
MID

Cohen, Capt E.J.N.
MC

Cohen, Dvr Ephraim
RASC
MID (*Gazette* 19.7.45)

Cohen, Flt/Lt G.
RAF
MID (New Year Hons 1.1.43)

Cohen, Pte G.
MID

Cohen, Capt Gaston Armand (aka Collin)
MC
Croix de Guerre
Chevalier de la Legion D'Honneur
French Resistance Medal

Cohen, Lt.
Croix de Guerre
(Sister of Gaston Armand Cohen)

Cohen, Capt Geoffrey Lewis
Guernsey
REME
MBE

Cohen, Capt George Stuart
Rifle Bde
MID (*Gazette* 4.4.46)

Cohen, Flt/Lt Gerald
RAF
MID (*JC* 6.2.42)

Cohen, Pte H.
Pal, RE
MM

Cohen, Harold
RWAAF/Welch
MID

Cohen, WO2 Harry
Kings Own Regt
MID (*Gazette* 4.4.46)

Cohen, L/Cpl Harry
Black Watch
MID (*Gazette* 14.3.46)

Cohen, Pte H.
MM

Cohen, Sgt I.
SAF
MID (*Gazette* 19.9.46)

Cohen, Lt Jerrold George
Recce Corps
TA Medal (*Gazette* 12.8.47)

Cohen, WO2 Joseph
RAOC
MBE (*Gazette* 13.12.45)

Cohen, Joseph
RN
MID

Cohen, Sqdn/Ldr Julius
RAAF
DFC (*Gazette* 19.9.40)

Cohen, Kalman Jacob
MBE
King's Police Medal

Cohen, Cdr Kenneth
RNC
Order of St Michael, CMG, CB
(New Year Hons 1.1.43)
Legion D'Honneur
Croix de Guerre
Order of White Lion (Czech)
USA Legion of Merit
Officier de l'Ordre de la Couronne
(*Gazette* 30.4.44)

Cohen, Sgt Leonard
3rd Btn Kings Own Hussars
MM (*JC* 26.2.43)

Cohen, Sgt Leslie
RASC
MID (*Gazette* 23.3.44)

Cohen, Maj Leslie Bernard
SAF
MID (*Gazette* 30.12.41)

Cohen, W/Cdr Lionel
RAFVR
DSO, MC (WW1), DFC
MID (*Gazette* Jan 41, 2.6.43, 2.2.44)
Air Medal USA (WW2) (*Gazette* 15.10.46)

Cohen, Sgt M.
MID 29.12.40

Cohen, M.
KOR Regt
3707387
MID

Cohen, L/Sgt M.B.
AIF
MID (*Gazette* 30.12.41)

Cohen, Lt Marcus
African PC
MID (*Gazette* 29.11.45)

Cohen, W/Cdr Mark
RAF
OBE (*Gazette* & Birthday Hons 24.9.41, 14.6.45), MID

Cohen, Lt/Col Mordaunt
RA
MID Burma

Cohen, L/Cpl Norman
Sherwood Foresters
MID (*Gazette* 29.11.45)

Cohen, P/O Norman
RAF
DFM (*Times* 14.11.44)

Cohen, Capt Oscar
MBE

Cohen, Capt P.
RA
MID

Cohen, Sgt Paul
RA
MID (*Gazette* 19.7.45)

Cohen, Capt Peter
MID

Cohen, Phillip
RAF
CBE

Cohen, Lt Phillip Mansell
RN
MID Normandy

Cohen, Lt/Col Rex Arthur Lewis
KSLI
OBE (*Gazette* 1.2.45)
Orange Order of Nassau

Cohen, F/O Robert Simon
DFC

Cohen, Ronald Arthur W.
MBE
MID

Cohen, Capt Ronald
PC
MID (*Gazette* 9.5.46)

Cohen, Sqdn/Ldr Ronald Joseph
RNZAF
AFC (1.1.41)

Cohen, Capt S.A.
RAMC
MID

Cohen, Maj Vernon Henry
GM (16.6.43)
MID (4.4.46)

Cohen, Dvr V.J.
MID
30.12.44

Cohen, Capt Vincent Oswald
RA
MC (*Gazette* 11.10.45)

Cohen, Pte W.
MID

Cohen, Pte Y.
RASC Pal
MM (Gazette 29.11.45)

Cohn, Sqdn/Ldr Edward Laurence 'Pathfinder'
RAF
DFC (*Gazette* 10.10.43)

Coley, F/O Joseph H.
RAF
DFC (*JC* 22.10.43)

Colover, Sqdn/Ldr Jack
RAF
MID

Collins, Capt David
RAMC
MID

Collins, Lt/Col Joseph Hyman
RA
OBE (New Year Hons 1.1.46)

Collins, Flt/Lt S.C.
MID

Colman, A/Maj George Gershon
MID

Comay, Maj Michael
SAF
MID (twice)
Later Israeli Ambassador to UN and UK

Conisa, Cpl Leonard Frank
RE
MID (*JC* 17.4.45)

Conrad, Sgt Eric (aka Konrad)
Intel Corps
USA Bronze Star (*JC* 4.7.44)
MID

Conrad, Cpl Isaac John
RASC
MID (*JC* 30.3.45)

Conradi, E.
PC
Cert. of Gallantry

Conway, Flt/Lt A.G.
DFC

Conway, Coleman
MID

Conway, Marine Stewart
RM
MID D Day

Cooper, Lt Jack
Essex Regt
MC (*JC* 6.10.44)

Copeman, Maj Isadore
ADC
MBE (JC 9.3.45)

Coplans, Capt Samuel Hyman
ADC
Cert of Good Service

Corcos, C/Cdr Nathan M.
RA
MID (New Year Hons 1.1.46)

Cornfeld, Maj M.
Pal Regt
MID (*Gazette* 23.5.46)

Cornfield, Flt/Sgt Ivor
DFM

Coussins, Cpl Leslie
S Wales Borderers
MM (*JC* 4.5.45)

Cowan, Sgt Horace
Recce Regt
MID

Cowan, Capt Jacob (John)
RAMC
MC (*Gazette* 7.12.44), MID

Cowan, Mark
S Lanc Regt
Croix de Guerre

Cowan, Sqdn/Ldr N.L.R.
DFC

Cowen, Sgt Joseph
Maritime Regt RA
DSM (*JC* 26.3.43)

Cowen, Lt R.T.H.
W Surreys
MID

Cowen, Flt/Sgt Samuel E.
DFM

Cowley, Sgt L.A.
RAF
MID (*JC* 17.8.45)

Cramer, John Norman
RN
DSM

Cramp, F/O Douglas Louis
RAF
DFC (*JC* 19.1.45)

Crof-Cohen, Sqdn Ldr Adolphus
(WW1 RN), RAF WW2
MID twice

Crome, Capt Leonard
RAMC
MC (*JC* 4.8.44)
(Medical Director I.B.
Span. Civil War)

Crowne, Maj Joseph George
Chindits
MBE Apr 1945

Cullen, Flt/Lt Richard Nigel
RAF
DFC (1941)

Cullen, Lt/Col Paul
DSO+ Bar

Cullen, Capt George
OBE

Czertok, Capt Leon
Polish Forces
VM
KIA 31/12/44 Holland

Dab, Pte Jacob
Pal Regt
MM (*JC* 6.11.42)

Da Costa, Flt/Sgt A.
RAF
MID

Dafni, WO2 Reuben
Jewish Brigade
MID

Dale, Capt Leslie Maurice
Roy Fus
DSO, MC
(*JC* 10.12.43, *Gazette* 15.6.44)

Dalton, Maj Benjamin
Roy Sussex Regt
DSO
MID (*JC* 19.5.44)

Daniels, Sgt Donald
Intel Corps
MID

Daniels, Act Sec Off H.
WAAF
MID

Danischewsky, Maj Victor
RA
MBE (*Gazette* 24.1.46), MID

Dantzic, Nathan
ARP
OBE courage

Darewski, Capt B.R.
RA
MID

Darewski, Maj N.L.T.
DSO

Dattner, Flt/Lt David
RAF
AFC, OBE

David, Pte Joe
MID

David, M.
Pal
MID

Davidesko, Pte D.
MID

Davids, Sgt Edward Henry
SA Tank Corps
MM

Davidson, Lt A.
RN
MBE

Davies, Cecil
RAF
MID

Davies, J.
Middx
MID

Davies, Sgt Lillie
ATC
BEM (*Gazette* 10.4.45)

D'Avigdor Goldsmid, Brig Henry
RAC
DSO, OBE, MC, MID
(*JC* 11.8.44, Hons Lists 1944 and
1945)

**D'Avigdor Goldschmidt, James
Arthur**
MC

Davis, Sgt A.
RA
MID

Davis, Cyril H.
AFS
BEM

Davis, David H.
AFM
MID Battle of Britain

Davis, Gp/Capt Edgar John
RAF
TD (*Gazette* 16.5.42)

Davis, W/O Joseph G. Michael
RAF
BEM, MBE (*Times* 1941, 1942)

Davis, Capt L.J.
RE
MID

Davis, Lt Peter George
RM
DSC (*Gazette* 13.3.45)

Davis, Lt Walter
RN
DSC (*JC* 18.1.46)

De Friend, P/O Benjamin
RAF
DFM (*Gazette* 12.3.43)
MID (New Year Hons 1.1.45)

De Lange, Gnr Arthur J.
SAF
MM

De Lange, David
RN
MID

Delow, F/O Sydney
RAF
DFM (*JC* 12.7.46)

Denman, Maj E. Peter (aka Dent)
Spec. Forces SOE
MC, MBE

De Pass, Capt D.
RN
CBE

De Pass, Col G.E.
OBE

Dersch, Maj Mark
RAOC
MID (*Gazette* 19.9.46)

De Smith, Lt Stanley
RA
Croix de Guerre 1940.
Order Leopold II
(*JC* 30.5.46) MID

Desolla, F/O Henri
RAF
DFC (*JC* 5.5.44) MID

Devries, Pte Michael Stanislaus
DCM

Deyong, Capt Sidney
RPC
Knight of the Orange Order of Nassau with Swords (Holland)
MID (*Gazette* 18.7.47)

De Young, S.
RAF
Chinese Order of Banner

Diamond, Rfmn Arnold
Rifle Bde
MID (*Gazette* 1.11.45)

Dimson, Lt/Col Samuel Barnet
RAMC
MID (*Gazette* 19.7.45)

Dison, Capt Gerald
RAMC
MC (Feb 1944)

Distrowsky, Sgt T.
Pal, RA
MID

Dixon, Capt Gerald
MC

Djamour, Cpl Victor
RAF
MID and Cert of Courage

Doffman, Capt Emanuel
RAOC
MID (*Gazette* 13.1.44)

Doniach, Sqdn/Ldr N.S.
Bletchley Park
OBE

Doniger, Flt/Lt Norman Albert
RAF
DFC (*JC* 17.11.44)

Donner, Samuel H.
ARP
BEM

Doppelt, C.
Pal
MID

Dostrowsky, Sgt T.
Pal RA
MID

Drage, Capt John Maurice
Recce Corps
MID

Drapkin, Maj Stanley
RA
MBE (*Gazette* 2.12.44)
MID (*Gazette* 23.5.46)
Cert. of Gallantry

Durlacher, Cdr L.G.
RN
OBE, DSC

Dresner, Capt Ellis
RAMC
Cert Good Service
(*JC* 11.5.45)

Dreyfus, Capt John Gustave
RASC
MID

Dreyfus, Maj M.T.A.
MID twice

Du Parc Braham, Col J.
Order of Merit of Luxembourg

Dubinsky, B.
Ambulance Service
Commendation for Courage

Dunkelman, Maj B.
Canada
DSO

Durlacher, Lt J.S.
MC

Dworkin, Flt/Lt David Louis
DFC

Easterman, Flt/Lt Leslie
RAF
DFC (*JC* 12.7.45)

Eagleman, Flt/Lt Leslie
DFC

Echenberg, Col Samuel
Can Efficiency Dec
OBE

Edwards, David Rufus
RAOC
DCM

Edelshain, Maj Gerald
Roy Sussex Regt
MBE (*Gazette* 17.1.46)

Ehrman, Flt/Lt L.
DFC

Eiler, Kurt
RAF
MID

Eimerl, Surg/Lt Teviot Selwyn
RNVR
DSC (*Times* 7.1.42)

Eisenberg, Pte B.
Pal PC
MID (Pos *Gazette* 27.5.45)

Eisenberg, Sgt Max
PC
MM (*Times* 3.12.41)

Eisenhammer, L/Cpl George Mark
SA Tank Corps
MM (*JC* 1.5.43)

Eldod, 1st/Off Esta
WRNS
MBE

Elkon, Spl Solly
SAIF
MID (S A Deputies 23.9.42)

Elkin, A.
MM

Elliott, Flt/Sgt Arthur
RAF
DFM (*JC* 16.4.43)

Ellis, LACW Lillian S.
WAAF
MID, BEM

Ellman, Sub Lt Sam
RN Commando (SAF)
MID – probably Jewish

Engleman, W/O Samuel
RAF
MID

Entin, M.
RAF
MID 5.10.42

Ephraimson (Holden), Joan
WAAF
Cert. of Merit

Epstein, L/Cpl Louis
RCOS
MID (*Gazette* 16.9.43)

Epstein, F/O Julius
RAF
DFC (*Times* 14.11.44) + Bar

Epstein, M.
Pal
MID

Engelhardt, L/Sgt Rudolph
RCOS/Pal
BEM (New Year Hons 1.1.45)

Erben, F/O Hanus Jiri
DFM

Erdman, Lt Edward Louis
KRRC
MID

Erleigh, Maj The Viscount
Dragoon Guards
MBE, MC, MID
(*Gazette* 29.9.40, 1.10.45)

**Errington, Harry
(aka Ehrengott)**
AFS
GC

Eshell, Y.A.
Pal
MID

Esler, P/O Samuel E.
DFC

Ettlinger, Maj E.S.
MC

Even, J.
Pal
MID

Eveneray, Sgt Moshe
SAF
BEM

Ezekiel, Sqdn/Ldr Herbert
RAF
MBE (New Year Hons 1.1.45)

Ezekiel, N.N.
RAF
MID

Ezra, Maj Derek Joseph
RA
MBE
American Bronze Star
(*Gazette* 8.11.45)

Fainlight, Maj Sidney Maurice
TEM (*JC* 2.5.47)

Falk, Alan D.
ARP
BEM

Falk, L/Cpl Harry
RASC
Cert of Good Service
(New Year Hons Jan 45)

Falk, W/Cdr R.J.
AFC

Falk, LAC Richard
RAF (Rhodesian)
MID (New Year Hons 1.1.43)

Farb, F/O Herbert Reuben
RCAF
DFC (*JC* 29.2.44)

**Farrow, John P.
(aka Friedland, Joseph)**
Lincs/SOE
BEM

Fearn, Lt M. Samuel
MID

Fechtner, P/O Emil
Czech RAF
DFC
KIA

Feiler, Kurt
RAF
MID

Feinberg, Lt Louis Aaron
SAAF
DFC (*JC* 8.7.43)

Feitel, Maj M.
AIF
MBE (2.6.42) MID

Feldman, Sgt A.
RE Pal
MID (*Gazette* 1.6.44)

Feldman, P/O S.B.
DFC

Felix, Capt P.
Army
OBE

**Feltz, F/O Monty
(aka Felton)**
RAF
DFC (*JC* 25.9.45)

Fenner, J.
RF
MM

Fenton, Cpl Sylvia
WAAF
MID (*Gazette* 1.1.43)

**Fernand, Sqdn/Ldr Alan H.
(aka Felton)**
RAF
DFC + Bar (28.9.45)

Ferner, Tpr Hyman
RAC
MM (*JC* 5.3.43)

Ferstman, F/O A.N.
DFC

Fialker, N.
Pal
MID

Fichman, Pte Leib
Pal Regt
BEM (*Gazette* 31.1.46)

Fidler, Lt Kenneth
RAC
MC

Fielding, Capt A.
RE/Intel Corps
MID (*LG* 15.12.42)

Fienburgh, Maj Wilfred
Rifle Bde
MBE

Filar, Cpl J.
Pal Port Op. Coy
Gallantry Cert.

Finauer, Lt/Col E.M.
RE
OBE, MC

Finberg, Maj A.
MBE

Finch, J.
Ambulance Blitz
BEM

Fine, Maj H.
Leic
MID

Fine, Cpl Henry
QVR
C in C Cert

Fine, CQMS Hyman
RAMC
MID (*Gazette* 19.9.46)

Fineberg, Sgt Maurice
RAOC
BEM (New Years Hons 9.1.46)

Fineman, S/Sgt Harry
REME
BEM
(New Year Hons 9.1.46)
Cert Gallantry & Good Service
(2.8.48)

Finer, Maj David Isaac
RAMC
MID (*Gazette* 23.5.46)

Fink, Rfmn Harry
KRRC
MM (*Gazette* 15.3.45)

Finkel, Capt Isaac
Pal Police
Col. Police Medal

Finkelstein, Gnr Abraham
RA
MM

Finkelstein, F/O C.L.
DFC

Finkelstein, Sgt Simon
Cert Good Service (5.2.47)

Finklestone, Hadassah
PATS
MID

Firestein, Fus Jack
Royal Fus
MM (*Gazette* 23.3.43)

Fischbeiner, LAC L.H.
RAF
MID (5.10.43)

Fischel, Capt Benzion
Cross of Victory (Fr)
Cross of Gallantry (Fr)

Fish, A.
Pal
MID

Fisher, Eric Joseph
DFC

Fisher, John
RAF
BEM for gallantry as a
POW of the Japanese

Fisher, Lt Dr John Harry
RN
MID
Anzio

Fisher, Joseph
RN
MID

Fisher, Ldg Smn Leonard
MID

Fishman, Sgt Gerald
RASC
MID (*Gazette* 23.9.43)

Flach, Sgt Isaac Woolf
RCOS
MID (Birthday Hons 14.6.45),
BEM

Flamberg, Pte Gerald
Para Regt
MM (*JC* 12.10.45) Arnhem

Fleishman, P/O E.
DFC, AFM

Fleishman, QMS David
Somaliland Camel Corps Regt
MM (*Times* 12.2.41)

Flek, Dvr M.
MID

Flexer, Julian
MID

Fligelstone, Col Theodor Henri
RAOC
MC

Flowers, Sgmn Paul
RCOS
MID (Nov 44)

Forrest, H.G.
Commended in the Field

Forster, Donald
RAF
CBE

Forster, Lt/Col Walter Leslie
CBE
USA Legion of Merit (*JC* 28.4.44)
(destruction of Burma oil wells
during retreat)

Fort, W.G. (aka Fortung)
SOE
USA Cert. of Merit

Fossleitner, Sgt L. Victor
RAF 149 Squadron
BEM

**Foster-Maurne, Sam
(aka Morris)**
MM Cassino

Fox, Lt David Bernard
RAPC
MC

Frajteg, Henryk
Polish att 8th Army
Cross of Valour

Frampton, Maj George M.
Yorks & Lancs
TD, MID
(*Gazette* 19.7.45, 13.12.45)

Frank, Sgt B.
Pal Reg
MID (*Gazette* 19.7.45)

Frankel, F/O Bernard
DFC

Frankel, Maj Leopold
RE
MID

**Frankenburg, Sqdn/Ldr
Benjamin John**
RAF
MID (New Year Hons 1.1.46)

**Frankenburg, Sqdn/Ldr Edward
Emanuel**
RAF
MID (Birthday Hons 14.6.45)

Franklin, Phillip (aka Yeslovitz)
MID
POW Germany

**Franks, Cyril Dudley
(Frankenstein)**
RN
MID

Franks, Jack
RN
DSM

Franks, P/O Harold
RAF
MID (New Year Hons 1.1.45)

Franses, Capt Maurice
MID Kohima

Frazer, H.M.
MID

Freeden, P/O Sidney
RAF
DFC (*Gazette* 24.10.44)

Freedlander, S/Maj Max
SAF
MID

Freedman, Sgt Aaron
RASC
BEM (*Gazette* 11.10.45)

Freedman, Sqdn/Ldr A.
DFC

Freedman, Sqdn/Ldr Archibald
114265
DFC + Bar

Freedman, Capt Barnett
RM
CBE (Hons List 13.6.46)

Freedman, Capt Frank J.
TM (*Gazette* 2.5.47)

Freedman, Cpl Harold
RAF
MID (New Year Hons 1.1.43)

**Freedman, Flt/Lt Samuel
Isidore**
RAF
AFC (New Year Hons 1.1.46)

Freedman, LACW
WAAF
MID (*Gazette* 14.1.44)

Freeman, Capt Harold Benjamin
RA
MC (*Gazette* 25.6.45)

Freeman, Sqdn/Ldr Leslie
MBE

Freeman, Ralph
PC
Cert of Gallantry

Freeman, Cpl Sydney
SAF
MM (*JC* 12.6.42)

Freshwater, Maj G.W.
RASC
MID

Friedberg, Capt Julius
Pal Regt
MID (*Gazette* 23.5.46)

Friedenthal, Lt Jonathan
Pal Regt
MC (*Gazette* 12.12.45)

Friedland, Sgt H.
SAF
MID (*Gazette* 13.1.44)

Friedlander, L/Cpl Bernard
SAF
GM
MID (*Gazette* 13.1.44)

Friedman, Air/Cpl
SAAF
BEM

Friedman, Lt Jack
SAAF
MID (SA Dep 23.9.42)

Friedman, Flt/Lt L.A.
DFC

Friendly, Sgt Jocelyn
RAF
DFM (Nov 1940)

Fromberg, Cyril
MM

Fruchter, I.
Pal
MID

Frumkin, Capt Y.
RASC
MID (*Gazette* 24.6.45)

Fry, Maj Harold Sidney
RA
MID (*Gazette* 23.5.46)

Fryberg, T/Maj Abraham
AMF
OBE, MBE
(*Gazette* 16.4.42, JC 28.8.42)

Fuchs, Capt Paul
RAMC
MID (*Gazette* 14.9.46)

Fuchs, Capt S.
SAF
MID

Furman, Capt John
RA
MC (*JC* 1.12.44)
Silver Cross Royal Order George I
(Greece, *JC* 13.2.48)

Gafni, B.
Pal
MID

Gale, Flt/Lt Reuben
RAF
MBE (New Years Hons 1.1.46)
MID (Birthday Hons 8.6.44)

Galgut, Lt/Col Oscar
SAAF
MID (twice *JC* 6.2.42, 23.9.42)
OBE

Galkoff, Sqdn/Ldr Cyril
RAF Plastic Surgeon
Cert Meritorious Service (Jan
1946), MID

Galson, T/Sgt W.
US Army
British MM

Garb, Tpr Marius
SATC
MID

Garcia, Flt/Sgt Abraham
RAF
DFM (*Gazette* 15.9.44)

Garcia, Maj Judah
RAC
MBE (Hons List 13.6.43)

Garelick, Sylvia
Services to Army Legal Service
MBE Mil.

Garfunkle, Sgt M.
RASC
MID

Garretts, Sqdn Ldr Abraham
OBE 1963

Gassman-Sherr, Rosalie
AFS, BEM
(1st Woman BEM)

Gavourin, Maj Herbert Samuel
RAMC
MBE (New Year Hons 9.1.59)

Gavsey, Gloria (aka Kay)
WAAF
MID (twice: once for rescuing
wounded bomber crew from
burning crashed aircraft)

Gelber, I.
Pal
MID

Gelbhauer, WO M.
DFC, MID

Geller, Sgt David
RASC
MID (*Gazette* 4.4.46)

Gellor, CQMS
PC
Cert Gallantry & Good Service
(June 1943)

Gersekowski, Sgt A.R.
AFM, DFC

Gershaw, P/O Jack
174702 RAF
DFM

Gershon, Sgt B.
Queens
MID

Gershons, WO2 John Charles
RA
MID (*Gazette* 8.11.45)

Gerson, Maj Haim Victor
SOE
MBE, OBE

Gestenberg, Maj V.
RA
MID

Gesundheit, Spr S.
Pal. Port Op Coy
Gallantry Cert.

Gewelber, Cpl Jacob
RAF
MM (*Gazette* 13.4.45)

Gibbons, Flt/Sgt Michael Julius
RAF
DFM (*Gazette* 15.9.44)

Gilbert, Sgt E.
SOE
MM, MID

Gilbert, E.
MID

Gillespie, Jack S.
MID

Gilroy, F/O Norry (aka Goldstein)
RAF
DFC (*JC* 6.10.44) + Bar
AEA (*Gazette* 6.11.45)

Gilutz, Sqdn/Ldr Yehoshua
RAF
MID (Birthday Hons 14.6.45)

Gimpel, Cmdr Ernest Richard
SOE
MID

Gimple, H.
MID

Gingold, Maj R.F.
MBE

Ginsberg, Cpl H.
RCOS
MID

Ginsberg, Lt Henry
SASC
MID (twice 25.6.42)

Ginsberg, Sgt Leslie
MM (*Gazette* 25.4.41)

Ginsburg, Tpr A.
RAC
Cert. of Gallantry
Order of Orange (Dutch)

Ginsburg, Michael
(*To Malaya Air Force*)
MBE 1968

Ginzburg, Sgt S.
MID

Glanz, L/Cpl Eli
RE
MM (*Gazette* 19.4.45)

Glaser, Cpl L.
RAC
MID (*Gazette* 25.11.44)

Glass, Sgt Harry
RCAF
DFM (*Gazette* 2.5.44)

Glauber, Sgt Kurt E.
RA
King's Commendation for Brave
Conduct

Glazer, Lt A.
RCAF
DFC (*Times* 19.9.42)
MID (New Year 1.1.43)

Glickman, Sid
DFM

Glikin, L/Cpl Theodore
RAC
MID (*Gazette* 23.5.46)

Gluckstein, Capt Bruce Montague
DCLI
MID (Pos *Gazette* 11.1.45)

Gluckstein, Maj Louis H.
MP
MID (*JC* 3.1.41)

Glustein, Flt/Lt Aaron
DFC

Glynne (aka Goldstein)
RE
MID D Day

Goddard, Cpl Gerald
Imperial Lt Horse (South Africa)
DCM (*JC* 17.4.42)

Godfrey, G.
RAMC
MID

Godfrey, John
ARP
Commendation for courage

Gold, John Joshua
RTC
BEM

Gold, Cpl N.
RAF
MID (New Year Hons 1.1.45)

Gold, S/Sgt Philip
RAMC
MID (*Gazette* 23.9.43)

Gold, Gnr Reuben
RA
MM (*Gazette* 19.7.45)

Goldberg, Sqdn/Ldr David
DFC

Goldberg, Maj Dan Shlomo
Roy Warwicks Regt
MID (*Gazette* 23.5.46)

Goldberg, Cpl Edward
RASC
MID (*Gazette* 23.5.46)

Goldberg, Tpr Harold
SAF
MID (*Gazette* 24.6.43)

Goldberg, BQMS I.
RA
Cert Good Service (*JC* 2.4.43)

Goldberg, L/Cpl Isidore
RASC
MID (*Gazette* 4.4.46)

Goldberg, Flt/Lt Raymond Gershon
RAAF
DFC (*Gazette* 9.6.44)

Goldcrown, Flt/Lt John
RAF
USA Air Medal (*JC* 9.2.45)

Golden, Maj Louis
Paras
OBE Mil. (Arnhem)

Goldfeder, Christine Skarbeck Granville
SOE
GM, OBE
Croix de Guerre

Goldin, Cpl Michael
Polish KIA Falaise
VM

Golding, Maj A.V.
RAC
MBE

Golding, David
DFC
AEA

Goldfarb, CSM
RE Pal
MID (*Gazette* 29.1.45)

Goldman, A.N.
DCM

Goldman, Maj S.
FMSVF
POW Thai.
MID

Goldman, WO2 B.
RAC
MID

Goldman, P/O Brian Philip
RAF
DFC (*Gazette* 17.10.44)

Goldman, Sgmn Henry
RCOS
MID (*Gazette* 9.5.46)

Goldman, Sgt S.
HG
Cert Good Service (*JC* 10.4.42)

Goldman, Flt/Lt W.E.
DFC

Goldring, Sgt Alec
RCOS
MM

Goldsmid, P/O P.
DFC

Goldsmith, O.L.
RNZAF
DFC

Goldstein, A.
St John's Ambulance Cert. of Courage

Goldstein, Cpl A.S.
RAMC, SOE
MID

Goldstein, Brig Barnard Alfred (aka Goldston[e])
RAOC
OBE (1.1.41)
CBE (*JC* 2.1.83)

Goldstein, Lt I.
SAF
MC
Normandy

Goldstein, Lt Isaac
MC

Goldstein, Sgt Isaac
Int Corps
MID (*Gazette* 19.9.46)

Goldstein, Lt Jack
RAOC
MID (*Gazette* 24.8.44)

Goldstein, L.
RAF
BEM

Goldstein, Stwd Marcus
RN
MID (New Year Hons 1.1.45)

Goldstein, Pte Montague Cecil
SAF
MM (*JC* 11.12.42)

Goldstein, Moshe
Colonial Police Medal

Goldstein, Maj R.K.
IAOC
MID

Goldstein, Lt/Col Simon R.
SAS
MBE Iraq (New Year Hons, *Times* -.12.05)

Goldston, Capt Leonard
RE
TA Medal (*Gazette* 20.3.47)

Goldstone, Sqdn/Ldr
MID

Goldstone, Lt H.
SA Eng Corps
MID (Pos)

Goldstone, Capt Lionel Stanley
MC
(*Gazette* 10.2.44)

Goldwater, Sgt
OBE

Goldwhite, Cpl Wolf Jack
BEM as POW of Germans
(*JC* 23.7.48)

Gollop, (Rabbi) Lt/Col M.
RA Chap Div
TA Medal (*Gazette* 17.11.42)

Gompertz, Lt Richard
RAC
MID

Gonov, F/O Abraham
DFC

Goodman, Capt Cyril Joshua
Int Corps
MID (*Gazette* 23.5.46)

Goodman, G.E.
RAF Battle of Britain
DFC
(Israel) born in Haifa, possibly
Jewish origin

Goodman, W/Cdr Hubert R.
KIA
Royal Hellenic Air Force Cross

Goodman, J.
Cert. Merit

Goodman, Capt Louis
RE
MID (*Gazette* 11.1.45)

Goodman, Maurice V.
RAF Battle of Britain
DFC

Goodman, P/O R.M.
DFC

Goodman, Cpl W.J.
RE
MID

Goodwin, Air/Mech W.P.
SAAF
MID (23.9.42)

Gordon, H.
Cert. Merit

Gordon, H.G.
MM

Gordon, Capt Louis Lazarus
SAAF
DFC (*JC* 11.12.42)

Gordon, Lt Stanley E.
RF
MC

Gordon, A/Sgt Sydney
MM, MID

Gorendar, LAC
RAF
MID (8.11.43)

Gorfunkle, Mannie
RASC Air Despatch
MID

Gottlieb, Capt A.W.
Intel Corps
MID

Gottlieb, Lt Joseph
RAMC
MID for services as a POW

Gottwaltz, Sgt Bernard
49 Squadron
DFM

Goudvis, Capt Samuel
SAF
MID (*JC* 2.10.42)

Gould, L.H.
DFM

Gould, P/O T.
RN
VC (*JC* 13.7.42), MID

Goulston, Capt Stanley J.M.
RAMC
MC (24.10.42)
MID (*Gazette* 30.12.41)

Goulevitch, W/Op J.
DFC

Gourevitch, Maj Arnold
RAMC
MC (*Gazette* 12.5.46) MID

Gournis, W/Op Harold
DFC

Graetz, L/Sgt Helmut
RAOC
MID (*Gazette* 8.11.45)

Graham, CQMS A.
PC
MID

Graham, Const Ernest
Wartime Constabulary
BEM

Grant, Lt Alan, R.N.
SOE
MID

Grant, Col Ernest
5th Northants
MBE, MID twice

Grant, F/O Jacob
RAF
(19.5.43) DFC

Grant, Larry
RN
DSM

Grant, F/O S.
RAF
DFC + Bar
KIA Hampstead Memorial

Green, Cpl Frank
RE
Croix de Guerre

Green, Sgt Harry
N Africa 8th Army
MID

Green, Sgt Hyman
MID

Green, Sgt Leonard
RADC
DCM
(*JC* 26.11.43) – escaper award

Green, Maj M.
MID
Germany

Green, Cpl Solomon Charles
SAAF
MID (*JC* 5.2.42)

Greenbaum, Constable Emmanuel
Wartime Constabulary
BEM

Greenbaum, Sgt Joseph
RA
BEM

Greenberg, J.J.
RASC
POW of the Japanese, BEM

Greenberg, Cpl Leonard
SAF
MID (*Gazette* 26.6.45)

Greenberg, Flt/Lt Louis
RAF
DFC + Bar
(*Gazette* 14.3.44, 30.10.44)

Greenberg, Lt P.B.
MC

Greenberg, Maj Solomon
PC
MID (*Gazette* 4.4.46)

Greenblatt, Flt/Sgt Munro Morris
RAF
DFM (*Gazette* 17.7.45)

Greenboam, Cpl Bertie
RAF
MID (Birthday Hons 14.6.45)

Greenburgh, Flt/Lt Louis
DFC + Bar (14.3.44, 30.10.44)

Greenspan, Capt H.
MBE
(June 1941)

Grennan, Lt J.
MC

Grenners
MC

Grierson, R. (Griesman)
SAS, Paras
MID

Grizzard, Charles
RAF
MID

Grossman, WO2
Cheshire Yeomanry
MID (30.12.41)

Grossman, WO1 Davis
RE
MBE (Hons List 13.6.46)
MID (*Gazette* 22.2.45)

Grossman, Flt/Lt Frederick
RAF
MID (Birthday Hons 8.6.44)

Grossman, Lt H.
Pal Regt
MID (*Gazette* 23.5.46)

Grossman, WO2 Philip
SAF
MID (*Gazette* 15.12.42)

Grossman, R.
Pal
MID

Gruber, Sgt Myer
RASC
MID (*Gazette* 9.2.45)

Gruber, Flt/Lt S.
RAF
MID (New Year Hons 1.1.46)

Gruberman, L/Cpl Sydney Solomon
MM (*JC* 14.8.42)

Grunbaum, Lt Mieczyslaw
Polish Arnhem
VM

Gruniss, WO Harold
RAF
DFC (*Gazette* 17.10.44)

Guberman, L/Cpl Sidney
MM

Guggenheim, E.N.
ARP
Commendation for Courage, BEM

Gurari, G.M.
Pal
MID

Gurevitz, Sgt Raphael
RAOC
MID (*Gazette* 29.11.45)

Gutenberg, Cpl Levi
RE Pal
DCM (12.9.42)

Guterman, Flt/Sgt Jack
RAF
DFM (*JC* 16.5.43)
Dambuster Raid

Guthman, H.
RAF
MID

**Gyori/Giori
(aka Michael Trent)**
Palestinian Jewish SOE
Italian Partisan Medal

Haarsz, S.
Pal RA
MID

Hadad, N.
Pal
MID

Hagen, Sgt Louis (aka Levy)
AAC Glider Pilot
MM Arnhem

Hahn, Capt J.A.
DFC

Hahn, S/Sgt Joseph Herbert
SAF
MID (25.6.42)

Haigh, Sgt Eleanor
BEM (Birthday Hons June 1943)

Haimovitch, Capt B.
RE
MBE (*Gazette* 13.12.45)

Haimovitz, Maj Dov
MBE, MID

Haimes, Flt/Sgt Frank
MID, BEM

Halford, Capt M.C.K.
Yorks & Lancs
MID

Halperin, M.D.
Cert. of Gallantry

Halperin, P/O Ronald
RAF
DFC (*Gazette* 15.2.44)

Halpern, CQMS Leonard G.
RASC
MID (*Gazette* 19.7.45)

Halpern, Bdr P.
RA
Commendation C in C MEF

Halpern, Capt W.K.L.
Indian Army
MID

Halson, Sqdn/Ldr Harold
RAF
MID (New Year Hons 1.1.46)

Hambro, Sir Charles
Early Head of SOE
CBE

Hamerow, Cpl J.
MID

Hanau, Col Julius
SOE
OBE

Haniford, CPO Barnet
RN
BEM
MID (twice 24.9.45)

Hannah, Capt Eric
SOE (Pal)
DCM
OBE (Mil.)

Hanuch, A.
Pal
MID

Harari, Maj Max Ernest
RAC
MID (*Gazette* 23.5.46)

Harari, Col R.A.
OBE

Harari, Cpl Yehuda
Pal Regt
MM (*Gazette* 13.11.44)

Hardman, Cpl Joseph
KIA
MM

Harris, Lt Dennis
RN
DSC

Harris, Gnr F.D.
RA
MID

Harris, Harry
AFS
BEM

Harris, Capt Herbert 'Berty'
Chindits
OBE

Harris, Cpl Ian (Hajes)
3 Tp 10 Com
MM (6.4.45)

Harris, Jack
MID

Harris, L/Sgt Lionel
Cert Good Service (8.1.44)

Harris, L/Cpl Mark
SAF
MID (23.9.42)

Harris, Sgt Ralph
RB
MID/N. Africa

Harris, Sol
MID

Harris, L/Cpl Stanley
RAC
USA Bronze Star
(*Gazette* 7.12.44)

Hart, Flt/O Jacob M. Stanley
DFC + Bar

Hart, Maj B.
RE
MID

Hart, Sgt David Lloyd
MM (Dieppe) (*JC* 1.1.43)

Hart, Pte Harry
W Surreys
MM

Hart, Gp/Capt J.B.
OBE

Hart, Cpl Mary Maisie (aka Sinclair)
ATS
MID

Hart, Maj O.
RE
DSO, MID

Hartman, Sgt Leslie R.
RA
MM

Hausman, L/Cpl Fritz Sigmund
RASC/Pal
DCM (*JC* 8.9.44), MID – escaper award

Harvey, Alfred Levi Cecil
DSM
Scharnhorst sinking

Hazan, Capt Victor Hyam
S Lancs Regt, SOE
MBE (*Gazette* 30.8.45),
Croix de Guerre

Hazard, Sgt/Pilot J.
RAF
CGM (*JC* 2.4.43)

Heaps, Lt Leo
1st Paras, Arnhem
MC

Hecht, Flt/Lt C.J.
RAF
MID (Birthday Hons 8.6.44)

Hecht, M.
Pal
MID

Hechier, AC1 M.E.
MID

Hechter, Flt/Lt Joseph
DFC

Heilbron, Capt David G.
RCOS
MID (*Gazette* 6.11 45)

Heilbron, Lt/Col E.J.
ARP
OBE

Heilbron, Ch Stwd Emmanuel
MN
BEM

Heilbut, Col Alfred S.
RAOC
OBE (New Year Hons 1.1.46)

Hein, Sqdn/Ldr Georg,
(aka Stevens, Peter)
RAF
MC and escaper x 2

Heine, Maj Keith Robert
SOE
MID Far East

Helenberg, Dvr M.
MID

Hemelik, Flt/Lt Anthony John
RAF
DFC

Henriques, Lt/Col E.C.Q.
MBE

Henriques, E.F.Q.
OBE

Henriques, T/Brig Robert D.Q.
RA
MBE (Birthday Hons 2.6.43)
USA Silver Star (*Gazette* 21.9.43)

Henry, WAC Miss Faith
Cert Merit of USA

Herbert, Dennis
RAF
AFC

Herbert, Capt Leopold
RAMC
MC (*JC* 19.11.43)

Herman, Sgt E.
RAF
MID (24.3.43)

Herman, Lt Ernest Edward
RN
DSC

Herman, WO2 H.
RAOC
MID (*Gazette* 30.12.41)

Herman, Sgt H.E.
RA
MM, MID

Herman, Sqdn/Ldr Jack
DFC, AFC

Herman, Capt M.
RAMC
MID

Herrmann, Sgt J. (Miss)
PATS
MID

Hermer, Capt Benjamin Samuel
SAMC
MBE

Herschkovits, CSM Eliyahu
Jew Inf Bde
MM (*JC* 2.6.45)

Herschlowitz, W.
Pal RASC
MID

Herscovici, Dvr J.
MID

Hershman, Maj Claude A.
Q Yorks Dragoons
MC (*JC* 6.8.43)

Herson, Capt Bernard
ADC
MID (*Gazette* 8.11.45)

Herzog, K.
RAF
MID

Hes, Pte Joseph
RAOC
BEM (*Gazette* 16.4.42)

Hess, Ldg/Smn
DSM

Hilberg, Francis
RN
DSM (15.2.44)

Hillman, Capt F.
(Kennedy/Steiner)
SIG/SAS Commando
MC, MM

Hines, Col Alfred
RE
MC and Bar, MID twice,
Orange Nassau (Arnhem)

Hirsch, Cpl K.
RAF
MID (Birthday Hons 8.6.44)

Hirscheimer, Cpl H.
RAF/Pal
MID (*Gazette* 10.7.42.)

Hirschfield, Capt Bernard
(aka Harfield)
ADC
MC (*Gazette* 12.7.45)

Hirschfield, C.A.L.
RN
DSM

Hizschberg, Pte R.
MID

Hoenig, LAC A.
RAF
MID (New Year Hons 1.1.43)

Hoffman, Capt B.M.
RAMC
MID

Holden, W/Cdr Eustace
DFC Batt of Br.
(brother of Kenneth below)

Holden, Sqdn/Ldr Kenneth
DFC Batt. of Br.

Hollander, P/O J.R.
DFC

Hollander, Paul
Croix de Guerre

Hollenberg, Maj Charles
MBE

Honig, Sgt Amichai
RAF/Pal
DFM (*Times* 21.12.41)

Hollis, Pte Dennis
Glider Para
MM

Horne, Flt/Sgt Albert Elliott
RAAF
DFM (*Gazette* 20.4.43)

Hoffman, Harry
SAS, Paras
USA Purple Heart
Citation for Bravery

Horowitz, L/Cpl J.
RASC/Pal
MID (*Gazette* 29.11.45)

Hughes, Sgt A.E.
RASC
MID

Humphreys, Maj Sqdn/Ldr H.M.
(Belfast)
MID

Hunter, Sq Ldr John
DFC, AFM

Hurwitz, Sgt Samuel Moses
DCM, MM

Hyam, Sgt Lawrence F.
RASC
BEM

Hyams, Sgt C.C.
MM

Hyams, Bdr H.
RA
MID

Hyams, Cpl Joseph
RE
MID (*Gazette* 23.5.46)

Hyman, Capt Albert Isadore
RAMC
MID (*Gazette* 19.9.46)

Hymans, Capt Max
SOE
OBE

Hummel, Sgt C.S.
MM

Infield, Maj Harold C.
PC
MC

Instone, Lt Charles Rupert
RAC
MBE

Instone, 2nd Lt Gordon A.
RA
MM (*Gazette* 15.7.41)
MID (*Gazette* 20.9.45)

Ionides, Capt H.M.C.
CBE (tbc)

Isaacs Capt Bernard A.
Roy Fus/SOE
MC
MID (1953) Korean War

Isaacs, Pte G.A.
MID

Isaacs, P/O George A.
DFM
MID

Isaacs, Cpl Harold
RAOC
MID (*Gazette* 23.5.46)

Isaacs, Pte I.
OBLI
MID

Isaacs, Lt M.
RNVR
MC

Isaacs, Cpl S.
REME
MID

**Isaacs, Sgt Samuel G.
(aka Murray)**
Glider Pilot Arnhem
DFM

Isaacson, P/O Peter Stuart
RAAF
DFM, DFC, AFC
(*Gazette* 30.3.43, 27.8.43)

Isenberg, F/O Melville
DFC

Israel, Lt/Cdr Neil Frederick
RNR
MID (*Gazette* 23.11.43)
DSC (New Year Hons 1.8.44)
Bar to DSC (*Gazette* 11.8.45)

Israel, Capt Solomon J.
MBE

Jackson, P/O Abraham S.
DFM

Jacobi, S.
Pal
MID

Jacobovitch, Gnr Samuel
RHA
MM (July 1941)

Jacobs, Col B.
OBE, MC

Jacobs, Lt Benjamin
RA
MC

Jacobs, Maj Bert
DCLI
MC

Jacobs, WO B.M.
RAF
MID

Jacobs, Cecil Dennis
RN
DSM

Jacobs, Maj Gideon
RM, SOE
OBE Sumatra

Jacobs, Cecil Isadore
MM, OBE

Jacobs, Charles
DSM

Jacobs, AC1 C.R.
RAF
MID

Jacobs, Lt D.A.
Intel Corps
MC, MID

Jacobs, L/Cpl David
Middx Regt
MID (*Gazette* 8.11.45)

Jacobs, Bdr Denis
RA
MM

Jacobs, Lt D.F.
DFC

Jacobs, Flt/Lt D.J.
DFC

Jacobs, Sgt E.
RAMC
MID

Jacobs, Edward William
HMS *Whisted*
DSM

Jacobs, Pte Frank Kenneth
RAMC
MM

Jacobs, Tpr Harold Montague
R Scots Greys RAC
MM (*JC* 2.2.45)

Jacobs, Flt/Lt Henry
RAF
DFC + Bar
AFC Batt. of Br.
(*Gazette* 9.10.42, 3.11.43)

Jacobs, Rfmn H.G.
Rifle Bde
MID

Jacobs, Sgt Jack
RAOC
BEM (New Year Hons 9.1.46)

Jacobs, Sgt J.D.
RE
MID

Jacobs, F/O Joseph
RAF
MID (*Gazette* 17.9.43)

Jacobs, Maj Julius
RAMC
MC (*Gazette* 6.4.46)

Jacobs, W/Cdr Lewis
RAF Meteorologist
USA Medal of Freedom with Palm

Jacobs, P/O Louis Harold
RAF
DFC (*Gazette* 19.10.43)

Jacobs, Capt Michael D.
W Yorks
MID

Jacobs, Cpl Moses
RASC
MID

Jacobs, Capt P.
IAMC
MID

Jacobs, Capt Richard Albert
RASC
MID, MC

Jacobs, Capt Ronald Harry
DFC

Jacobs, Sgt Sam
MM

Jacobs, Capt Simon R.
Queens
MC

Jacobs, W.
RAF
MID

Jacobsen, Sgt I.
RAF
MID
(Birthday Hons 14.6.45)

Jacobson, Cpl Cyril
Roy Fus
MID (*Gazette* 23.5.46)

Jacobson, Capt Dennis A.
Intel Corps
MID (*JC* 9.3.45)

Jacobson, Maj Sidney
Middx Regt
MC (*Gazette* 21.6.45)

Jacques, Capt Nicholas
Croix de Guerre (21.1.45)

Jaffey, Maj
Canadian Forces
OBE Korea

Jame de Pinto, Maj Richard
CMP
MC

Janikoun, Lt/Col S.H.
RAMC
OBE (*JC* 29.1.60) Malaya

Jankel, Lt Herbert
REME
MBE

Jedwab, Janek and his brother (?)
Polish Cross of Valour and Bar
Italy

Jekel, Cad/O Abraham
Polish VM
Cassino

Jellinek, Lt Lionel
RA
MC

Jellinek, Lt Robert Peter
SOE
MBE

Jellishevitz, A.
Pal
MID

Jembner, Sqdn/Ldr Medmergan
American Bronze Star, MID twice

Jerushalami, C/Sgt Aharon
RE/Pal
MM (*Gazette* 1.3.45)

Jessel, Lt C.J.
RAC
MID

Jessel, Maj R.G.
SLI
MID

Jessel, Cdr Richard Frederick
RN
DSO, DSC, OBE
(*Times* 7.1.42, 27.5.42)
Bar to DSC (3.10.42)
MID (*Gazette* 24.4.45)
Knight 1st Class St Olav, Norway
(*Gazette* 2.7.46)

Jiminez, Lt Anthony J.
AMPC
MC

Jockelson, Maj John Jacob
KSLI
MC (*Gazette* 8.3.45)

Joel, Ldg/Sig George T.
RN
DSM

Joel, H.M.
MM + Bar

Joel, W/Cdr L.S.
DFC + Bar

Jole, Henry
RN
MBE

Jonas, Capt Philip Griffith
RA
MC Sicily

Jones, J.
RA
MM

Jordon, Pte F.
Pal/Regt
DCM (*JC* 14.5.43) – escaper
award
Killed Israel War of Indep. 1948

Joselevicius, Dvr S.
MID

Joseph, F/O Abraham Alfred
RAF
DFC (*Times* 14.11.44)

Joseph, L/Col Alexander Keith
RASC
OBE (*Gazette* 23.9.43)

Joseph, Capt D.
SOE
MC
MM + Bar (tbc)

Joseph, Capt Edward Albert
SAAF
MID

Joseph, Sqdn/Ldr Edward Walter
RAF
OBE (New Year Hons 1.1.45)

Joseph, George
RN
MID

Joseph, Capt Ivor
RAMC
MC (*JC* 17.9.43)

Joseph, Capt Keith (Later Sir Keith, MP)
RA
MID (*Gazette* 11.1.45)

Joseph, Capt Maurice Roy
RAMC
MID (June 1940)

Joseph, Lt Michael
DSC

Joseph, Maj N.
MID

Joseph, Col N.C.
HG
CBE (Birthday Hons 2.6.43)

Joseph, Maj Norman S.
ACC
USA Bronze Star (*Gazette* 17.10.46)

Judah, Flt/Lt F.D.
DFC

Julius, T/Maj Allen A.
RE/SAS
MID (Dec 1958)
(later Brigadier)

Kaczan, Will
Polish RAF
Cr of Valour, Cr of Mil Valour,
Cross of Courage

Kahana/Kahan, Y.
Pal PC
MID

Kahanoff, Maj A.E.
RASC
MID (*Gazette* 23.5.46)

Kahn, LAC Bernard B.
RAF
MID (New Year Hons 1.1.45)

Kahn, S/Sgt Jacob
SAF
Gazetted for valuable services

Kaiser, CQMS M.
MID

Kaiser, M.
PC
MID

Kalinsky, Dr David (aka Collins)
RAMC
MID twice

Kalwesky, Cpl Abe
SAF
MID

Kamenkowitz, L/Cpl Z.M.
RE/Pal
MID (1.3.45)

Kaminash, Gnr Pincus
RA
Cert of Merit (1944)

Kaminsky, J.J.
RN
DSM

Kaminsky, Pte Maurice
Argyll & Sutherland Highldrs
MM (*Gazette* 26.10.44)

Kamsler, Sgt Emanuel William
RAF
BEM (New Year Hons 1.1.46)

Kantey, Capt Basil
SAF
MBE (*JC* 24.12.43)
MID

Kantoruwicz, Pte
RAMC/Pal
MID (*Gazette* 29.11.45)

Kaplan, LAC Isadore
RAF
MID (New Year Hons 1.1.45)

Kaplan, Jerry S.
SAAF
MID

Kaplan, Sgt N/H?
RA
MID

Kaplanskis, Sgt A.
Pal
USA Silver star (*JC* 20.3.41)

Kaplansky, Flt/Lt B.M.
DFC

Kaputa, Bdr H.
RA
MID (*Gazette* 29.11.45)

**Kardonsky, Sgt Horace/Harry
(aka Kardo)**
RAMC
BEM (*Gazette* 13.12.45), MID

Karlin, Sgt Rafel
SAAF
MID (23.9.42)

**Karminski, Lt Otto
(aka Simon)**
SOE
MID

Karo, Maj Max
MBE

Karpovsky, 2nd Lt Haim
RE
MID (*Gazette* 15.12.42)

Karstaedt, Capt Gabriel
MC (*Gazette* 29.3.45)

**Kasp, Sgt Yechiel
(aka Kasap, U.)**
Pal/Cdo
DCM, MM
KIA Greece

Kassis, S.H.
RAF
MID

Katanka, LAC M.
RAF
MID

Kathein, R.
Pal
MID

Katz, Sgt Arieh
Pal/Regt
BEM (*JC* 12.2.42)

Katz, L/Cpl Herman Lionel
SAF
MID

Katz, C/Sgt Simon
Queens Roy Regt
BEM (New Year Hons 1.1.48)

Katz, Pte Ted
Queens
MID
Died of Wounds

Katzin, Capt Alfred George
SASC
MID

Kaufman, Flt/Lt G.H.
MID

Kaufman, Gnr Joseph
RA
BEM (New Year Hons 9.1.46)

Kaufman, Leslie
RN
MID

Kaufman, Capt Ronald Benedict
RAOC
MID (*Gazette* 9.8.45)

Kaufman, Pte Sidney
Queens Roy Regt
MM (*Gazette* 19.8.43)

Kay, Leila
WAAF
MID

Kay, W/Cdr Leslie Herbert
DFC
KIA, 2.2.45

Kay, Cpl Sidney
RAF
BEM (*JC* 16.1.53) Suez

Kaye, Sgt Harry
RAF
KIA
DFM (*Gazette* 12.1.43)

Kaye, Flt/Lt Henry
MID

Kaye, W/Cdr Marcus Michael
RAF
OBE
MID (*JC* 19.1.45, Birthday Hons
14.6.45)

Kemper, W/Cdr Joseph
RAF
OBE, MBE (Birthday Hons,
8.6.44), MID

**Kemper, Flt/Lt Myer Julian
Isadore**
RAF
MBE (New Year Hons 1.1.46)

**Kempner, Sqdn/Ldr Morton
Philip**
RAF
USA Bronze Star (*Gazette*
19.11.46)
MID (twice, *JC* 22.11.46)

Kempner, Lt W.J.
RN
DSC, MID

Kenneally, John (aka Lesley)
Irish Guards
VC North Africa
See autobiography 'Kenneally VC'

**Kenrick, Hendrick, Sgt Bernard
(aka Goldman)**
RAF
DFM (29.10.43)

Kershaw, Sgt D.
Gren Gds
MM

Kestler, P/O Oldrich
Czech RAF
Czech MC
KIA

Ketlarofsky, Sgt Mark
RAF
MID (New Year Hons 1.1.45)

Keymer, Capt Phillip Nathaniel
Yorks & Lancs
MC

Keyser, Maj C.
Recce Corps
MID *(Gazette* 29.11.45)

Keyzor, Ldg/Smn R. Frank
RN
MID

Keyzor, J.E.
RN
DSM

Khan, Capt M.V.
RA
MID

Khouri, Pte M.K.
PAL12771
PC and SOE 'Force 133'
MM + Bar

Khytovitch, L/Sgt Eric
6 Commando
MM
KIA

Kimmermann, Wladislaw
Polish VM
Cassino

King, Capt Robert Sydney
RCOS
MID (15.9.42)

**Kingsley, Lt (Loewenstein)
R.J./O.J.**
10 1A Commando
MID Germany

Kirshner-Smalback, Pte M.
RASC/Pal
MID *(Gazette* 29.11.45)

Kisch, Lt Edward Ellis
RA
MC (*JC* 23.2.44)

Kisch, Brig F.H.
CBE, DSO, Com of Bath
MID (twice, *Gazette* 30.12.41,
24.6.43)
KIA Bomb disposal North Africa

Kisilenko, Pte Keva
Middx Regt
Croix de Guerre + Palm
(*Gazette* 17.10.46)

Kisner, Capt Cyril David
SAMC
MID

Kissen, F/O Manuel
RAF
MID (*Gazette* 17.9.43)

Kisroui/Kisray, Maj Rene
SIS
MBE

Kitchener, Sgt Isidore
RAF
MID (Birthday Hons June 1945)

Klar, Lt Ralph
RA
MC (*JC* 18.5.45)
Croix de Guerre (*JC* 27.7.45)

Klass, Maurice
RN
MID

Klauber, Maj George
SOE
MID

Klayman, Chaskiel
Polish VM
Falaise

Klein, BQMS Alfred
RA
MID (11.4.46)

Klein, Capt D.
RAMC
MID (twice, *Gazette* 28.5.44)

Klein, F/O Gerald
RAF
DFC (*Gazette* 10.9.43)

Klein, Flt/Sgt Hilda Minnie
WAAF
BEM (New Year Hons 1.1.46)

Klein, Sgt Louis
Hants Regt
MID (*Gazette* 29.11.45)

Klein, Lt P.F.J.
MID

Klein, Lt Paul F.
PC
MID

Klein, Lt Ralph
RA
MID (*Gazette* 11.4.46)

Klein, Zygmunt 'Joe'
Polish RAF
Battle of Britain KW and Bar
(Cross of Valour)

Kleinlerer, Michael Mordechai
Polish bravery award unknown

Klepetar, R.
Pal
MID

Klepfish, Michael
Posthumous VM
Warsaw Ghetto Uprising

Kliger, Cpl L.
MID

Kline, Lt Harry
RE
MC

Klioth, L/Cpl B.
Pal Port Op Coy
Gallantry Cert.

Klosser, Capt Arnold J.
RCOS
MC

Klugmannn, Lt Col James
SOE
MID

Knobovitch, F/O Harry
DFC

**Koen, Gnr G.R.
(aka Coehn)**
SOE Crete
DCM, MID

Koenigsbert, Maj L.
PC
MID

Kofler, Sgt A.
BEM

Kofler, Lt Alfred
Pal Regt
BEM

Kohan, Lt/Col Charles
PC
OBE

Kohen, Sgt Bernhard
Pal Regt
MM (*Gazette* 13.11.45)

Kohen, Pte Daniel
Pal Regt
MM (*Gazette* 13.12.45)

Kohut, P/O J.
DFC

Komrower, Maj Arthur Geoffrey
Commandos
DSO (*Gazette* 27.1.44)

Kon, Sgt S.
RAF
MID (24.3.43)

Kopel, WO2 P.
RASC/Pal
MID (*Gazette* 29.11.45)

Koplewicz, C.
Pal
MID

Koplovitch, Cpl Henry
RAOC
Cert of Merit (*JC* 18.5.45)

Koretz, Capt H.A.
RAMC
MID (*JC* 24.9.43)

Korman, WO Abraham Isaac
RCAF
DFC (*Gazette* 4.8.44)

Kornfeld, Capt Walter
RASC
MID (*Gazette* 4.1.45)

Korts, Lt C.T.
Roy Scots Fus
MID

Krakauer, Spr J.
RE
MID

Krakowsky, F/O Max
DFC

Krakowsky, F/O Morris Solomon
DFC

Kramer, Flt/Lt Marcus
RAF
DFC (10.7.40) Bat. of Brit.

Kramer, S/Sgt T. Mayer
MM

Krantz, Pte Hyman
PC
MID (*Gazette* 4.4.46)

Krasniansky, Dvr E.
MID

Krauze, Pte E.
PC Pal
MID (*Gazette* 24.5.45)

Kreengle, L/Cpl Nathan
RCOS
MID (*Gazette* 4.4.46)

Kretschmer, P/O R.E.
MID

Kretzer, Sgt Ernest
9th Queens Lancers
MM

Kriegel, Capt A.A.
RCOS
MID

Krish, Capt Ivan Raymond
OBLI
MBE (*Gazette* 24.1.46)

**Kronfield/Kronfeld, Sqdn/Ldr
Robert**
Glider expert
AFC

Kruyer, Rfmn Jack (Isaac)
MID Italy

Kubrik, A.
Pal
MID

Kuperman, Flt/Lt Amiel
RAF Pal
DFC (*JC* 31.8.45)

Kupewitz, Sgt Molly
WAAF
MID

Kupferman, Capt David
Polish 2nd Corps
MC

Krohn, Brig V.R.
MC CBE

Kvitzer, F/O Solomon
DFC

Kyte, Constable Bernard
Wartime Constabulary
BEM

Lachman, Capt Jean
RASC
MID (*Gazette* 11.1.45)

Lachs, W.
RAF
MID

Landau, L/Cpl Alan Aaron
MID

Landau, Cpl Edward Joseph
RCOS
MM
Cert of Merit (*Gazette* 12.7.45)

Landau, Lt G.B.
MID

Landau, Noel
AFS
BEM

Landberg, Frank
RN
DSM

Lander, F/O Israel
Croix de Guerre

Landerman, L/Sgt Harry
KRRC
MM (*Gazette* 12.7.45)

Landes, Maj Roger (Aristide)
SOE
Cr De G, Leg. D'Honneur
MC + Bar (*JC* 3.12.43, 24.8.45)

Landon, Pte Walter
(aka Lewy-Lingen)
Cert of Gallantry
KIA Arnhem

Lane, Lt George (Lanyi)
3Tp 10 Com
MC

Langley, Maj E.E.
MID

Lapish, AC2
RAF
MID

Lappin, Capt S.
SAF
MID (*JC* 1.5.42)

Lassman, Capt Laurence Philip
RAMC
MID
(*Gazette* 22.3.45)

Lassman, AB Lionel
RN
MID (*Gazette* 18.9.45)

Latner, Capt Marcus
RAMC
MID (*Gazette* 29.11.45)

Latutin, Capt Simmon
Somerset LI
GC (Somalia 11.9.46)

Lavan, Norman
(aka Levy)
40RM Commando/SBS
MM (Malaya)
Also N.Ireland, S. Arabia – 1966–79

Laver, L.G.C.de
DFM

Lawson, Capt Ernest
SOE
MC

Lawson, R/Adm Frederick
(aka Levy)
DSC + Bar

Lawson, Cpl Vivienne
WAAF
MID (Birthday Hons 23.6.44)

Lax, WO2 Karl Werner
Essex Regt
BEM

Layton, Lt/Col Julian David
OBE

Lazarus, P/O A.G.
RN (HM Submarines)
DSM

Lazarus, David
HG
GM (*Times* 12.2.41)

Lazarus, Lt/Col Miss H.M.
CBE

Lazarus, Maj K.H.
RE
MBE, MID

Lazarus, Capt Ken
LRDG
MBE

Lazarus, Sgt Sam
SAF
MID (*Gazette* 24.6.43)

Lazarus, Capt Dr Sydney
MBE

Leaman, Sgt Nathan Harold
RAF
MID (*JC* 7.2.47) – escaper award

Leapman, Cpl Moss
RASC
Commended Gallant Conduct

Leavey, Lt Maurice Henry
Essex Regt
MC (*JC* 1.12.44)

Lebosky, L/Cpl David
RASC
MID (*Gazette* 19.9.46)

Lee, Pte Fred
21st Indep Paras Arnhem
Dutch award

Lee, Capt Lionel
(aka Levy)
SOE
MC (*JC* 9.2.45)
MID, Croix de Guerre

Lee, Cmdr W. Asher
OBE

Lehahn, Miss B.
Pal ATS
MID

Leibling, WO1 Harry
RASC
MBE (New Year Hons 1.1.46)

Leigh, Sgt Eric (aka Levy)
RAF/ Paras
MID (Birthday Hons), MBE

Leigh, L/Sgt J.C. (aka Labsofsky)
RE
MID (twice, *Gazette* 24.8.44)

Leiper, LAC A.
RAFVR
MID

Leiser, A.
Pal
MID

Lelyveld, Sgt Asher
BEM
(New Year Hons 9.1.46)

Lendler, Pte S.
PC Pal
MM 1941

Lenson, P/O Ben
DFC
(Later Israel War of Ind)

Lentzer, Capt Joseph Gerson
SAEC
OBE (July 1941)

Leon, Capt Henry Cecil
Queen's Roy Regt
MC (*Gazette* 25.2.43)

Leon, Maj Hyman Appleby
MBE

Leon, W/Cdr Lionel Edward
RAF
DFC + Bar, DSO
(*JC* 24.12.43, *Gazette* 8.9.44)

Lerer, Cpl Leib
SATC
MM, MID

Lerner, Section Ldr Harry
Heavy Rescue
BEM

Lerner, Cpl Monty
RAF
MID (Birthday Hons 14.6.45)

Lerman, S/Sgt Isaac
RAOC
MID (*Gazette* 8.11.45)

Lesselbaum, Surgeon Dr H.P.
RNVR
MID

Lester, Brig Benjamin
CBE

Lev, Capt Jacob
Pal RE
MID

Levene, Lt Eugene
SOE
Posthmous MID

Levene, Pte Joshua
Chindits
DCM

Levene, LAC Victor
RAF
MID
(New Year Hons 1.1.46)

Levenson, Lt/Col Reuben
RAOC
MID (*Gazette* 23.5.46)

Levente, W/Cdr Dick
OBE

Lever, Sgt Emanuel
RASC
MID (*Gazette* 4.4.46)

Lever, Pte Morris
RAOC
MID (*Gazette* 11.1.45)

Leveson, Maj Ivan M.B.
RAMC
MID (*Gazette* 23.5.46)

Leveton, Sgt J.H.
RASC
MID

Levey, Lt C.V.
RAOC
MID

Levey, Lt Leonard A.
RNVR
MID

Levey, Lt M.E.
R Sussex Regt
Croix de Chevalier de l'Ordre de la Couronne (Belgium)
(*JC* 17.9.48)

Levi, Renato
PC
MM

Levi, Maj Hon Samuel Gershon
MBE

Levien, Gp/Capt Eric
DFC, MID

Levin, Gnr D.
RA
MID (*Gazette* 23.9.43)

Levin, Lt Henri
Gen List
DSO

Levin, F/O M.H.O.
MC

Levine, Albert
RAF Intel. Att. Foreign Legion
Fr. MM

Levine, Cpl David
RAF
MID (*JC* 27.3.42)

Levine, Capt Harry
RAMC
MID (*Gazette* 745)

Levine, Lt Kenneth Aubrey
S Wales Borderers
MC (July 1945)

Levinkind, Lt/Col Disraeli Hyman
SAEC
MBE, MC

Levinson, Lt Solomon Isaac
RA
MID (*JC* 17.8.45)

Levitan, Flt/Lt Nathan
DFC

Levitt, Flt/Sgt Frederick
RAF
DFM

Levitt, I.
Pal
MID

Levitt, Maj Reginald Nathaniel
RASC
MBE (*Gazette* 13.12.45)

Levy, Lt Ben
RA
MC (Dec 1943)

Levy, Lt Benn Wolfe
RNVR
MBE (New Year Hons 1.1.45)

Levy, Lt/Col C.A.
RAMC
MID (twice: *Gazette* 30.6.42, 6.4.44)

Levy, Cpl C.W.A.
Intel Corps
MID

Levy, Lt David
RE
MBE (*Gazette* 23.9.43)

Levy, Capt Gordon Lewis
Essex Regt
MID (*Gazette* 10.1.46)

Levy, Capt Herbert Gershon
RASC
MID (*Gazette* 29.11.45)

Levy, Capt Rev Isaac 'Harry'
Chaplain
OBE

Levy, Cpl J.
REME
MID

Levy, Joseph
ARP
BEM

Levy, Karl E. (aka Lincoln, Ken)
10 Commando
BEM 1947

Levy, Lt L.
Intel Corps
MID

Levy, L/Sgt L.C.
RA
MID (*Gazette* 6.4.44)

Levy, Flt/Lt Mark
RAF
DFC
MID (Birthday Hons 3.6.43, JC 6.11.45)

Levy, Maj Michael Meyer George
Malaya Force 136/SOE
MID

Levy, Pte Moss W.M.
Hants Regt
MM (*Gazette* 13.12.45)

Levy, Maj P.B.
NZMF
MID (Pos *Gazette* 15.12.42)

Levy, Capt R.
RAMC
MID

Levy, R.A.
RE
MID

Levy, Flt/Sgt Raymond A.
BEM

Levy, P/O Reginald
RAF
MID (*Gazette* 23.5.44)
DFC + Belgian Ordre de la Couronne
Pilot of Sabena 707 hijacked 1972 to Israel – part in rescue

Levy, W/Cdr Robert Camille Samuel
RAF
MBE (Birthday Hons 14.6.45)

Levy, Sqdn/Ldr Reuben
MC

Levy, Flt/Lt R.V.
Tempsford Spec Ops
DFC
KIA 1944

Levy, L/Sgt S.
Pal Regt
MID (*Gazette* 29.11.45)

Levy, S/Sgt Sidney Daniel
RASC
MID (*Gazette* 30.12.41)

Levy, 2nd Lt Vivian David
PC
MID (*Gazette* 6.4.44.)

Levy, W.
Pal
MID

Lewando, Lt/Col Jan Alfred
RAOC
USA Legion of Merit (*Gazette* 16.1.47)

Lewin, Maj Woolf
SAMC
MID

Lewis, Barnett (aka Karbatchnik)
GM, ARP

Lewis, Gnr D.J.
RA
MID

Lewis, Gnr E.S.
RA
MID

Lewis, Lt/Cdr Sir George, Bart
RN
OBE
(Pilot of aircraft in which Admiral Ramsey was killed in Jan. 1945)

Lewis, Gnr Jack
RA
MM (*Gazette* 1.6.43)

Lewis, BQMS Maurice
RA
MID (*JC* 12.11.43)

Lewis, Ralph
DFM

Lewis-Barnet, Maj de S.H.
RAMC
MC
MID (*Gazette* 4.4.46)

Lewisohn, Lt H.A.
Beds & Herts Regt
MID

Lezard, Capt Hugh Grant
SAF
MID (*JC* 1.5.42)

Lichtenstein, Capt Hans
RAMC
BEM Malaya

Liefman, L/Cpl W.
MID

Liepmann, Sgt M.
RAFVR
MID

Liepmann, M.M.
RAF
MID

Lifshitz, (Rabbi) Capt Jacob
Chaplain RA and Jewish Brigade
MID (*Gazette* 23.5.46)

Liknaitsky, Sgt Raphael
SAF
MID

**Likwornick, Wolfgang
(aka Lee, Wilfred)**
Gordon Highlanders
Cert. of Gallantry

Lincoln, Lt/Cdr Ashe
RNVR
Commendation for Bravery, Bomb
disposal
MID (*JC* 27.10.44)

Lindo, Flt/Lt H.L.
DFC

Links, W/Cdr Joseph Gluckstein
RAF
OBE (New Year Hons 1.1.46)

Lintern, R..
PC
MID

Lion, Ernest
Recce Regt
MID

**Lipawasky, Capt Gordon
Benjamin**
SAAF
DFC Korea 1953

Lipert, Lt Col Joseph
Essex Regt
OBE

Lipkin, Maj Leon Raphael
RASC
MBE
MID (*Gazette* 24.8.44, 24.1.46)

Lipman, Flt/Lt D.D..
DFC

Lipshitz, Sgt Arthur
RAF
DFM (*JC* 16.5.43)

Lippman-Kessel, Capt A.W.
RAMC
MBE
MC Arnhem

Lipson, Sgt Zena
WAAF
MID (New Year Hons 1.1.46)

Lipton, Flt/Lt John
RAF
DFC (*Gazette* 26.10.45)

Lipton, Lt/Col Marcus
(MP)
RAPC
OBE

Lipton, W/Cdr Maurice
RCAF
MID (*JC* 17.7.42)

Lipton, Capt Montague
MBE

Lipton, Capt Sydney John
RA
MID (*Gazette* 19.7.45)

Lissner, Flt/Lt Maurice
RAF
DFC (*Gazette* 17.11.44), AEA, MID

Liston, Maj David Joel
RCOS
MBE
MID (*JC* 14.9.45)

Littleton, Maj H.D.
MBE, MID

Livingstone, Maj Cyril
RAMC
Cert. of Gallantry, Imphal 1944

Livingstone, Sqdn/Ldr Norman
RAF
MBE (*JC* 26.11.43)

Lodge, R. (aka Friedlander)
SAS SOE
DCM, MID

Loewe, Lt Raphael James
RAC
MC (*Gazette* 8.7.43)

Loewenthal, Morris
LRDG/PPA
MM

Loirie, Col Saul Henry Cecil
OBE

Lopatin, Pte Judah Hersch
London Scottish
MID (Sept. 1945)

Lorie, Maj Gen Reginald Henry
CBE, CB (*JC* 8.1.43)

Lotinga, Maj Jack Leslie Harry
MC

Lotinga, Capt P.B.
MID

Lottenberg, Lt Louis Henry
Middx Regt
MID (*JC* 30.6.44)

Louis, Capt Percy
MID, Arnhem

Louis, W/Cdr Philip
RAF
OBE (*Gazette* 1.1.53)

Lowenstein, Cpl F.
RAF
BEM (Rabbi Brodie information
18.8.43)

Lowenstein, Sgmn H.
RCOS
MID (*Gazette* 4.11.46)

Lowenstein, Sgt H.
Pal
MID

Luby, Col M.
RE
DSO, MC

Ludmer, Maj H.H.
MBE (TJFF)

**Lyons, Sqdn/Ldr Emanuel
Barnett**
RAF
DFC
Netherlands DFC (*JC* 10.5.45,
9.6.47)

Lyons, Flt/Lt Kenneth
DFM

Lyons, Lt Reginald Ashley
PC
MID (*Gazette* 9.8.45)

Magnus, F/O Errol Henry
RAAF
DFC (*JC* 23.2.44)

Magnus, Capt H.F.S.
Gen Service
MBE, MC

Magrill, Capt G.
PC
MID

Magrill, Saul
RAF
MID

Makin, Capt Myer
RAMC
MID
Croix de Guerre
Silver Star (USA)
(*Gazette* 22.2.45, JC 8.6.45)

Makower, Capt Charles Abel
RE
MC (*Gazette* 24.8.45)

Makower, Capt John M.
Intel Corps
MC, MBE
MID twice
Awarded Bronze Star, USA by
President
(*Gazette* 15.12.42, *Times*
20.2.43)

Malins, F/O Michael
RAF
DFC (*Times* 14.11.44)

Malkoff, Capt Yoel
RE
MID (*Gazette* 19.7.45)

Mancroft, Lt Col Lord
RA
MBE, Croix de Guerre
MID twice

Mandel, M.
Pal
MID

Manderstam, Leopold Herman
SOE
MBE

Mandleberg, Col L.
Lanc Fus.
CBE 1939

Manierka, Sascha
Pathfinder, RCAF
DFM

Mann, Maj Bertram
RAMC
MID (*JC* 12.7.46)

Mann, Maurice
RAF
DFC

Mannheim, Maj Emmanuel M.
MID

Manson, WO2 David Leslie
RASC
BEM (Hons List *JC* 15.2.46)

Manstoff, Flt/Sgt Alfred
RAF
DFM (*Gazette* 10.11.44)

Manuel, Flt/Sgt Joseph
DFC

**Marcon, WO1 Mark Leonard
Leven**
SAEC
MBE (*JC* 6.11.42)

Marcovitch, Gnr John
RA
MID (*Gazette* 4.3.46)

Marcus, Lt Harold
SAF
MBE (*JC* 24.12.43)

Margo, Capt Cecil Stanley
SAAF
DFC (*JC* 1.11.43), DSO

Margolis, Cpl Abraham
RAMC
MID (*Gazette* 11.1.45)

Margolis, Sgt M.
MID

Margolis, S/Lt Sydney
RNVR
C in C Commendation (*JC*
31.12.43)

Marix, Air Vice Marshal R.I.G.
DSO, Belgium Croix de Guerre
MID (3), CB, Polish Order

Markowe, Lt/Col M.
RAMC
MID (*Gazette* 4.4.46)

Markowitz, Dr Jacob
RAMC
MBE for Gallantry as doctor
POW of Japanese

Marks, Flt/Sgt Alec
RAF
DFM (*Gazette* 4.12.45)

Marks, Cpl Bernard
Kings Dragoon Guards
MM (*JC* 27.4.45)

Marks, Cpl G.H.
MID

Marks, Flt/Lt Geoffrey Davis
RAF
MID (Hons List 1.1.45)

Marks, Maj Harry
RTC
MID

Marks, Lt Harry Victor Harris
RNVR
MID (Hons List 8.6.44)

Marks, W/Cdr J.H.
DSO, DFC

Marks, Maj John Emile
MID

Marks, Flt/Lt Joseph Frederick
RAAF
DFC (*JC* 29.12.44)

Marks, Bdr L.
RA
MID

Marks, Cpl Lawrence Wyndham
Middx Regt
MID (*Gazette* 29.11.45)

Marks, Leo
SOE (Chief of Codes)
MBE

Marks, Maj R.L.
RAMC
MID

Marks, Flt/Lt Robert Alan
DFM

Marks, Constable Samuel
BEM courage

Marks, Samuel
Loyal Regt
MID for services as a
POW of the Japanese

Marks, Flt/Sgt Solomon
RAF
BEM
MID (Hons List 1.1.45, 1.1.46)

Marks, Capt Tom Leopold
OBE, Dunkirk
MID

Martyn, WO2 Isidore Bonnie
REME
MID

Marx, Capt Frank Ralph
SAS
MC

Masel, Capt P.
AIF
MID (information from Chap
Goldman 2.6.42)

Masheyakh, Cpl M.
MID

Mason, Sqdn/Ldr Ernest Mitchelson
RAF
DFC

Maxwell, Capt Robert
MC Normandy
(later newspaper tycoon)

Mayer, Berthe
SOE Madagascar
MBE
Wife of Percy, below

Mayer, OS Eric G.
RN
MID

Mayer, Maj J.H.
RAMC
MID (*Gazette* 24.6.43)

Mayer, Percy
SOE Madagascar
OBE

Mayer, Stanley
101 Squadron
CGM

Mayo, Lt/Col Stanley
DSO, DFC

Medine, Capt Myer Michael
RCAMC
MBE
MID (*Gazette* 16.4.42, 23.3.44)

Meerloc, Maj John
HG
MBE (*JC* 27.12.44)

Mehlman, Gnr Barnett Lewis
RA
Commendation (*Gazette* 2.2.45)

Meidner, Cpl Hans
SAEC
MID

Meiszner, LAC Isaac
RAF
BEM (Hons List 1.1.45)

Meleck, Surg/Lt
RN
MBE

Mellins, CQMS Maurice
RCOS
MID (*Gazette* 16.4.4)

Mellish, Jack
French Foreign Legion
Croix de Guerre

Melzer, Maj Lionel
SAAF
MC (*JC* 6.2.42), OBE

Mendel, WO2 Alfred
Kenya Regt
BEM Kenya 1956

Mendels, Lt/Col Meyer M.
OBE

Mendelsohn, Sgt A.
MID

Mendelsohn, Lt Dominique A.E.
General List
DSO

Mendelssohn, Maj Clive
RA
OBE (Hons List 1.1.45)

Mendelssohn, Capt Gerald
RE
MID (*Gazette* 24.6.43)

Mendoza, Phillip
MSM

Menkin, CSM Hyman
PC
DCM (information from Rev Lew –
Chaplain)

Menzies, P/O G.J.
DFC

Mer, Lt/Col Gideon
RAMC Pal
OBE
MID (*Gazette* 5.11.45, 19.9.46)

Meredith, W/Cdr Hubert Angelo
RAF
MBE, OBE
(Hons List 8.6.44)

Merton, Maj Cecil
Burma Z Force
MC + Bar

Merton, Derek
SOE/IC
French bravery award

Meyerowitz, Cpl Leo M.
SAF
MM (SA Deputies 25.6.42)

Michael, Sgt Alfred
HG
Mention in Hons List (*JC* 16.7.43)
MID

Michael, Flt/Lt Emanuel S.
DCM

Michaelis, Percival G.
RA
MBE

Michaels, John Lewis
Roy Worcs.
MM, KIA

Michaels, Pte Maurice
RAOC
MID (*Gazette* 24.6.43)

Micholls, Col W.H.
MC, CBE

Mikardo, Lt Sidney
RASC
MID (*JC* 27.8.43)

Mileikowsky, Lt Elisha
RE
MID

Milewitz, Y.
Pal
MID

Miller, David
RN
MID

Miller, Sgt Joseph
Pal Police
Col. Police Medal

Miller, Capt Joseph E.
RAMC
MC

Miller, Monty
RAMC
MID twice

Milstein, Capt Benjamin Bethel
RAMC
MID (*Gazette* 9.8.45)

**Mimcovitch/Mimcowitz, S.
(aka London)**
PC
MID

Minchom, Sgt Maurice
RA
MID

Mindel, Sgt Monty
RA
BEM (*Gazette* 10.4.45)

Mindelsohn, Capt Alan
RASC
MID (*Gazette* 13.1.44)

Minkoff, Sgt Robert
Rifle Brigade
MM (*Gazette* 20.9.45)

Mirwis, WO2 Solomon
SAF
MID (twice)

Misell, Flt/Lt Julian H.
RAF
MID (Hons List 8.6.44)

Mitchell, James
22nd Indep Paras
BEM

Mito, Lt L.
MC

Mittelman, Inspector Pinchas
Pal Police
Col. Police Medal

Mocatta, Lt/Col Alan Abraham
RA
OBE (New Year Hons 1.1.45)

Mocatta, Col V.E.
CBE

Monks, Police Const
BEM

Montagu, P/O C.S.B.
DFC

**Montagu, Lt/Cdr Hon Ewan
Edward S.**
RNVR
OBE (Hons List 8.6.44)
('The man who never was')

Montefiore, Flt/Lt A.
AFC

Montefiore, L/Cpl A.S.F.
RAVC
MID

Moorin, Bdr Aaron Harry
RA
DCM (*JC* 20.10.44)

Mordecai, P/O H.
RAF
MID

**Morgan, Dr Maj Fred
(aka Morganbesser, Bedrich)**
RAMC
MID

Morofsky, L/Sgt Abraham
PC
BEM (Hons List 13.6.46)

Morris, Emmanuel
ARP
OBE

Morris, Brig F.
KIA -.3.42
OBE, MC

Morris, Capt Isaiah
RAMC
MC (*Gazette* 11.10.45)

Morris, Bdr Joseph
RA
MM (*Gazette* 19.4.45)
(Later killed in Israel's War of Ind.,
1948)

Morris, Lt Nathan Phillip
RN
Commended

Morton, Peter John (aka Meyer)
Intel Corps
MID

**Moses, M.
(aka Maynard)**
PC
MID

Moses, F/O Moses
DFM

Moss, Lt Cyril Herbert
MID

Moss, Lt Edgar
RN
DSC

Moss, Cpl E.G.
Middx
MID

Moss, Capt Graham B.
RAC
MC

Moss, Surg/Lt Solle David
RNVR
MID (*Gazette* 1.12.42)

Moss, Lt/Col Vernon
RA
Efficiency Decoration, MC
USA Bronze Star
(*Gazette* 30.8.45, 8.11.45)

Muller, Salomon
RAF
BEM
1962 N. Ireland

Murkis, N.
Pal
MID

Myer, Jnr Cmdr Lily
ATS
Cert of Commendation for
Courage

Myers, Bessie
1940 Ambulance Driver (*JC*
article)
Croix de Guerre with Palm

Myers, Capt Colin S.E.
RAMC
MBE

Myers, Col Edmund Wolf
DSO (*Gazette* 22.4.43)
CBE (*Gazette* 6.1.44)
Bronze Lion, Netherlands
(*Gazette* 20.3.47)
MID (*Gazette* 10.10.52) Korea
American 'Legion of Merit'

Myers, F/O Geoffrey Selim
RAF
MBE (New Year Hons 1.1.45)

Myers, Lt Col Harry
SAF
OBE (*Gazette* 18.2.43)

Myers, Henry
MID

Myers, Pte Leslie
RASC
MID (*Gazette* 15.6.44)

Myers, Pte Myer
RAPC
Cert of Gallantry (*JC* 29.1.43)

Myers, P/O Philip
RAF
DFM (*Gazette* 17.4.45)

Myers, Maj Philip
RCOS
MID

Myers, Cpl Richard
RN Fus
MM

Myerson, Capt Alec
RA (Chaplain)
MID (*Gazette* 4.4.46)

Myler, Olive
*SIS/Royal Observer Corps radio
detection*
BEM

Nabarro, A.N.
AFS
GM

Nabarro, Sgt Derrick David
RAF
DCM (*Gazette* 19.1.43)
DFC + Bar (escaper)

Nabarro, Maj J.D.N.
RAMC
MID

Nabarro, Cpl N.
Recce Reg
MID

Naftalin, Cpl Isidore
RAMC
Cert of Merit (*JC* 26.4.46)

Nagle, W. Louis
ARP
GM

Nahmias, Capt Yossef Saul
PC
MID (*Gazette* 11.1.45)

Nahum, Lt Baron Sterling
KSLI
MBE (Rev Joseph testimony
27.4.45)

Nahum, S/Lt Dennis Efraim
RNVR
MID (*Gazette* 19.10.43)

Naliert, Sgt J.D.
RAF
MID (30.7.41)

Nardell, Lt Col Sydney
POW Japanese
MID

Nathan, W/Cdr Bernard G.D.
DSO

Nathan, Cdr Ronald Keith
RN
Greek War Cross

Nathan, Sgt W.
MID

Nathan of Churt, Col Lord Harry
RA
TD (*Gazette* 12.4.45)
MID (twice)

Nathan of Churt, Roger
MID
(son of Harry)

Nathan, Cpl Joe
SAF
MID (*JC* 1.5.43)

Natoff, Lt Cyril
RASC
Croix de Guerre

Negrine, Sgt Samuel
Pal Regt
MM (*Times* 31.12.41)

Nelson, F/O W.H.
DFC
Bat. of Britain

Nessim, W/O Maurice S.
RAF
DFC (*Gazette* 30.10.45)

Nestor, Samuel
RS Fus
MM

Neubroch, Hans
Bomber Command
OBE

Newgass, Cdr Harold
RNVR (Bomb Disposal)
GC

Newlands, Keith
(aka Neuburger, Kurt)
WW2 and after Intelligence
OBE 1976

Newman, Lt Ellie
SAAF
MID (*JC* 6.111.42)

Newman, David
MM

Newman, Capt Isidore
SOE Intel Corps
MID, MBE (*Gazette* 31.1.46)
Croix de Guerre
Murdered Mauthausen

Newman, Cpl I.J.
RAMC
MID (twice, *JC* 17.8.45)

Newman, Stuart Samuel
Black Watch
DCM

Nieto, Lt L.
MC

Nightingale, Cpl Frank
41 RM Commando
DCM

Niman, Sgt Mark Alfred
RAF
DFM (*Times* 7.6.41)

Nissem, Maj Edward
MC (*Gazette* 17.11.42)

Nissenbaum, Lt Abraham
RE
MID (*Gazette* 29.11.45)

Norris, Dr G.S.
ARP Doctor
Kings Comm for Bravery

Novelli, Sgt G.
WAAF
MID

Novick, F/O W. Hyman
DFC

Nyburg, Lt/Cdr Arnold G.
RN
DSC

Nyburg, Maj Henry N.
RAC
Amer. Bronze Star

Ochmanoff, Pte S.
MID

Offstein, Sgt Maurice Bernard
RA TA 1939
Croix de Guerre

Olsberg, Lt Harold
RNVR
MID
(*Gazette* 11.12.45)

Oppenheim, Henry John
HMS Argus
DSM

Oppenheimer, Lt/Col Frank
RAMC
OBE

Oppenheimer, Flt/Lt G.F.
MID

Oppenheimer, Maj H.
Burma Aux Force
CBE

Oppenheimer, Lt Col Phillip
Dutch Bronze Cross

Orenstein, Brig A.J.
CMG, CBE, CB

Orkin, Lt Hyman John
SAF
MID

Orr, Sgt Adam
(aka Opoczynski)
Commandos/SOE
MID
KIA

Orton, Pte
Cert of Merit

Ortweiler, Mrs Winifred
ARP
BEM courage

Osborne
MM

Oshry, Capt Marcus
SAF
MID (*JC* 1.5.42)

Ospalek, Maj Dennis B.
RAC
MID (*Gazette* 26.5.46)

Ostry, Maj Edward Ivan
MBE

Oxenburgh, Flt/Sgt James
(aka Owen)
RAF
DFM (*Gazette* 29.10.43)

Oxenburgh, Sgt Paul
RAF
MID (*JC* 17.7.42)

Page, Sqdn/Ldr Gerald G.
Greek DFC

Palace, Sgt Sidney
RCOS
MID (*Gazette* 23.5.46)

Patashnik, Maj Israel Myer
PC
MID (twice, *Gazette* 23.5.46)

Pearlman, L/Cpl Cyril Solomon
AIF
MM (*Gazette* 9.5.41)

Pearlman, Maj Maurice
RA
MID (*JC* 31.1.47)

Pedretti, Lt/Col L.
OBE

Pegler, Lt Herbert R.D.
RAC
DCM, MM

Peniakoff, Col Vladimir
Founder, Popski's Private Army
(PPA)
DSO, MC
Croix de Guerre

Pepperman, Pte Joe A.
RAMC
MID (*JC* 10.11.44)

Pereira, Pte J.
RASC
MID

Pereirta, Flt/Lt R.N.
DFC

Peters, F/O Lazar
DFC

Perez, Cpl Woolf
RAF
MID (New Year Hons 14.6.45)

Perowitz, Pte Samuel
Middx Regt
MID (*Gazette* 29.11.45)

Peterman, Barnett
RAMC
MID

Pertschuk, Lt Maurice
Intel SOE
OBE (*Gazette* 15.11.45)
Croix de Guerre
Legion D'Honneur
MID

Philipp, Sqdn/Ldr Elias
RAF
MID (New Year Hons 1.1.46)
Legion D'Honneur (Chevalier)
1971

Phillips, Lt Eric
RAC
MC (*JC* 11.5.45)

Phillips, Capt Henry Ellis Isidore
MBE (*Gazette* 13.9.46)

Phillips, Flt/Lt Humphrey
Bernard
RAF
MID (twice)
DFC (*Gazette* 15.9.44)

Pilkington, Gnr William
RA
MID

Pillemer, Sgt Sydney
SAAF
MID (SA DeP 25.6.42)

Pinhas, Cpl
RAF
MID

Pinto, Capt Cyril J.
IAMC
MC

Placks, S/Sgt Solomon
REME
BEM (*Gazette* 21.12.44)

Platzko, Lt Karel
Pal Regt
MID (*Gazette* 23.5.46)

Pliatsky, Lt Leo
RAOC
MID (*Gazette* 23.5.46)

Polishuk, T.
Pal
MID

Pollack, P/O E.R.H.
MC

Pollack, Lt H.
Paras
MC

Pollack, Pte Joseph
Pal Regt
DCM (*Gazette* 9.11.44)

Pollen, Sgt Harold F.
RAF
MID (*JC* 4.8.44)

Pollock, Sqdn/Ldr Sidney Joseph
RAF
DFC (*Gazette* 20.7.45)

Porter, Maj Phillip
MC

Portnoy, Col Ben
RAMC
TD

Posament, 2nd Lt Philip V.
KRRC
MM (*Times* 20.2.43), MID

Posner, F/O Samuel W.
DFC

Pozner, Capt Harry
RAMC
MC (*Gazette* 27.7.44)

Prager, Flt/Lt H.E.J.
DFC

Press, L/Cpl Victor
DCLI
DCM
MID (*JC* 19.1.45, 25.8.44)

Preuss, Capt G.
RASC
MID (*Gazette* 11.1.45)

Prooth, John D.
Rifle Bde
DCM

Rabin, Flt/Lt Y.L.
RAF
MID (twice: *Gazette* 17.9.43, Hons List 8.6.44)

Rabinovitch, Pte Israel
Jewish Inf Bde
MID (*JC* 22.6.45)

Rabinowitz, Constable Abraham
Colonial Police Medal

Rabinowitz, Capt Adam/Adolph
SOE
Croix de Guerre
MID, OBE

Rabson, K.L.
DFM

Radberg, Cpl M.
Intel Corps
MID

Raphael, Sqdn/Ldr Alfred Sydney
RAF
DFC (*Gazette* 13.8.43)

Raphael, Capt G.L.
DSO, DFC Bar, MID
KIA

Raphael, Lt Col R.A.
Roy Warwicks
MC

Raphael, Sqdn/Ldr Ralph
RAF
MID (Birthday Hons 2.6.43)

Rapoport, Maj Aaron
SOE
Force 136 Burma
MBE

Rapoport, Maj Isaac
RE
MBE
MID (*Gazette* 20.9.45, 29.11.45)

Rapoport, Stanislaw
Polish RAF
Virtuti Militari

Rath, Maj J.
PC
MID

Rath, F/O Richard
DFC

Rauf, Pte Hilton
RAOC
MID (*Gazette* 1.1.45)

Rayner, R.M.S.
Bat. of Br.
DFC

Reading, Brig Lord
KC, CBE, MC, TD
(*Times* 2.2.45, *Gazette* 12.4.45)

Rebick, F/O Irwin
DFC

Redner, Flt/Sgt Aron
RAF
DFM (*JC* 25.9.45)

Ree, Harry
SOE
DSO, MC, OBE
Legion D'Honneur
Croix de Guerre
(Father Jewish)

Reed, Leslie
MID

Reed, Sgt Stanley Eric
RAF
MID
BEM (*JC* 9.8.46)

Rees, Flt/Lt Frank Leon
RAF
MID (*JC* 30.3.45)

Regulant, Sgt K.
MID

Rehfish, W/Cdr W.J.
AFC

Reichman, Sgt Jacob Herman
SAF
MID (*Gazette* 24.6.43)

Reichman, Capt R.
RA
MID

Reinhart, W.L.
DFM, DFC

Reiselson, Pte Nathaniel
RAMC
MID (*Gazette* 24.8.44)

Reiser, L/Cpl S.
Pal Port Op Coy
Cert. of Gallantry

Reith, Pte Joseph
MID

Resnick, Capt J.R.
SAF
MC

Reuben, H.
King's Police Medal
Fire Service Medal

Reuben, Hyams
RAMC
MID

Reuben, Capt Isidore
RAMC
MID

Reuben, Lt Louis Joseph
Royal Welch Fusiliers
MC (*Gazette* 2.8.45)

Reynolds, Capt G.
RAMC
MC

Reynolds, Lt J.
MC

Reznick, Capt J.R.
MC

Richards, Lt. Col T.
MID (twice)

Richardson, Maj A.N.
PC
DSO, MC

Richardson, Cdr Justin
RNVR
OBE (*JC* 23.2.45)

Richberg, Cpl Samuel
RASC Pal
DCM

Richlie, Joseph,
(aka Leslie Marius Gilbert)
SOE
MM, MID

Riesenfield, F.
PAL
MID

Rivlin, Flt/Lt Arthur Bernard
RAF
MID (New Year Hons 8.6.44)

Robins, Maj Gerald
RASC
MBE
MID (Gazette 27.12.46)

Robinson, Maj A.A.
PC
MC, DFC

Robinson, Cpl R.
RAF Pal
MID (*JC* 10.7.42)

Robinson, Maj T. Malcolm
RAMC
MBE Malaya 1953

Rochberg, Cpl Samuel
Pal
DCM

Rodner, Sgt H.
MM

Rogozinski, L/Cpl S.
MID

Rolfe, Pte C.
(aka Rofe)
MM

Rollins, C.R.
DFM

Romain, Lt David Robert
RNVR
MID (*Gazette* 21.11.44)

Romain, Lt H.A.
Royal West Kent Regt
MID (*Gazette* 19.7.45)

Romer, Sax
MID

Rooz, Lt Itzchok
RE Pal
BEM (Hons List 14.6.45)

Rose, Flt/Sgt Benjamin
RAF
BEM (New Year Hons 1.1.45)

Rose, W/Cdr Eliot
(aka Rosenheim)
American Legion of Merit –
Bletchley Park

Rose, Sgt F.
BEF
MID

Rose, Gerald
RN
DSM

Rose, H.K.
MID

Rose, Jack
DFC, MBE, CMG
Bat. of Britain

Rose, Lt J.H.
RAMC
MID

Rose, Maj Lionel Sidney
RAOC
MBE (*Gazette* 13.12.45)

Rose, Louis
REME 8th Army
MID 23/5/46

Rose, Flt/Lt Norman L.
DFC

Rose, Stanley Gordon
RN
MID

Rosen, Flt/Sgt Abraham
RAF
DFM (18.7.43)

Rosen, Sgt Abraham
RAAF
DFM (*Gazette* 13.7.43)

Rosen, Capt L.
MID

Rosenbaum, P/O Eli M.
AFC

Rosenberg, A.J.B.
RN
DSM

Rosenberg, 2/Off Isaac
SS Gibel Kebir, Tobruk
M Navy
OBE + Bar

Rosenberg, Sgt L.
RAF
MID

Rosenberg, Lt Mark
PC
MID (*Gazette* 11.1.45)

Rosenberger, Sgt P.
MID

Rosenblatt, Dvr L.
RASC
MID (*Gazette* 21.6.45)

Rosenbloom, Sgt
T Coy 1st Paras Arnhem
MM

Rosenbloom, Sgt Jacob
RAF
DFM (*Gazette* 17.8.43)

Rosenburg, Sgt John
AAC Arnhem
MM

Rosenfield, Cpl Maurice
The Loyals
MM (*Gazette* 15.6.44)

Rosenheim, Maj Charles Leslie
Welch Regt
MC (*Gazette* 12.4.45)

Rosenstein, Pte Meyer
RAOC
BEM (New Year Hons 9.1.46)

Rosenthal, Lt/Cdr A.R.
RAN
DSO (information from Chap
Goldman) + Bar

Rosenthal, Lt Jean Pierre
SOE
MC

Rosenthal, Pte L.
KOSB
MID (*Gazette* 8.11.45)

Rosenthal, S/Lt Maurice Samuel
RCNVR
MID (*JC* 17.7.42)

Rosenthal, Capt V.J.
MID

Rosenthal, W.
RAC
MID

Ross, Lt David
R. Bde
MID

Rossdale, Jnr Comdr Joyce G.
ATS
Cert. of Commendation

Rosser, Lt H.A.
RE
Cert. of Gallantry

Rosslyn, Stanley
Intel
MID

Rotenberg, Gnr Bernard
RA
MID (*Gazette* 9.5.46)

Rotenberg, Cftmn Jacob Edward
REME
MID (*Gazette* 11.1.45)

Roth, Lt Col A.A.
OBE, MID 3 times

Rothenberg, Harold
OBE

Rothler, Cpl H.
MID

Rothschild, Lt/Col Lord Nathan
Intel Corps
GM, MID
USA Legion of Merit
+ Legion of Honour
USA Bronze Star – Bomb disposal

Round, P/O
RN
DSC
American Silver Star,
Tirpitz, Pacific

Rowson, Flt/O Vera
WAAF
MID (*JC* 17.7.42)

Rozen, L/Cpl
10 IA Coy
MM Italy

Rozenberg, Lt/Cdr John
RN
MBE

Rozenstein, Solomon
Colonial Police Medal

Ruben, W/O2 Jacob
RASC
MBE (*Gazette* 1.2.45)

Ruben, Sqdn/Ldr M.S. Jacob
MBE

Rubens, Flt/Lt Charles Lewis
RAF
MID
(New Year Hons 1.1.46)

Rubenstein, Sgt Alan
RAF
MID (twice: *Gazette* 8.6.44, 1.1.46)

Rubenstein, WO2 F.
AFM
MID (*Gazette* 23.12.43)

Rubenstein, Maj Richard Arthur
RA, SOE
MC (*Gazette* 7.11.46), MID
Croix de Guerre

Rubin, F/O Harold
DFC

Rubin, P/O Hector Bernart
RCAF
DFC (*Gazette* 14.5.43)

Rubinovitch, C.
5th Paras
MID

Rubinstein, Maj Samuel Eric
RAC
MBE (*Gazette* 24.1.46)

Ruda, Pte Albert Mervin
SAF
MM (*JC* 11.7.41)

Rumney, Capt David
RAMC
MC (*JC* 10.12.43)

Russell, Sqdn/Ldr Alexander
RAF
OBE
MID (twice: *JC* 10.11.44, 6.7.45)

Russell, H.
(aka Reifenberg)
MID

Rustin, Clive
RAF
AFC 1967

Rustin, Maj Maurice Edward
REME
MC (*JC* 9.3.45)

Sachs, Lt A.
SAAF
DFC (6.3.44)

Sachs, Lt John
Force Z Commandos AIF
MM
Executed by Japanese

Sack, Flt/Lt Jack F.
DFC, AFC

Sack, Maj Myer (Michael)
RASC
MID (*Gazette* 23.5.46)

Sackman, Gnr Leonard
RA
MID (*Gazette* 1.3.45)

Sacks, Sqdn/Ldr Abraham
OBE

Sade, Sgt L.
RE Pal
MID (information from Rev Hooker
1.3.43)

Sadofsky, L/Sgt Aubrey
RCOS
BEM (New Year Hons 9.1.46)

Sadow, Capt Harvey
RAOC
MID (*Gazette* 17.8.45)

Saffron, W/Cdr Barnett
RAF
OBE
MID (New Year Hons 1.1.45,
1.1.46)

Saffron, W/Cdr Tony
RAF
OBE
(1913–2005, b. Bushey Jewish
Cem)

Sager, Sqdn/Ldr A.H.
DFC

Salaman, Capt O.
RA
MC

Salaman, Sqdn/Ldr
MID

Salinger, Maj Donald
SOE
MID (*Gazette* 7.11.46)

Salinger, Capt Frederick
Rowland
RA
MC (*Gazette* 24.1.46)

Salman, Capt H.M.B.
RAOC
DSO

Salmon, Maj F.A.
ACC
MID (*Gazette* 8.11.45)

Salmon, Sqdn/Ldr Julian
RAF
OBE (Hons List 2.6.43)

Salomon, Sgt Marguerite
WAAF
MID (New Year Hons 3.8.45)

Salomon, Cpl P.
PC
MID (*Gazette* 19.5.45)

Saloschin/Saunders, Cpl
George
No.3 Troop 10 Commando
MID

Samek, A.
REME
OBE

Samiri, Cpl Vladimir
Pal Regt
BEM

Sampson, Lt Charles
RN
DSC

Sampson, Joseph
RN
MID

Sampson, Solomon
RN
MID

Samson, L/Sgt Bernard Asher
RE
BEM (Hons List 13.6.46)

Samson, Capt Hyman Harold
SAF
MBE, MID

Samson, F/O Jon Frederick
RAF
DFC, DFM, USA Air Medal
(*Gazette* 29.10.43, 20.3.45)

Samson, F/O Rudom
RAF
MID (Hons List 14.6.45)

Samuel, Lt/Col C.M.
Paras
MID twice
MBE 4.7.64 (Aden)

Samuel, Capt David H.
RA
MID (*Gazette* 22.8.46)

Samuel, George Henry
RN
DSM

Samuel, Sgt H.M.
RAC
MID

Samuel, Maj Hon Marcus
Warwicks Yeomanry
TD (*Gazette* 25.1.45)

Samuel, Flt/Lt Maurice
RAF
MID (New Year Hons 1.1.45)

Samuel, Sqdn/Ldr Norman D.
DFC
KIA 14.11.45

Samuel, Maj Hon Peter M.
Warwicks Yeomanry
MC
MID (*Gazette* 19.7.45)

Samuel, CPO Stuart
RN
MID

Samuel, Cpl V.D.
RTR
MM (*Times* 23.7.43)

Samuels, WO1 Alexander
REME
MID (*Gazette* 10.5.45)

Samuels, Cecil Maxwell
RN
MID

Samuels, Dorothy M.
Red Cross award for gallantry in ME

Samuels, Maj F.A.L.
RAC
MID

Samuels, Maj Jeffrey George
RCOS
MBE (*JC* 15.2.46)

Samuels, Capt Leslie Joseph
RAMC
MC
MID (*Gazette* 24.8.44, 23.9.43)

Samuels, Lt L.H.
Rajah Rifles
MID

Samuels, Sqdn/Ldr Norman P.
DFC

Samuels, Capt Rupert Cecil
RE
MM

Samuelson, Capt Bernard F.M.
RA
MID

Samuelson, Capt John P.
Buffs
MC

Sander, Lt Gustav 'Gus'
Arnhem/Korea
MID
KIA Korea

Saphir, Maj Emanuel
RAC
MID (*Times* ? 7)
MBE (*Gazette* 1.2.45)

Saphir, Lt Col Joseph H.
CBE

Sapire, Sgt Max
SAF
MID

Sapiro, CQMS Wallace
RASC
MID (*Gazette* 9.8.45)

Sardi, Pte Hannah
Pal ATS
MID

Sarfaty, Sgt J.
RE
MID

Sarif, Maj Arthur
MBE (Hons List 1.1.45)

Sarudinsky, Lt Meir
Pal Regt
MC

Saunders, Sgt Harry John
(aka Holzer, Dietrich)
SOE (tbc)
MM

Saunders, Lt/Cdr Rafael
RN
MID, DSC

Sayers/Szauer, Gordon J.
3/10 Commando
Croix de Guerre

Schayek, Lt David Moshi
Sassoon
Inniskilling Fus
MC (*Gazette* 10.2.44)

Schidlovsky, Cpl Samuel
Colonial Police Medal

Schiff, Gnr David
RA
MID (*Gazette* 23.9.43)

Schifrin, Lt A.E. (Barson)
MM, Croix de Guerre
KIA 26.6.44

Schindler, Lt A.J.
MC

Schindler, WO1 A.W.
RE
MID

Schindler, Werner
Polish Forces
Gold Medal of Merit

Schlein, Capt W.
RASC
MID

Schlesinger, Sgt Robin Arthur
RAF
MID (New Year Hons 8.6.44)

Schlisinger, Brig Bernard
Edward
RAMC
OBE (New Year Hons 1.1.46)

Schneider, D.B.
REME
MID

**Schneider, Max
(aka Peter Shelley)**
Cameronians
MM

Schneider, Sgt R.
SAF
MID (*Gazette* 8.4.44)

Schnek, Maj F.
BEM, MID

Schoen, L/Cpl Herbert
PAL23173 RE/SOE 'Force 133'
BEM

Schrire, Capt I.
RAMC (Colditz)
MID

Schugurensky, Maj Abraham
Pal Regt
MID (23.5.46)

Schryver, Maj O.M.
MC

Schwab, Capt Harry
RASC
MID (*Gazette* 29.11.45)

Schwab, Sqdn/Ldr L.G.
DFC

Schweilly, Isaac
Colonial Police Medal

Scott, Cdr Gerald J.
RN
DSC (*JC* 30.7.43)

Seager, Flt/Lt C.M.
DFC

Sebag-Montefiore, Maj E.C.
DLI
MID (*Gazette* 23.5.46)

Sebag-Montefiore, Maj Geoffrey
DOAS
MBE

**Sebag-Montefiore, Lt Col
Thomas H.**
RA
DSO, MC

Sebba, Capt Samuel
KSLI 6th A/borne, SAS
MID (*Gazette* 10.5.45)

Seeley, Frank Levi
RN
MID

**Sefton, Capt W. (aka
Szafirsztejn)**
RE
MID

Segal, Lt Heinz
Croix de Guerre

Segal, F/O Isaac Ivor
RAF
DFC (*Gazette* 17.4.45) + Bar

Segal, Capt J. 'Ben'
LRDG
MC (*JC* 8.1.43)

Segal, Joseph
51st ME Commando
MID

Segal, Maurice E.
RA
MID

Seidenberg, Surgeon Dr J.
Blitz Doctor
MBE, Commendation for Courage

Seifert, Maj R.
RE
Cert of Merit (*JC* 2.7.43)

Selby, Maj C.H.
AIF
MID (information from Rev
Goldman, 9.42)

Seligman, Lt/Cdr A.C.C.
SAS Levant Schooner Flotilla
DSC

Seligman, Maj R.S.
MC
(Brother of above)

Sellick, J.B.
RN
DSM

Selman, P/O C.L.
DFC

Selman, Fl/Lt Harry
RAF
MBE – tbc

Semenowsky, Cpl K.
RAF
MID (Hons List 14.6.45)

Shackman, Sqdn/Ldr Laurence
RAF
MID
AFC (*Gazette* 1.9.44)

Shammy, Yehoshua
Pal Police
Col Police Medal

Shapero, Sgt G.A.
Intel Corps
MID

Shapero, Lt I.
MID (information from Rev
Wagner 6.2.46)

Shapiro, F/O Harry
RAF
DFC + Bar (*Gazette* 6.11.42,
Times 11.6.43)

Shapiro, WO2 Jack
Intel Corps
MID (*Gazette* 19.9.46)

Shapiro, Capt Louis
SAEC
MID

Shapiro, Pte Meyer
SAF
MM (*JC* 6.11.42)

Sharman, F/O H.R.
AFC Bat. of Britain

Sharony, L/Sgt M.
Pal Regt
MID (*Gazette* 29.11.45)

Sharp, Sgt David
RNF/SAS Malay Scouts
BEM for bravery as a Korea POW
1954

Shashoua, Cpl Victor
RAOC
MID (*Gazette* 24.6.43)

Shaverin, Lt David Benjamin
RN
MID (twice) Dieppe

**Shaw, Pte Sidney
(aka Schwartz)**
Green Howards
MM (*JC* 8.6.45)

**Shemtov-Reading, Capt Saul
Alan**
SIS
MBE

Sherrard, Surg/Lt M.
RNVR
MID (*JC* 7.9.45)

Shieldhouse, Sgt Barnett
RAOC
MID Italy 29.11.45

Shields, Maj Stanley Neil
RA
MC (*JC* 8.3.46)

Shmith, Cpl R.A.
AIF
MID (Chap Goldman 2.6.42)

Shmorak, Maj B.
RASC
MID (*Gazette* 23.5.46)

Shnejurson, M.
RAF
MID

Shnider, Flt/Lt Maurice
DFC

Shooster, B.
5439803
6th Sussex
DSM

Shopono, G.
Pal
MID

Shulemson, F/O Sydney Simon
RCAF
DFC
DSO (*Gazette* 18.2.44)

Shulman, P/O Cecil John
RAF
DFM (*JC* 9.4.43)

Shutz, L/Cpl H. Jack
MM

Shutz, L/Cpl S.
RASC
MID (*JC* 17.4.45)

Sidlin, L/Cpl S.
RASC
MID (*JC* 17.12.43)

Sieff, Lt/Col Marcus Joseph
RA
OBE (*Gazette* 23.3.44)
MID (*Gazette* 6.4.44)

Sieff, Capt S.
MID (*Gazette* 13.1.44)

Siegenberg, Pte H.M.
SAF
MID

Siegler, Sgt Norman M.
Princess Royal Kensington Regt
Polar Bear Medal, Iceland (June
1943)

Sievers, Maj Myer
RAMC
MID

Silberbauer, Maj H.L.
MC, MID

**Silberberg, Pte Moshe (aka
Zilberberg, Yosef)**
Jewish Inf Bde
MM (*JC* 22.6.45)

Silberbusch, Sgt Jacob
Pal Regt
MM (*Gazette* 10.5.45)

Silberman, CSM E.
Pal Port Op. Coy
Cert. of Gallantry

Silberman, Sgt L.
Pal Regt
MID (*Gazette* 19.7.45)

Silberman, Pte S.
Pal Regt
MID (*Gazette* 30.5.44)

Silkin, Lt Col Rt Hon Samuel,
RA
MID

Silver, CQMS Alec
PC
BEM (*Gazette* 1.2.45)

Silver, WO2 Meyer
RCAC
MID

Silver, Ronald M.
Roy Sussex Regt
MID (*Gazette* 29.11.45)

Silver, W.I.
RASC NW Europe
MID

Silverman, P/O David M.C.
RAF
DFC
DFM (*JC* 22.10.43)

Silverman, E.R.H.
RUR
MID

Silverman, L/Sgt Mark
RA
MID (*Gazette* 23.5.46)

Silverstone, Sgmn Alfred
RCOS
MID (*Gazette* 24.1.43)

Simitch, Alexander
PC
MM Middle East

Simmons, F/O Benjamin
RAF
MID (*JC* 9.3.45)

Simmons, RSM D.
RA
Cert. of Merit (June 1943)

Simmons, Maj John S.G.
Royal Warwickshires
MBE (*Gazette* 11.10.45)
OBE, MID

Simmons, WO1 Joseph Benjamin
Queens Regt Burma
MC

Simon, C.R.
RAC
MID Middle East

Simon, Capt O.J.H.
REME
MID (*Gazette* 9.5.46)

Simons, F/O Harold
RAF
DFC (*Gazette* 14.9.43)

Simons, L/Cpl S.A.
KOSB
MID

Sinauer, Lt/Col Esmond Morton
OBE, MC

Skosov, F/O Morris Norman
DFC

Slavid, L.
RA
MID Holland

Sless, Lt H.
Merchant Navy
DSC, MBE
Russian Medal of Honour

Slipman, Joseph
ARP
BEM

Sloman, AS Lionel M.
RAN
MID (*Gazette* 23.3.43)

Slovin, Sgt Zalman
Colonial Police Medal

Slutsky/Slater, Ian/Israel
RN
MID Russian convoys

Smith, L/Sgt Isadore
RA
Cert of Merit (*JC* 26.7.46)

Smith, J. Leonard
RASC
MID

Smouha, W/Cdr Edward R.
OBE, MID

Smulian, Flt/Lt Philip Keith
RAF
AFC (Hons List 2.6.43)

Soffer, Supt Solomon
Pal Police
Colonial Pol Medal

Soldinger, Capt Dr Phillip
MBE

Soloman, Maj D.A.
RNZAF, Caledonian Islands
OBE

Soloman, Capt W. Alexander
RE
MID

Solomon, Maj David Abraham
OBE

Solomon, E.M.
RASC
MID Italy

Solomon, Capt Frank
SAAF
MC (*JC* 6.2.42)

Solomon, F/O Joseph Wilfred
MBE

Solomon/Scott, Cpl Lawrence
Metropolitan Police
former Arnhem Paratrooper
GM 1964

Solomon, Sgt Leonard
RAMC
TD, Cert of Merit (*JC* 16.3.45)

Solomon, Lt Martin H.
RNVR
DSC + Bar
(Mar 1941, *Gazette* 10.11.42)
MBE (*Gazette* 14.8.45)

Solomon, Capt Robert B.
RA
MC

Solomon, Woolf
BEM 1946 for Fire Guard and Civil
Defence work,
Grimsby/Cleethorpes

Solomons, Fus Samuel
Roy Fus
MM (*Gazette* 13.1.44)

Somen, Lt Col Israel
RASC
MBE, MID – Ethiopia/Somalia

Sonick, Capt Charles
RAMC
MC (*JC* 8.9.44)

Spector, Flt/Lt Hyman
DFC

Spector, Maj Sidney S.
RCOS
MID (*Gazette* 9.5.46)

Spencer, Sgt Cyril
DLI
MID Normandy

Spiegel, N.
Pal
MID

Spiegel, W/O Sucher
MBE

Spielgelglass, Pte Mane
Para Regt
DCM (*JC* 8.12.44)

Spiers, Lt R.A.
DSC

Spiers, Capt Sydney P.
RAC
MC
MID (*Gazette* 13.12.45. 19.7.45)

Springer, CQMS
MID

Starr, Morris Cohen
ARP
GM

Steele, L.A.
ARP
Commendation for Courage, BEM

Steigrad, Col J.
AIF
CBE (Chap Goldman)

Stein, F/O Charles L.
DFC

Stein, David Malcolm
DSM

Stein, Richard
Polish Cross of Valour
Cassino

Steinberg, Sgt Edward R.
SAF
MID (*Gazette* 24.6.43)

Steinberg, P/O Otto
RCAF
DFC (*JC* 31.12.43)

Steinkopf, Capt M.B.S.
MBE

Stella, Cpl Charles
RAOC
Cert of Merit (*JC* 20.1.45)

Sterlin, F/O R.I.
DFC

Stern, Dvr Abraham
RASC
MM (*Gazette* 23.9.43)

Stern, Pte A.C.
MM

Stern, Capt A.M.
Grenadier Guards
MID

Stern, Lt David
MID (*Gazette* 23.9.43)

Stern, Capt David Laurence
Lancs Fus, SOE
MID (*Gazette* 30.8.45)
Croix De Guerre

Stern, S/Lt Kenneth J.
RNVR
MID

Stern, Capt Mervyn E.
RA
MID (*Gazette* 24.6.43)

Stern, Capt P.S.
RAMC
MID

Steyn, Maj Leopold S.
SATC
MBE

Stiebel, F/O J.H.
DFC

Stitcher, P/O Eric Marcus
RAF
MBE (*Gazette* 22.9.44)

Stockland, Col Maurice
HG/RNVR
BEM (1941)

Stopler, Cpl Leonard
Cameronians
MM (*JC* 17.3.44)

Stork, Maj C.
MBE, MC

Stormont, Lt Col Samuel (Lord Mancroft)
D-Day
MBE, Croix de Guerre
MID twice

Strauss, Capt C.A.
Polish Cross of Valour

Strawbaum, WO1 Leon Isaac
RCOS
MBE (New Year Hons 1.1.43)

Strump, Lt/Col R.
RE
MBE
MID (*Gazette* 5.4.45)

Stuppel, Maj R.
RAMC, SOE
MID (*Gazette* 1.3.45)

Sucharov, Maj Bert
RCE
MBE (*Times* 1.1.43)

Sugar, M.
Pal
MID

Sugarman, Capt William
E Yorks Regt
MC (*Gazette* 31.8.44)

Sumeray, Capt Monty
RASC
MID
(*Gazette* 29.11.45)

Sumray, LAC Hyman
RAF
GM (*Times* 9.6.42)

Sunshine, S. (aka Isaac)
MID

Sussman, Lt Alan Irwin
SAF
MID (*Gazette* 30.12.41)

Sutro, 2nd Lt J.L.
MC

Sutton, Capt Frances George
MC Cassino

Swerdlow, Lt Philip R.
SAMC
MID

Switzer, Harry
RN
DSM

Sylvester, Flt/Lt Leslie Arnold
RAF
MID (*JC* 16.2.45)

Taggar, Sgt Shalom
Pal 11638
MID Greece, 15.12.42 LG

Taglight, O.K.
RAF
MID

Talan, Monia
Pal SOE
MBE

Tallerman, Capt Kenneth H.
RAMC
MC

Tanburn, W/Cdr Harold J.
RAF
OBE (*JC* 10.3.44)

Tarragano, S/Sgt Moshe
REME Field Security
MID

Tauman, Spr
RE
MID

Taylor, F/O Henry Victor
RAF
DFC (*JC* 1.12.44)

Taylor, Sgt J. (Schneider)
DCM

Taylor, Reuben Derek
RAF
MID

Teich, Cpl M.
RAF
MID (*JC* 13.7.42)

Telfer, Thomas
HM Submarines
DSM + Bar, MID

Temkin, LACW Karina
WAAF
MID (Hons List 14.6.45)

Tendler, Cpl Arthur
Rifle Bde
MID (*JC* 18.2.44)

Tenenblatt, L/Cpl N.
MID

Teplicki, T.
Pal
MID

Tesler, S.
St John's Ambulance Cert. of
Courage

**Thomas, Capt Michael
(aka Hollander, Ulrich)**
OBE

Thomas, Capt Ralph P.
Queens Roy Lancers
MC (*JC* 18.2.43)

Tobias, L/Bdr Harry
RA
MM (*Gazette* 12.7.45)

Tobias, Dvr M.
MID

Tobias, Flt/Lt W.V.
DFC

Tondovsky, B.
Pal Regt
MID

Torontow, P/O Cyril
AFC

Trebitsch, Spr J.
Pal Port Op Coy
Cert. of Gallantry

Treger, F/O William
RAF
DFC (*JC* 19.12.41)

Trocki, Lt Adolf
Polish VM

Tuck, Sqdn/Ldr A.H.
DFC

Tuck, Robert R. Stanford
Bat. of Britain
DFC+ Bar, DSO
USA DFC

Uhlmann, F.
Pal
MID

Ulmann, Cpl G.
PC
MID (*Gazette* 11.11.43)

Unger, Jack
MM

Ungerman, F/O David
DFC

Uzielli, A.
Pal
MID

Valdeberg, Cpl H.
PC
MID (*Gazette* 24.6.43)

Valek, Col Charles
Czech RAF
Medal of Merit and Bravery Medal

Van den Bergh, Sqdn/Ldr C.J.
MBE

Van den Bergh, Lt/Col Donald
MID (*Gazette* 11.11.43)

Van den Bergh, Maj Robert H.C.
RCOS
TD
MID (*Gazette* 14.6.45)

Van Gelder, Cpl Bernard
KRRC
MM (*Gazette* 25.11.43)

Vangelder, Sgt M.
RAMC
MID

Van Mentz, F/O Brian
RAF Bat. of Britain
DFC

Van Praag, Sgt Lionel M.
RAAF
GM (*JC* 2.10.42)

Van Praagh, Gnr William
London Scottish
MM

Van Zwanenberg, Capt Hugh A.
RA
USA Bronze Star (*Gazette*
30.5.46)

Vardy, Pte J.
MM

Vernon, C.K. (aka Kurt Werner)
RN
Croix de Guerre

Vidcosky, Lt Sidney
RA
MID (*JC* 17.8.45)

Vilensky, Maj S.
RE
MID

Vinacour, A.
RAF
MID

Vogelman, Capt Nathan
Paras
MC

Wadia, Surgeon Dr Richard
RN
MID

Wagner, Maj M.S.
MBE

Wajsblat, I.
Pal
MID

Waldenberg, Lt/Col Albert
RAOC
MID (*Gazette* 9.5.46)

Waley, Maj E.A.
RA
OBE

Waley, Lt Col E.G.
RA
OBE

Waley, Lt Frank R.
Intel Corps
MC

Waley-Cohen, Capt Matthew Henry
Order of Nassau (*Gazette* 16.1.48)
MID

Wallace, Cpl Joseph
MM

Wallach, Lt C.W.
DSO

Wallan, Sgt Harry (aka Wallack)
MID

Wallis, L/Cpl Joseph
SAEC
MM

Walls, Pte R.A.
Pal
Palestine Police Medal 1944

Warndorfer, Lt August
SOE
MID KIA

Warshaw, Maj Aubrey C.
RASC
MID (*Gazette* 9.8.45)
Knight Officer Order of Orange, Netherlands (*Gazette* 18.7.47)

Wartensleben, Cpl K.
MID

Waxman, F/O J.H.
DFM

Wayburne, Capt Samuel
SAF
MID (*JC* 1.5.42)

Wayman, Flt/Lt M.M.
DFC

Webber, Flt/Lt N.W.
GM

Weber, Flt/Lt Jack
RAF Bat. of Britain
MID (Hons List 14.6.45)

Weber, P/O Joseph A.
DFC

Wechsler, Maj Theodore M.
RASC
MBE (*Gazette* 23.3.44)

Weil, Lt Daniel
RN
Commended twice Air Ops. Iraq 2008

Weil, Flt/Lt Theodor O.
DFC

Weinberg, Rolfe
Intel Corps
Fr. MM
Croix de Guerre, FFI

Weinberg, Maj Walter
KSLI
Croix Militaire (*Gazette* 14.5.48)

Weiner, Lt Dennis P.
RA
MID (*Gazette* 26.4.45)

Weiner, Maj P.
RAMC
TD (*Gazette* 14.6.45)

Weinstock, Flt/Lt G.D.
RAF
MID (Hons List 14.6.45)

Weinstock, Maj Leslie M.
RAC
TD (*Gazette* 13.6.47)

Weiser, F/O William
RCAF
MBE, DFC + Bar
(*Gazette* 15.10.43, *JC* 2.6.44)

Weiss, Pte Abraham
SATC
MM (Dep 23.9.42)

Weiss, Pte David Solomon
MM

Weiss, Capt Gerald A.
SW Borderers
MC

Weiss/Weisz, Peter
SOE
MID

Weissberg, Solomon
Palestine Police
BEM 1938

Weitzman, Capt David
RAMC
MID (twice: *Gazette* 27.11.45, 23.5.46)

Weldon, P/O Aubrey
RAF
DFM (*JC* 5.12.41)

Welensky, Flt/Sgt D.L.T.
DFM

Wenger, Capt Morris A.
PC
MBE (*Gazette* 29.3.45)

Werner, O.
Pal
MID

Wiberg, Capt J.
W Yorks
MID

Wideberg, B.
Ambulance Service
Commendation for Courage

Wien, Maj Sol
RAC
MBE
MID (twice: *Gazette* 4.4.46,
JC 3.7.45)

Wiener, Maj G.L.
RASC
MBE, MID

Wientrobe, Solomon
GM (fire rescue)

Wilk, F/O Lionel
RAF
DFC (21.7.44)

Wilkes, Maj Eric
RCOS
MBE (*JC* 20.7.45)

Wilkes, Maj Lyall
Middx Regt
MID (*JC* 20.7.45)

Wilks, Gnr Arnold
RA
MID

Winawar, H.M.
Polish Cross of Valour

Winberg, Lt/Col J.R.
RAC
MID (*Gazette* 15.12.42)

Winestein, Dvr Hyman
RASC
MID (*Gazette* 19.7.45)

Wingate, Lt John S.
RAC
MC
KIA 25.2.44 – remembered
Willesden; b. Anzio

Winter, Flt/Lt Simon
RAF
MBE (Medical)

Wise, Flt/Lt C.
MID

**Wiseman, Sgt Pilot Edward
Wolf**
DFM

Wiseman, Maj John M.
SAS
MC, MID
Croix de Guerre (*JC* 4.5.45)

Wiseman, P/O Michael M.
RAF
DFM (*Times* 9.5.41)

Wiseman, Sgt Ralph
RCOS
MID (*Gazette* 10.5.45)

Wisser, Pte S.E.
Beds & Herts Regt
MID

Witkin, Capt P.
Lancs Regt
MID Burma

Witzenfeld, Sgt S.
RAF
Cert. of Merit (*JC* 26.7.46)

Wolchak, B.
St John's Ambulance Cert. of
Courage

Wolf, Flt/Sgt Leslie
RAF
DFM (*Gazette* 6.6.44)

Wolfe, Capt H.L.
RAMC
MID

Wolfe, Sgmn N.
RCOS
MID

Wolfe, Lt R.T.
DSC

Wolfe, LAC Robert
RCAF
BEM (*Gazette* 27.10.44)

Wolfers, Capt David
RA
MC

Wolff, Sgt F.
MID

Wolfson, Flt/Lt Frank D.
RAF
DFC (*Gazette* 21.9.45)

Wolfson, Soloman
GM – bravery in ARP

Wolfson, Cmdr V.
RN, SOE
OBE

Wolfson, Capt V.H.
RA
MID

Woodburn-Bamberger, Lt L.A.
RA
MID (*Gazette* 22.3.45)

Woolf, P/O Basil
RN Commando
MID (*JC* 3.1.45)

Woolf, Capt Bernard M.
RAC
MC

Woolf, Lt/Col Donald S.
RAOC
OBE (New Year Hons 1.1.46)
TD (*Gazette* 20.3.47)

Woolf, Pte D.F.
SAF
MID (Gazette 24.6.43)

Woolf, Capt F.
MID

Woolf, Lt Ivan Justin
General List, SOE
MID

Woolf, LAC Joseph
RAF
MID Balham tube rescue 1940

Woolf, Gnr Lawrence
RA
MID (*Gazette* 10.3.45)

Woolf, Flt/Lt Ray
RAF
MBE (New Year Hons 1.1.46)
USA Bronze Star twice
MID (twice: *JC* 8.2.46)

Woolfe, Flt/Lt D.A.
MID

Woolfson, Capt Joseph
RAOC
MID (*Gazette* 4.4.46)

Woolfson, S.
ARP
GM

Wrisberg, Maj/Gen F.G.
CBE

Wynbourne, Lt/Col F.T.
RE
MID (*JC* 8.2.44)

Yershaw, Sgt J.
DFM

Yofe, D.
Pal
MID

Yofe, Maj J.
RAMC
MID

Young, Maj Benjamin
W Surreys
MBE Somaliland

Yudelman, Lt Montague M.
SAAF
DFC (*Gazette* 16.2.43)

Yenis, Willie
MID

Zacks, Lt Elias
Gold Coast Regt
MC (July 1941)

Zadik, M.G.
Pal
MID

Zagerman, Flt/Lt Cecil M.
RAF
AFC (*Gazette* 21.9.45) DFC

Zalsberg, Sgt Lewis
RAF
DFM (Sept 1941)

Zangen, Capt Ferdinand
RAMC
MC (*JC* 26.5.44)

Zarhi, B.
Pal
MID

Zassman, Sgt Jack
RA
MID (Rev Hooker 2.11.43)

Zeff, Capt Bernard
RAOC
MID (*Gazette* 11.1.45)

Zeff, Lt Edward
SOE
MBE, Croix de Guerre

Zeidman, Pte A.
Pal Regt
MID (*Gazette* 29.11.45)

Zeitlyn, Rad/O Oriel
RN
Gazetted for Valuable Service
(*JC* 7.1.44)

Zemla, Lt Israel M.
The Buffs
MID (*Gazette* 23.5.46)

Zemmil, Gnr Nathan
Roy Horse Arty
MM (*Gazette* 15.10.42)

Zenftman, Sgt L.
Recce Corps
MID

Zibman, Cpl J.
RAF
MID (Rabbi Brodie 8.11.43)

Zieleznik, I.
RWAAF
MC, MID

Ziera, J.
Pal
MID

Zigmond, W/Cdr Walter
RAF
Air Efficiency Award (6.6.45)

Zilberbaum, A.
Pal
MID

Ziller, R.
RAF
MID

Ziman, AC1 Officer Thelma
WRNS
MBE (Hons List 13.6.46)
Bletchley Park

Zimmerman, LAC J.
RAF
MID (*JC* 13.7.42)

Zimmerman, Sgt Cyril
DLI
MID D-Day

Zorea, Capt M.
Jewish Brigade
MC

Zuckerman, Surg/Lt Cyril Arthur H.
RN
Commended

Zweig, Sgt W. (aka Nelson)
10 1A Commando
Cert. of Commendation

Zukerman (Zukermanova), Edita (Marianne)
FF agent
Ordre de L'Armee de Merite
Croix de Guerre with Palm

A Different May Day

Henry Morris

There it was again: 'Killed in action at sea, 1st May 1943'. I was checking the print-out for the Roll of Honour in my book, *We Will Remember Them* and, again and again, this entry followed the names of men killed while serving with the Royal Army Service Corps of the Palestine Regiment. I counted them. There were 148, all killed on the same day, the greatest loss suffered by the Palestine Jews who fought and served with the British Army. 'How did this happen?' I asked myself, and I learned the answer with the help of the Israel Ministry of Defence, the RASC Regimental Museum in England, records held by Israel military historians, the Israel War Veterans League and survivors of the tragedy who subsequently settled in the USA.

462 Company RASC had been part of the forces surrounded by the German Afrika Korps in the siege of Tobruk and had then taken part in the battle of El Alamein. In his book, *Soldiers from Judea,* Rabbi Rabinowitz, Senior Jewish Chaplain MEF, writes: 'In the victorious advance of General Montgomery five RASC units took part: 462 GT Company commanded by Major H. Yoffe, a South African Jew, 178 Company commanded by Maj Wellesley Aron, a British Jew, 11 Water Tank eventually commanded by Maj B. Adelman, a Canadian Jew, 5 WT commanded by Maj Y. Frumkin and 179 GT, commanded by Maj I. Boganov'.

After performing heroically throughout the North African campaign, in April 1943, three weeks before the fall of Tunis, 178 and 462 Companies were informed that they had been chosen for 'highly operational work of the first importance'. 178 Company went to Tripoli and 462 went to Alexandria. It was intended that they should go on to Malta where 'the George Cross Island was to be changed from a battered place of siege to a base of attack'. But it was not to be – the flower of Palestine Jewish youth was to perish in less than five minutes.

During February and March of 1943, together with other Jewish forces, they were in Bengazi. In April they were sent to Egypt. There, in Tahay Camp, they organized for a new mission while enjoying the Passover holiday. After two weeks they transferred to Ameria Camp in Alexandria and awaited their departure. On 29 April they sailed on the 5,000 ton World War One Indian Merchant ship, the *Erinpura*. She was the flagship of a convoy of twenty-seven excluding escort. On board were 334 officers and men of 462 Company and 700 Basuto soldiers from Africa. On Friday evening, 30 April, the Commanding Officer, Maj Yoffe, informed his men that they were on their way to Malta.

From information received from survivors and the official report submitted by Maj Yoffe, I was able to piece together the story of what happened on that fateful night.

On the evening of the 1 May the convoy was approached by an enemy aircraft. Here I have varying reports of what followed. One claims that it was Italian and was driven off by anti-aircraft gunfire, another says it was a Heinkel that dropped a torpedo that failed to hit and was shot down. There is a third version saying it was an unidentified German plane that flew too low for the guns to attack. Such is the confusion of an air raid at sea. The official report writes that, following this opening move, 'In accordance with Ship's Standing Orders, Action Stations' had been ordered. All men without duties had been ordered below deck.

At about 20.10 hrs on 1 May 1943 there was an attack by enemy aircraft and, although bombs were dropped, the ship was not affected. About 20.50 there was a second aircraft attack. It was a very heavy raid and many bombs were dropping all around. At 21.05 Maj Yoffe was at his command position on the saloon deck, where he was immediately available and could employ maximum control, when a terrific explosion occurred forward of the bridge and he was knocked over by an enormous wave. When he recovered, the ship was going down at the bows. Orders came from the bridge to abandon ship. Attempts were made by officers to get the men up from below – many may have been dead already – but all ladders and gangways had been smashed by the explosion. A large number of men were still below when the bows were completely under water, within two minutes of the explosion. The ship was listing badly, making it impossible to lower boats. Of the two that succeeded, one capsized. Every raft and anything that floated had been thrown overboard and the men were ordered to jump. Taking all the circumstances into consideration, Maj Yoffe gave the opinion that everything possible had been done to evacuate the ship.

The light was failing when the ship went down and the convoy was out of sight of land. By the time the men had been in the water for ten minutes it was completely dark. The ship sank in about four minutes. It was not certain whether it had been struck by a torpedo or an aerial mine. One survivor told me he was in the water for several hours before being picked up, as the convoy was not allowed to search and rescue. He relates that the Basuto soldiers in the water added their voices in song to the Hebrew songs being sung by the Jewish soldiers.

Another survivor wrote that he spent all night clinging to a piece of wood and was picked up by a Greek destroyer. The Captain and the soldiers manning the guns were the last to jump. The attack continued and there are reports of the men in the water being machine gunned. Sgt Bijovsky, a survivor, reports: 'The rescue was very difficult, many of us did not know how to swim, it was dark, they did not manage to get down the lifeboats, the cries of the drowning were terrible. Our commander, Maj Yoffe, was all the time with us, he did not leave his soldiers, he could be proud of our behaviour.' The British and Greek sailors from the rescue ships did all they could to save the men in the water.

The survivors were taken by the British minesweeper *Santa* to the port of Bengazi and by the Greek warship *Adrias* to Tripoli, while others went to Malta.

One hundred and forty-eight soldiers of 462 Company died in the disaster, many others were wounded and hospitalized. After a period of recovery they were transferred to Egypt and, eventually, to live in Eretz Israel.

In July and August of 1943 the RASC unit commanded by Lt/Col Charkham OBE was reinforced by the survivors of 462. This unit was undergoing training for the D-Day landing on Pestume Beach, Salerno. The reconstituted 462 Company, led by Maj Yoffe, also took part in the landings and subsequently assisted at the beach head, Anzio, until the final breakout, where they suffered casualties in men and equipment. As part of the 8th Army in Italy they had returned as liberators to the continent which many had left as hunted and despised refugees, veterans of the desert, sons of Jewry in whom we take great pride.

At the Military Cemetery on Mt Herzl in Jerusalem there is a monument in the form of a ship inscribed with the names of those brave men who died on 1 May 1943.

Hevel Yami Le'Yisroel (Israeli Merchant Navy)

In memory of nineteen seamen of the *Har Zion* ship of the Merchant Navy of Eretz-Israel before the establishment of the State of Israel.

Har Zion, owned by Eretz-Israel Maritime Lloyd, had sailed in the Mediterranean Sea during the years 1934–39.

Upon the outbreak of World War Two, the ship was mobilized, together with her crew, to the service of the British Navy war effort, and was used to transport supplies. It was sunk by the German Navy during an attack on a convoy of ships in the Atlantic Ocean, on the eve of 1st September 1940.

Among the 34 crew members, nineteen were Jewish seamen from Eretz-Israel who went down to the depths of the sea and were not brought to burial.

The extract above was sent to me by Shimon Behar of the Israel War Veterans.

Henry Morris

PART FOUR
POWs and Other Lists

British and Commonwealth Jewish POWs of the Germans, 1939–1945

The experience of British and Commonwealth Jewish POWs of the Germans was a mixed but generally non-violent one. Most eye-witness accounts describe the treatment of Jewish POWs as the same as everyone else. But what is true is that at the beginning, the Germans did try to separate Jewish POWs with a view to deporting them elsewhere, perhaps to death; however, the immediate resistance of the Senior British Officer (SBO) or the Man of Confidence (MoC, senior NCO or OR – Other Rank – in other camps) rapidly put a stop to this. They insisted that all Jewish soldiers were British/Commonwealth soldiers and any attempt to mistreat Jewish prisoners would reach the ears of London and result in possible retaliation. These facts are lifted from comments in many published first-hand POW stories. The records show that little discrimination was therefore shown.[1]

One reason for this generally equal treatment is that many of the guards and commandants of German camps were elderly First World War veterans, or soldiers who were considered politically less reliable by the Reich; some were simply not Nazis. Circumstances, however, varied greatly over time and place. But more importantly, the Germans had signed the Geneva Convention and there were many Germans in Allied hands. In addition, many Jewish NCOs and ORs – unbeknown to the Germans – spoke Yiddish at home and thus could understand German quite well.[2] As a result, a disproportionate number of Jewish POWs became Men of Confidence in POW camps, or factories, farms and mines where many Allied POWs were sent to work, and usually were able to obtain better conditions and food for all the men, and became quite friendly with the guards. Sgt Jack Goldwhite, as just one example, was awarded the BEM for his work as a POW in the honours after the Second World War.[3] However, if it became known that a MoC was Jewish, they were often discarded by the Germans, as the personal testimony of Alf Bird and Lew Dorff shows.[4] Also there is one recorded incident of successful segregation of British Jewish POWs at Stalag Luft 1 in January 1945.[5] The knowledge of German among

Jewish Palestinian POWs was even greater as many had originally come to British Palestine as refugees from Europe.

Many Jewish personnel made home runs from camps and there is material at the Museum on this. For example, Nat Leaman, RAF, MID (a second-cousin by marriage to the author) was one of the famous 'Sergeant Escapers' with Dixie Dean, and the scrounger in the film *The Great Escape* (played by James Garner) is believed to be modelled on him. Palestinian Jewish POWs were especially in demand as escape partners because many spoke several European languages and even knew the geography of the escape areas from their pre-war days in Europe.[6]

The following anecdote was told by former POW Alec Jay (aka Jacobs), Rifle Brigade, in the magazine of the Hendon Reform Synagogue in 1978 (with thanks to his son John for bringing this to the author's attention). It is a moving story of solidarity. 'At a parade of (British) officers in a camp in 1940, an order was given by the Germans that any Jews should take two paces forward. The initial response by one Lt Clifford Cohen was to move forward, but hardly had he completed his two steps, when every other officer on the parade moved forward two paces to close ranks with him. Net result, no action from the Germans.' Lt Cohen was awarded an MC for gallantry at Dunkirk and after the war became a judge and Deputy Lord Lieutenant of County Durham. He died in 1973.

There were some notable and horrific exceptions to all this, however. After the collapse of Greece, approximately twelve British Palestinian Jewish POWs were found with their throats cut and hands tied behind their backs in a cave near Kalamata in 1941; this was witnessed by the SBO in the area and is described in a letter to AJEX from the British Brotherhood of the Greek Campaign. Jewish POW Morris Stodel (RCOS) had the unnerving experience of being closely questioned at Kalamata about whether he lived in Whitechapel by a German officer who spoke perfect English and claimed he had lived among Jews in the East End of London before the War.[7]

At Colditz, French POW officers openly discriminated against their own Jewish officers, demanding they be segregated. The British responded to this by openly expressing their disgust and immediately sided with the Jews. Orderly Fusilier Solly Goldman was beaten and abused by German guards and Capt Julius Green was verbally insulted by a British Chaplain POW.[8]

Norman Rubinstein from Cardiff was captured at Calais in 1940 and spent five years as a POW. A German speaker, he acted as Camp Interpreter in several camps. In his book, *The Invisibly Wounded*[9] he tells of two incidents where three Palestinian Jews were recaptured after escaping, and then taken by the Gestapo and never seen again, despite diplomatic efforts to find them. Norman himself overheard a group of German doctors, on another occasion, discussing whether to murder a wounded Jewish POW, but another doctor intervened. Norman himself was verbally abused and severely beaten by German guards on a number of occasions when they discovered his name and knew him to be Jewish.

Early in 1943, one Palestinian Jewish escaper was recaptured and then murdered by a German policeman in Upper Silesia.[10] A work to be consulted on this issue is by Yoav Gelber.[11] At Berga camp near Buchenwald[12] many ethnic Americans – mostly Jewish GIs – were separated out and subjected to the type of brutality usually associated with slave labour camps and concentration camps like Dachau. And at Teschen and Teklowicz, Jewish POWs were separated but apparently not ill-treated.[13] On the other hand, Palestinian Jewish POWs in Poland – Cracow, for example – who died of illness or attempting to escape, were given full military funerals by the Germans, with Star of David grave markers. This is extraordinary when not many miles away millions of Jewish women and children were being murdered by the Germans in Auschwitz and Treblinka. Conversely, there is a suspiciously large number of Palestinian Jewish soldiers recorded as having been killed attempting to escape in both Greek and Polish camps; further detailed research into the exact circumstances of their deaths is needed.

The *Jewish Chronicle* reported on 14 November 1941 that French Jewish POWs were also discriminated against by the Germans, and it is generally known that Polish and Russian Jewish POWs were especially ill-treated and often murdered.

On a related issue, some researchers found that relations between British and Palestinian Jewish POWs were not always good, partly because, as the Jews often spoke German, they were able to trade with Germans, obtain items through bribery, and get jobs as interpreters. This caused some resentment among the other British POWs in Greece/Crete, for example,[14] and even some outright anti-Semitism elsewhere.[15] However it should be remembered that there was already little love lost between the two groups as the British behaviour in the Palestine Mandate favoured

Arabs and severely restricted the immigration of European Jews to Palestine – in effect condemning them to death in the Holocaust. There were first-hand reports circulating of British troops who were fleeing Greece and Crete refusing places on lorries and boats to Palestinian Jewish soldiers, thus condemning a higher proportion of them than most other Empire groups to long incarceration in German hands.[16] It should be noted, however, that the British also had an antipathy for the many Cypriot POWs who were able – due to their knowledge of Greek – to trade with locals in Greece/Crete. Other British POWs, however, testified that they may well not have survived without the extra food the Palestinian Jews and British Jews managed to scrounge from the Germans and locals,[17] and openly admired the way they refused to be intimidated by the special Nazi hostility towards them.

Attempted Deportation of POW Palestinian Jews in the British Forces

Gelber's research revealed that the attorney of the German 12th Army in Greece attempted to find a judicial way to prosecute as traitors those Palestinian Jewish POWs who were of German/Austrian origin. However, he could not get round the fact that those men were Palestinian citizens as stated in their pay books and records. He then sought to harass them by searching for any with a criminal record in Germany/Austria, so as to prosecute them as criminals; this too failed. Thereafter the British authorities ordered the deletion of nationality and place of birth from the army documents and pay books of all Palestinian Jewish volunteers to ensure their proper treatment as POWs.[18]

Segregation and Attempted Segregation

In July 1941 in camps in Wolfsburg and Marburg, Palestinian Jews of German/Austrian origin in British Forces were segregated and forbidden to go on work detachments. In addition, a serious attempt was made to force them to wear a special badge like the German Jewish Yellow Star. But Order 11 of the German POW Main Office OKW of 11 March 1942 eventually was issued and stated that this was not to be permitted, as the laws in Germany were for civilians only.[19] The Germans then hoped the British and French POWs would separate themselves from Jewish or Palestinian Jewish POWs – but in this they were gravely disappointed (see above).

The information for the POW list comes from Henry Morris's two splendid books,[20] the 60,000 Jewish Chaplains cards kept at the AJEX Museum, the war-time issues of the *Jewish Chronicle* – with special thanks to Harold Pollins and the Gerald Bean survey – and numerous books and articles and other varied sources. However, as many Jewish Servicemen changed their names and listed themselves as Church of England in case they were ill-treated by the Germans if captured, the full picture may never be known.

Approximate Numbers of Jewish POWs

- RN – 9
- Army – 604
- RAF – 75
- Palestine Jews – 195 named but believed approx. 1,500
- Canadian – 85 in *Canadian Jewry at War* (Montreal: Canadian Jewish Congress, 1947/48)
- Australian – 19
- South African – at least 750 but approximately 260 named

Epilogue

Many POWs died or were killed on the notorious 'Forced Marches' in the winter of 1944–45 but are listed as killed in action or on active service; we will never know the true number. Also, many Palestinian Jews listed as missing may indeed have been murdered after capture in Greece, Crete and Poland. Awards mentioned are for gallantry whilst a POW, or for escaping. A *Jewish Chronicle* report of August 1941 asserted that about 1,500 Palestinian Jews were POWs.

Martin Sugarman

Notes

1. See also S.P. Mackenzie, *The Colditz Myth* (Oxford: Oxford University Press, 2005), index, who describes incidents at Lamsdorf camp, Stalag VIIIB, Warburg and Stalag Luft VI, where SNCOs, SBOs and the rank and file categorically and openly opposed the Germans in trying to segregate British or Empire Jewish POWs – especially the stands taken by Sidney Sherriff and Dixie Dean.
2. Yiddish, though written in Hebrew, sounds the same as German as many German words were incorporated into it as it developed as a Jewish lingua franca in Europe from the ninth century.
3. Personal file at AJEX Museum.
4. See AJEX POW archive recording.
5. Mackenzie, *The Colditz Myth*, p.289 n.18.
6. See Yoav Gelber, 'Palestinian POWs in German Captivity', *Yad Vashem Studies* 14 (1981), p.128 n.7.
7. AJEX Museum Archives.
8. Mackenzie, *The Colditz Myth* , p.282; and M. Sugarman, 'Jews in Colditz', *JHSE*, 39 (2004), pp.178–82; M. Booker, *Collecting Colditz and its Secrets* (London: Grub Street, 2005), Ch.12.
9. Norman Rubinstein, *The Invisibly Wounded* (Hull: J. Lennard, 1989).
10. Mackenzie, *The Colditz Myth*, p.237 – but names are not given.
11. Gelber, 'Palestinian POWs in German Captivity'.
12. M. Bard, *Forgotten Victims* (Boulder, CO: Westview Press, 1994).
13. Personal testimony from South African Jewish POWs in SAJEX, *The South African Jewish Book of Honour* (Johannesburg: Eagle Press, 1950), pp.106–8.
14. See Mackenzie, *The Colditz Myth*, index.
15. Mackenzie, *The Colditz Myth*, p.275 and anti-Semitic remarks by Air Gunner R. Watchorn, RAF at Fallingbostel Camp, R.P. Evans at Hohenfels and R.A. Wilson at Lamsdorf.
16. See recently published books on the Battle for Greece and Crete in 1941.
17. Mackenzie, *The Colditz Myth*, p.90, n.55.
18. Gelber, 'Palestinian POWs in German Captivity', p.101.
19. See Gelber, 'Palestinian POWs in German Captivity', pp.107–8.
20. Henry Morris, *We Will Remember Them* (London: Brassey, 1989) and *The Addendum* (London: AJEX, 1994).

Navy

Adler, Marine A.P.

Adler, Marine H.

Caplin, Richard
MN for 35 years
Repatriated 1943, lived in Swale
Street/Hind Grove, Stepney (*East
London Advertiser* 1943)

Friedlander, Marine S.

Israel, Marine T.G.

Jessel, Capt R.F.
DSO, DSC
POW Vichy Fr, Algeria 4/42,
escaped 12/42

Joel, OS O.A.
HMS *Voltaire*

Rosenthal, I.J.
HMS *Voltaire*

Shenker, OS Harold Jeffrey

Army

Aaron, Pte A.A.A.
Died as POW Italy

Abel, Sgt A.C.
RAMC

Abensur, V.I.
RA

Abrahams, A.
KRRC

Abrahams, Rfmn Alec
KRRC

Abrahams, Pte A.T.
Beds & Herts

Abrahams, Gnr David
RA

Abrahams, F.
Dorsets

Abrahams, Harry
Manchester Regt
Escaped from Maginot Line via
Spain

Abrahams, Tpr J. Cyril
(aka Baler)
Commandos
POW Sicily

Abrahams, M.
RAOC

Abrahamson, Pte M.
RASC

Abram, Rfmn Cyril H.
Commandos
POW Colditz, then murdered
Sachsenhausen

Addlestone, M.
Seaforths

Adler, D.
R. Warwicks

Adler, Lt Gabriel (aka Gabor)
SOE
Shot as a POW

Ahronson, E.A.K.
Queens

Ancill, RSM Samuel
Irish Guards

Arbib, Lt John R.

Astrovsky, Ben
Repat 1944

Backner, Nathan
Lancs Fus

Balch, Joseph
RWK

Banks, Pte Phillip (aka Levy)
10th Paras
POW/WIA Arnhem
Twice escaped

Barder, Gnr Geoffrey L.

Barnet, Lt J.M.
RE
POW Colditz

Barnett, Pte Bernard C.
RAMC

**Barnett, Tpr Horace
(aka Blumenthal)**
RAC

Barnett, Ralph M.
RASC Crete

Becker, Capt Fritz (aka Benson)
SOE
POW and murdered

**Becker, Lt Rudolf "Butch"
(aka Baker-Byrne)**
SOE
POW

Beckerman, Harry
Escaped to Switzerland

Behr/Beher, Gilbert Max
RAC

Behrens, H.A.
SWB

Behrens, Capt Louis Aubrey
Coldstream Guards

Behrman, Daniel
RASC

Beja, Robert
FFF

Bender, I
Falaise

Benjamin, H.J.
RE

Benjamin, L/Cpl R.A.
Norfolks

Bensusan, G.C.
E. Surrey Regt

Berger, H.
Black Watch

Berkeley, Capt Allan
RAMC

Berkowitz, Leslie
Killed after escaping Italy

**Berliner, Capt Frederick M.
(aka O'Hara aka Chirgwin)**
SOE
POW and murdered

Berlofsky, Gnr Daniel

Berman, Gnr J.

**Bernstein, L/Cpl Cyril
(aka Benton)**
11th Paras
POW/WIA Arnhem
Attempted escaper

Bernstein, 6970513 Harold
RB

Bernstein, I.
Worcs Regt

Bernstein, Pte Isaac M.
Worcs Regt

Bernstein, L.
RE

Bindler, Joseph
RB

Binnick, Sgt Norman (Sonny)
21st Indep Paras at Arnhem
POW/WIA

Bird, Alf
RB
('Man of Honour')

Blatt, Cpl Rudy
Commandos
Escaped

Blick, Sgt L.KRRC

Blint, Wolf/David
Commando/Airborne
POW

Bloch, Lt Andre (aka Boyd)
SOE
Murdered by Nazis after POW

Bloch, Denise
SOE
Kings Comm, Croix de Guerre
Murdered Ravensbruck

Blofeld, S.
RA

Bloom, Capt Harold
RAMC

Bloom, Harry
DLI

Bloom, Capt Marcus,
SOE
POW murdered Mauthausen

Bloomberg, H.
Cameronians

Bloomberg, Leonard John
KOYLI

Bloomfield, A.W.
RA

Bloomfield, Pte H.S.
RAMC

Bluestein, Pte Emmanuel
REME

Boder, Gnr J.
RA

Boris, Anthony P.
RA

Borstein, Sydney
Italy

Botoshaner, J.
RA

Boxenbaum, Harry
Commandos

Braverman, Dvr Sidney
RA
Escaped Italy

Brazil, Sydney
RE

Brazil, W.
Irish Guards

Breyer, Alf
6th Airborne
Rhine crossing 1945

Bromnick, Sgt Myer
1st Paras
POW/WIA Arnhem

Brooks, Dvr Temple
RASC

Brott, Pte Leonard
Anzio

Brown, Jack
Yorks & Lancs

Burgh, M. Stanley
RA

Cahill, Oswald
RE

Cahn, George
Glasgow (Rubinstein book)

Caplan/Caplin, Harold
RA

Carretta, Tony
RNF

Castle, Joe
Info. Harry Rose RAF

Charig, Stanley
RAC

Chickanofsky, Rfmn M.
KRRC

Clyne, Rfmn Albert

**Coehn, Cpl Gunther
(aka Cohn/Koen)**
SOE South African
POW

Cohen, Clifford
Brother of Lt D.L. Cohen,
later a judge
MC, POW at Dunkirk

**Cohen, Pte Abraham
(aka Conn)**
Green Howards

Cohen, Arnold Alex
Essex Regt

Cohen, 2nd Lt C.T.
DLI

Cohen, D.R.
RA

Cohen, Gnr Frank
RA
POW Tobruk
Escaped Italy with partisans,
recaptured to Germany

Cohen, G.
R. Berks

Cohen, Sgmn H.
RCOS

Cohen, Dvr Harold
RE

Cohen, Harris
T150397
Escaped 1943 Italy

Cohen, Hyman
6919399
Recce Corps
WIA/Repat. 1944

Cohen, J.
The Queens Regt

Cohen, J.M.
Green Howards

Cohen, Jack
Brady Club

Cohen, Cpl Joseph
RB

**Cohen, Capt Kenneth J.
(aka Smith aka Komrover?)**
6 Commando/SBS

Cohen, L.
RA

Cohen, Rfmn Leonard
London Irish
Died as POW

Cohen, R.A.
RB

Cohen, Rfmn Ralph
KRRC

Cohen, S.
RB

Cohen, S.
RB

Cohen, Rfmn Samuel
KRRC
POW Colditz

Cohen, W.J.
Dunkirk

Cooper, Pte Harry
Para Glider Arnhem
POW

Cooper, M.
RAMC

Cooper, Monty
RB

Coster, Sgt Sam C.
1st Paras
POW Arnhem, later escaped

Cowen, J.
RAMC

Cowen, Ralph
KRRC

Crietzman, M.
RA

Cuckle, Pte Lionel
11th Paras
POW/WIA Arnhem

Cutner, Tpr Lionel Joshua
RAC

Dale, Stephen (aka Guenther Spanglet, aka Turner, aka Ziba)
SOE
POW

Daniels, Dvr R.T.
RASC

Dansky, Victor
DLI

David, Lt John Edward
R Berks

Davidovitch, Sgt A.
RE

Davis, Pte G.R.
RWK

Dembinsky, Fus Sydney
Roy North Fus

De Haan, Sid (Sol)
RAMC Crete

Deman,Capt Erwin (aka Dent)
SOE
POW 1940
Escaped to UK

Desmond, Sgt H.W.
1-6th Queens
POW N.Africa

De Young, Rfmn Alfred
KRRC

Diamond, Rfmn Arnold
RB
MID as a POW

Diamond, Rfmn Phillip
T Hamlets Rif

Dobkin, Rfmn Jessel
Escaped Italy

Dorff/Dorfmann, Louis
RAC
('Man of Honour')

Dorlin, Danny (aka Dorlinski)

Dov, B.L.
Buffs

Dresser, Bernard
Paras
POW escaped Arnhem

Duboff, Cpl S.
RAOC

Edwards, David Rufus
DCM
Escaped

Eglash, Pte Ivor
RAMC

Eisen, Monty
RNF

Emden, Abraham Alf
RCOS

Emmanuel, Pte R.G.
Welch

Epstein, Lewis
RB

Fagelson, Pte Morris
POW Normandy
Escaped, recaptured

Fay, 2nd Lt Dennis Henry
RCOS

Feidelman, Gnr Morris

Ferguson, L/Cpl Leslie
Cameronians
Repatriated 1943

Field, Nicholas (an alias)
Escaped Dunkirk, interned Spain,
returned via Gibraltar

Fierstein, Fus Jack
MM

Fineman, Lt H.
RA
POW 15 mins
N Africa – ESCAPED!

Fink, F.G.
Green Howards

Finkel, Tpr Harry
RAC

Finn, Maurice
RCOS

Fisher, Emmanuel
RA

Fisher, Sgt Leonard

Fishman, Cpl S.
POW Tobruk and never seen again

Flamberg, Pte Gerald
156 Paras
WIA/POW Arnhem

Fleisig, Spr Dennis
Repat.

Frankenberg, Lt John
Cheshires

Franks, Sgt Ronald
Glider Pilot Arnhem
Died of wounds as a POW

**Fraser, L/Bdr Kenneth
(aka Fleischman, Kurt)**
POW/WIA Arnhem

Freedman, Dvr A.
RASC

Freedman, A.
RCOS

Freedman, M.
RASC

Freedman, Dvr S.

Freshwater, Rfmn Harry A.
POW then shot at El Aronsa, N
Africa

Freud, Capt Anton
SOE

Fridkin, Dvr Harry

Fried, Freddy

**Friedlaender, Rudolph
(aka Robert Lodge)**
SAS
DCM
Escaped, shot as a POW

**Friedland, Sgt Morris
(aka Farrow)**
SOE

Friedlander, E.
RASC

Friedlander, Maurice
Liverpool

Friedlander, S.
RASC

Furman, Capt John
RA
MC and Greek Order for 5
escapes

Futter, Capt Leonard
WIA/POW Arnhem

Gasson, Ron
RASC
POW N Africa

Geduld, Louis
KRRC

Geller, Rfmn Samuel
KRRC

Gerscovitch, Israel
RAOC

Gilbert, Sgt Mark
RASC

Gino/Sino, Morris 'Patsy'
Queens Regt

Glazier, C.N.
Gordons
POW Holland

Gleek, Cpl Mark
RAC

Goldberg, Dvr Abraham
RE

Goldberg, Pte Frank
POW Arnhem

Goldman, L.
Devons

Goldman, M.W.
RCOS

Goldman, Sidney
RNF
Repatriated 10/43

Goldman, Fus Solomon
POW Colditz

Goldrein, Eric
POW Normandy

Goldsmith, Rfmn Harry
KRRC
Escaper Libya and Italy

Goldstein, Sgt Ben
156 Paras
WIA/POW Arnhem
Brother of Samuel

Goldstein, E.W.
The Glosters
Escaped

Goldstein, Percy
RASC

Goldstein, Samuel
7016113
Paras
Brother of Ben

Goldstein, Sam
RA
Escaped

Goldstein, Pte Sidney
1st Paras
POW Arnhem

Goldstein, Cpl Woolfe

Goldwhite, Sgt Jack
BEM for gallantry as a POW
('Man of Honour')

Goodman, Pte
Essex
Died as POW in Italy

Goodman, Capt David
POW then liberated in N Africa

Goodman, Simon
RWK Desert Rats
POW Italy

Gordon, Isidore
RAOC

Gordon, Joseph
RASC
Repatriated

Gordon, Sydney Mark
DLI

Goschen, John
RHA
Escaped

Gottlieb, Lt Joseph
RAMC

Goulding, D.
Grenadier Guards
Escaped

Gourevitch, Capt A.
RAMC
MC
POW escaped with Crete
partisans
MID for this

Grabini, Abraham G.
PC
Escaped

Green, Cyril
DLI
Brother of Phillip

Green, Sgt Harry

Green, L/Sgt Jack
RA

Green, Capt Julius
Colditz POW – author of book

Green, Pte Leonard
RASC
DCM
Escaped – author of book

Green, Pte Phillip
DLI
Bother of Cyril

Green, Pte Samson
POW Salonika

Greenbaum, Sgt Frank A.
AAC Glider Pilot
WIA/POW Arnhem

Greenberg, J.
RAC

Greenberg, R.
Buffs

Gross, H.
RCOS

Grossman, H.B.
RF

Halfin, Rfmn Solomon Dennis
POW Colditz

Harris, Edward Arthur
E Yorks

Harris, Pte John

Harris, Marcus

Harris, Victor
Camerons

Harrison, Pte Norman
RAMC
Repatriated

Hart, Cpl M.E.
RAC

Hass, Gnr Lawrence
RA

Heaps, Capt Leo J.
POW Arnhem, escaped

Hecker, Morris
Essex Regt

Henriques, R.B.
AAC

Hess, Otto (aka Peter Giles)
SOE
POW murdered

Hoffman, Harry
Paras Blackpool
Escaped 3 times

Hoffman, Nat
RAC
POW Dunkirk

Hootman, Cpl Jack
KRRC

Houthaker, Sgt Harold Samuel
KRRC

Hudaly, Dvr Stanley Bernard

Hughes, W. (aka Walter Sachs)
Para
POW D Day plus 1

Hyams, K.L.
RB

Hyams, M.
AAC

Hyams, M.J.
AAC

Hyman, Capt Eric
RAMC

Iduas, Sydney
A&SH
WIA/POW D Day

Infield/Infeld, Lt Gerald M.
POW Arnhem

Ingram, Capt Barry B.
POW Arnhem

Instone, Gordon
RA
Escaped

Isaacovitch, Michael
Tobruk

Isaacs, A.V.
RA

**Isaacs, Maj Bernard Arthur
(aka Irvine)**
Korea Special Forces
MC, MID twice
USA Citation
POW/WIA, escaped

Israel, Dvr G.D.

Izon, Sgt Charles
WIA/POW Arnhem

Jacobs, Cpl F.H.
RAC

Jacobs, J.H.
E Surreys

Jacobs, Rfmn Norman Cecil

Jacobsen/son, Lt Isaac
RAMC, S Africa
Repat.

Jacobson, A.
E. Yorks

Jay, Alec (aka Jacobs)
RB, BEF
POW Calais
Escaped 5 times to Czech
partisans

Joel, 2nd Lt John H.
Green Howards

Joel, A.
RA

Joseph, Alfred Gordon
RA
POW Italy
Escaped, recap

Josephs, Pte Daniel
POW Arnhem

Jublitsky, Woolf
6th Airborne D Day

Kalikoff, Sgt Maurice
Paras
Died of wounds as POW after
Arnhem

Kalinsky, Reginald
RB/Queens

Kalman, Rfmn P.H.

Kandler, Rfmn Solomon
Escaped Italy (brother POW
Japanese)
With Corporal Perkoff

Karpf, Lt Anthony
Polish, lived UK
POW Colditz

Katz, Jack
Black Watch

Kauffman, Pte Harry
Green Howards
Escaped

Kaufman, F.
RWK

Kaufman, I.
Queens Regt

Kaufman, Sidney
Queens Roy Regt
MM

Kayne, Lt Dennis B.
POW Arnhem

Kemp, C.
RAMC
Repat.

**Kessel, Capt Surgeon Alexander
Lippman**
POW, Arnhem
Escaped

Khan, Dvr R.J.
RASC
Died as POW

Kirsch, J.M.
RCOS

Klein, B.
RAC

Kohler, C J.
RCOS

Komrower, Lt Donald
RAC
Liberated N Africa

Konisberg, Bdr Sydney
RA

Kosky, Dvr Leonard
RASC

Kosloff, Capt
RAMC

Koslover, Pte Samuel
RWK

Kottka, V. (aka Jones)
3-10 Commandos

Kramer, J.L.
RA

Kraus, L.
Green Howards

Kupferblatt, Gnr Eleazar
RA

Kurasch, Louis
RB/RNF

Kushelevsky, Pte Morris

Labinsky, Cpl Jack
RASC

Lambert, Jack
Glasgow

Landa, Godfrey
RA

Landes, Marcel

Landsberg, W.
Scots Guards

Landsman, J.H.
KRRC

Lanyi, Lt George (aka Lane)
3 Troop, 10th Commandos
POW pre D-Day landings

Lawton, Merton
RMP
Dunkirk

Lazarus, Lt Arnold A.
Intel Corps

Lazarus, Tpr Arnold
RTR

Lee, Pte Harry
POW Arnhem

Lee (Levy), Capt Lionel
SOE
POW
Murdered Gross-Rosen

Lemberger, Cpl M.
Yorks &Lancs
Later lost at sea

Lenel, Ernst (aka Lawrence)
3-10 Commando
Murdered as POW

Lerman, Abraham
R. Berks
WIA and POW
Repatriated 1943

Lerman, Leonard
RASC

Letwin, J.
RA

Letwin, Wolfe
Green Howards
Died as a POW

Levene, J.
RA

Levene, M.
Notts and Derby Regt

Lever, Pte Jeffery
RASC
Escaped

Levien, Lt Robert H.
POW Arnhem

Levine, Lt Edward/Eugene
SOE
Murdered Flossenburg

Levine, Rfmn H.
RB

Levine, H.
Life Guards

Levine, Rfmn R.
KRRC

Levitt, Pte Walter
Green Howards

Levy, Tpr A
783386 RAC

Levy, Pte Alfred
RAMC
POW Arnhem

Levy, Bert Myer
7382181 RAMC

Levy, F.C.
RA

Levy, Pte Harris
POW Arnhem

Levy, Capt Rev Isaac
'Rommel's Rabbi'
N Africa
Escaped after several days

Levy, Dr Isidore
RAMC
Glasgow

Levy, Tpr Isidore
RAC

Levy, John
RASC
Killed in bombing as a POW
Buried Durnbach

Levy, Maurice Jack
13808389 REME
POW Russians Jan 1952/release
May 1954

Levy, S.
A&SH

Lewis, David
POW Crete

Lewis, Julius
RAMC
Repatriated

Liebovitch, L.
RWK

Lifschitz, Pte Charles
Green Howards

Linden, Cpl Jack
Paras
POW Arnhem

Lindheimer, Pte W.
Pal
Killed in air crash on way home as
a recently liberated POW in
Germany

Linz, Cpl Joseph G.
Roy Berks
Anzio/Germany

Lipman, M.
REME

Liss, Jack
RASC

Listinsky, Fus Sol
Lancs Fus
Died as a POW

Litvinoff, Barnett
RAMC
Famous author

Lobell, Barry
(alias)
POW Korea

Losky, Pte Samuel H.
REME

Louisson, Charles
RNZ Arty
Died as POW 1945

Lowi, Sydney
RB
POW Dunkirk

Lucas, Anton I. (aka Lowenthal)
Paras
Escaped, recaptured Rhine
crossing
WIA

Luck, Donald
RA
POW Tobruk

Luck/Lucks, Pte Jack Isaac
Middx

Lyons, Fus Albert
Escaped Italy 3 times to
Switzerland

Lyons, Dvr Bernard
RASC

Madenberg, Harry Loewe
KRRC

Maier, Lt A.J.
RB

Makoff, Cyril
SLI

Mandelson, Lt George M.
Roy Dragoons
Escaped

Manstoff, Fus Leslie (Issy)
RF

Marcus, Dr J. (or M.)
RAMC (Rubinstein book)

Margolis, Solim
RAMC
POW Crete

Markham, David
RNF
Tobruk

Markovitch, Tpr David
Recce Corps

Marks, Pte Alfred David
Suffolks

Marks, Basil Louis
E Surreys
N. Africa

Marks, Pte D.
Glosters
POW Korea

Marks, Pte Lawrence
Dunkirk (Rubinstein book)

Marks, Sgmn Lionel
RCOS

Marks, Morris
Essex Regt (?)

**Marshall, Tpr Frank
(aka Silberstein)**
RAC

Master, Allen (Abraham)
DCLI

Masters, Monty (Morris)
RAMC
Crete

**Maxwell, Sgt Martin
(aka Meisels)**
POW Arnhem

Mayer, Marine
RN Commando
Murdered Sachsenhausen as
POW

Mayer(s), Lt Thomas
RB

Mayerbach, Arthur

Measure, Pte Philip
RAOC
Escaped 3 times

Mehlman, Sid
RAMC
Crete

Mehlmann, Pte Alfred
Kensington Regt

Mellish, Jack
RA Att. Foreign Legion

Melnick, Gnr I.

Mendelson, M.
RA

Meshkit/Maschit, Pte M.
Pal
Killed as returning POW in air
crash with
Lindheimer

Miller, Pte Bernhard
1940

Miller, Rfmn Hyman
KRRC

Milner, Sgt David
RB

Mindel, J.B.
RA

Mintz, M.
RA

Montefiore, A.S.F.
RAVC

Montrose, A.H.
RCOS

Mordecai, Pte E.V.
POW Arnhem

Mordecai, J.W.C.
RASC

Morris, Reginald

Morris,Pte S.
Camerons

Moscovitch, Morris
RAC

Moss, Rfmn Maurice
RB

Moss, Max
RASC
Crete

Mothio, Cpl Mark
RA

Muller, Dan
POW
Crete

Myers, Bessie
Ambulance Driver
POW Dunkirk
Escaped

Myers, Jack
RA
N Africa

Myers, Jack
RA
Tobruk, liberated by Americans
1942

Myers, Rfmn James
KRRC

Myers, Sgt Micky/Gerry
16th Paras Fld Amb
Arnhem
POW, escaped

Myers, Cpl V.J.
RB

**Nagel (Nagle), Pte Peter
(aka Newman (Bruneval Raid
aka Walker (St Nazaire Raid)**
SOE Commando
(Only Commando/SOE on both
raids)
POW St Nazaire
Escaped, recap

Nathan, Rfmn I.
6847737 RB
Pow Dunkirk

Nathan, W.A.
Worcestershire Regt

Nathanson, Lt Leslie
RA
Escaped to Switzerland

Newhouse, David Hyman
RA

Newman, Capt Isidore
SOE
MBE murdered at Mauthausen

Nyman, Arthur
KRRC

Nyman, H.
Dorset Regt

Nyman, Pte M.
RAOC

Oberman, Gnr Sidney
RA

Ofstein, Sgt Maurice
RA
(Brother of Wilfred)

Ofstein, Gnr Wilfred
RA
(Brother of Maurice)

Orr (Opoczynski), Sgt Adam
Commando SOE
POW
Escaped, later KIA

Osborne
Brother of B. Osborne, *RAF* POW

Oslof, Dvr M.

Ostroff, Myer/Mer
L. Irish

Ottolangui, M.
Wilts Regt

Pater, Rfmn John
RB

Pearlman, M.
RASC

Pereira, W.J.
S Staffs

Perkoff, Cpl Henry
Tower Hamlets Rifles
Escaped with Rfmn Kandler from Italy

Perrick, Harold W.
RA

Pertschuk, Lt Maurice
SOE
MBE
Murdered Buchenwald

Phillips, Capt E.J.
Beds & Herts

Phillips, Capt Henry

Phillips, Norman J.
RA

Phillips, Phineas Claude
RA

Pinkovsky, M.
RA

Pitkin, Pte Alec
RAMC

Pizer, C.
RA

Platter, Pte David
Italy

Podobransky, Sgt J.
RE

Pollack, Dr Robert

Powell, Jack (aka Pavodla)
Royal Sussex

Prager, Gnr Leonard
RA

Press, Harold
RNF

Press, L/Cpl Victor DCM
POW Normandy
Escaped

Pressman, Rfmn J.B.

Priestley, Peter (aka Egon Lindenbaum)
SOE
POW Italy

Pshygody/Schgodie, Cpl Sam
RF
POW Greece

Rabinovitch, Tpr David
RAC

Rabinovitz, Capt Adam/Adolphe
SOE
Croix de Guerre
Murdered by Nazis

Ramelson, Bert
POW N Africa
Escaped
Served Spanish Civil War

Rams, Max
Paras
Killed as a POW at Arnhem

Raphael, J.
RA

Raphael, M.
HLI

Rapperport, L/Cpl Victor
RASC

Redman, Lawrence
RE

Reinberger, Gnr D.

Reinhold, Arthur
HLI

Reynolds, Joseph
Liverpool Regt 1943

Riaj(g), Capt Clifford Beck

Richman, Woolf
RWK

Richter, D.
RAMC

Rimmon, Cecil
Paras
D Day

Roch, H.
RA
POW Tobruk

Rose, Dvr I.
BEF

Rose, Rfmn L.

Rosen, P.
Buffs

Rosenberg, Capt Hyman
RAMC

Rosenberg, Pte I.
RAMC

Rosenberg, J.
Buffs

Rosenberg, Pte L.

Rosenberg, Sgt S. (aka Ronald)
POW Arnhem

Rosenberger, W.

Rosenbloom, W.
RA

Rosenthal, Bernard A.
KRRC

Roth, Lt Col A.A.
RA

**Rothfarb, Gnr Max
(aka Rothbart)**
RA

Rothstein, Pte M.
RAOC

Rothstein, Sydney
RAOC

Rubenstein, Hyman
KRRC

Rubenstein, Norman
RA
Twice escaped – was in Terezin
Author *The Invisibly Wounded*

Rubin, Louis
RASC
Tobruk 1941

Rubinstein, Pte Sidney
POW Arnhem

Rustin, Capt Maurice
RAOC
Escaped

Sach, W.
E. Yorks Regt

Sacks, Bernard
Buffs

Sakol, Bernard
RASC

Salik, Sgt David
Polish Paras
At Arnhem
Had been POW in Russia

Saloschin (Saunders), George V.
*No 3 "Jewish" Troop 10
Commando*
Escaped 3 times

Saltman, Pte Jack
POW Arnhem

Samuel, L.
RAMC

Samuels, Lt A.
RA

Samuels, J.F.
Queens

Samuelson, Lt Alexander H.

Sander, Lt Gustav
Paras Arnhem
Escaped 7 times!
Later KIA Korea

Sarfaty, Sydney
RAOC
Repat. 10/43

Sassoon, H.F.
RF

Schalit, Tpr Leslie E.
Died attempting to escape in Italy
1944

**Scheinmann, Sgt Adi
(aka Anthony Eddy Sinclair)**
DCLI

**Schlesinger, Robert
(aka Bobby Shaw)**
POW Arnhem

Schneider, A.J.
Royal Sussex

Scholar, Wolf
KRRC

Schrire/Shire, Capt Isidore
POW Colditz from S African AMC
(author of a book)

Schwartz, A.
RAC

Schwartz, Joseph
(Rubinstein book)

Schwartz, R.H.
Staffs Regt

Segal, J.
RWK

Segal, J.
Queens Regt

Shama, 2nd Lt A.
Intel Corps

Shapiro, J.
KRRC

Sharp, Maj Derek
Special Forces
POW
BEM Korea & USA Special Award
('Man of Honour')

Sherbourne, Louis
Green Howards

Shilling, Tpr Ronald
City of London Yeo.

Shine, Isaac,
RA
POW Dunkirk

Shuell, Dvr Maurice

**Shufel/Schufel, Woolf
(aka William Scott)**
RASC
POW Dunkirk

Shulman, Sidney
Gordon Highlndrs

Silver, Joseph
AAC

Silver, P.
Rifle Bde, N Africa

Silver, Reuben
KRRC

Simmons, Rfmn Gerald
KRRC

Simon-Levy, R.
Duke of Well. Regt

Singer/Zhinger, Conrad
Spanish Civil War and Fr Foreign Leg
POW in N Africa

Singer, Dvr Cyril
RASC

Sino, Pte Morris
Queens

Sklan, Cecil
RA

Small, Gnr H.
RA

Smith, Jack

Snell, Capt E.
RAMC

Sobell, Joseph
RA

Sodikoff, Samuel
Roy Norfolks

Solomon, Gnr J.

Solomons, D.
RASC

Solomons, D.N.
RF

Solovitch, Pte Charles
RTR

Somers, Cpl A.W.

Speculand, Pte Alex
RASC

Spiegel, Dvr Charles M.

Spiro, L.
RASC
Escaped Italy

Steel, Gnr Joe
RA

Stein, D.
RASC

Stein, Pte M. Hyam
RAOC

Stein, Pte W.
RAOC
Died as POW in Germany

Stern, A.C.
Buffs

Stern, Alec
RB

Sternberg, L.
KORR

Stodel, Sgmn Morris
POW Crete

Stone, Capt Leslie D.
RAMC

Strong, Pte Michael
POW Dunkirk

Strouzer, Michael
RA

Strykowsky, Pte L.
RASC

Stuppel, Maj R.
RAMC, SOE
MID
Escaped Germans at Tobruk to fight with Tito
Killed as POW

Sugar, H.
Middx Regt

Sugarman, Cpl I.
RB
Escaped to Switzerland

Sumeray, Sgt Malcolm
11th Paras
POW Arnhem

Sunderland, Pte Arthur
13th Paras
POW Arnhem

Sussman, Louis
RA
WIA/POW

Swirsky/Switsky, Rfmn Max
Died as POW in Greece

Symons, Dvr Jack
RASC

Tannenbaum, Lt Albert L.
POW Arnhem

Taylor, David L.
6th Cameronians

Taylor, Norman
Glasgow

Temple, Arthur
Surreys
Dunkirk

Terry, Peter (aka Tischler)
3–10 Commando
POW Normandy
Escaped

Thomas, Dennis Russell
RASC

Turner, Lt Stephen Patrick
PC to Gen List
POW Italy 10/44

Valencia, Cpl Emmanuel
RF
Salerno

Valentine, Pte Al(bert?)

Van Buren, Hyman
Calais 1940
Brother of Leo

Van Buren, Leo
Calais 1940
Repatriated 1943
Brother of Hyman

Van der Linde, Sgt William
RAC
Repat.

Van Gelder, Bernard
KRRC

Van Gelder, John
RF

Vandenberg, G.D.
RWK

Wagenfield, Pte H.
W Yorks

Waller, Gnr Ben
RA

Webber, Fus Ralph
RNF

Weil, H.
RASC

Weinberg, Joseph
Welch Regt

Weinberg, Solomon
RE

Weiner, H.
RA

Weinstein, L.
Green Howards

Weiss, Abraham
R. Berks Regt

Weiss, Howard Dennis
RA

Weiss/Weisz, Sgt Peter
SOE (Pal)
MID
Murdered Dachau

Wertheim, G.
SAS
POW and murdered in France
1944
No known grave

Williams, Lt G.
RA

Williams, Sam

Wolfry, Joseph
RASC
Crete
(Info from Yeslovitz, below)

Woolf, Isaac Benjamin
RWK

Yeslovitz, Philip (aka Franklin)
MID for Gallantry rescuing
wounded POW in Crete

Zadik, Walter G. (aka Thompson)
3–10 Commando
POW escaped Normandy

Zeff, Lt Edward
SOE
Survived death camp at
Mauthausen

Zeffert, Tpr Henry
RAC
N Africa

Zenftman, Leon
Recce Corps

Zimmerman, N.
Lancs Fus

Zittman, Cpl Ernest A.
POW Arnhem

RAF

Abels, Sqdn/Ldr Alfred

Bendell, Abraham David
Escaped N Africa

Berger, P/O Jeffrey

Biderman, P/O David

Brenner, P/O Henry
DOW as POW

Canter, Herbert J.
Escaped

Chir, Sgt Bernard

Coen, P/O Oscar H.
American Eagle Squadron RAF
Escaped

Cohen, Flt/Sgt Murray
RCAF

Cooper, Sgt Eric Isaac

Deane, Flt/Sgt Arnold
Stalag 4B 21.1.44

Fischl, O.
101 Squadron

Frais, WO Eric B
POW Jan 1941

Gaum, Sgt Percy

Geisler, F/O Malcolm

Gershon, Eddie
USA serving RAF
(Info from Yeslovitz – Army POW)

Gevalber/Gewalber, AC Jack
33 Squadron
MM
Escaped

Gilbert, Jack

Goldfinger, Sgt Z.

Goldsmith, Ben
Escaped

Goldstone, Sgt A.A.

Goldwyn, Les
RAF
Escaped
Info Harry Rose

Goodman, P/O Gerald Mark

Greenberg, Lou
Escaped

Harris, LAC C. Hyman

Hecht, A.M.
Escaped

**Hein, Sqdn/Ldr Georg
(aka Peter Stevens) MC**
Escaped twice – book published
by son

Hemelik, Sgt David

Hirschbein, P/O Ivor

Horne, A.
Escaped

Isaacs, P/O David Samuel

Jacobs, Flt/Sgt Isaac David

Jacobs, John

Jacobs, Phillip
(Info from Yeslovitz – Army POW)

Jonas, Flt/Sgt Julian Gerald

Kayes, Ivan
85383

Lanzetter, F/O Harvey

Leaman, Nathan
MID as an escaper

Lenz, Aubrey

Levine, AC1 Isaac

Levy, A.J.D.
RAAF
Escaped

Levy, Harry
Escaped (author of book *Darker Side of the Sky*)

Luder, E.

Makowski, Flt/Lt M. Henry
Escaped

Manstoff, Fl/Sgt Alf
Escaped

Marantz, P/O Nathaniel
Eagle Squadron RAF

Meieran, Lt Sigmund
Norwegian RAF, Halifax Bombers
Escaped 6 times

Mondschein, P/O Jerzy
Polish RAF
Murdered at Sagan after 'The Great Escape'

Nabarro, P/O C.
15 Squadron
Escaped

Nabarro, Derrek D.W.
DCM
Escaped 4 times
First DCM awarded to an escaper in British Forces

Nagley, Flt/Sgt L. Wolfe

Osborne, Flt/Lt J. Bernard
Escaped

Phillips, Sgt Henry

Rattner, Cyril

Rofe, Peter (aka Rolfe)
Escaped; is this Cyril, MM who escaped and fought with Cossacks?
Author of a book

Rose, Sgt Harry
Escaped
Recaptured

Samson, Ronald
Escaped

Samuels, P/O Ian Israel

Samuels, Sqdn/Ldr Norman Philip
DFC

Samuels, Sgt B.E.
RCAF

Samuels, Sgt Dennis
RCAF

Shapiro, P/O M.B.

Shaw, LAC Wilfred

Silverstone(e), P/O Julius V.

Spagatner, WO Isidore

Spektor, Cpl

Starr, Flt/Sgt Joseph
RAF

Taylor, Flt/Sgt Harry (aka Doniger)

Tuck, Robert Stanford
B. of Britain
POW and escaper

Van-Hessen, P/O P.
Dutch RAF
Escaped

Wald, S.

Wayne, Harry (aka Wien)
Caterpillar badge
Escaped Sweden

Weizman, Andre

Wiseman, Andrew
POW Sagan

Wiseman, Sgt William

Palestinian Jews

Over 1,500 Palestinian Jews were POW and almost 300 escaped, many of whom joined the partisans in Yugoslavia and Greece; only some names have been identified here. See especially the research of Yoav Gelbar in Yad Vashem Studies 1981, *Palestinian Jewish POWs in German Hands.*

Abbadin, Pte K.A.
PC
Died POW Greece

Ackerman, Pte D.
PC
Died as POW

Almogi, Sgt Yosef (aka Karlenboim)
POW Greece 'Man of Confidence'

Altman, Spr Richard
RE
Shot trying to escape in Poland

Arad, Menachem (aka Edberg)

Armuzah, Abraham
Repatriated

Beckerman, Pte M.
RASC
Died as POW Greece

Begin, Sgt

Beili, Chaim

Ben Aharon, Lt Yitzhak

Bendava, L.

Ben Gershoni, Cpl
Escaped

Benjamin, A.

Ben Nadav

Ben Yaacov, Zvi Jindrich (aka Grunhut)
SOE
Murdered in Slovakia

Ben-Yacob, Sgt Yitzhak
Escaped

Ben-Yehuda, Spr Eliyahu
Died POW in Greece

Ben Zvi, Pte
(aged 47, former mayor of Binyamina)
Repatriated

Berdichev, Abba
(aka Robert Willis)
SOE
Murdered in Slovakia

Berger, Sgt John
Crete

Bernstein, Joseph MM
Pal RE
Escaped POW

Bitran, Spr Moshe
Died as POW in Greece

Blech, Pte Azriel
Lost his arm, Repatriated

Bleicher, Cpl Ludwig 'Vicky'
Escaped Greece by rowing to N Africa
Recaptured by Italians!

Bleifeder, Y.
Escaped

Bloch, Pte Oscar
PC
Died after liberation in Germany

Blueweis, David

Boim – TWO brothers

Bornstein, Sgt Leon
MM
Escaped Greece

Breier, Cpl Hyam M.
RE
Died attempting to escape in Germany

Chagigi, L/Cpl S.
RE
Died in POW camp Germany

Chanukah, M.

Charad, N.
PC
Died attempting to escape in Greece

Chrelenbaum, Yosef

Cohen, Sgt
Greece

Cohen, Pte Albert
PC
Died in German POW camp

Cohen, Cpl Cesar
Crete and Auschwitz Camp

Cohen, Y
Escaped

Davidovsky, H.

Digil, H.
Died as POW in Germany

Driki, Herman
Died escaping from POW camp in Yugoslavia

Drori, Cpl Avshalom
Raid on Rommel Op Flipper
POW later

Ehrman, Spr Aharon
RE
Shot attempting to escape in Germany

Eisenberg, Pte D. Berl
PC
MID (posthumous)
Shot attempting to escape in Germany

Elimelech, Spr Avraham
Shot attempting to escape in Greece

Elisha, Y.
Escaped and joined Paratroopers

Elkind, Sgt Y.
RE
Died of cancer
Buried full honours by Germans

El-Mishali, Spr M.
Died as POW in Germany

Fabian, Pte Y.
RASC
Died as a POW in Greece

Fenchel, Pte N.
PC
Died as POW in Germany

Fichaman
(aka Gideon Jacobson)
SOE
POW Survived

Field, Cpl Jonah

Filer, George
Escaped with Capt Roy Farran of the SAS

Filo, Spr Shimon
Died attempting to escape in Greece

Friedlander, David

Gavriel, Pte N.
PC
Died attempting to escape in Greece

Gelbart/Gilbert, Pte Avraham
PC
Died attempting to escape in Greece

Ghatatheh, Pte A.
PC
Died as POW in Greece

Glantz, A.

Gershuni, Lt Nathan

Glovinsky/Glubinsky, H.

Goldman
Escaped and then murdered

Goldreich, Theodor

Goldstein, Pte Asher
PC
Died attempting escape in Greece

**Goldstein, Henry Frederick
(aka Wilenski)**
1st SAS/SIG

Goldstein, Peretz/Ferencz
SOE
Murdered in Germany

Gonshirovsky, Pte H.
PC
Died as POW in Germany

Gottlieb, Pte E.
SAS/SIG
Murdered after capture in North
Africa with Haass/Hess

Graetzer, Paul
Pal 23139
Kalamta

Gutenberg, Pte Lev
DCM
Escaped twice

Haass/Hess, Cpl Peter
SIG/SAS
Murdered after capture in North
Africa
with Gottlieb

Haber, Z
Escaped and returned as British
Para

Hacohen, Lt Shimon
RE
POW Colditz
Author of book of drawings of
Colditz

Hagoel, H.

Hamadani, Pte Zion
PC
Died in Germany POW

Hammami, B.
Escaped

Hayon, Pte David

Herman, Pte Chaim
PC
Died of illness in POW camp,
Germany

Herzig/Herzog, Pte Zvi
PC
Died in Germany as POW

Hillebrand, Karl
Escaped with Rofe, RAF?

Hoffbauer/Landauer
Escaper

Holzer, Karl

Horn, Pte M.
PC
Died attempting to escape in
Germany

Israel, Pte Reuben
51st Middle East Commando
Escaped to SOE

Jechieli, Cpl

Jeffet, Pte Yehuda

Jerusalemi, Sgt Aharon
RE
MM as a POW escaper

Jordan, Pte Frederick Gustav
DCM
Escaped
KIA Israel War of Independence

Jordan, Fritz
Escaped – author of book on
escape

Kacenelenbeigen
Escaped with Rofe, RAF?

Kapun, Pte Jacob

Karter, Pte E.
PC
Died as POW in Germany

Katz, Sgt Ariyeh
POW Crete
BEM for gallantry
Escaped

Keller, Pte Moshe K.
PC
Died as POW in Germany

Klauber, George
POW Prague by Gestapo

Klein, Pte Joseph

Kolar, A.
Escaped

Kolman, Pte Y.
PC
Died as POW in Germany

Komfort, H.

Krause, Pte Eli
PC
MID (posthumous)
Died attempting escape in
Germany

Krause, Pte Shlomo

Kreitner, Pte J.
PC
Died as POW in Germany

Kutcher, Jack
POW Greece

Leiber, Cpl

Lerner, Dan
SOE
Escaped Balkans

Leshz, Haim

Levy, Pte Medinah

Levy, Cpl Meyer
PC
Crete/Stalag VIIIB

Lipman, Spr Perez
RE
Died as POW in Germany

Lobel/Arieli, Sgt Joshua

Lupesko, Ariyeh
SOE
Escaped Rumania

Lustig, Sgmn Norbert
RCOS
Died as POW in Germany

Luxemburg, Joseph
Escaped with Rofe, RAF?

Maabari, M.

Macaresco, Sgt Yitzak
SOE
Escaped, Romania

Marsh, Y.

Mayorcheck

Meichinsky, Pte H.
PC
Died as POW in Czechoslovakia

Menachem, Yitzhak
Escaped

Menasherov, Cpl Ephraim
PC
Shot attempting to escape in Crete

Meyer, Pte Franz, aka Lubowitz

Michaelovitz, Pte F.
PC
Died as POW in Germany

Mindel, Yehuda
Tunisia

Mizrahi, M.

Morganstern, B.

Mormorosch, Jakob

Opatowsky, A.
Escaped

Ornstein, Pte Morris

Nasser, Spr Ezra
RE
Murdered as a POW in Germany

Oprower, A.
(aka Oprover)
SIG/SAS
Murdered after capture in North Africa

Orbach, Pte Shaul
PC
Died as POW in Poland

Ossman, Peretz
Died as a POW in Germany

Palmay, Pte Alfred

Pessy, Spr J.
Died attempting to escape in Greece

Peys, Pte Leib
RASC
Died as POW in Germany

Pollack, Pte Joseph
DCM
Escaped twice

Popper, Sgt

Pritsch, Cpl Shlomo
Repatriated, died Switzerland

Rasiel/Raziel, Capt David
SOE
Murdered after capture after mission
in Iraq 1941

Reik/Reich, Sgt Chaviva
(aka Martinovic/Ada Robinson)
SOE
Murdered in Slovakia

Reiss, Peter/Stephen/Rafael
(aka Rice/Reisz)
SOE
Murdered in Slovakia

Reiss, Y.
Repatriated

Rochberg, Samuel
DCM
Escaped twice

Roer, J. (aka Rohr)
30777
SAS SIG
POW

Rosenbluth/Rosen, R.

Sachs
Three brothers all POW

Safanoff, Cpl

Salomon, Spr Y.
Died as a POW in Greece

Salpeter, A.

Schlap, Otto

Schoen, Herbert
SOE
Escaped Balkans

Schusterman, Coy/Sgt/Maj
Palestinian Jewish 'Man of Confidence' at Lamsdorf Camp

Segal, S.
Escaped

Selah-Slodash, S.

Senesh, Hannah (aka Szenesh)
SOE
Murdered in Hungary

Serbrani/Sarbonick, Pte V.
PC
Died as POW in Germany

Shalit, A.

Shetrit, Pte D.
PC
Died as POW in Greece

Shimon, Pte Eli
RASC
Died in Greece as a POW

Sigal, Sgt Hillel
PC
Died as POW in Germany

Silber
Died as POW in Greece

Sireni, Chaim/Enzo (aka Serini)
SOE
Murdered at Dachau or Auschwitz

Smudiak, Moshe
Brother of Ze-ev

Smudiak, Sgt Ze-ev
Jewish Brigade
POW Italy
Brother of Moshe

Soha, Yehuda
Greece

Spaak, Pte Menachem
PC
Died as a POW in Germany

Stern, Cain

Stern, Cpl Franz
RASC
Died as POW in Germany

Strogava, Isidore
(from Salonika)

Szechter, Cpl L.
PC
Died as POW in Germany

**Tieffenbrunner, Cpl Maurice
(aka Tiffen)**
SAS SIG
POW N Africa

Tovim, Pte Yaphet
PC
Died in Germany as a POW

Tsarfati, Cpl Shlomo
RE
Died escaping as a POW in
Greece

Tzabari, Saadia
PC
Killed escaping from POW camp
in Yugoslavia

Tzerjeck, Spr H.
Died attempting to escape in
Greece

Uziel, B.

Weiner, Hans Paul
RASC
POW Greece

Weisman, Pte Jacob

Weissbury, Pte Y.
RASC
Died escaping in Greece

Weissman, L/Cpl Aharon
RE
Died escaping in Greece

Weitzman, Cpl
KIA Israel War of Independence

Wilde, Sgt

Witner, Solly

Wissotsky, Pte Y.
PC
Died escaping in Greece

Yaacobi

Yaffe, L/Cpl Moshe
PC
Died as POW in Greece

Yeshua, A.
Escaped

Zasler, Sgmn Israel
RCOS
Died as POW in Germany

Zelberg, E.

Ziegler, Spr Arthur
Died as POW in Germany

Zucker/Sukari, Pte

Zundsiak, Isaak

Canadians

(See *Canadian Jewry at War*
[Montreal: Canadian Jewish
Congress, 1947/48], pp.119–33
for the 85 POWs.)

Australians

Dakers, Rex (VX33)
RAAMC
Stalag 3B
+ Auschwitz POW 95487

Traub, Alf
POW Greece attempted escaper

South Africans

It is estimated 750 South African
Jews were POW (SAJEX, *The
South African Jewish Book of
Honour* [Johannesburg: Eagle
Press, 1950], p.36), but only
some names have been found in
that book. Many of these names
below are from the book by Ike
Rosmarin, *Inside Story*, which
included a concise list of the
South African POWs at the Tobruk
disaster in June 1942 – they are
guesses using obvious Jewish
names, but no doubt many are not
included with anglicized or
ambiguous names.

Abraham, Pte Maurice A.

Abrahams, Sgmn Edward

Abrahamson, Capt Percy N.

Abramson, Bdr Jack

Alexander, Cpl Cecil
SAF

Alufowitz, Solomon
POW N Africa, esc Italy

Assaizky, Bdr Joseph

Auer, Bdr Oscar L.

Barnard
brother named below

Barnard, Lt Abraham
GM

Barnard, Bdr Ephraim L.

Behr, Pte Reuben

Berman, Harold

Berman, 2nd Lt Samuel L.

Bernstein, Pte Harold L.

Binder, Pte Montague A.

Bloch, Gnr Frank

Bloch, Gnr Kenneth H.P.

Blumenthal, Rfmn Eric B.

Blumenthal, L/Cpl Reuben R.

Bock, Walter
POW Tobruk

Boshoff, Pte Peter A.

Budlender, L/Cpl Reuben J.

Bussin/Bustin, Pte G. Lionel
SAILH

Caplan, Sgmn Samuel

Chorn, Pte Alec

Cinnamon, Gnr Maurice

Cohen, L/Bdr Dave

Cohen, Pte Ernest
Escaped

Cohen, Pte Isaac

Cohen, Gnr Jack

Cohen, Gnr Jack L.

Cohen, Cpl Philip

Cohen, Bdr Ralph

Cohen, Cpl Reuben

Cohen, Sgt Sam

Cousins, L/Cpl Emmanuel

Danielewitz, Cpl Daniel

Davids, Sgmn Solly

Dembo, Gnr Israel

De Tarnowsky, Gnr Paul G.

Dinkleman, Cpl O.

Dorfan, Sgmn Hymie

Eliasov, Cpl David

Falkson, Leon
Escaped

Fineberg/Feinberg, Sgt Louis A.
SAAF
Escaped

Flederman, Lt Alan
Escaped Italy
Author of book on his escape

Fineberg, Pte Maurice F.

Foreman, Alec

Freedberg, Pte Jack

Freund, Cpl Hans
Escaped N Africa dressed in German uniform

Friedlander, L/Cpl 'Bull'
GM

Friedman, Sgmn L.K.
Escaped

Friedman, Cpl Maurice

Friedman, Pte Monty J.

Friedman, Cpl Morris

Frootko, Herbert
Escaped, recaptured

Fuchs, H.E.
SAAF
Escaped

Futter, Cpl Leighton

Geffin, Sgt Aaron

Gershanov, Sgt Zelick

Gilbert, Sgt Solly
Escaped Italy

Glass, Gnr Cyril H.

Gluckman, Pte Joseph

Goddard, Pte Gerald
DCM

Goldberg, Sgmn Ernest

Goldie, Sgt Leslie

Goldin, Capt Dr
SAMC

Goldstein, L/Bdr Arthur M.

Golombik, Pte Louis

Goodman, Bdr Arnold V.

Goodman, Gnr Joe

Goodman, Pte Max P.

Greenberg, Sgt Bernard

Gurwitz, 2nd Lt Julius

Heerman, Capt Benjamin
Escaped

Hersch, Cpl Wilfred

Hilkowitz, Sgt Maurice

Hirschmann, Bdr Edward E.

Hirschmann, Pte John A.

Hirsowitz, WO Aaron K.

Hoffman, WO Abraham

Hoffman, Pte Daniel C.

Hotzman, Barney

Hyams, Cpl Danny G.

Israel, Sgt Asher L.

Jacob, Pte Louis

Jacobs, Pte Lewis T.

Jacobs, Lionel

Jacobson, Sgmn Esmond

Jacobson, Pte Hyman

Jacobson, Dr Isaac
RAMC
POW Dunkirk
Escaped

Jacobson, Sydney
Escaped twice to Partisans in Italy

Jacoby, Cpl Leonard W.

Jaffee, Gnr Cyril H.

Jaffer, Peter

Jassinowsky, Isidore

Jawitz, J.
SAA

Joffee, Cpl Abe

Jonas, Sgt Richard
SAMC

Joseph, Pte Lionel

Josselowitz, Sgt Israel

Judelsohn, L/Cpl Alec

Kamffer, Pte Samuel

Kannenberg, Pte Albert C.

Kaplan, Bdr Bernard

Kaplan, Pte Clarence

Kaplan, Pte Gerald

Kaplan, Gnr Norman M.

Kaplan, Capt Maurice

Karstaedt, Capt A.

Kassenbaum, Pte Arthur

Katzeff, Pte David

Katzenellenbogen, Gnr Isaac

Kay, Gnr Michael D.

Kirsch, Pte Ernest

Klugman, Lt Hirsch A.

Kossef, Pte

Kretschmer, Sgt Louie H.

Kupferman, Pte Kurt K.

Landsberg, Pte John A.

Landsman, Pte Wolf D.

Lazar, Sgt Harry

Lenz, Pte Herman

Levi, Cpl Cecil E.

Levin, Pte Jack

Levin, Pte Marcus
Escaped

Levin, Pte Maurice C.

Levin, Sgmn Neville

Levine, Basil
Escaped twice to partisans in Italy

Levinsohn, Pte Horace

Lewis, Pte Aubrey G.

Lewis, Simon

Loewenstein, Sgt Hans W.

Lourie, Cpl Harry
Escaped

Lubinsky, Pte David

Ludwick, Pte Robert J.

Lurie, Pte Morris E.

Margolis, L/Cpl Aaron

Marks, Samuel

Marsburg, Gnr Barney

Marx, Bdr David H.

Melamet, A.M.

Mendelsohn, Gnr Alexander

Meskin, Sgt Lionel

Michelsen, Gnr Colin

Milstein, Lt Samuel

Mintz, Sgt Sidney M.

Mirkin, Capt Leopold

Mofsowitz, Cpl Isadore

Morris, Sgmn Bennie

Mosenthal, Capt Dennis H.G.

Myers, Cpl Lewis
Escaped

Myerson, Pte Herbert

Neubert, Gnr Max F.

Nieman, Gnr Jerrry W.

Okey, Aron Geffin
North Africa
Later Springbok Rugby player

Orlin, Pte Barney

Perlstein, Gnr Fritz J.R.

Poliva, Sgt Simon
Escaped Italy

Potash, Cpl Max

Rabinowitz, Hymie
Rabinowitz, L/Cpl Joseph S.
Rabinowitz, Gnr Solomon
Three brothers

Rabkin, Capt Jerome

Raphael, Capt Maurice

Richter, Cpl Isaac

Rom, Billy

Rosenbaum, Pte Morris M.

Rosenbaum, L/Cpl Ronald L.

Rosenberg, Pte Edward W.

Rosenberg, Bdr K.C.

Rosenberg, L/Cpl Solomon J.

Rosenthal, Pte Nathan

Rosmarin, Sgt Ike

Rothschild, Pte M.H.

Rubenstein, Mark
Escaped

Sacks, Gnr Hymie

Sacks, L/Cpl Issy

Sacks, Gnr Phillip

Salzer, Gnr Leslie W.

Sandberg, Sgmn Gerald J.

Sandground, Pte

Sarapsky, L/Bdr Monty

Schaefer, Sgt Mervyn R.

Schenck, Sgmn Lionel A.

Schoenfeldt, L/Cpl Dudley E.

Schoenfeldt, L/Cpl Lester O.

Schonberg, Sgt Arthur C.

Schulman, Pte Bernard R.

Schulman, L/Bdr Royce

Schuster
2nd SA Div
POW Tobruk

Schuster, Capt Ernest F.

Schuster, Gnr Frank M.
Escaped

Schwartz, Rfmn Charles L.

Schwartz, Rfmn Cecil W.

Schwartz, Sgt John D.

Schwartz, Rfmn Robert A.J.

Schwartz, WO Sidney F.

Schwegman, Gnr Leslie W.

Segal, Pte Abe

Segal, Sgmn Hyman

Segal, Pte Louis

Segall, WO Ephraim L.

Shapiro, Sgmn Harold

Shapiro, Cpl Solly B.

Sheingold, Pte Trevor M.

Sheinuk, L/Cpl Barney

Sher, Gnr Abraham S.

Shum, Pte Colin N.

Silberbauer, Gnr Cyril F.

Silbert, Pte Neville

Silks, Gnr Ariel

Singer, Gnr Barney

Slott, Nick

Smollan, Sgmn Neville L.

Smuskowitz, Gnr Judel

Soffer, Pte Eliezer

Solomon, Capt Charles R.A.

Solomon, L/Bdr Gershon M.

Solomon, Bdr Laurence C.

Solomon, Gnr Louis I.

Solomon, L/Cpl Samuel

Solomon, Bdr William B.S.

Solomons, Sgt C.
Escaped Italy

Sonnenberg, Pte Stanley

Spitzglass, Gnr Barry

Stern, Sgt Alfred

Stolk, L/Cpl Daniel J.

Stork, Joe
RE
Escaped

Strelitz, Rfmn Emanuel

Susman, Sgmn Philip

Suttner, Gnr Adolph

Swart, Lt Jacob R.H.

Swarts, Pte Alfred T.

Swarts, Pte Charles

Swarts, Gnr Philip K.

Swartz, Tpr Benjamin

Vogel, Pte Frederick M.

Weil, Gnr Alfred

Weimer, Gnr Adam L.

Weinstein, Chaplain/Capt
Baruch/Simie

Wiesner, Gnr Tobias

Wirtz, Sgt Ivan W.

Wolf, Cpl Louis

Woolf, Cpl Jeffrey

Woolf, Pte Julius

Wolff, Gnr Heinrich L.E.

Zaiden, Gnr Leon
Tobruk

Ziman, Lt/Col David B.

Jewish POWs of the Japanese in the Second World War

How did Jewish soldiers fare in the struggle in the distant Far East tropics, in countries where Jews were hardly known and were certainly a tiny minority, confronting a fanatical enemy from a country where virtually no Jews had ever lived and where anti-Semitism was virtually unrecognized? We are moved and amazed by the images and true stories set in the terrible jungle conditions of the barbaric Japanese POW camps, of Jewish military personnel who came from Stepney or Leeds, Brooklyn or Sydney, Auckland or Ottawa.

The list below has several major sources. First, Henry Morris's first edition of *We Will Remember Them* and *The Addendum*.[1] Henry used the Jewish Chaplains' cards at the Museum[2] but also an AJEX survey which was conducted via synagogues and other Jewish institutions, and which captured information not noted on the Chaplaincy cards. Information also came from our large museum archives. I then examined, over a period of a year, all the Chaplains' cards, to seek out those possibly missed by Henry because not all the Jewish Community took part in the AJEX survey. However, an immediate problem is that researchers like Henry and myself know that the cards are an incomplete source.[3] This is not surprising given that not all Jewish personnel enlisted as Jews, and not all saw a Jewish Chaplain in order to have a card completed in their name. Furthermore, the information on the cards is only a snapshot – it may record several meetings with a soldier, for example, up till 1940, then nothing. There is thus no indication that the person may have gone on to serve in the Far East or anywhere else after the war with Japan began and perhaps been made a POW. This is stated only on those cards where such information came to light via families, newspaper reports or if it was communicated to the Jewish Chaplains via Regimental or Corps clerical staff. Indeed, many were posted as missing or believed killed when in fact they were POWs, and this was either not known till after the war, and possibly never recorded on the cards, or in some cases never discovered at all. Prisoner information given to the Red Cross and neutral governments by the Japanese – who had not ratified the Geneva Convention on POWs – was minimal and often inaccurate. Add to this the desire of the Japanese to hide the names and the numbers of POWs who died in their hands, in order to obstruct the War Crimes investigators, then it becomes clear that we will never truly know how many missing Jewish personnel died as POWs in the Far East.

Further limitations in using the cards include the fact that (like the CWGC records) many describe a death/missing in action after the beginning of the fighting with the Japanese, but do not specify whether this was as a POW; where it is not so specified, that name has been omitted, yet it may well be that the persons concerned did die as POWs; we may never know.

Rabbi Chaim Nussbaum's book[4] revealed many names of Dutch Jewish civilian internees as well as Allied soldiers, and some were named in Jack Caplan's book.[5] I have tried to include civilian Jewish internees but, according to Joseph Kennedy,[6] there were almost 500 Jews in the Sime Road camp alone in Singapore, and many German Jews not interned at all in Bangkok. The thousands of German and other Jewish refugees in Shanghai and other cities, and the members of the Jewish company of the Shanghai Volunteer Force[7] are also outside the scope of this study.

The indomitable David Arkush, retired Captain of the RADC, provided the author with his personal list of Jewish POWs he had known; these came from his personal notes kept at the time at great risk to his life.[8]

Researcher Jonathan Moffatt kindly supplied me with information from huge files he had scanned at the Imperial War Museum and The National Archives on Britons and other nationalities, including the resident Jewish community, in Malaya and Singapore at the time of the Japanese invasion, and who were interned. He also gave me lists of regimental personnel who were present, so enabling me to pick out further Jewish POWs. However, his research is far from complete and names of many more Jewish personnel are likely to emerge. Similar information came from the Far Eastern Prisoners of War Association (FEPOW), the Children of Far East Prisoners of War (COFEPOW) and Taiwan POW websites on the Internet.[9]

Behind every name there is a story and volumes could be written: Monty (Nat) Rakusen (of the famous Leeds family) was a POW after fighting in the Hong Kong Volunteers, incarcerated in Argyll Street camp and later sent to a coal mine in Japan in 1943. His wife claimed neutrality as she had a German father and Portuguese mother and she and her son Ronal were interned in Shanghai. Reunited after the war, the family lived in Hong Kong until Monty died in 1966 and he was buried there. Mrs Rakusen died in the UK in 1981 and Ronal, now retired, lives in France.[10] Hyman Weisberg, a Cambridge graduate, was a Senior Civil Servant in Malaya – his signature was on the bank notes. He always claimed he survived because he was short and the Japanese could thus relate to him! Post-war he lived in Wembley and taught himself Braille so he could teach mathematics to blind people.[11] The stories are endless.

I then went through all the *Jewish Chronicle* newspapers from December 1941 to December 1946, with the help of Harold Pollins in Oxford, and appropriate names on the CWGC registers on their website, to confirm or discover more names. But information on how men died can only come from personal testimony from family archives or surviving comrades – rapidly declining sources – or by consulting personal military records, which is a very expensive and sometimes impossible task as only next of kin are permitted access to such information. So meanwhile what follows must be the tribute to our men and women who were there.

Note: where death is not specified in the list of names, the POW is presumed to have survived the war. Any awards named are only for those given for gallantry whilst a POW. Those who died in Taiwan/Formosa were re-interred/commemorated in Hong Kong and elsewhere

Notes

1. Henry Morris, *We Will Remember Them* (London: Brassey, 1989) and *The Addendum* (London: AJEX, 1994). The Addendum was written in response to the clamour that arose from the community that relatives and comrades had been missed in Henry's first book.
2. There are over 65,000 of these stored at the Museum, kept by the Chaplains, mostly during the Second World War.
3. We are adding cards frequently when research reveals that personnel are missing.
4. *Chaplain on the River Kwai* (New York: Shapolsky, 1988).
5. *Gorbals to Jungle* (published privately, AJEX archives).
6. Joseph Kennedy, *British Civilians and the Japanese War in Malaya and Singapore* (London: Palgrave Macmillan, 1987).

7. See chapter in Martin Sugarman, *Fighting Back* (London and Portland, OR: Vallentine Mitchell, 2010).
8. His records will be kept at the AJEX Museum. Reuben Kandler kept a similar list which his family have kindly shared with us
9. Thanks to George Money of the Essex and Herts FEPOW Association.
10. Letter from Ronal, November 2003.
11. Letter from Ernest Shenton who knew him, November 2003.

Martin Sugarman

Navy

Biderman, WO George
RNVR
Died

Cohen, Rad/O Joseph
MN
MS *American Leader*

Drake, Ldg/Tel E.A.
RN
POW sinking of *Prince of Wales*

Goldberg, AB Solomon
Glasgow

Grossman, Lt Edward
HMS *Cornflower*
Hong Kong POW

Herman, AB Isaac
RAN HMAS *Perth*
Buried Kanchanaburi

Kaye, 1st Rad/O Eric
MN
Buried Kranji after dying as a
POW (??)

Mason, H.
PJX182275 HMS Stronghold
POW Celebes.

Webber, P/O Bertram
POW Hong Kong

Army UK & Dutch

(With thanks for the help of Peter Dunstan.)

Aaron, Tpr Abraham
The Loyals RAC
Buried Chungkai

Abas, S.
Dutch Inf
Buried Chungkai

Abel, Dvr Albert
RASC

Abraham, Pte Ezekiel
SVC

Abramson, Barnett/Ben
D of Wellingtons
Died 3.6.43

Angel, Bdr Eric
RA

Arkush, Capt David
RADC
Changi/Thailand

Auerbach, Gnr Harry Aaron
RA
Buried Labuan

Bachrach, Alfred G.H.
Liaison to Dutch Special Forces,
Far East.
Interned with wife and baby son
(who died) in 6 camps including
Changi. Post war Dutch spy in far
East – died Feb. 2010

Baker, Pte James Morris
Recce Corps
Buried Kranji (Sing. Vol. Corps)
Changi

Barcellon/Bareilon, Major Hector
RA

Barnett, Pte Bernard
RAMC, Alexandria Hosp, Sing
From Leicester

Baron, William
Norfolk Reg
Died 22.4.42

Basco, Gnr Lionel
RA
Buried Chungkai

Baum, Gnr Henry
RA
Buried Kranji

Beck, Capt Clifford
RASC

Bell, C.
Java

Benjamin, Aaron
Died POW 5.8.43

Benjamin, Pte Vivian
HKVDC
Died 21.9.45

Berkley/Berkeley, Capt Allan
RAMC

Berkovitch, Pte Frank/Len
13th Kings

Berner, Pte Jack/Isaac
2nd The Loyals

Bernstein, Dvr Joseph
RASC
Cantor in Synagogue, Changi
Glasgow

Besbrode, Cpl Mark
Middx

Besser, Pte Barnett
Recce Coy/Rifle Bde
Changi

Bialestock/Bialstock, Pte Charles
Norfolk Regt
Killed with Saunders

Birnbaum, David (aka Goldstein)
Toronto serving UK forces

Blitz, Cpl
Dutch army
Died?

Bloch, Cpl M.
RASC

Bloom, Rfmn John (aka Baker)
KRRC/RCOS
Sing. POW
Died 1964 aged 46

Bloom, Maj Dr Phillip M.
RAMC
From South Africa
Changi

Bluestone, Cpl W.
RCOS
Chungkai Camp – believed
character in film *King Rat* is based
on him.

Bolter, Gnr Max
RA Straits Settl. Vol. Force
Buried Chungkai

Braham, Capt Mark Gordon
RAMC
Died with Saunders

Brodie, Cpl J. or Leo

Brody, Louis
Singapore

Brownhood, Gnr Alec
RA
Died as a POW

Burton, Anthony Lewis
RA

Burton, Sgmn Joseph
RCOS

Caggan, Gnr Leon
RA Beds Regt
Buried Kranji

Caplan, Gnr Harold
RA

Caplan, Jack
RCOS
Glasgow. Survived

Caplin, Pte Ellis
13th Kings

Caun, Lt
Dutch POW interpreter on Burma
Railway

Child, Kenneth Joseph (aka Burleigh)
RCOS
MID

Chowan, Pte Stanley
(Probable)

Citroen, J.
Changi

Clayton, Pte David/Sid (aka Cohen)
Suffolks
Buried Formosa/H Kong, comm.
at Kranji

Cohen, Capt
Dutch Army Doctor
Java

Cohen, Gnr Harry
1099755
RA
Buried Kuala Lumpur

Cohen, Joseph
From Manchester
Changi

Cohen, L/Cpl Marcus Leonard
T181551
RASC

Cohen, Gen Morris 'Two Gun' (Retd)
Interned Hong Kong

Cohen, Pte Norman
Middx
Buried Yokohama

Cohen, Pte Sydney
1696896
RA

Cowen, Capt Harold Wolfe
RAMC

Cyfer, Adj J.
Dutch Artillery
Java

Da Costa, W/O B.
Dutch Army
Java

Davids, Pte
Dutch Army

Davidson, Sgmn A.
SSVF
Ilford

Davis, Bdr David
RA
Buried Kanchanaburi

De Louw, Pte
Dutch Army

Dicks, Claude Maurice
REME

Donn, Gnr Harry
RA

Dorfman, Cpl Louis
Field Sec. Intel Corps

Dykes, Bdr Robert
RA

Egalnick, Abraham/Alf Joseph
18th Recce/Rifle Bde
Changi

Ellis, Nurse Leontine
Hong Kong VDF
Buried Stanley CWGC Cem, Hong
Kong

Elze, Lt
Dutch Army
Died at Changi

Ernstone, Gnr Nathan
RA

Fay, Capt Dennis Henry
Ghurkas

Feldman, Gnr Louis
RA
Lost at sea as POW

Fine, Dvr Eli
RASC
Died at sea as POW
Brother of Nathan (*JC*)

Fine, Nathan
RA
Changi, brother of Eli (*JC*)

Finegold, Lt Martin
RIASC

Frank, Pte Leon
Chindit
POW

Franklin, Dvr Jacob
RCOS
Buried Kanchnaburi

Freedman, Bdr Morris S.
RA
Died Kuching, Sarawak

Freeman, Sgt Sidney
RA
Died Formosa. Buried Hong Kong

Gaffin, Cpl Merton Eugene
RCOS
Buried Thanbyuzayat

Gaisman, Lt Peter
Manchester Regt

Gareh, Pte M.
2nd Loyals

Gendleman, A.
Sherwood Foresters
From Shoreditch, POW Nong
Pladuk

Gershonblatt, David
Norfolk Regt

Getzels, Gnr A.
RA

Glaser, Lt/Col J.
Dutch Army

Glickman, Gnr Leonard
RA

Gold, Sgmn Benjamin
RCOS
Borneo

Goldberg, D.
5th Field Regt RA
Died Taiwan
FEPOW website
No more known

Goldenberg, Lt William
SVC

Goldfarb, Len
Royal Norfolks
Glasgow/London

Goldman, Maj S.
Sing./Thai.

Goldrich, Pte Samuel
Sherwood Foresters
Gp. 5 Nakon Ni/Taiwan

Goldstein, David
4th Norfolks
Changi

Goldstone, Pte Bernard
Manch. Regt
Died at Song Krai, buried
Thanbyuzayat

Gordon, Simmy
(info. from Sir Martin Gilbert)

Gotlieb, Gnr Gerald
RA
Buried Kanchanaburi

Goudsmit, Cpl
Dutch Army

Goulding, L/Bdr Harold B.
RA
Changi

Green, Pte Myer
Beds & Herts

Greenberg, Jack Joseph
(aka 'Aussie Pom')
T198268
RAMC
BEM for courage as a POW

Greenberg, S.

Greenstein, Gnr Harry
RA
Buried Kanchanaburi

Greenwood, Bdr Irvin Henry
(aka Greenburgh)
RA

Gubby, Nurse Susan
(aka Gabbay)
Hong Kong Def Force
Died, buried Hong Kong 17.5.42

Hecht, Capt C.
RAMC

Helpern, Len
From Manchester

Herzberg, Harry (aka Hart)
Leeds, Burma railway.

Hewitt, Jack (aka Reich)
Ox & St George Club
Died POW Malaya

Hirsch, Lt Derek
Java

Hirsch, Pte Joseph
RCOS
Changi/Siam
War artist

Hornstein, S.
Glasgow

Hyman, Pte Maurice
Notts & Derby
Died Changi, Buried Kranji.
From Hendon

Isaacs, Capt L.
FMSVF
Java

Jacoby, M.
Dutch (?)
Changi

Jacobs, Capt Noel
SVC

Jaffee, Nathan
2412 RNZN

Janis, Capt Morris
RASC

Kandler, Reuben
RA

Kant, Jack
RAOC - tbc

Kaplan, L/Cpl Alf
1st Cambs Regt

Katz, Tpr Nathan
RAC

Kaufman, Dvr Harry
RASC
Buried Chungkai

Kelmenson, Dvr W.
RASC

Kersh, Gnr Leslie
RA
Changi

Kitchener, G.L.
Glasgow

Kramsky/Kransky, L/Cpl
Swansea

Krieger, Pte Alfred
Notts & Derby
Buried Kanchanaburi
From Barnet

Lamkin, Dvr S.
RASC

Lander, Ronald Sidney
N Lancs Regt
Died 8.10.42
Poss. Jewish

Lapsky, Jack
Middx. Regt
Hong Kong

Lavender, Sgmn Leopold
RCOS

Leftwich, Cpl R.W.
Java

Leigh, Capt Mark
YMCA
Died as POW
Buried Kranji

Leslie, Pte Harry (aka Zilesnick)
Beds & Herts
Taiwan

Levie, Lt E.L.
Dutch Army
Java

Levinson, Sid/Solomon
Cambridge Regt
Suffolks

Levison, M.
Changi

Levitton, L/Cpl Henry Louis
RASC
Buried Chungkai

Levy, Lt

Levy, Cpl D.
RASC

Levy, Ronald
W. Surrey's Reg
Died 20.10.45 after liberation as
POW

Levy, Pte Walter
RA

Lichman, Sgmn Aubrey/Albert
RCOS

Lipman, Gnr Nathan
RA
Died in Fukuoka, buried Yokohama

Lisser, Yits
Dutch Army
Died

Litenstone, Capt Jack
Singapore

Lithauer, L/Cpl Ronald Louis
RCOS
Buried Yokohama

Loskey, Pte Henry Samuel
REME

Lucas, Lt Henry Arthur
RA
Killed as POW aboard a ship

Lyons, Pte C.
RAMC

Lyons, Henry
Changi

Macklin, Sgt Robert
RAEC
Buried Hong Kong
Wife survived

Magrill, L/Sgt Jack Harold
RA
Died on POW ship

Margolis, D.
1st Btn Manchester Regt

Marguleff, Sgt M.
SVC, formerly Pal Police

Marks, Pte R.
RASC
Java

Marks, Samuel
The Loyals
MID
Changi/Singapore
Seawalls/Burma Rly.

Markson, Pte Norman Gilbert
RAOC
Lost as POW at sea
Glasgow

Melek, Meyer
RE
Died

Mendelson, Pte Arthur Leonard
Middx. Regt
Died at sea as POW

Mendelson, Pte John
Brit. Att. Dutch army

Mendes Da Costa, Sgt N.
Dutch Army
Buried Kanchanaburi

Mendoza, M.
RCOS
Tottenham

Meninsky, Philip
British war artist Burma Railway

Minchom, Sgt M.
RA, Sunderland.

**Mincovitch, Sgt Maurice Hillel
(aka Minchom)**
RA

Morris, Pte G.
RAMC
Newcastle

Morris, L/Cpl G.L.
FMSVF
Java

Morris, Lt J.J.
Middx Regt

Morris, 2nd Lt Joseph
RASC

Morrison, Pte William
Glasgow

Moss, Gnr Alfred Aaron
RA
Died

Mossel, Pte
Dutch army
Died?

Mutsemaker, M.
Dutch Infantry
Buried Chungkai (?)

Nairnsey, Capt Coleman
RAMC

Nardell, Maj Sidney
IMS/RAMC

Nathan, Pte
Harrogate

Nemko, Sam
RCOS
Bethnal Green

**Nickolay, Gnr George Arthur
William**
RA
Buried Kanchanaburi

Novick, L/Cpl Harris David
Norfolk Regt
Died at sea with Saunders
Surrey

Nunes, Pte Morry
Sumatra.

Nussbaum, Rev Chaim
Dutch Army
Jewish Chaplain

Onderwyzer, Sgt Sam/L(?)
Dutch Army
Buried Kanchanaburi

Oppenheim, Pte Aaron Leonard
Australian 1st SSVF
Died Borneo 15.2.45
Kranji memorial

Orchant, Morris

Orenstein, Edwin
Changi

Paradise, Jack
Escaped to fight with Phillipino
guerillas, reached Australia
(see *JC* 5.6.42)

Paulden, Gnr R.F.
RA
Prestwich

Paulden, Pte S.
RAEC (?)
Trafalgar St., Salford

**Pearlman, L/Bdr Edward John
(aka Sunderland)**
RA
MIA/POW?

**Pearls/Perls, Lt Ormond Israel
Rodney**
RA
Died Malaya

Pepper, Pte Frank Robert
Norfolk Regt
Buried Chungkai

**Phillips, Capt (later Sir) Henry
Ellis Isidore**
Beds & Herts
MBE
Oxford

Polak, M.
Dutch

Popper, Cpl Barnett
Recce Coy/ Rifle Bde
Hackney

Posener, L/Cpl Alf
RCOS
Aldgate

Purdy, L/Bdr
RA
Died as POW

Rabbie, Michael/Myer

Rabin, M.
Java

Rabinovitch, Gnr Simon
RA
Buried Yokohama
From Clapton

Rabinowitz, Pte David
(aka Rabinoff)

Rakusen, Monty (Nat)
Hong Kong Vol
Argyll Camp & Japan

Redhill, WO Jack
(aka Roitenberg)
FMSVF Bandmaster

Roit, Pte
Dutch Army

Rose, Dvr A. Jack
(aka Harry Rosinsky?)
AASC
Buried Kranji
From London

Rose, L/Bdr C.
Cardiff

Rose, Dr J.
RASC AIF
Died 29.9.45 of illness on
liberation

Rose, Lt Lionel
Sherwood Foresters
POW 1943 crossing of
Chindwin/Chindits

Rosen, Gnr M.
RA
Returned to London

Rosen, Gnr Solomon
RA
Buried Labuan

Rosenberg, Gnr J.
1075156
RA
Buried Kanchanaburi

Rosenberg, Col. R.L.M.
RCOS
Died 3.3.42

Rosenthal, Capt Willi
RASC
Sing/Thai.
aged 50+
WW1 Croix-de Guerre (Paris)

Rosenwald, Capt Pieter
Dutch
Taiwan POW web site prob. Jewish

Roumania, Pte Abraham
1st Cambs
Lost at sea as a POW

Russell, M.L.
Intel Corps
Died of illness after liberation,
1946
Buried Kranji

Sammes, George
Dutch

Samuel, The Hon Phillip
Hong Kong VDF

Samsonovitch, Cpl P.
SVC

Samuel, Herbert
HKVDC
Died 25.12.41

Samuels, N.D.
5775466
Royal Norfolk Regt
MIA/POW
Hackney

Samuelson, Lt Alexander
Humphrey
RA

Saunders, Cpl Louis
Norfolk Regt
Lost at sea whilst being
transferred as a POW

Schwenk, H.
RASC
Died 10.4.42

Seebohm, Maj E.
Sing/Thai

Sefton, Capt Lou
RAMC Singapore

Segal, Gnr Mark
RA

Segal, Reuben 'Johnny'

Shapiro, Cpl
Lordship Park, Stoke Newington

Shapiro, Sgmn Israel
RCOS
Buried Kanchanaburi

Shoop/Shloop, Pte Judah
Beds & Herts

Shore, Pte T.
6472825
Roy Fus
Southgate

Shulman, Pte Sydney
Gordon Hghldrs

Silman, Capt Harry
RAMC
Changi and Burma

Silver, L/Cpl A.
Norfolk Regt

Silver, Gnr Samuel
Died as POW in Singapore

Silverstone, Pte Nat
RASC

Silverton, E.K.
RA
Saigon

Simon, Pte Charles
SSVF

Simon, Pte Moss
1447697
RA
Cardiff

Simons, Mark
Singapore – Burma Rly

Singer, Dvr Lewis
RCOS
Buried Kanchanaburi

Sluizer, Pte I.S.
Dutch Army
Died

Smith, Pte Jack
RAOC

Snell, Capt E.
RAMC

South African Jewish Doctor not named by Nussbaum

Spero, 'Doddy'

Steel, Pte Joseph
1829108
RA
Hendon

Steingart, Sydney
RA
Died 24.8.45

Stern, Capt Eugene
WW1 Austrian army in UK/AIF forces

Stern, Pte Nathaniel
Recce Coy/Rifle Bde

Sternfield, Sol
Dutch Medical Corps

Stockfisch
Dutch Army

Stolk, C.J.
Dutch Army
Java

Stone, Gnr Leslie
RA
Buried Kranji

Stone, Maj Leslie David
RAMC

Stone, Gnr Louis
RA
Buried Kuala Lumpur

Strauss, Capt Richard L.
HQ 11th Indian Div.
MIA/POW Sing/Thai

Sugar, Cpl Jack
Norfolks
(from Luton)

Sunshine, Edward
RA
Died 5.3.43

Swift, Pte Joseph
Rangoon Memorial

Symonds?
Java

Talan/Jalan, Lt Emmanuel
Hong Kong VDC

Taylor, Pte H.

Tiller, Gnr Morris
RA

Tobias, Pte E.
Sherwood Foresters

Tropp, Spr Alfred
RE

Turchin, John

Two undecipherable signatures on Changi Synagogue leaflet in Arkush Archive Aug 1945

Unterman, Frances
RA
Died 1.3.42

Van Gelderen, M.J.
Dutch (?)
Changi

Vas-Nunes, Sgt Maurice
RASC

Weill, Gnr Leon
Hong Kong Vol. Force

Weinblatt, Pte Raphael Leslie
Suffolk Regt
Buried Thanbyuzayat, Burma

Weinfass, Pte Leslie
Royal Norfolk
Taiwan

Weinman, L/Bdr W.
RA
Died 13.2.42

Weinstock, Wally

Weiss, Pte Harry
Luton
Mentioned in book, *Surviving the Sword*

Weissman, Geoffrey
Java

Wenzerul, Gnr Edward
Lost at sea as POW

Wernick, L/Cpl Cyril
Norfolk Regt
Died after liberation as POW in Singapore

Willenski, Pte Michael
Cambs Regt

Wince, L/Cpl David Leonard
2nd Cambs

Winter, L/Cpl Leonard E. (aka Ginsburg)
Middx Regt
Buried Hong Kong

Wolf, Pte
Dutch Army

Woods, Maj Everard
RIASC

Woolf, Robert 'Bobby' (aka Emmanuel Nathan Woolf)
RCOS
Taiwan

Young, D.
Glasgow

Yudkin, Abraham
RA
Lost at sea as POW

Zeehandelaar, Pte L.H.
Dutch Army
Java

Zimmer, Gnr Morris
RA
Lost at sea as a POW

Zimmern, Bdr A.
HKVDC
Died 18.12.41
Of Jewish origin

Zimmern, Sgt E.
HKVDC
Died 19.12.41
Of Jewish origin

RAF

Altman, LAC Lewis
Secretary to Col 'Weary' Dunlop
Java

Baker, Sgt Leonard Alfred
Java

Bloom, Pte Jack

Brogsall, A.
Glasgow

Camberg, David
Died 28.4.45

Circurel, P/O Richard Leon
Java

Colman/Coleman, Samuel Gerald
POW Batavia

Courts, AC2 Harry A.

De Lange, LAC George Ivor
POW Java
Buried Bandoeng

Fell, A.
Glasgow

Fisher, LAC John
BEM for courage giving medical services and interpreter for POWs

Goldberg, AC2 Charles
Died 29.11.43

Grunis, Cpl Abraham
Lost at sea as a POW

Harris, LAC C. Hyman

Hart, LAC Sidney

Kaplan, J.
Glasgow

Lawrence, LAC Sydney

Leigh/Lee, LAC Harold
Sandakan/Sarawak

Levinson, LAC Sydney Henry
Buried Kanchanaburi

Levy, LAC Alf/Sonny
Buried Kanchanaburi

Marks, AC1 Robert George
Kranji memorial

Nathan, LAC Gerald M.
Died Sandakan Death March

Prechner, AC1 Harold Joseph
Changi

Ruben, LAC S.A.
Leeds

Shenken, L.
Glasgow

Simmonds, AC2 Albert Bernard

Simmonds, LAC Joseph

Solity, AC2 Abraham Sidney

Stoll/Shaw (?), Dr F/O Basil

Warshawsky, AC1 Arthur Reginald
Changi/Java

Weiner, AC2 Louis (aka Wilton ?)
Changi

Welzer, LAC David

Palestinian Jews

Alster, Reuben/Rudolf
RAF 211 Squadron
KIA Israel War of Independence, 1948

Cohen, Mrs Moselle
Murdered by Japanese for assisting Sandakan marchers

Kissen, Abraham 'Kiki'
RAF 211 Squadron
Samarang, Haraku, Batavia

Unknown Third RAF probably Ehrmann, Leonard/Ludwig
RAF
Tel-Aviv (*JC*)

Canadians

(from *Canadian Jewry at War* [Montreal: Canadian Jewish Congress, 1947/48])

Allister, Sgmn William
RCCOS
Hong Kong/Tokyo

Brown, Rfmn Louis
Canadian Rifles
Hong Kong/Fukuaoka

Golden, Capt David Aaron
Grenad. Of Winnipeg
Hong Kong

Harrison, Capt Robert George
Manitoba Regt
Hong Kong/Osaka

Markowitz, Capt Dr Jacob
RCAMC
MBE for courage as a doctor POW
Malaya

Rose, Sgmn Jacob
RCCOS
Hong Kong/Tokyo

Zaidman, Rfmn Frederick 'Zeke'
Canad. Rifles
Hong Kong/Tokyo

USA – A Selection

Altman/Alterman

Bank, Capt Bert
Bataan/Cabu Philippines

Cohen, Sgt Larry Herman
USAAC
Captured Battaan, POW
Yokohama

Eckstein, Col A.
USN
Died Taiwan

Epstein, Cmdr Dr Abraham
USN
At the camp Bar Mitzvah
ceremony at Tamarkan

Garfinkle,Col A.
Taiwan

Kauffmann, Nelson Nissan
USAMC
Captured Philippines
POW Yokohama

Schneider, Capt Dr Leo

Schwartz, Dr
Philippines

Tenny, Lester (aka Tennenberg)
Bataan march, escaped,
recaptured

Weinstein, Dr Alfred A.
Philippines

*NB: Sources show that were a
huge number of US Jewish POWs
but this is beyond the scope of
this survey and sources are best
found in the USA.*

Australians

(some from '*Australian Jewry
Book of Honour*' (AJBH))

There are a dozen indecipherable
names from the Bar Mitzvah
Certificate written at Tamarkan
camp 27.9.44 (now in the
Museum of Australian Jewish
History), mentioned in the AJBH,
which has Australian, British,
Dutch, USA and even some
Japanese names on it, attending
the mock Bar Mitzvah ceremony
for the son (Leon) of Mark 'Gil'
Hayman, one of the Australian
POWs.

San = Sandakan Death March,
killed as POWs

Abrahams, Gnr
Java

Bard, Dr Solomon
Hong Kong Def. Force
Kowloon

Berman, Izzi

Bines, James
From USA in *AIF*

Blashki, Sgt Victor
Kranji memorial

Bliner, Sgt Sam

Boan, Sgt Clive H.
2/29 Inf
BEM
Changi

Brand, Capt Victor
2/29th Btn 8th Div
MC for courage as a POW

Cavanagh, Pte C.
22nd Pioneers AIF
Orbust,Vic

Cohen, Bmdr Arthur
Java

Danny (?)

Diamond, Lt Oscar
Taiwan

Goldburg, Arthur Leslie
AAOC
Died at Kanchanaburi 7.9.43.

Griff, Sgt B.G.
Java

Harris, Lt and brother
Sons of Major Sam Harris below

Harris, Maj Sam N.
Vic.
San

Hayman, Mark 'Gill'

Krantz, Maj Dr Sydney
RAAMC
Burma, Thailand, Changi

Marks, Pte F.J.
AIF
Died 20.7.43 Saigon

Milston, Sgmn Neville
8th Div.
Thailand

Montefiore, Sgt
Java (named by Col E. 'Weary'
Dunlop)

Nagelberg, Sgmn
Polish serving Australian Army

Nagle, Max
German refugee

Noble, Cpl C.H.
Bondi

Peck, Flt Lt
RAAF
Melbourne

Pierce, Pte J.
Alias as not in AJBH
Bondi

Rabinov/Rapinow, Alan

Relik, Sgt Schmuel
(written in Hebrew on Tamarkan
Bar Mitzvah certificate)

Rosenberg, Alf

Rosenberg, Gnr Allan
RAA NX23803
Buried Kanchanaburi

Rosenberg, Gerald

Rosenbloom, Alex

Sachs, Lt John
AIF 'Z' Force
Executed as POW

Samuelson

Sanders, Pte Harry
AIF
Buried Kranji

Schwartz, Capt
Java

Shadbolt, R.
Sydney

Sharp, W.
NSW
San

Shaw, R.
NSW
San

Silman, L.
Melbourne

Soffer, Pte S.
Melbourne

Solomon, A.
Melbourne

**Solonsch, Samuel (aka John
Douglas, aka Schmidt)**
Executed by Japanese as an
Australian Intell. whilst a POW.
Java 11.4.43 (Dunlop, p. 80)

Spielvogel, Sgt L.H./Speilvogal, F.
Balarat, Vic.

Stolarski, C/J
Vic.
San

Swartz/Schwartz, Pte J.
Lawley, W Aust.

Taylor, Joe
Rumanian refugee in *AIF*
Changi

Victorsen, E.L.M.
NSW/Qsd
San

Weinberg, Sgmn Coleman

White, Bernard
Vic.
San

Woolf, Dvr E.B.
AIF

Zinn, Spr Aubrey
Born in South Africa
Sent from Sandakan to Labuan

Ziporkin, Maurice
AIF

South African

Hefferman, AB Nelson Joseph
HMS *Encounter*
San; lost at sea as POW

Totals

Navy	9
Army	295
RAF	32
Palestinian Jews	4
Canadian	7
Australian	97
South African	1
Total	445

Civilian POWs of Japanese

This list includes military Volunteer
Force personnel. There are over
100 other Jewish-sounding
names on the list from J. Moffatt,
but we cannot yet verify religion.
By 7 April 1943 eye-witness
Thomas Kitching (surveyor of
Singapore) stated that there were
110 Jewish civilian POWs at
Changi Jail (C. Bayly and T.
Harper, *Forgotten Armies*
[Penguin, 2005], p.340).

Aaron, J.E.E. Salimon
Singapore

Aaron, H.R.
Estate agent Singapore

Abbott, Bill

Abbott, Shookee

Abdullah, Abraham Ezekiel
Died

Abett, I.B.
Pte 1st SSVF
Singapore
Died Burma railway 2/9/43
Buried Thambyuzayat; not on
CWGC

Abett, Stanley

Abraham, David Ezekiel Joshua
Died Shanghai camp 27.5.45

**Abraham, Rabbi name
unknown and his family**
Shanghai camp

Adler, E.S.

Albert, Elias
Died

Attias, Clara Adelina
Died Sime Rd Camp, Singapore
2.8.44

Bekhon/Bekhore, Yahya
Singapore

Bennett, Mrs Margaret
Aged 26 in 1942
Changi & Sime Rd

Bloom, Mrs Freddy
US wife of Dr Phillip (see POW
Army) 'Double Tenth' victim
Singapore

Bolter, Norman
Died at sea on transport

Bolter, Max

Brisk, Albert Wolfe
Died aged 62
Changi 19.12.42

Brisk, Buyeenish
Died Changi, 18.11.43
Buried Jewish Cem. Lim
Chu Kang

Brisk, Mrs E.R.
Singapore

Brisk, Mr I.A.

Brisk, Pte L.V.
1st SSVF

Brisk, Max
Changi & Sime Rd

Brisk, Mrs Rebecca
Wife of Max
Aged 47 in 1942
Changi & Sime Rd

Brown, Rev Mendel
(*SVC Chaplain*)

Citrin, Walter
Plus wife and two sons
Chapel camp, Hong Kong

Cohen, Mrs A.
Died at sea 4/42
Singapore

Cohen, Mr A.
Husband of above 4/42

Cohen, Flori Enid
Interned China, born Shanghai

Cohen, Isaiah Meyer
Interned China, born Shanghai,
Husband of Flori Enid

Cohen, Moses M.

Cohen, Silman
Died

Cohen, Mr Yahya
Changi & Sime Rd
Later professor of surgery post
war

Dabelstein, Winifred E.
Died Hong Kong camp 21.9.44

Daniel, Moses

Daniel, Sion Charlie

David, Jacob Moses
Singapore

David, Jack M.
Changi
Survived

David, Joe Brooke
Tin broker

David, L/Cpl Soloman
FMSVF
Died Sime Rd   27.8.45

Davis, S.
Changi
Singapore Jewish Community

Deborah, Albert
Died

De Leon, S.
(Dutch at Tamarkan Camp)
Dutch War Office civilian

Elias, A. Ezra
Changi & Sime Rd

Elias, Diana (nee Hardoon)
Interned Stanley Camp, Hong Kong
Survived

Elias, E.A.
JP
Interned Stanley Camp, Hong Kong
Survived

Elias, Helen

Elias, Jack M.
Interned Stanley Camp, Hong
Kong
Survived

Elias, Jacob
Changl & Slme Rd

Elias, Jonah
Changi & Sime Rd

Elias, Joseph
Changi & Sime Rd
Died

Elias, S. Moses
Changi & Sime Rd

Elias, Ezekiel Moses
Died

Elias, Zeki

Elisha, Meyer J.
Changi & Sime Rd

Elkins, Mrs K. Lena, née Cohen
Wife of Philip
Changi & Sime Rd

Elkins, Philip H.
JP
Customs and Excise Officer

Engels, Dr

Ezekiel, Abraham
Changi Rd. 10.5.43

Ezekiel, Elias
Died

Ezekiel, Maurice
Died

Frankel, David
JP
Singapore

Goldberg, Dr Mrs
Sumatra
Betty Jeffrey, *White Coolies*
(Angus & Robertson,
2001), pp.82, 113, 114

Goldenberg, Harry
Aged 57, Malaya

Goldman, Maj S.
FMSVF
MID POW Thailand

Goldman, B.
Changi & Sime Rd

Grand, Meyer

Green, Mr
In charge Singapore Electric
Company

Greenburg, Essie/Elsie
Wife of Walter
Stanley, Hong Kong

Guston, Mrs Thelma

Hardoon, Abraham Isaac

Hardoon, Charles Isaac
Hong Kong Police

Hardoon, Elizabeth

Hardoon, Isaac Silas
Died 1945 as a result of
internment

Hardoon, Jack/Jacob

Hardoon, John

Hardoon, Loulou/Lily
Wife of Isaac

Hardoon, Mattie/Mathilda
(MS)

Hardoon, Sophie

Hayim, R.E.J.
Changi & Sime Rd

Herman, Leo
Czech national
                            4.2.45
Died Omata Camp, Japan

Ingold, Felix

Jonah, Solomon
Died

Joseph, Albert
Changi & Sime Rd

Joseph, Dolly
Died Singapore Camp 11.8.45

Joseph, Elias
Died

Joseph, Sarah and 2 children
Died

Kauffman, Stella
                            28.2.42
Husband Bernard Maurice KIA at
sea MV *Rooseboom*

Komaroff, Charles David
Komaroff, Elsa (wife)
Son fought in Battle of Britain RAF

Kossick, David
of Newcastle
Died Hong Kong
Son Arnold KIA *RAF*

Landor, Dr Joseph Victor
Registrar Singapore General
Hospital Changi & Sime Rd

Lazarus, Mr. C.
                            29.6.42
Died Toungoo, Burma

Leiah, Albert
Born 1913
Changi & Sime Rd

Leiah, M.
As above

Levene
2nd FMSVF
POW

Levien, John Lawson
Lindenhafen, New Britain aged 57

Levy, Michael Meyer George
Escaped from Japanese in
Shanghai. Trecked 2000 miles
to British lines and became
SOE officer Malaya Force 126.
MID

Levy, Phillip Montague
Husband of Mable
Kavieng, PNG

Lewis, Max
Changi/Sime Rd

Macklin, Mrs R.
Hong Kong

Macmorine, Levers
Changi & Sime Rd

Macmorine, Mrs L.
As above

Manasseh, Alec

Manasseh, Elsie
Wife of Ezekiel
Sime Rd

Manasseh, Ezekiel S.
JP
                            17.5.44
Changi & Sime Rd

Manasseh, Jacob Isaac
Changi & Sime Rd

Manasseh, J.H.
Changi & Sime Rd

Manasseh, Maurice S.
Changi & Sime Rd

Manasseh, Sassoon
Changi & Sime Rd

Mandelson, Jack
Rubber Planter
Glasgow/Sumatra

Marshall, Pte David
SSVF
Singapore community

Meyer, Kew
Changi

Meyer, L.D.
Superintendant of Surveys,
Malaya

Mordecau, K.J.
Photographer
Changi

Morris, Pte Eric V.
13912 1st FMSVF
Singapore
Born 1907 POW
Wife Anna Estel Silvermann

Moser, G.A.
Kuala Lumpur

Moses, E.
Singapore

Moses, Hannah

Moses, Hayim

Moses, M.H.
Sime Rd
2.9.45

Moses, P.D.
Penang

Moses, Robert

Moses, Simon

Murad, W.K.
Changi & Sime Rd

**Nabi, David Abdul
(aka Davies, David)**
Java

**Naftaly family – Harry, Lilly,
Emil, Albert, Nancy**
Shanghai

Nassim family

Nathan, Eze

Nathan, Ivor,

Nathan, Isaac Elias
Died

Nathan R.

Nathan Meyer

Nathans, Esther
Wife of Max

Nathans, Maximillian
Husband of Esther
9.5.44
Malaya Sime Rd

Neufeld, Rebecca
Lunguha camp

Neufeld
Brother of above

Oppenheim, Prof Alec

Oppenheim, Pte L.R.
Later Chancellor Univ. of Malaya
Australian (?)

Pinhas, Abraham
Died

Raymond, Lazarus
Changi

Robin, Moses Nissim
Died

Ruben, Sol

Sadka, Sassoon

Saltoon, R.E.
Changi & Sime Rd

Sharbanee, David
Died

Sharbanee, E.M.
Changi & Sime Rd

Short
Brother of Zaida
Murdered by Japanese
First name not known

Short, Hilda
POW Sumatra

Short, Zaida
POW Sumatra
Sister of Hilda (Lavinia Warner and
John Sandilands, *Women beyond
the Wire* [Michael Joseph, 1982])

Silvermann, Ann Estel
Survivor Giang Bee, rescued HMS
Tapah,
POW Sumatra
Sec. Sir A. Young Malaya Emerg.,
later Mrs Powell of Shrewsbury

Silvermann, J.C.
Singapore Municipality
Changi & Sime Rd

Silvermann, S.B.
Changi & Sime Rd

Simon, Leon
Singapore Aux Police

Soloman, Edgar Samuel
Montevideo Maru at sea
1.7.42

Soloman, Moses David
Lost at sea
-.02.42

Solomans/Solomon, S.D.
Sime Rd
27.8.45, Changi aged 28

Storch, Adolph G.
Pte 1st FMSVF Labuan
22.1.45
Changi/Borneo

Tuck, Sharon Anne
Aged 10 months
Daughter of T.W. Tuck and Anna
Raphael Tuck
Died Shanghai camp

Waltz, Max
Died

Warmen, Mischa
Boy POW from HMT *Vyner Brooke*
later lived Shanghai (*Women
Beyond the Wire*)

Weinberg, M.
Changi

Weinberg, Simone
French
Changi

Wiseberg/Weisberg, Hyman
Changi & Sime Rd

Wuertzburger, Walter
Singapore camp

Zimmerman, Herbert
Husband of Sonia
Sumatra

Unidentified family of four killed in bombing in Joo Chiat Rd, Sing. – evidence of Eze Nathan

The following list of Commonwealth Jewish internees of the Japanese, all over South and East Asia, was drawn up by Brian Gander (himself a child internee from 14–17 years old) of ABCIFER – The Association of British Civilian Internees in the Far East – from their memorial book which is kept at St Michael's Church in Cornhill, City of London. For ease, in some cases, the family name has been listed and is then followed by the first names. Where an initial only was known, that has been given. Every entry, whether the same first name or not, or same initial or not, is a separate individual.

AARON
Abraham
Abraham
Benjamin
David
Eileen Dorothy
Helen Jena Margaret
John David
Jonah
Katherine
Margaret Elizabeth
Meda
Meyer G.
Moses
Pauline

ABRAHAM
Abraham
Abe
Abraham S.
Absalom
Aziza
Celia
Diana
Edgar S.

Elias Ezekiel
Ellis Michael
Emma Moses
Ezekiel
Ezekiel
Ezekiel R. D.
Ezra Gertie
Geulah
Hannah
Harry Ezekiel
Isaac S.
Isaac Reuben
Joseph Hayim
Julian
Katie
Katie Rahma
Leah
Louisa
Masie
Marjorie Aziza
Meda
Mildred Patricia
Moshe Hai
Mozelle
Mozelle
Mozelle Ruby
Nachama
Naomi
Patricia
Rachel
Rachel
Rahma Katie
Rebecca
Regina
Reuben David
Reuben
Rosie
Sarah
Sassoon Hai
Seema
Shulamith
Victoria
Yahya

ACKRILL, Reuben

AKERIB, Ezekiel Manasseh
AKERIB, Saul Manasseh

ALBERT, Ezekiel

ALBERT, Moses

BEKHORE
Dinah Diana
Flora
Hawa Hannah
Joseph Elias
Judah Freddy
Lily B.
Sally Sudah
Toba

BENGHIAT
Abraham Jacob
Fortuna
Lillian
Victoria

BENJAMIN
A.
B.
Benjamin David
Benjamin F.
David
Eileen Grace
Elsa Beate
Estelle Rosemarie
Eva Rahma
Isaac
Judah Ephraim
Liza Matilda
Said Ezekiel
Simon H.
Sophie Isaac
Sylvia Simha

BERAHA, Denise
BERAHA, Michael

COHEN
A.A.
Abraham Meyer
Aziza Meyer
E.P.
Elias Meyer
Florence Frances
Hilda
Hilda Katherine
Hubert
Jack Major

Joseph J.
L.
Mordecai
R.
Rachel Grace

DANIEL
Ellas Sion
Frederick
Jacob
Katie
Manasseh Sion
Menehem
Meyer Ezekiel
Mozelle Sion
Rachel Sion
Rebecca Remaah
Sion

DAVID
David B.
Dina
Evelyn
Ezekiel Haim
Flossie Flora
Jacob
Joseph Salem
Maurice
Samuel
Samuel Yahya

ELIAS
Abraham
Abraham
Benjamin
Clara Harry
Clara Reuben
Dinah Dorothy
Dinah Nassim
Dinah Ruben
E.
E.
Edward Leopold
Eleanor
Elias
Elias Jacob
Elias Nassim
Esther Reuben
Ezekiel
Ezekiel Ezra

Flora
Flora
Flossie Reuben
Grace Nassim
Hannah Katie
Haron
Harry
Harry Moses
Isaac
Isaac Brooke
Isaac Ezekiel
Jacob
Jacob John
Jacob Moses
Jacob Sasoon
Jonah
Jonah Jacob
Joseph Nassim
Joseph Reuben
Lily
Louise
Louise
Manasseh Nasim
Marina
Meda E.
Meda Nassim
Mollie
Moses Joseph
Moses Reuben
Natty
Olivia
Rachel
Rachel
Ramon
Raymond
Reuben Sassoon
Reuben Solomon
Rochelle
Ronald Jack R.
Rosalind
Rosie
Sarah Blanche
Sarah Catherine
Sarah Joseph
Sassoon Jacob
Saul
Sion
Solomon M.
Sophie
Victor

Victoria
Victoria
Violct

EMANUEL
A.
B.
C.
D.
D.A.
F.
G.
J.
J.F.
M.
M.
M.A.
P.

EZEKIEL
Aba Mannesh
Abraham Saul
Alfred
David
David Shalom
Elias Nissim
Ellis
Ellison S.
Elsie N.
Ezekiel Harry
Flossy Abraham
Hannah
Isaac Saul
Isadore Saul
Jacob Harry
Joseph
Julian Saul
Katie Abraham
Manasseh Nassim
Marguerite A.
Maurice
Meyer
Morris Saul
Moselle
Noel Elias
Rachel
Rachel
Rachel Sassoon
Raymond Aaron
Regina

Remah Abraham
Ritchie
Sassoon
Sasoon George
Saul
Sophie Abraham

EZMANIEL, Ari

EZRA
Densil Marcus
Edward
Ellis Isaac
Frederick
Grace K.
Hannah
Irene M.
Joseph
Judah Isaac
Lydia
Messiah
Rachel
Simon

ISAAC
A.
Aaron Jacob
Albert Solomon
Ezekiel
Freddie J.
George J.
Isaac N.
Jacob N.
Joseph N.
Kitty
Leah
Maurice S.
Mooda
Nahom N.
R.
Ose Moses
Rosie
S.

JACOB
Abraham
Amelia Cambell B.
Edward Fred Meyer
Ezekiel
Hil

Isaac E.
Jack
Jean Anne
Maisie
Majia
Matilda Meyer
Meda
Meyer Manasseh
Reuben
Solomon
Sophie
Sophie

JACOBS
Archibald Gordon
Aurelius Reuben
Beatrice Daisy
Bertram William
Ernest
Harry William Frank
Noel Stanley

JOSEPH
A.
A.
A. V.
Abraham
David George O.
E.
Ellis Menashih
Ezekiel
Ezekiel Sassoon
Flora
Flossie
Freddy H.
H. W.
Hannah
Hannah
John
Jonathan David
Joseph
Joseph Edgar
Judah
Manasseh
Mozelle
Nassim
Nassim Edward
Raphael
Raphael Judah
Rebecca

Sassoon
Solomon Saul
T.

JOSHUA
Elias
Ezekiel
Hannah
John
Katie
Moses
Moses
Nellie
Roy Moses
Sarah
Saul
Theresa

JUDAH
Albert Joseph
Cyril Ralph
David Bernard
Diana Evelyn
Elsie Rosemary
Ezekiel Joseph
Flossie
Gloria Jeanette
Joseph Edwin
Judith Jocelyn
Katie
Katieh
Manya
Moses Joseph
Rachel
Rameh Rosamond
Rebecca
Reva
Samson Albert
Valerie Marian
Valerie Nicholevna

KADOORIE
Elly Horace
Lawrence
Michael David
Muriel
Rita Laura

KLIENE
Bert

Dennis
Ron

LEHEM
Fortuna S.
Mazaltob S.
Solomon Marco

LELAH, Aaron Sion
LELAH, Charles Aaron

LEVENSPIEL, Octave

LEVI, Raphael Zabulon
LEVI, Renee Zabulon

LEVIS
Bonnie
Constance H.
Esther
Evelyn M.
Hazedella Louisa
Hebe
Isaac Abraham
Lilian
Luela Iris Suzanne
Rachel
Violet H.
John Hazedel

LEVISON
A.H.
Corina M.
Harold
Jacob

LEVY
Bertie Saul
David Ezra
Peter Cecil
Raphael Hyeem
Salam H. Rachel
Seemah

MANASSEH
Albert
Daisy
Ezekiel Hai
Ezekiel
Ezekiel

Flora Dolly
Gertrude
Hilda Kitty
Hone
Jackie
Lily
Liza
Louisa
Louisa Jacob
Mary
Mary Jacob
Meda
Moses Maurice
Sally
Sophie Poppy

MASRY, Esther
MASRY, Joseph Eskel

MENAHEM
David
Elias Saul
Esther Elias
Esther Reuben
Grace Elias
Katie Elias
Katy Reuben
Sarah

MENEHEM
Elia
Manahem
Margillet
Mary
Mesumer

MEYER
A.
E.
Elias David
Esther
Ezekiel
Ezra
Katie Elias
Kiaassen
Kitty
Morris
Mozelle
Rachel

Raymond Elias
Rebecca
Rueben
Sarah
Saul Snr.
Sophie Poppy
Toba

MOALEM
Daniel
Emma M.
Girgee
Grace K. E.
Hannah
Joseph
Joseph R.
Louise R.
Reuben Joseph
Simon Joseph
Sophia Shaker
Sophie Irene
William M.

MOSES
Aaron Ezra
Abraham Elias
Abraham Sassoon
Branita Edith
Cyril David
David Hya Ezra M.
Flora
Flossie
Helen Riddel
Hilda
Isaac Hayoo
Lionel
Lucy A.
Moses Simon
Nissim
Polly
Rachel Simon
Rebecca
Rosa Christina
Sarah
Sion Abraham
Solomon Simon
Sybil Simon
Victoria Simon
Violet

NASSIM
Abraham
Freddy Isaac
Menahem Aaron
Moses J.
Nassim A.
Sarah
Sarah Katie

NATHAN
Edward Jonah
Ezekiel E.
Ezekiel J.
Henry Bernard
Joseph A.

NISSIM
Dorothy
Flora
Matthew Albert
Matook Raymond
Nazira
Nissim Marcus M.
Nooriel Frederick
Rachelle S.
Rahma Nissima
Ramona Mamona
Salem Raphael
Saul Gabriel

RAPHAEL
Eleazar Freddy
Ezekiel
Flora
Flossie
Helen Marcus
Louise
Maurice
Meda
Tobs

REUBEN
Elias Y.
Ezekiel
Ezekiel Elias
Florence
Grace
Helen
Helen Ezekiel Hilda
Ezekiel Maisie

Ezekiel Morris
Nina Sassoon
Naim George
R. Saul
Rachel Yahya
Reuben N.
Reuben Saul
Rosalind
Rose Ezekiel
S.M.S.
Saul Felix Carrady
Shirley Solomon Ezekiel
Sophie Ezekiel
Violet Y.
Yahya

SASSOON
Abraham Albert
Abraham Ezra
Adee Lee
David E.
Elias Albert
Ezekiel Albert
Ezekiel Sassoon
Harry Meyer
Isaac Albert
Jacob
Matilda Albert
Sally Albert
Sassoon Albert
Solomon Albert

SAUL
David
Esther
Flora
Flora Ezekiel
Hannah Meyer
Hilda
Hilda Meyer
Joseph Joseph
Joseph Meyer
Katy Meyer
Lily Meyer
Meda Meyer
Naima Meyer
R. V.
Raymon Meyer
Sarah Ezekiel
Schimea Meyer

Sofia Ezekiel
Walter Emil Medhurst

SCHUKER
Hannah Joseph
Jack Meyer J.
Joseph Saul
Sadie Joseph
Saul Ray Joseph
Sydney H.
Thelma Joseph

SHALOME
Ezekiel I.
Gracie Ezekiel
Halka
Joseph Ezekiel
Menahem I.
Mozelle Ezekiel
Rosie Ezekiel
Victoria Ezekiel

SHEMTOB
Diana
Ella
Ezekiel Jacob
Flora
Gladys
Jacob Silas
Maisie
Rachel Jacob
Silas Jacob

SOLOMON
Aaron David
Abraham
Abraham George
Abraham S.
Betty Said
Daisy Sassoon
David
David Sassoon
Dinah Said
Eleanor Sassoon
Eleazar B.
Eleazar Hai
Ellis David
Emma Jacob
Ezekiel
Ezekiel Elias

Flora
Flora
Florence
Florence Sassoon
Freddy
Grace Sassoon
Helen
Helen Said
Isaac Jnr.
Isaac Snr.
Sophie Sassoon
Jacob
Jacob H.
Jacob D.
Jarnila
Judah
Juliett
Lulu Moses
Manasseh
Manasseh David
Mary Said
Menahem
Moses E.
Mozelle
Nassim E.
Rachel
Rachel
Rachel Mrs
Rahama

Rebecca
Rosie
Said
Sally
Sarah
Sassoon Eleazar
Sophie
Sophie
Sophie
Sophie Sassoon
Thelma
Victoria Jacob

ZAAB, Jacob Hyam

ZACHARIAS, Hans
ZACHARIAS, R. A.
ZACHARIAS, V. D.

ZELLENSKY, George Abraham
ZELLENSKY, Jacob

ZELLENSKY, Miriam

ZIMMERMAN, E.R.
ZIMMERMAN, Ernest
ZIMMERMAN, Kathleen
ZIMMERMAN, Vlademar

Dutch Civilian Jewish Internees

Armand (?)

Caun, Mr
(Interpreter for Japanese)

De Vries, Louis

Elburg, Rabbi and Family
Changi

Grunwald, Moses

Hollaender, Hans
Died

Joel, Henri F.
Journalist. Taiwan
Prob. Jewish

Nussbaum, Mrs Rachel
(wife of Rabbi Chaim) plus three
children: Motke, Brenda and
Shifra

Rapaport, Eddie

Rotenberg, Frank

Velmans, Lou

Jews Who Served in Special Forces in the Second World War and After

NB: Many who served in the units below were also Paratroopers (see separate list 'Paras and Commandos'). For those who served in the SOE, see Martin Sugarman, *Fighting Back* (London and Portland, OR: Vallentine Mitchell, 2010).

Special Air Service (SAS)

Angel, Mark

Birch, Lionel/Lee
SAS
N Ireland, MBE

Faust, Joseph Dan (aka Fauschleger)
2nd SAS 1944–51 and Paras

Friedlander, Sgt Robert (aka Lodge)
DCM
KIA France

Goldsmith, Sgt Ernest, MM
SAS
Probably Jewish

Goldstein, H. (aka Wilenski), Sgmn and LRDG
SIG Att. 1st SAS (Buffs)
1942 POW

Goldstein, Lt Col Simon
21st SAS
MBE Iraq 2005

Goodman, Mark
1990s N Ireland (from Hackney)

Griessman (aka Sir Ronald Grierson)
1st SAS att. 21st Indep Paras/SOE
MID
WIA

Hausmann, Cpl Fritz Sigmund
att. SAS
DCM Yugoslavia

Hillman, Capt Charles Leo (aka Kennedy/Steiner/Peter/Hefer/Gerber)
SIG/SOE
MC and Bar
Palestinian Jewish 'L'
Detachment, MM
Tobruk, SOE No. 6 Special Force
Italy & Austria

Hoffman, Harry
Paras att. SAS
POW, escaped 3 x MID, Purple Heart!

Julius, Brig Alan
SAS Malaya

Kahane/Cahann, Sgt Karl
SBS/SIG Att 'L' Detach
SAS
Palestinian Jewish 1941-45

Kalkstein, Pte Joachim
SAS
KIA France

Kasperovitch, Cpl Boris (aka King)
SAS
KIA France

Kauffman
more not known

Kennedy, S/Sgt Eric John
2nd SAS/Commandos 1943–45

Klein
more not known

Kruyer, Jack Isaac
Att SAS/LRDG/Rifle Bde

Levinsohn/Lewinsohn, Pte Michael (aka Lewis)
SAS
KIA France

Mann, Jack (aka Zachariah Zuckerman)
SBS/LRDG

Marx, Capt Frank Ralph
MC
2nd SAS France 1943–45

Orr/Opoczynski, Adam
att SSRF
see below

Reichenstein, Pte W.
13809152
PC to 2nd SAS 'Operation Archway' 1945
Germany

Rohr/Roer, J. (aka Berg)
SIG Palestinian Jewish

Rosen, Woolf
Australian Special Forces

Rosenstein, L/Cpl Natan
SAS
KIA N Africa (Palestinian Jewish)

Russell, Daniel
C Squadron 23rd SA
TA 1983-9

Sebba, Capt Samuel
6th Airborne att. SAS
MID

Sharp, Maj David
Malay Scouts Later 22nd SAS
POW Korea BEM, WIA

Strauss, Capt Cyril Anthony
also LRDG
Polish CofV
KIA

Tieffenbrunner/Tiffen, Maurice
SIG/1st SAS
POW
Palestinian Jewish

Tyler, John
SAS Territ. 2000

Wertheim, Pte Gerhard
Att. SAS
KIA France

Willmers, Capt John Geoffrey
(aka Hans Johann
Willmersdorfer)
10 Com att. SAS

Wiseman, Lt John
SAS
MC, Croix de Guerre
WIA

Zermati, Jacques
Algerian Jew
SAS France and Holland

NB. There are many Jewish names among the French and Belgian SAS squadrons KIA and the Belgian Piron Brigade. See www.alliedspecialforces.org for many others who served and survived; see also Commando list as many were attached SAS/SBS/LRDG/SOE.

Special Boat Squadron (SBS)

Benelisha, Samuel
KIA
Palestinian Jewish

Davis, Col Peter
RM att SBS CMF
DSC

Garber, Joseph
Army att. SBS Yugoslavia

Green, Freddy 'Gyppo'

Kahanne/Cahann
see SAS

Katz, Yehuda Victor
(aka Stavros Papadakis)
Pal. Jewish, served *Special Task Force (STF) Rhodes* ('Guns of Navarone' raid)

Lavan, Norman (aka Levy)
40 RM Commando/SBS
Malaya (MM)
Also N Ireland and Saudi Arabia

Seligman, Lt/Cdr Adrian
Founder Levant Schooner Fleet/Squadron
DSC

Solomon, Lt Martin
RN, att SAS/Commandos
DSC and Bar, MBE

Woolfson, Cdr V.
RNVR

Small Scale Raiding Force (SSRF)

Bentley, Sgt Frederick
(aka Bierer)
Raid on Herne/62 Commando

Leonard, Pte Richard
(aka Lehniger)
KIA France

Levin, Huburtus
(aka Miles, Patrick Hugh)
Raid on Herne/SOE/10 Commando

Orr, Sgt Adam (Orr, Anthony James?) (aka Abraham Opoczynski)
att. SAS from RAMC
KIA

Ritter, Henry
Ox. and St. George Jewish Club
Polish refugee

Tischler, (aka Peter Terry)
Att. 10 Commando/SOE/47th RM Commando
WIA

Weinberger, E.G. (aka Ernest George Webster)
10 Com/47th RM Commando

Long Range Desert Group (LRDG)

Bloom, Henry

Ehrlich, John (aka Peter/John Graham) (aka 'Darkie')
WIA twice – information from daughter Jane, with photo 'LRDG'

Federman, Gnr Herbert
Palestinian Jewish
KIA Rhodes raid

Herman, 2nd Lt B.

Lazarus, Lt Ken (aka Lawrence)
MBE Mil

Levy, Derek
Att. 30 Commando

Segal, Lt Judah Benzion (aka Seagrim)
MC

Seligman, Capt Robert
MC
Brother of Adrian

Shemtob Reading, Capt Alan
MBE raid on Rommel HQ

Urban, Richard
Palestinian Jewish att.

Zimmerman, J.
no. 1392

Popski's Private Army (PPA)

Loewenstein/Loewentahl, Morris
Also LRDG
MM

Lyon, Lt James Marcus
tbc

Peniakoff, Col Vladimir
Founder of PPA and CO
DSO, MC

Reece, L/Cpl Monty 'Titch'

Schwartzman, Capt Yohanan
Palestinian Jewish

Silverman, Tpr

Topkins, Joe
Prob. German Jewish from Palestine Mandate

Pacific Coastwatchers

These were Australian Special Forces, all volunteers, who were inserted by sea-plane or submarine onto isolated South West Pacific islands, with powerful radios. They would 'lay-up' and report Japanese air and sea activity to HQ, who would then direct Allied Forces by sea and air to destroy them. This was hazardous work.

Cohen, Sgt Bill

Kotz, Sgmn G.

British and Commonwealth Jews Who Served in the Commandos and Paratroopers in the Second World War

This list has been compiled from the AJEX Jewish Chaplains' cards, personal testimony, back issues of the *Jewish Chronicle* and *AJEX Journal*, and many other miscellaneous sources. Peter Leighton-Langer's book *HM Most Loyal Enemy Aliens* was an excellent source.

Awards or killed are shown. More research is required on the Palestine 51st Middle East (ME) Commando – only some have been named here. For more detail on Arnhem Paras and 3 Troop 10 Commando, see Martin Sugarman, *Fighting Back* (London and Portland, OR: Vallentine Mitchell, 2010).

Aaronsohn
6th Airborne

Aboud, Samuel Mordechai
13th Paras

Abrahams, H.
2nd Paras CMF

Abrahams, Sgt John Cyril (aka Baler)
Commandos
Lofoten/Dieppe/POW Sicily

Abrahamson, Martin (aka Amson, Martin Leslie)
Paras
KIA Wesel

Abram, Cyril H.
Commandos Norway
POW murdered Sachsenhausen

Abramovicz/Abrahamovitz (aka Arlen/Arnold, Richard George)
10 Commando
KIA D-Day

Abramowski, Wigdor
1st Paras AAC
From Palestine/Israel

Adam, Frank
12/13th Paras

Amoser, Hans
(Austrian)
Commando. Also SOE?

Anderson, Alfred Valentin (aka Arnstein)
10 Commando

Anikest, Pte Ezra
(Pal)
51st Middle East Commando
KIA Tobruk

Anson, Sgt Colin Edward (aka Claus L.O. Ascher)
10 Commando
WIA Italy

Arany, P.F. (aka Masters, Lt/Sgt Peter)
10 Commando

Arnold, Pte
Commandos

Arnstein, Hans Richard (aka Andrews, Harry)
10 Commando
KIA Normandy

Ashkenazy, Lt Karol Maximillian
1st Indep Polish Paras Arnhem

Askins, Isidore Jack
Paras Arnhem

Attersley (aka Rudiger, Otto Uhlrich Etzdorf)
1 Commando

Auerhahn, Werner (aka Wells, Peter Vernon Allen)
10 Commando
KIA

Backwitz/Bachwitz (aka Blakely, Chris)
Arnhem 21st Indep Paras

Bailey, Marine Jack
46 RM Commandos
KIA D-Day

Baker, Capt Albert
RAMC Paras
Bruneval

Baker, Pte Sydney
6107762
Paras

Banks (aka Levy, Philip)
10th Paras Arnhem
WIA
POW escaped twice

Banks, Michael (Monty)
Red Devons D-Day

Barblinger, Nicholas (aka Allington)
21st Indep Paras Arnhem

Barman, Roman
3rd Polish Paras Arnhem

Barnet, Capt David Solomon
RM Commando
WIA, MC, MID Italy

Barnett, Abraham
Paras Arnhem

Barnet, L/Cpl Phillip
T76558
RASC to 716 Airborne Light Composite Coy
D-Day
WIA

Barsh, Jack
Paras

Barth, Georg Alex (aka Streets, Cad George Bryan)
10 Commando
KOAS

Bartlett, Lt Kenneth W. (aka Billman, Karl Walter)
10 Commando

Bate (aka Oppelt, Gustav?)
Commando
KIA Dieppe

Bauer, Georg (aka Bower, G.)
10 Commando

Baum, Hans (aka Trevor, Charles Leslie)
10 Commando

Baumwollspinner, Gotthard (aka Barnes, Robert G.)
10 Commando

Behman, Sgt Phillip
1489303
Paras

Behrendt, Guenter (aka O'Brian, Gene, aka Behrendt, Gideon)
Paras

Benjamin, Harold (aka Bennett)
Commando Lofoten Is. Raid

Benstock, Pte Benjamin
22967236
Paras

Bentley, Sgt Frederick (aka Bierer, Frederic)
SSRF Herne/att 62 Commando

Bergbaum, Lt Harold
3 Commando Belgium/Germany

Berger, Pte Samuel
Canadian Commandos
KIA Dieppe

Bernstein (aka Benton, Cyril)
11th Paras
POW/WIA escaper

Bier, Anatol
1st Polish Paras Arnhem
KIA

Binick, Sgt Norman
Paras Arnhem
WIA/POW, MM

Blatt, Pte Rudy
Dutch Commandos att Brit SAS and SOE, Holland, Burma.
Escaped as a POW.

Bleach, Timothy Alexander (aka Bleichroder, Adolf)
21st Indep Paras Arnhem
KIA

Blint, David
Airborne
POW

Blint, Woolf
6 Commando
POW N Africa

Block, Peter
1st Indep Paras
WIA

Block, Sgt
Glider Pilot Arnhem

Bloom, Morris
Paras Arnhem

Blumenfeld, Ludwig George (aka Merton, Lt Michael James)
10th Polish Com/10 IA
Commando/2 Comm

Boorman, Sgt John Arthur
1st Glider Pilot Regt
KIA

Boroditsky, Sgt S.L.
Canadian Command
US Special Force "The Devils Brigade" – See film of same name
– JC 16.10.42.

Boxenbaum, Harry
Commandos
POW

Brand, Lou
21st Indep Paras Arnhem

Brett, Peter Isidore
(aka Bretzfelder)
RF, att Paras at Arnhem

Breyer, Alf
6th Airborne
D-Day, POW Rhine drop

Bright, Robert
(aka Leipziger, W.)
16th Paras India

Britenbach/Breitenbach, Sgt
John (aka Brighton)
1st Pilot E Squadron GPR Down
Ampney
D-Day/Arnhem
Lived Knaresborough post war
(From comrade Larry Goldthrope,
formerly of York – info. 3.4.10)
Also, see *Fighting Back*

Brodin, E. Nick
Paras N Af/It

Brodsky, Pte Walter
4753877 *Paras*

Bromnick, Myer
Paras Arnhem
WIA/POW MID twice

Brooks, Eric
12 Paras SEAC

Brooks, Harry (aka Bruchs)
(aka Steiner, Hans)
8th Paras, 6th Airborne D-Day

Brown, Pte D.H.
24099611 *Paras*

Brown, Sgt Henry
Commandos

Brown, W.
6th Airborne D-Day

Brownleader, Pte Joseph
3658705 *Paras*

Buchanan, P/O (alias)
RN Commando. SOE

Burley, Lt Leonard Charles
(aka Berlin, Ludwig Carl)
9th Commandos/att 10
Commando

Burman, Sydney
19th Airborne Signals

Burnett, Walter (aka Indlander)
10 Commando

Burt, Jason
1st Paras
KIA Falklands 1982

Busell, Judah
1st Airborne

Cahn, Helmut (aka Curtis,
Harry)
6th Airborne, Germany
Refused to serve Palestine, court
martialled

Cahn, Major
Arnhem Paras

Calman, Calan, C.
2 Commando

Canter, Maurice
Arnhem Paras

Carason, A.
Paras

Carr, Pte
Paras Arnhem
No more info.

Carson, Andrew Peter
(aka Carlebach)
10 Commando

Chencholsky, Samuel
13th Paras
KIA

Chub, Gnr Ernest
RA 6th A-Borne Div
WIA Normandy. From S. London

Clamp, Pte Sam
Arnhem Paras
(info. Gerry Flamberg)

Clarke, K.E.
(aka Goldschlaeger)
10 Commando
MID

Cobb, Harold M.
716 Light Composite Coy
Airborne
D-Day

Cohen, A.J. and Cohen M.S.
(brothers)
Commandos
JL (Jack Lennard) Archives

Cohen, Emmanuel Mendel
OBLI Airborne Recce
KIA

Cohen, H.
628477
4th Paras

Cohen, H.
14043107
Air Support Sigs. Paras

Cohen, Harry
Commandos
KIA

Cohen, Cpl Isaac David
45 RM Commando
PO/X3246
KIA D Day

Cohen, Jack
RUR
D-Day glider landings

Cohen, Pte Jack
OBLI att. Airborne Arnhem

Cohen, Capt Kenneth J.
(aka Smith, aka Komrover[?])
POW
C Troop 6 Commando SBS

Cohen, Leon
4399650
12th Paras

Cohen, Pte Leslie
6102997 *Commandos*

Cohen, Pte Lionel
Canadian Commandos
KIA Dieppe

Collier, Joseph
3rd Paras

Collins, F.T. (aka Cohen)
No 3 Troop 10IA

Conradi, Lt Gordon Henry
Airborne signals

Cooper, Pte Harry
Paras Arnhem
POW

Cossman, Gerhardt H.C. (aka Crawford, Peter)
Paras

Coster, Sgt Sam
1st Paras Arnhem
POW/escaped

Coyne, Cpl Ralph
2/2nd Indep. Coy. Australian Commandos

Craven, Malcolm
5th Paras

Cremlin, G.J.
6th Airborne

Crossick, Mervyn
23 Para Fld Amb

Curtis, F.H. (alias)
No 3 Troop 10IA

Cuckle, Lionel
11th Paras Arnhem
WIA/POW

Daikes (alias unknown)
10 Commando

Dale, Joseph
RM Commando 2000-4
Grandson of Lt Col M. Dale, DSO, MC

Dale, Leslie (aka Litvak, Eugen)
10 Commando

Dansky, Conrad
1st Airborne

Davies, Col Gordon
South African
Commandos/SOE?

Davis, Frank M.
OBLI Airborne

Davis, H.
1st Air Landing Bde

Delafuente, David
41st RM Commandos D-Day
WIA

De Liss/Delitz, Sgt George V.
Glider Pilot Arnhem

De Liss/Delitz, Joseph
Glider Pilot Arnhem
Brother of George

De Marco, Louie
1st Paras Arnhem

Denby-Dreyfuss, P.C.
Paras D-Day
KIA

**Descarr/Dossmar
(aka Dawson, Bernard K.)**
21st Indep Paras Arnhem

Dexter, L.H.
Paras 1965

Diamand, Lewis
Airborne Arnhem

Diamond, Len
RUR
D-Day glider landings

Dias, Michael H.
23rd Para Fld Amb. 1959

**Dickinson/Dickson, Geoffrey
(aka Dobriner, Max)**
10 Commando

Dickson, John
RM 7021 *RM Commandos*
Korea

Dickson, Max (an alias)
Indep. Paras
Kindertransportee

Dixon, Alfred W.
2nd Paras

**Dobrozynski/Dobrozyski/
Dobrovski, Frank P.**
1st Paras Arnhem
KIA
Cross on grave in error

Doffman, Sydney
Paras

Donda, J.
2nd Indep Paras
KIA

**Douglas, Cpl Keith (aka
Dungler, K.)**
10 Commando

Drage, Jerry
Paras Burma

Dresser, Bernard 'Ginger'
AAC Mortar platoon Arnhem
POW escaped

Drew, Sgt Harry (aka Nomburg)
10 Commando
WIA

Dubovitch, Michael
Paras D-Day
KIA

Dudley, L.A. (aka Hirsch)
No 3 Troop 10IA

Dudley, Percy
6 Commando

Duhig
Commando
(No more known)

Dungler/Dangler (aka Douglas, Keith)
10 Commando

Dunn, D.
No 3 Troop 10IA

Dwelly, Capt Vernon
(aka Goldschmidt, Werner)
10 Commando att 4 Commando

Eden, LAC Roffer James
RAF att Paras Arnhem
KIA

Edelstein, Lt Adolf
FIU (Forward Intel Unit) – German
Speakers POW questioning
e.g. Walcheren with Special
Forces

Edwards, Albert
5th Paras

Edwards, Charles E.
7th Paras

Edwards, Sgt Stanley Joseph
Glider Pilot

Edwards, Sydney (aka Kahn)
13th Paras SEAC

Eimerl, Siegfried (aka Edwards, Sidney)
13th Paras Europe and Far East

Eisner, Adalbert (aka Edwards, Albert)
6th Paras D-Day/Europe and Far East

Elisha, Y.
Palestinian Jewish escaper
Joined Paras

Ellis, Pte Leslie
9th Paras

Ellman, Sub/Lt Sam
RN Commando
MID
Probably Jewish

Emmanuel, George D.R.
10th Paras Arnhem
KIA

Emmerach, Rfmn P.
Raiding Support
Regt/Commandos

Emmett, Lt Bunny
Att 4 Commando/10 Commando

Envers, Hans Gunter
(aka Engel, John)
10 Commando/4 Commando
WIA

Erickson, Rusty
(aka Isaacs, Eric)
1st Paras Arnhem
WIA

Ettinger, Gerry S.
Paras

Evans, Abraham
18th Air Form. Sigs.

Eversley, David E.C.
(aka Eberstadt, Ernest K.E.)
10 Commando

Fagin, Herbert
Paras

Falck, Lt Rudolf Julian
Provost Paras Arnhem
KIA

Faltitschek, H.
Paras

Farley
10 Commando
name unknown

Farr, Ernst Herbert
(aka Freytag)
10 Commando

Fauschlager
(aka Faust, Joseph Dan)
Arnhem Paras
see *SAS*

Feigen, Sgt Harold
RAF Para instructor

Fenner, Jurgen
Airborne

Fenton, Abraham
(aka Feinstein?)
Paras Arnhem
KIA

Fenton, TSM Bryan Leslie
(aka Feder, Ernst Wolfgang)
10 Commando

Fenyce (aka Fenton)
1st Indep Paras

Ferguson, K.
9th Paras

Fersht, Joseph
6th Airborne

Fetterman, Pte Sal
4755254 Paras

Fijalkowski, Lt Jerzy Zygmunt
3rd Polish Paras Arnhem
WIA VM

Finch, WO Ernest (alias)
Airborne
Germany

Fincklestein
(aka Findlay, aka Ferguson)
Commandos

Fineberg, Solomon
1st Glider Pilot Regt

Fineberg/Feinberg, 'Tetley'
D-Day
from Leeds
info from Phillip Barnet (above)

Fink, Capt Merton
Intel Corps
Pre D-Day raids on France

Firth, Lt Anthony
(aka Fuerth, Hans Georg)
10 Commando

Firth, Charles
Airborne
KIA Burma

Fischer, Walter
6 Commando
WIA

Fisher, 1st Pilot Cyril
Glider Pilot D-Day/Arnhem
KIA

Flamberg, Gerald, MM
Paras Arnhem
WIA/POW

**Fletcher, Fred
(aka Fleischer)**
10 Commando/6 Commando
KIA D-Day

Flexer, A.E.
1st Canadian Paras
KIA D-Day

Ford (aka Farago, Viktor)
10 Commando

Foster, Pte R.
(an alias)
10 Commando

Fox (aka Fuchs, Paul L.)
7th Paras

**Frank, Max Guenther
(aka Franklyn, George)**
10 Commando
KIA D-Day

Frankenburg, Dennis
5th Paras SEAC

Franks, Ronald
Glider Pilot Arnhem
KIA

Franks, W.
1st Glider Regt

**Fraser, Evelyn Harold
(aka Frey, Hubert Clarence)**
10 Commando

**Fraser, Kenneth D.
(aka Fleischmann, Kurt)**
1st Airborne Arnhem
WIA POW

Freeman, A.E. (served as Ward)
Paras Arnhem

Freeman, B.
Paras

Freeman, Lt Phillip
6th Airborne
D-Day

Freeman, Maj Thomas
RAMC Paras

**Friedlander/Freidland/
Freedlander, Gerald Eliezer**
12th Paras
KIA   7.7.44

Friedlander, Leon
Paras

Friend, Cpl Ronald
1st Btn Paras
post war

Frimond, Walter Reginald
Paras Arnhem

Fropfmachen, N.
Paras

Fryman, Bernard
Airborne Sigs Arnhem

Fuchs, Franz
Palestinian
No 2 Commando Yugos. Paras

Futter, Capt Leonard
Paras/also Commandos Arnhem
WIA/POW

**Gaensler/Gansler, Friedrich
(aka Gordon, Frederick)**
22nd Indep Paras/Pathfinders
D-Day minus 1
First Jewish soldier down

Gardner, Freddy
Paras

**Garvin, Robert Kenneth K.
(aka Goldstern, Konstantin)**
10 Commando

Gaster, Sub/Lt Jack
RN Commando
Probably Jewish

**Gautier, Jean (aka Otto
Zivolava)**
No 3 Troop JL

Gelber, Lt Ludwik George
Polish Paras Arnhem

Gellert
Polish Commandos

Gershon, Israel
12th Paras

Gilbert, Lt I.
Airborne

**Gilbert, Ronnie
(aka Guttman, Hans Julius)**
10 Commando
WIA

Giles, Peter (aka Hess, Otto)
10 Commando SOE
KIA

Ginsberg, Sgt Bertie
Glider Pilot RAF AAC
Rhine Crossing

Ginsberg, Pte David
3656209 4 Commando

Ginsberg Samuel
Airborne Div

**Glaser, Kurt Joachim
(aka Griffith, Keith John)**
*CO of 3 Troop 10 Commando/
45 RM Comm*
KIA

Glatman, Capt Leslie
Glider Pilot

Godfrey, Benjamin
1st Airborne RAMC

Gold, Joseph
Glider Pilot 3rd paras AAC

Goldberg, Bernhard
Airborne Signals

Goldberg, Frank
Paras Arnhem
POW

Goldman, Alfred
4th Paras
KIA

Goldman, Harold

Goldman, Lt Sydney Elliot
Paras

Goldsmid/Rubinstein, Phillip
6th Airborne

Goldstein
KIA Arnhem
No more known

Goldstein, Ben
156 Paras Arnhem
POW/WIA
brother of Samuel

Goldstein, Lt Isaac
47th RM Commandos
MC Normandy/WIA

Goldstein, Sgt Len
Glider Pilot Arnhem

Goldstein, Samuel
Paras
Brother of Ben

Goldstein, Sydney
1st Indep Paras Arnhem
POW

Goldstone, Sgt J.
9th Paras Merville battery
D-Day

Goldstone, Louis
6th Airborne

Goldthorpe, Sqdn/Ldr
RAF Surgeon, Paras
Yugoslav Partisans

Goodman, Benjamin
Airborne 2nd Paras
Arnhem

Goodman, Cpl John
Commandos

Gordon, Arthur Jack
1st Airborne

**Gordon, TSM Henry E.
(aka Geiser, Kurt)**
10 Commando

Goschen, Lt Col John
Airborne
Bruneval etc.

Goulden, Lt Lewis
Arnhem
MBE

Graham, Cpl P.
2nd Glider Regt

**Grant, Sgt Hubert Brian (aka
Groves, aka Goldschmidt,
Konrad Levin)**
10 Commando/SOE
WIA

**Gray, Capt Freddy (aka Gans,
Manfred)**
*10 Commando att 41 RM
Commando*

Green/Grunen
3rd Paras Arnhem

**Greenbaum, Sgt Frank (aka
Ashleigh)**
Glider Pilot
WIA/POW Arnhem

Greenfield, D.
Commando
WIA

Greenwood, Pte W.
14441765 *Paras*

**Griessman (aka Grierson,
Sir Ronald)**
21st Indep Paras, att 1st SAS
MID WIA

Groman(u), Moszek
Polish Paras
KIA Arnhem

Gruber, Fred S.H.
6th Airborne

Grunbaum, Lt Mieczyslaw
WIA Arnhem/KIA Germany
VM

Gubbay, Lt Alan
Z Force AIF
KIA   13.4.45
Lae Memorial

**Gumpertz, Kurt Wilhelm (aka
Graham, Kenneth Wakefield)**
10 Commando/4 Comm D-Day
KIA

Guttman (aka Lewis)
No 3 Troop 10 Comm

**Guttman, Capt Tony/Anton
(aka Gordon)**
21st Indep Paras Arnhem

Haeffner, Lt Bruno
Glider Pilot Arnhem - tbc

**Hagen, Sgt Louis
(aka Haig/Levy, Lewis)**
Glider Pilot Arnhem
MM

Haikin, Bernard
Paras Arnhem
KIA

Hajtler, Cpl Nissan
1st Indep Polish Paras Arnhem

Halmer, Sgt Harold
Glider Pilot Arnhem

Halpern, Howard
Commando

Hamilton, Paul (aka Herschau)
12th Paras
WIA

**Hamilton, Robert Geoffrey
(aka Weich, aka Reich, aka
Weil, Robert Salo)**
10 Commando/41 RM Comm.
KIA

Harbert, Pte S.
Paras
KIA D-Day

**Harding, Henry
(aka Heindrich Getting)**
10th Paras Arnhem

Hardman, Sgt Ephraim David
Paras Arnhem

Harris, Harry
6th Airborne
KIA

Harris, Cpl Ian (aka Hajos, Hans Ludwig)
45 RM Commando/10 Commando
MM

Harris, Sgt
Paras Arnhem

Hartman, Sydney
Paras
KIA

Heaps, Capt Leo, MC
Paras Arnhem
POW Escaped

Helfgott, Paul
1st A-Borne Malaya/India

Henriques, Lt Col Robert David Quin
Commandos
MBE, Am. Silver Star

Henry, Capt John Miles
10th Paras Arnhem
KIA

Hepworth, Freddy (aka Herschthal, Fritz)
10 Commando/att 45 RM Commando

Hepworth, Walter Douglas (aka Herschthal, Walter)
10 Commando

Herman, Pte Mark Peter
13th Paras Ardennes
KIA

Herszkowicz, Israel
3rd Polish Paras Arnhem
WIA

Hines, Col Alfred John
Paras Arnhem
MC and bar
MID twice, Order of Nassau.

Hirschfeld, Cpl Henryk
Polish Paras Arnhem

Hoffman, H.
144th Airborne Burma

Hoffman, Hans Guenter Josef (aka Compton, David Michael)
21st Indep Paras

Hoffman, Harry
Paras att. SAS
POW, escaped 3 times
MID, Purple Heart

Hollaender, Ulrich (aka M.A.Thomas)
Commandos D Day

Hollis, Pte Dennis
Glider Para Rhine crossing
MM

Homer, Benjamin Harry
12th Paras
KIA

Hornig, Paul (aka Streeten, Paul Patrick)
10 Commando att 41 RM Comm
WIA

Howarth/Howard, Lt Eric William (aka Nathan, Eli/Erich Wolfgang)
RSM 10 Commando
KIA

Hudson, Stevern Keith (aka Hirsch, Stefan)
10 Commando

Hughes, W. (aka Sachs, Walter)
Para
D-Day minus 1
POW

Hurwitz, Samuel Moses
Canadian Commandos
DCM, MM
KIA

Hutton, Harry
6th Airborne 1945
Germany

Hutton, Pte Max (aka Horwitz)
13051609 *Paras*
WIA
Took part in attack on the Merville Guns, Normandy

Hyam, Eric
Lofoten Islands Commando raid

Hyams, M.
AAC

Hyams, M.J.
AAC

Hytner, Cyril
RAMC att. 48 RM Commando
WIA D-Day

Infield/Infeld, Lt Gerald M.
1st Btn Paras at Bridge, Arnhem
POW, with Frost

Ingram, Capt Barry Barnett
Paras Arnhem
POW attempted escape

Ingram, Lt Malcolm
Paras

Isaacs, Israel
1st Airborne Paras, Arnhem
WIA

Isaacs, Laurence L.
9th Airborne Anti-Tank

Isaacs, Sgt Samuel Gregory (aka Murray)
Glider Pilot Arnhem
DFM

Isaacs, Teddy
45 RM Commando
against insurgents, Malaya

Isaaman, Lawrence
1st Air Formation

Israel, Morris
Paras CMF

Israel, Pte Reuben
Pal
51st M East Commando, to SOE

Izon, Sgt Charles
Commandos/Paras Arnhem
WIA/POW

Jackson, Fred (aka Jacobus, Peter)
10 Commando

Jackson, Wally
6th Airborne D-Day

Jacobs, Abraham Solomon
Paras Arnhem
WIA

Jacobs, D.H.
Paras Fld Amb Arnhem

Jacobs, Maj Gideon F., OBE
SOE RM Commandos Paras
Sumatra

Jacobs, Sgt J.
Commandos
Yugoslavia
South African

Jacobs, Sgt Leslie
5th Paras
D-Day

Jacobs, S.
1st Airborne

Jaffa, Mark
Paras

Jessem, Ralph (aka Jensen, aka James, Rolf)
10 Commando

Joel, Israel
13th Paras

Jones, Henry Phillip
Airlanding Regt

Jones, Jack (aka Kottka, Vladimir)
10 Commando
POW

Joseph, Harry
RM Commando D-Day
WIA

Josephs, Pte Daniel
Paras Arnhem
POW

Jublitsky, Pte Woolf
5th Paras D-Day
POW

Julius, Brig Alan
Paras and SAS Malaya

Jung, Otto (aka Young, Thomas)
6th Airborne

Kaits, Cpl Henry
RAMC Para
KIA D-Day

Kalikoff, Maurice
2nd Paras Arnhem
WIA Died of wounds

Kallar, Cpl Saul/Sydney
Paras

Kantrovitch, Sgt Abraham
Airborne

Kaplan, Cpl Leslie Eli
6th Airborne

Karger-Stein, Eugen von (aka Fuller, Eugene 'Didi')
10 Commando/47 RM Comm
KIA D-Day

Karminski, Otto 'Putzi' (aka Simon)
10 Commando

Katz, Weinhart Paul Oscar (aka Heathcote, Michael Paul)
10 Commando

Kauffman, Henry B.C.
Capt 12th Paras
KIA Reichswald

Kauffman, Lt Martin
KOSB Arnhem Paras - tbc

Kayne, Lt Dennis Benjamin
1st Paras Arnhem
POW

Keen, Denzil Myer
10th Paras Arnhem
KIA

Kelly, Bernard
(an alias)
Paras-later Israel War of Independence

Kendal, Lt George Harold (aka Knobloch, Gunther Hans)
10 Commando/2 Comm/Belgian Comm/Ski Instructor

Kendall, Bob (aka Kraus)
21st Indep Paras Arnhem

Kenneally, Sgt John (aka Lesley)
Airborne 1945–48 (Israel)
VC

Kennedy, Eric J.
2nd SAS/Commandos

Kennedy, Robert (aka Koerpel, W.)
13th Paras
WIA

Kent, John
(an alias)
Indep. Paras?
Kindertransport

Keren
No 3 Troop 10IA – JL

Kersh, Max
Paras

Kershaw, Lt Andrew G. (aka Kirschner, Andre Gabriel)
10 Commando

Kessell, Capt/Surgeon Alex Lippman
Paras Arnhem, 16 Para Fld Amb
POW/escaped
MBE, MC

Khytovitch, Sgt Eric, MM
6 Commando

King, Mendel
Paras 1960s

**King, Ronald Michael
(aka Werner Oppenheim)**
22nd Pathfinders
D-Day minus 1
9th man down/F East

**Kingsley, Lt Roger James
(aka Loewenstein, Otto Julius)**
10 Commando/41 RM Comm
OBE, MID

Kingston, Morris (aka Cohen)
Paras Arnhem
KIA

Kirby, M.J. (aka Kellman, M.)
10 Commando

Kirsch, Harry
16th Paras Fld Amb. N Africa

Klemin, Dennis Phillip
2nd Airborne

Koenigswater
No 3 Troop - JL

Kohane, Lt Col M.
RAMC Paras Italy

**Komrower, Lt Col Arthur
Geoffrey**
3 Commando
DSO

**Kraussman/Krausen, Hans
Heinz (aka Aitchison, Harry)**
10 Commando

Kronfeld, Col/Sqdn/Ldr Robert
RAF Planner D-Day Glider expert
Killed 1948

Krugman, Cpl Kersch/Heszel
1st Indep Polish Paras Arnhem

Kruyer, Harry (Chaim)
Red Devons D-Day

Kunkel, Pte Robert
Paras
DOAS buried Cyprus 1956

Kurt, Pte Sydney
14060828 *Paras*

Kurzweil, Sgt Albert Leon
Polish Paras Arnhem

Kuttner, Alfred
8th Paras
KIA
Cross on grave in error

Laddy/Lewinsky, Max
10 Commando
KIA D-Day

Ladivitch, Sgt
D-Day

Lambert, Lt Gustav J.T.
Polish Paras Arnhem

Landau, Cpl Edward Joseph
5th Paras Rhine
MM, MID

**Landau, Ernst (aka Langley,
Ernest Robert)**
10 Commando
KIA

**Landon/Langdon Walter
(aka Lewey-Lingen)**
21st Indep Paras Arnhem
KIA MID
Cross on grave in error

**Landon, Walter (aka Landauer –
NOT Lewey-Lingen)**

Landsman, Lt Joseph
Commandos
WIA Anzio KIA

Lane, Lt George (aka Lanyi)
10 Commando
MC

Lang, Jack
4th Paras
KIA

**Langford, John (aka Lehmann,
Erwin)**
6th Airborne D-Day

**Langley, Lt E.R.F.
(aka Landau)**
*10 Commando and RM
Commando*

Laskey, Cpl Cyril
RM Commando
KIA Ravenna 18.4.45

**Latimer, Cpl Maurice
(aka Loewy/Levey, Moritz)**
10 Commando Dieppe
WIA

Latz, Sgt John
*Arnhem Paras Lonsdale Force 3rd
Btn*

**Lawrence, Sgt Ernest Richard
(aka Lenel, Ernst)**
10 Commando
KIA

**Lawton, Pte Brian
(aka Lauffer, Guenther)**
Commandos

Layton, Henry (aka Lachotsky)
6th Airborne

Lebor, Phillip
Paras Arnhem

Lee, Fred
21st Indep Paras Arnhem
Dutch award for courage

Lee, Pte Harry
Paras Arnhem
POW

Lehniger, Richard (aka Leonard)
SSRF/Commando
KIA

Leigh, Eric, MBE (aka Levy)
Paras Pathfinders
MID

Leigh, Gerald
Paras Arnhem

Leigh, O/Cad P.
13116178 *Paras*

Lenel, Victor
10 Commando
Brother of Lawrence

Lent, Pte L.
6288746 *Paras*

Levien, Lt Robert Hugh
2nd Paras Arnhem
POW

Levin, Hubertus (aka Miles, Lt Patrick Hugh)
SSRF Herne/SOE/10 Commando

Levison, John Oliver
Glider Pilot Arnhem
KIA
Cross on grave in error

Levy, Pte Alfred
Paras 133 Fld Amb Arnhem
POW

Levy, Lt Ben Wolfe
RN
Extracting/inserting agents N. Africa on yacht 'Sidi Ifni'

Levy, Sgt Bob
Glider Pilot
KIA

Levy, Derek
30 Commando att. LRDG

Levy, G.E.
8th Paras

Levy, Gerald E.
3rd Paras Lonsdale Force Arnhem

Levy, Pte Harris
Paras Arnhem
WIA/POW

Levy, Sgt Harry
Paras Arnhem

Levy, Sgmn Harry
2/2nd Indep. Coy. Australian Commandos

Levy, Israel
2nd Commando

Levy, L/Cpl John
RM Commando, Malaya

Levy, Julius
Glider Pilot
KIA

Levy, Karl Ernst (aka Ken Lincoln)
10 Commando

Levy, Louis
Glider Pilot Arnhem

Levy, Maj Michael Meyer George
SOE Force 136 Malaya
MID

Lewin, Sgt Martin David (aka Lewis)
21st Indep Paras Arnhem

Lewis, Michael
2nd Paras

Lewis, Sydney
2nd Glider Regt

Licht, Leopold Ernest
Polish Troop No 10 Comm
M Cassino
Named at Sikorski Museum, London

Liebel, Peter (aka Leigh-Bell)
No 3 Troop 10 Comm

Liebeschuetz, Capt Hugo
RAMC Paras

Liebman, Maj Joe
Formed Italian Comm behind lines

Light, Kenneth (aka Klaus Licht)
10th Paras 1950s

Lincoln, Lt/Cdr Ashe
RN att 30 RM Commando
Mediterranean

Linden, Cpl Jack
Paras Arnhem
POW

Lipman, Lt Eric
2/2nd Indep. Coy. Australian Commandos

Liss, Sgt Arthur
Canadian Commandos Dieppe

Lister, Pte

Long, Peter (aka Leven, Peter Gunther)
10 Commando

Lorch, Walter
Paras

Louis, Frederick Mac (aka Lewin, Siegfried)
10 Commando

Louis, Capt Percy
RAMC
133 Para Fld Ambul Arnhem
KIA

Lowy, Arthur F.
10 Commando
(alias not known)

Lowy, J.
6th Airborne

Lozdon, Pte Maurice
Canadian Commandos
KIA Dieppe

Lucas, A.I. (aka Lowenthal, Anton)
6th Airborne Recce
WIA/POW, escaped

Luchtenstein, Hans Guenther (aka Ludlow, John Hugh)
10 Commando

Lunzer, Peter
FIU
(see Edelstein above)

Lyon, Lt James Marcus
tbc
Paras, SOE, PPA
m. to Israeli artist Miriam (Marjorie) Danziger, d.2007

Lyons (aka Isaac, Phillip)
1st Glider Regt

Lyons, Lt Samuel A.
RA
Airborne Gliders D-Day
KIA 6.6.44

Makoff, Cyril
Glider Pilot
POW, escaped

Mannings, G.
6th Airborne Recce

Mapstone, Mark William
RM Commando PO33017R
Plymouth
from London, E1

Marks, Pte Sydney
3661016 *Paras*

Martin, W. Alias
10 Commando

**Maxwell, Sgt Martin
(aka Meisels)**
Paras Arnhem
POW

Mayer, Marine
April 1943 raid on Haugersund
fiord, Norway
6 British Commandos taken by
MTB to sink German ships by
Sub/Lt John Godwin. Commandos
captured, sent to Grini then
Sachsenhausen, then Mayer and
others executed.

**McManners/McManus (alias
poss. Mertz)**
Sgt 21st Indep Paras Arnhem

Melvin, P.H. (aka Mayer)
No 3 Troop – JL

**Mendelsohn, Heinz
(aka Melford, Johnny)**
21st Indep Paras Arnhem

Mendoza, Sam
Paras Arnhem

Merton, Maj Cecil, MC and bar
Z Force, Burma

Milgrom, Jacob Jack
Paras

Mines, J.
10 Commando

Mitchell, S/Sgt James
2nd Indep Paras
BEM

Modlin, Monty
BBC Corresp Att Paras D-Day

Monahan
(alias unknown)
10 Commando

**Moody, Peter
(aka Meyer, Kurt)**
10 Commando
KIA

Mordecai, Pte E.V.
Paras at the Bridge, Arnhem
POW

Morgan, Jack
1st Airborne

**Morris, Tommy (aka Vashilofsky,
Isidore)**
Para
In 2005 oldest surviving Para,
possibly in world!

Moscow, CSM Benjamin
Commandos
KIA France

Moss, J.
No 3 Troop - JL

Most, Marine Goodman
RM Commando POX126549
1947 (Glasgow)

Myers, Brig Edmund C. Wolf
CO Engineers at Arnhem
DSO, CBE, etc

Myers, Lt Peter N.
Paras Recce Corps
KIA Italy 1944

Myers, Sgt Micky/Gerry
16th Paras Fld Amb Arnhem
POW, escaped

Myers, Stanley
RA Paras
1953-61

**Nabarro, QMS
Ronald/Raymond/Rudolf**
Paras Arnhem

**Nagle, Peter (aka Newman,
aka Walker)**
*Paras/Commandos Bruneval/St
Nazaire*
POW

Naughton
10 Commando
KIA

Naughton
(alias not known)
10 Commando
KIA (possibly cousin of above)

Naumoff, Lt
Paras Bruneval

Needleman, Sgt Jack
Glider Pilot
KIA

**Nell, Heinz Herman
(aka Nichols, Capt Gerald Peter)**
WIA rescuing Lord Lovat

Neumann, Lt Ernest
Glider pilot

Nightingale, Frank
41st RM Commando
D-Day
DCM
Lives Australia

Niven, A.Z.
8th Paras

**Niven, Nevill
(aka Nussbaum, David)**
9th Paras Arnhem
WIA/POW, escaped

**Norton, Pte Ernest
(aka Nathan, Eli/Ernst)**
10 Commando/4 Commando
KIA

Norton, Edward
6th Airborne

Novick
8th Paras
(evidence H Brook)

Opoczynski, Abraham
(aka Orr, Sgt Adam)
SAS/SSRF
KIA
See under SSRF

Orgin, Joseph
6th Airborne

Ottolangui, Solomon
2nd Paras

Paiba, Dennis A.
44 RM Commando
Later a judge

Palmer (aka Peyer)
10 Commando

Patkin, Sgt Leo
Glider Pilot
KIA

Paton, Cpl

Peters, H.
(an alias)
10 Commando

Pick, A.
Commando ski instructor
KIA Walcheren
Buried Austria

Pinkus, Sgt A.
9th Paras Merville D-Day

Pirquet, Sgt P.
No 3 Troop JL

Platteck/Plattschek
(aka Platt, 'Bubi')
10 Commando
WIA Dieppe

Pollack, Lt H.M.
MC
Arnhem/Burma

Pollaschek, O. (aka Turner, A.C.)
10 Commando

Potter, Henry Frederick
Paras

Pozner, Maj Harry, MC
RAMC Paras

Pratt (alias not known)
10 Commando
KIA

Preger, George Harry
(aka Bruce)
21st Indep Paras Arnhem

Rabinowitch, Sgt David
(aka Rabin)
5th Paras D-Day
MID

Rakussen, Seaman Monty
KIA St Nazaire Raid

Ramenski/Ramel, John
(aka J. Ramsay)
Glasgow safebreaker
30 Commando

Rams, Sgt Max
Paras Arnhem
POW/shot

Rapaport/Rappaport, Cpl
Eliyahu (?)
Commandos
KIA

Rapaport, Capt Leon Sydney
Glider pilot

Redmond, Pte Harry
5443909 *Paras*

Reed, Mark
Paras, N Ireland 1989-92

Rees, N.
Dunkirk
Paras D Day and Rhine crossing

Regert, Alex M. (aka Anthony
Richards)
Paras

Reinhold, Cpl Joseph
1st Para Pal
KIA

Reiter, Pte Herman
13807393 *Commando*

Reutner, Robert (aka Rodney)
Dunkirk/6th Airborne D-Day/Israel
Paras

Rice
Dieppe Commando
KIA

Richman, Capt Harry
Commandos CMF and Pacific

Richmond, Pte Harry
5443909 *Paras*

Rimmon, Ivor
1st Airbone
N Africa, Italy, France

Ritter, Henry/Herman
SSRF Oxf & St Geo Club
Polish Refugee

Ritterband, Montague
Was in *Paras* in WW2,
SE Asia (Java/Sumatra)
KIA Korea

Rodgers, Gnr G.E.
33 Para Fld Regt Cyprus 1955

Rose, Roland
Glider Pilot
D-Day and Arnhem
WIA

Rosen
Polish Commandos
Cross of Valour Cassino

Rosenberg
Pal Jew on 'Operation Typical'
SOE May 1943
Para to support Tito

Rosenberg, Sgt John N.
MM
Paras Arnhem

Rosenberg, Sgt S. (aka Ronald)
Arnhem Paras
POW

**Rosenberg, Stefan
(aka Rigby, Stephen)**
*unknown Commando No 3 Troop,
10 Commando*
Did he exist?

Rosenbloom, Sgt
MM
Arnhem Paras sniper expert
He and Rosenberg J N refused to
serve Palestine

**Rosenfeld, Hans
(aka Rodley, Peter John)**
Paras Arnhem
KIA

**Rosenthal/Rosen
(aka Redferne)**
Arnhem Paras

Rosenthall, Sgt Abraham (?)
unarmed combat instruc. Paras

Rossdale, Sgt Harvey/Harry
Glider Pilot D-Day
WIA

**Rosskamm, Stephan
(aka Stephen Ross)**
10 Commando att 9 Comm Italy
WIA

**Rothbart, Erwin (aka Rivers,
Max)**
Paras Arnhem
KIA

Rothschild, Freddy
(alias not known)
10 Commando

Rozen, Cpl B.J.
10 Commando
MM

**Rubenstein, Sgt Theodore
Albert**
Glider Pilot Arnhem
KIA

Rubin, L.S.
181 Para Fld Amb Arnhem

Rubin, Leonard
2 Commando
KIA

Rubinstein, Pte Sydney
Arnhem Paras
POW

Sachs, Herbert (aka Seymour)
10 Commando
KIA

Sachs, Lt John
Australian Z Force
POW/executed by Japanese
MM

Salik, Sgt David
Polish Paras Arnhem

Salomons, Sgt Joseph Lowden
Airborne OBLI
KIA

**Saloschin, Victor
(aka Saunders)**
No 3 Troop, 10 Comm

Saltman, Pte Jack
Paras Arnhem
POW

Sampson, Sgt Fred
AAC

**Samson, Lt Alfred
(aka Shelley, Percy)**
*No 3 Troop, 10 Commando/att
RM Comm*

Samuel, Lt Col Clive Marshall
114 Paras Field Amb
DOAS Cyprus/Kenya/Aden
MBE bravery

Sander, Lt Gustav
Arnhem Paras
KIA Korea with *Middx* 10/50

Sanders/Saunders, L/Cpl
10IA

Saunders, Sgt Joseph Harry
5624611 *Paras*

Saunders, Ken
11th Btn Devons
Glider landing D-Day

**Schilling, Sgt
(aka Harold Bruce)**
21st Indep Paras Arnhem

Schivern (aka ??)
21st Indep Paras Arnhem

**Schlesinger, Robert
(aka Bobby Shaw)**
POW Paras Arnhem

Schlonovien
21st Indep Paras

**Schloss, Jakob
(aka Scott, Jack)**
10 Commando liason Tito on Vis

Scholem, Robert
2 Commando
KIA

Schubert-Stevens, Eric
21st Indep Paras Arnhem

**Schultz (aka Schulberg, Ellis
'Dutch')**
Arnhem Paras

Schwartz, Donald R.
7th Paras
KIA

Schwartz, Lt Ralph Harding
Paras Arnhem

Schweitzer, Dennis
*1st Airborne Af, lt; 6th Airborne
Palestine*
(Sheffield)

**Schwitzer, Tamas Gyorgy
(aka Swinton, Tommy)**
*10 Commando att 41 RM
Commando*

Scully, Pte Len
Commando St Nazaire
(Glasgow)

Sebba, Samuel
6th Airborne att SAS OBLI
D-Day
MID

Secter, Capt Jack M.
*Canadian US Special Force
'The Devil's Brigade' (see movie
of that name) JC 16.10.42*
MID

Selby, W.
13046307 *Commando*

Sevitt, Pte L.
23660546 *Paras*
Disch. 1958

Schneidermann, Sam
R Naval Frogman WW2
(from friend in AJEX)

Shaw, Harry
6th Airborne

Shaw, P.F. (aka Schonfeld)
3 Troop 10IA

Sher, Pte Greg
1st Australian Comm
KIA Afghanistan Jan 2009

**Sheridan, Melvin R.
(aka Saloman, Mendel)**
101A Commando

Sherman, Sgt Alf
*NX71356
2/5 Australian Ind Comm, New
Guinea*

Shotolinsky, Raymond David
Dunkirk and Paras
Buried in Cardiff

Shovel, Sgt Raphael
Glider pilot D-Day and Arnhem
WIA

Silifonts, Simon Aron
Paras/Commando
KIA Italy

Silver, Joseph
AAC

Silvert, P.
Paras
KIA D-Day

Simeon/Simon, Sgt Ernst
Paras Glider Pilot Arnhem
KIA

Simon, Capt R.H.S.
2nd Air Formation Signals

Simons, Mike
Commando

Singer, Alfred
6th Airborne Recce
WIA

Singer, Pte Ronald
Paras
Cyprus 1955

Smith
Commando
KIA Dieppe

Smith, J. (aka Sleigh?)
(an alias)
10 Commando

Smollan, Pte H.
7th Bat Paras
KIA 7.4.45
One of three brothers killed

Sobotka
21st Indep Paras Arnhem

**Solomon, Laurence
(aka Scott)**
21st Indep Paras Arnhem
Post war GM Met. Police

Specter, Maj J.M.
*Canadian Special Services
Bde/Commandos*
KIA Italy

Spencer, Frederick
10 Commando
Alias not known

Spiegelglass, Mane
Paras Arnhem
DCM KIA

Spielman, E.
Pal Driver/3 Troop, 10 Commando

Spiewak, Pte G.
13120163 *Paras*

**Stanleigh, Sgt John Hubert
(aka Schwartz, Hans)**
21st Indep Paras Arnhem

Steele-Baume, Lt Eric H.
*Cameronians
Arnhem Paras tbc*

Stein, Artur (aka Spencer, Tom)
10 Commando att 3 Comm

Stein, Cpl
Paras

**Steiner, Uli (aka Scott, Capt
Leslie)**
3 Troop 10 Commando last CO

**Stenham, Robert Eric
(aka Stern)**
*22nd P/Finders, D-Day 8th man
down*
WIA Rhine crossing

Stephens, Freddy
Paras

Stern, Sgt Erwin
Mountain Commandos CMF

Stern, Hans
8th Paras
Evidence H. Brook

Stern, John
2 Commando
Lived Warwickshire

**Stevens, Harry George
(aka Steiner, Heinz Georg)**
RM/RN Commando

Stevens, J.
(an alias)
10 Commando

Stevens, T.
(an alias)
10 Commando

Stewart, Lt David (aka Strauss)
10 Commando att. 45 RM Commando

Stewart, J.
(an alias)
10 Commando

Stone, Sgmn Bernard
Roy Nav Comm
Probably Jewish

Stringman, Pte J.
3964339 *Paras*

Stuppel, Maj R.
Commando/SOE with Tito
KIA Yugoslavia

Subak (aka Sharpe, John Herbert)
Paras

Subkovitch
Arnhem Paras

Sumeray, Sgt Malcolm
11th Paras Arnhem
WIA/POW

Sumray, Pte Hyman
13th Paras
KIA

Sunderland, A.
13th Paras Arnhem
POW

Sutton, Lt Frances George
10IA Commandos

Szauer, Gyula Jence (aka Sayers, Gordon Julian)
French Troop 10 Commando 4 Comm
WIA Croix de Guerre

Szreiber, Cpl Jozef
2nd Polish Paras Arnhem

Tannenbaum, Lt Albert Louis
2nd Paras Arnhem
WIA POW

Taylor, Alec Louis
Paras Arnhem
KIA

Taylor, B.
3 Commando
KIA   -.6.44

Taylor, John (aka Theilinger, Jan)
3 Troop 10 Commando, also Spanish CW
(info. from children)

Taylor, H.
13th Paras
KIA Ardennes

Tazgal, N.
9th Paras

Teichman, Col Phillip
2nd Paras
KIA

Telechowicz, C/E
13th Paras

Tenczowski, Michael
9th Paras

Tepper
22nd Ind Paras
Evidence H. Brook

Thornton
alias not known
10 I.A.

Tischler (aka Peter Terry)
10 Commando SSRF/SOE att 47 RM Commando
WIA

Tomkins, J. (aka Teisher, Julius)
6th Airborne

Trepel, Charles
10 Commando, French Troop

Trojan, Richard Walter (aka Tennant, Richard William)
10 Commando

Urich, Lt Dr Henryk
Polish Paras Arnhem

Valencia, L/Cpl Joseph
6020761 *Paras*

Verhoeff, Anthony William
10th Paras
KIA Arnhem

Victor, Capt Maurice
1st Airborne Arnhem
Order of Nassau

Villiers, Ernest Robert (aka Vogel, Egon)
10 Commando att 46 RN Commando
KIA

Vine, Norman Alexander
6th Airborne
KIA

Vogelman, Lt
Paras
MC
South African

Wallace, C. (aka Wapnitski)
253 Airborne Coy

Ward, G. (aka Woolf)
6436380
10 Commando

Warren, H.
(an alias)
10 Commando

Warwick, R.
(an alias)
10 Commando

Wasserman, O. (aka Watson, William Walter)
10 Commando
WIA

Waxman, John (aka Wolfgang Wachsmann, John Hayes)
6th Airborne
Formerly no 3 Troop 10IA Comm

Weikerscheimer, L. (aka Wallen, Leslie)
10 Commando

Weil, Lt G.R.
AAC Paras

Weinberg, Sgt K.
(aka Mason, Gary)
10 Commando

Weinberger, E.G.
(aka Webster, Ernest George)
10 Commando SSRF/47 RM
Comm
KIA

Weiner
(an alias?)
Paras Arnhem

White/Weiss, Adi (aka White,
Alan)
10 Commando

White, 'Ikey'
Glider Pilot

Wientrobe, Solomon, GM
Paras

Wilby, Sam (aka Wiseberg)
Paras
KIA N Africa

Wilmers, Capt John Geoffrey
(aka Wilmersdoerfer, Hans
Johann)
10 Commando att SAS

Wineberg, Pte I.
5891086
Paras

Wisebad, Sgt Julius
Glider Pilot
KIA Arnhem

Witko, Lt Paul Weitzen
Polish Paras Arnhem

Wolf, P/O Basil
RN Commando
MID

Wolf, Walter L. (aka Marshall,
Alan W.)
10 Commando
WIA Cassino

Woltag, Sgt Hyman 'Wally'
Glider Pilot D-Day/Arnhem
WIA

Woolfe, Raymond David
Paras

Wyss/Weiss, Capt Edward
Mariel
Paras
KIA Arnhem

Yallow/Yellow, Hyman
Para at Arnhem
Mentioned in *Ham and High*
article Sept 1946?

Yank, Capt Danny
148 Commando
Afghanistan 2010

Yapp, Francis 'Buster'
Paras
KIA Arnhem
Cross on grave in error

Yentis, Harry
Arnhem Para
No more known

Yetzes, Joseph
1st Airborne

Young, C.C.
5th Paras

Young, Pte Warner
14443944
Paras

Zadik, Walter Gabriel (aka
Thomson, Sgt Walter Gerald)
10 Commando att 4 Comm
POW

Zeff, Monty
Paras and instructor

Zimmerman, Harry
Paras Arnhem
KIA

Zittman, Cpl Ernest A.
Paras Arnhem
POW

Zivohlava, J. (aka Gautier, Jean)
French
10 Commando

Zucker, Desire D.C.
Arnhem Paras

Zweig, Werner (aka Nelson, Sgt
Vernon)
40 RM/46 RN Commandos
WIA Italy MID

Zwergfeld, Pte Herbert
14459206 *Paras*

Palestinian Jews

Agayev, AS Jacob
RN
Pal Jewish 'Ghost Commando'
Att SOE, served Greece
Survived

Benelisha, Samuel
SBS Motor Boat Coy/Commando
KIA

Ben Shiprut, AS Shmuel
RN
Pal Jewish 'Ghost Commando'
Att SOE, served Greece
Survived

Ben Yosef, Arye
51st ME Commando
KIA

Carmi, Israel (aka Weinman)
SIG
Col. Police Medal

Cohen, Dov
SIG
KIA Acre prison raid 1947, Israel

Drori, Cpl Avshalom
Commando
Raid on Rommel with Keyes, VC

Fisher, Morris
51st ME Commando
KIA

Furt, Moshe
51st ME Commando
KIA

Goldstein, H. (aka Wilenski)
SIG SAS/LRDG

Golomb, AS Yoel
RN
Pal Jewish 'Ghost Commando'
Att SOE, served Greece
Survived

Gottlieb, Eliyahu
SIG
KIA

Hass/Hess, Peter
SIG
KIA

Hausmann, L/Cpl Fritz Sigmund
2 Commando att. SAS
DCM Yugoslavia

Heckssher, Pte
Commandos

Hillman, Capt Charles Leo F. (aka Kennedy, aka Steiner, Peter/Hefer/Gerber)
SIG, SAS, Comm, SOE
Rommel Raid
MM MC

Hollander, Herbert Paul (aka Delmonte-Nietto)
SIG

Kahane/Cahanna, Karl
SIG/SAS/SBS

Kasap, Yechiel Asher (aka Kasp, Jechel Usher)
'A' Force to free POWs
DCM, MM
KIA

Kogel, Phillip (aka Schrager-Iser, Phillip)
SIG

Kohn
Airborne

Kostica, AS Shlomo
RN
Pal Jewish 'Ghost Comm'
Att SOE, served Greece
Survived

Lishinski, AS Mordechai
RN
Pal Jewish 'Ghost Commando'
Att SOE, served Greece
Survived

Lowenthal, Bernard
SIG

Oprover/Opprower/Ofover, A. (aka Weizmann)
SIG
KIA

Orlich, Pte
52nd ME Commando
KIA with Weinstein and Officer Frost

Osterman, Werner
51st ME Commando
KIA

Rappaport, Eliyahu
51st ME Commando
KIA

Roer/Rohr, J. (aka Berg)
SIG att SAS
POW/WIA

Rosenstein, L/Cpl Ernest Zeno
No 2 Commando Yugoslavia
KIA

Rosenstein, Pte H.
Commando
KIA

Rosenstein, Uri
Commando
KIA

Rosenzweig (aka unknown)
SIG

Segal, Joseph
51st ME Commando
MID

Shai, Ariyeh (aka Sheikin/ Sheinik)
SIG

Spector, AS Yitzhak
RN
Pal Jewish 'Ghost Commando'
Att SOE, served Greece
Survived

Spielman, Ernst
Commandos Italy

Swet, Zvi (aka Bruda, Vic)
2 Commando
WIA Italy

Tieffenbrunner/Tiffen, Maurice
51st ME Commando, SIG att SAS
POW

Ulrich, Yitzak
51st ME Commando
KIA

Urban, Richard
att LRDG

Weinstein, Sgt Shmaryahu
52st ME Commando
KIA

Wise, Samuel
51st M East Commando

Zentner/Zeitner, Dolph
SIG

Zwik, Mordechai
51 M East Commando
KIA Eritrea

Jews Who Served with Wingate's Chindits in Burma

My thanks go to the Chindit OCA and all the veterans who helped me compile this list by contacting me through the various advertisements I placed in the *Jewish Chronicle*, *British Legion Journal*, *Dekko* (journal of the Burma Star Association), *Wartime News*, the *AJEX Journal* and other publications. Without their help, this work would not have been possible. I am especially grateful to Colonel Orde Wingate, the late General's son, for contacting me with some useful information. I am also grateful to the courageous American veterans of the USAAF Commando who provided names of their comrades who took part in the airlifting in and out of supplies and men on the two Chindit raids.

The list is clearly incomplete and this research would surely have revealed an astonishingly greater picture of the contribution of Jewish troops to the Chindits had it been completed twenty years ago when more eyewitnesses would have been alive. (NB: Further details on these can be found in Martin Sugarman, *Fighting Back* [London and Portland, OR: Vallentine Mitchell, 2010].)

Asher, Sgt
S. Staffs
KIA attack on Mogaung 23.6.44
See P.D. Chinnery, *March or Die*,
pp.215–16
Probably Jewish; no AJEX card.

Berkovitch, Pte Len Frank
*378027 13th King's Liverpool
Regiment*
From Manchester
POW with Frank (listed below) in
Rangoon Jail – info from Frank.
He survived.

Berkovitz, A/Sgt Pte Sam
*13091795 2nd/13th Btn
Sherwood Foresters & SEAC
Lancs Fus/Border Regt*
Served in Calvert's Chindit column
as a Bren gunner.
Born East End of London,
30.3.06, died 30.10.98

Bick, Sgt Gabriel 'Gaby'
*6095498 2nd Queen's Own RW
Surrey/Essex Regt/Chindits Sig
and Intel*
Died post-war in Ramat Gan,
Israel
Named in D. Moore, *GI Jews*,
p.114

Bresler, Lewis
13043873 RWF

Broder, Pte Harry Leon
*7369228 180/215th Field
Ambulance RAMC*
Served Col. 45 with Chindits

Broomkin/Bloomkin, Monty (?)
Duke of Wellington's, att. Chindits

Camp, A.L.
*5952706 'D' Coy, 5th Beds &
Herts Regt*

Caplan/Kaplan/Caplin, Pte Sid Ellis
3780118 13th King's Liverpool Regiment
POW with Frank – info. from Frank. Survived.

Chadwick, Fus Michael (aka Freedman)
4202412 10th Btn RWF, later att. 23rd Bde Chindits
(Info. from M. Cohen, listed below)

Chester, Alfred
Poss. Pte R. Chester, 14203953, Warwicks Regt

Cohen, Pte Mendel/Manny
3602186 4th Btn Border Regt
23rd Bde Chindits under Brig Fergusson
Served India/Burma 1942–45

Cross, Cpl John Denis
6827042 HAC/Royal West Kent/Essex Regt
Born 9.1.18, died 1972
Son of H.B. Cross, 38th Jewish Btn RF WW1

Crowne, C/Cdr Maj Joseph George
Brigade Sig Off, formerly Beds & Herts Regt.
7th Nigerian Regt/Gold Coast – WAF GHQ
MBE for 'gallant and distinguished service with the Chindits'
JC, 6.45 with photo

Da Costa, Capt Darnley Peter Lamont
121576 7th Leics Regt
KIA 14.7.44, buried Taukkyan 6 F 1, Burma
Brother Patrick in 1st Irish Guards, also KIA 30.1.44

Dubora, Sgt John (Julius)
6149595, 6th E. Surreys att. 6th Nigeria

Davis, Pte Ernest 'Dave'
6022982 Essex Regt

Duque, L/Cpl Shimshon (Samson)/Simon S.
14203623 1st Btn King's Liverpool Regt/
15th Btn Queen's Roy Regt
– 81 column, 77th Brigade, Chindits
KIA 'Blackpool' stronghold 15.5.44, aged 21
Buried Rangoon.
Son of Rabbi I.D. Duque, Bevis Marks

Englhardt, Maj Charles L.
0-729107 1st Air Commando USAAF/Chindits

Farber, Pte Hyman
3781622 13th Btn, King's Liverpool Regt/Chindits
MIA/KIA 8.5.43, aged 32
Commemorated Rangoon Memorial, Myanmar,
Taukkyan War Cemetery, north of Rangoon, face 5

Feldman, Sgt Abraham (Alf)
6898926 35 Column Intel NCO det. from 8th Btn Black Watch to 7th Nigerian Regt

Finestein, Gnr David
1090904 RA
60th Field Regt att. Chindits, 23rd Bde column, 2nd exped.
'Batman' to Lt L. Grove

Frank, Pte Leon
3780682 13th Platoon, 13th Btn, King's Liverpool Regt
On Operation Longcloth 1943, Column 7
POW, 21.4.43 in Rangoon

Franks, RSM Leslie S.
6092321/10020606 Queen's RW Surrey Regt

Franks, Sgt (later Maj) Ralph
3781685 King's Regt

Freedman, Sgt Arthur Isidore
S/14269034 RASC
Chindits Intelligence HQ.

Freedman, Pte Joseph
4200940 2nd KOR Regt, Lanc.
KIA 25.5.44, aged 27; Rangoon Memorial, face 5.

Glassman, Pte Harry
5339452 1st Beds & Herts Regt
KIA 12.6.44, aged 27; buried Gauhati, India, 4 C 11.

Gordon, Pte Hyman
3534963 10th Btn Loyal Regt/Border Regt
WIA aged 29 (*JC*, 27.4.45)

Green, Sgt Arthur
7668275/1523050 W. Yorks/ RA HAA, 296 Battery, att. Chindits
Recommendation for MID, not given

Greenberg, L/Cpl Harry
3781716 13th Btn, King's Liverpool Regt
Died of illness/wounds, 20.8.43, aged 30
Buried St Mary's Cemetery, Madras

Harris-Taylor, Captain Herbert 'Berty', OBE
140674 Liverpool Regt/2nd Btn Duke of Wellington's att. Chindits 2nd expedition

Isaacs, L/Bdr Peter George
11410057 RA

Lempert, Pte Jacob
6479057 Roy Fus/1st Btn S. Staffs/Chindits
KIA 23.6.44, aged 31
Field burial at Mogaung, later buried at Taukkyan,
plot collective row, grave 14, grave E, 1–8
Memorial plaque in the Sandys Row Dutch Syn., Whitechapel, E1

Levene/Levine, Pte G./James or Josh 'Lefty', DCM
3777022 77th Bde under Brig Mike Calvert/
1st Btn King's Liverpool Regt
Awarded DCM at Battle of Mogaung, Burma 1944
Liverpool Echo, 27.4.45; *LG*, 26.4.45, p.2212
Buried at Allerton RC Cem, 23.12.48: father Jewish

Levene, Cpl Morris,
3779294 13th King's Liverpool Regt

Levy, L.
45 Recce Regt
(possibly Leslie 6476761)

Lindo, Jack J.
Liverpool Regt
Of Jewish origin

Luck, Pte Basil Michael
6026356 formerly 26th Hussars/ 2nd Btn Yorks & Lancs/Essex Regiment
14th HQ Brigade
WIA 18.4.44

Marks, Brig Neville
Special Forces, Chindits
KIA

Milgrom, Jacob 'Jack'
14517215 Essex Regt
Also served with *Paras*

Pavlotsky, Pte Morry
4808743 2nd Yorks & Lancs Regt
Died 26.4.44, aged 36
Buried Taukkyan, Burma, 14 C 10.

Pennamacoor, John Jacob
22224506 No. 9 RAMC
Regular soldier until 1952

Rodrigues, Pte M.
2035089 1st Btn Essex Regt

Rome, L/Cpl Maurice 'Monty'
5953142 Beds/Herts/Essex Regt
Served Egypt, Palestine, Ethiopia, Sudan, Iraq, Syria, India and Burma with Chindits under Brigadier Perowne (HQ Signals section),

Rose, Lt Lionel
214106 Sherwood Foresters
HQ Staff Coy with Wingate and CO of the Gurkha HQ Defence Platoon.
MIA 9.4–1.5.43
POW Rangoon

Rosenberg
44 or 56 Column, 2nd expedition
From Leeds

Rosewood, Pte Nathan
5260505 1st South Staffs
Killed 17.3.44, aged 21
Buried Taukkayan, Burma, 6 B 16

Saffer, 2/Lt Neville Nathan
5979048/162342 'B' Coy, 14th Platoon
13th Btn, King's Liverpool Regt
KOAS with Chindits, 28.8.42 (?)
Buried Ramna Forest Pathania, India

Sampson, Cpl Alf
6023036 Essex Regt/1st Btn DLI
2nd Chindit Campaign
Artist and soldier

Samuels, Capt Jessel
Chindit/Army HQ liaison officer

Samuelson, Lt (later Maj) Sir Michael, MBE
HAC/Leicesters
att. Chindits under Colonel Lockett
Of German Jewish origin

Schieferstein, R.J.
1st Air Commando, USAAF
Of Reading, Pennsylvania

Segal, Maj Harry C.
23rd Brigade HQ

Shaw, Willy

Simmons, Pte Henry
1092769 51st Field Regt, RA
WIA Tobruk, then to Ceylon and India, and to 'White City' by Dakota with Chindits, under Major Fergusson, 2nd Chindit expedition

Sonnenfield, Gnr Bernard
1111578 RA
1st Expedition with Colonel Fergusson

Specterman, Alfred
RA
With Henry Simmons, listed above

Stupack, L/Cpl Bernard
2347255 Royal Signals

Summers, Dvr Morris
222851 RASC
Father, Samuel, served 39th Jewish Btn RF in WW1

Taylor, WO/AG Basil
1113615 RAF

Werthizer, Joseph (aka Velsizer/Worth)
14517316 RE att. Essex Regt

Winston, Pte Dvr 'Myer' Harry (aka Winstein)
7651768 RAOC/REME, att. Chindits
Also served North Africa, Madagascar and India

Zeigler, Col C.E.
1st Air Commando USAAF
Of Alexandria, Virginia

British and Commonwealth Jews in the Korean War

For help in compiling this list of almost 100 names I would like to thank Sidney Goldberg, former Vice-Chair of AJEX, and Henry Morris, AJEX Museum Curator, for all their encouragement. I would also like to especially thank the many veterans and their families, Jewish and non-Jewish, who wrote to me from all over the world – including Canada, the USA and Israel – with information. Without their assistance the work could never have been started.

As with all such studies this list will always be incomplete. Information can come only from surviving veterans who make themselves known through appeals in Korean War veterans' journals, and other magazines and journals. I placed appeals in the *AJEX Journal*, the *Jewish Chronicle*, Korean War veterans' groups' journals, the *British Legion Journal* and other related publications.

Major Isaacs (see below) testified to the author that there were many Jewish servicemen serving with him among the Royal Fusiliers in Korea, and several killed whom he helped to bury. We both concluded that they must have attested to being C. of E. and/or changed their names on being called up for National Service, as records of burials and other rolls or casualty lists reveal very few Jewish names. We will thus never really know the full extent of the Jewish community's contribution. However, by scanning the War Diaries of the Royal Fusiliers at TNA, I discovered many names, cross-referenced with the AJEX Jewish Chaplain Cards, of Jewish lads who served (indicated as PRO-RF in the text). We know that not all the cards are complete, and hence it is always the case that some veterans' cards cannot be found.

The *JC* of 31 July 1953 stated that there were 4,000 Jewish servicemen and women serving in the Allied Forces in Korea, mostly American.

Alt, Walter
Royal Canadian Corps of Signals
Formerly British Army, WW2
(Possibly 13120004 Abraham Alt
as per Jewish Chaplains Cards)

Abingold
From Liverpool
Named as serving in Korea in *JC*,
8.5.53, p.18.

Apter, Capt Isidore
421996 RADC

Babot, Pte Anthony
22168031 Middx Regt
JC, 23.5.52, p.32.

Back, Spr David
22759423 RE

Balcon, Maj Michael Arnold
349943 RA/1st Btn Roy Warwicks

**Bamberger, Sqdn/Ldr Cyril
Stanley, DFC + Bar**
116515 RAF Intelligence, Korea
RAF WW2, Bat of Britain ace

Bellman, Bernard
2430125 RAF
AT Control, also Berlin Airlift

**Benjamin (now Bennett), Harold
Gershon**
2328455 RCOS
WW2 veteran of Lofoten Islands
Commando raid, Iceland, North
Africa

Bentley, Cpl (later Dr) H.
22943686 RAMC
IDF in Six-Day War

Bernstein, Pte Aubrey
22985360 RASC

Brice, Geoffrey
FAA; HMS Glory

Carson, Pte Frank Frederick
22611667 RAPC
In the BAOR, posted to Korea in
1951 (PRO-RF)

Charig, Lt Brian
Died December 2006 – obituary,
JC.

Cohen, Bernard
FAA
HMS *Glory*

Cohen, Pte Victor
22992559 RAOC – 1st Comm. Div

Cohen, Sgt Julius
14452236 KSLI

Cohen, David
Info. from L. Keene; no more
known.

Cohen, Fus H.
22493698 1st Btn, Roy Fus
(PRO-RF)

Cohen, Maj Elliot L., OBE
*CO 'B' Coy, 1st Btn Roy Canadian
Regt*
At Hill 355 (Little Gibraltar) in
October 1952
JC, 31.10.52, p.24

Cohen, Pte Gerald
22650106 1st Btn, Roy Fus

Cornell, Tpr Frank
7893184 RAC

Collins, Spr Malcolm
22937819 RE

Dickinson, Capt K.
427856 RAMC
Possible MC

Dickson, John
RM7021 45 RM Commando
Also served Malaya

Dickson, Joseph
RN
Brother of John Dickson above.

Dixon, Capt Graham Gershon
*ZD10253 Canadian Roy 22nd
Regt, Infantry*
Regular soldier for 16 years

Driberg, Tom, MP
War correspondent

Drogie, L/Cpl Conrad Percy
*S/22637658 38/39th Platoon,
RASC*
JC, 24.4.53

Dubow, Sgt Vivian
*22933997 'E' Trp RCOS of 19th
Fld/Regt, RA*

Ellerman, A/Sgt Howard Peter
23093366 'C' Coy, RAMC
12.54–12.56, Japan and Korea

Ellis, Pte Alfred
22860834 Roy Irish Fus
to 1st Btn Commonwealth Div

Engelsman, Capt Henry
433532 RADC

Feinstein, Fus Jack
*22650111 1st Btn, 'D' Coy,
12 Platoon, 3 Section, Roy Fus*
Bren gunner, served at battles of
Inchon, The Hook, Hill 355

Fineberg, Pte Samuel
*2239370 29th Field Ambulance,
RAMC*

Freedman, Sgt Alec 'Moishe'
'B' Coy, 1st Btn Leicestershires
Battle of Italy Hill (Hill 317)
Later resident at Royal Hospital
Chelsea

Gabriel, Pte Bertram
23022452 RAOC
1954 Korea and Japan

**Gilmour/Gilmore
(aka Ginsburg/Ginsberg)**
RADC

Goldstein, Fus A.
22594482
PRO-RF

Greenbaum, Fus E. Teddy
22650113 1st Btn Royal Fus

Hearne, Dvr Sidney
T22911049 RASC

Herman, Pte Dennis
22868160 RAOC

Hyams, Tpr H.
22457395 5th Dragoon Guards

Isaacs, Maj Bernard Arthur (aka Irvine)
22361530/414377 KRRC/1st Btn KSLI/1st Btn Roy Fus
MC, MID twice, US Citation
21 years' service
WIA and POW

Jaffey, Maj, OBE
Canadian Forces

Karsberg, Cpl Barry
S/22451246 RASC/Roy West Kent Regt
HMT *Empire Pride* to Japan and Korea
JC, 17.10.52, p.13

Katz, Sgt Stanley
2435534 RAF Bomb Disposal 42 Group Maintenance

Katzin, Col Alfred G.
Personal representative of
UN Secretary General Trygvie Lee
JC, 21.7.50.

Keene, Pte Leon
23171332 1st Btn Roy Sussex Regt
and ACC

Kisch, Lt Michael S.
413358/2234477 2nd Field RE
Son of Brigadier Kisch, KIA in WW2

Kosmin, Pte Gerald Emmanuel
22943980 Royal Signals
Radio mechanic

Krimholtz (now Kaye), Cpl Lionel
22493234 RAOC
Base Ammunition Depot, Zong Zang, near Pusan

Langdon, Pte Godfrey
6631255 RCOS
Formerly S/Sgt WW2, France & N. Africa
Recommended for MID

Lehrer, Pte Leon
S/227443822 RASC

Levy, Lt A.
From Istanbul
ADC to Commanding Officer of Turkish Brigade

Levy, A/Sgt H.
1485439 RWK att. RF
WIA 27.6.53
PRO-RF roll

Levy, Lt Meyer Michael George
Princess Patricia's Canadian LI, 'D' Coy, 10th Platoon
Formerly SOE 136 Force Malaya 1944–45
MID

Lipawasky, Capt Gordon Benjamin, DFC
SAAF
Shot down but survived

Lobell, Barry (not real name)
POW of the Chinese

Manasseh, Spr Jonathan Ellis
22318551 RE

Marks, Pte D.
21127179 Gloucestershire Regt
MIA/POW 26.4.51

Marks, Pte D.H.
Duke of Wellington's (West Riding) Regt
WIA 6.6.53

Marks, Lt Col R.L.
26th Field Ambulance, RAMC

Mazin, Pte Maurice Martin
22307199 RAOC, 1st Comm. Div

Miller, L/Cpl H.
22559891 BAOR
Posted to Korea
On PRO-RF roll

Myers, Col E.C. Wolf
Engineers
MID for gallantry, Jan–June 1952
JC, 17.10.52, p.13
Served at Arnhem and in SOE in Yugoslavia in WW2

Myers, Lou
2201375 Combined Operations
WW2 RM in N. Africa
Israel Machal 1948–50
Korea 1950–52

Myerthall, Cpl Solly
22541117 RASC

Orbaum, Sgt Eric Jack
22859663 RASC

Ottolangui, Pte Morris
22576845 ACC att. RF, 'D' Coy, 1st Btn
PRO-RF roll

Phillips, Pte Peter
Roy Fus

Phillips, L/Cpl Sam
22929428 RAMC, 26th Field Ambulance
Served in Japan and 9 months in Korea, British and Commonwealth Comms Zone Medical Unit
UN Korea Medal

Rairu, Pte Joe
Roy Fus

Rapaport, Cftmn Louis
22616095 REME and 1st Btn DLI

Renack, P/O John 'Jack'
FX584695 FAA
Also WW2

Rondell, A/Sgt Issy (aka Reynolds)
22943905 29th Brigade, RA
Born Poland, survived Nazi death camps

Ross, Sgt Harold Colin
22895132 26th Field Ambulance,
1st Commonwealth Div
Section commander Battle of The
Hook and Stand of the
Gloucesters

Schwartzman, Pte Arnold M.
23179534 1st Btn Roy Sussex
Regt/RAEC

Shaffer, Fus A.
22508074 1st Btn Roy Fus/BAOR
Posted to Korea
PRO-RF roll

Share, Stanley
22928876 15th Coy, RASC

Sharp, Intel Sgt (later Maj)
David, BEM
14472846 Served 1st Malay
Scouts, later 22 SAS Malaya/ HQ
29th Indep Inf Bde Group
att. 1st Btn Roy Northumberland
Fus
Captured at Imijin River, 25.4.51,
three times wounded
Last (946th) POW to be released
9.53, aged 25
JC, 13.4.53 and 11.53; *Daily*
Express, 7.9.53
BEM and US Gallantry Award
Recommended for GC but passed
over

Silver, Gnr Neville
22387810 RA 14/24th Bty 61st
L/Regt
Hong Kong and Korea
Served 12.51 to 4.52

Silver, Pte Phillip M.
22700971 RASC

Solomon, Fus Maurice
2258037 BAOR
Posted to Korea – PRO-RF

Sonsky, Pte Eddie
23271186 1st Btn Roy Sussex
Regt

Steinberg, Fus Ivan
22409862 Roy Ulster Rifles/Roy
Irish Fus

Summers, Lady Sybil
ATS/Army

Sylvester, Pte Joel
23136318 RASC

Szapira, Spr R.L.
22521609 RE, 55 Field Squadron

Taylor, Fus Michael Micky
22622159 'B' Coy 1st Btn, RF

Tyler, Lt/Cdr Alan
RN
Served WW2 and worldwide post-
war, including Malaya

Wainstein, Sgt R.
22244052 APTC att. RF
PRO-RF

Weinberg, Fus Harold
22622146 1st Btn, RF

Wolff, Lt Michael
22486122/421197 Platoon 2,
'C' Coy, 1st Btn, RF
PRO-RF roll

Zetter, L/Cpl Norman
23081754 RAOC att. S. Staffs.
Regt

Unidentified.
KOSB, 1st Btn, 'A' Coy
Was Coy Clerk, KIA in Korea
Previously served in Palestine and
Hong Kong

Killed in Action

Albrecht, Lt Andrew J.
414788 RIDG (Dragoons)
  tbc 20.6.52
Buried Pusan, grave 22-4-1450.

Arno, Pte Harry
E. Yorks Reg.
Memorial Wall, Pusan

Levison, Lt Joseph Yehudi
Princess Patricia's Canadian L/I
20.5.51
KIA at Munsan, seven miles south
of Panmanjon
Canadian Book of Remembrance

Lipschild, Cpl. Barnett
2277176 RE
13.5.53
Born Nkana, N. Rhodesia
Buried Pusan, grave 39-83-399 –
so symbol on grave in error

Ritterband, Cpl Montague
22290920 'B' Coy, 1st Btn KSLI
Formerly 14422233 2nd Btn,
RB/att. AAC in WW2
Age 26   17.11.51
JC, 7.12.51
Served Sumatra and Israel War of
Independence. Memorial Cem,
Pusan, 23-6-1616
On War Memorial, Abington
Square, Northampton

Sander, Lt Gustav 'Gus'
370959 Cmndr 6th Platoon, 'B'
Coy, Mddx Regt
30.10.50
Served at Arnhem with Paras
MID, KIA in Tae-Dong village, near
Chongju
On memorial to those with no
known graves at Pusan WG Cem

Two un-named Hungarian Jews
medical orderlies with the
Allies KIA – JC, 7.12.51

British and Commonwealth Jews in Kenya

Austin, 2nd Lt Clive
23098445 *RAPC*
18 Parkholme Rd, London E8

Baker, Capt Harvey
441920 *RAMC*
161 Zetland Rd, Doncaster

Berliner, Sgmn David
22727701 *Roy Sig*
42 Mornington Rd, Greenford

Brackman, AC1 Arnold Lewis
2458360 *82nd Squadron*
128 Holmleigh Rd, N16

Brazil, AC2 Alan L.
2713949
Kibbutz Zichron Yeshayachia,
Hurst Grange, Reading

Brogin, LAC Malcolm Geoffrey
2499509
In Bulawayo, S Rhodesia
242 Evering Rd, E5

Burack, Capt Malcolm
449631 *RAMC*
67 Westbourne Gdns, Hove

Cohen, Capt Charles
431327 *RAMC*
3 Brookside Terr., Sunderland

Colman, Sgmn Dennis
22331194 *Roy Sig*
18 Ashfield Dr., Frazinghall,
Bradford

Fader, AC2 Paul
2560709
95 Langdale Mansions, Cannon St
Rd, E1

Fisher, Pte Norman A.
22940568 *RAMC*
283 Menlove Ave, Woolton,
Liverpool

Freeling, Capt Paul
RAMC

Gillary, B.S.
23354736 *Roy Fus*
5 Lukin St., Commercial Rd, E1

Goldberg, Ronald
22692447 *Roy Inniskillen Fus*
12 Felix Hse, Forbes St., E1

Halpern, Sgmn Michael
22971059 *Roy Sig*
28 Garth Dr., Liverpool

Haring, SAC Alan
2785262

Harris, 2nd Lt Paul M.
463472/23609568 *Roy Sussex*
3 Palmeira Sq., Hove

Harrison, Cftmn David John
22505010 *REME*
73 Nightingale Lane, Bromley,
Kent

Isaacs, Sgt Ernest
4388509, *Green Howards*
Lived in Nairobi

Jacobs, Ethel S.
W/211285, *WRAC*
43, Hove Manor, Hove St., Hove
Also in Malaya (see below)

Julius, Maj A.A, MID
SAS
Also served Malaya – see below

King, Rfmn Benjamin
23170778 *1st RB*
29 Raven Row E1
Also served Malaya (see below)

Kleiman, 2nd Lt Henri
443706/23018209 *Ox & Bucks*
att. Kings African Rifles
23 Oslo Ct, St Johns Wood, NW8

Lawson, Capt Jack P.
450037 *RAMC*
14 Grosvenor Rd, Southport
Also served Cyprus

Lever, 2nd Lt Jeremy Frederick
421701/22586262 *RA*
Pyghtle Cottage, Denham, Bucks

Levine, Cpl David
22654756 *RAMC*

Lewis, Pte Leslie
S/22759666 *RASC*
17 Casson Hse, Hanbury St., E1

Lipson, Lt Col Leslie D.
Also served Malaya (see below)

Lucks, Rfmn David M.
23201225 *RB*
21 East Bank, N16

Mann, Pte David
22512759 *RAMC*

Marks, Sgt H.P.
1896416 *RAF*
Also served Cyprus

Mendel, WO2 Alfred, BEM
Special Branch Kenya Regt.
From Nairobi
JC April 1956

Moss, Pte H.
23559893 *Kings Regt*
124 Downham Cres., Prestwich,
Lancs

Nayton, Cftmn Gerald E.
23858621 *REME*
Lived in Kenya

Rees, Fus Leonard
22731375 *Roy Innis Fus*

Rosenblatt, Cpl A. Lionel
21055629 *RAPC*
164 Stepney Green E1

Reuben, LAC F.
RAF
42 Firsby Rd, Stamford Hill, N16

Ruben, Capt Lewis A.
459696 *RAMC*
461 Lordship Lane, Dulwich

Rubin, Sgt Peter
Army Field Intel.
From Surrey

Samuel, Lt Col. Clive Marshall
RAMC Paras
MBE Aden, Kenya, Cyprus

Schaffer, LAC Gerald
2700635 *RAF*
72 Gower Rd SW11

Stevens, Pte L.
23616310 *RAOC Military Police*

Style, Cpl Peter Louis
22706186 *RASC*
Mallory Rd, Hove

Weisberg, Pte Mark H.
22931327 *RAMC*
28 Enid St, Salford

White, Gnr Terry
22329575 *RA*
Lived in Kenya

British and Commonwealth Jews in Malaya

Aber, Capt Geoffrey M.
435055 *RAMC*

Abrahams, AC1 Mark John
2494562 *RAF*
38 Edgeworth Cl., NW4

Abrahams, Gnr Michael
23823491 *RA*
36 Ellesmere Rd, Bow

Abramovitz Pte Leon
22700796 *1st Btn Manchester Regt*

Alouf, AC2 Marco Albert
3126087 *RAF*
18 Springfield Rd, Leicester

Andrews, SAC David
2760717 *RAF*
119 St Marks Rd, W10

Antick, Cpl Boris
22686779 *RAOC*
2 Iffley Flats, Shoreditch

Apel, Pte Denis

Asher, Sgt Alan D.
RAMC
54 York Rd, Southend

Ballon, LAC Gordon
5041339 *RAF*
16 Vaughan Gdns, Ilford

Bamary, Pte Miss E.
Q1000269 *QARANC*

Barbenel, Capt Joseph Cyril
467402 *RADC*
25 Kyneston Rd N16

Baron, Capt Jeremy H.
450613 *RAMC*
37 Ashley Lane, NW4

Bazar, LAC Adrian
2575394 *RAF*
Manchester St., Cheltenham

Becker, LAC Gerald
5068388 *RAF*
83 Southwood Gdns, Ramsgate

Benson, Pte George
RAMC
4 Woodlands Ave, Wanstead

Billing, Miss Estelle
WVS att. 13/18 Hussars
61 Ditton Rd, Surbiton

Black, Pte Frank Raymond
22684284 *REME*
31 Shore Rd, Hackney E9

Black, Michael William
2578206 *SAC RAF*
97 St James St., Manchester

Bliss, Sgt Alfred M.
22912158 *RAOC – Police Special Branch*
84 Chambers Lane, NW10

Blumenthal, Capt Leonard
P/168272 *RASC*

Boxer, Rfmn
SLI

Boyask, Sidney
2578278 *SAC RAF*
65 Sidney St, E1

Boyask, AC1 Stanley
2761782
22 Thurlestone Ave, Ilford

Brodsky, Dvr H.
T/22472899 *RASC*

Brunswick, AC2 Gary Simon
2480430 RAF
20 Priory Ct (?)

Charkham, 2/Lt Stephen Julian
431896/22856918 *SLI*
9 Brunswick Gdns, W8

Cohen, Alan
4184154 *SAC RAF*
21 Kenmare Rd, Liverpool 15

Cohen, Cpl Debroy
22737281 *1st Btn Queens Regt*
7 Dunstans House, E1

Cohen, Pte Jeffrey
23057235 *RAPC*
21 Ellingfort Rd, Hackney, E8

Cohen, Cpl Neville
22933465 RAMC
4 Wilton Pl., Sheffield

Cohen, Phyllis H.
2823044 WRAF/SACW
193a Lower Clapton Rd, E5

Cohen, AS Saul
RN

Collis, Cpl Gerald L.
22971515 *REME*
12 Greenhill, Wembley Pk

Content, Lt J.J.
RAMC
29 Copley Pk, SW16

Corper, Hyman Alexander
4037503, *SAC RAF 60 Squadron*
c/o Mrs P. Ellis, 2119 East Pratt St., Baltimore, USA

Cowan, LAC Harris H.
4141903
15 College Gdns, E4

Curtis, AC1 Harris
2311597 Movement Control
24 Ellesmere Gdns, Redbridge

Davies, Maj P.E.
RM

Dean, LAC Alan
5036131 *RAF*
24 Lilford Ave, Liverpool 9

Decent, Lt R.
447675 *RE*

Dickson, John
RM7021 45 RM Commandos
35 Kensington Drive, Woodford
Green

Donn, Sgmn Maurice J.
22132787 *RAOC*
11 Downs Rd, Clapton, E5

Duke, Sgmn David
23381193 *Roy Sig*
23 Haslemere Gdns, Finchley, N3

Eban, Lt R.E.
418511 *RAMC*

**Eidelstein (Edison), AC1
Lawrence Joseph**
3109366 *RAF*

Elkes, Capt Z.
411425 *RAMC*

Endfield, Pte Arnold
23410742 *RAOC*
39 Cumberland Ave, Liverpool

Epstein, Pte Maurice
23392375 *RAMC*
23 Borough St, Brighton

Feldman, Capt Maurice G.
431858 *RAMC*
99 Ninian Rd, Cardiff

Feldman, Pte Philip M.
22651717 *1st E Yorks*
21 Kingswood Gdns, Leeds 8

Feldman, Sgt Stephen T.
23339835 *REME*
20 Gunton Rd, Clapton, E5

Fellman, S/Sgt Harold H.
22250688 *RAPC*

Fiber, Sgt Alan E.
23146295 *Field Security Intel
Johore*
39 Mapesbury Rd, NW2

Fielding, Capt A.
IC
MID WW2

Fischl, Capt Robert Arnold
431322 *RAMC*
45 Arkwright Rd, NW3

Fletcher, Pte C.
22608051, *1st E Yorks*
17 Savile Rd, Leeds 7

Forres, Lt Miss M.C.
406744 *QARANC*
The Uplands, Fimfield,
Wolverhampton

Fox, Capt Anthony David
428908 *RAMC*
11 Seagry Rd, Wanstead

Fox, Capt Harold
458369 *RAMC*
33 Stanley Rd, Salford

Freedman, Pte Frank A.
23036593 *RAMC 19th Field Amb*
6 Broom Lane, Salford

Freedman, Capt Murray Philip
419516, *RADC*
195 Chapletown Rd, Leeds

Friend, Cpl Ronald
23490857 *1st Btn Para Regt*

Gardner, Lt J.
RAOC

Gee, Fl Lt Nathan J.
503548 *RAF*
45 Ossulton Way, N2
Died of polio OAS 1956
Buried Changi

Gillman, Pte Morris Reuben
22851762 *RAMC 19th Field Amb*
71 Stanley Rd, Bootle

Golder, LAC David S.
2591124
20 Mowbray Rd, Edgware

Goldin, Fl Lt Sam
RAF

Golding, Pte Michael E.
23578070 *RAPC*
47 Boyne Ave, NW4

Goldman, Capt Ian E.
461758 *RAMC*

Goldman, Sgt Simpson M.
22563065 REME

**Goldring, Sgt James (Alec?),
MM**
6153636

Goldschmid, Pte Kurt
23402505 *RAMC*
70 Fleetwood Rd, NW10

Goldstein, SAC Sidney
3151263 *RAF*

Grace, SAC Frederick S.
1943009
Grandfather in Aden

Grand, SAC Reuben
2707711 *RAF*

Grant, 2nd Lt Alec A.
418571/22451428 *RA*
5 Mayfield Ave, Finchley

Guedalla, Cpl Richard S.
RAC 13/18th Hussars
9 Harley Rd, NW3

**Gurney, SACW Leonora (later
Gosling)**
W/2836807 *WRAF*
24 St Leonard's Rd, Hove

Haase, Pte John
23059083 *1st Btn Queens*
35 Ferncroft Ave, NW3

Hajioff, SAC Maurice
5031612
43 Durley Rd, N1

Herman, Tpr Irving
3rd Carbineers

Hirshall, LAC Ernest
3127764 *RAF*
29 Shannon St, Glasgow

Hope-Stone, Capt Harold Francis
422707 *RAMC*
147 Dartmouth Rd, NW2

Hyams, Pte Ben
23636688 ACC
54 Bethnia Hse, Harford St, E1

Hyman, Cpl. Dennis
22681556 *RAOC*
39 Woodland Rd, Manchester

Isaac, Capt Geoffrey Henry
422213 *RAMC*
40 Lyndale Ave, NW2

Isaacs, Rfmn A.
23359662 *Rifle Brigade*

Isaacs, Teddy
45 RM Commando

Isaacson, Lt Henry Percy
420658 *RAMC*
3 Yewlands Ave, Fulwood, Preston

Israel (aka) Lasalle, Cpl Alan
23175622 *RAOC*
41 Gascony Ave, Kilburn

Jacobs, LAC Albert
4053470, *110 Squadron*
8 Grants Lane, Calcutta, India

Jacobs, Ethel S.
W/211285 *WRAC*
43 Hove Manor, Hove St., Hove
Also in Kenya (above)

Jagerman, Capt Kurt
438159 *RADC*
11 Vincent Ct, Green Lane, NW4

Janikoun, Lt Col Samuel H.
221581 *RAMC*
OBE Military, Malaya (*JC* 29/1/60)

Jeffery, Pte Peter
23639558 *Sherwood Foresters*
4 St James Mans, West End Lane, NW6

Joseph, Tpr D.
23742730, *RAC 1st Btn Roy Dragoons*

Josephs, Pte Gerald
22944648 *RAPC att 1st Btn Hants*
929 Finchley Rd

Julius, Maj (Brig) Allan Aubrey
390923/373629 *RE, SAS*
MID Gallantry Malaya
Also served Kenya

Kalb, LAC Manfred
2718172 *RAF*
31 St Frances/James (?) Rd, Leicester

Kamin, Pte Frank
23416086 *RAOC*
82 Buxton St, Vallance Rd, E1

Kampéner, Lt Frederick B.E.
420314 *RAMC*
c/o L. Kemp 110, Banbury Rd, Oxford

Kanitz, Sgt F.
Intel Corps
Also WW2

Karmel, 2nd Lt Nigel L.
463814/23623558 *RAC 13th & 18th Hussars*
28 Addisland Ct, W14

Kemp, Sgt Melville
22141576 *Green Jackets*
16 Caledon Rd, Nottingham

Khan, Capt Louis
423609 *RAMC*
188 Langside Rd, Glasgow

King, Rfmn Benjamin
1st Btn Rifle Bde
29 Raven Row, E1
Also served Kenya

Kliman, Cpl David M.
23378233 *RAMC 16th Field Amb*
15 Lister Cres., Liverpool

Kocen, Capt Roman S.
456862 *RAMC*
22 The Green, Leeds 17

Koffler, Jnr Tech. Ivor B.
5059831 *RAF*
11 Waterpark Rd, Salford 7

Kurer, Capt H. Gus
431091 *RADC*

Langsman, Pte Stanley
22448091 *RAOC*
34 Newmarket St, W1

Lavine, Capt Michael J.
457506 *RAMC*
1 Westland Rd, Hull

Lee, LAC Anthony
5059824
262 Waterloo Rd, Manchester 8

Lerner, Lt Maurice A.
419065 *RAMC att. Gurkhas*
902 Scotts Hall Rd, Leeds

Lestner, Pte Gerald
22855057 *W Yorks Regt*

Levene, Cpl David
22654756 *RAMC*

Levene, Capt Leslie Joseph
412974 *RAMC*
78 Manor House Rd, Newcastle

Levene, Cpl Maurice
22737305 *1st Btn Queens Regt*
75 The Highway, E1

Lever, AC2 Alan
2541942 *RAF*
38 Ruislip Ct, Ruislip, Middx

Levy, SAC Barry F.
5061195 *RAF*
233 Wigan House, E5

Levy, Pte Clifford
23770041 *East Anglia Regt*
157 Balmoral Dr., Borehamwood, Herts

Levy, Capt Harold D.
433032 *RADC*
400 Cheetham Hill, Manchester

Levy, SAC Ivor
2776875 *RAF*
14 Highfield Gdns, Westcliff on Sea

Levy, L/Cpl John
RM Commandos

Levy, Norman (aka Lavan)
40th RM Commandos
MM, SBS, Malaya

Levy, Cpl Sidney M.
22607468 *1st Btn Queens*
52 Upper Tooting Rd, SW17

Lewis, Pte Elliot E.
22766677 *1st Btn Queens Regt*
101 Christchurch House, Streatham

Lewis, Cpl Kenneth A.
22820534 *RE 11th Ind Fld Squadron*
102 Inverness Ave, Westcliff

Lichtenstein, Capt Hans E.
429376 *RAMC*
BEM for distinguished service

Lipson, Lt Col Leslie D.
186038
Also served Kenya

Lopian, Capt Jacob
431483 *RADC*
96 Terrace Drive, Perth, Austral

Lovatt, AC2 Ivor
2514602 *RAF*
54 St Andrews Dr., Glasgow

Lurie, Capt Israel R.
455685, *RAMC*
214 Anlaby Rd, Hull

Manning, LAC Leslie
2503654 *RAF*
15 Hawkins St, Leeds 7

Mendel, Capt Dennis
RAMC

Mendick, Lt Norman
419998 *RAMC*
39 Marchmont Rd, Edinburgh

Midda, Sqdn Ldr Marshall
507434
105 Lorraine Mansions, Holloway
(Dentist)

Milman, Cpl Michael
22479576 *RAC 13th/18th Hussars*
40 Westcliffe Rd, Southport

Mitchell, Cpl E.
415714 *RAF*

Morris, AC2 Henry
2380243 *RAF*
41 Stoke Newington Rd, N16

Morris, AC1 Joe Leslie Sanikoff
4042506 *RAF*
309 Randwick Park Rd, Plymouth
Son of Mrs A. Horton

RADC

Nieman, LAC2 Marks
2488343 *RAF*
12 Flanders Rd, Chiswick

Noar, Lt A.
419438
RAMC

Noyeek, David Phillip
1940927 *RAF*
25 Neville Rd, Dublin, Eire

Order, LAC R.
2595875 *RAF*
59 Cecilia Rd, Dalston, E8

Pash, Capt Raphael
462557 *RAMC*
12 Hollypark Gdns, Finchley

Paul, Pte M.B.
22436359 *Manchester Regt*
64 Breck Rd, Liverpool

Phillips, Tpr Cyril

Rabin, SAC Michael Sidney
2744926 *RAF*
386 Seven Sisters Rd, N4

Raffman, Lt David
Staffs Regt

Reefe, Pte Lawrence A.
23770042 *East Anglia Regt*
92 Ashurst Dr., Ilford

Rhodes, Capt Alan Abraham
418088 *RADC*
c/o M. Rosenstraugh, 23 Cavendish Rd, Salford

Rich, AC2 Leonard
2515361 *RAF*
67 Coke St, Salford 7

Robinson, Capt C.R.
428849 *RAMC*

Robinson, Pte Nevil
22736031 *RAMC*
19 Broad St, Blaenavon, Mon.

Robinson, Maj T. Malcolm
RAMC
MBE military ops Malaya
'Valhalla', Blaenavon, Mon.

Rodin, Capt Philip
443144 *RAMC*
11 St Andrews Grove, N16

Rosenbaum, Cpl Norman L.
23188440 *RADC*
30 Gubssens Rd, Welwyn Garden
City

**Rosenberg, Pte Michael
Emmanuel**
22177293 *RASC*
16 Palace Ct, Finchley

Ross, Pte Barrie
RAMC
3 jungle patrols against
Communist insurgents

Ross, Capt Oswald
424959 *RAMC*
12 Thistlethwaite Rd, Clapton E5

Ross, Cpl Robin H.
22594608 *RASC*
32 Lyndale Ave, NW2

Ruben, Pte M.
22399286 *Kings Regt*
53 Woodsorrel Rd, Liverpool

Rudnick, Tpr Murray
22903832 *RAC 11th Hussars*
70 Salisbury Rd, Liverpool

Russell, LAC Stanley Lionel
2568256
94 Geary Rd, NW10

Sackwood, Lt M.
419101 *RAMC att. Gurkhas*

Salkin, LAC Brian
5023120 *RAF*
231 Albion Rd, N16

Salkin, LAC Michael
4115823 *RAF*
9 Hollis Field, WC1

**Saloschin/Saunders,
Superintendent George**
Malaya Police Formerly No 3
Troop 10 Commando

Sampson, Pte Coleman
21039849 *RASC*
26 Bernard House, Toynbee St, E1

Samuels, Cpl Gerald
22418744 *RE*
5 Mafeking Rd, Tottenham, N17

Sassoon, Sgt V.
RAF

Sebag-Montefiore, Maj David
302612 *RA Rocket Troop, RHA*
Church House, Shrewton, Wilts

Sharp, Surgeon Lt Larry
RN

Shimbart, Louis Phillip
4038933 *RAF*
12 Bailey's Rd, Southsea

Shine, Sgt David Bernard
4034037 *RAF*
Finchley

Shrensky, Pte Lawrence M.
23437756 *RAOC*
19 Norcott Rd, N16

Silver, SACW Alma
2810152 *WRAF*
46a Commercial Rd,
Bournemouth

Silver, Pte Cyril L.
23124199 *RAPC*
168 Golders Green Rd, NW11

Silver, Cpl Martin
23583576 *RAMC*
9 Spearpoint Gdns, Ilford

Silverman, SAC Basil
2564779
70 Hackney Rd, E1

Simmons, Sgt Aubrey
14988354 (*Army*)
3060664 (*RAF*)

Singer, Spr Michael
22718265 *RE*
153 Highbury New Park, N5

**Singleton, LAC Stanley
Frederick**
2504720 *RAF*
75 Alexandra Rd, Manchester 16

Smiler, Pte William
22542454 *Essex Regt*
41 Ashville Rd, E11

Smith, SAC Stuart
1944994 *RAF*
Gainsborough Dr., Southend

Solden, Pte D.
22060271 *RAPC*
Leeds

Solomon, Pte Leon Ezra
22571828 *RASC*
198 Colindeep Lane, NW9

Solomons, LAC Gerald
5013044 *RAF*
28 Valentine's Rd, Ilford

Stanway, Cpl Arthur F.
4252240 *RAF*
19 Warnsford Rd, Boscombe East,
Bournemouth

Stein, Cpl Lionel
22017709 RAMC

Stephens, Cpl Miss Alma
2810152 RADC
Ruislip, later 1 Cornerways, Park
Rd, NW4

Stern, Sgt Henry
22250650 *1st Btn Lincolns*
53 Arle Rd, Cheltenham

Stevelman, WO2 Harry Joseph
Roy Sig
31 Hill Rise Mansions, Hornsey,
N19

Stibbe, SAC Michael M.
4270950 *RAF*
54 Cuckoo Dene, Hanwell

Sugar, Pte Derek Stanley
22731717 *RAOC*
16 Woolmer House, Upper
Clapton, E5

Summers, Major Lady Sybil
WRAC
(also Korea)

Sutton, Lt S.E.
421089 *REME*

Sykes, Pte Miss F.
Q1000229 *QARANC*

Taylor, Fus Michael Sidney A.
22622159 *Roy Fus*
44 Hodford Rd, NW11

Thornfield, LAC Anthony
2747720
57 Donnington Ct, NW10

Toke, Capt Eric
422220 *RAMC*
6 Argyle Rd, Liverpool

Topaz, Charles
(Newcastle)

Tyler, Lt Alan
RN

Veltman, AC1 Isaac S.
2322502 *RAF*
3 Lailworth St, E1

Wagerman, Flt/Lt Peter
504968 *RAF*
40 Bergholt Cres, N16

Weissberger, 2nd Lt E.C.J.
23307865 *RAPC*
14 Oakleigh Gdns, Edgware

Whitehill, Bdr Edward
23166410

Wilmot, Sgt B.A.
13116482 RPC MP
Edinburgh

Woodrow, Jnr Tech Michael M.
4171397 *RAF*
32 St Margarets Rd, Wanstead

Woolf, Sqdn/Ldr Dr (?) A.J.
500948
32 Ambrose Ave, NW11

Zermansky, Sgt Victor D.
22933451 *RASC*
31 Sandhill Oval, Leeds

Zuck, Lt J.

Jewish Personnel Who Served in Cyprus during the Emergency

Information only from the Jewish Chaplains' cards kept at the AJEX Museum

Adler, Cpl David J.
RE

Ansell, LAC Aubrey
RAF

Ashley, LAC Barry Phillip
RAF

Atkins, Sgt Harold
RAF

Babsky, F/O Michael Leon
RAF

Bailey, SAC Ronald
RAF

Barnett, Pte Michael D.
Essex Regt

Benardout, LAC Maurice
RAF

Bendon, AC2 Jeffrey P.
RAF

Benn, Pte Martyn
RASC

Berlinsky, Gnr Bernard
RA

Bernstein, SAC Stanley L.
RAF

Bliss, AC1 Alec
RAF

Borsack, Geoffrey
RAF

Braham, Spr Bernard
RE

Breur-Weil, SAC Peter
RAF

Brodie, AC1 R.H.
RAF

Brown, Pte Harvey
ACC

Burke, AC1 Anthony M.
RAF

Caplan, SAC Arthur
RAF

Castello, Gnr Simon J.
RA

Chinn, SAC Sefton W.
RAF

Clifton-Samuel, Capt Anthony D.
RADC

Cobden, SAC Eric J.
RAF

Cohen, Sgt B.
RAF

Cohen, Jun/Tech Gerald
RAF

Cohen, SAC Gerald Sidney
RAF

Cohen, Pte Ellis I.
RAOC

Cohen, Pte Norman Victor
RASC

Colaco-Osorio, Gnr L.R.
RA

Collis, Pte Norman N.
Middx

Cooper, SAC Barry
RAF

Cowan, Sgt Michael L.
RAMC

Cowen, LAC Maurice Graham
RAF

Crown, Pte Michael K.
RCOS

Cytrynbaum, Pte Sarah R.
QARANC

Davis, Sgt M.
REME

Davis, Cpl Phillip M.
RAF

Dean, Pte Montague
SLI

De Leon, Cpl Albert S.
RAF

Denningberg, Spr Malcolm Myer
RE

Drapkin, LAC Abraham A.
RAF

Epstein, Pte Lionel
Middx

Etherton, LAC David
RAF

Feld, SAC Michael R.
RAF

Felston, Pte Brian C.
RAMC

Fenton, Pte Harry
(also at Suez)

Field, F/O E.O.
RAF

Fineman, SAC Anthony G.
RAF

Finesilver, SAC Brian
RAF

Finn, L/Cpl Lewis D.
RAC

Fisher, Cpl David Ballie
ACC

Fisher, David
Infantry
Also N. Ireland

Flater, L/Cpl Lionel B.
RAMC

Flitman, SAC Alan M.
RAF

Forman, Flt/Lt Arthur D.
RAF

Forrest, Pte Anthony C.
RAOC

Frank, Sgmn Steven
RCOS 1955

Freedman, LAC Ivor
RAF

Freedman, L/Cpl N.
RASC

Freeman, Cpl Paul E.
DLI

Friedman, Pte C.
RAOC

Fuller, LAC L.
RAF

Fulner, AC1 Brian Michael
RAF

Galan, Gnr Michael J.
RA

Garson, Cpl Arnold
RAF

Genis, Spr Roy M.
RE

Geraldie/Lazarus, Gnr R.K.
RA

Gillis, SAC Frank
RAF

Ginsberg, Pte Michael
RWK

Godfrey, SAC Harry
RAF

Gold, AC1 Ronald
RAF

Goldblatt, Spr Daniel
RE

Goldblatt, LAC Leonard
RAF

Goldenfeld, LAC Leonard C.
RAF

Goldman, Capt Gordon L.
RADC

Grant, Capt Lionel
RAMC

Grant, LAC Maurice Isaac
RAF

Gross, Capt Maurice
RAMC

Halpern, Lt Theodore L.
RAPC

Haring, SAC Alan P.
RAF
Also in Kenya

Harling, Pte R.
RAOC

Harris, AC1 M.
2773278
RAF

Harris, AC1 M.
RAF

Hart, LAC Colin C.
RAF

Hart, David
Army

Hart, Pte D.B.
RAMC

Hartzberg, Cpl L.
RAF

Hayman, Cpl N.J.
RAF

Homburg, SAC Lionel
RAF

Horn, Lt John

Hurst, Gnr Ian S.
RA

Hyatt, Pte Anthony A.
RAMC

Isaacs, LAC Adrian Maurice
RAF

Isaacs, Pte David H.
RASC

Isaacs, LAC H.
RAF

Isaacs, SAC M.
RAF

Isbitsky, AC1 Gerald
RAF

Isenberg, Pte Brian M.
RAMC

Jackman, Maj John David
Special Service; also Congo

Jones, Cpl S.
RAF

Joseph, SAC A.E.
RAF

Judah, Pte David H.
RADC

Kane, L/Cpl Herbert
Northants

Kaplin, Pte Ivor P.
RAPC

Karat, Maj Basil
RAMC

Keal, Sgt A.
RAEC

Krolick, L/Cpl Ivan
Field Security (Intel)

Kunkel, Pte Robert
Paras
DOAS 1956

Lackmaker, Jnr Tech Jack
RAF

Lang, LAC David F.
RAF

Lawson, Capt Jack P.
RAMC

Leaman, Cpl
RAF

Lee, LAC A.M.
RAF

Lee, SAC David
RAF

Lee, LAC Howard
RAF

Lee, AC1 Jack G.
RAF

Lee, Pte Norman
RADC

Levene, Cpl B.
RAF

Levin, Dr Capt Ronald
RAMC

Levy, Anthony

Levy, Capt Brian G.
REME

Levy, Lt Brian John
RASC

Levy, Sgt Kalman
RAF

Lewis, LAC Lawrence
RAF

Lewis, Capt Norman G.
RAMC

Lewis, Pte Philip
RAOC

Life, SAC M.A.
RAF

Lincoln, Rfmn Jack
Cameronians
Later served in Israeli army

Lingel, L/Cpl Melvin R.
RASC

Lishner, LAC Stuart T.
RAF

Lyth, AC2 Frederick I.
RAF

Massing, LAC Benny
RAF

May, SAC D.
RAF

May, Lt J.
RE

Mayson, SAC Bryan J.S.
RAF

Mendleson, L/Cpl J.S.
RAMC

Michaels, SAC Ivor
RAF

Miller, SAC Henry D.F.
RAF

Miller, AC1 Stanley
RAF

Milne, Nathan
RAF

Minkin, SAC Lewis
RAF

Mitzman, Pte Martin
RAPC

Montefiore, Capt David G.
RAMC

Myers, Dvr Martyn
RCOS

Nathan, SAC David
RAF – 27517677 – 1956–57

Newman, Flt/Lt Claude
Medical

Noye, Lt Jolyon E.
RE

Orlans, Capt D.M.
RAMC

Parker, SAC Alan K.
RAF

Patashnik, LAC Lawrence
RAF

Penpraz, Lt Ian H.D.
RAEC

Phillips, Sgmn Stanley
RCOS

Pincus, Sgt
DP Camps 1948

Press, SAC Brian
RAF

Prince, SAC Gerhard S.M.
RAF

Proctor, Pte Stuart
RCOS

Rainbow, L/Cpl Michael J.
REME

Randall, SAC Anthony D.
RAF

Reuben, Cpl Harvey L.
RAF

Richardson, Pte Ronald
RAPC

Richenberg, F/O Cecil Simon
90 Group 2551105 – 1952–54

Robin, LAC Brian Sydney
RAF

Robinson, LAC Michael
RAF

Robinson, Roger
Intel Corps

Rodgers, Gnr J.E.
33 Para Fld Regt

Rose, Sgt Colin L.
RAPC

Rose, LAC Joseph
RAF

Rose, Gnr Melvin
RA

Roseman, Cpl Peter
RAF

Rosenberg, Pte Jack H.
RAMC

Rosenberg, Pte Sidney
Middx

Rosenthal, Cpl Harry
RAF

Ross, L/Cpl Peter A.
RE

Roth, Pte Theodore
RASC

Sackwood, Pte S.
RASC

Sampson, Colin
REME

Samuel, Col Clive Marshall
RAMC/Paras
MBE (Aden)

Samuelson, Cpl Maurice
RCOS

Sargon, Pte Isaac
RAOC

Sass, Cpl Brian S.
RAF

Schlesinger, Pte I.
Suffolks

Schrier, AC1 John A.
RAF

Schupak, Pte Roger P.
RCOS

Sebag-Montefiore,
Lt Nathaniel C.
RA

Sewell, Capt Maxwell
RAMC

Sheeter, SAC Eric
RAF

Silver, SAC David S.
RAF

Silver, SAC Gerald
RAF

Silverman, Lt Lawrence
RA

Simon, Pte David
RAPC

Simon, Pte Donald
23057248 – 1956

Simon, Pte Harvey I.
ACC

Singer, Cpl William,
RAMC

Singer, Pte Ronald
Paras

Solomon, Cpl Daniel
RAF

Solomon, LAC S.
RAF

Steingold, L/Cpl Norman
RAMC

Strong, Sgt H. Edward
RAF

Sykes, Pte Murray G.
RAOC

Talbot, Pte Harry
RAPC

Thomas, SAC Anthony S.
RAF

Tierney, Pte L.
Middx

Turk, Capt John L.
RAMC

Ullman, L/Cpl Joseph
Middx

Valman, Capt Hyman B.
RAMC

Van Praag, Pte Anthony/
Aubrey C.
RASC

Volinsky, Pte Joseph
RAMC

Wassenberg, L/Cpl William
RAPC

Weisberg, SAC Michael D.
RAF

Weiss, Technician Jeremy
RAF

White, L/Cpl R.
Middx

Wiener, Pte Philip B.
RCOS

Woad, LAC D.A.
RAF

Woolf, Pte Sidney
RAPC

Zalsberg, SAC Julian
RAF

The VCs and GCs
Arthur Louis Aaron, VC

'In my opinion, never, even in the annals of the RAF, has the VC been awarded for skill, determination and courage in the face of the enemy of a higher order than that displayed by your son on his last flight.' Thus wrote Sir Arthur Harris, Commander-in-Chief of RAF Bomber Command, to the parents of Flight Sergeant Arthur Louis Aaron DFM in November 1943.

Though of small consolation for the loss of a beloved son, Harris's sincere tribute was heartfelt, and shared by all who had witnessed Arthur Aaron's superlative courage. Grievously injured, Aaron's single-minded determination to preserve the lives of his crew overrode all other considerations in his last hours, exemplifying the close bond of comradeship amongst the bomber crews, and epitomizing the heavy responsibility borne by so many youthful bomber captains.

Born in Leeds on 5 March 1922, Arthur Aaron was the son of an Englishman, Benjamin Aaron, who had married a girl originally from Switzerland, but who had come to Scotland before the First World War to the family of the Rector of Aberdeen University, Adam Smith. From his earliest years young Arthur became fascinated by two things, mountains and flying – a tragically prophetic combination of interests. His absorption with mountains – possibly inherited from his mother's background – found expression in many rock-climbing expeditions, while the boy's first ecstatic taste of the pure joy of flying came with a short flight with one of Alan Cobham's travelling aerial 'circuses' near Penrith.

Educated at Roundhay Secondary School, Aaron won an art scholarship in 1939 and entered Leeds College of Architecture as the start of his intended career. Still keen on flying, he joined the Leeds University Squadron of the Air Defence Cadet Corps (later renamed Air Training Corps) and, eventually, enlisted in the RAF for pilot training on 15 September 1941. In early December he was sent to the USA and commenced flying instruction at No.1 (British) FTS, Terrell in Texas, graduating as a Sergeant Pilot on 19 June 1942.

Figure 343. Arthur Louis Aaron, VC.

Returning to England, Aaron underwent further advanced instruction at No.6 (P) AFU and No.26 OTU, before being sent to No.1657 Heavy Conversion Unit (HCU) to acquire experience in handling the giant four-engined Short Stirling bomber. Finally, on 17 April 1943, Aaron joined his first operational unit, 218 Gold Coast Squadron based at Downham Market in East Anglia.

From his first operational sortie, a 'soft' trip dropping mines in the Bay of Biscay, Aaron, quiet and mild-mannered on the ground, exercised a firm discipline over his crew in the air. His constant aim was efficiency in the bombing role and, towards this end, he insisted that each crew member gained some experience of other members' jobs. It meant improved understanding and cooperation – knitting each member into a cohesive whole, as a team, ready to cope instinctively with any untoward situation which might arise. Promoted to Flight Sergeant on 1 May 1943, Aaron's authority over his crew was, nevertheless, not due to his rank but by his status as the crew skipper; age or rank seniority held little meaning for an operational crew when actually flying.

During the following three months Aaron and his crew completed twenty sorties over Europe, bombing a wide variety of targets in Germany and enemy-occupied territory. An early indication of the young pilot's streak of determination came on the night his Stirling was partly crippled by flak on his approach to the target. Undeterred by the damage, which had left his aircraft only marginally controllable, Aaron continued his sortie, bombed the objective, and then brought the Stirling home again safely. His action that night brought him the award of a Distinguished Flying Medal (DFM) (Gazetted 19 October 1943).

In the afternoon of 12 August 1943, Aaron and his crew were briefed for their twenty-first operational sortie. The target was Turin, their first trip to Italy. Piloting Stirling EF452, HA-O, Aaron took off from Downham Market into the lowering sun of a warm summer evening, lifting the nose of the bomber which, like some winged dinosaur, laboured upwards, struggling to gain height with full petrol tanks and a maximum bomb load. Inside its fuselage the crew automatically busied themselves, preparing for the long haul across France to Italy – by now an experienced crew whose teamwork ran like clockwork. Navigating was Sergeant Bill Brennan, a Canadian, while the bomb aimer, another Canadian, was Flight Sergeant Allan Larden. At the wireless set sat Sergeant T. 'Jimmy' Guy and, nearby, the flight engineer Sergeant Malcolm Mitchem. In the mid-upper gun turret Sergeant J. Richmond, having tested his guns and turret, was settling down to the constant vigil he would need to maintain for many hours to come; as was Sergeant Thomas McCabe, a Manchester man, seated in the cramped lonely rear gun turret.

All had been well briefed and were pleased with the target – a combined attack wherein the Stirlings were to bomb Turin, while Halifaxes of 6 Group were attacking Milan. Crossing the French coast near Caen at 10,000 feet, Aaron continued to coax the overburdened Stirling upwards, gaining height steadily in the brilliant moonlight. Reaching a comfortable 14,000 feet ceiling, Aaron levelled out and continued southwards, passing Le Creusot and eventually approaching the Alps. He was well used to the Stirling's lack of a safe ceiling by now, but he was not particularly worried, the sheer beauty of the Alps bathed in clear moonlight to port capturing his and his crew's admiration. To Aaron, fascinated with mountains since childhood, the grandeur of the scene was breathtaking. Pointing to Mont Blanc, he remarked, 'Boy, would I like to climb that'.

Then the crew's attention was brought back to the job in hand: Turin had loomed into view ahead and below.

Aaron called for the bomb doors to be opened; Allan Larden slithered down into the nose position to prepare for dropping the bomb load; Mitchem climbed into Larden's vacated seat, his fingers poised over the bombing panel switches – smooth, trained movements, carried out instinctively without fuss.

Richmond's voice from the mid-upper turret crackled over the intercom: 'Watch that bloke up front, Art.'

Aaron leaned to his right and saw, on the starboard side, another Stirling of the main stream, slightly below and wallowing rather too close for comfort. 'OK, Ritch', replied Aaron.

Hardly were the words out of his mouth than Richmond's voice came back, yelling, 'Christ, he's firing at us!' Below their starboard wing tip, the rear gunner of the other Stirling had opened fire and, at about 250 yards range, was raking Aaron's aircraft from starboard wing to port and back again.

'Fire back at him, Ritchie.'

'I can't, the wing tip's in the way.' The time was 1.20 a.m. on Friday 13 August. Lying in the nose, Larden was startled to see half a dozen finger holes suddenly appear in the fuselage two feet from his face to the right. Back inside the fuselage, Brennan collapsed in a cascade of maps, pencils and instruments as one bullet went clean through his heart and he died instantly.

Larden was then stung into action by the voice of Mitchem shouting, 'My God, fellows, look at Art. Oh, poor Art. Give me a hand, Allan.'

Swinging up into the cockpit Larden saw Aaron hunched over to his left and covered in blood from a gaping wound in the face, his right arm dangling useless and limp, held on by only a few tendons. The instrument panel was a shambles of blood-flecked glass and torn metal, while the pilot's side of the front windscreen was blown apart. Both inboard engine throttle levers were smashed and bent and, by now, the Stirling was in a powered 250 mph dive, with Mitchem in the right-hand pilot's seat fighting the controls to straighten the plunging bomber, and throwing agonised glances at his grievously injured skipper in the other seat.

As Mitchem slid out of the co-pilot's seat, Larden took his place – an instinctive, trained movement, needing no conscious thought and the Canadian gradually regained control of the diving Stirling and levelled out between the menacing Alpine peaks at about 4,000 feet. Meanwhile Mitchem and two others gave Aaron morphia injections and bundled him amidships between the spars. Before accepting this rough first aid treatment however, Aaron – still, astonishingly, conscious – insisted on knowing Larden's intentions for getting the bomber to safety.

Unable to speak, he scratched a message with his left hand on the back of the dead navigator's log, telling Larden to head for England. Larden gave him an OK sign, and only then did Aaron permit medical aid to be given.

In point of fact, Larden had no choice, for the moment, but to continue flying southwards through the surrounding mountain peaks, having constantly to fight for control of the crippled bomber. The automatic pilot was inoperable, cables for the trimming tabs dangling broken from the roof, hydraulic lines ruptured thus rendering the rear turret useless and slopping oil in the fuselage mid-section. Added to all this, the starboard inner engine was threatening to overheat, and there was still a full bomb load aboard. Taking stock of all these items, Larden began to head eastwards over the lower mountains towards Austria, but then, as he cleared these lower peaks, he turned through south to head westward, hoping to reach British-occupied territory in Sicily. Baling out among the snow-covered peaks was considered briefly and rejected: apart from almost certain death by freezing in the mountains, the crew would not risk further injury to Aaron.

At his wireless set, Jimmy Guy continued to transmit to base but the response was virtually inaudible. It meant that the crew was ostensibly alone in the sky without a position fix or accurate course to fly, and with little idea of their precise location.

After what seemed an age, the Stirling crossed the Italian coast at Spezia where Larden promptly jettisoned the bomb load into the harbour area. Mitchem, having checked the state of the engines and fuel, relieved Larden at the controls while the latter went aft. Moving Brennan's body from the gangway, he told the other crew members to check their parachutes and aircraft dinghies for damage, and then prepare them for use. This done, Richmond went forward to take a spell at piloting the bomber, relieving Mitchem, and Larden had a brief 'conference' to decide what to do on arrival in Sicily.

Guy informed him that Group in England had finally faded out of range and then sent out a plain language distress call to Bone airfield in North Africa; an emergency call which paid off when he received a reply telling him not to land in Sicily but to try to make it to Bone across the Mediterranean.

By this time, Larden and Mitchem had realized that they had both had narrow escapes from the original 'attack' by the unknown Stirling's rear gunner. Larden had two bullets in his right buttock, while Mitchem's right flying boot had been cut in two at the ankle by three bullets; two of which had scraped the bone. Telling McCabe to sit facing the flight engineer's instrument panels, Mitchem told the rear gunner to yell out when the first warning indicator came on; then Larden returned to the front cockpit and took over the two pilot seats while Richmond went back to stay with Aaron.

Desperately weak from loss of blood and the waves of shock, Aaron rallied sufficiently to scratch out a question, 'How navigate?' Guy and Richmond reassured their skipper that they were on course for Bone airfield, and had a map bearing to get them there. Aaron lay back again, exhausted even from this brief effort to ensure his crew's safety.

For nearly four hours the Stirling droned on across the moon-dappled surface of the Mediterranean with Larden, under Mitchem's skilled guidance, alternating engine power and carefully extracting the last drop of precious petrol from each tank in turn. Then Larden saw ahead two searchlight beams form an inverted 'V' which were then joined by a third, forming a marker tripod of light. Still unable to contact Bone by R/T, the Canadian was not sure if the lights indicated friend or foe, but homed right over the beams and let Guy obtain a reciprocal. Two miles out to sea Larden turned again and came back over the airfield. Below him, the strip was lighted but there were mountains at the back of the aerodrome, making any landing hazardous for a novice pilot.

Yawing round in a jerky right-hand circuit, Larden prepared to land, only finally to receive a message from the aerodrome warning him of a crashed Wellington bomber at the end of the main runway. Larden decided to make a wheels-up landing alongside the runway, but at that moment fate stepped in. Aaron regained consiousness as the effect of the morphia wore off and, alerted instinctively by the (to him) crude manoeuvring of the aircraft, asked Guy what was happening. Guy told him they were about to land.

With a face practically shot in two and black with caked blood, and his right arm dangling by the tenuous support of a few tendons, Aaron immediately started to crawl foward to take command of the landing. As Larden remarked later: 'Who could deny such an indomitable spirit?'

As the two gunners helped their skipper into his seat, Larden slid into the co-pilot's seat, and Mitchem went back to his instrument panel.

Aaron had only his left arm to operate controls and, being unable to talk, could only indicate his wishes by nodding his head. Unaware of the wrecked Wellington at the far end of the main runway, Aaron automatically lined up the Stirling for a normal landing approach, ignoring Larden's shouts (if indeed he heard him). It could only have been sheer experienced instinct which made Aaron aware that the let-down was wrongly placed, and he nodded to Larden to open throttles and go round again.

On his second approach Aaron was, again, dissatisfied and signalled to Larden to open up and circuit. Automatically obeying his skipper's unspoken order, Larden advanced the throttles – to the dismay of Mitchem, who yelled that they would have to land this time: the petrol was virtually gone.

The Stirling made its third approach but, at only 500 feet above the runway edge, Aaron indicated to Larden to go round yet again. Larden shouted that there was no fuel for another circuit – they must land. Aaron, his mind possibly impaired by his awful pain, seemed unable to comprehend this and began to pull on the throttles. In sheer desperation Larden swung his arm and thumped Aaron across the chest to make him release the controls and Aaron collapsed completely, only his eyes glaring at his co-pilot in an unforgettable reproach.

With the bomber at stalling point and the port wing beginning to drop, Larden pushed the control column hard forward and held tight as the desert sand rushed up towards him; then heaved back sharply. The aircraft tobogganed in for a belly-landing, scooping earth and sand in a monstrous tidal wave as it careered to an eventual halt. They were down. The time was 6 a.m.

As the dust settled, Arthur Aaron was quickly removed and taken to the base hospital, where surgeons operated to remove bullets from the pilot's right chest cavity (probably those which had near-severed his arm). The rest of the crew were medically checked over and treated for their various minor wounds.

It was only after this that they learned that the Stirling's bomb bay still contained one of its bombs which failed to release over Spezia. Larden was presented with the safety buckle of his Sutton parachute harness. Two bullets had struck this, jamming the mechanism in the 'released' position. Had he decided to bale out he would have fallen straight through the harness.

All through the day the survivors prayed silently for the skipper and, indeed, at first he appeared to be responding well. Then, in the early evening, they learned that he had finally succumbed to his appalling injuries at approximately 3pm. He was buried, with full military honours, in Bone Military Cemetery.

On 3 November 1943 the *London Gazette* published the official citation for the award of a posthumous Victoria Cross to Arthur Louis Aaron, its narrative discreetly attributing the attack on the Stirling to 'an enemy nightfighter'. For their own parts in this epic of courage, Allan Larden was awarded a Conspicuous Gallantry medal (CGM) and Mitchem and Guy each received a Distinguished Flying Medal (DFM). On 25 February 1944, Aaron's parents received their son's awards at a Buckingham Palace investiture and, shortly afterwards, Benjamin Aaron was present at a mass parade of ATC cadets in Wellington Barracks, London, where the ATC Commandant, Air Marshal Sir Leslie Gossage read out the VC citation of their most distinguished ex-cadet.

Two years later, in August 1946, the parents' house was burgled and all Aaron's medals stolen, but after a police appeal the medals were returned through the mail anonymously. In December 1953, Aaron's father presented his son's medals to the Leeds City Museum for permanent public display.

Arthur Louis Aaron was born in Leeds. His grandparents, Isaac and Tamar Aaronson, were Polish or Russian Jews. His father, Ben Aaron was married to a non Jew, so that, according to strict Jewish Law (halacha), he could not claim to be a Jew. Hitler did not make this distinction so I am satisfied to include him in this Roll of Honour.

Most of this article has been reprinted with the kind permission of RAF, Hendon.

Henry Morris

Tommy Gould, VC

Thomas 'Tommy' William Gould was born in Dover on 28 December 1914, the son of Reuben Gould who served in the Boer War and was later killed in action in the First World War in 1916. He joined the Navy in 1933 and the submarine service in 1937. Tommy often visited his Jewish uncles in Dalston, Hackney, as boy and man.

He attended the Hackney Synagogue in Brenthouse Road on several Remembrance Days post war and in July 1946 he marched with AJEX when protesting the British Government's policy on restricting Jewish immigration into Palestine. He was very active in AJEX affairs and always in the wreath party of the Annual National Parade in Whitehall until he was too ill to attend

London Gazette
9 June 1942

Figure 344. Tommy Gould, VC.

On 16 February 1942, in daylight, HM Submarine *Thrasher* attacked and sank a heavily escorted supply ship. She was at once attacked by depth-charges and was bombed by aircraft. The presence of two unexploded bombs in the gun casing was discovered when, after dark, the submarine surfaced and began to roll. Lieutenant Roberts and Petty Officer Gould volunteered to remove the bombs, which were of a type unknown to them. The danger in dealing with the second bomb was very great. To reach it, they had to go through the casing, which was so low they had to lie full length to move it. Through this narrow space in complete darkness they pushed and dragged the bomb over a distance of some 20 feet until it could be lowered over the side. Every time the bomb was moved there was a loud twanging noise as of a broken spring, which added nothing to their peace of mind. This deed was the more gallant as HM Submarine *Thrasher*'s presence was known to the enemy: she was close to the enemy shore and in waters where his patrols were known to be active day and night. There was a very great chance, and they knew it, that the submarine might have to crash dive while they were in the casing. Had this happened they must have drowned.'

In his book, *The Victoria Cross at Sea*, John Winton provides a much more detailed account of this incident:

'About midday on 16th February 1942, HM Submarine *Thrasher* (Lieutenant H.S. Mackenzie) on patrol off Suva Bay, on the north coast of Crete, torpedoed and sank an Axis supply ship of some 3,000 tons,

strongly escorted by five anti-submarine vessels. The escorts counter
attacked, with support from aircraft, and dropped 33 depth-charges,
some of them very close indeed. *Thrasher* survived the attacks and,
that evening after dark, surfaced to recharge batteries. Later, in the
early hours of the morning, when *Thrasher* altered course across the
swell and began to roll more heavily, some unusual banging noises
were heard from the deck above, as though some heavy object was
loose and rolling about. It was found that there was a bomb between
three and four feet long, five to six inches in diameter, probably
weighing about 100 lb, lying on the submarine's casing in front of the
four-inch gun mounting.

'Lieutenant P.S.W. Roberts, the First Lieutenant, and Petty Officer
Gould, the Second Coxswain, volunteered to go on deck and remove
the bomb. As Second Coxswain, Gould was in charge of handling wires
when entering or leaving harbour, and of the care and stowage of gear
inside the casing (which was a light metal free-flooding structure,
erected as an upper deck, on top of the Submarine's pressure hull;
normally there was about two or three feet of clearance between the
casing and the hull, enclosing a tangle of pipes, wires and other gear).

'At any moment the bomb might roll off the casing on to the saddle
tank below and detonate. While Gould held the bomb still, Roberts
fetched an old potato sack, which they put round the bomb and tied
with a length of rope. The bomb was too heavy to be thrown clear of
the saddle tanks, so they manhandled it 100 feet forward to the bows
and dropped it overboard, whilst *Thrasher* went full astern to get clear.

'Looking more closely at the casing they found a jagged hole in the
metal and, inside, another bomb was resting on top of the pressure
hull. There was no possibility of handling the bomb up through the hole
it had made. The only approach was through a hinged metal grating
trap-door about twenty feet away. The two men lowered themselves
through the trap-door and wriggled on their stomachs to where the
bomb lay.

'If the bomb exploded, they and the submarine would be lost. Furthermore, *Thrasher* was off an enemy coast, and the enemy knew there was an Allied submarine in the area. If a surface vessel or aircraft were sighted now, Mackenzie would have to dive, and the two men would be drowned.

'Gould lay flat on his back with the bomb in his arms. Roberts lay in front of him, dragging him by the shoulders as he crawled along. By the faint light of a shaded torch, the two of them worked the bomb through the narrow casing, easing its weight around obstacles and up through the trap-door. Now and then, the bomb made a disconcerting twanging noise as it was moved. It was forty minutes before they had the bomb clear and could wrap it in the sack, carry it forward and drop it over the bows like its predecessor.

'Understandably, both men were recommended for, and awarded, the Victoria Cross.'

Tommy Gould died in December 2001 aged 86 years and his funeral ceremony was conducted by a Jewish and a Christian Naval Chaplain . His medals are at the AJEX Jewish Military Museum in London. He and John Kenneally (Irish Guards, died 2000) were the last surviving Jewish holders of the VC.

John Patrick Kenneally, VC

The scenario for the bloody and hard fought battle in which Lance Corporal Kenneally was wounded could have been written for a film epic, but this was reality, in which many men, on both sides, were killed and wounded.

Serving with the First Battalion of the Irish Guards, he had landed at Bone, a French port in Algeria. The night sky was clear and moonlit and the days were sunny and hot. They took up their position by Recce Ridge, which was covered in German mines and heavy machine guns and supported by anti-tank guns, heavy mortars and artillery. It was here that Rommel's Desert Army had chosen to make its stand.

Preceded by an artillery barrage, the British attacked the ridge, climbing the hill through the mines, but were met by heavy enemy shelling, grenades and machine gun fire; the probe failed completely. It was a forlorn action that should not have been

KENNEALLY VC

He fought with two of the world's finest regiments
But first he had to desert and change his name.

THE TRUE STORY OF A REMARKABLE LIFE

Figure 345. John Kenneally, VC.

attempted. After many further attacks in which there were heavy casualties, the Scots, Irish and Grenadier Guards serving as an infantry force advanced across the minefields, facing the Hermann Goering Division, battle-hard veterans of Stalingrad, who were supported by artillery and mortars. On 21 April 1943 Kenneally in No.1 Company, under cover of darkness, moved forward through the minefields under enemy flares, rifle and machine gun fire and succeeded in taking its objectives.

On 27 April the Germans began shelling again, when Kenneally sighted a number of the enemy unloading equipment. He charged forward quite alone, firing his Bren gun from the hip. Pursued by No.1 Company, the Germans fled in all directions and were fired on as they ran. Later that morning, he broke up a machine gun position and forced a German unit of three tanks to retreat. On 30 April, the Germans made their final attack with bombardment, armour and massed infantry.

Kenneally returned to the scene of his first single-handed attack to find that the enemy had returned. Together with a sergeant carrying a Sten gun, he attacked the Germans firing his Bren gun. They were followed by No.1 Company firing rifles and grenades until the enemy retreated. Kenneally was wounded deep in his right leg, but fought on. It was a fierce battle with 'grenades flying through the air like snowballs'. The battle eventually descended into close combat until the Germans broke, the British in pursuit. There were 700 enemy dead; only eighty men of the 1st Battalion Irish Guards survived.

The Citation for the award of the Victoria Cross read: 'The magnificent gallantry of the NCO on these two occasions under heavy fire, his unfailing vigilance and remarkable accuracy were responsible for saving many valuable lives in the days and nights in the forward positions. His actions also played a considerable part in holding these positions and this influenced the whole course of the battle. His rapid appreciation of the situation, his initiative and extraordinary gallantry in attacking single handed a mass body of the enemy and breaking up an attack on two occasions was an achievement that can seldom have been equalled. His courage in fighting all day was an inspiration to all ranks.'

Kenneally was born on 15 March 1921. He was the son of Gertrude Robinson, daughter of a Blackpool pharmacist, and Neville Leslie Blond. Blond was born in 1896, the son of a Jewish father and mother, Bernard and Rachel. Kenneally met his father only once in the late 1920s, but it is understood that his mother did receive help from the Blond family. He originally enlisted in the Royal Artillery, in which he served until February 1941. At some point, he deserted and worked in Glasgow. There he obtained an identity card in the name of John Patrick Kenneally. With the money provided by Mrs Blond, he was able to buy some clothes. Sometime later he enlisted in the Irish Guards. Later in the war, he took part in the fiercely fought Anzio landings where his battalion lost 741 men. On his return to the United Kingdom, he received his Victoria Cross from King George VI at a Buckingham Palace investiture. He took part in the Victory Parade and was then posted to the Rhine Army. He then joined the 1st Guards Parachute Battalion and served in Palestine as part of the 6th Airborne Division.

In Palestine he saw a great deal of action preserving order between Jewish villagers and Arab attackers. His last task was to defend a Kibbutz in northern Galilee against Arab marauders using grenade launchers. He was asked to stay in Palestine with the possibility of joining the Haganah. As a Jew and an Englishman, he might have accepted, but he chose to return to his wife and two children.

With acknowledgements to John Colvin (Lions of Judah)

Harry Errington, GC

Harry Errington was born in Soho on 20 August 1910, son of Solomon and Bella Ehrengott, Polish Jewish immigrants from Lublin who had come to live in Poland Street in 1908. One of four children, he went to Westminster Jewish Free School and won a trade scholarship to be an engraver, but his parents decided this was an unhealthy business owing to the chemicals involved, and so he went to work at his uncle's tailoring shop.

Figure 346. Harry Errington, GC.

Harry remained in the business – a master tailor – as Errington and Whyte in Saville Row until 1992, but his true passion in life was amateur basketball, playing and later coaching the team from Regent Street Polytechnic, one of the best in the country. He was involved with the 1948 British Olympics team and travelled widely to promote the game.

When war broke out Harry joined the Auxiliary Fire Service (AFS) – most of whose members worked at their normal jobs by day and then became firemen at night, providing an indispensable back up for the National Fire Service (this is why they were not overwhelmed by the Blitz).

Just before midnight on 17 September 1940, during an air raid, Harry was resting with other volunteers in the basement of a three storey garage next to the fire station in Soho, when it received a direct hit and the building collapsed, killing twenty people, including six firemen in the basement where Harry was.

Thrown across the basement by the blast, Harry recovered, finding fierce fires around him. As he dashed to the exit he heard the cries of a comrade trapped beneath the debris, so he turned back and, wrapping himself in a wet blanket, clawed at the burning rubble with his bare hands as the fire worsened and the masonry creaked above him, threatening to collapse further. He dragged his colleague along the ground and then up a narrow, smoke-filled staircase to a courtyard and into the relatively safer street. Despite the damage to his burnt hands – and thus his livelihood – he returned to the building to bring out another injured fireman who he had seen pinned to the ground by a heavy radiator, on his way out! He also dragged and carried him to safety.

All three men had serious burns but recovered and returned to duties some months later. For his gallantry and selflessness in saving the lives of his two comrades, Harry was awarded the GC in August 1941, receiving it from the King in October 1942, the only AFS man to be so honoured in the Second World War. One of the men saved became Sir John Terry and both the men and their families stayed in touch with Harry for years after.

Harry continued to serve with the AFS throughout the war. In later years he became treasurer of the VC & GC Association and the Westminster branch of the Association of Jewish Ex-Servicemen and Women of the UK (AJEX), often attending the Annual Jewish Parade in Whitehall. He was present when the Queen unveiled the VC and GC Memorial in Westminster Abbey in May 2003. He also became vice-chair of the UK Amateur Basketball Association and later a life vice-president, maintaining his interest with them right up until his death.

He was always a welcome and honoured visitor to Soho fire station and in 2000 they gave him a splendid 90th birthday party. His photograph hangs with pride in the watch room. He was especially proud of the fact that the Fire Services College at Moreton-in-the-Marsh had named a road on its site after him. Harry never married and was the last Jewish holder of the George Cross.

A gentle, dignified and modest man, Harry died aged 94 on 15 December 2004 and when he was buried at Cheshunt Jewish cemetery, a full guard of honour of firemen with their fire engines attended the funeral. His medals are at the Jewish Museum in Camden and the miniatures at the AJEX Museum in Hendon.

Figure 347. Harold 'Pop' Newgass, GC.

Harold 'Pop' Newgass, GC

Harold Reginald Newgass was born on 3 August 1896, son of Benjamin and Maria Regina Newgass of The Round House, Wiston, Steyning, Sussex. A monocled country gentleman, he served in the Royal Artillery, TA from 1918–34 and in September 1940 was commissioned as Temporary Sub Lieutenant in the Royal Navy Volunteer Reserve (RNVR), assigned to the Torpedo and Mining Department.

Throughout the 1930s he was also a Governor of the Board of the Oxford and St George Jewish Youth Club in Stepney, where he was given the nickname 'Pop', and was a regular contributor to its magazine *Fratres*.

On 29 November 1940, a large German parachute mine penetrated the roof of a gas storage tank at Garston, Liverpool, where it hung unexploded in seven feet of foul water. Newgass was sent for. The records noted that 'not only was the defusing of the mine one of the most delicate and dangerous assignments of its type carried out during the war, but had it exploded, the gasworks, Garston docks and a good deal of local industry would have been put out of action'. 6,000 people were evacuated from homes, factories and railways and the area was paralysed. The gasholder contained two million cubic feet of gas and the fuse of the mine was pressed against a roof support; the mine had to be rotated before work could begin.

Newgass worked alone, wearing oxygen equipment, and had to continually return to the surface to replenish his air as the containers only gave a half-hour of supply. He lashed the mine to stop it slipping, and turned it to the required position, a Herculean task in that apparatus.

Suffering increasingly from fatigue (he was 44 years old), he successfully removed the fuse, primer and detonator, and then after two days, the clock. Had the clock started during this time, nothing could have prevented a devastating explosion.

On 13 December 1940, Newgass was promoted to Temporary Lieutenant and on 4 March 1941 was Gazetted for the George Cross, with the citation reading: 'The King has graciously pleased to approve the award of the GC, for great gallantry and undaunted devotion to duty to Temporary Lieutenant Harold R. Newgass, RNVR'. He received the medal from the King on 8 July 1941.

Newgass's extraordinary heroism and skill also earned him a gold cigarette case from the gas company and a set of cufflinks from the employees. He particularly treasured the gifts given him by local residents for saving their homes. For their assistance to Newgass, George Kermode and Ernest Saxon were awarded the GM, William Norris and William Brown the MBE and Alec McRae and Albert Kemp the BEM.

After the war Newgass lived in Dorset and became involved in local government; he was also a revered figure in the Association of Jewish Ex-Servicemen and Women. He died at West Stafford, Dorchester on 17 November 1984 aged 88 (an obituary appeared in the *Jewish Chronicle*) and cremated, with his ashes spread at sea as he wished. His medals are at the Imperial War Museum, and on 25 November 1990 a plaque to his memory was unveiled at St Michael's Church, Garston.

Captain Simmon Latutin, GC

It is not on the battlefield alone that acts of heroism and self-sacrifice are performed, although it is gallantry in action that most often receives tangible recognition. The 'undaunted selflessness' of Captain Simmon Latutin's rescue of two comrades in a fire at the Training School of the Somalia Gendarmerie in December 1944 at the cost of his own life was recognised by the posthumous award of the George Cross, the highest recognition available for gallantry not in the face of the enemy.

The citation reads:

> It was on December 29th, 1944, that a fire occurred at the Training School Store, Somalia Gendarmerie, Mogadishu, while some Italian rockets and explosives were being taken out for another unit about to hold a New Year's entertainment.

Captain Simmon Latutin, together with one officer, a Company Sergeant Major, and a personal boy, were in the store selecting explosives, Captain Latutin standing in the main doorway. For some unexplained reason, a fire broke out and almost simultaneously, a great number of rockets began to explode and burn. There were some seventy cases in the store. The force of the explosion and the fire turned the store into an inferno.

Regardless of the detonating rockets, the intense heat of the fire and the choking clouds of smoke, Captain Latutin plunged into the storeroom and succeeded in

dragging out the officer who was almost unconscious due to his burns. By this time, Captain Latutin's clothes were alight, but unhesitatingly, he rushed again into the inferno and rescued the Company Sergeant Major, who, by this time was quite naked. The body of the personal boy was recovered later, but was unrecognizable due to its charred condition.

Figure 348. Acting Major Simmon Latutin, George Cross, SLI, attached Somalia Gendarmerie; taken in 1944. He is wearing the SLI collar badges and the cap badge of the Gendarmerie

The heroism of Captain Latutin was outstanding as he fully realized the acute danger he was in as he entered the blazing building. His unquenchable determination to succour the injured is illustrated by his second entry into the store, even though his own clothes were alight.

His action was illustrative of the finest degree of British courage and a magnificent example of undaunted selflessness.

Captain Latutin died the next day as a result of his injuries.

The full story of Captain Latutin is told by Martin Sugarman in *Fighting Back* (London and Portland, OR: Vallentine Mitchell, 2010).

Appendix

Post-War Deaths in Service/Action and Suez 1956

The following names of British Jewish military personnel who were killed or died on active service after the Second World War, are from the Armed Forces Memorial at Alrewas, Staffordshire and from the accompanying database. We believe they are Jewish, but evidence is difficult to obtain in some cases. Further details on some of these personnel are available on www.forcesmemorial.org.uk.roll-of-honour.asp.

It *excludes* the Falklands War and some other casualties since 1945, who appear in the earlier sections of this book because they were known of some time ago. AJEX and the Jewish Military Museum would welcome further information from readers. The year given is year of death. The letter b. means 'buried'; a (?) means possibly Jewish. The authors wish to thank Saul Issroff and Nigel Grizzard for their superb assistance.

Arno, Pte Harry
E. Yorks Regt
Killed   1951
UN Memorial Wall, Pusan (?),
Korea

Arno, Pte Robert G.
Roy Sigs   1948
b. Ramleh, Israel

Bahin, Lt/Col Raymond J.
Devon and Dorset
                                            1964

Bankier, Cpl. Robert
Roy Green Jackets
1971
N Ireland; killed by a sniper

Belsom, AB Robert
RN, HMS *Dolphin*
                                            1973
b. Sittingbourne

Benjamin, L/Cpl Anthony
REME
                                            1982
b. Augustwise, Germany

Benjamin, Cpl Harold
Roy Lancers
                                            1973

Burstein, P/O Irving L.
RAF   1952
b. Willesden Jewish cemetery

Cohen, P/O John Alexander
RAF   1955
b. Cardiff – crashed in a Gloster
Meteor jet

Fischer, Pte Michael Walter
Queens Roy Regt
                                            1957

Frieze, O/Cadet Sarah Jane
                                            1995
b. Croydon

Gee, Flt/Lt Nathan John
RAF
                                            1956
b. Changi Jewish cemetery,
Singapore

Gee, Pte Raymond
KOYLI
                                            1945,
b. Penang, later exhumed

Gleiwitz, Pte Alfred
Worcs Regt
                                            1949

Gold, Spr Leslie Ivan
RE
                                            1949
b. Kuala Lumpur, Cheras Rd

Goldblatt, Pte Michael Isaac
Beds and Herts
1948

Grundman, ERA1 Alan Frederick
RN, HMS *Chichester*
1967
b.Grimsby

Hauser, P/O Grahame Otto
RAF
1955
b. Birmingham

Hesselberg, SAC Simon A
RAF
1952
b. Birmingham

Hofman, Sub Lt Graham Peter
RN, HMS *Seahawk*
1962 (?)

Hofman, Capt Geoffrey P.
Northants Regt
1948
b. Ibadan, Nigeria

Hoffman, Sq/Ldr William F.
RAF
1953
b. West Zoyland, Somerset (?)

Isaacs, Sgt Godfrey Stanley
RAEC
1948

Jacobson, WO2 Joseph Rigall
RASC
1963

Kahan, P.O. Richard F.
RAF
1948
b. Cambridge

Keyser, P/O Richard
RAF
1952
b. Ohlsdorf, Germany

Klein, Pte Albert
S. Lancs Regt
1948

Kreiner, WO2 Michael
RE
1982
b. Chatham

Kunkel, Pte Robert
Paras
1956
b. Cyprus

Kyte, F/O Dudley Harold
RAF
1955
b. Cambridge

Landau, R/Off Mark Jonathan
RN, HMS *Sirius*
1984
b. Hereford

Leitner, Cpl Martin Isidore
RAF
1987
b. Aberdeen

Margoliouth, Lt Joseph Maurice
RN HMS *Fulmer*
1955
b. Yeovilton

Meyers, Capt Ernest
RCT
1978
b. Germany

Mocatta, Capt Peter Charles
Lincs Regt
1958

Moss, Sgt Norman Emmanuel
RAF
1951
b. Marlow Rd Jewish cemetery

Pickholz, 2nd Lt Wladyslaw P
Polish Forces in UK
DOAS   27.01.47
Son of Leon and Maria Liss
b. Chester British cemetery, grave
165, as a Catholic; father was
Jewish from Tarnopol

Polikoff, Pte Leslie
RAOC
1948

Reuben, Spr Raymond Ivor
RE
1956

Rosen, Surgeon/Lt Leon
RN, HMS *Mercury*
1952

Samuel, Lt/Col Clive MBE, MD,
Para
30.6.69

Selman, Flt/Lt Harry MBE
RAF
1950
b. Cheshire (?)

Shurman, F/O Charles
RAF
1952
b. Newton-on-Ouse

Silver, WO2 Reuben Philip Barnett
KRRC
1961
b. Berlin

Solomon, L/Cpl Edward John
RE
1960
b. Hanover

Spiers Pte Albert,
Roy Berks
1948
b. Moascar, Egypt

Spiro, Pte Mark
Roy MP
1976

Stein, Cpl Derek Louis
RAPC
1957
b. Willesden Jewish Cem

Stern, Sgt Herman
RA
1953
b. City of Westminster Cem

Tagger, AC1 Derek
RAF
1956
b. Leeds

Tapper, Flt/Lt Jonathan
RAF (?)
1994
b. Belfast

Tobias, Maj John
Intel Corps
1994
b. West Herts (?)

Zissman, Gnr Irwin
RA
1951
b. Wrexham (?)

Known to have served in Suez 1956

Borsack, Jeffrey
RAF

Boxer, Clive
Army

Butler, Alex
RAF

Cohen, Murray

Davis, Mark

Fenton, Harry

Garretts, Capt Morris
RAMC

Hines, Col Alfred John MC and Bar,
RE, Paras at Suez
MID twice

Lang, LAC David F.
2768667 RAF

Reuben, Victor

Robinson, Roger
Intel Corps

Falklands War

Bradman, OS Tony
RN Task Force

Burt, Pte Jason
Paras
KIA 12.6.82

Australian Jewish POWs of the Japanese

ABRAMOVITCH, Capt Gershom S., Malaya

ALTSHULER, Sgt Evan, died at sea

ASHER, Pte Keith R., died at sea

BERLINER, Pte Leon A., executed

BERNSTEIN, Pte Harry, died at sea

BERNSTEIN, Pte Philip, Malaya

COHEN, Pte Lewis S., Changi

COHEN, Pte Norman M., Changi

COHEN, Sig Ronald L., Tokyo

DAVIS, Gp/Capt Reginald H.S., OBE, RAAF, Manchuria

DE GROEN, Sgt Geoffrey, Fukuoka

DEANE, Dvr Nathan, Timor

EDELSTEN, Dvr Ivor, Rabaul, died

FALK, Gnr Harry, Timor

FALK, Sgt Norman, Changi

GOLDMAN, Pte Samuel, Changi

HAYMAN, Sgt Marcus, Tamarkan

JACOBS, Sgt Peter A., Ambon, died

JACOBS, Pte David T., Malaya, died

JACOBS, L/Cpl Harold, Malaya

JONAS, Cpl Lewis, Changi

JOSEPH, Pte Leonard, Singapore

KEMPLER, L/Cpl Edward, Java

KRASNOSTEIN, Pte Leslie, Malaya

LANGFORD, Pte Alfred E., Java

LAZARUS, Lt Samuel A., Ambon

LETWIN, Pte Gerald, Malaya, died

LEVEY, Pte Robert E., Borneo

LEVINSOHN, Sgt Harold A., Changi

LEVY, WO2 Patrick R., Malaya

MANSFIELD, Lt George J., Changi

MORITZ, WO Abraham, RAAF, Java?

MORRIS, Cpl Alan, Ambon, died

NORMAN, Sgt G. Solomon, Changi

PYKE, Lt R. Elias, Changi

RAPHAEL, Lt Geoffrey A., Malaya, died

ROSEBERY, Sgt Norman J., Osaka

ROSTKIER, Pte Samuel, Changi

SEGAL, Sgmn Norman E., Timor

SILVERMAN, Capt. H. Nathan, Executed, Rabaul

SOLOMON, Gnr Neville L., Malaya, died

STONE, Pte Joseph E., Malaya, died

VAN DER SLUYS, Pte Aaron, Java

WOOD, Sgt Francis E., Changi

Australian Jewish POWs of Germans

BENJAMIN, Sgt Sydney C., Greece

BERCOVE, Pte Solomon D., Crete

CREMER, Sgt Samuel, Crete

FINKELSTEIN, Pte Harry, Crete

GREENSTEIN, Cpl Wolfe, Crete

JACOBS, Pte Joseph, North Africa

JOSEPH, Pte Louis, Crete

KALIK, Pte Max, Crete

LAPIN, Lt Abraham Allenby, Crete

LOFFMAN, Cpl Philip, North Africa

MARKS, Pte Albert H., Greece

PATKIN, Sgt Robert, Crete

PHILLIPS, Sgt Mark, Crete

ROBERTS, Pte R. Alexander, Crete

ROSEN, Pte Alex Eli, Crete

SILVERSTONE, Maj Jessel, North Africa

SOLOMONS, Pte Phillip, Crete

We appreciate that it is likely that further names will be identified in the future and would ask that any names be forwarded to AJEX where they will be inserted on the AJEX website in their Record of Honour (http://www.ajexroh.org.uk).

Location of Cemeteries

Algeria
Bone War Cemetery, Annaba
Canrobert Cemetery, Algiers
Constantine Civil Cemetery
Dely Ibrahim War Cemetery
El Alia Military Cemetery, Maison
  Carée, Algiers
Le Petit Lac Cemetery
Oran, American Military Cemetery
St Eugene Jewish Cemetery,
  Algiers

Australia
Fawkner Memorial Park Cemetery,
  Victoria
Northern Territory Memorial
Toowoomba Cemetery, Queensland

Austria
Klagenfurt Military Cemetery

Belgium
Antwerp Military Cemetery
Adegem Canadian War Cemetery
Bruges, Canadian Cemetery
Bruges Civil Cemetery
Burg Leopold Cemetery
Esquelmes War Cemetery
Evere Cemetery, Brussels
Gent City Cemetery
Ghent Military Cemetery
Heverlee War Cemetery, near
  Brussels
Hotton War Cemetery
Oost-Dunkerke Communal
  Cemetery
Ostend Cemetery
St Martens-Voeren Churchyard
Schoonselhof Cemetery, Antwerp
Tongaloo-Westerloo Cemetery
Veurnes Communal Cemetery
Warneton (Waasten) Communal
  Cemetery
Wevelghem Commonwealth
  Cemetery

Wihogne Communal Cemetery,
  Liege

Canada
Baron de Hirsch Cemetery,
  Carterville, Montreal
Calgary Jewish Cemetery, Alberta
Halifax Memorial, Nova Scotia
Lethbridge Hebrew Cemetery
Ottawa Memorial Cemetery,
  Ontario
Toronto (Dawes Road) Cemetery,
  Ontario
Toronto (Mount Hope) Cemetery,
  Ontario
Toronto (Roselawn) Hebrew
  Cemetery

Ceylon
St Stephen's Cemetery,
  Trincomalee

Cyprus
Famagusta Military Cemetery
Margo Jewish Cemetery
Nicosia War Cemetery

Denmark
Aabenraa Cemetery
Esbjerg Cemetery

Egypt
Alexandria Jewish Cemetery
Alexandria (Chatby) Military and
  War Memorial Cemetery
El Alamein War Cemetery
El Gharbaniyat War Memorial
  Cemetery
El Hamman Military Cemetery
Fayid War Cemetery
Geneifa War Cemetery
Heliopolis Military Cemetery
Hadra Military Cemetery,
  Alexandria
Ismailia War Memorial Cemetery

Kantara Military Cemetery
Moascar War Cemetery
Old Cairo War Memorial Cemetery
Port Said War Cemetery
Suez War Memorial Cemetery
Tel-El-Kebir Military Cemetery

Eritrea
Asmara (St Michele) War
  Cemetery

Far East
River Kwai Cemetery, Chung Kai,
  Thailand
River Kwai War Cemetery,
  Kanchanburi, Thailand

Taukkyan War Cemetery,
  Rangoon, Burma (Myanmar)
Thanbyuzayat War Cemetery
Rangoon War Cemetery, Burma

Hong Kong Jewish Cemetery
Hong Kong Sai Wan Memorial
  Cemetery

Lae War Cem, Papua New Guinea
Port Moresby War Cemetery,
  Papua New Guinea

Kranji War Cemetery, Singapore

Ambon Memorial, Indonesia
Jakarta War Cemetery, Indonesia

Yokohama, Commonwealth
  Cemetery, Japan

France
Banneville-La-Campagne British
  Cemetery
Bayeux Military Cemetery,
  Normandy
Bethune Military Cemetery, Pas de
  Calaisance

Boulogne East Cemetery
Bretteville-sur-Laize Canadian War Cemetery
Breux-sur-Avre
Brouay War Cemetery
Cambes-En-Plaine War Cemetery
Chaumont
Cherbourg Old Communal Cemetery, Manche
Cholay War Cemetery
Cugny Communal Cemetery, Aisne
Dunkirk Municipal Cemetery
Epinac Les Mines Cemetery
Escoublac-la-Baule War Cemetery
Hermanville War Cemetery
Hottot-Les-Bagues War Cemetery
Jerusalem War Cemetery, Chouain, Calvados
La Delivrande War Cemetery, Douvres, Calvados
Le Paradis War Cemetery
Lille Southern Cemetery
Marquise Cemetery, Pas de Calais
Maubeuge Centre Cemetery
Meteren Communal Cemetery
Metz Jewish Cemetery
Moussey Churchyard, Vosges
Nord, Maubeuge-Centre Cemetery
Paris, City Cemetery
Pihen-Les-Guines War Cemetery
Poix de Picardie Churchyard, Somme
Pornic War Cemetery
Ranville British Military Cemetery, Normandy
Rebrechien Communal Cemetery, Loiret
Romescamps Churchyard, Abancourt
Ryes British Military Cemetery, Normandy
St Charles De Percy British Cemetery, Calvados
St Desir British Military Cemetery
Saint Germain Cemetery, Paris
St Laurent-Sur-Mer Churchyard
St Leger Ryes British Military Cemetery, Normandy
St Manvieu War Cemetery, Calvados
St Pierre-Du-Vauvray Communal Cemetery
St Requier Cemetery near Lille
St Sever Cemetery, Rouen
St Valery en Caux Cemetery
Secqueville War Cemetery, Calvados
Tilly-sur-Seulles, Normandy

Germany
Becklingen War Cemetery, Soltau
Berlin British Military Cemetery
Dusseldorf Military Cemetery
Durnbach Military Cemetery
Flensburg Military Cemetery
Hamburg Military Cemetery
Hann-Stohen Dispenau Russian Cemetery
Hanover War Cemetery
Kiel Military Cemetery, Schleswig-Holstein
Kleve British Military Cemetery
Kolpin-See Mecklenburg
Munster, Standort Lagvett
Reichswald British Cemetery
Rheinberg British Cemetery
Risznow, Pomerania (former East Germany)
Tecklenburg, Scheirloh Cemetery
Sage Cemetery, Oldenburg
Soltau British Cemetery Becklingen

Greece
Phaleron War Cemetery, Athens
Rhodes War Cemetery
Salonika Allied Military Cemetery

India
Bombay Jewish Cemetery
Calcutta Jewish Cemetery
Delhi War Cemetery, India
Ganhati Military Cemetery, Assam
Kamptee Military Cemetery, Nagpur
Karachi Jewish Cemetery
Kirkee War Cemetery, Bombay
Kohima Military Cemetery
Madras War Cemetery, Chennai
New Delhi Jewish Cemetery, India

Poona, St Sepulchre Cemetery, India
Ranchi War Cemetery
St Mary's Cemetery, Madras
Trimulgherry Cemetery, India

Iraq
Basra War Cemetery
Mosul War Cemetery

Israel
Beersheba Cemetery
Gaza War Cemetery
Mount Scopus Cemetery, Jerusalem
Khayat Beach War Cemetery
Ramleh Military Cemetery
Ramleh Memorial Cemetery
Tel Aviv (Nahlat Yitzhak) Cemetery

Italy
Ancona War Cemetery
Anzio British Military Cemetery
Arezzo War Cemetery
Argenta Gap War Cemetery (78 Div Cemetery)
Assisi War Cemetery
Bari War Cemetery
Bologna War Cemetery
Bolsena War Cemetery
Camp Verano Cemetery
Canadian Cemetery, Riccioni
Carvignano British Military Cemetery
Caserta War Cemetery
Castel-Del-Rio, Santerno
Castelforte
Catania British Cemetery, Sicily
Cesena War Cemetery
Coriano Ridge Miramore di Romagna War Cemetery
Faenza British Cemetery
Florence British War Cemetery
Forli War Cemetery
Fort Capuzzo Cemetery
Gradara British Military Cemetery
Milan War Cemetery
Minturno War Cemetery
Naples Military Cemetery
Ravenna War Cemetery

Roccamonfina British Military
    Cemetery
Rome War Cemetery
Sessa Arunca Military Cemetery
Salerno War Cemetery
Sangro River Cemetery
Syracuse Military Cemetery, Sicily
Taranto British Military Cemetery
Vairano Military Cemetery, near
    Cassino

Kenya
Nairobi Jewish Cemetery

Korea
Memorial Cemetery, Pusan, South
    Korea

Libya
Derna Cemetery, Benghazi
Belhamed War Cemetery, Tobruk
Benghazi Mil Cem
Bir-Hakim British Cemetery
Knightsbridge War Cemetery,
    Acroma
Sollum Halfaya War Cemetery,
    Tobruk
Sollum Italian Burial Ground,
    Tobruk
Sollum Sidi Aziz Cemetery, Tobruk
Sollum-Tobruk Military Cemetery
Tripoli Military Cemetery

Madagascar
Diego Suarez War Cemetery

Malaysia
Kuala Lumpur Protestant
    Cemetery, Malaya
Labuan War Cem, North Borneo
Penang Jewish Cemetery

Malta
Marsa Jewish Cemetery
Military Cemetery
Naval Cemetery

The Netherlands
Arnhem British Military Cemetery
Bergen-op-Zoom War Cemetery

Crooswijk General Cemetery,
    Rotterdam
Ede General Cemetery, Holland
Eelde General Cemetery,
    Groningen
Eindhoven Jewish Cemetery,
    Holland
Goirle, Tilburg, Holland
Groesbeek Memorial Cemetery
Harderwijk Cemetery, Holland
Holton, Canadian War Cemetery,
    Holland
Milsbeek War Cemetery
Mook Military Cemetery, Holland
Moskowa cemetery, Rosendaal,
    Holland
Nederweert War Cemetery
Nijmegen, Holland
Roosendaal-en-Nispen General
    Cemetery
Sittard War Cemetery
Texel (Den Burg) War Cemetery,
    Holland
Veendam Cemetery, Holland
Venlo Military Cemetery
Venray British Cemetery
Vianen Protestant Cemetery

New Zealand
Auckland (Waikumete) Cemetery

Norway
Trondheim (Stavne) Cemetery

Pakistan
Rawalpindi War Cemetery

Poland
Cracow Rakowicki Cemetery
Cracow British War Cemetery

Serbia and Montenegro
Belgrade War Cemetery

Sierra Leone, West Africa
Freetown Military Cemetery, Sierra
    Leone

South Africa
East London Cemetery
Johannesburg Cemetery
Wuppertal Jewish Civil Cemetery

Sri Lanka
Trincomalee War Cemetery

Sudan
Khartoum War Cemetery
Khartoum Memorial Cemetery

Sweden
Malmo Jewish Cemetery

Syria
Damascus British War Cemetery

Tunisia
Beja War Cemetery
Borgel Jewish Cemetery Tunis
Enfidaville British Military
    Cemetery
Infida War Graves Cemetery,
    Sousse
Massicault Military Cemetery
Medjez-El-Bab
Sfax War Cemetery
Sousse Military Cemetery
Tabarka Ras Rajel War Cemetery

United Kingdom
Beck Row (St John) Churchyard
Blackley Cemetery, Manchester
Brookwood Cemetery, Surrey
Cheltenham Cemetery
Chester RAF Cemetery
East Ham Cemetery, London
Ecclesfield Jewish Cemetery,
    Sheffield
Emel Burial Cemetery, Glasgow
Failsworth Jewish Cemetery
Finningley Churchyard,
    Nottingham
Glenduffhill Jewish Cemetery,
    Glasgow
Hazelrigg Jewish Cemetery,
    Gosforth
Kingston Cemetery, Portsmouth
Leeds, Geldard Road Cemetery

Lingen Jewish Cemetery,
Herefordshire
Liverpool (Walton) Jewish
Cemetery
Llandilo Churchyard,
Carmarthenshire
Middlesbrough Cemetery
Milltown Cemetery, Belfast
Moor Top Cemetery, Farnley,
Leeds
Rainborough Cemetery,
Manchester

Rainsough Jewish Cemetery,
Lancashire
St Denys Cemetery, St Austell,
Cornwall
St Mary's Cemetery, Walthamstow
Sunderland Jewish Cemetery,
Bishopwearmouth
West End Chessed V'ameth
Cemetery, Rowan Road,
London SW16
Willesden Cemetery, London
Witton New Cemetery,
Birmingham

United States
Detroit (Hebrew Memorial) Park
Florida, US National Cemetery,
Saint Augustine
Texas, RAF Cemetery, Terrel

Zimbabwe
Bulawayo (Athlone) Jewish
Cemetery

Glossary of Abbreviations

2/Lt	Second Lieutenant
2 Arm/Bde	2nd Army Brigade
A&SH	Argyle & Sutherland Highlanders
A/T	Anti-Tank
AAC	Army Air Corps (Gliders)
AB	Able Seaman
AC	Aircraftsman
AC1	Aircraftsman 1st Class
AC2	Aircraftsman 2nd Class
ACW	Aircraft Woman
ADFC	American Distinguished Flying Cross
AFC	Air Force Cross
AFS	Auxiliary Fire Service
AFU	Advanced Flying Unit
AG	Air Gunner
AIF	Australian Imperial Force(s)
Air/Mech	Air Mechanic
AMF	Australian Military Force(s)
AO	Apprentice Officer
AOC	Air Officer Commanding
Armd	Armoured
ARP	Air Raid Precautions
Arty	Artillery
Asst Stwd	Assistant Steward
ATA	Air Transport Auxiliary
ATC	Air Training Corps
ATS	Auxiliary Territorial Service (later WRAC: Women's Royal Army Corps)
Att	Attached

Bde	Brigade
Beds & Herts Regt	Bedfordshire and Hertfordshire Regiment
BEM	British Empire Medal
Bdr	Bombardier
BQMS	Battery Quarter Master Sergeant
Brig	Brigadier
Brit	British
Btn	Battalion
Bty	Battery
Buffs	Royal East Kents
C in C	Commander in Chief
C/Sgt	Company Sergeant
Cad/O	Cadet Officer
Capt	Captain
Cdr	Commander
Cem	Cemetery
Cert	Certificate
Cftmn	Craftsman
CGM	Conspicuous Gallantry Medal
Ch Eng/O	Chief Engineering Officer
Chap	Chaplain
CMF	Central Mediterranean Force
CMG	Companion of the Order of St Michael and St George
Col/Sgt	Colour Sergeant
COS	Chief of Staff
Coy	Company
Cpl	Corporal
CPO	Chief Petty Officer
CQMS	Company Quarter Master Sergeant
CSM	Company Sergeant Major
DCLI	Duke of Cornwall's Light Infantry
Devons	Devonshire Regiment
DFC	Distinguished Flying Cross
DFM	Distinguished Flying Medal

Div	Division
DLI	Durham Light Infantry
DoW	Died of wounds
DSO	Distinguished Service Order
Dvr (RN & RM)	Diver
Dvr	Driver
E Surrey Regt	East Surrey Regiment
E Yorks Regt	East Yorkshire Regiment
Eng	Engineer
ERA	Engine Room Artificer (RN)
F/O	Flying Officer
FAA	Fleet Air Arm
Fed	Federation
FFF	Free French Forces
Fld/Regt	Field Regiment
Flt/Eng	Flight Engineer
Flt/Lt	Flight Lieutenant
Flt/O	Flight Officer (WAAF)
Flt/Sgt	Flight Sergeant
FM	Field Marshall
FMSVF	Federated Malay States Volunteer Force
FTS	Flying Training School
Fus	Fusilier
Gdsmn	Guardsman
Glos	Gloucester
GM	George Medal
Gnr	Gunner
Gp	Group
Gp/Capt	Group Captain
GSC	General Service Corps
GTC	Government Training Centre
HAA	Heavy Anti-Aircraft
HAC	Honourable Artillery Company
HCU	Heavy Conversion Unit

HG	Home Guard
Highldrs	Highlanders
HKVDC	Hong Kong Volunteer Defence Corps
HLI	Highland Light Infantry
HMCS	His Majesty's Canadian Ship
HMIS	His Majesty's Indian Ship
HMML	His Majesty's Motor Launch
HMS	His Majesty's Ship
Hon	Honourable
Hons	Honours
HQ	Headquarters
10 IA	10th Inter-Allied Commando
Indep	Independent
Inf	Infantry
Intel Corps	Intelligence Corps
JC	Jewish Chronicle
JL	Jack Lennard archive, AJEX Museum
KAFR	King's African Rifles
KAR	Kenya African Rifles
KIA	Killed in Action
KOSB	King's Own Scottish Borderers
KOYLI	King's Own Yorkshire Light Infantry
KRRC	King's Royal Rifle Corps
KSLI	King's Shropshire Light Infantry
L/Bdr	Lance Bombardier
L/Cpl	Lance Corporal
L/I	Light Infantry
L/Sgt	Lance Sergeant
LAA	Light Anti-Aircraft
LAC	Leading Aircraftsman
LACW	Leading Aircraftswoman
Ldg/Smn	Leading Seaman
Lib	Liberal
LRDG	Long Range Desert Group

LSBA	Leading Sick Bay Attendant
LST	Landing Ship tank
Lt	Lieutenant
Lt/Cdr	Lieutenant Commander
Lt/Col	Lieutenant Colonel
Maj	Major
Maj/Gen	Major General
MBE	Member of the British Empire
MC	Military Cross
Mddx	Middlesex
MEF	Middle East Force
MID	Mentioned in Despatches
Mil	Military
MM	Military Medal
MN	Merchant Navy
MSM	Meritorious Service Medal
MV	Motor Vessel
Nav	Navigator
NZEF	New Zealand Expeditionary Force
NZF	New Zealand Forces
O/C	Observer Corps
O/Cad	Officer Cadet
O/Eng	Officer/Engineer
O/Sig	Observer Signalman
OBE	Order of British Empire
Obs	Observer
OC	Observer Corps
OCA	Old Comrades Association
Ops	Operations
OS	Ordinary Seaman
OTU	Operational Training Unit
Ox & Bucks LI (OBLI)	Oxfordshire and Buckinghamshire Light Infantry
P/O (Navy)	Petty Officer
P/O (RAF)	Pilot Officer

Pal	Palestine Jewish
Para	Parachute
Para/Regt	Parachute Regiment
PATS	Palestine Auxiliary Territorial Service
PC	Pioneer Corps
Pos	Posthumous
POW	Prisoner of War
PPA	Popski's Private Army
Pte	Private
QARANC	Queen Alexandra's Royal Army Nursing Corps
QMS	Quarter Master Sergeant
Queen's Roy Regt	Queen's Royal Regiment
Queens R Lancers	Queen's Royal Lancers
QVR	Queen Victoria Rifles
R/Adm	Rear Admiral
R Scots Greys	Royal Scots Greys
R/T	Radio Telegraphy
RA	Royal Artillery
RAAF	Royal Australian Air Force
RAC	Royal Armoured Corps
Rad/O	Radio Officer
RADC	Royal Army Dental Corps
RAEC	Royal Army Education Corps
RAF	Royal Air Force
RAFVR	Royal Air Force Volunteer Reserve
RAMC	Royal Army Medical Corps
RAN	Royal Australian Navy
RAOC	Royal Army Ordnance Corps
RAPC	Royal Army Pay Corps
RASC	Royal Army Service Corps
RB	Rifle Brigade
RCAF	Royal Canadian Air Force
RCNVR	Royal Canadian Navy Volunteer Reserve
RCOS	Royal Corps of Signals

RE	Royal Engineer
Recce	Reconnaissance
Regt	Regiment
REME	Royal Electrical and Mechanical Engineers
Rev	Reverend
Rfmn	Rifleman
RHA	Royal Horse Artillery
RIH	Royal Irish Horse
RM	Royal Marines
RN	Royal Navy
RNC	Royal Naval Commando
RNVR	Royal Navy Volunteer Reserve
RNZAF	Royal New Zealand Air Force
RNZAMC	Royal New Zealand Army Medical Corps
RNZCOS	Royal New Zealand Corps of Signals
RNZN	Royal New Zealand Navy
Roy Fus	Royal Fusiliers
Roy	Royal
RPC	Royal Pioneer Corps
RSM	Regimental Sergeant Major
RTR	Royal Tank Regiment
RUF	Royal Ulster Fusiliers
S Lancs	South Lancashire
S/Lt	Sub Lieutenant
S/Maj	Sergeant Major
S/Sgt	Staff Sergeant
SAAF	South African Air Force
SAC	Senior Aircraftsman
SACOS	South African Corps of Signals
SACW	Senior Aircraft Woman
SAMC	South African Medical Corps
SAEC	South African Engineering Corps
SAF	South African Forces
SASC	Small Arms School Corps

SATC	South African Tank Corps
SEAC	South East Asia Command
Sgmn	Signalman
Sgt	Sergeant
Sgt/Ag	Sergeant Air Gunner
Sgt/Nav	Sergeant Navigator
Sgt/Obs	Sergeant Observer
SIG	Special Interrogation Group
Sgmn	Signalman
SIS	Secret Intelligence Service
SLI	Somerset Light Infantry
SNS	Special Night Squads
SOE	Special Operations Executive
Spec Ops	Special Operations
Spr	Sapper
Sqdn/Ldr	Squadron Leader
SS	Steam Ship
SSRF	Small Scale Raiding Force
SSVF	Straits Settlement Volunteer Force
St	Saint
Stkr	Stoker
Stkr/I	Stoker First Class
Stwd	Steward
Surg/Lt	Surgeon Lieutenant
SVC	Shanghai Volunteer Corps
SWB	South Wales Borderers
T/Brig	Temporary Brigadier
T/Maj	Temporary Major
TA	Territorial Army
TD	Territorial Decoration
TD	Tactical Division
TJFF	Trans Jordan Frontier Force
TM	Territorial Medal
Tpr	Trooper

UDF	Union Defence Forces (South African)
US	United States
USA	United States of America
USAAF	United States Army Air Force
VC	Victoria Cross
VM	Virtuti Militari (Polish "VC")
VR	Volunteer Reserve
W/Cdr	Wing Commander
W Lancs Fus	West Lancashire Fusiliers
W Yorks Regt	West Yorkshire Regiment
WAAF	Women's Auxiliary Air Force
WO (Army)	Warrant Officer
WO (RAF)	Wireless Operator
WOl	Warrant Officer/1
WO2	Warrant Officer/2
Worc Regt	Worcestershire Regiment
WRAC	Women's Royal Army Corps
Yorks & Lancs Regt	Yorkshire and Lancashire Regiment

'And he shall judge among the nations, and shall decide among many people: and they shall beat their swords into plowshares, and their spears into pruning hooks: nation shall not lift up sword against nation, neither shall they learn war any more.' (Isaiah, 2:4)

וְשָׁפַט֙ בֵּ֣ין הַגּוֹיִ֔ם
וְהוֹכִ֖יחַ לְעַמִּ֣ים רַבִּ֑ים וְכִתְּת֨וּ חַרְבוֹתָ֜ם לְאִתִּ֗ים וַחֲנִיתֽוֹתֵיהֶם֙
לְמַזְמֵר֔וֹת לֹא־יִשָּׂ֨א ג֤וֹי אֶל־גּוֹי֙ חֶ֔רֶב וְלֹא־יִלְמְד֥וּ ע֖וֹד
מִלְחָמָֽה׃